PRAYER IN THE CATHOLIC TRADITION

PRAYER
in the
CATHOLIC
TRADITION

A HANDBOOK OF
PRACTICAL APPROACHES

ROBERT J. WICKS, GENERAL EDITOR

Franciscan
MEDIA
Cincinnati, Ohio

Ronald Rolheiser's "Struggling in Prayer" is excerpted from *Prayer: Our Deepest Longing* (Franciscan Media, 2013), used by permission. James Martin, SJ's "The Easiest Prayer Ever" originally appeared in *The Word Among Us* magazine, reprinted by permission. All other chapters appear in print here for the first time.

Cover and book design by Mark Sullivan

LIBRARY OF CONGRESS CATALOGING-IN-PUBLICATION DATA
Names: Wicks, Robert J., author, editor.
Title: Prayer in the Catholic tradition : a handbook of practical approaches / Robert J. Wicks, general editor.
Description: Cincinnati, OH : Franciscan Media, 2016.
Identifiers: LCCN 2016022194 | ISBN 9781632530325 (hardcover)
Subjects: LCSH: Prayer—Catholic Church—Handbooks, manuals, etc. | Prayer—Catholic Church—Study and teaching.
Classification: LCC BV215 .H755 2016 | DDC 248.3/2088282—dc23
LC record available at https://lccn.loc.gov/2016022194

ISBN 978-1-63253-032-5

Published by Franciscan Media
28 W. Liberty St.
Cincinnati, OH 45202
www.FranciscanMedia.org

Printed in the United States of America
Printed on acid-free paper
16 17 18 19 20 5 4 3 2 1

For Pope Francis
whose spirit of prayer and compassion
calls us to follow Jesus's command
to "go and do likewise"

CONTENTS

the former seminary for the north of England. He has also presented workshops and retreats in areas related to psychology, human development, sexuality, ministry, and spirituality throughout Europe, Africa, Australia, and Latin America. As well as being the author of numerous chapters and articles, he is coeditor of *The Christian Handbook of Abuse, Addiction and Difficult Behavior*, *Sexual Issues: Understanding and Advising in a Christian Context*, and *The Dark Night of the Catholic Church*, on the clergy sexual abuse crisis.

Chapter 5 ~ Contemplation | 65

Mary Frohlich, RSCJ, is Associate Professor of Spirituality and Director of the Ecumenical Doctor of Ministry Program at Catholic Theological Union in Chicago. She has written widely, especially on topics related to Carmelite spirituality, ecological spirituality, and the study of spirituality. Edited books include *The Lay Contemplative* and *St. Thérèse of Lisieux: Essential Writings*.

Chapter 6 ~ Spiritual Direction and Prayer | 77

William A. Barry, SJ, has been a Jesuit for sixty-four years and a priest for fifty-two. He has taught at the University of Michigan, Weston Jesuit School of Theology, and Boston College and engaged in administrative work in the Society of Jesus. He gives retreats and spiritual direction at Campion Renewal Center, Weston, MA, and elsewhere, and is the author of twenty books including (with William J. Connolly) *The Practice of Spiritual Direction* and *Praying the Truth: Deepening Your Friendship with God through Honest Prayer*.

Chapter 7 ~ Struggling in Prayer | 89

Ronald Rolheiser, OMI, is a speaker and writer whose books are popular throughout the world and whose weekly column is carried in more than seventy newspapers worldwide. He is President of the Oblate School of Theology. His books include *Sacred Fire*, *Prayer: Our Deepest Longing*, and the modern classic, *Holy Longing: The Search for a Christian Spirituality*.

Chapter 8 ~ Marian Prayer | 99

Mary Catherine Nolan, OP, is an Adrian Dominican Sister, a teacher, spiritual director, retreat director, and member of both the Mariological Society of America and the Ecumenical Society of the Blessed Virgin Mary. She is the author of *Mary's Song: Living Her Timeless Message* and contributed a chapter, "Mary and Islam," to *Mary for the Love and Glory of God*, as well as "The Magnificat" to *Mary: God-Bearer to a World in Need*. Currently retired, she continues to lecture and write.

Sacred Theology from the Pontifical Gregorian University in Rome. His concentration in theological studies was in Augustinian spirituality.

Hung Trung Pham, SJ, is assistant professor of Ignatian Spirituality at the Jesuit School of Theology of Santa Clara University in Berkeley. He received his Doctor of Sacred Theology (STD) from Commillas Pontificia Universidad de Madrid. He has published on various Ignatian topics as well as topics in Vietnamese Christianity and spirituality for immigrants. For the last twenty years, he has directed the Spiritual Exercises in Canada, Spain, the United States, Thailand, and Vietnam.

Rosemary Jeffries, RSM, a Sister of Mercy, is President Emeritus of Georgian Court University, Lakewood (NJ) where she served for fourteen years. She has a doctorate in Sociology from Fordham University and a Master's from Princeton Theological Seminary. She has served in various administrative and leadership roles for the Church and her religious community.

Keith J. Egan, TOC, is the Aquinas Chair in Catholic Theology Emeritus at Saint Mary's College, Indiana, where he founded its Center for Spirituality. He has been an Adjunct Professor of Theology at the University of Notre Dame since 1983. For his doctorate at Cambridge University, he studied under Dom David Knowles. He is also a fellow of the *Institutum Carmelitanum*, Rome, and a charter member of the North American Carmelite Forum. He has lectured in North America, England, and Rome and has written widely on Carmelite spirituality.

Constance FitzGerald, OCD, is a contemplative theologian and a member of the Carmelite Community in Baltimore, where she has served as prioress, formation director, archivist/historian, treasurer, and a long time spiritual director. She is a founding member of the North American Carmelite Forum and the National Association of Contemplative Sisters. She is known for her interpretation of the writings of Saint John of the Cross, particularly her essay, "Impasse and Dark Night," and her address to the Catholic Theological Society of America, "From Impasse to Prophetic Hope: Crisis of Memory."

Barbara Jean LaRochester, OCD, has been a religious sister for over sixty years. She is a member of the Baltimore Carmel, a seasoned spiritual director, prayer counselor, and retreat director. A Founding Mother of the National Black Sisters Conference, she is also the author of articles on the spiritual life.

Leopold Glueckert, OCarm., is the author of *Desert Springs in the City*, a concise history of the Carmelites. He contributes to the Carmelite Institute with lectures, articles, and retreats. A historian by training, he has taught for Loyola University, Catholic University, Lewis University, Loyola-Marymount University, and DePaul University, as well as at the Washington Theological Union.

Anthony J. Ciorra was ordained a priest in 1973. He is the author of *Everyday Mysticism*, coauthor of *Moral Formation in the Parish*, and editor of *Vatican II: A Universal Call to Holiness* on the occasion of the fiftieth anniversary of the Council. His latest book is *Beauty: A Way to God*. He is Assistant Vice President for Mission and Catholic Identity and Professor of Theology at Sacred Heart University. Prior to that, he was Dean of the Graduate School of Religion and Religious Education at Fordham University.

Lisa M. Cataldo is on the faculty of the Graduate School of Religion and Religious Education at Fordham University. She is a psychotherapist in private practice and writes in the area of psychology and religious experience as well as conducts retreats and workshops in psychology and spiritual life. She lived in the L'Arche Daybreak community with Henri Nouwen from 1995 to 1996 and was in spiritual direction with him.

Laurence Freeman, OSB, serves the World Community for Christian Meditation, a global contemplative family. Within this "monastery without walls" he travels to teach and lead retreats. He has also initiated the *Meditatio* program, which brings the fruits of contemplation to the wider, secular world. He is the author of several works, including *Jesus: The Teacher Within* and *Sensing God*, as well as a quarterly letter and a "daily wisdom" mailing. He is a monk of the Benedictine Olivetan Congregation.

Leslie J. Hoppe, OFM, is the Carroll Stuhmueller Distinguished Professor of Old Testament Studies at Catholic Theological Union. He is also the general editor of the *Catholic Biblical Quarterly* and associate editor of *The Bible Today*. He has written several books and numerous articles on biblical topics and biblical archaeology.

Paul Giblin, PhD, is Associate Professor Emeritus of Pastoral Counseling at Loyola University Chicago, the Institute of Pastoral Studies, where he began and directed the MA Program in Pastoral Counseling. His research, writing, and teaching have focused on marital spirituality, marital counseling, marital enrichment, counseling men, and the intersection of sexuality and spirituality.

F. Richard Spencer is Auxiliary Bishop of all the US military chapels (and US State Department embassies) in Europe and Asia for the Archdiocese, Military Services, U.S.A. Bishop Spencer served for thirty years in the active military forces, retiring as an Army Chaplain, Colonel. He has deployed to Iraq six times and to Afghanistan twice. His military awards include the Combat Action Badge for specific combat actions in Iraq on bloody Good Friday, April 9, 2004.

Michael Rubeling is currently a seminarian and transitional deacon at the Pontifical North American College in Rome.

Joyce Ann Zimmerman, CPPS, is the Director of the Institute for Liturgical Ministry in Dayton, Ohio. She is also Adjunct Professor of Liturgy at the Athenaeum of Ohio and has served as Theological Consultant to the USCCB Committee on Divine Worship, is recipient of the Notre Dame Center for Liturgy 2008 Michael Mathis Award, the 2010 Georgetown Center for Liturgy National Award for Contributions to the Liturgical Life of the American Church, and the Federation of Diocesan Liturgical Commissions 2015 Frederick R. McManus Award.

Joseph Tetlow, SJ, directs and preaches retreats and writes on Ignatian spirituality. His handbook *Choosing Christ in the World* has been widely applied for thirty years in languages as diverse as Portuguese and Chinese. His other books include *Making Choices in Christ* and *Finding Christ in the World*. He has been tertian instructor and was secretary for Ignatian spirituality in Rome. He is now writer-in-residence, Jesuit Hall, at St. Louis University.

Geraldine Fialkowski has taught in the MS and PhD Programs in Pastoral Counseling at Loyola University, Maryland, for twenty-five years. A licensed professional and board-certified Counselor with advanced degrees in Theology and Pastoral Counseling, her personal and professional interest is the integration of Spirituality and Psychology. In addition to her work with counselors, she is a retreat director and has lectured in Thailand, Chile, and Ireland.

Kieran Scott is Associate Professor of Theology and Religious Education at the Graduate School of Religion and Religious Education at Fordham University. His publications include a series of essays in the volume, *Critical Issues in Religious Education* (edited by Oliver Brennan), *Perspectives on Marriage*, 3rd ed. (edited with Michael Warren), and *Human Sexuality in the Catholic Tradition* (edited with Harold Daly Horell).

Kathy Coffey is the author of such books as *Hidden Women of the Gospels, Women of Mercy, God in the Moment, Mary, Immersed in the Sacred, When the Saints Came Marching In*, and numerous articles. She taught for fifteen years at the University of Colorado, Denver, and Regis Jesuit University and is the recipient of sixteen awards from the Catholic Press Association, as well as the Foley Poetry Award from *America* magazine, the Independent Publishers Book Award, and the Associated Church Press Award for Editorial Courage.

Encountering the Amazing Richness
of Catholic Prayer

A Brief Introduction to the Development
and Use of this Handbook

One of the most rewarding experiences for Catholics happens when they begin to discover the amazing scope of the approaches to prayer in the Catholic tradition. Oftentimes, they encounter a prayer form in another tradition or the secular world and turn to theirs to ask, "Where is an approach similar to this in *my* faith tradition?" and find it in a very rich form. For instance, if someone were to learn about mindfulness meditation and use it as a lens to see how a Catholic variant has been employed in the history of our Church, they would find a treasure trove in the writings of the fourth century desert mothers (*ammas*) and fathers (*abbas*) as well as in the more contemporary writings on centering prayer. In doing this, they would also learn what is different about this form of prayer when we use it as Catholics (meditation as a way of seeking to be one with God).

An insight into the depth and breadth of prayer in the Catholic tradition may also occur when people are on retreat and hear a presentation on Celtic prayer or involve themselves more deeply in Marian prayer, attend a novena for the first time, or read a book on how to pray with a particular saint like Teresa of Ávila or modern spiritual figures such as Thomas Merton and Henri Nouwen. And so, the ways Catholics can enter through the portals to greater spiritual intimacy is both far-reaching and fortuitous. Yet, there is often a lack of awareness of such avenues.

With this in mind, the idea behind the development of this handbook came from a desire to respond to the question: What if there were a *single* resource that both adult Catholics and those who minister to them (priests, vowed religious, seminarians, permanent deacons, lay pastoral ministers, chaplains, spiritual directors, and others) could have to better learn, practice, and share some of the major approaches used by Catholics through the centuries? In response to this question and the current lack of a broad, inclusive resource, *Prayer in the Catholic Tradition* was developed. Given its broad scope, in the following pages, there will be discussions of ways to approach prayer to match the different spiritual traditions, personalities, cultures, genders, and other differences all contained *within* the Catholic Church.

Is the coverage in the following chapters comprehensive? Most definitely. Is it exhaustive? Certainly not. The hope, instead, in gathering people familiar with the approaches they write on (and often have written a book or major article on as well), is to provide a resource that represents a respectable beginning to understanding through varied spiritual tributaries on the journey toward meeting and experiencing God. In addition, in creating this work, a goal was to be able to capture under one cover, leading and upcoming voices in the current Church who represent wisdom that can easily be lost when the books or articles they have written are no longer readily available and their conferences or homilies no longer given.

With these overarching intentions, the forty-five contributions in this book have been organized thematically into the following nine sections:

I: Welcoming and Deepening Our Prayer Life

II: Praying with the Gospels

III: Praying with Different Catholic Spiritual Traditions

IV: Praying with Classic and Contemporary Spiritual Guides

V: Praying through the Transitions and Challenges of Life

VI: Praying with the Old Testament

VII: Prayer among Different Types of Groups

VIII: Liturgical Prayer and Praying During the Liturgical Seasons

IX: Going Forward: Creative and Brief Reflections on Prayer

Since *Prayer in the Catholic Tradition* is a sourcebook, it is not meant to be read straight through from beginning to end (although certainly do so if you wish!). Instead, you are invited to begin in whichever section or with whichever chapter strikes a particularly welcoming chord at this point. To help with this decision, a short description of the contributions is presented at the beginning of each section.

Scholarly, pastoral, and experiential portals to a greater appreciation of prayer in the Catholic tradition are contained here. Some will be more relevant for you now given your current desires, needs, personality, spirituality, and maturity. This is as it should be. However, at some point, going beyond your current attractions to certain aspects of prayer is also recommended. In addition, every Catholic, every Christian, should be interested in certain sections ("Praying with the Gospels") no matter where they are in their spiritual journey.

A final suggestion in the use of the material in this book is tied to the desert wisdom that advises each of us to take on spiritually what we can and more will be given to us. The selections are meant to be read slowly, reflectively, and given time to be absorbed. In addition, they should lead to a change in how you approach God, the service of others, and your own life. If this book doesn't lead to greater love for God, others, and your own self, then of what real import is it? The knowledge you can gain *about* prayer in this book is significant. Yet, only with an attitude of humility will the experience of the contents of this book be truly fruitful for you. When you take the knowledge you learn in this book and add humility, you will get wisdom—and when you take that very wisdom and add it to the compassion God calls each of us to express, you will get love, and God is love. This is certainly worth remembering as you prayerfully read the following pages.

PART ONE

Welcoming and Deepening Our Prayer Life

PRAYERFULNESS

TRADITIONAL CATHOLIC PRAYER

GRACE AND PRAYER

DISTRACTIONS IN PRAYER: NUISANCE AND GIFT

CONTEMPLATION

SPIRITUAL DIRECTION AND PRAYER

STRUGGLING IN PRAYER

MARIAN PRAYER

This book appropriately begins with a chapter on Prayerfulness—being in the present with our eyes wide open to the presence of God within and around us. We are called to see prayer not solely as words to say but as a fruitful life to be lived. Beginning with Christ's invitation to experience a threefold attitude of presence, this opening chapter addresses the fruits of true prayerfulness, provides information on how we can strengthen our spiritual sensitivity, and offers reflections in responses to common questions about prayerfulness.

The second chapter of this first section is Dennis Billy's Traditional Catholic Prayer. He aptly notes, "The phrase 'traditional Catholic prayer' can mean different things to different people and therefore requires some explanation. If it is to be of any use in understanding the role it plays in the liturgical and devotional life of the Church, it must have a clear set of boundaries to set it apart from the prayer forms of other Christian and non-Christian traditions. The three words that make up the phrase— 'traditional,' 'Catholic,' and 'prayer'—offer a clue about how to proceed." He then proceeds to discuss fully what he means. He also reminds us of the complementary value of both Eastern and Western traditional prayer forms as being (in the words of Pope—now Saint—John Paul II) "the two lungs with which the Church must breathe," explores the often overlooked value of vocal prayer, and provides a discussion of how "traditional Catholic prayers often form key elements of large Catholic gatherings [assembled] to seek to deepen the faith of believers and galvanize their commitment to the Church."

In Grace and Prayer, Brian McDermott relates grace and prayer to each other "the same way oxygen and our lungs are related." To accomplish this, he reviews grace in Catholic tradition, provides an especially helpful section on "the kinds of grace when one is praying," points out how we can open ourselves to seek and receive God's grace, and addresses the theme of "cooperative grace" through a discussion of the experience of Teresa of Ávila's experience in what she terms the "seventh mansion."

In Distractions in Prayer: Nuisance and Gift, Brendan Geary focuses on a reality many of us have encountered in seeking a rich prayer life, namely, "having good intention to create a space of stillness in our lives is not a simple task." In response to this difficulty, Geary wants to "explore the experiences of people who choose to remain in silence for a dedicated period of time." He does this by sharing his own personal experiences, examining assumptions many bring to prayer, working with our bodies in prayer, examining difficulties that may arise in our minds during periods of alone time, reflecting on ways that distractions can actually be gifts, unmaking unrecognized idols in prayer, confronting the "darkness, embarrassing, or more disturbing parts of our own selves," and appreciating how the spiritual experience of Thérèse of Lisieux illustrates some of these major themes. The information in this chapter is a gift to both the novice and seasoned contemplative.

Contemplation by Mary Frohlich, then, guides us through an early understanding of the word *contemplation* to the contributions certain contemplatives and mystics have made to our current understanding of this form of prayer. Following this, Frohlich helps us appreciate how to weave contemplation into our daily lives rather than see it simply as representing a few moments apart from the bustle of our schedules. She concludes by presenting a simple contemplative practice, offering an appreciation of contemplation as a "fruit of spiritual maturity," discussing the paradox of the eruptive contemplative experience, and reflecting on contemplation as a mature stage in the life of prayer.

William Barry undertakes the important topic Spiritual Direction and Prayer. With a recognition that most of us at times wish we had someone to speak with about our prayer life, Barry discusses the history of spiritual direction since Vatican II. He then defines what he means by the term *spiritual direction*, addresses helping others with prayer by offering us illustrations, discusses the need for spiritual direction to help directees make better sense of their experiences, and shares his conviction that "God wants a personal relationship with us as human beings." Steeped in Ignatian spirituality and mindful of the seminal work on spirituality he wrote with Connolly, Barry helps us see both prayer and the process of spiritual direction as directing us to a greater personal friendship with God.

Ronald Rolheiser's Struggling in Prayer helps us understand the challenges of seeking to be prayerful in our complex and task-filled world, how to understand and address boredom in prayer, and ways to appreciate what false notions we might have of prayer as well as, in his view, how to address them (for example, "The solution is not so much new prayer forms and more variety, but rhythm, routine and established ritual.") He closes by addressing misleading feelings, inappropriate expectations, and occurrences of shame when they arise in prayer. He also discusses how the predominant culture around us needs to be unmasked for its "conspiracy against interiority."

The final chapter of this section then offers us an opportunity to return to some of our beautiful contemporary prayer roots as Catholics. Marian Prayer by Mary Catherine Nolan helps us appreciate anew how and why Mary is a model of true contemplative prayer. Discussion of how Mary is an intercessor and protector, inclusion of classical Marian anthems (*Salve Regina, Regina Caeli, Ave Maria Stelli, Stabat Mater*, and the *Angelus*) as well as popular devotions to Mary (with special mention of the rosary), are included. Even those familiar with Marian devotions are sure to learn something new.

CHAPTER ONE

Prayerfulness

~ Robert J. Wicks ~

> Every moment and every event of every person's life on earth plants some-
> thing in his soul. For just as the wind carries thousands of winged seeds,
> so each moment brings with it germs of spiritual vitality that come to rest
> imperceptibly in the minds and wills of [people]. Most of these unnum-
> bered seeds perish and are lost, because [people] are not prepared to receive
> them: for such seeds as these cannot spring up anywhere except in the *good
> soil* of freedom, spontaneity, and love.
> —Thomas Merton, *New Seeds of Contemplation*

In one catechism for African children, the answer given to the question, "Why did
God make you?" is "Because He thought you might just like it." If, as people of faith,
we lived more completely in this belief on a daily basis, we would better understand
both the Gospel and how to pray.

As Catholics, most of us wish to have a little more peace in our lives, experience
some joy, be able to understand ourselves better, and, if possible, lead a more meaningful, compassionate life. Surprisingly, even though Jesus has offered us "fullness,"
often we settle for so much less. How sad and unnecessary this is—especially since
at some level we sense there is so much more to a faith-filled life. Of course this is
nothing new. It can be traced back to the time of Christ.

For instance, in the beginning of John's Gospel, Jesus helps future disciples recognize what is essential to live more fully. He sees their need for meaning and asks,
"What are you looking for?" Later on he invites them to "Come and see," and then
chapter one closes, as does the end of John's Gospel, with the call, "Follow me."[1]
However, what the disciples will see in doing this is not what they expect or hope for,
and Jesus will teach them, on their way to greater faith and a richer life, that

- in place of power, the call is to friendship and service
- in place of success, the call is to faithfulness
- in place of certainty, the call is to face their doubts and
- in place of retribution, the call is to forgive and love

In essence, we are called now, as the disciples were then, to a new type of living. The
call Jesus had for them is the same call meant for us to take to heart now.

One of the primary ways we can respond to this call to live abundantly is by developing an attitude based on a rich sense of *prayerfulness*—that is, being in the present with our eyes wide open to the presence and reflection of God in all things, including ourselves. Given this, a true attitude of prayerfulness can be seen as *the* portal to a full, rewarding life. Yet, sadly, being prayerful is often poorly understood, so the gate to a life marked by meaning, joy, peace, and compassion isn't entered into by many of us—even those of us who claim we are religious.

Instead, many think they are being prayerful only when they are undertaking "religious" practices, usually on Sunday or in acts like grace before meals that are often performed in a perfunctory way. It is true that such acts are beneficial if they are done with the right intention, and they are certainly part of the process of inviting God into our lives. However, prayerfulness is much more encompassing than a series of acts. As a theologian once noted, "Jesus didn't call us to a new religion; he called us to life." And so, prayerfulness helps us discover a new center of gravity in our lives—one that will lead to closer divine intimacy, greater compassion, and a richer sense of self.

William Paulsell, in *Rules for Prayer*, recognizes this when he writes:

> It may be that you consider prayer as being more than simply just asking God for things you want.... You may have developed certain disciplines, setting aside time for prayer on a regular basis. You now pray frequently, having integrated prayer into your normal routine... You offer prayer of praise, thanksgiving, confession and intercession. You have also begun to meditate on scripture and to ponder more carefully things you have often taken for granted or practiced by rote.
>
> But still something is lacking.... [You're] doing all the right things and making a sincere effort, often at the sacrifice of the elements that once were important in your life. However, God still seems very distant, and while you feel good about yourself for living a more disciplined religious life, you still wonder if there is something more that ought to be happening.

A serious spiritual life is more than just following the rules and doing things the proper way. More fundamental is the attitude with which we enter into and carry on our quest.

A Three-Fold Attitude of Presence

Jesus offered us the framework for such an attitude of prayerfulness in his response to the oft-asked classic rabbinical question, "What is the greatest commandment?" Like other rabbis, he reached into Torah for the answer and selected from Leviticus and

Deuteronomy. And, like other rabbis, he used the approach of putting people at ease with the first half of his response and then spiritually pulling the rug out from under their complacency through the second part of his answer!

In the first part, he selected a heavy precept from one of the 613 precepts adhered to by Pharisees of the day by stating, "You must love God with your whole heart, your whole mind, and your whole soul." In response, it is easy to imagine the people listening and nodding their heads in assent. After all, if you were religious, how could you disagree with such a statement? Then, as they were taking in the familiar, he reached down and grasped a lighter precept and held it up *on the same level* as the heavier precept and said, "*and* you must love your neighbor as yourself."

In emphasizing the love of neighbor of course he was reemphasizing the message that Moses received from God during the Exodus that the Israelites must not only find God vertically in prayer but also horizontally through each other. However, he was indicating that this also must be a circular movement by emphasizing that we must love our neighbor *as ourselves.* True compassion includes *self*-compassion. After all, why would you treat yourself any different than God would treat you? We must recognize that one of the greatest gifts we can share with others is a sense of our own inner peace and a healthy perspective, but we can't share what we don't have.

And so, an attitude of prayerfulness must include a balance of the right sense of presence to God, others, and self. To open ourselves to this occurring naturally and continually, as John of the Cross would note many years later, we also need to seek to make space for God in constantly new and different ways. This involves recognizing that often in the darkness, God is making new space in us to experience the Divine at a deeper level. As in the case of the apostles present at the Transfiguration, for us to welcome God in such moments, we must be "awake" to experiencing God in our lives. In this way, what is being offered us that is new or unfamiliar can be recognized and responded to with a sense of openness, passion and compassion.

The gifts for us, and those whom we touch in life, are too great to be missed. In prayerfulness, when theonomy (God's will) and autonomy (our will) intersect, true freedom, peace, and joy become possible. Then we can receive and freely share with our unique God-given gifts (what theology would speak of as our charisms and psychology would refer to today as "signature strengths"). Prayerfulness becomes transformed from something we "do" or "add" to our lives into a new vision of life in which the daily events are part of an actual ongoing pilgrimage. We welcome Jesus's desire to "make all things new" each moment rather than leaving Jesus's words of conversion as merely a Sunday wish unable to produce real fruit.

What Are the Fruits of an Attitude of Prayerfulness?

Following Jesus's call to love God, others, and self, the goal of prayerfulness is to see as clearly as possible what God is gifting us with each day so that we, in turn, may "go and do likewise" and reach out to others. This spiritual journey is aided to some extent by keeping our "psychological fingers" on the pulse of our cognitions (ways of thinking, perceiving, and understanding) in order to be as clear as possible as to what the motivations of our behavior are each day. In this way we can really appreciate more accurately what the fruits of our outlook and actions are. You see, sometimes what appears to be initially good really turns out to be something else, but with a prayerful attitude in place we are more apt to take note of it.

It is easy to miss what God is calling us to be and do when we are lost amid the fog of our own intentions and desires, even though they seem good. For instance, a very religious Catholic woman once consulted me about her life. She admitted to being a worrier, upset about the negative reactions from her children (some of them already young adults) to her hovering over them, and her confusion about not enjoying what she considered the good life she had. After speaking with her for a while, I responded, "You seem to be a woman of commitment and prayer. Am I correct in assuming that?"

"Yes, I'd like to think so," she replied.

I then commented, "Well, that is what confuses me. I wonder why you are leaving out an important prayer."

"Which one?" she asked.

"Well, let me illustrate by telling you a story that leads to a question. There was once a young girl who was given a gift for her birthday. What would be the best way she could thank the person who gave it to her? She could say 'thank you' and that would be lovely. Or she could fully enjoy the gift given to her and then freely share it with her friends. Which act of gratitude would be more profound, do you think?"

"Probably the response that was more than words."

"Yes, I agree, and the same is true of the life we have been given by God. Our prayer of gratitude for the beautiful life we have is to enjoy and share it freely, not looking for the results *we* want. An attitude of prayerfulness is so important because, really, when you come down to it, the quality of our lives depends upon it. As physician and Catholic novelist Walker Percy once wrote, 'What if life is like a train, and I miss it?' When we lack a sense of prayerfulness, this becomes more possible than we might imagine, especially when we are seeking the best for others."

What I shared with her was in line with the basic philosophy of prayerfulness that calls us to love God deeply, do what we can for others, and please, take good care of ourselves.

An attitude of true prayerfulness helps straighten out our thoughts on how to best do this. One way is by keeping a gentle, clear eye on the *fruits* of our prayer life to see *if* our prayer is really true. Sometimes this can be difficult for us to accomplish. For example, a professor involved in the ministry of spiritual formation once approached me about how to assist a young man who seemed to be very negative in his response to others at the school. The first thing I asked is whether the youth spent quiet time alone each day with the Lord. (As Henri Nouwen noted in his book *Way of the Heart* time in silence and solitude with God can straighten out our thoughts.) He responded by saying, "Oh yes, he is very dedicated in spending an hour before the Blessed Sacrament in prayer in our chapel. But as soon as he comes out, he gossips about the faculty and those with whom he is studying."

From these negative fruits, we recognize that, for the most part, he is probably not spending time alone with God but mistakenly with his own inflated ego. He is not in silence listening to God but to his own opinions and because of this remains quite self-righteous rather than having the opportunity to be truly righteous, which would be evidenced by his own humility and compassion toward others. The fruits of true prayerfulness are clear. (See Table 1.) By recalling them, we can better monitor ourselves as well as be able to bring them up for discussion in spiritual direction or in informal discussions about our prayer life with wise, trustworthy friends.

TABLE 1 | THE FRUITS OF TRUE PRAYERFULNESS

Prayerfulness can

- lift us out of stagnant, obsessive thought patterns
- alert us to when we are not living the experience of life but merely wandering around in an envelope of thought, thinking we are alive
- move us out of the thicket of preoccupations, fears, anxieties, and worries about the past or future by having us "simply" be where we are
- help us to appreciate that *all* things/people/situations change
- give us the space to step back and get unglued from our desires, demands, and attachments so we can have the freedom to flow with what is
- enable us to get in touch with the invisible bonds of shame, loneliness, secrets, addictions, hopes, and other places in our hearts where we have expended a great deal of energy in avoidance
- help us forgo the comfort of denial and avoidance for the peace that allows us to fear nothing but instead welcome all of our emotions, cognitions (ways of thinking, perceiving, and understanding), and impulses with compassion and clarity

- open up true space for others by opening it up in ourselves
- help us to imitate Jesus and others we admire by reaching out to others who are in need
- enable us to see our defenses, failures, and growing edges as opportunities for new wisdom and openings to life (because rather than judging, we are intrigued by them)
- ask us if we are relating to ourselves with kindness and clarity
- awaken us to our habitual, possibly deadening styles of thinking, believing, and behaving
- allow us especially to become freer by taking "the sacred pause" spiritual guide Tara Brach suggests when confronted with suffering (this pause is made up of a desire to recognize what is happening, allowing it, and experiencing it rather than trying to jut figure out or control it)
- help us see that permanent problems are so because of the way we formulate them, thus teaching us that loosening our grip on such ways of seeing our world makes all the difference
- set aside the way we have created meaning so all things can be made new
- increase our appreciation of how little things can produce emotional peaks and valleys on our lives
- develop our respect for both formal prayer (meditation) and informal approaches (prayerfulness and spiritual mindfulness) that increase our awareness of "the now" during the day
- incorporate simple practices, such as taking a few moments to notice something enjoyable, appreciate our own small, beautiful acts, and slow down when we are caught up in a sense of mindless driven action
- encourage us to wonder more about what thoughts, emotions, and events help us create peace rather than suffering
- teach us that being spiritually aware is more natural when we don't seek it aggressively or with expectations or fear that it won't produce dramatic results
- have us welcome and learn from, rather than label and reject, so-called negative experiences such as boredom
- help us to be clear and sort things out as well as deepen ourselves
- encourage humility, help us see our foibles, and over time increase the enjoyment we have in being with ourselves and with God
- result in less dependence on reinforcement by others while at the same time setting the stage for taking a healthier part in community

- protect our inner fire by helping us see when we need to withdraw for time alone and also uncover time within our daily activity where we can take a few breaths and center ourselves, rather than be disturbed that we are being delayed or postponed in our travels or activities
- make us more in tune with the voice of God that is continually being drowned out by society and our own habitual voices

Slowly reflecting on the above fruits can help us to better notice and more fully embrace them.[2]

Once again, prayerfulness is being in the now with our eyes open to the presence of God. An attitude of true prayerfulness helps us to be more open and attuned to what God is teaching us, especially during those moments that face us with our own failings and help us embrace humility. When we are truly prayerful, we recognize that sin is not the final word, but *instead* it may be the flashpoint for new deeper self-knowledge and the freedom it brings. The reason for this is that when you take knowledge and add humility you get wisdom, and when you take that wisdom and add it to compassion you get love. And God is love. Also, as the fourth- and fifth-century desert fathers and mothers teach us: Humility helps us constantly become aware of the need for God's grace.

I think an awareness of this was behind the following well-loved prayer by Thomas Merton (from *Thoughts in Solitude*):

> I have no idea where I am going. I do not see the road ahead of me. I cannot know for certain where it will end. Nor do I really know myself, and the fact that I think that I am following your will does not mean that I am actually doing so. But I believe that the desire to please you does in fact please you. And I hope that I will never do anything apart from that desire. And I know that if I do this, you will lead me by the right road, though I may know nothing about it. Therefore will I trust you always, though I may seem to be lost and in the shadow of death. I will not fear, for you are ever with me, and you will never leave me to face my perils alone.

STRENGTHENING OUR PRAYERFULNESS

Anything that increases our awareness of the presence of God is part of a rich rule of prayer. (See Table 2.) Most important, we need to have the right way of looking for the reflections of God in our lives and within ourselves. To do so, we must be nonjudgmental, clear, honest, and gentle. Rather than seeing life as we would like it, we can be open to how it truly is so we can respond to it in ways that appreciate what we are being taught by God. A prayerful attitude is the key to discernment. It helps us see who God is calling us to be and what God is asking us to do *now*. By following these insights step by step we can, with God's help—like the flashlight on a dark night illumining the path right in front of us—eventually find our way.

....

TABLE 2 | KEY ELEMENTS OF A RULE OF PRAYER (PARTIAL LISTING)

Liturgy

Meeting God in the Eucharist, the Word, and in each other on Sunday and during the week is a great opportunity to receive a new insight from preparing or hearing the homily, finding an opportunity for intimacy with God, and encountering or sharing the presence of God with, and in, others.

Faith sharing

These are conversations with others that are not only about God, Mary, the saints, and the church, but also about goodness, mercy, and meaning. These are all ways of sharing our living faith.

Formal prayer

Praying the psalms, Liturgy of the Hours, contemporary prayers, spiritually themed poetry, and employing a classic prayer form like the rosary, are all ways of using formal prayer gifted to us, especially when we ourselves are lost for words.

Reflection during the day

Racing through our life, attending to small details, chores, and demands seems both natural and practical. But how reasonable is it to rush to our grave and miss our own life? During the day, we can take mini prayer breaks when we have a cup of coffee, stroll down the hallway, do the laundry, walk to the bathroom, or take a moment between when the phone rings and we answer the call. All those times are ideal moments to say even one word ("Lord," "gentle," "compassion," "love"…) to remind us who we are called to be and what we are called to do in a world often compulsively racing in another direction.

Spiritual reading

Sharing in the spiritual wisdom of others is a beautiful way to encourage us to live a deeper, more fulfilling, and compassionate life. The list of people and writers we can turn to for insight, support, new perspectives, and challenges are endless. A regular visit to a Catholic bookstore and online visits to various Catholic publishers are good ways to find books that will enhance our sense of prayerfulness.

Sacred Scripture

Theologian Karl Barth suggested that when we read sacred Scripture our own identity should be on the line so that when we ask "What is this book saying?", it will challenge us in return with the question, "Who is it that is asking?" Reading

Scripture regularly—even for just a few moments—allows us to enter into the history of God's relationship with the world and the discernments, both faithful and not, people have made in response to situations. By imaging ourselves in the story we can find ourselves in new ways. Without a deep knowledge of sacred Scripture we run the risk of faith becoming too general, our relationship with God too vague.

Journaling and theological reflection

So much can be learned at the end of the day when we jot down our thoughts and feelings and prayerfully sit quietly with them. In a theological reflection, we look at the objective (what happened) and the subjective (what I thought and felt about them) and in light of the Gospel and our spirituality, we seek to learn and change in an effort to be more responsive to God in concrete ways. Love as a general principle is worth nothing; love lived out in the Spirit is everything.

Prayer in silence and possibly solitude

Prayer in which we seek to empty ourselves of all thoughts and images (*apophatic*) and those quiet times where we image God in rich and creative ways (*kataphatic*) are essential cornerstones of the spiritual life. In silence, and possibly solitude, we have the opportunity to listen to the Lord and be quiet in our hearts with God. Prayer in silence and solitude can straighten out our thoughts and help distance us from what is aching our hearts at the moment. Even two minutes a day in silence and solitude can make all the difference in how we both enjoy and live our lives in rewarding ways. Regularity is more important than length of time, although hopefully more time will be seen as attractive and necessary in the search to embrace the reality of God's friendship. Such prayer is the royal road to spiritual wisdom and a centered life in the Spirit.

Hospitality

How we welcome people we meet in our life is a significant part of prayerfulness. If we say all kinds of religious words and make sacrifices and spiritual proclamations but are not generous with those we meet, then we are not being prayerful. After all, how can we say we love God if we treat God's children poorly? Even those we meet briefly are worthy of respect and attention.

Seeing God as a CEO rather than a friend will not be helpful on this road. Anything we can do to take to heart Jesus's words "You are my friends" (John 15:14), is essential. If God is love and we are seeking God, one of the royal roads to true divine encounter lies in being a loving person ourselves. This involves a willingness to open our eyes to *receiving* love as well as freely offering love to others.

Receiving love is difficult for some and a task at times for all of us. We must see that an ability to be prayerfully receptive aids us in our ability to be compassionate. Pope John XXIII said that whoever has a heart full of love always has something to share. It is also cross-cultural. The Catholic Ibo of Nigeria have a saying, "It is the heart that gives; the fingers just let go." Friendship with the Lord and others is a "circle of grace" that is at the heart of prayerfulness. So two essential prayerful questions are, "How are we opening ourselves to receive love?" and, "What within us prevents us from encountering God everywhere?"

Some of the answer to these questions can be found when we examine our spirit of gratefulness. Brother David Steindl-Rast suggests that we open our eyes so we can uncover and enjoy what is already around us that is gift. He says the problem with many of us today is that we leave the house with a mental list and on that list is what we will be grateful for. He suggests throwing away the list in order to welcome all of the gifts from God already in our lives that we have failed to recognize and embrace.

Prayerfulness is not designed to pull us away from life; it allows us to enjoy it fully, recognize and appreciate our own God-given talents rather than put them under a bushel basket, and like the good Samaritan, "Go and do likewise" by giving freely not expecting *anything* in return (not a smile, thanks, following our suggestions, appreciating our efforts…*nothing*!) As far back as Ezekiel, we are told that it is not being successful that matters, it is faithfulness. And to be truly faithful is not possible until we embrace the reality of prayerfulness—which once again is being in the present with our eyes wide open to experiencing the presence of God *everywhere*: in the Eucharist, the Word of God, in ourselves, others, nature, joy, peace, and even failure, loss, and suffering.

Prayerfulness is *a way of being*. In silence and solitude (which are essential), prayer becomes much more than breaking away from life for a few moments, hours, or days. Instead, it is a time to let the dust of the day and our minds settle so we can see more clearly and celebrate the gift of our birth, the opportunity for compassion, and an appreciation of everything without being attached to any of it. A spirit of prayerfulness is metaphorically like the air we breathe and the water we drink: so necessary for life but runs the risk of being taken for granted or not being attended to as it should. As Teresa of Ávila advised her sisters, prayerfulness takes determination, persistence, a commitment to grow, and a dedication to be friends with God by nurturing healthy concrete relationships with others. And the theocentric living that Teresa and a spirit of prayerfulness encourage allow us to enjoy life without being captured by elements of it—be they positive or not. When we live this way, we can both see life clearly and flow with it in the best way possible.

We recognize this in people who are naturally in tune with the Spirit of God. Robert Lax, minimalist poet, convert to Catholicism, and best friend of Thomas Merton, is a good example. Merton shared in his autobiography *The Seven Storey Mountain* that Lax "had a kind of inborn direction to the living God." S. T. Georgiou, in a memoir of his interactions with Lax during the time Lax lived on the isle of Patmos (*Way of the Dreamcatcher*), said, "Those who left him broke into warm and carefree smiles, having been uplifted by an energy born of a lifetime of theocentric living.... I remember how after spending long evenings with Lax, I would leave his hermitage and feel as though I had landed on the earth for the first time."

In response to one of Georgiou's questions, Lax's reply reflected his deeply prayerful approach to life. He said, "Try to live as purely and simply and as gently as you can. Relax. Be flexible. Be forgiving. Be creative. Be loving. You are a peacemaker. Those who cross your path may need you, as you may need them." At another point he amplified this guidance further by adding, "First you come to see where you are in the world, where others are, and then you begin to take care of all things that come your way, as many as you can." Lax reflects the reality that prayerfulness is the music to a fulfilling life and that each of us in our own way of living a spirit-filled life are called to provide unique "lyrics" for living it out. His words are certainly worth emulating. We can sense the theocentric source of them, that God was his moving force.

When we live with God at the center of our lives, we start to see that even the traps and pitfalls of the spiritual life can be met with a sense of intrigue rather than with self-blame or projecting our lacks onto the behavior of others. And so, we become interested in ferreting out our

- failure to see all God is offering us
- blocks to listening carefully to what we are being given and told *now* so we may live and share life more fully in the present moment
- blindness to how we are in rivalry with God or seeking to tie the hands of God— sometimes in the name of "good"
- lack of appreciation of what others can teach us about ourselves so we can be more open to encountering the living God in a deeper way
- not attending to those times when the veil between the physical and the spiritual is thin so we can experience a sense of wonder and awe

When we face ourselves constantly, honestly, and with understanding, we even see sin differently. As Jack Kornfield notes in *A Path with Heart*, "We must fully allow each difficult state we have rejected…to come and tell their story until we know them all and let them back into our heart…. The purpose of the spiritual life is…to see the ways we get trapped by our fears, desire, and anger, and to learn directly our capacity for freedom…. [Our very issues are the] 'manure for enlightenment.'"

With this in mind, my own book *Prayerfulness: Awakening to the Fullness of Life* identifies some of the essential characteristics of prayerfulness that can help us mature spiritually as well as break open the dramatic and daily occurrences of our lives. Knowing them is essential for us to welcome the Spirit of God's activity in deeper, more creatively nourishing ways. They include

- a clear awareness of what you are experiencing, thinking, or feeling without judging yourself or others
- a sense of intrigue about yourself and others without projection (blaming others), self-condemnation, discouragement, or unrealistic expectations
- more interest in discovering the presence of grace—namely the wonderful gifts of God—rather than merely focusing on your accomplishments
- an appreciation of being in the now and a willingness to return to the present when you are drawn into the past or begin to be preoccupied by the future
- a spirit of "unlearning" and a willingness to see life differently that is inspired by the Lord's call to "making all things new"
- a non-ego-centered approach to life that recognizes it isn't all about *me*
- a willingness to recognize, embrace, and flow with change
- a spirit of receiving life as it is without reaction or rejection
- a gratitude and an openness to being nourished by God in everyday life
- a focus on those activities that create well-being instead of suffering for others… and *ourselves*
- an appreciation of the beauty of patience and enjoying the *process* of life rather than solely looking forward to completions or successes
- an interest in letting go of the "secular training" we have received in grasping, being envious, angry, and unkind and developing instead an openness to sharing without an expectation of getting anything in return, being intrigued by our responses so we can learn from them rather than responding by being defensive or self-indicting, and slowing down rather than straining toward goals (even "good" ones)
- an avoidance of comparing ourselves favorably or unfavorably with others
- a greater desire to be sensitive to how our words and actions affect others
- an openness to "spiritually touching" all of our denial, loneliness, shame, and negative feelings about ourselves with compassion, rather than running away from them

- an allowance of information, negative and positive, familiar and unfamiliar, to flow to us without being obstructed or modified by our ego or fears
- an increased desire for transparency and being persons without guile in the way we live so we can help purify—rather than contaminate with our defensiveness —the spiritual atmosphere in which we and others live

Practicing, not simply knowing about, these elements of prayerfulness allows us to receive from God the gifts meant for us. In addition, we will be able to both face and benefit from our gray and dark times as well as be a gift to those with whom we come into contact. This is theocentric living at its best. No one ever masters prayer or gains, once and for all, the perfect attitude of prayerfulness. But interest in expanding and deepening one's appreciation and practice of prayer and a prayerful attitude is a true cause for celebration.

Act upon your desire to be intentionally prayerful. Otherwise, you run the risk of stepping on that Grace. As Flavian Burns, Thomas Merton's final abbot and my own spiritual mentor, once told me, "When you receive the Grace to pray, Bob, you can turn to other things—a phone call, reading, maybe another task, and they will be blessed. Yet, when you return to being intentionally prayerful again after doing these things, the Grace to meet, not simply know about, God in prayer may be gone for the moment. Be sensitive to those gifted moments and act upon them in ways you can when they are there." What he was pointing out is that the veil covering the spiritual source of life may be very thin at times. When this occurs, we must look, see, and take in the vision of God's presence in new, transforming ways. Promptings to experience life differently may be sometimes strong and sometimes weak, but our response to them can allow us to experience each new day as an opportunity to be more open to the possibility of a beautiful change. Life no longer becomes simply a series of activities that must be done but becomes a pilgrimage to experiencing God in the common and unusual.

Prayer doesn't usually change the events of life, even though intercessory prayer may in fact lead to such change. But prayer infuses the events of life with new light so we are able to see people and things more clearly in ways that might not have been possible before. If you have ever lived or spent an extended time in another country, you may have experienced something similar to this sort of prayerful awakening. As Peter France wrote in *Patmos: A Place of Healing for the Soul*, "Living abroad changes you. There is, first of all, the continual learning process of coming up against local people who are different, who see the world through different eyes and respond to it in ways that have been shaped through generations of different conditioning. Then there is the experience of meeting people who are also abroad and whose behavior, on that account is changed." Living a prayerful life is like this because we begin to see life in many different, new ways. We become open to being conditioned by God and not the world, in the narrow sense of this term.

COMMON QUESTIONS ABOUT PRAYERFULNESS

Prayerfulness is predicated on a threefold sense of *presence*:

- Presence to God: prayer
- Presence to others: compassion
- Presence to self: fullness

To close this introduction, I want to recount a number of common questions asked of both classic and contemporary spiritual mentors, organized according to these three senses of presence. Comments provided after the questions are not meant to provide *the* answers. Their purpose is to prompt the development of one's own more personal, complete response. In doing this, the ownership for new motivation, thinking, and action by you can more readily lead to a more encompassing and personally owned attitude of prayer and prayerfulness going forward. This ownership will also then increase your motivation to act upon, not merely think about, the key elements of a rich life of prayerfulness.

PRESENCE TO GOD: PRAYER

To shift from the sense of prayer I have now to something greater seems attractive. However, when I realize all the ways I can move ahead in my prayer life, I feel almost overwhelmed. Is there a natural place to begin?

Abba Macarius provided good advice when he said, "Don't try to understand everything. Take on board as much as you can and try to make it work for you. Then the things that are hidden will be made clear." Simply look at "the rule of prayer" provided in this chapter, pick something from the list that you are already involved in and ask yourself, how might I deepen it? So, if you are attending Sunday Mass, what might you do to deepen your presence there? Also, might you participate in liturgy at other times? Then, pick something else out of the list that you are not doing at present, possibly reading sacred Scripture on a regular basis, and select a time to read one chapter from one of the Gospels and sit with it for a few moments.

I hear and read about other people's spiritual experiences that seem so rich, but I don't seem to have these experiences myself. Am I doing something wrong?

One of the reasons people who are seeking to lead a more vibrant and meaningful life and don't experience what is spiritual or God-given more readily is because their view is too narrow. Thomas Merton felt the presence of God by placing himself in front of God during periods of silence and solitude. He tried to empty himself and not expect anything but be open to what happened. To paraphrase his advice, "Don't sit in the silence waiting for God to speak, let the silence speak for God." He was also aware of God's reflection in the changing of the seasons—for instance, by being in tune with God when reading the psalms or listening to the rain on the roof.

Some of us wake up well rested on a Saturday morning. Our mind is alert, the sun is shining, and we feel at peace and grateful. That is a form of prayerfulness in which we can sense God's hand holding ours if we are open to seeing it that way.

Start recalling moments of calm, surprise, relaxed friendship, or the voice of a beautiful choir or the insight given into Scripture in hearing or preparing a homily, and you will see all these things as spiritual reflections. Moreover, they will help you be attuned to others in the forthcoming days. Rabbi Abraham Joshua Heschel wrote in *God in Search of Man*, "We teach children how to measure, how to weigh. We fail to teach them how to revere, how to sense wonder and awe. The sense of the sublime, the sign of the inward greatness of the human soul and something which is potentially given to all [people] is now a rare gift." If we are to pass these gifts on to our Catholic children, we must first seek to enhance the gift of sensitivity in ourselves.

Spiritual awareness may be something obvious, such as witnessing construction workers remove their hats when the church they are building is having the crucifix raised above the altar. It could be something subtle such as seeing snow falling or hearing children laugh. Whatever it is in us or nature or circumstances, prayerfulness teaches us to have the eyes to see and ears to hear. As Henri Nouwen noted in *Making All Things New*, "The beginning of the spiritual life is often difficult not only because the powers which cause us to worry are so strong but also because the presence of God's Spirit seems barely noticeable. If, however, we are faithful to our discipline, a new hunger will make itself known."

What should I do when I sit in silence and solitude? Most of the time I find my mind is wandering or I am bored.

A spiritual master recognized this reality for all of us and said, "You try and you try and then you go deeper." Part of our problem in such situations is that we come to meditation (formal prayer) with expectations and see prayer almost like a lottery in which, if we are lucky, we will win a spiritual prize or awakening. The discipline and approach to time in silence with God is simple: find a quiet place, read a bit of Scripture if you wish, take a word or phrase that you can repeat quietly to yourself as a centering prayer, and relax with the Lord. If and when your mind wanders, simply come back to the word. This time is meant for you to relax with God. During that time, God will relate to you in different ways. Your only job is to be present. Moreover, during this time, the elements of your life will wind up taking their proper place.

In *The Genesee Diary*, Henri Nouwen said that Abbot John Eudes Bamberger, who was his spiritual director at one point, taught him,

> When you are faithful in [silent meditation]…you will slowly experience yourself in a deeper way. Because in this useless hour in which you do nothing 'important' or urgent you have to come to terms with your basic powerlessness, you have to feel your fundamental inability to solve your or other people's problems or change the world. When you do not avoid that experience but live through it, you will find out that your many projects, plans, and obligations become less urgent, crucial, and important and lose their power over you. They will leave you free during your time with God and take their appropriate place in your life.

What parts do passion and patience play in prayerfulness?

When we are privileged to encounter someone whom we would see as prayerful, we are drawn to their sense of holiness and their attitude of trust in the Lord that comes from a sense of centeredness. This arose, in part, because they had the eyes to see the importance of letting God pervade their lives. Consequently, they had the passion that translated into discipline to keep a rule of prayer. However, they also had the patience to appreciate that wisdom coming from joining humility with knowledge takes a lifetime. They were willing to learn, relearn, and overlearn the lessons put forth in sacred Scripture, spiritual writings, and the example or mentorship of others. The question for us is: Are we willing to do the same?

What really is the benefit of having a "rule of prayer"?

The purpose of a rule of prayer is to create the conditions within ourselves so we will be more awake to movement of the Holy Spirit. We can be quite intelligent or street wise; many of the saints were certainly that way; but without a rule of prayer, we run the risk of becoming more ego driven. Whereas, when we seek to be in connection with God, there are opportunities to be free from egotism and more open to new knowledge and a spirit of simplicity that will have us center ourselves on what is freeing, calling us to more readily live out of this spirit.

A rule of prayer can also help us recognize and experience a spiritual yearning for what this calling truly is: a desire and willingness to take actions to become more alive and share the joy of life with others.

Presence to Others: Receiving and Offering Friendship and Compassion

Friendship would seem to be a natural part of prayerfulness. Specifically, are there some essential elements for me to be aware of in this regard?

Receiving and offering friendship is an essential element of prayerfulness. For our part, we need a rich faith community: one that includes friends that challenge, encourage, tease, and inspire us. It is important to have such voices in your life. Accessing them by visiting, calling, e-mailing, or writing on regular basis is not a luxury but a necessity. At the other end of the spectrum, take care with those who would laugh, belittle, or do things that may seek to consciously or unconsciously erode your faith. Even if it is not malicious, this can cause harm, because if I drop a rock on your head on purpose or by mistake, you still will get a bump!

Is having a spiritual director or mentor important?

Psychiatrist Carl Jung once asked, "Where are the wise and wonderful [persons] of old who did not merely talk about life but actually lived it?" We need people like that in our lives and others might turn to us to accompany them on the spiritual journey as well. It is especially important to have someone we can turn to during periods of physical transition or when moving to a new phase of spiritual maturity that requires us to let go of what might be familiar.

As a spiritual friend to others, what are some of the things I need to keep in mind?

There are a number of key themes to reflect on when being a spiritual presence for others either formally or, more often than not, informally.

- Possessing simple values in line with the Gospel, rather than what the world says, is important. So being rich means possessing spiritual insight; being successful means being faithful in our efforts to be compassionate; being accomplished means having some sense of self-knowledge and self-control. This is very different from how the world sees these values playing out in people's lives.

- Being intrigued by both our strengths and growing edges or weakness, rather than trying to cover these by blaming others, picking on or unduly praising ourselves, or by becoming discouraged.

- Being serious about taking some alone time each day.

- Seeing life as a pilgrimage in which we don't simply know about God but have a passion to experience reflections of the divine everywhere—even in, *especially* in, the darkness we encounter.

- Appreciating that what good we can do comes from the stillness with God that serves as a center of gravity for each of our days.

- Not wasting energy on what we cannot change (aging, sickness, death...) but focusing on what we can change (our perception of life and what we can do for others).
- Recognizing that prayer is not simply sitting in church saying words out loud or to ourselves but is manifested in our character and the way we live out each day.
- Accepting people where they are at and calling them to be all they can be.
- Being able to laugh at ourselves and know more readily when our ego is in play.
- Not asking others to have faith in us but instead manifesting in our way of interacting with them that we have faith in them.
- Appreciating the reality of impermanence—in other words, that we may die at any moment and will surely die at some point—so that we can more fully value the people and gifts in our life *now*.

There are so many demands in my life, I am not sure that I have the space for compassion to more people than are looking to me now. Does that make sense?

A minister who became famous was asked by his sister to help a man in need. He replied that he was already overwhelmed by all of the activities in his life and that he was not able to help any more people. "Even God is not that busy," his sister said.

Often the drain on us is not because we are doing too much but is because of how we view what we are already doing. When we are concerned about success, worried about how we will look to others, or discouraged that what we do doesn't have the impact we wish, it can be very draining. Instead, what we need to focus on is how we can be faithful in doing what we can in situations and then letting God take care of the residue. We talk a lot about grace but are often closet Pelagians. By that I mean we believe in our hearts that it *all* depends on us. This is a form of grandiosity that can lead to an erosion of a compassionate heart.

PRESENCE TO SELF: FULLNESS

When I think about all that I have and the needs of others, I wonder whether it is all right for me to take out time for myself or even enjoy what I have?

This question indicates a possibly distorted view of one of the most elusive gifts in the spiritual life: gratitude. Starting out the day with a prayer of gratitude does many wonderful things for us and those with whom we interact. For instance, eyes of gratitude allow us to actually see all we are being given. We don't prejudge what is good but anticipate encountering it in new ways. Second, when we feel grateful we give more freely without strings being attached. This allows us to use our bounty in ways that feeds others in need. Because it is natural, doing it without guilt, duty, or fear makes a difference not only to us but to those on the receiving end.

It is easy for me to delude myself. How might I see my sins or shortcomings more clearly?

One of the best ways is to *first* look at your gifts. We have each been given many talents to enjoy and share with others. When we are clear about them, it provides us with the security and interest to look further at how we may fall short in some areas or under what circumstances our very gifts become growing edges that we need to address. For instance, if we are passionate about what is good, that is wonderful. However, under certain circumstances, we may feel insecure, and instead of being passionate, we may become egotistical and seek to draw attention to ourselves and our deeds.

Self-knowledge seems important in the spiritual life. Are there some key ways to foster self-awareness?

There is an axiom about the spiritual life: the more you know about yourself, the more you can know about God; the more you know about God, the more you know about yourself. Self-knowledge is essential, and there are many ways to enhance it:

- Take a longer period of quiet time to make resolutions regarding how you will lead your life in slightly or dramatically differently ways so you are more responsive to the Spirit. This can be done on your birthday; New Year's Eve; just before September, when the year begins for most people who are in school, have children in school, or feel that the fall represents the start of the year after vacation time during the summer; or at other junctures when change is afoot.
- Have a circle of friends who will give you clear feedback in a helpful way.
- Seek formal or informal spiritual direction or, when needed, short-term counseling/mentoring/coaching.
- Be sensitive to the information that arises during prayer.
- Keep the psychological fingers on the pulse of your emotions and then check your cognitions (ways of thinking, perceiving, and understanding) so you can see what is giving rise to such feelings.

ONE FINAL NOTE

Attending to how we live in the life of the Spirit is essential. However, in our efforts to have discipline, be attentive, and be both responsible and responsive to the call to live fully and share our life freely, we must not fall into the trap of being overly concerned about progress. In the words again of Thomas Merton:

> Do not be too anxious about your advancement in the ways of prayer because you have left the beaten track and are traveling by paths that cannot be charted and measured. Therefore leave God to take care of your degree of sanctity and contemplation. If you yourself try to measure your own

progress you will waste your time in futile introspection. Seek one thing alone: to purify your life in God more and more, to abandon yourself more and more perfectly to His will and to love Him more exclusively and more completely, but also more simply and more peacefully and with more total and uncompromising trust.

This, I think, is grand advice for all of us!

---

1. All Scripture quotations are from the *New Revised Standard Version of the Bible.*

2. Robert J. Wicks, *Prayerfulness: Awakening to the Fullness of Life* (Notre Dame, IN: Sorin, 2009), 100–103

CHAPTER 2

Traditional Catholic Prayer

~ Dennis J. Billy, CSsR ~

Prayer is nothing but "the raising of one's heart and mind to God or the requesting of good things from God."[1] It is necessary for salvation and has been called "the great means of salvation."[2] As Alphonsus de Liguori points out: "What profit is there in sermons, meditations, and all other means pointed out by the masters of the spiritual life, if we forget to pray?"[3] Traditional Catholic prayer is often the faithful's first exposure to this transforming spiritual exercise. Its origins lie in Jesus's instructions to his disciples on how to pray.

Jesus taught his disciples to address God as "Abba, Father" and encouraged them to open their hearts and minds to God as a child would to a loving parent.[4] The Our Father, the prayer he taught them and which Tertullian calls "a summary of the whole Gospel," is one of the most traditional forms of Christian prayer.[5] Deeply rooted in the Catholic tradition, it rests at the center of the Scriptures and prayer of the Church. Thomas Aquinas calls it the "most perfect of prayers," since it contains in essence everything the heart wishes to say to God.[6] It has found its way into the heart of the Church's liturgy and informs many of the traditional forms of Catholic prayer that have evolved over the centuries. Traditional Catholic prayer takes its inspiration from these simple, childlike words of Jesus to his heavenly Father. In one way or another, they all cry out, "Abba, Father."

THE ROOTS OF TRADITIONAL CATHOLIC PRAYER

The Church is a vital mystical organism with its origins in the person of Jesus Christ and the outpouring of his Spirit on the nascent community of believers at Pentecost. This living organism both traverses and transcends history; it remains the same in the midst of change and throughout its earthly sojourn seeks to keep its focus on its heavenly homeland. The Second Vatican Council teaches us that the Church is on a pilgrim journey and that prayer is one of the means by which the people of God sustain themselves.[7] In its many forms, traditional Catholic prayer supplies a substantial part of this daily spiritual diet.

From its earliest days, the community of believers devoted itself to the teaching of the apostles, the communal life, the breaking of the bread, and the prayers (see Acts 2:42). Although these early prayers reflected those of the Jewish religion in which the Christian faith has its origins, they evolved within the believing community as it adapted itself to new cultural contexts and became enculturated into the life of the peoples it was seeking to evangelize. As the Church's prayer evolved over time, the Lord's Prayer provided believers with some basic guidelines for distinguishing authentic prayer from false, inauthentic, and even harmful forms. Jesus, in other words, taught his disciples that authentic prayer (1) viewed God as personal, (2) was dialogical in nature, (3) offered praise and adoration to God, (4) surfaced authentic needs and petitions, (5) embraced every dimension of our human makeup, (6) was both communal and personal, (7) reverenced both words and the silence between them, (8) had an eschatological, "already but not yet" dimension, (9) emphasized complete and utter dependence on God, and (10) sought first and foremost the will of God. Jesus taught his disciples how to pray, not merely by giving them words to say (he warned them not to babble on as the pagans [see Matthew 6:7]), but by praying before them and showing them how to converse with God intimately and familiarly as a child speaks to a loving parent.[8]

What is more, the Lord's Prayer would make its way into the very heart of the Eucharistic liturgy, ensuring that personal prayer was intimately related to the Church's liturgical worship—and vice versa. The presence of the Lord's Prayer in such traditional Catholic prayers as the rosary, meditations, visits to the Blessed Sacrament, and novenas confirms this orientation of private devotional prayer forms to the Church's liturgy and highlights the cohesive role it plays in the Church's life and worship. The Lord's Prayer, in this respect, is one of the earliest forms of traditional Catholic prayer, one that the early community of believers learned to pray together and alone, and one that had special significance for them in the breaking of the bread. Its two Gospel versions may very well have taken their final shape within a liturgical setting of the early believing community and been preserved in the New Testament canon with a wide array of other liturgical hymns, prayers, and formulas.[9]

Its Universal Sense

The phase "traditional Catholic prayer" can mean different things to different people and therefore requires some explanation. And if the explanation is to be of any use in understanding the role that Catholic prayer plays in the liturgical and devotional life of the Church, it must have a clear set of boundaries to set it apart from the prayer forms of other Christian and non-Christian traditions. The three words that make up the phrase—*traditional, Catholic,* and *prayer*—offer a clue about how to proceed.

The word *traditional* suggests that these prayer forms are embedded in popular piety and devotion, structured according to set guidelines, and rooted in the living tradition of the Church. The word *Catholic* implies that they are closely associated with one of the many theological and liturgical rites within the Catholic Church, the largest of which are the Roman and Byzantine rites. The word *prayer* indicates that they address a personal God, are fundamentally dialogical in nature, and focus on one or more key aspects of human existence: the physical, the mental, the spiritual, and the social. When properly understood, "traditional Catholic prayer" flows out of the living tradition and public worship of the Church and embraces a wide range of accepted approaches to the divine, the three most celebrated of which are *oratio* (vocal or embodied prayer), *meditatio* (meditation or mental prayer), and *contemplatio* (contemplation or wordless prayer).[10] These various prayer forms are deeply rooted in Catholic life, spirituality, and practice and must be included in any comprehensive catalogue of traditional Catholic prayer forms.

When taken in its larger, more general sense, the phrase "traditional Catholic prayer" speaks of any approach to prayer that has become clearly identified with Catholic faith and recognized by the faithful as a legitimate devotion to be practiced on a regular basis as a means to growth in virtue and holiness. Because the Church is a vital, living organism, one that develops and matures over time as a sapling sprouts from a small seed and grows into a mighty tree, these prayer forms have appeared at different moments in Church history to meet the needs of the faithful and enable them to continue their pilgrim journey. When seen in this light, traditional Catholic prayer embraces a wide spectrum of set vocal, meditative, and contemplative practices. In its more specific sense, however, it refers to certain popular devotional practices that, at various points in the Church's history, have seized the Catholic imagination and accompanied the faithful in their spiritual journey.[11]

PRAYING WITH BOTH LUNGS

These traditional prayer forms resemble one another in that they propose certain set spiritual practices that immerse Catholics in the mysteries of the faith and seek to shape their minds and hearts to reflect the mind of Christ and the Gospel values he espoused. They differ from each other, however, in their Eastern or Western spiritual provenance and in the particular emphasis they give to the external expression of truths of the faith.

In the Catholic West, for example, these traditional prayer forms include such practices as Eucharistic adoration, the rosary, the Sign of the Cross, novenas, stations of the cross, Ash Wednesday ashes, Lenten fast and abstinence, visits to the Blessed Sacrament, the litany of the saints, grace before meals, the morning offering, and chaplets—to name but a few. In the Catholic East, by way of contrast, they focus on such practices as the veneration of icons, the devotional use of prayer ropes, and the vocal, meditative, and contemplative use of the "prayer of the heart" or Jesus Prayer: "Lord Jesus Christ, Son of God, have mercy on me, a sinner."[12] Wherever they come from and whatever their particular emphasis, these prayer forms have generally been actively promoted by the Church magisterium and embedded themselves so deeply into popular Catholic imagination that they have become closely tied to its identity.

Pope John Paul II once described the Eastern and Western Christian traditions as the two lungs with which the Church must breathe.[13] Although this statement refers to the importance of working toward the unity of the Catholic and Orthodox churches, it pertains equally well to those Eastern Christians who have always maintained unity with the Church of Rome. In the context of "traditional Catholic Prayer," the pope's statement highlights the complementary nature of these prayer forms despite their subtle differences in approach. As the Western liturgy tends to be more kataphatic and the Eastern more apophatic in their approaches to the divine mysteries, the traditional prayer forms flowing from these liturgical traditions follow suit.

If the Western forms emphasize the role of the passion and death of the crucified Lord in humanity's redemption and the Eastern forms highlight the process of *theosis* in humanity's divinization, the two complement each other in profound ways and can be used by Catholics from both traditions to deepen their relationship with God and foster a spirituality that is truly one, holy, catholic, and apostolic. By being sensitive to the wide range of traditional prayer forms within the Catholic faith, the community of believers will deepen its understanding of Jesus's prayer that "all may be one" (see John 17:21) and will be able to breathe with two lungs, walk on two legs, and fly with two wings to their spiritual homeland.

Its Characteristics

Regardless of their origin in time or place, the various forms of traditional Catholic prayer share a number of distinctive characteristics that set them apart and make them clearly identifiable. The following list, while in no way exhaustive, draws out their main contours and offers some keen insights into their makeup and relation to one another. Its purpose is to show that prayer forms as diverse as Eucharistic Adoration, the rosary, the Sign of the Cross, novenas, stations of the cross, Ash Wednesday ashes, Lenten fast and abstinence, visits to the Blessed Sacrament, chaplets, the veneration of icons, and the Jesus Prayer, share more in common than one may commonly think and make the same kind of contribution to Catholic spirituality.

To begin with, the traditional Catholic prayer forms cited above are distinct from the Church's liturgical worship, yet intrinsically oriented toward it. The notion that they in some way are in conflict with official Catholic worship is a gross misperception and overlooks the important way in which private devotions flow from the liturgy and lead their devotees back to it. Although abuses are always possible, they are more often than not the exception rather than the rule. Although some traditional prayer forms are more closely associated with the liturgy than others (Eucharistic Adoration, the veneration of icons), each of them seeks to deepen a person's relationship with God so that he or she may be able to participate more fully and thus share more deeply in the fruits of the sacraments. This important link between traditional Catholic prayer and the liturgy flows from the Catholic understanding of the Eucharist as "the source and the culmination of all Christian life" and sees no conflict between authentic devotion and the Church's official public worship, since both are rooted in and flow from the same redemptive, re-creative, and sanctifying mysteries of the Christ event.[14]

These traditional Catholic prayer forms are generally repeated at regular intervals in a set pattern that conforms to the rhythmic nature of the spiritual life. In this respect, they parallel the cyclical pattern of the Church liturgy (the liturgical seasons, Sunday Mass, the seven hours of the daily office) and are meant to instill in the faithful a habit of prayer that shapes their awareness of the presence of God. This repetitive nature fosters in the lives of the faithful a spirituality of practice that allows their actions to rise from deep within their hearts. It recognizes that a regular regimen of prayer impacts a person's attitude, thoughts, and actions for the better. In doing so, it helps a person to integrate faith and reason, spirituality and morality, contemplation and action in a way that, at one and the same time, is honest, human, and thoroughly Catholic. The repetitive character of these prayers, however, also carries with it an important spiritual caveat. If care is not taken, they can devolve into merely rote, external exercises devoid of spiritual meaning and done merely to get through them. In such instances, they can impede a person's progress in the spiritual life and actually do harm to his or her soul.

Traditional Catholic prayer plays an important role in the imagination of the faithful as bearer of the Catholic identity. Such diverse prayer forms as Corpus Christi processions, devotions to Our Lady, and intercessory prayers to the saints (to name but a few) allow the faithful to take ownership of their faith and give concrete expression to it in their daily lives. They enable those participating in them to embrace their Catholic identity, enter into relationship with the communion of saints, and claim for themselves a deeper sense of corporate belonging. Practices such as Ash Wednesday ashes, Lenten fast and abstinence, the blessing of throats on the feast of St. Blaise, perpetual adoration, visits to the Blessed Sacrament, and the Eucharistic Holy Hour accentuate key aspects of Catholicism that set it apart from other Christian churches and ecclesial communities. Moreover, in those times when, for whatever reason, the lay faithful had little opportunity to participate in the liturgy, these devotions gave them an opportunity to play a more active role in the celebration of their faith. When the Second Vatican Council encouraged more active participation of the faithful, it placed these traditional forms of devotion in perspective by emphasizing their orientation toward the liturgy.[15] If they decreased in popularity for a time, they are now being retrieved and discovered anew as genuine bearers of the Catholic identity.

In helping to sustain this identity, traditional Catholic prayer forms have also helped to preserve unity in the midst of cultural diversity. Being both one *and* universal, the Catholic Church extends to all corners of the earth and has embraced a multiplicity of peoples from a wide variety of cultural, racial, and ethnic backgrounds. Traditional Catholic prayers have been one way in which the Church has enabled the faithful to incorporate their cultural background into their Catholic identity. This phenomenon is seen most clearly in the Catholic devotion to Mary, whom the faithful venerate under a number of titles, many of which are tied in a special way to a particular people or nation (for example, Czestochowa for Poland, Lourdes for France, Fatima for Portugal, Aparecida in Brazil, Guadalupe for Mexico). The people of these nations take great pride in their national Madonna, while also recognizing that she is a gift to the universal Church and, indeed, for all humanity. Something similar also occurs with the devotion to patron saints in certain cities or nations (such as San Gennaro in Naples, St. Patrick in Ireland, St. Anthony in Italy) or of certain professions, diseases, or situations (St. Joseph for carpenters, St. Peregrine for cancer, St. Jude for hopeless cases). These popular devotions help to preserve the Catholic identity by giving the faithful a deeper sense of belonging to the communion of saints, assuring them that they have intercessors with God on their behalf, and the hope that they too might one day become "friends of God."[16]

Traditional Catholic prayer can assume many forms. They include private practices such as wearing a devotional scapular or a medal of Our Lady, reciting set vocal prayers like the morning offering or grace before meals prayers, blessing oneself with holy water as a person enters or exists a church, or a making a short heartfelt prayer such as "O God, come to my assistance" and "Lord, make haste to help me."[17] They also can include group services such as Forty Hours Devotion, novenas in honor of the Blessed Mother, and processions celebrating the patron saint of a local church or parish community. Group devotions often incorporate set prayers such as the Our Father, Hail Mary, and Glory Be, and Sign of the Cross, along with various hymns into the rhythm of their time together. Some traditional Catholic prayers such as the rosary and the divine mercy chaplet can be prayed either in private or a group setting, either silently or aloud, and in a fast-moving or more meditative manner. Since they are rooted in the living faith of the faithful, these private and group devotions arise at different moments in the history of the Church and typically evolve over time. They are not considered obligatory by the Church but often weave themselves into the daily rhythm of life of the faithful.

Traditional Catholic prayers stem from a sound Christian anthropology that affirms the physical, mental, spiritual, and social dimensions of human existence. They address the physical by engaging the various senses through the use of gestures, movements, incense, art, colorful vestments, singing, and other means. They embrace the mental by immersing their adherents in the mysteries of the faith and encouraging them to ponder the relevance of these mysteries for their lives. They look to the spiritual or contemplative by incorporating moments of silence at appropriate times and by ensuring that these devotions are prayed with reverence. They emphasize the social by conducting these devotions in common and orienting them toward the Church's celebration of the sacraments, especially the Eucharist. While some of these traditional prayers may emphasize one or more dimension over the others, the most popular ones, that is, those most deeply ingrained in the Catholic imagination, are flexible enough to address and engage them all. The rosary, for example, is typically fingered on a string of beads (the physical), it proposes specific mysteries upon which to meditate (the mental), it uses the words simply to focus the mind so that the spirit might rest contemplatively in the Lord (the spiritual), and it can be prayed in a group setting to emphasize the community of the faithful (the social). Other traditional prayer forms such as the visits to the Blessed Sacrament, the stations of the cross, and divine mercy chaplet are also very adaptable and can easily engage the person on every level.

Traditional Catholic prayer is both Christological and ecclesial. It understands that prayer is rooted in an act of faith, which is a gift of God made possible by the saving action of Christ's incarnation and paschal mystery. Whenever the faithful pray to God with sincere minds and hearts, they pray through, with, and in Christ, in the unity of the Holy Spirit, who vivifies and sanctifies the Church through her life and sacraments. Traditional Catholic prayer is fundamentally oriented to Christ and his body, the Church, and its sacraments. It recognizes that Christ continues to live out his paschal mystery in the lives of the faithful and understands that prayer is the key to remaining united to him at all times. The attraction of traditional Catholic prayer lies in its deep roots in the living faith of the faithful and in the awareness it imparts of Christ's continuing presence among them. These prayers bind the faithful together not merely in their Catholic identity, but also to Christ and his mystical body. This intimate union with Christ and his Spirit allows them to enter into the presence of the Father and underscores the reality of God's love for humanity.

Although fundamentally oriented toward the liturgy, traditional Catholic prayer can survive without it. Since it operates in the realm of popular piety and does not absolutely require partaking in the sacraments, it can exist apart from the hierarchical priesthood upon which the administration of the sacraments is dependent. This independence enables these prayer forms to sustain the faith in those times when the faithful, for whatever reason, do not have easy access to the sacraments and must depend on their own courage and resiliency to sustain the faith. When seen in this light, such prayers are a major means by which the Catholic faith, in the absence of the ordinary means of salvation, can be passed on from one generation to the next. In this respect, they complement the sacramental life of the Church and provide a cushion of spiritual practice upon which it can rely in times of persecution and hardship. The Church needs structures and mechanisms that enable it to continue its mission in the harshest of circumstances. In the past, these traditional prayers have sustained the faithful in the most dire circumstances and helped them to survive (and even thrive) when access to the Eucharist was rare and, at times, even nonexistent. There is every reason to believe that, should the occasion arise, they will do so in the future.

Because of its popular tone and emphasis on vocal prayer, there has, at times, been a tendency to downplay traditional Catholic prayer and relegate it to a level of secondary importance. Such an attitude fails to recognize the true value of such prayer and overlooks the basic spiritual principle that God meets his people where they are and then gives them a little more. It also reveals an unhealthy spiritual prejudice that those seemingly further along the way can look down on popular prayers and devotions as practices for the ignorant and unlearned, not for those of the spiritual elite who have left such childish practices behind. Such an attitude forgets that the true masters of the spiritual life have always had a place in their hearts for such prayers and often returned to them as the "meat and potatoes" of the spiritual life. It also represents a blatant misunderstanding of spiritual progress in thinking that a person must leave such practices behind as he or she becomes more familiar with the ways of discursive mediation and contemplation. Rather than abandoning such practices, those interested in the spiritual life should recognize their intrinsic worth, acknowledge them as authentic forms of prayer recognized by the Church, and seek to find ways of integrating them into their lives in a balanced way.

Finally, traditional Catholic prayers often form key elements of large Catholic gatherings that seek to deepen the faith of believers and galvanize their commitment to the Church. Events such as retreats, missions, pilgrimages, and marches utilize these prayers to give the faithful a single voice in their prayer to God. The vocal and social nature of prayers such as the rosary and the divine mercy chaplet, hymns such as the *"Salve Regina"* and the *"Tantum Ergo,"* and paraliturgical practices such as Benediction and various novenas allow large groups to join together in prayer with little preparation or rehearsal. Moreover, many traditional Catholic prayers such as the Hail Mary, the Our Father, the *Gloria Patri*, and the Sign of the Cross are so deeply ingrained in the Catholic imagination that they do not require printed versions for distribution among the people but can be prayed spontaneously. They are also generally simple prayers that can be easily taught, remembered by heart, and passed on from one generation to the next both within the family and through local Catholic institutions such as schools and orphanages, as well as various guilds and sodalities. Taken together, these prayers forge a sense of solidarity that orients the Catholic faithful toward the Church's mission. As such, they are instruments of conversion for a person's mind, heart, and soul in the spirit of the Gospel.

These characteristics do not exhaust the meaning of traditional Catholic prayer but merely seek to underscore its value for spiritual life and offer some general features for understanding and better appreciating its place in the Church's life and worship. If nothing else, they reveal the main contours of how these simple prayers embody profound truths and are an important means through which the faith has been passed on from one generation to the next.

CONCLUSION

In one way or another, traditional Catholic prayer accompanies the faithful throughout their lives. It is not an inferior form of prayer to look down on or hope one day to outgrow, but a staple food of the spiritual life that nourishes every dimension of a person's makeup. It does not conflict with the Church's liturgy but is intrinsically oriented toward and thoroughly fed by it. It encompasses many shapes, adapts to a variety of contexts, and orients the faithful toward the transcendent through a set of religious practices. It supports a focused "spirituality of practice" that has captured the heart of the faithful, shores up their Catholic identity, enables believers to take ownership of their spiritual lives, and gives their faith a marked personal imprint.

As with any spiritual practice, traditional Catholic prayer can sometimes fall short of its intended purpose. Such a tendency is usually due not to the prayer itself, but to the way it is practiced. If care is not taken, the faithful can concentrate too much on its external dimensions and lose sight of the way it shapes their souls and prepares them for a deepening of their interior lives. Its orientation to the liturgy can also be overlooked or even set in competition with it. For this reason, its various forms and practices need to be examined at times to insure that the faithful understand its proper place in the life of the Church and the important role it plays in their spiritual lives. They also need to be adapted to the changing circumstances of Catholic life and practice.

Although traditional Catholic prayer is sometimes taken for granted, it is a mainstay of Catholic life and practice and plays an important role in forging popular Catholic culture. Some of these prayers are the first ever learned by the faithful and often the last to leave their lips in their dying moments. Taken together, they seek to deepen the faith of the Catholic community and encourage them in their journey through life. They are simple, easy to learn, repetitive, petitionary, and deeply rooted in the Catholic imagination. They represent an important means by which the faithful nourish their spiritual lives and grow in their relationship to Lord. What is more, they are humble prayers, ones that take to heart the Church's teaching that those who pray will be saved. Considered valid complements to the Church's liturgical worship, they carry the faithful to the threshold of the sacred and help to mediate the process of conversion of mind and heart that is central to the Catholic faith and its ongoing call to discipleship.

1. St. John Damascene, *De fide orthodoxa*, 3.24 (PG 94.1098C) cited in *Catechism of the Catholic Church*, 2559 (Vatican City: *Libreria Editrice Vaticana*, 1994), 613. See also "Catechism of the Catholic Church," The Holy See, http://www.vatican.va/archive/ENG0015/__P8Z.HTM.
2. Alphonsus de Liguori, *Prayer, The Great Means of Obtaining Salvation and All the Graces Which We Desire of God*, in *The Complete Works of Saint Alphonsus de Liguori*, ed. Eugene Grimm, vol. 3, *The Great Means of Salvation and of Perfection* (Toronto: Redemptorist Fathers, 1927), 23–28. See also Dennis J. Billy, *Plentiful Redemption: An Introduction to Alphonsian Spirituality* (Liguori, MO: Liguori, 2001), 91–104.
3. Liguori, *Prayer, The Great Means of Obtaining Salvation*, 20.
4. See Mark 14:36. All quotations from Scripture come from the *Holy Bible: New Revised Standard Version with Apocrypha* (Oxford: Oxford University Press, 1989). *Abba* is Aramaic for "Father." See *New World Encyclopedia*, s.v. "Abba," http://www.newworld encyclopedia.org/entry/Abba.
5. Tertullian, *De oratatione*, 1 (PL 1.1155), cited in *CCC* 2761.
6. Thomas Aquinas, *Summa theologiae* II–II, q. 83, a. 9, resp, cited in *CCC* 2762.
7. Second Vatican Council, *Lumen Gentium* (The Dogmatic Constitution on the Church), 48–51, in *Decrees of the Ecumenical Councils*, ed. Norman P. Tanner, vol. 2 (Washington, DC: Georgetown University Press, 1990), 887–891.
8. See *CCC* 2759–2865. See also Servais Pinckaers, *The Sources of Christian Ethics*, trans. Mary Thomas Noble (Edinburgh: T&T Clark, 1995), 155–158; Dennis J. Billy, *The "Our Father": A Prayer's Power to Touch Hearts* (Liguori, MO: Liguori, 2012), 7–110.

9. See Matthew 6: 10–13; Luke 11:2–4. For the roots of the Our Father in liturgical prayer, see John Chrysostom, *In Matthaeum homiliae*, 91.4, cited in *CCC* 2767–2772.

10. See *CCC* 2700–2724.

11. For a thorough listing of the various forms of traditional Catholic prayer, see *Daily Roman Missal*, 7th ed. (Woodridge, IL: Midwest Theological Forum, 1993–2011), 2260–2480. See also "Traditional Catholic Prayers" at Loyola Press, http://www.loyolapress.com/traditional-catholic-prayers.htm.

12. For an extensive treatment of the Jesus Prayer, see *The Philokalia: The Complete Text*, trans. and ed. G.E.H. Palmer, Philip Sherrard, and Kallistos Ware, 4 vols. (Boston: Faber and Faber, 1979–1995). See also Denis J. Billy, *The Way of a Pilgrim: Complete Text and Reader's Guide* (Liguori, MO: Liguori, 2000),75–99.

13. John Paul II, *Ut Unum Sint* (encyclical letter On Commitment to Ecumenism, May 25, 1995), 54, http://w2.vatican.va/content/john-paul-ii/en/ encyclicals/documents/hf_jp-ii_enc_25051995_ut-unum-sint.html.

14. Second Vatican Council, *Lumen Gentium*, 11 in *Decrees of the Ecumenical Councils*, 2:857. See also http://www.vatican.va/archive/hist_councils/ ii_vatican_ council/documents/vat-ii_const_19641121_lumen-gentium_en.html.

15. See Second Vatican Council, *Sacrosanctum Concilium* (The Constitution on the Sacred Liturgy), 26–32 in Tanner, *Decrees of the Ecumenical Councils*, 2:826–27.

16. For more on the saints as the "friends of God," see Peter Brown, *The Making of Late Antiquity* (Cambridge, MA: Harvard University Press, 1978), 54–80.

17. Rooted in the psalms (70:1), such brief, passionate prayers for help were favored by the Desert Fathers and made their way into the monastic recitation of the psalms and opening prayers of the Church's Liturgy of the Hours. See, for example, John Cassian, Conferences, 10.10, Classics of Western Spirituality (New York: Paulist, 1885), 125–140.

CHAPTER 3

Grace and Prayer

~ Brian McDermott, SJ ~

Grace and prayer are related to each other the same way oxygen and our lungs are related. The dependence is absolutely necessary if prayer, like our lungs, is to survive and flourish. With this in mind, this brief chapter will explore various ways in which grace supports, orients, and fulfills personal prayer in the Catholic Christian life.

GRACE IN THE CATHOLIC TRADITION

God relates to what is not God in two distinct but profoundly interrelated ways. God creates what is not God every moment of its existence. While Scripture gives priority to God's act of creating in the past, every second that a creature exists God is causing its existence. Creation is a totally free act on the part of God. It is abundantly appropriate that God creates, because goodness is diffusive of itself and God is infinite Goodness. But, nevertheless, the existence of each and every creature and all creatures viewed as a vast system is pure gift from the divine other.

The second gift, transcending and enveloping the gift of causing a creature to exist, is the gift of God's own life and love, God's own self, to creatures. This is called the gift of divine self-communication, divine self-donation. This gift is grace properly so called. From the first moment of their existence, creatures are the recipients of God's self-communication to them. This affects their situatedness from the beginning, prior to any decision on the part of creatures (should they be blessed with freedom as we humans are).

God's self-communication to creation is Trinitarian in form. The primordial, invisible abyss and source of all that is (God the Father) pours God's self out on creation through the sending of the incarnate Word of God and through the pouring out of the Holy Spirit, the bond of love between the Father and the eternal Word. The Holy Spirit, thus poured out, capacitates creatures to receive the Father through the sending of the Word incarnate by liberating creatures from sin and drawing them into the divine life and into the mutual relationships that constitute the triune God.

This second gift also involves any and all ways in which God's self-communication transforms created realities blessed with freedom: by purifying and forgiving them (healing grace), by raising them up into deep intimacy with God through Christ in the Spirit (elevating grace), and by bringing them to final consummation (grace as final glory). Prayer has everything to do with grace thus described, for both are all about relationship.

It is important to recognize that we never experience grace as such in our daylight explicit consciousness. Grace is not a thing or object or item in the field of our awareness. It is more like an attunement, or an atmosphere, horizon, or tonality, of our awareness. Karl Rahner, the great German Jesuit theologian, reminds us that grace shows up in our experience at times when we seem to live beyond our ordinary limits, when we hope beyond all particular worldly hopes, when we sacrifice ourselves and our safety and comfort for our neighbor, or when we yearn for the cause of truth and justice. Christian faith discerns the presence and impact of grace at work in times of self-transcendence such as these.[1]

KINDS OF GRACE WHEN ONE IS PRAYING

Every time that it occurs to me to quiet down and remember that I am in God's presence and to turn to God in praise, thanksgiving, or need, God's grace was silently and invisibly working in me prior to my consciously turning to God. This is God's grace—the Holy Spirit—working as *prevenient* grace in me, that is, working in me without my cooperation (*in me sed sine me*, as the tradition puts it: "in me but without me").

While I am praying, God's grace is at work in me as well. The Holy Spirit "comes to the aid of our weakness; for we do not know how to pray as we ought, but the Spirit itself intercedes with inexpressible groanings. And the one who searches hearts knows what is the intention of the Spirit, because it intercedes for the holy ones according to God's will" (Romans 8:26–27).[2]

In John's Gospel Jesus tells us, "whatever you ask in my name, I will do" (John 14:13). I take this to mean that our prayer is answerable when and to the degree that we allow the Holy Spirit to fashion us into Jesus's relational identity, that is to say, into our being sharers in Jesus's relationship of surrender to the Father and submission to the persuasive sway of the Holy Spirit. When we pray thus formed, our prayer will be begging God for those primary realities that Jesus invited us to pray for: the hallowing of God's name, that is, the gathering of all people into the peace of God's kingdom, the coming of God's reign, the doing of God's will on earth as in heaven, enough sustenance for the day, the gift to forgive others as the coming to fruition of God's forgiveness of us, and the gift of not being put in situations where our faith might crumple but rather being protected from the evil one. Considered this way, our creaturely prayer for graces is rooted in the uncreated grace that is the Holy Spirit at work in our hearts.

The Catholic tradition appreciates this grace in a special way. It is called "cooperative grace," and St. Bernard of Clairvaux gave it signal expression.[3] According to this wise author, every good act which fosters our growing union with the Father through Christ in the Spirit and our deepening love for our blessed and broken world is brought about totally *by* God's grace and totally *in* human freedom. This is a wonderful example of good theology expressing a gracious humanism. God and creatures are not in competition. God does not have to carve out a space in creation for God to act. God's action in our midst spells the enhancing of the human, of the creaturely. As Father Rahner liked to say: "The creature grows in healthy autonomy vis-à-vis God not despite but precisely because of the creature's growing dependence on God."[4] This is grace *in me et cum me* ("in me and with me," with my cooperation).

Thomas Aquinas wrote that the fruit of cooperative grace is called merit.[5] Thus understood, merit is not some claim my prayer has on God; it is not some debt God owes me in justice because I pray this way or that way. No, merit properly understood is the new situation of intimacy and partnership that has come to existence by virtue of God's free involvement in my praying and my free involvement in that same praying. (If only Martin Luther had known this Thomistic understanding of merit!) Prevenient grace desires to become cooperative grace.

Cooperative grace, at work in us pilgrims, seeks in turn to become *consummating grace*, which comes to pass when we are gathered totally and definitively into the Trinitarian life with all those who died as friends of God. This will be the resurrection of the dead and the transformation of this heaven and this earth into the new and thoroughly fulfilled heaven and earth, when God will be all in all. We stammer when we try to say much about this final condition of blessedness.

Petitionary Prayer: Seeking God's Grace

Asking for healing of body or psyche is a fundamental faith conviction of Christians that God as creator and self-communicator desires the making whole of all persons, communities and the planet earth. In the light of this divine desire, when I ask God for my friend to be healed of her cancer, a number of things are going on. I bring to God my desire for my friend to become free of the cancer. Bringing that desire to God is part of the honesty of my engagement with God.

I also need to seek the grace to align myself with God's will for me and for this person. In terms of the Gospel, this is an act of desiring to pray in Jesus's name. It is important that I ask God to align me with what God desires in this situation. I am also called to trust that God and Jesus want what is ultimately best in this situation. Thus, it is important that I pray for trust in Jesus's desire for my friend, his desire for the very best flourishing of my friend. I need not assume that I possess that trust in Jesus; I can and ought to ask for it to become strengthened in me.

Many things can happen now with regard to my friend: the cancer can stay the same for a long time, it can go into remission, or it can get worse. If the cancer stays the same or gets worse, I am not called to believe that God positively desires those outcomes. Cancer arises, grows, or diminishes because of many worldly factors and influences. What I am called to believe is that God wants on the deepest level that my friend—and I—grow in ever-deepening union with God. That is the ultimate good, the ultimate flourishing, in God's eyes, and it is supposed to be my ultimate good as well.

There is a big element of mystery in all this. God is infinite mystery. God's relationship to creatures as creator and self-communicator is mystery. How my prayer affects the web of creaturely relationships and how it opens up "thin places" (as Celtic spirituality expresses it) for God's grace to work are also mysterious: we cannot get on top of all that. Sometimes prayer seems to contribute to the healing (as far as we can see). Sometimes it seems as though it does not have an effect on the level of creaturely interconnections. We cannot fathom this. But in God's eyes, it seems that the most important results are the sick person's and my growing in union with God, with God taking over us more and more, as our deepest and most lasting blessedness.

We are invited to pray for the physical gift of healing or of cure of the cancer. We are called also to pray for the psychological well-being of the person, that he or she stay centered in all that is happening. Finally, we are called to pray for the spiritual flourishing of the sick person, that is, for the growing union of that person with God the Father, in companionship with Jesus and by the power of the Holy Spirit. Here we are asking for *grace* in the strict sense, the one thing necessary.

Physical health is not an absolute; it is a good but a relative good. And death ultimately comes to all of us. Physical healing is a temporary stay against inevitable death. We are called "to care and not to care" (T. S. Eliot) about our friend becoming healthy (as we understand that). "To care" because we love our friend and want what is best, proximately and ultimately. "Not to care" in the sense that our ultimate concern is not directed to the (temporary) health of our friend but the eternal blessedness of that friend. That is the only abiding good for my friend (and for me).

In the language of grace, our seeking for God's healing for another's body or psyche involves both asking for the return of a person to their earlier well-being and asking for deeper union for the ill person and the petitioner with God in and through the situation of sickness or unwellness. This is asking for grace in the strict sense.

Asking for grace as grace is an example of prayer that focuses on desiring and requesting grace. Strictly speaking, this occurs prominently in the *Spiritual Exercises* of St. Ignatius of Loyola. In each of the four weeks of the exercises, the one making them orients his or her prayer by asking for a specific grace. Ordinarily, a person remains in that week until the grace has been given in a way that the one making the exercises can begin to integrate into their lives. In the first week, the grace is three-fold: first, light from God to reveal what God desires to liberate, heal, or change in the individual; second, an experience of contrition for the damage the retreatant has been doing to his or her own goodness, to the goodness of others, and to their relationship with God; and third, a deep desire for change in attitude and behavior on the part of the person.

In the second week, the grace requested is to grow in interior knowledge of Jesus, to love him more ardently, and to follow him by sharing in his mission more generously. Involved here is a growing appreciation for the humanity of Jesus as revelatory of his profound, indeed unique, relationship with Abba and the Holy Spirit.

In the third week, the retreatant asks for the grace of accompanying Jesus with faithful and compassionate love as he walks the path of suffering and death out of fidelity to Abba and out of deep solidarity with the betraying and fearful disciples, the tormenting Romans, and those Jewish authorities who conspired with the Romans against Jesus. This is a tough grace, for when it is given, it sustains the retreatant in dryness of prayer, and the anguish of witnessing Jesus, whom one now freshly loves thanks to the second week, undergoing so much suffering in a dreadful loneliness.

The fourth week emerges when the retreatant waits at the tomb with others who loved Jesus, such as Mary, Mary of Magdala, and John, the beloved disciple. The retreatant waits on grace, not using Scripture except perhaps for psalms of longing, until some signs of new life are offered by God. The grace of this week is sharing in the consolation of Jesus's resurrection and being sent by the risen one to preach the joy of the Gospel.

When a retreatant prays for these graces, the individual is praying in Jesus's name. Each of these graces is something Jesus wants to give us and only needs our openness to receiving them for them to be experienced. Here, there is deep alignment of Jesus's desire to grace us and our desire for grace.

Active Prayer and Passive Prayer

Earlier I spoke about Bernard of Clairvaux's insight about cooperative grace. He was convinced that, in any decision we make that increases our union with God, our freedom is involved 100 percent and God's grace is also at work 100 percent. But the Catholic tradition of prayer also affirms what many Christians have experienced, namely, that at some stages of the spiritual journey the person is explicitly aware of engaging very actively with God. The first three of the seven stages of St. Teresa of Jesus's *The Interior Castle* would be an example of this. (In her allegory, each stage depicts a set of mansions or dwelling places in the soul, and moving from one stage to the next means that one is growing closer to God.) In older terminology, this would be termed the ascetical phase of praying.

At other stages of union with God, things are very different. The person experiences the invitation to let go of previous ways of praying, and what he or she is doing in the prayer becomes very obscure. A sense emerges that God is asking the person to allow him to take over the prayer more and more. The individual tries simply to show up and let God do whatever work he desires to do in and through the person praying. Classically this has been called the mystical phase of the prayer journey. In *The Interior Castle*, the last four stages articulate Teresa's growing receptivity or passivity in relation to God's actions in her, as God increasingly purifies and stretches her soul so that she can become more united with and moved toward Christ.[6]

In terms of cooperative grace, what is going on here? I would suggest that even though the *experience* of prayer shifts from greater activity on the part of the pray-er to greater passivity, on the deepest level of the person, God's grace and human freedom are both engaged 100 percent in both the ascetical and mystical phases of prayer. Whenever God's work in the person succeeds in uniting the individual more deeply to God, the person's core freedom is fully engaged, saying a profound "yes" to what God is doing. It is important to remember that all union with God and a human being involves their joining on the personal level, that is, as persons who relate to each other not organically but precisely as free subjects.

I believe this way of viewing cooperative grace is validated by Teresa's experience in the seven mansions of profound mutuality and equality with Christ, and through Christ, with Abba and the Holy Spirit. This mutuality and equality are signs of true friendship, what Jesus affirmed in John's Gospel at the Last Supper. At the same time, Teresa experienced in the last mansions the complete coming together of Martha and Mary, of loving engagement in the world, and her profound surrender to the Holy Mystery we call God. All this is divine grace's doing, but it is always also the doing of human freedom understood as grounded in grace and therefore truly itself. To allude to Father Rahner's thinking one last time, in the deepest reaches of prayer and union with God, this side of the beatific vision, dependence on God's action and our healthy autonomy exist in direct and perfect proportion.

1. Karl Rahner, "Reflections on the Experience of Grace," in *Theological Investigations*, vol. 3 (Baltimore: Helicon, 1967), 86–90.
2. All scriptural citations are from *The New American Bible rev. NT* (Iowa Falls, IA: World, 1991).
3. Bernard of Clairvaux, *Grace and Free Choice*, trans. Daniel O'Donovan (Kalamazoo, Mich.: Cistercian, 1988), 106.
4. Karl Rahner, "Thoughts on the Possibility of Belief Today," in *Theological Investigations*, vol. 5 (Baltimore: Helicon, 1966), 12.
5. Thomas Aquinas, *Summa Theologica*, Prima Secundae, q. 111, art. 2.
6. St. Teresa of Ávila, *The Interior Castle: Study Edition*, trans. by Kieran Kavanaugh, OCD, and Otilio Rodriguez, OCD, prepared by Kieran Kavanaugh, OCD, and Carol Lisi, OCD (Washington, DC: ICS, 2010).

CHAPTER 4

Distractions in Prayer: Nuisance and Gift

~ *Brendan Geary, FMS* ~

The English poet George Herbert described prayer as "Softness, and peace, and joy, and love, and bliss."[1] It is hard to imagine anyone not wanting these things as part of their life. It has become a truism to talk about the frenzied pace of contemporary life, the constant intrusion of noise, finding ourselves the accidental auditors of one-sided telephone conversations, the omnipresent Muzak in public spaces, and the prominence given to television sets in places where people meet and relax. There is plenty of interest in meditation and prayer, and there are many organizations and methods available to those who seek to find stillness, quiet, insight, and contact with God as part of their lives.

The problem, as many people have discovered, is that having good intentions to create a space of stillness in our lives is not a simple task. Many find that far from encountering peace and the "still, small voice of calm," as another poet has put it,[2] they find themselves restless, bored, daydreaming, and aware of thoughts that cause them to feel anxious or upset. It is not unusual for people to abandon the enterprise at this stage and to consider themselves failures in the area of prayer.

In this chapter, I do not intend to discuss the different understandings of words like *meditation, contemplation,* or *lectio divina.* I am interested in what happens when people dedicate time in their lives to the activity that we call personal prayer. I am not concerned here with public prayer, liturgical prayer, public or private devotions, or the prayer of intercession. I want to explore the experience of people who choose to remain in silence for a dedicated period of time with the intention of deepening their spiritual lives. I hope that reading this will be a source of encouragement in your ongoing commitment to draw closer to God and to learn how to listen to your experiences of prayer in order to find God there.

I will begin with my own early experience of trying to meditate and will discuss assumptions many people bring to prayer and some of the difficulties they encounter. I will then continue with the physical reality that we are embodied people and reflect on ways of working with our bodies in prayer. This leads naturally to a discussion of the difficulties that can arise in our minds. Further sections offer reflections on ways that distractions can be gifts that lead us to know ourselves better and can draw us ever closer to the true God we wish to worship by gradually unmasking the gods we are in fact worshipping. From this point, the chapter will explore our feelings, particularly when we are confronted with the darker, embarrassing, or more disturbing parts of our selves. I will end by reflecting on a significant spiritual experience of St. Thérèse of Lisieux, which neatly illustrates some of these themes.

BEGINNING TO PRAY

I well remember my own experiences of trying to spend time in personal prayer when I entered the Marist Brothers' novitiate. I felt drawn to the idea of prayer but had no idea how to go about it. After a few introductory talks I remember going to the chapel at 9:00 AM, facing the tabernacle as a focal point, and choosing to pray meditatively on the Magnificat. I took time to center myself, then slowly took each verse in turn. I intentionally read each verse, extracted whatever message appeared to strike me, and then moved on to the next. In between times, I was aware of a number of distracting thoughts that presented themselves, ranging from thinking about which hymn I would choose for night prayer to work I had left unfinished in the garden. Before finishing my time of prayer, I read over the text again. At that point, I was fairly sure that thirty minutes must have passed. I felt quite pleased with my first efforts. But then I was deeply discouraged to look at my watch and discover that it was exactly 9:10 AM.

As I look back on those early efforts, I realize that I brought a number of expectations and preconceptions to my prayer: an assumption that choosing the right location and creating the right atmosphere would lead to inner stillness, a hoped for sense of enlightenment or insight, and an expectation that the time would pass without difficulty. I suspect that anyone who has persevered with a life of personal prayer has had to disabuse himself of similar assumptions. Such experiences are echoed by Kevin Culligan, a Carmelite friar who, reflecting on his early experiences of trying to meditate, wrote that, "The periods of mental prayer had now become two boring, restless, distracted often painful hours in my day."[3]

There are a number of misconceptions that people can bring to meditation. There can be an expectation that the experience will be full of fervor or some kind of spiritually focused nirvana. The old title of "mental prayer," also may have led to a belief that prayer could be achieved through concentration and will power. Others can be left with the impression that all that is required is a mix of dedicated time, a quiet space, and a religious focus, and that as a result of this time-honored recipe, stillness will simply fall upon them without any effort. Somehow, the voice of God will make itself heard, though how this will happen is seldom explained. The quotation from Herbert can contribute to this expectation, as can the kind of spiritual writing that highlights the benefits of personal prayer without describing the kind of discipline required to (one hopes) experience such special, graced moments. As the editor of this volume, Robert Wicks, has written, "We read about the vibrant prayer of others in books and wonder what is wrong with ours."[4]

Many people can feel a compelling need for greater simplicity in their lives. They yearn for closeness to God and want to create a space for the Spirit in their lives. They are sufficiently aware of the traps, addictions, and compulsions of modern living to want to carve out a space where they can listen to the voice of God and grow spiritually. So often, the rock on which they perish is summed up in the word *distractions*. Gerard Hughes, the Scottish Jesuit writer, described distractions as the heart's restlessness, echoing St. Augustine's famous insight from the *Confessions* that our hearts are ever restless until they rest in God.[5] Distractions can be a nuisance and can cause discouragement and distress, but as I hope to show, they can also be the spiritual equivalent of the royal road to growth, maturity, and insight.

Dealing with Distractions

Essentially, distractions are any thoughts or feelings that appear to prevent us from staying focused on the main purpose of prayer, "The raising of our mind and heart to God," to use the old *Catechism* definition. Distraction has been defined as "attention pulled away from that which is important."[6] As I learned from my own experience, it is almost impossible to stop our minds from thinking and wandering. In a sense, that is what our minds are designed to do. Matthieu Ricard notes that it is not possible nor even desirable to suppress the mind's natural activities.[7] Michael Harding, an Irish writer who wrote humorously about his own attempts to meditate, noted that the mind, like an elephant, will go anywhere—unless it is trained.[8] The first lesson that people learn when they want to begin a life of personal prayer is to do what they can to work with their bodies and train their minds.

Our Bodies

There are many books which provide guidance on how to pray, and they almost all begin with the body. The first and most important issue related to our bodies and prayer is to accept—and value—the fact that we are embodied persons. Many people will remember being scolded in childhood for not sitting still. Being physically restless, finding oneself in an uncomfortable posture, or being preoccupied with an itch or source of pain is not conducive to finding inner stillness.

Introductory chapters on prayer often recommend that the person sit in a relaxed position. Some people like to use prayer stools or a stool without a back to lean on, as this encourages you to adopt a posture that promotes being physically centered. Others may choose a comfortable chair with or without arm rests. The important point is to be able to sit (or kneel) in a posture that is conducive to stillness, without being distracted by physical discomfort. Experience has taught some to sit with their feet side by side on the floor, with their hands on their lap. It can be helpful to become aware of one's body, to notice any points of tension, constrictions in footwear or clothes, and to flex and relax muscles to enable the body to be rested and still, letting go of any tension being stored in the body.[9]

The next stage can involve becoming aware of any sounds that can be heard. We notice them and then let them go. This can refer to the ticking of a clock, the gentle hum of an electrical appliance, the wind in the trees or other noises that can catch our attention and interrupt us, like traffic or music in the distance. The key part of these introductory exercises involves awareness of our breathing. From becoming aware of the pattern of our breathing, we can choose to breath in, drawing in God's Spirit (breath—*ruah*—means "spirit" in Hebrew), and breathing out, releasing anything that might separate us from God. There are a range of breathing and stillness exercises which can be used in order to facilitate the physical stillness that is important for prayer. Ricard provides many useful exercises in his book *Happiness*, including one for people who are beginning the practice of meditation.[10]

A second aspect of the role of our bodies in prayer is to understand that bodies can be instruments of prayer. The Western Catholic tradition has given an honored place to the posture of kneeling before God in a way that indicates worship or supplication. This is not the only posture that can be used. In the early Church, Christians often stood to pray. This had a double significance for them. First, only free people could stand in each other's presence. Standing together reminded believers that whatever their social status outside of the gathering, while there, they were all free in Christ (Galatians 3:28).[11] At the same time, standing conveyed readiness for doing God's work. Some people take a time to stand at the beginning or end of their time of prayer, as a way of reminding themselves of their dignity as a son or daughter of God. This action becomes a prayer. Similarly, various postures involving hand and arm gestures can communicate different dispositions in prayer, from openness to longing, from praise to supplication.

St. Paul reminds us, "The Spirit too comes to help us in our weakness," and that when we cannot find words, that the Sprit can express our pleas to God (Romans 8:26). In the same way our bodies can be instruments that express the meaning of our prayer, whatever might be happening inside our heads. Our posture, if chosen intentionally, can bring us back to the focus of our prayer, when our minds have been taken elsewhere. One of the dangers of our Western tradition is that we can come to see prayer as something that takes place in our minds. Reminding ourselves that our bodies are on our side, learning how to prepare them and working with them to support our prayer, can help us when we encounter difficulties with distractions.

OUR MINDS

The human mind is remarkable. Whether we consider it from the perspective of its size and development compared to other animals, its left and right hemispheres and their different and complementary functions, its plasticity, capacity for memory, inventiveness, and even dysfunction, it is unquestionably fascinating in itself.[12] From the perspective of the practice we call prayer, the mind is often viewed as an obstacle or hindrance rather than an asset. Many authors who write on prayer note that the "mind rarely leaves us long in peace."[13] The mind has been designed to roam freely, make connections, reflect, be curious and solve problems. It would be strange if these capacities could be shut down after a few minutes of physical stillness and deep breathing.

Accepting that the mind has been designed to present thoughts and reflections to the person is not the same thing as saying that there is no place for discipline or training regarding how to engage ourselves in prayer in a mindful, focused, and attentive way. We know about the importance of exercise, disciplined eating, and attentiveness to our bodies as part of healthy living. It would be odd if the same learning could not be of use when it comes to working with our minds.

Time itself can be a distraction, as I learned from my early attempts at meditation. Trying to fill thirty minutes with meditation was quite a challenge. Two years after I entered the novitiate, I had the good fortune to spend a week in Fr. Henri Caffarel's House of Prayer in Troussures, France. In order to minimize the distracting effect of the constant movement of other retreatants in and out of the chapel, Fr. Caffarel arranged for a gentle bell to be rung every fifteen minutes. This was a signal that people could enter or leave the chapel. This small innovation meant that it was not necessary for me to look at my watch, as I knew that the bell would ring after fifteen minutes. Over the years I became more practiced at reading my internal rhythms during times of prayer and became better able to judge how long I was spending in prayer. One of my colleagues who prays for an allocated one hour each day uses a small timer to inform him when he has five minutes left. As long as such a practice does not disturb others, it can be a good way to remove the distraction of worrying about time.

The first point that can be made is that we can learn how to use our breathing to slow down our pulse rate. This practice prepares and disposes the body and mind to the kind of stillness that favors meditative practice. There is a difference between accepting that our minds were designed to be curious and to offer thoughts and solutions to problems, and allowing our minds to daydream, plan future activities or strategies, problem-solve, reminisce, work out clinching comments in imaginary arguments, or indulge in self-pity over past hurts. We will return to these issues later, but for the moment, it is important to be clear that such mental activities are not conducive to the kind of receptivity that enables us to benefit from prayer.

There are various techniques for helping the mind to stay focused. Gerry Hughes, SJ, recommends having a journal beside you so that if a pressing concern presents itself that you know you have to follow up on later, you may note it down so that you can then leave the concern until after your prayer is over.[14] If a persistent thought—or piece of music—keeps presenting itself to your mind, a simple solution is to count to ten or to fifty, doing it backward if necessary, or to distract yourself by deliberately choosing to think about something else.

Another helpful way to begin a time of prayer is to take a simple repetitive chant or hymn which requires little effort to bring to our minds and to let it repeat itself. Over the years I have been drawn to the Taizé chants as a way to engage my mind in the service of my prayer. I often begin with *Laudate omnes gentes*, as a way of beginning, by praising God. At other times, I begin with "In the Lord I am ever thankful" as a way to begin with a sentiment of gratitude. I have always been drawn to the chant that invites us to look into the darkness inside us: "Within our darkest night, you kindle the fire that never dies away." Starting with this is a way of gently asserting my belief that not even darkness can separate me from God. These chants help me to become more centered and to invite the kind of disposition that I want to make part of my prayer. I also find that as I begin to let the chants play in my mind I become aware of the tempo—which is usually too fast for the kind of meditative state I want to achieve. I have learned how to slow down the pace along with the breathing exercises to arrive at a gentler pace. Gradually the chants tend to recede and fall into the background.

If the mind is stuck in a negative groove, a helpful way to shift emotional gear is to reflect on our lives to identify things for which we can be grateful.[15] I remember once driving away from a particularly unpleasant meeting with a member of my religious order. I could not stop reflecting on what had happened and being affected by my sad feelings about the encounter, wondering what I could have done or said differently. I decided that being stuck in this pattern of thought was not helping me feel better. I could not change the brother, his attitude, his past experiences, or the meeting, but I could change what I was thinking about. I scanned my mental horizons and decided to think about some forthcoming things I needed to attend to that offered me stimulation for creative problem solving. On this occasion my tactic worked.

The second piece of advice that writers often give is that trying to overcome distractions is like King Canute telling the waves to go back to the sea. The advice that is often given is to notice the thought with detached curiosity, note how we feel with this particular thought, and then let it go. Some people use mental imaging, for example having a sort of "mental shelf" where such thoughts are deposited, possibly to be returned to later. Others can almost ritually acknowledge the thought, say hello to it, thank it for presenting itself, and then bid it farewell. This approach requires a capacity to be tolerant of one's thoughts and to be as nonjudgmental as possible. In this way, we can observe the thoughts as they arise, but establish a personal non-proliferation treaty with ourselves to arrest their spread. As we will see later, it is important to avoid judging our experiences and thoughts or, perhaps better, to note when and how we judge them, as this gives us vital information regarding our inner world with its values, fears, and dreams. Vilma Seelaus notes that "for the most part distractions are to be endured not dealt with, at least during the time of prayer."[16]

Psychologists have noted that attempts to suppress a thought often only leads to strengthening it and making it more difficult to change one's thoughts or to find peace. This has also led to the idea of "thought surfing." This is important when a thought or urge seems to take possession of us. If the person can *notice* the thought without *becoming* the thought, almost like a detached stranger, then it becomes more manageable to *tolerate* the thought or urge and to wait until the intensity of the desire or obsessive thought recedes and hopefully disappears.[17] This can be a helpful strategy with distractions as it engages our curiosity without leading us to spend our time following daydreams, angry thoughts, hurts, disappointments, ambitions, or grandiose plans, or rehearsing conversations where we always have the best lines, the winning arguments, or the smartest put-downs.

Ricard notes that simplicity of mind leads to clarity of thought.[18] We need to train our minds in order to find ourselves at a deeper level of awareness than is possible when we allow our minds to take us for walks. This training is possible, particularly if we benefit from courses in spirituality or mindfulness. The current development of the practice of mindfulness has led to various strategies and programs to enable people to slow down breathing, attend to thought processes, have an attitude of curiosity rather than judgment, and perhaps more important, avoid feelings of failure because of aspects of mental behavior that are normal, part of our humanity, and which can, as we shall see, lead us to the kind of self-awareness that can be a significant part of a prayerful life and attitude.

The Gift of Distractions

Prayer is often spoken of as a means of hearing the voice of God in our lives. However, the experience of many is that it is not God's voice that they become aware of, but their own. Ronald Rolheiser confirms this when he writes, "What is common in prayer is the tendency to talk to ourselves rather than God."[19] This can be a source of discouragement for many. If, however, we take seriously the Ignatian principle that we can find God in all things, then we need to ask how God may be presenting himself to us in the thoughts and feelings that present themselves to us in our time of prayer.

The title of Vilma Seelaus's excellent book on St. Teresa of Ávila's teaching on distractions in the *Interior Castle* is *Distractions in Prayer: Blessing or Curse?*[20] This subtitle captures the paradox; distractions seem to tell us that we are failures in the art of prayer, and yet, as we shall see, they can also be gifts that enable us to grow.

The Importance of Self-knowledge

It is often said that self-knowledge is the foundation of wisdom and personal growth. Life experiences, both successes and failures, offer opportunities to come to know ourselves. People who are closed, defensive, and brittle can make uncomfortable companions, whereas those who can laugh at themselves and allow themselves to be teased are easier people with whom to live and work. Most people live busy lives, which leave little time to stop, reflect, and take stock of what is happening beneath the surface of their concerns and obligations. Some religious traditions have encouraged people to create a space for a personal retreat, or sabbatical time so that they can suspend their daily activities and responsibilities to attend to what is happening in their lives. We know that Jesus himself often left the crowds and the apostles and disciples to "go to a lonely place" to pray (Mark 1:35).

If we take time to center ourselves in the ways described in the first part of this chapter, and then focus on a line of Scripture, an icon, or being present to God, we can still find our minds becoming filled with a range of thoughts. This can be material that sits in what psychologists refer to as our preconscious, that is, ideas that sit just outside ordinary awareness, but which are ready to present themselves to our awareness when we are not asking our minds to be busy and focused on other things. In this way, we can become aware of what is actually important to us as opposed to what we might like to think is important to us. Ricard notes that we are often afraid to look inward because we are afraid of what we might see there. It may not reflect the self we want to see.[21]

There is a well-known story about Sir Winston Churchill, the prime minister of Great Britain during WWII. In 1954 the British Parliament commissioned Graham

Sutherland to paint a portrait of the war leader as a gift from parliament. Churchill hated the painting and described it as a "work of British modernism," which provoked laughter in Westminster Hall at the unveiling ceremony. The problem with the painting was not its modernism, but that it painted Churchill as he was, rather than as the great war leader whom Churchill wanted to see looking back at himself. Churchill's wife famously destroyed the painting.[22] Churchill did not want to see himself as he was, and the destruction of the painting is the equivalent of refusing to allow ourselves to look within in order to attend to and learn from what we see and hear.

When we are praying, we may not realize that we are distracted until we become aware that we are involved in a particular train of thought. At that point, we can either gently return to the focus of our prayer, or we can ask ourselves what has taken our attention. As Michael Harding discovered when he tried to meditate, we can find ourselves thinking about anything from a theological problem to a recent dinner party. Having said that, it is not unusual to find that our concerns, hopes, ambitions, self-pity, revenge, entitlement, anger, hurt, or sexual desires can take pride of place. Joseph Schmidt wrote that distractions offer us a way to pray our experiences and asks where our distractions lead us.[23] Our distractions can lead us to the kind of dreams that have more to do with our sense of grandiosity than any realistic appraisal of our capacities. Some of our thoughts can lead us to judge, condemn, and blame others for hurts and disappointments in our lives.

At this point, we can stop and ask ourselves which God we are worshipping. We may like to think that we are worshipping the living God of Jesus Christ but can discover that, in fact, we are worshipping a God made in our own image and likeness. Our distractions, perhaps more than anything else, have the capacity to reveal us to ourselves. Rolheiser describes this practice rather pithily as "self-adoration before the Blessed Sacrament."[24] In a similar vein, Robert Wicks writes:

> To be unrelentingly open with respect to oneself is the lifelong goal of self-knowledge and self-esteem. I believe that from a psychological perspective one of the most serious sins is to ignore, deny or worship our own personalities rather than to prize them, find out all about them, and seek to express them naturally and freely with a sense of mitzvah (giving and expecting nothing in return).[25]

Rather than blocking and avoiding such thoughts, memories, and feelings, as Churchill's wife did by destroying the unflattering portrait, we can advance spiritually and humanly by noticing our distractions and listening to what they tell us about our real selves. They can tell us about our true values—status, pride, attention, respect, achievement, sexual pleasure, comfort—and the things that we are attached to and hold precious.[26]

Jesus told us that the truth would set us free (John 8:32). The capacity to take time to pray alone, notice what fills our mind, and in the presence of God, look at ourselves with fresh eyes, can free us from the deceptions and defensive postures that prevent us from getting close to God. The fears, emotions, desires, and attachments that disturb us come from within ourselves. It is only in noticing them and acknowledging that they are part of us that we can ever become free of them. Schmidt notes that human beings have a curious desire to be angelic and that our distractions have the wonderful gift of returning us to our humanity.[27] St. Paul, in the Second Letter to the Corinthians wrote, "You yourselves are our letter…written…not on tablets of stone but on the tablets of human hearts" (2 Corinthians 3:2–3). Our distractions can be God's letters to us which reveal what is written in our hearts.

Distractions also challenge us to grow through the purifying process of self-knowledge, which leads to humility. Such self-knowledge invites us to conversion of heart. Paradoxically, if we want to empty ourselves of our false selves, we need to pay attention to our actual selves, and this can happen when we allow our distractions to be our teachers.[28] Wicks notes that before the truth sets us free, it might make us a bit miserable. However, he also notes that the energy we no longer have to use in protecting a false self that doesn't actually exist can be used in bringing compassion sensitivity, creativity, and generosity to the world.[29]

WHICH GOD?

In the book of Exodus, Yahweh says to Moses: "But…you cannot see my face; for no one can see me and live" (Exodus 33:20). One way to understand what happens during our time of prayer is that it is a way to gradually unmask the false god that we are worshiping in order to get closer to the true God whom we wish to see face to face. In that sense, our distractions become the pillar of fire which God can use to lead us to a place we did not know.[30]

How can we know when we are worshipping a false god? One of the surest guides is when we notice ourselves feeling self-righteous, like the Pharisee in the Gospel parable (Luke 18:9–13). The world of the Pharisee was stable and unchanging; he knew where virtue lay and he thought he could confidently identify the sinners who merited God's judgment. Whenever we find ourselves judging or condemning someone, we can be sure that this is not the attitude of a loving Father to this person. One of the practices I have developed in prayer whenever I find myself being angry or judgmental about another is to imagine God holding the person in the palm of his hand. I then ask myself how God views him or her and find that this always leads to a change in my own attitude. It is difficult to be judgmental when imaging God in this way. My distraction leads me to compassion and puts me in the presence of the God of love and mercy.

Another indicator that we are not worshipping the true God is when we find ourselves self-indulgent or narcissistic in our thoughts and fantasies. We may find ourselves dreaming about a wonderful future where we will be successful, receive recognition, qualifications, or honors and be sought for our wisdom. We can notice the things we are attached to: our possessions, reputation, sexual behaviors, positions of importance, and so on. While these things are not necessarily bad, when they become the focus of what is happening in our time of prayer, they reveal to us that we may be worshipping at the foothills of our own ego and not in the approaches to Mount Zion, where we can worship God in freedom and truth. Within our distractions we can "catch glimpses of our own idolatry."[31]

THE DISTRACTIONS IN THE DESERT

After Jesus's baptism, we are told that he was "led by the Spirit out into the desert to be put to the test by the devil" (Matthew 4:1). The desert had symbolic importance in Jewish religious tradition as the place where Yahweh could speak to the heart (Hosea 2:16). In St. Matthew's account, Jesus is confronted with three temptations. The devil tempts Jesus to turn stones into loaves, then to throw himself down off of the parapet of the Temple, and finally to receive all of the kingdoms of the world in their splendor if he worships at the feet of the devil. Jesus replies to each of these temptations by quoting Scripture and putting the focus on God. He says, for example, "The lord your God is the one to whom you must do homage, him alone you must serve" (Matthew 4:10).

As we read this narrative, it is not difficult to understand these temptations, which come at the beginning of Jesus's public ministry, as a summary of a process that had gone on inside him as he grew into maturity. We know from the Gospels that Jesus spoke with authority, that he inspired people to follow him, that he was focused and deliberate in his actions, and that he was an intelligent and a gifted teacher. It is possible to imagine the narrative of the temptations as the distillation of the distractions that Jesus confronted in his prayer as he matured and came to understand his vocation. What were the dreams that filled his mind as he grew and matured? What desires did he have when he saw how he could influence people? What rewards did he seek as a young man growing up in Nazareth as the son of a locally respected carpenter? The temptations in the desert reveal that the temptations to power, status, wealth, glory, and control were demons that Jesus had to confront before he could begin his public life. He needed to know that he was focused on worshipping the living God of Abraham, Isaac, and Jacob, and not the God that would satisfy his own ego.

Reconsidering this story as a narrative of distractions helps us to see how the process of attending to our own distractions, noticing them, and allowing ourselves to be converted by them can help us to grow in self-knowledge, and to unmask the false gods we are tempted to worship in order to find ourselves closer to the true God. Our distractions can be gifts and not only nuisances or stumbling blocks on the path of prayer.

SITTING IN THE DARKNESS: TEMPTATIONS AND DESIRES

St. Ignatius of Loyola left his followers a text entitled the *Spiritual Exercises*, which he used to invite them to a deep conversion of heart leading to their commitment to follow Christ. The text begins with the "Principle and Foundation," which acts as an introduction. Ignatius wrote, "We ought to desire only that which is more conducive to the end for which we were created," adding that we are created to "praise, reverence and serve God, our Lord."[32] While we might like only to desire things that lead to serving God, the reality is that our hearts contain other desires and temptations.

It is not unusual to find hatred and anger against others arising during our time of prayer. The problem with hatred is that it feeds on its own energy and becomes a prison from which we cannot escape. It is usually fueled by self-pity and righteous anger, with a desire to punish the other. People who are prisoners of their own hatred become trapped in rigid thinking. As noted above, we can indulge ourselves in blaming others for our hurts and misfortunes. We can also find greed and other "deadly sins" lurking in the various caverns of our hearts.

A close neighbor of hatred is resentment. This can simmer away inside us as we can feel overlooked, slighted, not valued, or treated with disregard. While there may be truth in the behaviors that led to the painful memory and feeling of hurt, remaining in a place of resentment is not healthy, humanly or spiritually. The danger with such feelings, especially where there is some sense of entitlement, is that we can feed the feeling instead of allowing God's purifying presence to lift us out of the negative pit where we find ourselves. We read in the Psalms, "By your light we see the light" (36:9). Prayer can be an opportunity to allow the distraction that has revealed aspects of our negativity to ourselves, to be touched by God's light, which dispels the darkness.

ALLOWING OUR SEXUALITY TO BE PRESENT

For some people, sexuality and sexual desire can be particularly problematic. For most of Christian history the Church was very suspicious of this whole area of life. In recent years, there have been efforts to present human sexuality in a more positive light. Sexuality is one of God's gifts to us, but it can also be a part of our lives where we experience distress, hurt, anxiety, shame, embarrassment, failure, and guilt. If we want to approach God as we are, and not as the angelic beings we might like to be, then we need to allow our sexual histories and desires to be present as part of our prayer also. In the first place, we need to acknowledge the sexual desires that exist within us. We need to be attentive to desires and fantasies that can arise during prayer and, if we can avoid rushing to judge them, to let them teach us about ourselves. Can we be honest with ourselves about experiences of masturbation, sexual orientation and preferences, our lack of fidelity to our commitments, the desires that might surprise us or disturb us, or aspects of ourselves that we would prefer to keep hidden? These parts of our lives can help us to remain earthed and in touch with our humanity. They can also offer spaces for ongoing conversion and trust in God's grace in our lives. We need to find a delicate balance between accepting ourselves as we are and allowing God to lead us to places of health in our sexual selves.

Rolheiser says that an integrated sexuality is one where we live with our commitments. He later added that the soul cannot tolerate moral duplicity for long.[33] If there is dishonesty in our sexual lives, as opposed to the simple reality of human weakness, then it is likely that this will present itself to our awareness in times of prayer. It is common for people to avoid personal prayer as a way of avoiding the confrontation with their sexual selves. Like Adam and Eve, they want to avoid the discomfort that comes from bringing their desires and history into the presence of God. Sexual distractions can be gifts that enable us to see our true selves and do not have to be problems that prevent us from encountering God.

One of the goals of prayer is to move us ever closer to interior peace. As Ricard reminds us, greed and desire cannot coexist with inner freedom.[34] Our distractions invite us to welcome the truth about ourselves—the attachments, desires, contradictions, inconsistencies, and paradoxes—to enable us to recognize them, acknowledge them, own them as our own, and not be imprisoned by them.

SCRIPTURE AS PART OF PRAYER

Many people make use of sacred Scripture as part of their prayer. In order to avoid the temptation to return continually to favorite passages, some spiritual directors recommend making use of the passages offered to us each day as part of the Mass or which form part of the Liturgy of the Hours (such as Morning and Evening Prayer). This has the advantage of enabling us to pray with the rhythm of the Church's life, as well as opening us to a greater range of Scripture than we might choose ourselves. Wicks describes this advice that was given by the well-known spiritual writer Henri Nouwen:

> Each day in the morning, get up about twenty minutes earlier. Read a few lines of Scripture or the readings of the day that the Church suggests.... Once you have read the Epistle and Gospel readings, put the book aside and simply sit silently for about twenty minutes. Your mind will wander but just let the thoughts run through you like a train. Don't try to suppress, hide or entertain them. Simply come back in your mind, your heart really, to the themes that struck you from the Epistle and Gospel of the day. Do that each day and your balance and passion will return more quickly.[35]

The Ignatian tradition recommends that the person who is praying should note which lines lead to an emotional response, be it peace, curiosity, anxiety, excitement, sadness, or joy. I can remember, at a time when I was in a position of leadership, an occasion when I was very angry at someone who had pushed me beyond my limit by obsessively pursuing a topic which I thought we had agreed to let go. I was annoyed at the person's insensitivity, but I also felt disappointed that I had not been able to manage my own response to this provocation. Over the next few days, the readings at Mass were from the First Letter to Timothy, which is not a book of the New Testament that I would instinctively look to for prayerful reflection, and I found myself focusing on the following line:

> In every place, then, I want the men to lift their hands up reverently in prayer, with no anger or argument. (1 Timothy 2:8)

This line invited me to reflect on my anger and to find a way to avoid engaging in a futile argument. The other person was determined to push for a particular outcome which I had made clear, after many consultations, was not going to happen. Having said that, I was still upset by the experience. On the following day I read the following lines: "The president must...[not be] hot tempered, but gentle and peaceable" (1 Timothy 3:2–3).

During those days I was struggling with my own anger and was not thinking kind or peaceable thoughts. As the "president" (leader) in the province, I felt challenged by Scripture to reflect on my recent experience. Rather than simply allow my mind to be filled with distracting thoughts about the interaction which had upset me and allowing the anger to take over my prayer, I found the space to reflect on my feelings and reactions and, through the lines from St. Paul, brought them into dialogue with my values. This led to a shift in my feelings and in my attitude. After a few days, I was feeling less punitive and had found a better sense of balance in my response to the person whose behavior had upset my equilibrium. This practice of reading and meditating on Scripture, while letting the passages weave their way through the events of our lives, can lead us to our better selves, where our values and our faith in Jesus Christ can gradually involve us in a process of conversion and healing.

Scripture can become a mirror through which we see ourselves and dialogue with our experiences. Wicks recounts the story of a young man who wanted to become a rabbi and who was advised to read the Torah. The young man returned and told the Rebbe that he had been through the Torah ten times, to which the Rebbe replied, "Yes, but how often has the Torah been through you?"[36] Prayerful reading of Scripture, and allowing it to flow through our experiences, can be a source of personal conversion. This cannot happen unless we allow the light of the Scripture passages to illuminate the thoughts that distract us, inviting us to increased self-awareness and spiritual growth.

Addressing Our Feelings

Up until this point, our emphasis has been on the thoughts that accompany our feelings: memories, desires, dreams, hopes, attachments, and so on. David Matsumoto, a psychologist, wrote the following about our feelings: "Feelings color our life experiences. They inform us who we are, what our relationships with others are like, and how to behave. Emotions give meaning to events. Without emotions, those events would be mere facts in our lives."[37]

Often the feelings themselves can be a source of distraction, particularly negative feelings. People can experience joy, contentment, excitement, and longing in prayer. These, however, are often the kind of emotional experiences that we aspire to, and which we more easily label as "spiritual experiences." Negative emotions, on the other hand, can feel like unwelcome intrusions which appear to be far from what we hoped would happen when we took time to pray.

Gerry Hughes described negative feelings as the "nudgings of God," because God's treasures are often hidden in our negative feelings, if we can find the courage to look there.[38] Guilt, for example, often leads to discouragement in prayer. But if we can tolerate the feeling of guilt, it may reveal an aspect of our behavior that God invites us to change, or it may remind us of something we have done that calls us to apologize to another person or make amends, thereby restoring peace to a relationship that has been damaged in some way. Hughes goes on to say that feelings that are not integrated into our lives will act like stray sheep.[39] Feelings such as bitterness, anger, resentment, or jealousy require honest self-appraisal.

I remember at one stage in my life feeling angry at people who I believed had hurt me. No matter what I did, I was not able to shake free of these strong feelings. At one point, I asked myself what I would recommend to another person in my situation. Finally, during a time of prayer, I engaged in an exercise in which I wrote down all the words I could associate with the situation. I then leaned back and looked at this large sheet of paper and eliminated the less important words. Eventually a word struck me forcefully which was not on the paper: revenge. It was a distinctly unpleasant moment as I did not think of myself as a vengeful person. Allowing this word to emerge had led me to readjust my sense of self. At the same time, it was a moment of liberation as the power of my negative feelings gradually dissipated once I could confront the true feeling that was lurking inside of me, driving my hurt and anger. The feelings that had been distractions for months led me to a place of freedom—but first I had to swallow a bitter pill in terms of my sense of myself.

One of the dangers associated with negative feelings is that people can distance themselves from prayer because of a sense of personal unworthiness. Guilt and shame can be particularly problematic, as can feelings of jealousy or revenge. As we saw above, sexual thoughts and arousal can also be difficult for people. Given the negative attitude that existed in the Church toward sexuality for so long, people can have an unstated hope that the practice of prayer will rescue them from the intensity of sexual desire. Often it works the other way. Sexual desire is such a strong part of us that it would be strange if it did not present itself to us when we allow ourselves the space to be quiet in order to attend to what is happening within. The first step toward integration involves acknowledging that this is part of our selves, without choosing to indulge whatever fantasies are presenting themselves. A second step involves being grateful to God for the passion that burns within us, and which impels us to creativity, connectedness with others, compassion, and pastoral action. A third step involves the acceptance that, as Karl Rahner wisely observed, here in this life, all symphonies remain unfinished. The hunger of sexuality reminds us of our incompleteness.[40]

St. Ignatius on the Topic of Feelings

St. Ignatius offered his followers a system for discerning spirits to help them to better understand where God was leading them. Based on his own experiences, he drew up a list of feelings that come from God and from the devil. Hugo Rahner presents the list as follows:[41]

The good spirit	The evil spirit
Interior peace	Disturbance of peace
Spiritual joy	Sadness
Hope, faith and charity	Longing after base things
Tears	Aridity
Elevation of mind	Distraction of mind in base things

Every person who has begun to seriously engage with personal prayer knows that we live with an inner restlessness that reveals itself in our distractions. The Ignatian system invites us to ask if our feelings are consistent with our values and whether or not they are leading us to God. The experience of disturbance, aridity, or sadness can be an invitation to grow or change. These feelings are not signs of failure and should not lead to discouragement. God wants us to experience peace and well-being, and the feelings we experience can be like signposts that direct us along the road God wants for us.

The Example of St. Thérèse of Lisieux

St. Thérèse of Lisieux is one of the most popular Catholic saints. In recent years her relics have been taken on pilgrimage to various countries, and crowds have attended special liturgies where the casket is venerated. In England the casket was even brought to Wormwood Scrubs, a famous prison in London, where, at the time there were three hundred Catholic inmates.[42] St. Thérèse spent her short life in an enclosed Carmelite convent in the north of France. In her autobiography she describes an experience of prayer that illustrates many of the themes discussed in this chapter:

> During my meditation, my desires caused me a veritable martyrdom, and I opened the epistles of St. Paul to find some kind of answer. Chapters 12 and 13 of the First Letter to the Corinthians fell under my eyes. I read there, in the first of these chapters, that all cannot be apostles, prophets, or doctors that the Church is composed of different members, and that the eye cannot be the hand at one and the same time. The answer was clear, but it did not fulfill my desires and gave me no peace.

We can imagine St. Thérèse beginning her time of prayer with hopes of being present to God, only to find that she was wrestling with her desires. She described the experience as a "veritable martyrdom." She chooses a passage of Scripture in the hope of finding a way out of her discomfort. She found an answer, but it still did not bring her peace. She continued:

> Without becoming discouraged, I continued my reading, and this sentence consoled me: "Yet strive after THE BETTER GIFTS, and I

point out to you a more excellent way. And the Apostle explains how all the most PERFECT gifts are nothing without LOVE. That Charity is the EXCELLENT WAY that leads most surely to God.

I finally had rest…. Charity gave me the key to my vocation…. Then in the excess of my delirious joy, I cried out: O Jesus, my Love…my vocation, at last I have found it…MY VOCATION IS LOVE![43]

This is a deeply moving passage, where we are given the opportunity to eavesdrop on a significant moment in a soul's journey toward God. St. Thérèse was attentive to the thoughts and feelings that were taking place inside her. She was aware of her restlessness and tried to find an answer in Scripture. She found an answer but was still restless. It was only as she stayed with this restless spirit, without allowing herself to be put off and discouraged, that her mind found its way to the invitation to strive for the better gift of love. When this insight touched her mind and heart, she experienced profound joy, which, following the system of St. Ignatius, she immediately interpreted as a sign that God's Spirit was with her.

CONCLUSION

Distractions are often a significant problem for people who set out on the road of personal prayer. There is a difference, though, between daydreaming or following every thought that presents itself to us, as we do while driving or on a long journey, and being aware of stray thoughts and feelings that emerge into our awareness while we are praying. People have also learned that struggling against distractions and trying to fight or overcome them through force of will only exacerbates their power.

Schmidt wrote that "distractions may be a nuisance, but they need not separate us from God."[44] Distractions can lead us to self-awareness, without which spiritual progress is not possible. It enables us to see the gods we are actually worshipping, and when we confront these false gods, we are able to come closer to see and experience the living God whom we seek. We cannot stop our minds from thinking, and we cannot stop having feelings. We can, however, learn how to listen to our thoughts and feelings in order to hear how God is speaking to us. As we confront the darkness and negativity that is within us, we can free ourselves to experience the peace and happiness that God wants for us. We can also use Scripture as a way to bring our values to our life experiences so that what we experience as distractions can actually lead us to conversion of heart and fidelity to our vocation.

Far from being a problem, distractions can be the Spirit's opportunity to draw us to God. The distractions which can leave us feeling like failures in the spiritual life can turn out to be a rich resource for spiritual growth. We may not always have fervent, emotionally uplifting experiences of tranquility and joy, but we can arrive at a place in our lives where we know that we have been engaged in a worthwhile activity and that the various thoughts, feelings, and desires that distract and annoy us and appear to take us away from God can be the unplanned and unsought route that brings us closer to the God we wish to experience and whose voice we want to hear.

1. George Herbert, "Prayer I," Poetry Foundation, http://www.poetryfoundation.org/poem/173636.
2. John Greenleaf Whittier, "Dear Lord and Father of Mankind," various editions. http://www.hymnary.org/text/dear_lord_and_father_of_mankind.
3. Kevin Culligan, "Learning How to Meditate: Fifty Years in Carmel", in *A Better Wine*, ed. Kevin Culligan (Washington, DC: ICS, 2007), 279–302.
4. Robert J. Wicks, *Seeds of Sensitivity: Deepening Your Spiritual Life* (Notre Dame, IN: Ave Maria, 1995), 106.
5. Gerard Hughes, *God of Surprises* (London: Darton, Longman & Todd, 1988), 58.
6. E.H. Hoffman and C.D. Hoffman, *Staying Focused in the Age of Distraction* (Oakland, CA: New Harbinger, 2006), 14.
7. Matthieu Ricard, *Happiness: A Guide to Developing Life's Most Important Skill* (London: Atlantic, 2003), 126.
8. Michael Harding, *Hanging with the Elephant* (Dublin: Hachette, 2014), 109.
9. P. Nicholson, SJ, *Growing into Silence* (2010), published by the Society of Jesus (British Province), 114 Mount Street, London, W1K 3AH. www.growingintosilence.com.
10. Ricard, 57.
11. All Scripture cited in this chapter from *The New Jerusalem Bible* (London: Darton, Longman & Todd, 1985).
12. Elaine Fox, *Rainy Brain, Sunny Brain* (London: Arrow, 2012).
13. Hughes, 43.
14. Hughes, 48.
15. Hoffman and Hoffman, 34–35.
16. Vilma Seelaus, *Distractions in Prayer: Blessing or Curse?* (New York: St. Paul's, 2005), 39.
17. http://www.mindfulness.org.au/urge-surfing-relapse-prevention/.
18. Ricard, 165.
19. Ronald Rolheiser, *Prayer: Our Deepest Longing* (Cincinnati: Franciscan Media, 2013), 39.
20. Seelaus, iii.
21. Ricard, 45.
22. Jonathan Jones, "Winston Churchill, Graham Sutherland (1954)," *The Guardian*, November 3, 2001. http://www.theguardian.com/culture/2001/nov/03/art.
23. Joseph F. Schmidt. *Praying Our Experiences* (Frederick, MD: The Word Among Us, 2008), 32.
24. Rolheiser, *Prayer*, 40.
25. Robert J. Wicks, *Spiritual Resilience* (Cincinnati: Franciscan Media, 2015), 48.
26. Seelaus, 2.
27. Schmidt, 67.
28. Seelaus, 52.
29. Wicks, *Seeds of Sensitivity*, 110.

30. Schmidt, 75.

31. Hughes, 153.

32. George E. Ganss, *The Spiritual Exercises of Saint Ignatius* (St. Louis: Institute of Jesuit Sources, 1992), 32.

33. Ronald Rolheiser, *Sacred Fire: A Vision for a Deeper Humanity and Christian Maturity* (New York: Image, 2014), 66, 262.

34. Ricard, 125.

35. Robert J. Wicks, *Conversations with a Guardian Angel* (Cincinnati: Franciscan Media, 2015), 70.

36. Wicks, *Seeds of Sensitivity*, 113.

37. David Matsumoto, *Culture and Psychology* (Pacific Grove, CA: Brooks Cole, 1996), 243.

38. Hughes, x.

39. Hughes, 93.

40. Karl Rahner, quoted in Ronald Rolheiser, *The Holy Longing* (New York: Doubleday, 1999), 204.

41. Hugo Rahner, *Ignatius the Theologian* (London: Geoffrey Chapman, 1964), 152.

42. Carolyn Davies, "Saint Who Loved Sinners to Visit Wormwood Scrubs Inmates," *The Guardian*, July 5, 2009. http://www.theguardian.com/artanddesign/2009/jul/05/wormwood-scrubs-saint-therese.

43. St. Thérèse of Lisieux. *The Story of a Soul*. 3rd ed., trans. John Clarke, OCD (Washington, DC: ICS, 1996), 193–194. (All caps are used by translator John Clarke.)

44. Schmidt, 92.

CHAPTER 5

Contemplation

~ Mary Frohlich, RSCJ ~

A good place to start a reflection on Christian contemplation is Luke's story about Jesus's friends Martha and Mary (Luke 10:38–42). Biblical scholars strongly caution us, however, to avoid the common misinterpretation that divides the two women into stereotypes of Martha the activist and Mary the contemplative. Both women are deeply committed to being present to Jesus, and both are called to radically deepen that presence. Mary, who sits still and listens with great attention to the teaching of Jesus, has chosen the more classic pose of contemplation. Martha, on the other hand, receives an unsettling call from Jesus to a form of contemplation emerging in the very midst of her service: to discern the "one thing" that is needed (Luke 10:42) and, on that basis, to release rancor in favor of flowing joy.[1] One chooses to practice contemplation; the other discovers a surprising invitation to contemplation erupting into her busy life. The commonality between the two is that their center of attention, vitality, and joy must shift from themselves to Jesus, the Word of God. These two images of contemplation—the one immersed in God in stillness, the other discovering God in the midst of active discipleship—are both essential models for the Christian.

CONTEMPLATION: WORD STUDY

As a term, *contemplation* means quite different things in different contexts, and it certainly has meant many different things over the course of Christian history. A starting point for exploring its meaning is to examine the word itself for a clue to its field of reference. The core of the Latin word *contemplatio* is *templum*, which also lies behind the English word *temple*. We begin our exploration of contemplation with a reflection on the common root and diverging connotations of these two words, *temple* and *contemplation*.

It seems that the original Roman meaning of *templum* was "a space or time set apart for the interpretation of signs from the gods." The Romans wanted their public policies to be aligned with the will of the gods, so they designated special officials called augurs, who were trained in the practice of interpreting the gods' messages. The augur's role was to ritually mark out the space and time of the *templum*, then to carefully observe and discern such phenomena as thunder, lightning, and the activities of birds or other animals. Thus, *templum* referred to a place where specially appointed people sought divine presence and guidance on behalf of the whole community.[2]

While originally these spaces were strictly associated with the ritual activities of the augurs, rather than with any specific building, as time went on, the concept developed into a broader reference to "a consecrated space" or "a house of the gods." From this comes the meaning familiar to us: a temple is a building consecrated for prayer, meditation, or worship.

Contemplatio originally referred to what the augur did while in the *templum*. His charge was to exercise great solemnity and care in observing the phenomena that were believed to bear within them the message of the gods, to recognize this message, and to convey it to those responsible for public policy so they could act accordingly. In this context, *contemplatio* refers especially to that act of reverent, intense attention that searches for the divine presence and communication within the consecrated space. On this basis, the word gradually took on more general connotations such as focused attention, careful observation, or deep pondering, whether in sacred or secular contexts. The original reference to the ritual activity of a consecrated person in a consecrated space, on behalf of the community, dropped away. What remained was a more metaphorical meaning of "space," usually connoting a movement inward to an inner stance of presence to the depths of reality.

Today, many people may be inclined to forget the link between temple and contemplation. Contemplation is often seen as an individual, inner practice that one can do on one's own and in one's own way, while temples represent the externalized practice typical of institutionalized religions. The relevance of this review of ancient etymology to our present interest in becoming practitioners of contemplative Christian prayer is that it recalls us, right at the start, to the essential connection between an inner contemplative stance and responsibility within a community. In its earliest meaning, contemplation was understood to be practiced not for the sake of individual fulfillment or salvation, but to assist the community in finding and following its divine vocation. As we begin to examine the Christian meaning of contemplation in relation to some key biblical texts, this link will be further strengthened.

SOME BIBLICAL PERSPECTIVES ON CONTEMPLATION

While the word *contemplation* does not appear in the Bible, the temple as a key image in both the Old and New Testaments can offer a bridge to a Christian understanding of contemplation. In the Old Testament the Temple was a building constructed and consecrated as a meeting place for God and God's people. Most of the people, however, were consigned to the courtyards of the Temple; only priests and royalty could enter the sacred inner space where God was to be encountered. The New Testament shifts the Temple imagery in several profound ways. Jesus is reported as having said that he will destroy the temple and raise it up in three days. After his death—followed, in AD

70, by the actual destruction of the temple building by the Romans—Jesus's followers believed that his saying meant that his resurrected body will be the new temple.

Paul then developed this into the foundations of a contemplative spirituality as he affirmed that the ecclesial community is the body of Christ and the temple of God. Both the social body of the ecclesial community and the physical body of each individual Christian are manifestations of the new temple within which the living God dwells in the Spirit. He writes, "Do you not know that you are the temple of God, and that the Spirit of God dwells in you?" (1 Corinthians 3:16). Then, spelling it out more fully, he expounds:

> You are fellow citizens with the holy ones and members of the household of God, built upon the foundation of the apostles and prophets, with Christ Jesus himself as the capstone. Through him the whole structure is held together and grows into a temple sacred in the Lord; in him you also are being built together into a dwelling place of God in the Spirit. (Ephesians 2:19–22)

Thus, Paul depicts the indwelling of the living God as the root of both communal worship and personal contemplation.

Although the explicit language of Trinity is postbiblical, there are many biblical sources for the assertion that Christian contemplation is necessarily Trinitarian. The centrality of Jesus's own *Abba* experience, as well as his affirmation, "I am in the Father and the Father is in me" (John 14:11), ground all Christian experience in the first person of the Trinity. The Johannine parable of the vine and the branches (John 15:1–10) stresses that all Christian life flows from vital union with Jesus, second person of the Trinity. As noted above, Paul links the indwelling of God in Christians to the Holy Spirit, third person of the Trinity. These are only a few among a great many biblical texts that would need to be plumbed to write a full exposition of the Trinitarian character of Christian contemplation. What we can observe from even these few references, however, is that the essential theme is mutual indwelling and the sharing of life at the most fundamental level. The doctrine of the Trinity teaches that God's own being is a flowing communion of love; to contemplate that being, then, is to be completely filled with and encompassed by that same flowing communion.

So a basic definition of Christian contemplation is that it is the radiant embodied awareness of mutual indwelling with God and with God's people. The implication of being the temple of God is that God has consecrated this space for such a radical encounter between God and God's people. Christian contemplation is this encounter brought to its fulfillment in an encompassing experience of participation in divine life. Although it is the most deeply inward and intimate of experiences, it is also an enlivening of community from its roots in God's personal love of each and every one. Thus Christian contemplation is, paradoxically, both solitary and communal, joy-filled, yet alive to the anguish that permeates the world, radically dependent on the transcendent God, yet fully embodied.

THE CONTRIBUTION OF CONTEMPLATIVES AND MYSTICS

By delving into the Bible we have gained a basic theology of Christian contemplation, yet the description remains somewhat abstract. When contemplatives write from their own experience, their language is full of intense emotion and vibrant imagery. For example, here is the outpouring of an anonymous, but not atypical, fourteenth-century German mystic as he encourages a disciple to pursue contemplation:

> O deep treasure, how will you be dug up? O high perfection, who may attain you? O flowing fountain, who can exhaust you? O burning Brilliance; outbursting Power; simple Return; naked Hiddenness; hidden Security; secure Confidence; simple silent One in all things; manifold Good in a single silence; You silent Outcry, no one can find you who does not know how to let you go.[3]

This excerpt illustrates a characteristic that scholars note in mystical language across traditions, namely, that rather than using logic and direct reference to *describe* an experience, mystics often prefer to employ paradox, excess, and unsettling metaphors to *evoke* an experience.[4] In other words, the writer's way of using language shocks the reader's mind into letting go of the usual discursive level of thinking and perceiving so that she or he can glimpse, at least for a moment, the transcendent ecstasy of participation in God. This is why reading the writings of experienced contemplatives and mystics is an important practice to nurture one's contemplative growth.

The chief characteristic of contemplation is radical experiential participation in God. Within Christian (as well as in Jewish and Islamic) traditions, a common metaphor for this is the "spiritual marriage" of God and the human soul. Marriage is a physical, moral, and spiritual union, yet it also retains the "twoness" of the partners. Here is how Jeanne Guyon expressed it in her commentary on the biblical Song of Songs:

> The marriage takes place when the soul falls dead and senseless into the arms of the Bridegroom who, beholding her more fitted for it, receives her into union. But the consummation of the marriage does not come to pass until the soul is so melted, annihilated, and freed from self that it can unreservedly flow into God. Then is accomplished that admirable fusion of the creature and the Creator which brings them into unity, so to speak, though

with such an infinite disproportion as exists between a single drop of water and the ocean. The drop has become ocean, but it remains forever a little drop.[5]

Thus, in the culmination of contemplative experience the small "drop" that is human consciousness flows completely into the infinite ocean of God, paradoxically both losing its boundaries (so that it becomes the ocean) and retaining them (so that it remains just a little drop).

Guyon describes the limited case of contemplation, yet in the journey of contemplative practice, few spend the majority of their time at such a peak of intensity. In the following three sections, I will discuss the meaning of Christian contemplation in three aspects: contemplation as a chosen style of prayer and of life, contemplation as an eruptive spiritual event in the midst of life, and contemplation as a mature stage in the development of a life of prayer.

A Style of Prayer and of Life

In the midst of a busy, demanding life, it is not uncommon to hear people say, "I would like to be more contemplative." Often what they mean is that they long to have time to slow down, sit quietly without the demand of an immediate task, and let the reflections of the mind float freely. Calling this "contemplative" is correct insofar as simple practices like these can signal the beginning of a turn from a heavily task-oriented way of life to one that has space for breathing with God. For example, try pausing in the middle of a busy day to take a fifteen-minute outdoor stroll with eyes, ears, and nose alert to the wonders of creation, or simply put aside your work for five minutes, close your eyes, and invite remembrance of God's presence. Yet for such an aspiration to blossom into a genuinely contemplative way of life, one's repertoire of contemplative practices must expand and become woven deeply into daily life.

In this aspect, we identify a contemplative person as characterized by long-term commitment to practices that actively encourage a deep, inward attentiveness to God's movement in self and world. Stillness, silence, focused awareness, and reflective attentiveness to the world around are examples of contemplative practices. The contemplative person also typically values a rhythm of life that includes regular periods of solitude and withdrawal from outward activity. A daily practice of at least one or two periods of twenty to sixty minutes devoted exclusively to quiet prayer or meditation is normative. As noted above, Mary of Bethany in Luke 10:39, who "sat beside the Lord at his feet listening to him speak," is a model of this sort of chosen practice.

A contemplative style of prayer deemphasizes rituals, words, active imagination, and discursive thinking in favor of simple, wordless presence to God. This does not mean that contemplative people never engage in those more active forms of praying;

they do, and indeed they must—for "wordless presence" can sometimes degenerate into an aimless mind wandering about banal thoughts! The difference in the contemplative style is a readiness, even an eagerness, to shift gears from the active motion of the mind into deep attentiveness to God in wordless silence. For some, this shift is facilitated by body practices such as attention to breathing, Tai Chi, or yoga. Learning from the meditation practices of Buddhists, Hindus, or Sufis has also been helpful to many. Two Christian movements that explicitly teach a contemplative style of prayer are Contemplative Outreach/Centering Prayer (Basil Pennington, OCSO, and Thomas Keating, OCSO) and the World Community for Christian Meditation (John Main, OSB, and Laurence Freeman, OSB).

Some people seem to be drawn, even from a young age, to this style of prayer, while other committed Christians may never find this approach attractive. A friend of mine gives the example of herself and her husband of forty years: she has long been committed to practicing contemplative prayer, while he is a deeply committed social justice advocate who finds God primarily through action and social participation. Personality and temperament are among the factors that may incline a person to the quiet, inward, and regular rhythm of the contemplative style. Yet we cannot stereotype contemplative prayer as strictly for introverts, because some gregarious people are also drawn to it.

Attraction to the contemplative approach seems to become more common, however, as people grow older. Psychologist Carl Jung suggested that this is because the task of the first half of life is to build a strong ego through active achievements, while the task of the second half of life is to let go of the ego as one explores the inner world and seeks spiritual wholeness. Other factors may simply be that people have more freedom to let go of other demands in later years or that a slower, quieter style becomes more appealing as the body ages.

A small minority of people discover a vocation to become full-time contemplatives by joining a contemplative religious order or becoming lay hermits. Many others maintain a contemplative rhythm while carrying on ordinary lives including jobs, family, and social commitments.[6] Even full-time contemplatives usually work several hours a day as well as deal with a variety of normal human relationships. The difference is that they build the structure of their days by starting with the priority of contemplative practice, while most of us seek to build a rhythm of contemplative practice into a life already structured by work and relational commitments.

This section has focused on contemplation as a style of prayer and a way of life that may be attractive to some people because of temperament, personal gifts, stage of life, or the discovery of a need for balance in an overfilled life. In this aspect, contemplative prayer does not necessarily require unusual gifts or maturity in the life of prayer. The practices of contemplative prayer can be chosen and cultivated by anyone, regardless of their vocation, lifestyle, or stage of life.

CONTEMPLATION AS AN ERUPTIVE SPIRITUAL EVENT

A contemplative spiritual *event* is characterized by a breakthrough of intense awareness of communion with God and/or nature. A contemplative moment may occur spontaneously and "by surprise" in the midst of almost any sort of activity, or while a person is engaged in an intentional practice of prayer. In either case, it is a transforming moment because one feels that one has been awakened to life at a vastly deeper and fuller level than before. It can also be a disturbing event because it invites—or even impels—a reassessment and restructuring of the way one has previously been living. If asked, many people are able to recount one or more such events as a memory to which they return frequently to refresh their core sense of identity and meaning.

As a spontaneous event, such contemplative moments can take place at a very young age. Edward Robinson's *The Original Vision* records many such cases. A woman described the following experience when she was four or five years old:

> My mother and I were walking on a stretch of land in Pangbourne Berks, known locally as "the moors." As the sun declined and the slight chill of evening came on, a pearly mist formed over the ground.... Suddenly I seemed to see the mist as a shimmering gossamer tissue and the harebells, appearing here and there, seemed to shine with a brilliant fire. Somehow I understood that this was the living tissue of life itself, in which that which we call consciousness was embedded, appearing here and there as a shining focus of energy in the more diffused whole. In that moment I knew that I had my own special place, as had all other things, animate and so-called inanimate, and that we were all part of this universal tissue which was both fragile yet immensely strong, and utterly good and beneficent.[7]

Such an event has sometimes been termed "nature mysticism" or "extraverted mysticism," since it occurs while engaged in activity (walking) and outward perception (seeing). More significant than the context, however, is the psychological character of the event. Whereas ordinary experience is fundamentally organized by the distinctions between self and other, subject and object, such eruptive contemplative events soften or even temporarily eliminate these distinctions. The experiencer's sense of self shifts into an enchanted awareness of profound interconnection with the world around, accompanied by the conviction that this way of being is more real, substantial, and sacred than the ordinary perception of self that has preceded it. Such an experience can become a lifelong foundation of identity, as evidenced by the same woman's statement: "The vision has never left me...the whole of this experience has ever since formed a kind of reservoir of strength fed from an unseen source."[8]

Psychologists have proffered a variety of theories about what might make a person susceptible to such a spiritual breakthrough. While it is not possible to take time here to adequately survey this complex field of study, one commonality in many of these theories is the idea that the normal strength of a person's self-boundaries was already undergoing some challenging stress when a seemingly minor event tipped the balance toward the softening or collapse of these boundaries. Stress may come from a life-stage transition, such as adolescence, mid-life, or retirement; from social dislocation, as when someone loses a job or migrates to a new country; from a traumatic event, such as an experience of violence or severe loss; or from a preexisting psychological instability derived either from heredity or from early life experience. In the example given above, as well as others from Robinson's *Original Vision*, childhood itself may be seen as a predisposing condition since a child's self-boundaries have not yet firmed up to adult strength.

It is important to note that such a sudden shift of self-boundaries carries risks and, in some cases, could even be psychologically pathological. If loss of the subject-object boundaries leads to violent reactions, intense negative emotions, or ongoing patterns of disorganized thinking and behavior, it is likely to be a sign of pathological breakdown rather than of positive contemplative breakthrough. Those who teach contemplative practices of prayer and meditation often caution that for a small minority of people with notably fragile mental health, the encouragement of contemplative practice is inadvisable.[9] Even for the person of average mental health, the psychological impact of the contemplative restructuring of consciousness sometimes may be a protracted period of turmoil as one's core sense of identity, vocational choices, and relationships undergo painful readjustment. The conviction that an experience is fundamentally spiritual and growth-enhancing does not preclude the possibility that psychotherapeutic consultation may be needed for a time.

This very brief psychological discussion points to another paradox of the eruptive contemplative experience; that is, a kind of weakness frequently accompanies the breakthrough that leads to a powerful contemplative refounding of the self. The strong, successful, well-adjusted adult may be less prone to such transformative contemplative moments, which are more likely to visit children, the suffering, the marginalized, or those who feel they have lost their way. On the other hand, an apparently strong person may be unaware of the chink in their own armor—the "weak point" in the success-seeking self, lying in wait to provide an opening for the unsettling attack of divine life. Then the question becomes whether one will cling to the current successful contours of one's life or find the courage to embark on the risk-filled journey of reformation that taking the contemplative vision seriously will demand.

Again, to return to the story of Martha of Bethany (Luke 10:38–42), we do not hear how she responded to the eruptive contemplative invitation. Such an experience may be dismissed as no more than a puzzling aberration, or it may initiate a process of search and new commitments that leads to a profoundly different way of life. For the negative case, one may think of the rich young man in the gospels who turned away sad when Jesus offered him a radically different perspective on what constitutes a life of joy. For the positive case, we can think of famous conversion stories such as those of Paul (Acts 9:1–22) or of St. Augustine (*Confessions*, VIII, 7–12), in which the initial breakthrough was eventually integrated into a mature and fruitful Christian life.

A Mature Stage of the Life of Prayer

Finally, contemplation can be a *stage* in a dedicated life of prayer, characterized by a permanent shift to a different level of God-awareness. The sign of transition to this stage is a growing conviction that prayer practices that keep one's focus primarily on the mental or emotional level are inadequate to the urgent inward attraction one is experiencing. In most cases this stage is only reached after a person has engaged for several years in a disciplined practice of prayer that includes more active methods such as reflection on Scripture and imaginative conversation with God. The person in the contemplative stage feels compelled to spend the majority of their prayer time in a deep and wordless awareness of the presence of God.

St. John of the Cross provided the classic list of signs for discerning when a person is being invited to make the transition to the contemplative stage in the life of prayer. John distinguished between discursive meditation, which engages actively in point by point reflection on holy topics, and contemplation, which responds to a divine lure toward wordless mutual indwelling. In his time, discursive meditation was the commonly recommended method of prayer for ordinary folk, and many spiritual directors insisted that their directees continue to practice it even if they found it very difficult. John aims to provide guidance to both seekers and spiritual directors when he asserts that the following three signs indicate that the time is ripe to abandon discursive meditation in favor of contemplation:

First sign: "The realization that one cannot make discursive meditation nor receive satisfaction from it as before."

Second sign: "An awareness of the disinclination to fix the imagination or sense faculties upon other particular objects, exterior or interior." Though the imagination wanders, one does not want to fix it on anything.

Third (and surest) sign: "A person likes to remain alone in loving awareness of God, without particular considerations…he prefers to remain only in the general, loving awareness and knowledge we mentioned, without particular knowledge or understanding."[10]

John emphasizes that all three signs must be present since any one or two of them without the others could be an indication of some other condition such as laziness, distraction, exhaustion, or illness. He acknowledges that making this discernment is not always easy, especially since "at the beginning of this state [of contemplation] the loving knowledge is almost imperceptible." John indicates that there is something truly new emerging in this stage—a profound depth and intensity of awareness of divine life permeating one's whole being and drawing one into a consciousness beyond all thought and imagination. The first harbingers of this new level of prayer experience are very delicate, but they must not be neglected because the gift of contemplation is of such high value. As John puts it, "a little of this pure love is more precious to God and the soul and more beneficial to the Church, even though it seems one is doing nothing, than all other works put together."[11]

The essential underlying issue for discernment during the transitional period is whether God is moving in a person's being in such a way that he or she perceives experientially that the contemplative process has passed from one's own control to that of God, whose ways are essentially ungraspable. A classic image for this paradoxical awareness is the "cloud of unknowing." The anonymous author of the fourteenth century book of that name writes:

> For when you first begin to undertake [this contemplative path], all that you find is a darkness, a sort of cloud of unknowing.…This darkness and cloud is always between you and God, no matter what you do, and it prevents you from seeing him clearly by the light of understanding in your reason, and from experiencing him in sweetness of love in your affection.[12]

The advice to the aspiring contemplative is to "beat with a sharp dart of longing love upon this cloud of unknowing which is between you and your God."[13] In another place he adds, "So now labor earnestly for a short while, and beat upon this high cloud of unknowing, and then take your rest."[14] This phraseology captures the combination of active, focused longing, and more passive "letting go into the darkness" that characterizes the prayer of one moving into the contemplative stage. The person has a deep certainty that God is actively at work in the "cloud" that obscures the inner dwelling place, but can do no more than eagerly turn attention in that direction and let God do as he will.

The character of the contemplative stage can perhaps best be summed up by Galatians 2:20: "It is no longer I who live, but Christ who lives in me" (NRSV). The phrase preceding this sentence is "I have been crucified with Christ," and it is important to note that for some contemplatives this radical participation in Christ involves a period of deep suffering that John of the Cross called the "dark night of spirit."[15] For John, as for the author of the *Cloud of Unknowing* and a number of other Christian teachers of contemplation, darkness is a multifaceted symbol that stands for the romantic night of love as well as for the radical unknowability of God, which may engender deep psychological distress. The "dark night of spirit" refers particularly to a phase in which the deeply dedicated person of prayer feels as if God has completely disappeared from his or her life. John calls this a "purgation" that ultimately prepares the contemplative for a union with God that lets go of all dependence on feelings, expectations, and images, and instead rests only in God's own life and movements.

In reality, most people take a somewhat circuitous route to the contemplative stage and are well advised to keep active prayer practices in their repertoire rather than abandoning them permanently. John of the Cross's three signs do not apply only to a onetime process of transition to a new stage, but rather can be employed as ongoing discernment criteria. The three signs emphasize that it is not enough to feel that active prayer is fruitless; this must also be accompanied by a conviction that "loving awareness" is active within one, even though faint and ungraspable. This conviction is what distinguishes the "dark night" from psychological depression.[16] It requires sensitivity and patience on the part of both seeker and spiritual director to discern the occasions when the precious gift of contemplation is best nurtured by "doing nothing" from the occasions when it is wiser to take some gentle measures to keep mind and imagination prayerfully focused.

Fourteenth-century Flemish mystic John Ruusbroec provides an intimate portrait of the inner life of the mature contemplative, describing it as a "storm of love":

> God's touch and his giving of himself, together with our striving in love and our giving of ourselves in return—this is what sets love on a firm foundation. This flux and reflux make the spring of love overflow, so that God's touch and our striving in love become a single love. Here a person becomes so possessed by love that he must forget both himself and God and know nothing but love. [17]

Ruusbroec also masterfully articulates the intrinsic links between activity and rest, innerness and outgoingness, prayer and social responsibility that characterize the mature contemplative, who "goes toward God with fervent interior love through his eternal activity, enters into God with his blissful inclination toward eternal rest, remains in God, and nevertheless goes out to all creatures in virtue and righteousness through a love which is common to all." Ruusbroec affirms that "this is the highest point of the interior life."[18] His words provide an excellent conclusion to our reflection on Christian contemplation, again reminding us that its fruit is a divine enlivening of the whole embodied and social person in all their inward and outward engagements.

1. *The New American Bible* rev. ed. This is the translation used for all quotations from Scripture in this chapter.
2. On the role and practices of Roman augurs, see Mary Beard, John A. North, and S.R.F. Price, *Religions of Rome* (New York: Cambridge University Press, 1998), 21–23.
3. Bernard McGinn, ed., *The Essential Writings of Christian Mysticism*, Modern Library Classics (New York: Modern Library, 2006), 141.
4. Michael Anthony Sells, *Mystical Languages of Unsaying* (Chicago: University of Chicago Press, 1994).
5. James W. Metcalf, *The Song of Songs of Solomon with Explanation and Reflections Having Reference to the Interior Life by Madame Guyon* (New York: A.W. Dennett, 1879), 102.
6. See Virginia Manss and Mary Frohlich, eds., *The Lay Contemplative: Testimonies, Perspectives, Resources* (Cincinnati: St. Anthony Messenger Press, 2000).
7. Edward Robinson, *The Original Vision: A Study of the Religious Experience of Childhood* (New York: Seabury, 1983), 32.
8. Edward Robinson, 32–33.
9. See, for example, Mary Garden, "Can Meditation Be Bad for You?," *Humanist* 67, no. 5 (September 2007): 20–24; Thomas Merton, "The Inner Experience: Some Dangers in Contemplation," *Cistercian Studies* 19, no. 2 (1984): 139–150.
10. John of the Cross, "Ascent of Mount Carmel," in *Collected Works of St. John of the Cross*, rev. ed., trans. Kieran Kavanaugh, OCD, and Otilio Rodriguez, OCD (Washington, DC: ICS, 1991), book 2, 13.
11. John of the Cross, "Spiritual Canticle," in *Collected Works*, verse 29.
12. James Walsh, ed., *The Cloud of Unknowing*, Classics of Western Spirituality (New York: Paulist, 1981), chap. 3.
13. Walsh, chap. 12.
14. Walsh, chap. 26.
15. John of the Cross, "Dark Night," in *Collected Works*, book 2, 1, 1.
16. It is also possible that dynamics of both spiritual dark night and psychological depression can be active at the same time. For discussion, see Kevin G. Culligan, "The Dark Night and Depression," in *Carmelite Prayer: A Tradition for the 21st Century* (New York: Paulist, 2003).
17. Jan van Ruusbroec, *John Ruusbroec: The Spiritual Espousals and Other Works*, Classics of Western Spirituality (New York: Paulist, 1985), 115.
18. Ruusbroec, 135.

CHAPTER 6

Spiritual Direction and Prayer

~ William A. Barry, SJ ~

People who take prayer seriously often wish that they had someone with whom to talk about their prayer. Prayer, after all, means communicating, in some fashion, with God, and God is a mystery. Questions arise. How do I know whether I am talking to God or just to myself? Is the way I pray the right way? Are there better ways of praying? Are the experiences I am having in prayer crazy or real? These and many other questions beg for answers. Where do we turn? Throughout history, men and women have sought out other people who seem to know something about prayer in the hope that they can get some answers to questions such as these. Most often the people to whom they turned were called spiritual directors or spiritual companions. In this article, I want to explore the relationship of spiritual direction to the development of a solid prayer life.

THE EXPANSION OF SPIRITUAL DIRECTION

The time after the Second Vatican Council has been a watershed in the history of spiritual direction. Before the Council, spiritual direction was by and large the province of Roman Catholic clergy, and those who sought it out were mostly Roman Catholic, and mostly what one might call religious professionals, that is, priests, seminarians, members of religious congregations. What these seekers sought and received was mainly direction on how to deal with various problems that came up in their prayer and moral life. Rarely was there a discussion of actual experiences of prayer. There were, of course, exceptions to this depiction, but I dare say they were few and far between. However, after Vatican II when Roman Catholic religious congregations were counseled to go back to their roots to find the sources of their spirituality in order to adapt themselves and their spiritualties to modern needs, many members of religious congregations discovered that a tradition of spiritual direction that took seriously God's desire for a personal relationship with us human beings had somehow been neglected in favor of a rule-based spirituality. Among those who discovered such a tradition were the members of the Society of Jesus (the Jesuits), who found out that the *Spiritual Exercises* of their founder, Ignatius of Loyola, were originally given to individuals by individual directors. This direction meant talking with those making the *Spiritual Exercises* about their experience of prayer in the previous day and then deciding with them how they should proceed with prayer after this session. It was, for many Jesuits and others, a revelation to find out how helpful this kind of spiritual direction could be. Beginning in the late 1960s and early 1970s, more and more people came into contact with this kind of spiritual direction that took seriously that God was real and was really encountered.[1]

For a century or more prior to the Second Vatican Council the phrase "Spiritual Exercises" meant listening to four or five talks a day, each one followed by time for personal prayer. The talks stressed asceticism and moral living to a great degree. The retreat director was so taken up with giving talks that there was little time for personal discussions with those making the exercises about their experience in prayer. Moreover, since Ignatius himself had defined his spiritual exercises as aimed "to overcome oneself and to order one's life, without reaching a decision through some disordered affection,"[2] it was no wonder that many people, both directors and recipients and readers of the text, believed that the exercises were more a manual for ascetical training than a way to meet God in an intimate and personal manner. The discovery of the individually directed spiritual exercises changed this perspective almost overnight. It was understood that Ignatius himself had come to believe through his own experience that God communicated personally with him, sinner though he was. Hence, he presumed that God was communicating with everyone in order to lead them into a transforming personal relationship that would enable them to live as the images of God they were created to be.

With this discovery of the individually directed retreat after Vatican II, many people besides Jesuits began to make the Spiritual Exercises in various formats and then to receive training in order to give them. Soon those who were not Catholic began to make the exercises and to seek training in order to give them.

At the same time, in many quarters people began to seek regular help with their relationship with God apart from retreats.[3] Modern spiritual direction began to spread like wildfire not only in the United States but throughout the world. In 1990 a national meeting of people from various training programs for spiritual directors was held in the Mercy Center in Burlingame, California. At this meeting the idea of starting an international association for spiritual directors was floated and ratified. Spiritual Directors International was founded and has in the past twenty-five years grown into an organization of 6,800 active members on six continents and from different faith traditions who have an annual conference and publish a quarterly journal, *Presence*.[4]

For present purposes, I offer the definition of spiritual direction given by Barry and Connolly in *The Practice of Spiritual Direction*, first published in 1982 and revised for a new edition in 2009:

We define spiritual direction...as help given by one believer to another which enables the latter to pay attention to God's personal communication to him or her, to respond to this personally communicating God, to grow in intimacy with this God, and to live out the consequences of the relationship. The focus of this type of spiritual direction is on experience, not ideas, and specifically on the religious dimension of experience, i.e., that dimension of any experience that evokes the presence of the mysterious Other whom we call God. Moreover, this experience is viewed, not as an isolated event, but as an expression of the ongoing personal relationship God has established with each one of us.[5]

Connolly and I made clear that our definition of spiritual direction derived from our experience of the Ignatian spiritual exercises. Since the book has become something of a primer for programs training spiritual directors throughout the world and has been translated into twelve languages as of this writing,[6] it appears that the definition resonates with many people of different spiritual traditions. The definition presumes that God is personal and wants a personal relationship with every human being. It states that God is personally communicating with us. Hence it also presumes that God is somehow encountered by us, that there is a religious dimension to our experience if only we become attuned to that dimension. Just as there are physiological, psychological, sociological and cultural dimensions (among others) to every human experience, so too there is a religious dimension for those who are open to it. Indeed, one of the tasks of a spiritual director is to help directees pay attention to their experience and to discern within it what is of God from what is not. The definition states that God's communication involves a desire for an ongoing and developing relationship, a relationship which, in another context, I have likened to a friendship.[7] Finally, the definition underlines the fact that this relationship is initiated by God, not by us.

THE RELATIONSHIP BETWEEN SPIRITUAL DIRECTION AND PRAYER

With this definition, we already touch upon the relationship of spiritual direction to prayer since prayer is, quite simply, the working out of this relationship. A personal relationship with anyone, including with God, can only be sustained by mutual communication, another word for prayer.

Not everyone, of course, believes in a personal God, and those who don't often want to nourish a spiritual life as well. Since Spiritual Directors International is home to many different spiritual traditions, not all of which believe in a personal God or a personally communicating God, it is clear that people of these traditions also seek spiritual direction. It is simply important to note that there are many kinds of spiritual direction on offer through SDI and other venues, beyond those that I am focusing on, here. My focus is Judeo-Christian.

The Judeo-Christian tradition presents a God who not only creates this universe out of nothing but also creates, at least on the planet Earth, human beings in God's image and likeness (Genesis 1). According to this tradition, God demonstrates an ongoing interest in what human beings are doing and how they are faring. The Jewish and Christian Bibles together can be read as the ongoing story of God's dealings with human beings, attempting always to convince them to live in this world as God's image. Indeed, one can make a case for the idea that God's hopes for the world depend on human beings acting as images of God. In this story the initial harmonious relationship between God and the first human beings is broken when the human beings disobey God in order to become like God and live forever, something that they already had by God's good gift and promise (cf. Genesis 3). The ensuing downward spiral seems to reach a nadir in the eleventh chapter of Genesis when, at the tower of Babel, human beings lose the ability to communicate with one another. But chapter 12 begins a new venture in God's efforts to show us how to live when God calls Abram and Sarai to leave their native land and go with God in trust to another land. The Abraham saga can be read as a story of growing intimacy between God and Abraham and then with Abraham's family. God and Abraham, one can say, become friends, and Abraham becomes the father of a people chosen for special intimacy with God, but an intimacy that was ultimately for the good of the whole human family and, indeed, for the good of the whole planet. In their better moments, the Israelites knew that they were chosen not because of their special goodness or might, but only because of God's love for the world.

I won't take the space, here, to develop this way of reading the Bible. I only want to highlight that in this story, God continually engages in a personal relationship with people and asks their willingness to engage in this personal relationship. God initiates this relationship; we respond. Prayer is the result of God's initiative, but because of God's desire, the relationship is one of mutuality. God cannot have what he wants without our cooperation. So God wants us to engage in something like the mutual communication friends have with one another.[8]

How Spiritual Directors Help Others in Prayer

Anyone who has engaged in friendship knows that mutual communication is not easy, even when the two people are visible to one another. Since God is neither visible nor even comprehensible to human beings, it is no wonder that over the centuries people have looked for help with developing a personal relationship with God. How does a spiritual director help someone who comes for help with this relationship?

Spiritual direction is a form of pastoral counseling, I believe, and is distinguished from other forms by its focus. The definition cited earlier makes the focus of spiritual direction the experience of seekers when they are consciously trying to be in relationship with God. This focus on what that definition calls the religious dimension of experience sets the context for the agreement that spiritual directors and directees make about what they will talk about when they meet. Spiritual directors agree that they will offer help to others to develop a mutual personal relationship with God. Directees agree to try to pay attention to their attempts to engage in a mutual relationship with God, for example, to pray, and to talk about what they notice in prayer.

Most people who begin spiritual direction need help to pay attention to their experiences. First of all, they have to learn their experience is important, because only in their experience can they come to know God in a personal way. So directors have to work patiently and with empathy with directees in order to convince them of the worthwhileness of their experience. Only in their experience do they meet God who personally communicates with them. In other words, directees have to come through experience to the realization that God is real for them.

Robert Marsh explains well what I mean here by God being real and how his spiritual director helped him:

> One phrase became something of a mantra for me during my theology studies: how would I do *this* if I believed God were *real*. By "this" I meant theology, but I also included all the other things I did as a Jesuit at the time—preach, preside at Eucharist, give spiritual direction, *be* a Jesuit. How would I do all these things if I believed God were really real? And by "real" I meant present, interested, involved, available for real interaction: and more than that—initiating, acting, relating, desiring and responding—pick your verb.

He had come to these questions because, in his continuing theology studies after ordination, he had a spiritual director who did believe in God's reality and kept asking him about his experience of God. "When she asked what the God of my prayer was like, she expected me to be capable of answering in straightforward terms rather than in abstract notions." In the early stages of this new kind of spiritual direction it dawned on him that he did not know nor expect to know what his God was actually like. He goes on:

Over several months, my director's gentle perseverance and belief in God's reality (not to mention her insight and skill) paid off: I began to have glimmers of answers to her questions about my experience of God; I began to know what my God was like; and I began to trust that knowledge. I came face-to-face with God and God became real to me. It was an opening of the eyes for me, with repercussions beyond my own prayer....I hadn't been able to do spiritual direction in a way that trusted that God would be there in other people's experience. That began to change too: once I *expected* God to be there in someone else's life I found God was—as long as I was, in my turn, patient and persistent enough to allow such experiences to emerge and be noticed.[9]

Marsh's spiritual director gently, but insistently kept asking him to talk about his experience and, by using personal terms, conveyed to him that she expected that he was encountering God who could be described in concrete terms. To be this kind of spiritual director, she herself had to have encountered God as real and really interested in a personal relationship and have come to believe that God wanted to be encountered in this way by others. She would need to be patient with the stumbling efforts of beginners to pay attention to and to speak about their experience. Clearly, Marsh's spiritual director was patient, but insistent with him.[10]

Second, directors help directees to make sense of their experience. Not everything we at first believe is an experience of God is that in reality. How do we tell the difference? With this question, people enter that phase of their personal relationship with God called, in the Christian tradition, the "discernment of spirits." They want to sift the wheat from the chaff, as it were, in their experience. But note that this sifting requires that they have experiences that need sifting. If they do not first take their experience seriously as the locus where they meet God, they will never have to worry about which experiences are of God, which ones not of God.

The term "discernment of spirits" may conjure up ideas of some mysterious realm, but in reality it refers to something that happens all the time. Imagine yourself walking in a cemetery at night; suddenly you hear a strange noise that sounds like a moan. You jump with alarm and look around, fearful that you are about to be accosted by a ghost, and start to run for the nearest exit and your car. When you get to the car and are safely inside with the doors locked, you begin to wonder what just happened. You are asking yourself a question of discernment. Did I just escape a disaster or was I deluded by the darkness and the fact that I was in a very quiet cemetery? When the tradition speaks of discernment of spirits, it is referring to questions like this, only the questions now refer to the various interior movements that occur as we try to engage with God.

In his "Reminiscences," sometimes called his "Autobiography," Ignatius of Loyola relates how he began to become a discerning person. He was a young nobleman interested in gaining glory and renown as a soldier and courtier who had been badly wounded in his legs by a cannonball. As he recuperated at the Loyola castle, he asked for some books to read, hoping to be given some of the romance novels of the period. The only books available, however, were a life of Jesus and a book of the lives of saints which he began to read with some relish. He was a great daydreamer whose dreams now kept shifting. In one set of daydreams he was a dashing courtier who did feats of daring in order to win the favor of a great lady. He enjoyed these very much. After he started to read the life of Christ and the lives of saints, he alternated a new kind of daydream in which he imitated the great saints, even doing greater deeds of asceticism than they had done. He also enjoyed these very much. However, he did not, for a relatively long time, notice a difference, namely that after the dreams of doing great knightly deeds he felt "dry and discontented," but after the dreams of following Christ, he remained "content and happy." He paid no attention to this difference, he says, "until one time when his eyes were opened a little, and he began to marvel at this difference in kind and to reflect on it, picking it up from experience that from some thoughts he would be left sad and from others happy, and little by little coming to know the difference in kind of spirits that were stirring: the one from the devil, and the other from God."[11] This story can take some of the mystery out of the term "discernment of spirits." Ignatius came to believe that God could use daydreams to teach him something about the ways of God and the ways of Satan, whom Ignatius often called the "enemy of human nature."

Here is an example of how a spiritual director might help a person to decide whether he or she is experiencing God or not. A young man who had been engaging in spiritual direction for some years told his director, with some animation, that he had experienced a warm and tender feeling of being loved in a special way by God. The director asked him to say more about the experience. He said that he was walking in a wooded area, thinking about his life and about what God might have in mind for him when he was suddenly overcome with a sense of being deeply loved by God. The director asked him to describe his feelings and other reactions. He said that almost as soon as he had the experience of feeling deeply loved, the thought flashed through his mind, "How do I know this is God?" He spent the next few minutes trying to answer the question and then decided to go back to his apartment for dinner. The director asked him if he had talked with God about the experience and his question. He had not. Instead, he had begun questioning a number of his prayer experiences and had gotten quite discouraged. As the two of them looked at what happened at the time of the experience, it became clear that an experience that could have led to a deepening of his relationship with God had been sidetracked by the nagging question, "How do I know this is God?"

The director said that he had a chance here to try to answer his question, one that many people who take the relationship with God seriously have to answer. The director then helped him to look more carefully at the sequence. The young man noted that when he felt the love of God, he was filled with joy and great hopes, but the question had quickly put a damper on those feelings and led to discouragement and self-doubt. The director reminded him of the first two rules for discernment of spirits in Ignatius of Loyola's *Spiritual Exercises*.[12] He had used these rules before to good effect but had not thought of them at this time. In these first rules, the orientation of the person toward God and God's ways is used to determine whether a movement is from God's Spirit or from the evil spirit. If a person is trying to lead a good life in union with God, then "the enemy" tries to derail the person by raising doubts and questions whose only purpose is to keep him disquieted and self-absorbed; when one pays attention to such movements, one notices that they lead to endless questions and to self-absorption. The "good spirit," on the other hand, encourages the person, gives peace, joy, and hope. As the two talked about this rule, the directee saw clearly that his initial experience was most likely from God and was encouraged to have a conversation with God about the event and its aftermath.

Spiritual directors help others with their prayer by helping them to take seriously questions of discernment. In an age when the very existence of God, let alone a self-communicating and personally interested God, is questioned on all sides, anyone who engages in a relationship with God will face questions of discernment. Spiritual directors are guides who have themselves faced such questions and know how to try to answer them as honestly as possible. Modern seekers of a personal relationship with God do well to seek out wise people who can help them to pay attention to their experience and to make sense of it.[13]

Prayer and a Personal Relationship with God

I am convinced that God wants a personal relationship with us human beings. It may sound as though I am belaboring an undisputed point. The issue, however, is not what people say about prayer but what they do when they pray. I have met too many people for whom prayer is a matter of talking to God without any expectation of a personal response. Of course, when they ask for something, such as their daily bread or a good outcome to a diagnosis of cancer, they hope that God will give them their daily bread or a cure for the cancer. But they do not expect to have something like a conversation with God; prayer, in other words, is a monologue in practice, not a dialogue.

I know from experience that those for whom prayer is essentially a monologue often include men and women whose profession is connected with religion, for example, priests and ministers and members of religious congregations, as well as spiritual directors. About five years ago, I gave a workshop for trained spiritual directors who, in their training programs to become spiritual directors, had read thoroughly and discussed *The Practice of Spiritual Direction*, the book mentioned earlier. In that workshop, I stressed that God wants something like a friendship and used examples and cases to illustrate how this notion of friendship facilitated the work of spiritual direction. I was surprised to find out that many of the participants felt that this was the first time they had heard that God wants a personal relationship. Earlier I mentioned the article by the Jesuit Robert Marsh, "Teaching Spiritual Direction as If God Were Real." Marsh notes that before he met a spiritual director who took seriously God's desire for a personal relationship and thus began to take God's reality seriously, he had twice made the full thirty-day Spiritual Exercises, given them in various formats and trained spiritual directors. After he had caught on that his spiritual director seriously expected that he was encountering a personally communicating God, he reread *The Practice of Spiritual Direction* and found that the authors "had been talking all the time about noticing the experience of God, but *I* hadn't noticed."[14] So I do not believe that I am barking up the wrong tree here.

For whatever reason, we have lost sight of the fact that the Judeo-Christian tradition constantly tells stories of God's concern and personal communication with human beings. God speaks tenderly, cajoles, warns, threatens, and even seems to get down on metaphorical knees (see Micah 6:3–5) to convince us to live as images of God and in a close personal relationship with God, with one another and with the whole world. Human beings speak back to God, thanking, praising, begging, expressing sorrow, but also laughing with God, arguing with God, even telling God how to be God (see the Abraham cycle in Genesis). What comes across is a story of a very close relationship indeed, one that can be likened to a friendship. For Christians, Jesus then ups the ante by calling us friends and showing us how to live as an image of God (cf. John 15:12–15).

Those who grasp that God wants their friendship find that their way of praying changes. They begin to share their feelings, desires, and dreams with God. After a while, they wonder about God's reactions to what they are experiencing and to what is happening in the world, and they ask God about them. They notice responses from

God and feel gratified and grateful. Prayer becomes rather easy and attractive. Just as any friendship goes through stages as it develops and gets deeper and more personal, so does the friendship with God. At first, our conversations with God are relatively superficial as we test the waters, just as new friends do. But gradually we go deeper and share more and more of our thoughts and feelings, dreams, and hurts. In the beginning there is a period that I have likened to a honeymoon period when all goes swimmingly. But no friendship, including that with God, can sustain this period for long. We think of things that we are ashamed of and question whether God could really love us. Life has dealt many people deep hurts, and they feel anger and wonder where God was when these things happened. Will we speak honestly to God of these shames and hurts and anger? Our past sins can suddenly plague us and cause a disruption in our friendship with God. "Who am I kidding? God can't want my friendship after the things I have done to offend him." As with any friendship, such disruptions will only be overcome by taking the chance of speaking honestly and asking for God's response. At times like these, people are greatly helped by a spiritual director who encourages them to speak frankly to God and to ask for a response. When we tell God the whole truth about our sins and shameful realities and find God forgiving and even grateful for our honesty, then a great burden is lifted from our hearts, and we want to spend more time with God in friendship. It can be a time of great healing of the hurts and sins of life and often leads a person to want to join God in the great work of bringing about a world where everyone lives in harmony and friendship with God, with one another, and with the whole world. For Christians, this new period of growth in friendship means becoming a close friend of Jesus and a disciple.[15]

Then, as friendship with God develops, prayer changes, naturally. For one thing, events in our world that impinge on us and on those we love continually change, so we have different things to talk about with God. Also, as we age, we have different experiences to share with God. As in any friendship, there are always new things to talk about. If God seems absent, we might be experiencing what St. John of the Cross called the "dark night of the soul," but this does not mean that we have to like it; we can tell God that we don't like it and want to experience his presence again. Finally, as with any close friendship, we will find that with God, the need to talk may recede, and we can just be with one another without much need for words. Spiritual directors are prepared to guide their directees through these experiences.

To conclude, we can see that the kind of spiritual direction I am advocating can help people develop a personal relationship with God analogous to a friendship. On this account of the nature of spiritual direction, this ministry deserves to be considered profoundly needed in our day and providentially brought to light, at least for Roman

Catholics, in the aftermath of the Second Vatican Council. I still agree with what Connolly and I wrote many years ago: "Indeed, spiritual direction may be considered the core form from which all other forms of pastoral care radiate, since ultimately all forms of pastoral care and counseling aim, or should aim, at helping people to center their lives in the mystery we call God."[16]

1. For an insightful indication of what I mean here by God being real, see Robert R. Marsh, "Teaching Spiritual Direction as if God Were Real," *The Way*, 53, no. 4 (October, 2014): 57–67.
2. *The Spiritual Exercises of Saint Ignatius: A Translation and Commentary*, trans. and ed. George E. Ganss, SJ (St. Louis: The Institute of Jesuit Sources, 1992), 31. Hereafter cited as *Sp. Ex.*
3. For examples from other traditions, see Tilden Edwards, *Spiritual Friend: Reclaiming the Gift of Spiritual Direction* (New York: Paulist, 1980); and Kenneth Leech, *Soul Friend: The Practice of Christian Spirituality*, rev. ed. (Harrisburg, PA: Morehouse, 2001). The previous edition was originally published in Great Britain in 1978.
4. Spiritual Directors International can be contacted at its website, SDIworld.org.
5. William A. Barry and William J. Connolly, *The Practice of Spiritual Direction*, 2nd ed. (New York: HarperOne, 2009), 8–9. The phrase "the mysterious Other we call God" was frequently used by Karl Rahner, SJ, in his writings.
6. *Spiritual Exercises* has been translated into Portuguese, French, Italian, Polish, German, Swedish, Norwegian, Czech, Spanish, Vietnamese, Hungarian, and two different Chinese translations.
7. William A. Barry, *A Friendship Like No Other: Experiencing God's Amazing Embrace* (Chicago: Loyola, 2008).
8. I have developed the notion of speaking intimately with God in *Praying the Truth: Deepening Your Friendship with God through Honest Prayer* (Chicago: Loyola, 2012).
9. Robert R. Marsh, "Teaching Spiritual Direction," 57–58.
10. For more on how spiritual directors help people to pay attention to and to talk about key interior facts, see Barry and Connolly, *The Practice of Spiritual Direction*, chapters 4 and 5.
11. St. Ignatius of Loyola, "Reminiscences," *Personal Writings*, translated with introductions and notes by Joseph A. Munitiz and Philip Endean (New York: Penguin, 1996), 15.
12. "Rules for the Discernment of Spirits," *Sp. Ex.*, 121–128.
13. For further reading on discernment, see Maureen Conroy, *The Discerning Heart: Discovering a Personal God* (Chicago: Loyola, 1993); Timothy Gallagher, *The Discernment of Spirits: An Ignatian Guide for Everyday Living* (New York: Crossroad, 2005); and *Spiritual Consolation: An Ignatian Guide for the Greater Discernment of Spirits* (New York: Crossroad, 2007); and Jim Manney, *What Do You Really Want? St. Ignatius and the Art of Discernment* (Chicago: Loyola, 2015).
14. Marsh, "Teaching Spiritual Direction," 58.
15. For a longer development of how friendship with God develops, see Barry, *A Friendship Like No Other*, chapters 3 and 4.
16. Barry and Connolly, *The Practice of Spiritual Direction*, 12.

CHAPTER 7

Struggling in Prayer

Ronald Rolheiser, OMI

Too Busy to Bow Down

We are not, by choice or ideology, a culture set against solitude, interiority, and prayer. Nor are we, in my opinion, more malicious, pagan, or afraid of interiority than past ages. Where we differ from the past is not so much in badness as in busyness. Most days, we don't pray simply because we don't quite get around to it.

Perhaps the best metaphor to describe our hurried and distracted lives is that of a car wash. When you pull up to a car wash, you are instructed to leave your motor running, to take your hands off the steering wheel, and to keep your foot off the brake. The idea is that the machine itself will guide you through.

For most of us, that's just what our typical day does to us. We have smartphones and radios that stimulate us before we are fully awake. Many of us are texting friends, checking Facebook and e-mail, watching the news, or listening to music or talk radio before we even shower or eat breakfast. The drive to work follows the same pattern: Stimulated and preoccupied, we listen to the radio, talk on our cell phones, and plan the day's agenda. We return home to television, conversation, activities, and preoccupations of all kinds. Eventually, we go to bed, where perhaps we read or watch a bit more TV. Finally, we fall asleep. When, in all of this, did we take time to think, to pray, to wonder, to be restful, to be grateful for life, for love, for health, for God?

Moreover, prayer is not easy because we are greedy for experience. The spiritual writer Henri Nouwen said this well: "I want to pray," he once said, "but I also don't want to miss out on anything—television, movies, socializing with friends, drinking in the world." Because we don't want to miss out on any experience, prayer is truly a discipline. When we sit or kneel in prayer, our natural craving for experience feels starved and begins to protest.

Ironically, most of us crave solitude. As our lives grow more pressured, as we grow more tired, and as we begin to talk more about burnout, we fantasize about solitude. We imagine it as a peaceful, quiet place, where we are walking by a lake, watching a sunset, or smoking a pipe in a rocker by the fireplace. But even here, many times we make solitude yet another activity, something we do.

Solitude, however, is a form of awareness. It's a way of being present and perceptive within all of life. It's having a dimension of reflectiveness in our daily lives that brings with it a sense of gratitude, appreciation, peacefulness, enjoyment, and prayer. It's the sense, within ordinary life, that life is precious, sacred, and enough.

How do we foster solitude? How do we get a handle on life so it doesn't just suck us through? How do we begin to lay a foundation for prayer in our lives?

The first step is to "put out into the deep" by remaining quietly in God's presence in solitude, in silence, in prayer. If it is your first time doing this, set aside fifteen minutes for prayer. In time, you might be able to manage thirty minutes.

Remember: Your heart is made to rest in God. If St. Augustine is right, and he is, then you can count on your restlessness to lead you into deeper prayer—the kind of prayer that leads to profound transformation, the kind of prayer that will not leave you empty-handed.

Struggling with Boredom

Prayer has a huge ebb and flow. When we try to pray, sometimes we walk on water, and sometimes we sink like a stone. Sometimes we have a deep sense of God's reality, and sometimes we can't even imagine that God exists. Sometimes we have deep feelings about God's goodness and love, and sometimes we feel only boredom and distraction. Sometimes our eyes fill with tears and we wish we could stay in our prayer place forever, and sometimes our eyes wander furtively to our wristwatches to see how much time we still need to spend in prayer.

We nurse a naïve fantasy both about what constitutes prayer and how we might sustain ourselves in it. What often lies at the center of this misguided notion is the belief that prayer is always meant to be interesting, warm, bringing spiritual insight, and giving the sense that we are actually praying. Classical writers in spirituality assure us that, though this is often true during our early prayer lives when we are in the honeymoon stage of our spiritual growth, it becomes less and less true the deeper we advance in prayer and spirituality. But that doesn't mean we are regressing in prayer. It often means the opposite.

Here's an analogy that might encourage you when you are struggling with boredom and the sense that nothing meaningful is happening.

Imagine you have an aged mother who is confined to a retirement home. You're the dutiful child and, every night after work, for one hour, you stop and spend time with her, helping her with her evening meal, sharing the events of the day, and simply being with her as her daughter or son. I doubt that, save for a rare occasion, you will have many deeply emotive or even interesting conversations with her. On the surface your visits will seem mostly routine and dry. Most times you will be talking about trivial, everyday things. "The kids are fine." "Steve dropped in last week." "Mom, your food really is bland. How can you stand all that Jell-O?" "No, we didn't get much rain, just a sprinkle." Given that you're busy and preoccupied with many pressures in your own life, it is natural that you will sneak the occasional glance at your watch.

But if you persevere in these regular visits with your mother, month after month, year after year, among everyone in the whole world, you will grow to know your mother the most deeply, and she will grow to know you the most deeply. That's because at a deep level of relationship, the real connection between us takes place below the surface of our conversations. We begin to know each other through simple presence.

Prayer is the same. If we pray faithfully every day, year in and year out, we can expect little excitement, lots of boredom, and regular temptations to look at the clock. But a bond and an intimacy will be growing under the surface: a deep, growing bond with our God.

FALSE NOTIONS OF PRAYER

Why is it so difficult to pray regularly?

Some reasons are obvious: overbusyness, tiredness, and too many demands on our time. But there are other reasons too, suggested by monks and people we think of as mystics. The problem we have in sustaining prayer, they say, is often grounded in the false notion that prayer needs to be exciting, intense, and full of energy all the time. That is impossible! Nothing is meant to be exciting all the time, including prayer and church services, and nobody has the energy to be alert, attentive, intense, and actively engaged every minute.

Like eating, prayer is meant to respect the natural rhythms of our energy. As we know from experience, we don't always want a banquet. If we tried to have a banquet every day, we would soon find coming to the table burdensome, and we would look for every excuse to escape, to sneak off for a quick sandwich by ourselves. Eating has a natural balance: banquets alternate with quick snacks, rich dishes with simple sandwiches, meals that take a whole evening with meals we eat on the run. We can have high season only if we mostly have ordinary time. Healthy eating habits respect our natural rhythms: our time, energy, tiredness, the season, the hour, our taste.

Prayer should be the same, but this isn't generally respected. Too often we are left with the impression that all prayer should be high celebration, upbeat, with high energy. The more variety, the better. Longer is better than shorter. No wonder we often lack the energy to pray and want to avoid church services!

The solution is not so much new prayer forms and more variety, but rhythm, routine, and established ritual. For monks, the key to sustaining a daily life of prayer is not novelty or the call for higher energy, but rather a reliance on the expected, the familiar, the repetitious, the ritual. What's needed is a clearly delineated prayer form that does not demand of you an energy you cannot muster on a given day.

There are times, of course, for high celebration, for variety and novelty, for spontaneity, and for long ceremonies. There are also times—and these are meant to predominate just as they do in our eating habits—for ordinary time, for low season, for prayer that respects our energy level, work pressures, and time constraints.

It is no accident, I suspect, that more people used to attend daily church services when these were shorter, simpler, and less demanding in terms of energy expenditure, and gave people attending a clear expectation as to how long they would last. The same holds true for the Office of the Church and all common prayer. What clear rituals provide is prayer that depends precisely upon something beyond our own energy. The rituals carry us: our tiredness, our inattentiveness, our indifference, and even our occasional distaste. They keep us praying even when we are too tired to muster up our own energy.

False Feelings in Prayer

Prayer, as one of its oldest definitions puts it, is "lifting mind and heart to God." That sounds simple, but it is hard to do. Why?

Because we have the wrong notion of what that means. We unconsciously nurse the idea that we can pray only when we are not distracted, not angry, not emotionally or sexually preoccupied. We think God is like a parent who wants to see us only on our best behavior. So we go into God's presence only when we have nothing to hide, are joy-filled, and feel we can give proper attention to God in a reverent and loving way. Because we don't understand what prayer is, we treat God as an authority figure or a visiting dignitary—as someone to whom we don't tell the real truth. We don't tell God what is really going on in our lives. We tell God what we think God wants to hear.

Because of this, we find it difficult to pray with any regularity. What happens is we go to pray, privately or in church, feeling tired, preoccupied, perhaps even angry at someone. We bracket what we are actually feeling and instead try to crank up praise, reverence, and gratitude to God. Of course it doesn't work! Our hearts and heads (because they are preoccupied with our real issues) grow distracted. We get the sense that what we are doing—trying to pray—is not something we can do right now and we leave it for some other time.

But the problem is not that our prayer is unreal or that the moment isn't right. The problem is that we are trying to lift to God thoughts and feelings that are not our own. If we take seriously that prayer is "lifting mind and heart to God," then every feeling and every thought we have is a valid and apt entry into prayer, no matter how irreverent, unholy, selfish, sexual, or angry that thought or feeling might seem.

Simply put, if you go to pray and you are feeling angry, pray anger; if you are sexually preoccupied, pray that preoccupation; if you are feeling murderous, pray murder; and if you are feeling full of fervor and want to praise and thank God, pray fervor. Every thought or feeling is a valid entry into prayer. What's important is that we pray what's inside of us and not what we think God would like to see inside of us.

What's so unfortunate is that, most often, because we misunderstand prayer, we stay away from it just when we most need it. We try to pray only when we feel good, centered, reverent, and worthy of praying. But we don't try to pray precisely when we most need it; that is, when we are feeling bad, irreverent, sinful, emotionally and sexually preoccupied, and unworthy of praying.

But all of these feelings can be our entry into prayer. No matter the headache or the heartache, we need only to lift it up to God.

FALSE EXPECTATIONS IN PRAYER

What does it mean to be holy or perfect?

There are two classical concepts of perfection, one Greek and the other Hebrew. In the Greek ideal, to be perfect is to have no deficiencies, no faults, no flaws. Perfection, to the Greek mind, means to measure up to some ideal standard, to be completely whole, true, good, and beautiful. To be perfect is never to sin.

The Hebrew ideal of perfection is quite different. In this mind-set, to be perfect simply means to walk with God, despite our flaws. Perfection here means being in the divine presence, in spite of the fact that we are not perfectly whole, good, true, and beautiful.

Our concept of holiness in the West has been, both for good and bad, very much shaped by the Greek ideal of perfection. Hence, holiness has been understood as a question of measuring up to a certain benchmark. In such a view of things, a view with which many of us were raised, sanctity is understood as achieving and maintaining something—namely, moral goodness, and integrity.

Such a view is not without its merits. It is a perpetual challenge against mediocrity, laziness, giving in to the line of least resistance, and settling for what is second best. Such a view of perfection (and the spirituality it engenders) keeps the ideal squarely in view. The flag is always held high, ahead of us, beckoning us, calling us beyond the limits of our present tiredness. We are always invited to something higher. This can be very healthy, especially in a culture that is cynical and despairing of ideals.

But such a concept of perfection also has a nasty underside. Nobody measures up. In the end, we all fall short, which leads to a whole series of spiritual pitfalls. First of all, we beat ourselves up with the false expectation that we can somehow, all on our own, through sheer will power, fix all that is wrong with us. Will power, as we now know, is powerless in the face of our addictions. Because we don't recognize this, we often grow discouraged and simply quit trying to break some bad habit. Why try when the result is always the same? The temptation then is to do what we in fact so often do, namely, split off holiness and project it onto to a "Mother Teresa" type of figure. We let her carry holiness for us because we believe we are unable to become holy ourselves.

Worse still, when perfection means measuring up, we find it hard to forgive ourselves and others for not being God. When the dominant idea of holiness is something that only God can measure up to, it is not easy to give others or ourselves permission to be human. We carry around a lot of discouragement, guilt, and lack of forgiveness because of this.

Hence, despite the positives that are contained in the Greek concept of perfection, we might well profit from incorporating into our lives more of the Hebrew ideal. Perfection here means walking with God, despite imperfection.

All on our own, we can never measure up. We can never be perfect in the Greek sense. But that is not what God is asking of us. What God is asking is that we bring our helplessness, weaknesses, imperfections, and sin constantly to him, that we walk with him, and that we never hide from him. God is a good parent. He understands that we will make mistakes and disappoint him and ourselves. What God asks is simply that we come home, that we share our lives with him, that we let him help us in those ways in which we are powerless to help ourselves.

OUR SHAME AND NAKEDNESS

"Shame on you! You should know better!" How often have we heard those awful words? How often have we seen them, unspoken, real, in another's eyes? Perhaps there are no words, but the message is clear: "You should be ashamed of yourself!"

That's raw hurt—a whip on bare flesh!

Shame is part of life. Most of the time we connect it to a particular quality about ourselves. We are ashamed of something. Something about us is not quite right: our ignorance, our selfishness, our sexual darkness, our laziness, our loneliness, our past, our poverty, our lack of sophistication, our hidden phobia, our height, our fatness, our complexion, our hair, our birthmark, our smells, our addiction. We are all ashamed of something.

The importance of this should never be understated, not just for psychology but also for spirituality and prayer. If we are ever to become whole and spiritual—if we are to take seriously the first words that came out of the mouth of Jesus: "Change your life and believe in the good news"—then the coldness and distrust brought upon us by shame must be overcome.

Change will not be easy. Shame is powerful. Its bite is deep, the scars permanent. Although the scars of shame are permanent, they are not necessarily fatal. We are powerfully resilient, capable of living warm and trusting lives, beyond shame. But the power to live beyond shame does not lie in some easy solution. As a wise axiom has it, not everything can be cured or fixed, though it should be named properly. This is critical in the case of shame. It must be named properly.

There is a growing body of literature today, much of it in popular psychology circles, that tries precisely to do this, to name shame properly. Unfortunately, to my mind, it often does not name it very well. It talks about cultures of shame and religions of shame and, all too quickly, lays much of the blame for shame at the feet of those who insist on duty and on those who are less liberal sexually. Duty and sexual restraint, in this view, are the culprits.

Whatever the truth of that, it misses the deeper point. We are not most deeply shamed and hurt for the first time when we are made to feel bad on account of some unfulfilled duty or because religion and culture have not given us permission to feel good about sex and our own bodies. No. Long before that, we are shamed at a deeper level. We are shamed in our enthusiasm. We are made to feel guilty, naïve, and humiliated about our very pulse for life and about our very trust of each other. Long before we are ever told that sex is bad or that our body isn't quite right or that we have failed in our duty somewhere, we are told we are bad because we are so trusting and enthusiastic. Trust and enthusiasm are our nakedness, our bare flesh.

Remember as a child the number of times you ran up to somebody, someone you trusted—a parent, a teacher, a friend? Completely trusting, full of life, you tried, with a nakedness you can never bring yourself to risk again, to share something you were excited about: a leaf you had found, a drawing you had made, your report card, a story you wanted to tell, a fall you had just taken, something that was very important to you. Try to recall the warmth, trust, and spontaneity of that moment. Try to bring that feeling into your prayers with God, a God who delights in you, a God who has no use for crippling shame.

A Conspiracy against Interiority

Our culture is a powerful narcotic, for good and for bad. It is important that we first underline that there's partly a good side to this. A narcotic soothes and protects against brute, raw pain. Our culture has within it every kind of thing (from medicine to entertainment) to shield us from suffering. That can be good, but a narcotic also can be bad, especially when it becomes a way of escaping reality. Where our culture is particularly dangerous, I feel, is in the way it can perpetually shield us from having to face the deeper issues of life: faith, forgiveness, morality, and mortality. It can constitute, as theologian Jan Walgrave has said, "a virtual conspiracy" against the interior life by keeping us so entertained, so busy, so preoccupied, and so distracted that we lose all focus on the deeper things.

We live in a world of instant and constant communication, of mobile phones and e-mail, of iPods that contain whole libraries of music, of television packages that contain hundreds of channels, of malls and stores that are open twenty-four hours a day, of restaurants and clubs that stay open all night, of sounds that never die and lights that never go out. We can be amused, distracted, and catered to at any time.

While that has made our lives wonderfully efficient, it also has conspired against depth. The danger, as one commentator puts it, is that we are all developing permanent attention deficit disorder. We are attentive to so many things that, ultimately, we aren't attentive to anything, particularly to what is deepest inside of us.

This isn't an abstract concept! Typically our day is so full (of work, noise, pressure, rush) that when we do finally get home and have some time when we could shut down all the stimulation, we are so fatigued that what soothes us is something that functions as a narcotic: a sporting event, a game show on television, a mindless sitcom, or anything that can calm our tensions and relax us enough to sleep. It's not bad if we do this on a given night, but it is bad when we do it every night.

What happens is that we never find the space in our lives to touch what's deepest inside of us and inside of others. Given the power of our culture, we can go along like this for years until something cracks in our lives—a loved one dies, someone breaks our heart, the doctor tells us we have a terminal disease—or some other crisis suddenly renders empty all the stimulation and entertainment in the world. Then we are forced to look into our own depth, and that can be a frightening abyss if we have spent years avoiding it.

Sometimes we need a narcotic. But we have to know when it is time to unplug the television, turn off the phone, shut down the computer, silence the iPod, lay away the sports page, and resist going out for coffee with a friend, so that, for one moment at least, we are not avoiding making friends with that one part of us, the deepest part, that someday will accompany us into the sunset.

CHAPTER 8

Marian Prayer

~ Mary Catherine Nolan, OP ~

From earliest Christian times, Mary, Mother of the Lord, has been remembered with love and affection. Historically, little is known of her life after the resurrection and ascension of Jesus. Yet, our Catholic tradition is rich in memories of her. The final scriptural image of Mary comes to us from Luke's account of Pentecost in the Acts of the Apostles 1:14.[1] There, we find Mary, the first disciple, together with men and women disciples of her Son, gathered in continuous prayer. Mary is thus present when the Holy Spirit descends upon the disciples and gives birth to the Church.

Mary, Mother of Jesus, was the first to receive the fullness of the Holy Spirit. When sent by God to visit Mary, the angel, Gabriel, addressed her as *kecharitomene*, which means, "one already transformed by grace."[2] Mary received the message that God had chosen her to be mother of the long-awaited Messiah with a discerning heart. Entering into dialogue with the angel, she asked for clarification of what was being asked of her, a virgin. Gabriel assured her it was through the action of the Holy Spirit that she would conceive the Son of God. Truly full of grace, Mary responded to God's messenger, "Let it be done to me as you say" (Luke 1:26–38). Once Mary understands her situation, she totally surrenders to God's will.

MARY, MODEL OF CONTEMPLATIVE PRAYER

Mary, then, became for us, a model of prayer. She listened; she pondered; she believed; she responded with trust in God's power and love for her. After the annunciation by Gabriel, Mary visited her cousin Elizabeth, who greeted and affirmed her in her divine motherhood. Mary replied to Elizabeth's greeting with a psalm prayer expressing joy and gratitude for God's blessings. This prayer, Mary's Song, also is known as the Magnificat:

My soul magnifies the Lord
And my spirit rejoices in God my Savior,
For he has looked with favor on the lowliness of his handmaid.
Surely, from now on all generations will call me blessed.
For the Mighty One has done great things for me,
And holy is his name.
God's mercy is from generation to generation for those who fear him.
God has shown might with his arm;

He has confused the arrogant in the conceit of their hearts.

God has pulled down the powerful from their thrones,

And lifted up the lowly;

He has filled the hungry with good things,

And the rich he has sent away empty.

God has come to the help of his servant Israel,

Remembering his mercy,

According to the promise he made to our ancestors,

To Abraham and to his descendants forever. (Luke 1:46–55)

Mary's song is sung or recited today in churches, convents, and monasteries as an integral part of Vespers, the liturgical evening prayer of the Church. For almost two thousand years, this song has rung out in joyous praise and gratitude to God. We can join our voices with the voice of Mary by making the Magnificat our own song.

To enter into the mind and heart of the Mother of God, praying as she prayed, is a way to ground oneself in the disposition for true and faith-filled prayer. In praying Mary's Song, we do not pray alone but join our voices with the countless men and women throughout the ages who have praised God in these words. As members of the communion of saints, we are part of a community that spans the centuries and today circles the globe, transcending all languages and cultures. Entering into the interior disposition of Mary in prayer requires an attitude of attunement to the Spirit and a letting go of distracting anxieties which turn us in on ourselves. Mary trusted the divine graciousness of God and so should we. All that we fear or cringe from in ourselves can be left in her hands as we enter with her into her song of joy.

St. Ambrose encouraged the early Christians to pray, saying, "Let Mary's soul be in each of you to proclaim the greatness of the Lord. Let her spirit be in each to rejoice in the Lord. The Lord is magnified not because the human voice can add anything to God, but because he is magnified in us."[3]

Centuries later, the great Scripture scholar known as the father of modern critical interpretation of Scripture and founder of the Ecole Biblique in Jerusalem, Pere Marie-Joseph Lagrange, OP, wrote of his grief when as a young Dominican seminarian he was told of his beloved father's imminent death. He threw himself in fervent prayer at the feet of Mary. "To an extraordinary degree, I joined myself to the interior dispositions of this great Christian," he wrote in his memoirs.[4] To unite one's heart to the Immaculate Heart of Mary is surely a graced way of praying that leads to acceptance of God's will in all things.

The birth of Jesus is surrounded by angelic manifestations of the identity of this child who is the long awaited Messiah. As for Mary, we read, "She treasured all these things and reflected on them in her heart" (Luke 2:19). Words are not necessary for contemplative prayer, but a deep consciousness of the Divine. In this interior treasuring and pondering of the Divine Presence and action, Mary is the model of contemplative prayer.

An important fruit of contemplation is action. When a woman in the crowd to which Jesus was preaching raised her voice in praise of Mary, Jesus replied, "Blest are they who hear the word of God and keep it" (Luke 11:27). Mary pondered the Word of God and acted on it. The medieval Dominican mystic and preacher, Meister Eckhart, taught that Mary conceived the Word of God in her heart before she conceived him in her body. He further preached that all the grace that was in Mary is also in us, and we must all be mothers of God, meaning we are called to bring Christ into the world. Pondering God's blessings as Mary did leads us to share in her happiness.[5]

MARY AS INTERCESSOR AND PROTECTOR

In Catholic prayer tradition, Mary is considered a mother who intercedes with God for her children. There are numerous Catholic prayers requesting Mary's intercession. The *Catechism of the Catholic Church* states, "When we pray to her we are adhering with her to the plan of the Father who sends his Son to save all men" (*CCC*, 2679.) The best known and most widespread Marian prayer is the *Ave Maria* or *Hail Mary*:

Hail Mary, full of grace, the Lord is with you.

Blessed are you among women,

and blessed is the fruit of your womb, Jesus.

Holy Mary, Mother of God, pray for us sinners,

now and at the hour of our death. Amen.

The first verse of the Hail Mary consists of the salutations to Mary by the angel Gabriel at the time of the annunciation (Luke 1:28) and by Elizabeth at the time of the visitation (Luke 1:42). This verse has been found in liturgies dating back as far as the fifth century. The second verse, coming later, added a prayer of petition to the ancient prayer. The present form of the *Hail Mary* has been used since the fifteenth century. This prayer has been translated into almost every known language around the globe. There are 150 known versions.

The earliest written prayer of intercession to Mary that has been found is an early Greek version of the Latin prayer, *Sub Tuum Praesidium*. It was found on a fragment of papyrus which may be dated as early as the third century AD. An English version of this prayer is:

We turn to you for protection, Holy Mother of God. Listen to our prayers and help us in our needs. Save us from every danger, glorious and blessed Virgin.

Another prayer similar to this is known as the Memorare. An earlier version has been attributed to St. Bernard of Clairvaux. There are variations of this prayer, the following being a well-known one.

Remember, O most gracious Virgin Mary, that never was it known that anyone who fled to your protection or sought your intercession was left unaided. Inspired by this confidence I fly unto you, O Virgin of Virgins, my Mother. To you I come; before you I stand, sinful and sorrowful. O Mother of the Word Incarnate, despise not my petitions but in your mercy hear and answer me. Amen.[6]

That Mary was widely invoked as a protector in both the Latin and Greek Churches is attested to by the many icons and other medieval images depicting her with mantle or veil spread out widely to shelter her clients beneath it. The images are known by various names, such as Mother of Mercy, Virgin of Mercy, and Our Lady of Protection. Under Our Lady's cloak can be found various groups depending on the origin of the image. There are, for example, medieval images of Mary sheltering Dominicans or Franciscans or Augustinians. The city of Regensburg in Germany has to this day a lovely wood carving example of Mary with the city magistrates gathered under her mantle. The image of Mary, Mother of Mercy, is a visual reminder that those depicted under her cloak or veil have chosen her as patron and protector. As a loving mother, she can be trusted to shield her children from evil.

In my long years as a teacher and also as a spiritual director, I have listened to many accounts of a person praying to Mary for help in a dangerous or even desperate situation and attributing their safety or help to Mary's intercession. One well-documented incident of turning to Mary for help happened during the devastating Wisconsin forest fire of 1871. People finding themselves trapped by the raging flames of the fire took refuge on the grounds of a small shrine to Our Lady of Good Help, located in the Green Bay diocese of Wisconsin. As they fervently prayed, the wind shifted, and those at the shrine, who had been in the path of this intense fire, were saved. Mary is invoked for large favors and small ones. One student reported that he was terrified because he felt unprepared to take an important examination. As he begged Mary to help him, words came into his mind, "I'll help you this time, but after this, you will have to study." He passed the test.

Mary, Help of Those in Need is a prayer sometimes sung as an antiphon before the singing of the Magnificat at evening prayer:

> Holy Mary, help those in need, give strength to the weak, comfort the sorrowful, pray for God's people, assist the clergy, intercede for religious. Mary, all who seek your help experience your unfailing protection. Amen.

CLASSIC MARIAN ANTHEMS

Evening or night prayer services traditionally are concluded with an anthem honoring Our Lady. These anthems, sung or chanted, differ according to the liturgical season. In some places, a procession takes place following the prayers of Vespers or Compline, during which the anthem is sung and the presider sprinkles the congregation with holy water. Four anthems, referred to by their Latin names, are *Salve Regina*, sung during ordinary time; *Alma Redemptoris Mater*, used during Advent; *Ave Regina Caelorum*, the Lenten anthem; and *Regina Caeli*, sung during the Easter season.

The *Salve Regina* (*Hail, Holy Queen*) dates from the eleventh century and is often sung at liturgical services, especially in the evening. It is the custom of some religious, including Dominicans, to gather at the bedside of a sister or friar who is very ill or dying and sing the *Salve*.

> Hail, holy Queen, Mother of mercy, hail, our life, our sweetness, and our hope. To you we cry, exiled children of Eve; to you we send up our sighs, mourning and weeping in this vale of tears.

> Turn, then, most gracious advocate, your eyes of mercy toward us; and after this our exile, show to us the blessed fruit of your womb, Jesus. O clement, O loving, O kind Virgin Mary.

Alma Redemptoris Mater, which dates from the eleventh century, was traditionally sung after Night Prayer during Advent:

> Loving mother of the Redeemer, gate of heaven, star of the sea,
> Assist your people who have fallen yet strive to rise again.
> To the wonderment of nature you bore your Creator,
> Yet remained a virgin after as before.
> You who received Gabriel's joyful greeting,
> Have pity on us poor sinners.

During the Lenten season, the antiphon, *Ave Regina Caelorum* (Hail, Queen of Heaven) may be used liturgically after Night Prayer or for other prayer services.

> Hail, Queen of heaven;

Hail, Mistress of the Angels;

Hail, root of Jesus,

Hail, the gate through which the Light rose over the earth.

Rejoice, Virgin most renowned and of unsurpassed beauty.

Farewell, O most beautiful one,

And beseech Christ for us.

Regina Caeli (*Queen of Heaven*) is the joy-filled anthem used after Evening Prayer during the Easter season. It has been used since the thirteenth century. The Easter antiphon is filled with shouts of *Alleluia*, which has not been used during the preceding season of Lent but is sung with exuberance during liturgies at Eastertime. We share Mary's joy in the resurrection of her Son, as we sing out *alleluia* in this Easter anthem.

O Queen of Heaven, rejoice, alleluia! The Son whom you merited to bear, alleluia, has risen as He said, alleluia! Pray for us to God, alleluia!

Rejoice and be glad, O Virgin Mary, alleluia! For the Lord has truly risen, alleluia!

Ave Maris Stella (Hail, Star of the Sea) is another ancient and much loved hymn. It is often sung in processions at Marian shrines and during the liturgy of Marian feasts. It is used to pray for travelers that they may arrive safely at their destination. Mary, as Star of the Sea, is a sign of hope and a guide in the journey of life.

Hail, you Star of Ocean!

Portal of the sky,

Ever Virgin Mother

Of the Lord most high.

O! by Gabriel's Ave,

Uttered long ago,

Eva's name reversing,

Establish peace below.

Break the captive's fetters;

Light on blindness pour.

All our ills expelling,

Every bliss implore.

Show yourself a mother,

Offer him our sighs,

Who for us incarnate

Did not you despise.

Virgin of all virgins!
To your shelter take us;
Gentlest of the gentle!
Chaste and gentle make us.
Still as on we journey,
Help our weak endeavor,
Till with you and Jesus
We rejoice forever.
Through the highest heaven,
To the Almighty Three,
Father, Son and Spirit,
One same glory be.

STABAT MATER

There are joys in life, but also, there are times of suffering. The image of Mary standing at the foot of the cross upon which her Son is dying (John 19:25) speaks volumes of her suffering. Anyone who has lost a child to violence can identify with Our Lady of Sorrows. The *Pieta* is one of the most common subjects in the history of Western art, perhaps best known in Michelangelo's famous sculpture of Mary holding the body of Jesus taken down from the cross. Mary's pain is united to that of her Son's in his agony. Pondering this, we are able to trust that Mary understands our own pain and suffering. She holds us as a loving mother whose compassion is born of suffering.

Similarly, the Marian hymn *Stabat Mater* gives voice to those who identify with Mary in her suffering. This hymn, consisting of twenty verses, originated in the thirteenth century and may have been written by the Franciscan poet Jacopone of Todi. It is usually sung as part of the Catholic devotion of walking the *via dolorosa* or "way of the cross," stopping briefly for meditation and prayer at each of fourteen stations. It is also used liturgically in the Office and Mass for the feast of Our Lady of Sorrows on September 15. Powerful, poetic images, together with the distinctive rhyme scheme and meter of *Stabat Mater* have inspired great musicians to compose versions for chorus and orchestra. During the Renaissance, Palestrina composed an elaborate polyphonic version. Haydn, Verdi, Rossini, Schubert, Dvorak and others have contributed to musical renditions of this prayer.

Stabat Mater begins with a description of Mary as the sorrowful mother grieving at the foot of the cross as she beholds her Son, Jesus, suffering and dying. It ends with petitions to Mary to be with us, her children, at our deaths and to plead for our salvation:

At the cross her station keeping,
Stood the sorrowful mother weeping.
When her Son was crucified.
While she waiting in her anguish,
Seeing Christ in torment languish,
Bitter sorrow pierced her heart.
With what pain and desolation,
With what noble resignation,
Mary watched her dying Son.
Ever patient in her yearning
Though her tear-filled eyes were burning,
Mary gazed upon her Son.
Who, that sorrow contemplating,
On that passion meditating,
Would not share the Virgin's grief?
Christ she saw, for our salvation,
Scourged with cruel acclamation,
Bruised and beaten by the rod.
Christ she saw with life-blood falling
All her anguish unavailing,
Saw him breathe his very last.
Mary, font of love's devotion,
Let me share with true emotion
All the sorrow you endured.
Virgin, ever interceding,
Hear me in my fervent pleading;
Fire me with your love of Christ.
Mother, may this prayer be granted;
That Christ's love may be implanted
In the depths of my poor soul.
At the cross, your sorrow sharing,
All your grief and torment bearing
Let me stand and mourn with you.
Fairest maid of all creation,
Queen of hope and consolation,
Let me feel your grief sublime.
Virgin, in your love befriend me,

At the Judgment Day defend me.
Help me by your constant prayer.
Savior, when my life shall leave me,
Through your mother's prayers receive me.
With the fruits of victory.
Virgin of all virgins blest!
Listen to my fond request;
Let me share your grief divine.
Let me, to my latest breath,
In my body bear the death
Of your dying Son divine.
Wounded with His every wound,
Steep my soul till it has swooned
In His very Blood away.
Be to me, O Virgin, nigh,
Lest in flames I burn and die,
In His awe-full judgment day.
Savior, when my life shall leave me,
Through your mother's prayers receive me
With the fruits of victory.
While my body here decays
May my soul your goodness praise,
Safe in heaven eternally. Amen, Alleluia.[7]

Today, victims of war, displacement, persecution, or prejudices of many kinds may look to Mary to understand their plight, just as the author of the *Stabat Mater* did during the late Middle Ages. Mary's compassionate heart has been forged from suffering with love.

THE ANGELUS

A well-loved oil painting by the French artist Jean-Francois Millet entitled *The Angelus* depicts a peasant couple with reverently bowed heads at prayer in their field as twilight falls. Millet painted the picture in 1859, and it was instantly recognized as the familiar scene of devout farmers and townspeople throughout Europe used to respond to church bells signaling each day when it was time to pray. Some Catholic churches and institutions with bell towers still traditionally ring the bells three times a day, in the morning about 6:00 AM, at noon, and in the evening at 6:00 PM. This is a call to recite the prayer known as the *Angelus*. The practice recalls the Incarnation of the Lord and has at least medieval origins. A traditional version is:

The angel of the Lord declared unto Mary
And she conceived of the Holy Spirit.
Hail Mary…
"I am the handmaid of the Lord:
Be it done to me according to your word."
Hail Mary…
And the Word became flesh
and dwelt among us.
Hail Mary…
Pray for us, O holy Mother of God
that we may be made worthy of the promises of Christ.
Let us pray:
Pour forth, we beseech you, O Lord, your grace into our hearts, that we, to whom the incarnation of Christ your Son was made known by the message of an angel, may by his passion and cross be brought to the glory of his resurrection, through the same Christ, our Lord. Amen.

The development of the *Angelus* has a long history, from a custom of saying three Hail Marys during the tolling of a church bell at sunset in medieval times to the form it has today. The practice was promoted by the first Franciscans during St. Francis's time and was widespread in France as well. Bells were also rung at dawn, and by the fourteenth century, the practice of saying three Hail Marys at the sound of the bells in the morning as well as in the evening was observed in Rome. The midday bell ringing was ordered by King Louis IX of France to remind the people to pray for the peace of the realm, and Pope Sixtus IV endorsed this practice. From at least the time of the Crusades, church bells have been rung, calling the faithful to pray for peace in times of war. The *Angelus* scene painted by Millet is one of tranquility, but it can be contrasted to the scenes of devastation and destruction caused by war in our own day. Pausing three times a day to pray for peace and safety is still a good practice, especially if prayer moves us to act in the interests of peace and justice. Mary is wisely invoked as Our Lady of Peace.

OTHER POPULAR DEVOTIONS TO MARY

Throughout the many centuries of Christianity, devotion to Mary became widespread in the multiple cultures and languages in which the Church was present. Prayer to Mary now takes many forms, such as litanies, which invoke her under her many titles with the response, "Pray for us," as each title is announced. Pilgrimages to Marian shrines around the world are also an expression of faith and show trust in Mary's power of intercession with God to heal the wounds of human existence. The shrine at Lourdes, France, is well known as a place of healing and is visited by hundreds of thousands of pilgrims every year. In England, the famous shrine of Our Lady at Walsingham, rebuilt after the Protestant Reformation, is also the site of ecumenical pilgrimages. Fatima in Portugal is a shrine visited by pilgrims longing for world peace. In October of 1942, as World War II was raging, Pope Pius XII pronounced an act of consecration of the world to the Immaculate Heart of Mary in an address to a gathering of Fatima pilgrims. In Poland, in 1956, a time of political oppression, over a million people from all over Poland witnessed to their Catholic faith by gathering at the shrine Our Lady of Czestochowa.

Prayers are offered before statues, pictures, or icons which have special meaning to various groups. I have a favorite statuette of Our Lady made of Waterford crystal. When the sun strikes it, the rainbow colors of the prism are reflected. Mary is not a goddess but one who reflects the radiance of God's love which shines through her. Statues, icons, tapestries, medals, and many other images of Mary are symbols which draw us to consciousness of her loving presence among us and lead us to ponder the inner reality of who she is for us.

The image of Our Lady of Guadalupe, preserved on the tilma (or long, outer garment) of St. Juan Diego in the cathedral of Mexico City, is much loved due to its miraculous origin and the gracious message of Mary's love for the people which accompanied it. Our Lady of Guadalupe has been proclaimed the patroness of all the Americas. Mary is patroness of the United States under her title the Immaculate Conception. The National Basilica of the Immaculate Conception in Washington, DC, contains chapels commemorating the special devotion to Our Lady held by the diverse ethnic groups that form the fabric of the people of our land.

THE ROSARY

Although praying the rosary is more important than knowing its origins, the history of how it came to be a much loved and familiar prayer of the faithful is an example of the living tradition of the Church. The rosary has been referred to as the poor person's psalter. Its origin reaches far back into the mists of early medieval Christian prayer practices. The probable beginning was in the desire of the people, who were not able to read the psalms or who could not be present at the praying of the psalms during the celebration of the canonical hours of the Divine Office, to join their hearts and minds to those who were gathered at prayer. Thus, a Lord's Prayer would be substituted for each psalm. These prayers could be counted on a string of beads or on the knots of a cord. Later, the first part of the Angel's greeting to Mary was used, also. The

Bible contains 150 psalms in the psalter. These are divided into five books of psalms, each collection ending in a psalm of doxology. Thus, the 150 Hail Marys, replacing the 150 psalms of the Bible developed into a prayer mantra, and eventually into the rosary.

The rosary is a prayer, both Gospel and contemplative. As early as the twelfth century, reflections were being made upon the events of Christ's life as experienced by his mother while chaplets of *Aves* were recited. Over time, the principle salvific events accomplished in Christ from the incarnation through his passion, death, resurrection, ascension, and the outpouring of the Holy Spirit at Pentecost were recalled and meditated upon. Added to these Gospel mysteries were events of Mary's life, her assumption and glorification. By the early fifteenth century, phrases identifying these gospel events had been added to the recitation of 150 *Aves*, which had been grouped into fifteen decades of *Aves*. Each decade was preceded by a *Pater*. The Carthusian and Dominican rosaries were structured this way. Dominican preacher Blessed Alan de la Roche founded the first Confraternity of the rosary in 1470 and did much to spread the practice of this devotion in his preaching and writing.

Pope Pius V, also a Dominican, shaped the rosary into the prayer form with which we are now familiar and officially approved it in 1569. The second part of the Hail Mary was added to the angel's salutation and the doxology: "Glory be to the Father" was included after each decade. To each of fifteen decades a mystery recalling a salvation event was attached. There were three sets of mysteries, the Joyful, the Sorrowful and the Glorious. When Christendom was threatened by invading Turkish forces, Pius V sent out an urgent call for prayer, and in gratitude for the Christian victory at Lepanto, which he attributed to Our Lady's intercession, he established the feast of Our Lady of Victory in 1571. Shortly afterwards, this became the feast of Our Lady of the Rosary and is celebrated on October 7.

The rosary can be prayed alone or with others at any time or in any place except during a liturgical celebration. Families are encouraged to pray the rosary together. Bringing the family together in prayer builds bonds of love and harmony among its members. It is a custom to daily recite five decades of the rosary while contemplating a set of mysteries. In 2002 Pope John Paul II, wishing to present a wider group of reflections upon the salvific events of the Gospel, added five new mysteries to the traditional fifteen. The original 150 Hail Marys was then expanded to 200. The new mysteries are referred to as the Mysteries of Light or the Luminous Mysteries. In his apostolic letter The Rosary of the Virgin Mary the pope calls the rosary "an exquisitely contemplative prayer." It starts with Mary's own experience and helps one meditate on the mysteries of the Lord's life as seen through the eyes of she who was closest to the Lord.

It is suggested that the Joyful Mysteries be meditated upon on Mondays and Saturdays, as well as on Sundays of the Christmas Season; the Luminous Mysteries on Thursdays; the Sorrowful Mysteries on Tuesdays, Fridays, and Sundays during the Lenten season; the Glorious Mysteries on Wednesdays and all other Sundays. A phrase from Scripture which pertains to each mystery may be read to assist in meditation on that mystery.

THE JOYFUL MYSTERIES OF THE ROSARY:

The Annunciation (Luke 1:26–38)

The Visitation (Luke 1:39–56)

The Nativity (Matthew 1:18–25; Luke 2:1–20; John 1:1–14)

The Presentation of Jesus in the Temple (Luke 2:22–38)

The Finding of the Child Jesus in the Temple (Luke 2:41–50)

THE LUMINOUS MYSTERIES OF THE ROSARY:

The Baptism of Jesus (Matthew 3:13–17; Mark 1:9–11; Luke 3:21–22)

The Wedding Feast at Cana (John 2:1–12)

Jesus's Proclamation of the Kingdom (Matthew 4:23–25; Mark 1:32–34; Luke 4:14–22)

The Transfiguration (Matthew 17:1–8; Mark 9:2–8; Luke 9:28–36)

The Institution of the Eucharist (Matthew 26:26–29; Mark 14:22–25; Luke 22:17–23)

THE SORROWFUL MYSTERIES OF THE ROSARY:

The Agony in the Garden (Matthew 26:36–46; Mark 14:32–42; Luke 22:40–46)

The Scourging at the Pillar (Matthew 27:26; Mark 15:15; Luke 23:14–16)

The Crowning with Thorns (Matthew 27:27–31; Mark 15:16–20; John 19:2–3)

The Carrying of the Cross (Matthew 27:32; Mark 15:21; Luke 23:26–32)

The Crucifixion and Death (Matthew 27:33–56; Mark 15:22–41; Luke 23:33–49; John 19:17–30)

THE GLORIOUS MYSTERIES OF THE ROSARY:

The Resurrection (Matthew 28:1–10; Mark 16:1–8; Luke 24:1–11; John 20:1–10)

The Ascension (Mark 16:14–20; Luke 24:50–53; Acts 1:6–11)

The Descent of the Holy Spirit (Acts 2:1–4)

The Assumption of Mary into Heaven (John 14:3)

The Coronation of the Blessed Mother (Revelation 12:1)

MARY IN THE MYSTERY OF CHRIST AND THE CHURCH

In all of these many ways, veneration of Our Lady, Mother of God, is always linked to the mystery of Christ in the Incarnation and to the liturgical worship of the Church. She is likewise remembered in the celebration of the Eucharist and in the prayers of the Divine Office. Feast days dedicated to Mary were established to commemorate important events in her life and her influence in the living tradition of the Church. Historical evidence of Marian feasts is inconclusive, but the earliest seems to have been linked to the Christmas liturgical cycle and celebrates Mary's divine mother-hood. After freedom was granted to the Church (making it legal for the first time to be a Christian) in the fourth century, there is evidence of the emergence of other feasts at various times and places.

Participants of the Second Vatican Council, convened by Pope John XXIII, approved a document, *The Constitution on the Sacred Liturgy*, in 1963. Article 103 of this document affirms Mary's place in the liturgy, as it states:

> In celebrating this annual cycle of the mysteries of Christ, Holy Church honors the Blessed Mary, Mother of God, with a special love. She is insep-arably linked with her son's saving work. In her the Church admires and exalts the most excellent fruit of redemption, and joyfully contemplates, as in a faultless image, which she herself desires and hopes wholly to be.

The bishops deliberated vigorously over how to present Mary in the context of Church renewal, and it was finally decided not to write a separate document about Mary but to include her in the document *Lumen Gentium*. Chapter seven of *Lumen Gentium* discusses our place in the communion of saints and the veneration that the Church has always given to apostles, martyrs "together with the Blessed Virgin Mary and the holy angels, with a special love and has asked piously for the help of their intercession" (*Lumen Gentium* 50). The statement goes on to explain that this veneration "in no way diminishes the adoration given to God the Father, through Christ, in the spirit; on the contrary, it enriches it" (*Lumen Gentium*, 51). Chapter 8 of *Lumen Gentium* is entitled "The Blessed Virgin Mary, Mother of God, in the mystery of Christ and of the Church." This chapter sets forth the function of the Blessed Virgin in the plan of salvation, the relationship of the Blessed Virgin and the Church, and the cult of Mary in the Church and Mary's presence as a sign of true hope and comfort for us. The spiritual motherhood of Mary is a central theme of the chapter.

Marialis Cultus, an apostolic exhortation for the right ordering and development of the cult of the Blessed Virgin Mary, was then written by Pope Paul VI in 1974. It discusses devotion to Mary since Vatican II and gives guidelines for renewed devotion and practices in their biblical, liturgical, ecumenical, and anthropological aspects. In his exhortation, the pope expresses his esteem for the pious practice of praying the rosary, calling it "the compendium of the entire gospel." He notes the rosary's suitability for fostering contemplative prayer, as well as prayer of praise and petition, also recalling its "intrinsic effectiveness for promoting apostolic life and commitment" (*Marialis Cultus,* 42). The pope points to liturgical prayer as different from the practice of the rosary but not in opposition to it. The rosary harmonizes with the liturgy "because it is of a community nature, draws its inspiration from Sacred Scripture and is oriented toward the mystery of Christ. Yet, it is a mistake to recite the rosary during a liturgy" (*Marialis Cultus,* 48).

CONCLUSION

From the earliest ages of Christianity, Mary, Mother of the Lord Jesus, has been remembered and cherished. The Council of Ephesus in 431 proclaimed her to be *Theotokos,* God-bearer. A woman of faith and courage, Mary freely gave her "yes" to God's plan of salvation. In Mary's womb, the Word of God took flesh, and the reign of God broke into human history.

In Catholic tradition, Mary is Mother of God, Mother of the Church, and spiritual mother of all members of the Church. She who bore the joys, hopes, dreams, and sufferings of the human condition is a trusted mentor and guide along the path of life. The lowly, the poor, the powerless, the politically oppressed, and all who suffer loss or diminishment can join their voices with Mary's voice in singing her Magnificat, praising God for their own blessings, and finding in her prayer a future full of hope. She is the sister who walks beside us and intercedes for us as we move toward our final end, transforming union with God for all eternity.

1. *The New American Bible,* 1971 version, is the translation used for biblical quotes in this chapter with the exception of the words of Mary's Song, Luke 1:47–55, which is the author's translation from the Greek text.
2. At a Dominican symposium held in Huissen, Holland, in 1990, Edward Schillebeeckx, OP, presented a lecture in Mariology in which he addressed Mary's role in salvation. He affirms Mary's position as standing on the side of those redeemed by her Son as first to receive redemption. Schillebeeckx opposes the position that because of her relationship to the Holy Spirit, Mary was not in need of redemption.
3. This comment by St. Ambrose is taken from the Office of Readings during Advent on December 21.
4. *Pere Lagrange, Personal Reflections and Memoirs,* trans. Rev. Henry Wansbrough (New York: Paulist, 1985), 225.

5. The Marian thought of Meister Eckhart is found in sermon five. The sermon with a commentary can be found in Matthew Fox, *Breakthrough: Meister Eckhart's Creation Spirituality in New Translation* (Garden City, NY: Doubleday Image, 1980), 91–101.
6. These and other traditional Marian prayers can be accessed online at the website of the International Marian Research Institute, https//www.udayton.edu/imri/.
7. This English translation of the original Latin *Stabat Mater* was taken from the IMRI website which credits *The Collegeville Hymnal* (Collegeville, MN: Liturgical, 1990).

PART TWO

Praying with the Gospels

PRAYING WITH THE GOSPEL OF MATTHEW

PRAYING WITH THE GOSPEL OF MARK

PRAYER AND PRAY-ER IN THE GOSPEL OF LUKE

PRAYER IN THE GOSPEL OF JOHN

If there is a heart to *Prayer in the Catholic Tradition*, it is this section on praying with the Gospels. These four chapters are written by Scripture scholars who also offer a strong pastoral presence through what they have written. As we read through their writings, we can sense the dangers of our becoming unconnected to Christ when we are not grounded in the Gospels. In addition, we can begin to appreciate again or anew, how each gospel offers a unique insight into the life of Christ and our life in prayer with him.

In Praying with the Gospel of Matthew, "the most 'Jewish' of all four Gospels," Donald Senior reminds us that Matthew wanted to affirm "Jesus's Jewish roots and his mission." To accomplish this, Matthew draws heavily on the Old Testament, and Senior notes that "Jewish tradition at the time of Jesus was steeped in prayer" and then unpacks key elements of and stories from this Gospel to illustrate this. His sections on "Jesus at Prayer," which brings to the fore Jesus's Jewish piety, the instructions on prayer including the structure of Jesus's direct teaching on it (the Lord's Prayer), and Senior's closing four lessons are invaluable guides to praying with the Gospel of Matthew.

In Praying with the Gospel of Mark, Thomas Stegman begins by reminding us that Mark's Gospel is "challenging and enigmatic in many ways" and invites us to "prayerful encounter with the text." He then sets the stage by offering four lenses through which to view Mark: "Jesus as Pray-er," "Being with Jesus," "Listening to Jesus on the Way," and "The New Temple: House of Prayer for All." Prayerful attention to Jesus as model of prayer, as well as prayerful discernment and action, are made more vibrant for us, given the scholarly and pastoral portals Stegman offers.

In the next chapter on Prayer and Pray-er in the Gospel of Luke, John Donahue shares with us insights that many have had the honor of hearing in his retreats and workshops on this Gospel. None of the Gospels reveal Jesus at prayer more than

Luke, and each of the authors in this section discuss Jesus at prayer, but this explains why Donahue's title is slightly different from the others. After an overview of prayer in Luke, he points to a number of passages for us to examine, reflect upon, and pray over, and then highlights special texts on prayer in Luke including the infancy narratives, the prayers of Jesus, prayers during the passion of Jesus, Jesus's prayers on the cross, and a discussion of the parables on prayer in Luke. Through all of this, Luke becomes a guide for us in prayer.

In the final chapter in this section, we move away from the synoptic Gospels with Jude Winkler's Prayer in the Gospel of John. He emphasizes the theme of relationship and notes, "Prayer is one means of reinforcing that relationship [of Jesus with the Father] and inviting others into it." To accomplish an understanding of this, the themes of "Prayer and Life," "A Prayer for Glory," "The Last Supper Discourse," and "Ask in My Name" are employed to focus our attention on what John is trying to tell us about prayer and relationship. In Winkler's words, "When Jesus prays and teaches his disciples how to pray, he is using words to make present and intensify a profound reality: his relationship with the Father and theirs with us." To a great extent, that is what *Prayer in the Catholic Tradition* is all about. And as with all of them, this last chapter is worth reading slowly again and again. Otherwise, once again, we lose a sense of prayer's reality in our lives for what it truly should help us seek: becoming one with God so we can reflect that presence in our relationship with others.

CHAPTER 9

Praying with the Gospel of Matthew

~ Donald Senior, CP ~

What can a Christian learn about prayer from a study of Matthew's Gospel? From the earliest decades of the Church, Matthew's Gospel has been considered to be a catechism for Christian life, and the teaching of this Gospel catechism on prayer is profound. In considering prayer, the focus of the Gospel is, not surprisingly, fixed on the figure of Jesus—his example and his teaching.

THE JESUS OF MATTHEW'S GOSPEL AND THE JEWISH TRADITION OF PRAYER

The Gospel of Matthew is the most Jewish of all four Gospels. At a critical time of transition in the early Church, the evangelist wanted both to affirm the Jewish roots of Jesus and his mission and open his Jewish Christian community to extending the Christian mission to the gentile world. At the outset of his ministry as described by Matthew, Jesus declares that he has not come to "abolish the law or the prophets.... But to fulfill" (Matthew 5:17) and that fundamental principle is reflected throughout Matthew's narrative.[1] Matthew draws heavily on the Old Testament, citing it explicitly and frequently to illustrate the meaning of Jesus's mission. Matthew's account of Jesus's conception and birth is steeped in Old Testament quotations and allusions. What happened to Israel happens to Jesus: threatened by a despot, driven into exile, saved, and brought home through God's intervention. All through the Gospel, Jesus is portrayed as God's obedient Son, faithful to God's Word, attentive to God's will, and revealing the ultimate meaning of God's saving intent for Israel and the nations. The Matthean Jesus has sharp conflicts with various Jewish religious leaders—Pharisees, Sadducees, scribes, and priests—but this cannot be read as a rejection of Judaism itself, but rather is reflective of a struggle for authentic fidelity to the covenant forged by God with Israel. In Matthew's Gospel, Jesus during his earthly ministry restricts his mission to his beloved Israel. In the Gospel's mission discourse, Jesus instructs his disciples: "Do not go into pagan territory or enter a Samaritan town. Go rather to the lost sheep of the house of Israel" (10:5–6). Only after the resurrection and the beginning of a new age of salvation does Jesus send his disciples into the whole world (28:16–20).

This Jewish character of Matthew certainly comes to the fore in the matter of Jesus's prayer. Jewish tradition at the time of Jesus was steeped in prayer. There was the formal liturgy in the Temple of Jerusalem, which was the object of yearly pilgrimage feasts of Tabernacles, Passover, and Pentecost, drawing to Jerusalem thousands of devout Jews from all over the Mediterranean world, and there were additional days of intense fasting and reflection, such as Yom Kippur, along with daily prayer and worship in the Temple precincts. The neighborhood and village synagogues that existed in Jesus's day were also places of prayer and instruction, although the sacrificial cult was restricted to the Jerusalem Temple. There is no doubt Jesus frequented both on a regular basis, as is clear in Matthew's account (see Matthew 9:18; 12:9; 13:54).

Matthew portrays Jesus responding to a lawyer's attempt to test him by drawing on the rich tradition of prayer that permeates the Hebrew Scriptures, instinctively citing the *Shema*—the so-called daily creed of Israel drawn from Deuteronomy 6:4–9, calling upon Israel to be alert and attentive to God's presence and to respond in love with all one's being: "You shall love the Lord, your God, with all your heart, with all your soul, and with all your mind." (Matthew 22:37). Jesus's zeal for the Temple leads him to drive out those who are presented as defiling it by quoting from Isaiah and Jeremiah: "'My house shall be a house of prayer' but you are making it a den of thieves" (Matthew 21:13). In the final days of his mission, Matthew portrays Jesus teaching in the temple area, challenging his enemies and speaking of the final destiny of Israel (Matthew 21:23—24:1). On the night of his arrest, Jesus celebrates Passover with his disciples and joins them in singing hymns at its conclusion (Matthew 26:17–30).

JESUS AT PRAYER

Even more significant, throughout Matthew, Jesus exemplifies those attitudes and perspectives that underwrite all expressions of authentic Jewish piety in the Scriptures. First and foremost, the Jesus of Matthew's Gospel has a profound reverence for the holiness of God his Father. When Satan tries to lure Jesus away from his mission, he rebuffs the demon with quotations from the Scriptures: "One does not live by bread alone, but by every word that comes forth from the mouth of God" (Matthew 4:4, quoting Deuteronomy 8:3) and "The Lord, your God, shall you worship and him alone shall you serve" (Matthew 4:10, quoting Deuteronomy 6:13). Doing the will of the Father is a constant emphasis. The Sermon on the Mount concludes with Jesus's declaration: "Not everyone who says to me, 'Lord, Lord,' will enter the kingdom of heaven, but only the one who does the will of my Father in heaven" (Matthew 7:21).

It is clear that the Jesus of Matthew's Gospel has a close bond with God his Father ("Father" is the favored address of Jesus to God in Matthew). This breaks out into the open in Jesus's prayer of praise in 11:25–27, a remarkable passage that some have called the "Johannine meteor" since it evokes the kind of language that Jesus uses in John's Gospel. But this prayer fits perfectly into Matthew's portrayal of Jesus as well:

I give praise to you, Father, Lord of heaven and earth, for although you have hidden these things from the wise and the learned you have revealed them to the childlike.

Yes, Father, such has been your gracious will.

All things have been handed over to me by my Father. No one knows the Son except the Father, and no one knows the Father except the Son and anyone to whom the Son wishes to reveal him. (Matthew 11:25–27)

Other times in the Gospel, Jesus also prays—on the mountain top alone (Matthew 14:23), as he is about to distribute the rations of bread and fish to the multitudes (Matthew 14:19; 15:36), praying over the children the crowds bring to him for a blessing (Matthew 19:13), and urging the disciples to pray for laborers for God's harvest (Matthew 9:38).

It is not surprising that Jesus's prayer in Matthew is most intense as he stands on the brink of death. Jesus's characteristic spirit of trust is reflected in Matthew's version of the Gethsemane prayer, but here the mood is one of anguish as Jesus prays in the face of impending death: "My Father, if it is possible, let this cup pass from me; yet, not as I will, but as you will" (Matthew 26:39). But no moment of prayer in Matthew's Gospel is more poignant and challenging than the final prayer of Jesus at the moment of his death. Matthew, similar to Mark's account, has Jesus at the very last moment of his life "crying out with a loud voice" and praying the opening words of Psalm 22: "My God, my God, why have you forsaken me?" (Matthew 27:46). This is one of the great lament psalms of the Old Testament. The one who laments cries out to God from an experience of isolation and anguish—"Why so far from my call for help, from my cries of anguish? My God, I call by day, but you do not answer; by night, but I have no relief" (Psalm 22:2–3). The underlying motif of the lament is to search for God's abiding and sustaining presence in the midst of threat and great suffering. Several times in the first half of this great prayer the psalmist cites God's past trustworthiness in the midst of suffering: "In you our fathers trusted; they trusted and you rescued them.... In you they trusted and were not disappointed" (Psalm 22:5–6).

There is a dramatic turn in the mood of the lament when the one who cries out to God is ultimately heard. "[You] did not turn away from me but heard me when I cried out" (Psalm 22:25). This leads to a sense of triumph and ecstasy at the conclusion of the lament psalm, with the psalmist acclaiming that "all the ends of the earth will worship and turn to the Lord; all the families of nations will bow low before him." (Psalm 22:28). Even those who have died and who "sleep in the earth" will "bow low before God; all who have gone down in the dust will kneel in homage" before the God who has rescued them from anguish and death.

Many interpreters of Matthew's Gospel believe that the evangelist structured the entire account of Jesus's crucifixion on the pattern of Psalm 22. The underlying issue is of one of trust—is trust in God able to endure through experience of death? Will God be present and faithful to Jesus, his Son, at the very moment of death? Matthew underscores this by having those who mock Jesus at his dying hour pose this very challenge to him: "He saved others; he cannot save himself. So he is the king of Israel! Let him come down from the cross now, and we will believe in him. He trusted in God; let him deliver him now if he wants him. For he said, I am the Son of God." (Matthew 27:42–43; words also echoed in Wisdom 2:12–20 which also alludes to Psalm 22). But Jesus, the obedient Son of God, does not give way to despair but in the midst of the assault of death, cries to God in prayer, and at the very moment of death gives up his spirit to his Father whom he would trust even in the face of death (Matthew 27:50).

The powerful events that immediately happen after Jesus's death in Matthew's account confirm the efficacy of that trust and echo the triumphant conclusion to Psalm 22: the veil of the temple is split in two; there is an earthquake that splits the rocks and opens the graves of those in Sheol, and they will appear in triumph in Jerusalem in the wake of Jesus's own resurrection; and finally, the very soldiers that carried out the crucifixion of Jesus acclaim him as the Son of God (Matthew 27:51–54).

Thus Matthew portrays Jesus as one who had lived his entire life in a spirit of reverent trust in God his Father and concludes his earthly life in the same manner, crying out to God in the midst of torment and defeating the power of death

Jesus's Teaching on Prayer in Matthew

The spirit and manner of Jesus's own prayer in the Gospel of Matthew is also reflected in Jesus's explicit instruction on prayer, particularly in the Sermon on the Mount, a collection of Jesus's characteristic teaching found in chapters 5—7 of Matthew's narrative. Through the Sermon, Jesus instructs his disciples, and through them the crowds, who gather from all points of the compass, including those who are sick and longing for healing (Matthew 4:23—5:1). The first major section of the Sermon (Matthew 5:21–48) presents Jesus's key teachings which "fulfill" the revered Jewish Law: on reconciliation, on sexual integrity, on marriage, on honest speech, on nonre-taliation, and a climactic teaching on love of enemies. Each of these powerful teachings is contrasted with traditional interpretations of the Jewish law that were less radical and less internalized.

A new section of the Sermon begins with chapter 6 which will deal with the traditional expressions of Jewish piety: prayer, fasting, and almsgiving. A general principle stands at the beginning of this section: "Take care not to perform righteous deeds in order that people may see them" (Matthew 6:1). This warning about false piety will be a strong motif throughout this section of the Sermon, including Jesus's instruction on prayer. The disciples are not to pray "like the hypocrites who love to stand and pray in the synagogues and on street corners so that others may see them" (Matthew 6:5). In contrast, he instructs the disciples, "Go to your inner room, close the door, and pray to your Father in secret. And your Father who sees in secret will repay you" (Matthew 6:6). This does imply that Jesus is against all prayer in public—he himself prayed in the presence of his disciples (Matthew 11:25–27) and frequented the synagogue and the temple. The point is, rather, to underscore the spirit of integrity and modesty that should be the context for prayer. Prayer, whether in public or in private, is a moment when one is in communion with the heavenly Father—posturing or seeking one's own praise is totally out of character with the meaning of authentic prayer.

Matthew's Jesus also criticizes those who, like the pagans, think that an abundance of words will gain them a hearing with God. Here Matthew's Jesus again reflects a Jewish perspective, characterizing the long incantations of some pagan rituals as "babbling" and without impact. Attempting to manipulate God in this way is useless because "your Father knows what you need before you ask him." (One thinks of the famous confrontation of the prophet Elijah with the priests of Baal in 1 Kings 18:21–40, in which the pagan priests pray and chant most of the day to ignite the fire of sacrifice but without result, while God hears Elijah's prayer and answers right away!).

All of this leads up to Jesus's direct teaching on how to pray, exemplified in the "Lord's Prayer" (Matthew 6:9–15). "This is how you are to pray" (Matthew 6:9) Jesus tells his disciples. There are two versions of the Lord's Prayer in the gospels, one in Luke 11:2–4 (presented as Jesus's response to his disciples' request, "teach us to pray just as John taught his disciples") and this one in Matthew's Gospel. Luke's version is briefer than Matthew's—the latter may reflect some elaboration of Jesus's prayer in the context of Christian worship. But each version reflects the direct and authentic tone of Jesus's own prayer.

The structure of the prayer is clear: After an address to God as "Our Father in heaven," there follow three "you" petitions acclaiming God ("hallowed be your name," "your kingdom come," "your will be done") and three "we" petitions asking God's help ("give us today our daily bread," "forgive us our debts, as we forgive our debts," and "do not subject us to the final test but deliver us from the evil one"). Each of these segments bears reflection as fundamental components of authentic Christian prayer.

Address to God

As noted earlier, Jesus in Matthew's Gospel typically addresses God as "Father"—also a hallmark of Jewish prayer that viewed God as the author of life and one whose love for his "son" Israel never dimmed. Biblical Judaism viewed God as both awesomely transcendent (and therefore out of reverence, devout Jews would never directly say the name of God) and yet infinitely tender (and thus able to speak in intimate terms with God). This same spirit is present in the prayer Jesus teaches his disciples. Jesus addresses God as "*my* Father" some eighteen times in Matthew's Gospel and speaks to his disciples seventeen times about "*your* Father." (By contrast Jesus refers to God as his Father only three times in Mark's Gospel.) It is striking in the address of the Lord's Prayer, Jesus speaks of "*our* Father"—the only time in the Gospel this is used. The disciples share in the bond of Jesus with his Father, reflecting the ardent prayer of Matthew 11:25–27, in which Jesus exclaims, "No one knows the Father except the Son and anyone to whom the Son wishes to reveal him" (Matthew 11:27). The disciples whom Jesus has chosen share in the unfathomable bond of love between Father and Son and are able to address the transcendent and almighty God as "our Father." Yet this Father who is immediately present to the disciples in prayer remains a mysterious and unfathomable presence—"our Father who is *in heaven.*"

The "You" Petitions

Each of these petitions praise and acclaim the God who is both present ("our Father") and beyond our grasp ("who is in heaven"). The Greek text has a strong symmetrical pattern—each of the petitions begins with a verb: "hallowed be" (*hagiastheto*), "come" (*eltheto*), "be done" (*genetheto*). The first petition prays that God's name be "hallowed." This captures the meaning of the Greek verb *hagiastheto*, literally that God's name be revered as "holy." Obviously this is not praying that God would be holy—since God epitomizes what holiness means—but that among humans, God's name would be reverenced and acknowledged as infinitely holy. Here again we see the influence of Jewish piety. Because the name of God revealed the very identity of God, it was to be absolutely reverenced. As noted earlier, traditional Jewish piety would not permit one to say the name of God and even where the name of God (Yahweh) was written in the biblical text, the reader was to substitute in public readings an alternate name such as "My Lord" (in Hebrew, *adonai*, a practice that continues in contemporary Judaism). It should be noted that the early Christians apparently also followed this practice—nowhere in the New Testament does the name of God appear, but alternatives such as "Lord" (*kurios*) or, in the case of the Lord's Prayer, "my Father in heaven."

The second "you" petition has a similar spirit: "your kingdom come." The advent of the reign or kingdom of God was the keynote of Jesus's own ministry (see Matthew 4:17; also Mark 1:14–15). The "kingdom of God" (or as Matthew's Gospel often refers to it as "the kingdom of heaven"—also a euphemism for the name of God) was a motif with deep Jewish roots—a longing that God would come to Israel and finally achieve what the human efforts of centuries could not effect: bringing healing, justice, and ultimate peace. The words and actions of Jesus's ministry presented in Matthew's Gospel anticipate the values and spirit of God's reign. Several of Jesus's parables define the meaning of the kingdom and its anticipated yet unexpected arrival (see the collection of parables in the parable discourse of Matthew 13). When Jesus's opponents challenge him and suggest that his healing power derives in fact from a demonic spirit, Jesus sharply refutes them and declares: "But if it is by the Spirit of God that I drive out demons, then the kingdom of God has come upon you" (Matthew 12:28). Being liberated from evil and experiencing healing are anticipations of the flourishing of human life that will characterize life within the reign of God. Thus the disciples are instructed by Jesus to earnestly pray that God's kingdom will come and bring redemption to the world.

The third "you" petition continues this line of thought: "your will be done on earth as in heaven" (6:10). Obedience to the will of God is one of the characteristic motifs of Matthew's Gospel. At the temptation in the desert, Jesus turns back the lures of Satan by repeatedly affirming his obedience to the Word of God (4:1–11). The Sermon on the Mount will conclude with the declaration that those "who do the will of my Father in heaven" will enter the kingdom of heaven (Matthew 7:21). Jesus defines his true family: "Whoever does the will of my heavenly Father is my brother, and sister, and mother" (Matthew 12:50). In the community discourse of chapter 18, Jesus reaffirms his mission to the "lost sheep" by anchoring it in God's will: "It is not the will of your heavenly Father that one of these little ones be lost" (Matthew 18:14), just as it is also the will of the Father that "each of you forgives his brother or sister from one's heart" (Matthew 18:35). And in a parable unique to Matthew's Gospel (21:28–32), where one son at first refuses his father's request to work in his vineyard but later repents and goes to work, and the other son initially responds yes but then fails to go to work, Jesus asks, "Which of the two did his father's will?" And when his opponents reluctantly admit that the first son did so, Jesus replies in a stern fashion: "Amen, I say to you, tax collectors and prostitutes are entering the kingdom of God before you."

Perhaps most significant of all, in Matthew's version of the Gethsemane prayer, Jesus twice echoes this petition of the Lord's Prayer: "My Father, if it is possible, let this cup pass from me; yet, not as I will, but as you will" (Matthew 26:39), and, "My Father, if it is not possible that this cup pass without my drinking it, your will be done"—the latter the identical phrase as in this petition of the Lord's Prayer (Matthew 26:42, *genetheto to thelma sou*). The Jesus of Matthew's Gospel himself prays as he had taught his disciples.

To a certain degree, the concluding phrase of this petition—"on earth as it is in heaven"—could be applied to all of the "you" petitions. The disciples are to pray that life on earth will reflect the reality of God's own realm. This is a fundamental dynamic of New Testament thinking. The reverence due to God's name, the transformation of the world through the advent of God's reign, and obedience to God's will should reflect and be in harmony with the ultimate reality of God's own life and presence. At work here in the Lord's Prayer, as it is in so much of Jesus's teaching, is what could be called an "eschatological" perspective—a longing for the definitive future realization of God's purpose in creating the world and the human person. The heart of New Testament ethics is the conviction that the disciple is to live now by the future one most earnestly desires to see. Thus the "you" petitions take their cue from the longed-for future that God will bring, but these petitions are also directed to the present—praying that the attitudes and actions of God's reign will have an impact now on those who are disciples of Jesus and live by his teaching and example.

The "We" Petitions

The three "we" petitions ask for fundamental human needs and, as did the "you" petitions, reflect the spirit of Jesus's teaching. The first of these petitions poses a challenge to interpretation. Literally it reads: "Give to us today our daily bread." The precise translation for the word *daily* is the problem. The Greek word *epiousion* as an adjective linked with bread is found only in the Gospels of Matthew and Luke and nowhere else in Greek literature. Depending on how one interprets the Greek components of the word, it can have various meanings:

1. The bread "necessary for existence," understanding *epiousian* to be derived from *epi* ("for") and *ousian* (meaning power or strength or vitality). With this meaning, the "bread" asked for is the sustenance necessary for one to live.

2. Or linking it with the word "today," it could mean the bread necessary for the current day, that is, "today."

3. Or similarly, it could mean the "bread for tomorrow," in the sense that we ask the Father to give us today the daily portion we need for tomorrow.

4. Finally, if the components of the word are taken to be derived from the Greek verb *epienai*, meaning to "be coming," then the petition would be to give us today the "bread that is coming" or the "bread of the future."

How to decide among these alternatives? There are two fundamental directions included in these options for the word *epiousian*. One set of meanings refers to the reality of bread needed to exist or the daily ration of bread sufficient to sustain life. Thus we petition God to give us the food we need to keep us alive, expressing our fundamental dependence on God for the gift of life. The other in speaking of the "bread of the future" or the "bread that is coming" may refer to bread in a metaphorical way as the bread of God's kingdom for which we long. Texts such as Isaiah 25:6–9 spoke of the future as a great banquet, filled with choice wines and rich food. And in the Exodus account, God feeds Israel with bread, that is, manna, provided miraculously to sustain the people on the way to the Promised Land. In Jesus's encounter with the centurion of Capernaum, this gentile's great faith causes Jesus to foresee that "many will come from the east and the west, and will recline with Abraham, Isaac, and Jacob at the banquet in the kingdom of heaven" (Matthew 8:11).

There is no reason why this petition could not include both levels of meaning. We ask God to give us our daily bread needed to sustain our life today, but we also long for that heavenly banquet of the future, where we will be filled with the bread of God's loving presence, nourishment already signaled in the life-giving rations we receive each day.

The second "we" petition asking for forgiveness also reflects a strong current of Matthew's Gospel. Literally, we ask God to "take away" or "forgive" our sins as we forgive others. The Greek word Matthew uses for sin—*opheilemata*—is accurately translated as "debts" while the parallel petition in Luke's version uses the word "sins" (*harmatia*) for the first part of the petition (Luke 11:4a). The meaning of the two versions is equivalent but Matthew's use of the term "debt" has more of a Jewish character. A widespread notion in Judaism was that sin accrued "debt" with God, a debt that had to be paid off in righteous acts and repentance. The petition thus links God's forgiveness of our debts with our willingness to forgive others who "owe us debts."

The experience of forgiveness and reconciliation is found in other prominent places in Matthew's Gospel, including the verses that immediately follow the Lord's Prayer: "If you forgive others their transgressions, your heavenly Father will forgive you. But if you do not forgive others, neither will your Father forgive your transgressions" (Matthew 6:14–15; see a similar saying in Mark 11:25). Here, the Greek term for *sin* is *parapatomata*, which is accurately translated as "transgressions" and has the connotation of "taking a false step" or straying from the proper course of action. Earlier in the Sermon, Jesus had urged his disciples to seek reconciliation with one who has "anything against you"—even to leave their gift at the altar and "go first be reconciled with your brother and then come and offer your gift" (Matthew 5:23–24). And the climactic contrast statement in the series of Jesus's teachings in Matthew 5:21–48 concludes with the exhortation to "love your enemies, and pray for those who persecute you" (Matthew 5:44)—a reconciling act that makes one like the "heavenly Father, for he makes his sun rise on the bad and the good, and causes rain to fall on the just and the unjust" (Matthew 5:45).

In the community discourse of chapter 18, the parable of the unforgiving servant—found only in Matthew's Gospel—is in effect a commentary on this petition of the Lord's Prayer (18:21–35). The parable is told by Jesus in response to Peter's question about the limits of forgiveness regarding a member of the community who "sins against me" (the verb *harmatesei* is used). The story recounts the behavior of a servant who is forgiven an enormous debt by his king who could have thrown him in prison but instead was "moved with pity" for the man and dissolved his entire debt. Here, as in the petition of the Lord's Prayer, the discussion has to do with "debts" owed (a "debt of ten thousand talents"—a staggering amount in the economy of the time, equivalent to the totality of taxation collected by Herod in one year!). The servant asks for "more time" but instead is forgiven the entire debt by his master. Then in turn, the servant goes out and without pity demands that a fellow servant pay his owed debt of 100 denarii (a relatively insignificant sum). Because of the servant's cruel behavior to his fellow servant, he experiences severe judgment from the king. Jesus draws the conclusion to this parable: "So will my heavenly Father do to you, unless each of you forgives his brother from his heart" (Matthew 18:35).

Thus this petition of the Lord's Prayer works on the dual level we have seen in other parts of the prayer. We ask God's forgiveness for our sins but are also made aware that the mercy and forgiveness we rightly expect from our Father must also be reflected in our way of life as well—we, too, must forgive as we are forgiven. Otherwise, we can expect that ultimately God will judge us for our misdeeds—the motif of judgment being a strong emphasis in Matthew's Gospel. (See, for example, the series of "judgment" parables in chapter 25, climaxing with Matthew's parable of the sheep and the goats where the just are blessed for their good deeds done to the least, in verses 25:31–46.)

The final "we" petition and the conclusion of the prayer itself turns to the end-time of human history. Literally, the petition asks that God "not subject us to the final test." The word *test* accurately translates the Greek term *peirasmos*, which comes from the verb connoting struggle and a test of strength. Translating this word as "temptation," as is sometimes the case, may give the wrong impression of its meaning. "Temptation" in English has the connotation of a lure or seduction to do something wrong. The "test" or "struggle" implied in the term *peirasmos* refers to the final struggle between good and evil that in the Gospels' view will characterize the final destiny of humankind. In the opening scenes of the Gospel, Jesus himself is "tested" by Satan (Matthew 4:1, 3), and in the course of his ministry, his opponents try to "test" him as well (Matthew 16:1; 19:3; 22:18, 35). Such tests anticipate the final testing that will occur in the last days, as predicted by Jesus in Matthew 24:1–28.

The petition concludes by asking the heavenly Father to "deliver us from the evil one." The Greek term for "the evil one" is *to poneros*, and it could be used in a neutral sense to mean simply "evil," but previously in Matthew's Gospel, Jesus clearly speaks of *to poneros* as the "evil one," as in the parable of the sower, in which the "evil one" comes and takes away the seed sown in the heart of the one who hears "the word of the kingdom without understanding it" (Matthew 13:19) and, similarly, in the parable of the wheat and the weeds, the weeds themselves are "the children of the evil one" (Matthew 13:38).

While the direction of the prayer is toward the final struggles of the end time, it is also clear that in this petition, as in the others, the future destiny of humankind plays out in the present. So we pray that God the merciful Father would protect us from overwhelming evil and not place us in mortal jeopardy either now or in the future. This final petition has an innate sense of humility, acknowledging that there are situations suffused with evil that could test us beyond our capacity and overwhelm us spiritually and physically. Just as a previous petition asked that God "give us today our bread for the future"—"bread" that would also be the final sustenance for us—we also need bread now, this day, in order to sustain our lives. So just as we count on our merciful and loving God to protect us and lead us through to him at the moment of our final journey, so now we trust God to protect us on our daily path.

CONCLUSION

What, then, do we learn from Matthew's Gospel about prayer?

First of all, the Gospel's rich teaching reminds us through the example of Jesus himself of the need for profound reverence for our God "who is in heaven"—the God whose will Jesus continually seeks and faithfully observes. Such fidelity to God's will is the fundamental condition of discipleship (Matthew 12:50). At the same time, Matthew's Gospel teaches us that this same awesome God is "our Father"—close to us so we may speak to God, merciful as the love exhibited by the best of human parents reflects, compassionate for us as "sheep without a shepherd (Matthew 9:36), seeking us when we stray (Matthew 18:14), and forgiving our sins no matter how enormous they might be (Matthew 18:35). Thus our prayer should be shot through with praise for God and thanksgiving for God's mercy and infinite beauty.

Second, prayer directed intimately to such a loving God should be authentic, without artifice, never drawing attention to ourselves, never put on for show, but the kind of prayer that one might say in the private of one's inner room hidden from everyone else. The things we should pray for are fundamental and genuine: bread, forgiveness, protection.

We learn, too, that prayer must be linked to action. What we ask of God should also be reflected in our own life. If we ask for forgiveness, then we must be ready to forgive. If we ask for bread, then we must feed the hungry. If we ask for deliverance, then we must work to protect others.

And, finally, our prayer should reflect our deepest and most noble desires: for the coming of God's kingdom and its gift of genuine healing and peace in our world, for the glorification of God's holy name on everyone's lips and in every part of our universe, and for God's presence with us, sustaining us, and protecting us.

These are the lessons about prayer that Jesus's example and teaching in the Gospel of Matthew gives. All of this is embodied in the model prayer that is Jesus's gift to us: the Lord's Prayer. A prayer that reaches deep into our Jewish heritage and a prayer that epitomizes the mission of Jesus himself.

---

1. All biblical quotations are taken from the *New American Bible*.

CHAPTER 10

Praying with the Gospel of Mark

~ *Thomas D. Stegman, SJ* ~

The Gospel of Mark is challenging and enigmatic in many ways. Mark depicts Jesus as the *mystērion* ("mystery") of the kingdom of God, as a mighty healer and exorcist who warns people—the healed and witnesses alike—not to tell others of his power, and as a Messiah who must suffer and die (and be raised from the dead). The Markan Jesus calls his disciples to carry their cross and to strive for greatness by becoming slaves. Mark frequently portrays the disciples as failing to comprehend Jesus and heed his teaching. In fact, the original ending of this Gospel has the women who encountered the empty tomb running away and saying nothing to anyone, for they were greatly afraid. Challenging and enigmatic, indeed.

These features, among others, demand that Mark's Gospel be studied with great care. Even more, as a privileged expression of God's Word, they invite prayerful encounter with the text. Such prayerful encounter will be greatly rewarded. We will see that, in the first place, Mark presents Jesus as a model pray-er, as one whose fidelity to prayer allows him to discern God's will and gives him the wherewithal to carry it out. Second, a unique aspect of Mark's portrayal of discipleship is his emphasis on the necessity of being with Jesus; for present day disciples, being with him is made possible by prayer. Third, Mark highlights the necessity of listening to Jesus, especially as he journeys toward Jerusalem in the "way section" (Mark 8:22—10:52), wherein he reveals the essence of discipleship; as we will see, the type of listening called forth here leads to obedience. Last, Mark suggests that the community of Jesus's followers are, in effect, a new temple, a "house of prayer" open to all, characterized by robust faith and mutual forgiveness.

JESUS AS PRAY-ER: DISCERNING AND ENACTING GOD'S WILL[1]

An underappreciated facet of Mark's Gospel is his depiction of Jesus as pray-er. To be sure, Mark does not list as many instances of Jesus at prayer as, for example, Luke. Nevertheless, Mark's placement of such occurrences at critical points in the narrative —within the prologue (1:9–13), in his description of a representative day in Jesus's ministry (1:35–39), at a significant moment near the midpoint of the Gospel (6:46), at the beginning of Jesus's passion (14:32–42), and in the moments before his death (15:34)—attests to their importance more than the quantity of instances might, prima facie, indicate. As we will discover, Mark suggests that Jesus's fidelity to prayer helps him to discern God's will and strengthens him to enact it.

1:9–13—Jesus's Baptism and Testing

Just as the infancy narratives in Matthew (1:1–2:23) and Luke (1:1–2:52) and the prologue in John (1:1–18) set forth each evangelist's particular understanding of Jesus, so do Mark's introductory verses (Mark 1:1–13).[2] Mark's prologue has details that intimate the importance of Jesus's prayer. His account of what happens immediately following Jesus's baptism—the rending open of the heavens, the descent of the Spirit like a dove, and the divine voice (Mark 1:10–11)—is unique in one important respect. While the other evangelists convey the public character of (at least some of) these phenomena, Mark implies that Jesus alone saw the vision and heard the heavenly voice. His version therefore homes in on Jesus's *private* experience of God's communication with him.[3] To be sure, Mark does not explicitly declare that Jesus was praying at the baptism (compare Luke 3:21), but the emphasis on the private, intimate quality of the experience suggests a context of prayer.

Two elements of God's declaration to Jesus in Mark 1:11—"You are my beloved Son; in you I have taken delight"[4]—are also worth noting. First, God's calling Jesus "beloved (*agapētos*) Son" evokes the story of Abraham and Isaac in Genesis 22, where Abraham is directed to sacrifice his only son. Three times he refers to Isaac as "beloved son" (Genesis 22:2, 12, 16). Thus, at the outset of the Gospel, Mark already foreshadows the cross, the sacrifice of God's Son. Second, "in you I have taken delight" is an allusion to Isaiah 42:1, a passage in which God's servant is anointed with the Spirit and commissioned to bring forth justice. Evocation of the Isaian servant also points to Jesus's suffering. (See Mark 10:45, another allusion to the Isaian servant.)

Following Jesus's baptism, the Spirit of God leads him into the wilderness (*erēmos*; Mark 1:12). In the biblical world, the wilderness is a place of privileged encounter with God (see, e.g., Hosea 2:16). It is also a place of testing.[5] Indeed, Mark indicates that Jesus was "tempted by Satan" for forty days (Mark 1:13). He then immediately declares that Jesus "was with the wild beasts." Though commentators differ on their interpretation of the presence of "wild beasts," it is best understood as pointing to the restoration of creation's original harmony (see Isaiah 11:1–9).[6] That is, Mark portrays Jesus as the new Adam who, by his obedience to God in the face of testing, reverses the deleterious effects of the first Adam's disobedience. Unlike Adam who failed when tempted by the serpent (Genesis 3:1–7), Jesus was steadfastly faithful to God when "tempted by Satan." And unlike Adam who, after succumbing to temptation, shrank away from God's presence (Genesis 3:8), Jesus remained in the divine presence as obedient Son.

Pulling together the various elements, including the biblical allusions, from the Markan prologue, the following themes emerge: Jesus is depicted as having an intimate encounter with God the Father; he is empowered by the Spirit and given a mission by God, one that will involve suffering and death; and he remains faithful to God in the face of testing. Just as the overture of a symphony sounds forth notes and motifs to be developed, so Mark is setting the stage for later elaboration of these themes. And in doing so, he will make explicit that Jesus's *prayer* is the linchpin that holds them together.

But before pressing on with the analysis, I want to linger a moment on Jesus's experience of hearing God the Father name him "beloved" and express delight in him. Observe that this occurs *before* Jesus has begun his public ministry. Jesus is loved, first and foremost, for *who* he is. This is worth pondering. We who are God's children by adoption, by virtue of our baptism, are likewise invited to hear God name us his "beloved son" or "beloved daughter," and to grow in the realization of his wondrous delight in us, first and foremost, for *who* we are. Prayer enables us to so experience God's love. Such prayerful encounter helps build a strong foundation for persevering in fidelity to God's will for us.

1:35–39—TYPICAL DAY OF JESUS'S MINISTRY

Mark's first explicit statement that Jesus withdrew for solitary prayer appears in 1:35: "And early in the morning, when it was still dark, he arose and left [the house]. And he went away to a wilderness place and there he was praying." Jesus's early morning prayer brings to completion a twenty-four–hour period of ministry in Capernaum. On the previous day, Jesus taught in the synagogue and cast out a demon (1:21–28); upon leaving the synagogue, he healed Peter's mother-in-law (1:29–31); and after sunset, he cured many who were sick and cast out several demons (1:32–34). Many commentators correctly note that Mark's description of Jesus's activity in 1:21–34 is intended to convey a typical day in his ministry. Fewer scholars, however, rightly point out that Mark's report of Jesus at prayer is *also* meant to be regarded as his typical practice.[7]

The locus of Jesus's prayer is *erēmos topos* (literally, "wilderness place"; Mark 1:35). This phrase has puzzled exegetes, many of whom observe that the area surrounding Capernaum is cultivated (thus, for instance, the RSV renders the phrase "a lonely place"). Mark's reference to *erēmos*, however, points the reader back to the conclusion of the prologue (Mark 1:12–13). As we saw in the previous section, the wilderness is a place of encounter with God, as well as of testing. Just as Jesus was depicted in the opening verses as steadfast in obeying God, even in the face of being tested, so is the case in Mark 1:35–39.

What is the nature of Jesus's "test" in this instance? A hint is given by the verb *katadiōkō* in 1:36. Simon and other disciples "pursued" or "tracked down" Jesus. This verb has hostile or negative connotations.[8] That the disciples are in pursuit of Jesus, having their own agenda—and not "following" (*akoloutheō*) him, as they were called to do (Mark 1:17, 20)—is an indicator that something is amiss. Upon finding Jesus, they comment, "Everyone is looking for you" (Mark 1:37). The implication seems to be that, given the success of Jesus's ministry the previous day, he should return to Capernaum in order to continue it there.[9] But as the following verses make clear, Jesus regards their idea—inspired by the flush of success and the people's acclamation—as an instance of thinking not from God's perspective, but rather from a human point of view (cf. Mark 8:33).

Jesus then reveals, in Mark 1:38, the knowledge and resolve that result from his encounter with God in prayer. He declares, "Let us go (*agōmen*) elsewhere, into the neighboring towns, in order that I might preach there as well." Following the arrest of John the Baptist, Jesus entered Galilee and began his ministry of "preaching the good news" (Mark 1:14). In the present passage, Jesus not only confirms that his God-given mission is to preach; he also insists that God is now calling him to proclaim the good news *beyond* Capernaum. The allure of success and popularity do not hold Jesus back from responding positively to the will of his Father.

Jesus's final comment in Mark 1:38—"For this is the reason I have come out"—can and should be read at two different levels. At the level of the story, it reinforces Jesus's determination to "come out" from (i.e., leave) Capernaum in order to proclaim the good news elsewhere. At the level of theology, Jesus's words indicate that he has come forth from God both to announce and inaugurate the coming of his kingdom. Jesus's prayer brings him knowledge of God's will and the commitment to obey it—both in terms of a particular situation early in his ministry, as well as in terms of his overall mission.

6:31–32, 46—JESUS'S PRAYER ON THE MOUNTAIN...

The image of Jesus's typical practice of prayer should be kept in mind as we work our way through Mark's Gospel, including his account of Jesus's Galilean mission (chaps. 1–6).[10] In other words, we are to understand that Jesus's ministry of teaching, casting out demons, and healing manifests his prayer-grounded obedience to God. These are the very activities by which he proclaims "the gospel of God" and inbreaks God's kingdom (Mark 1:14–15). With this in mind, we arrive at a crucial juncture in Mark's Gospel, where Jesus invites his disciples to come away with him to "a wilderness place" (Mark 6:31–32) and where, following his feeding of five thousand men (not to mention the women and children who were there), he "went away to the mountain in order to pray" (Mark 6:46).

What is the significance of Mark's second explicit notice of Jesus at prayer? That Jesus decides to retreat to "a wilderness place" (*erēmos topos*), mentioned two times in 6:31–32, is an important clue. This is the same phrase Mark used in 1:35, which in turn evokes his reference to *erēmos* in 1:12–13. While many commentators struggle to make sense of Mark's geographical markers in 6:31–53, it is more productive to focus on the symbolic significance of "wilderness place"—that is, as a place of encounter with God as well as of testing. Jesus's encounter with God in prayer, however, is not recounted until the end of the day (6:46). In the meantime, the immediately preceding context suggests how Jesus is "tested" here.

In Mark's telling, Jesus's withdrawal into the wilderness is catalyzed by the unjust and brutal murder of John the Baptist (6:17–29).[11] John was the divinely appointed forerunner of Jesus who announced his coming and prepared for it by calling people to repent (Mark 1:2–8). It was John's faithfulness to his vocation that led to his death. His challenge to Herod to repent of his unlawful marriage provoked the ire of Herodias (Mark 6:17–19), who took advantage of the former's shameful promises at his birthday party to have the Baptist beheaded. This sequence of events—in which John's God-given mission ultimately led to his being put to a violent death—likely triggered in Jesus a realization and question: was his God-given mission to announce and inaugurate the kingdom of God leading to a similar violent ending?

That John's death functions as a pivotal moment in Jesus's discernment of God's will is confirmed by Mark 9:12–13. Immediately following Jesus's transfiguration—a scene that anticipates Jesus's resurrection and glorification following his suffering and death—he interprets John's death as prefiguring his own fate; moreover, both deaths are linked to God's mysterious plan for salvation.[12] Of course, John's death is not the first suggestion that Jesus's mission will culminate in his death. Recall the allusion to the story of the sacrifice of Isaac, the "beloved son," in Mark 1:11. In addition, Mark has inserted several "passion pointers" in the text up to this point, such as the plot by the Pharisees and Herodians to "destroy" Jesus (3:5).[13] Even the feeding of the multitudes with the five loaves foreshadows Jesus's later self-description as one who "came not to be served but to serve, and to offer his life as ransom for many" (Mark 10:45). Though seeking quiet and rest with his disciples, Jesus responded with compassion to the needs of the assembled crowds. It is hardly accidental that Mark employs explicitly Eucharistic language—"taking," "blessed," "broke," and "gave" (6:41)—to describe Jesus's feeding the crowds. (See Mark 14:22–25 and the description of the meal on the night before he died.)

These contextual markers are essential for interpreting Mark's notice in 6:46 that Jesus, after first dismissing the disciples and then the multitudes, "went up on the mountain to pray." Just as the phrase *erēmos topos* ("wilderness place") has symbolic resonances for Mark, so does *oros* ("mountain"). It is a locus of special encounter with God. (See, for example, Exodus 19:3–6; 24:12–18 [Moses]; 1 Kings 19:9–18 [Elijah].) While Mark does not relay the content of Jesus's prayer in this instance, the latter's subsequent words and actions (esp. in the "way section," Mark 8:22—10:52) make clear that he understands that he "must" (*dei*; Mark 8:31) go to Jerusalem, where he will suffer and die; Jesus's resolute journey to the Holy City also manifests his obedience to God. Such knowledge and commitment are, I suggest, the fruit of his sustained prayer (he does not leave until the fourth watch of the night [Mark 6:48]) on the mountain, as well as of his ongoing prayer.

14:32–42—GETHSEMANE

The next explicit notice of Jesus at prayer in Mark's Gospel is the poignant scene in Gethsemane on the night before his death. Jesus ascends another mount to pray, the Mount of Olives (Mark 14:26). In contrast to his imperturbable resolve during his journey to Jerusalem and in the preceding days, Mark now portrays Jesus's fear and distress as "the hour" draws near (14:33). Indeed, Jesus confides to his inner circle of disciples (Peter, James, and John), "My soul is deeply grieved, to the point of death" (Mark 14:34). Most commentators rightly see here an allusion to Psalms 42–43 (esp. Psalms 42:5, 11; 43:5).[14] These were originally a single psalm, more specifically, an individual lament psalm. Such psalms express the quandary, fear, and sense of abandonment felt by the one who is suffering. But just as important, they also give voice to the sufferer's faith and trust in God to deliver from affliction (e.g., Psalm 42:4, 8; Psalm 43:2–3). Moreover, some lament psalms even relate the sufferer's thanksgiving to God in anticipation of his answering the prayer for deliverance (Psalm 43:4). These characteristics of lament psalms will assist in interpreting not only Jesus's words and actions in Gethsemane, but also the final words he will utter on the cross.

Jesus's posture during his prayer at Gethsemane draws attention. Mark dramatically describes him as falling prostrate on the ground (14:35). Lying down on his face is an expression of both Jesus's reverent submission before God's presence and his desperate plea for help. The latter point raises a crucial question: Does Jesus experience God's presence and receive divine assistance during this prayer? Because a direct answer is not given, it is necessary to press some details in the text.

Jesus's prayer in Mark 14:36 divides into four parts. First, he addresses God as "Abba" (Mark is the only evangelist who records the Aramaic term; see Romans 8:15 and Galatians 4:6). With this form of address, Jesus expresses his filial intimacy and love for the One who has named him "beloved Son" (Mark 1:11; 9:7). Second, Jesus renders to God his reverence and praise: "all things are possible to you." Rather than express some abstract theological principle concerning divine omnipotence, Jesus's confession of God's power reflects his conviction, borne from experience, that God holds and sustains his life—indeed, *all* life—in his hands.[15] Used in conjunction with his address to God as "Abba," Jesus's confession of God's power is "shot through with obedient trusting."[16]

Third, Jesus offers a prayer of petition that God remove the cup of suffering from him. At first glance, this request seems to call into question Jesus's willingness to submit obediently to the divine will. How is this to be reconciled with the preceding analysis that insists on the importance of prayer for him in determining and then acting on God's will? To be sure, Mark does not flinch to portray the *pathos* of the situation: Jesus hesitates and expresses his horror in the face of the gruesome suffering of crucifixion. Yet, his intimate relationship with God allows him to express himself with complete honesty and transparency. Jesus's petition should also be understood in light of what was said above about lament psalms. That is, just as his statement to the disciples that his soul is deeply grieved evoked the plight, terror, and feeling of isolation of the innocent sufferer of Psalms 42–43, so now his plea echoes the psalmist's cry for deliverance (see Psalm 43:1). Not to be lost sight of is that, in the first two parts of his prayer, Jesus has *already* demonstrated his trust in God—another feature of lament psalms.

Fourth, and here we arrive at the climax of Jesus's supplication, he prays, "But [I ask for] not what I want, but instead [I ask for] what *you* want."[17] These final words of Jesus's prayer trump the previous petition. Despite his understandable hesitation and fear in the face of suffering, Jesus now commits himself to carry out wholeheartedly the divine will. And in doing so, his prayer in Gethsemane "taps the deepest current in Jesus's life as presented by Mark." It is cut from the same cloth as the prayers in Mark 1:35 and 6:46, wherein Jesus emerges with resolve to enact God's plan for him. Now, similar to Isaac the "beloved son," he obediently entrusts his life and future into the hands of the One he lovingly calls "Abba."[18]

Is Jesus's determination the result of experiencing God's presence and aid? The passage ends with the notice that Jesus returns to his disciples and declares, "Get up. Let us go. Behold, the betrayer has drawn near" (Mark 14:42). Jesus's posture and demeanor are markedly transformed from lying prostrate in desperation to resolutely taking charge. Moreover, the phrase "[L]et us go" renders *agōmen*, the very same word Jesus employed when rising from prayer in Mark 1:38 as he declared his commitment to heed God's call to him to proclaim the gospel to "the neighboring towns." In these ways, Mark signals that Jesus did gain strength from his prayer, and that he did encounter the divine presence and succor in Gethsemane. Although the evangelist records no words from God here, his narrative strongly suggests that the Father was neither absent nor silent.[19]

15:34—JESUS'S FINAL WORDS ON THE CROSS

Following his arrest in the garden, Jesus says very little in Mark's Gospel (14:62; 15:2). His final words are uttered after he has endured the agony of the crucifixion for six hours. Jesus prays the opening line of Psalm 22: "My God, my God, why have you forsaken me?" To be sure, these words convey Jesus's heart-wrenching pain and feelings of discouragement as he hung on the cross. But his cry ought not to be reduced to expressing only despair.[20] Psalm 22 is another song of lament. This particular psalm alternates between cries of complaint (22:1–2, 6–8, 12–18) and expressions of hope and trust in God (22:3–5, 9–11, 19–21); moreover, it culminates with an extended thanksgiving to God for deliverance (22:22–31, esp. 22:24: "[The LORD] did not hide his face from me, but heard when I cried to him" [NRSV]). That Mark intends Jesus as praying the *entire* psalm—and that the original audience would have interpreted him thus—is strongly suggested by the evangelist's allusions to various parts of Psalm 22 throughout the passion narrative.[21]

Thus, as was the case with the prayer in Gethsemane, the key to understanding Jesus's prayer in 15:34 is the movement—one might say the theology—of the lament psalm. While Mark retains Jesus's sense of terror and pain, as evident not only in the cited words of Psalm 22:1 but also in the two-fold reference to Jesus's crying out with a "loud voice" (Mark 15:34, 37); nevertheless, he also implies that Jesus's prayer expresses trust in God to vindicate his faithfulness in carrying out the divine will (see esp. Psalm 22:9–11).

Mark's narrative goes on to indicate that God *did* in fact respond to Jesus's self-offering. In 15:38, immediately following Jesus's death, Mark reports that the curtain of the temple "was rent apart."[22] God's mercy and forgiveness of sins are now mediated through the cross, through Jesus's self-offering in love in obedience to God. Furthermore, as the women went to the tomb on the third day, Mark relates in 16:4 that the large stone that sealed Jesus's tomb "was rolled back," which is then followed in 16:6 by the heavenly messenger's announcement that Jesus "has been raised." In all instances, Mark employs passive voice verbs, indicating *God's* agency.[23] God has vindicated Jesus's obedient self-offering by raising him from the dead to the fullness of life over which death has no more power. Indeed the resurrection of Jesus, God's "beloved Son," gives texture and definition to the eschatological deliverance portrayed in Psalm 22:27–31.

Mark thereby presents Jesus as the new Adam, through whose obedience unto death God has brought about a new creation, life in the Spirit that will culminate in the resurrection from the dead, of which Jesus is the first fruits (1 Corinthians 15:20–28). At pivotal points in his narrative, Mark has shown that it is through fidelity to prayer that Jesus comes to know God's will and receives the strength to enact it. But Jesus's prayer is only one side of the coin of Mark's teaching about prayer. The other side is the importance of prayer for Jesus's followers.

"Being with" Jesus[24]

What are the implications for the prayer life of the community—both Mark's original community and believers today—that exists in this new creation? In addition to presenting him as the model pray-er, Mark reveals that the risen Jesus (along with God the Father) is the one to whom our prayer is to be directed. A key to appreciating how Jesus's followers are called to pray is found in four texts that bear special Markan emphases (3:14; 6:31–32; 4:11; 16:1–8). As we will see, Mark presents us with a concrete way of "being with" the risen Jesus—namely through our prayerful contemplation of the Gospel text itself.

Jesus the Pray-er as Paradigm for God's "New Family"

Mark's portrait of prayer functions, at the level of the Gospel's narrative, to show how Jesus discerned God's will and was empowered to obey it. At another level—at what might be called the exhortative level—the evangelist holds him up as a model pray-er for us to emulate.[25] This paradigmatic aspect of Jesus's prayer is essential for Mark because of the way he sets forth what constitutes the heart of discipleship: seeking and doing God's will. Jesus makes this clear when he is approached by members of his family who think he is out of his mind because of his frenetic ministerial activity; he responds, "Who is my mother? Who are my brothers?... Whoever does the will of God is my brother, and sister, and mother" (Mark 3:33–35). Jesus thereby introduces the image of "family" to describe the community of his followers.

Mark's Gospel suggests a four-fold logical sequence in connection with these points. First, the distinctive characteristic of the family of faith gathered around Jesus is the commitment to do God's will. Second, prayer is the chief way by which we discern the divine will and are empowered to obey it. Third, prayer of this type is exemplified by Jesus, God's beloved Son. And fourth, we thus express our filial relationship with God the Father and our solidarity with Jesus by imitating his prayer. John R. Donahue admirably captures this solidarity between Jesus and the new family gathered around him:

> Jesus is Son because he hears and does the will of God, because, though loved by God and chosen to proclaim the mystery of the kingdom, he struggled with finding and doing the will of God. Mark's gospel, therefore, does not widen the distance between Jesus and the believer. In calling Jesus, "Son of God," Mark's community affirms solidarity with him and their consciousness that, in doing the will of God, they are to Jesus, brothers and sisters.[26]

(The Risen) Jesus as Addressed by the Community in Prayer

While Mark's Gospel expresses solidarity between Jesus and his followers, he also sets forth the former's exalted status vis-à-vis the family of faith. For instance, in his prologue—wherein he sounds notes to be amplified later in the text—Mark ascribes to Jesus the divine titles "Lord" (1:3; cf. 12:35–37) and "mightier one" (1:7).[27] In addition, Jesus is described by John the Baptist as having the power to dispense the gift of God's Spirit (Mark 1:8). As Son of Man, Jesus pronounces the forgiveness of sins (Mark 2:10), exercises authority over the Sabbath (Mark 2:28), and will participate in the future (and final) judgment (Mark 13:26–27), all of which are divine prerogatives. Moreover, Mark dramatically narrates Jesus's power to quell the destructive forces of a storm at sea (4:35–41), of a legion of demons (5:1–20), of untreatable illness (5:25–34), and—most spectacularly of all—of the power of death itself (5:21–24, 35–43). No wonder that figures like the Gerasene demoniac, Jairus, and the hemorrhaging woman fall at Jesus's feet (Mark 5:22, 33) and worship him (Mark 5:6)!

Mark thereby presents a paradox in terms of the prayer life of the new family gathered around Jesus. On one hand, he holds up Jesus the pray-er—the one who in prayer addresses God as "Abba"—as a model for us to imitate. On the other hand, he intimates that Jesus—especially in light of his resurrection and exaltation—is now worthy to receive our prayer. That is, the risen and exalted Jesus (along with God the Father) is to be addressed in prayer, both by individuals and by the gathered community.[28]

Four Key Texts with Unique Markan Emphases

In order to work through Mark's paradox, let's look briefly at four passages which, when compared to parallel texts in Matthew and Luke, highlight Markan themes that are often underappreciated by commentators. The first text is Mark 3:13–15, Jesus's calling the twelve and empowering them for ministry. Luke's account of this event is streamlined; Jesus "chose from them twelve, whom he named apostles" (Luke 6:13). Matthew's telling puts the accent on Jesus's bestowing on the twelve the power to cast out demons and heal infirmities (Matthew 10:1). Mark's version has Jesus appointing the twelve "in order that they might be with him (*hina ōsin met' autou*) and in order to be sent to preach and to have authority to cast out demons" (Mark 3:14–15). Notice that *prior* to sending the twelve on mission, Mark highlights the notion of "being with" Jesus. For him, "being with" Jesus is the primary task of those who are called by him; it is the sine qua non of faithful discipleship.

Not only does Mark's syntax in 3:14–15 suggest this emphasis on "being with" Jesus; it is also indicated by the arrangement of the ensuing narrative. That is, the twelve are not actually sent on mission until Mark 6:7. In the meantime, they are privy to listening to Jesus teach about the kingdom of God in parables (Mark 4:1–34) and to watching him in his ministry (Mark 4:35–5:43). "Being with" Jesus therefore entails learning from his words and deeds about how to be faithful proclaimers, healers, and agents of God's liberating mercy.

While "being with" might seem to be the special privilege of the twelve who enjoyed Jesus's physical presence, Mark offers hints of both a wider call and a broader mode of access. In terms of a wider call, Mark does not emphasize—especially in comparison with Luke—the special role of the apostles. In his Gospel, the line separating the twelve from a larger group of disciples is fluid and often blurred.[29] Hence, "being with" Jesus is an essential trait of *all* of his followers and not just the prerogative of the twelve. But granted this observation, is not "being with" Jesus in order to listen to him and observe him in action still limited to the characters in the Gospel, to the disciples who actually accompanied him?

The second key text, Mark 6:31–32—Jesus's invitation to the twelve to come by themselves to a "wilderness place" (*erēmos topos*)—is where Mark suggests a broader mode of access to Jesus. The context of this passage is the twelve's return from their missionary work that was marked by hectic activity (cf. "all that they had done and taught"; 6:30). Looking at the parallel texts once again sheds light on what Mark is up to. In Luke 9:10, Jesus and the apostles withdraw to a "city" (*polis*), while in Matthew 14:13, only Jesus withdraws to a "wilderness place." (The disciples come onto the scene at Matthew 14:15, *after* the crowds have found Jesus.) What is unique about Mark's account is that Jesus directly invites his followers to accompany him into the wilderness.[30]

As we saw above, the wilderness is a place of encounter with the divine (Mark 1:12–13, 35). I suggest that Mark 6:31–32 functions as a *perennial* invitation by Jesus to his followers, including those of us in the present day, to take time out from the (often chaotic) busyness of our lives to "be with" him in prayer. That is, the passage calls us to come to a place of sacred encounter, one that sets us in the presence of the risen Lord. Indeed, it is with good reason that many retreat directors assign this text to their directees at the beginning of a retreat.

One reason why "being with" Jesus in prayer is crucially important is suggested by the third key passage, Mark 4:10–12, where he answers the question posed to him by his disciples about why he speaks in parables. Again, comparison with Luke and Matthew illuminates a particular Markan emphasis. In the former, Jesus tells his disciples, "To you it has been given to know the mysteries [*mystēria*] of the kingdom of God/heaven" (Luke 8:10; Matthew 13:11). Both Luke and Matthew emphasize the disciples' knowledge and the object of their knowledge, namely the "mysteries" or "secrets" (plural) of the kingdom. In Mark's telling, Jesus's focus is different: "To you have been given the mystery [*mystērion*] of the kingdom of God." Observe that there is no reference to the disciples' being bestowed with particular knowledge. Even more significant is that Mark stresses they have been given the mystery (singular) of God's kingdom.

What is this mystery of God's kingdom? While that is the natural question to ask, it turns out to be on the wrong track. The better question is "Who?" The mystery of God's kingdom is Jesus himself, "the holy one of God" (Mark 1:24).[31] As noted in the introduction, Mark's portrait of Jesus is both difficult and enigmatic. Throughout his narrative, only God and the demons fully recognize who he is. It is challenging enough that Jesus manifests the power of God in ways that evoke wonder and awe (see Mark 2:12; 4:41; 5:42; 6:51; 7:37). But, as we will see momentarily, it is in the "way section" of Mark's Gospel (8:22—10:52) that the mysterious quality of Jesus's revelation is most evident.

Another way to express that, for Mark, Jesus is the mystery of God's kingdom is to refer to him as "the parable of God."[32] Just as parables with their open-ended nature elude exhaustive comprehension, so it is with Jesus. Such is to be expected of one who reveals the mysterious love and power of God. It is thus necessary for us to constantly heed Jesus's invitation to "come away" with him to "a wilderness place," to "be with" him in prayer. Allowing Jesus to fully reveal himself and teach the depths of what is entailed in discipleship is a lifelong task. It is also a necessary task if we are to discern God's will in our lives. The family of faith, those whom Jesus calls his brothers and sisters, must draw close to him. Intimacy with the risen Jesus—which *does* include understanding him more and more—is the sine qua non for discerning and enacting God's will.

How does the prayerful encounter with the risen Jesus, "being with" him, take place for contemporary disciples? The original ending of Mark's Gospel (16:1–8), the fourth key passage, suggests one privileged way this can happen. When the women come to Jesus's tomb to anoint the body, they find the stone covering the tomb rolled back. Instead of a corpse, they encounter a mysterious figure (*neaniskos*; "young man") dressed in white who reveals to them that Jesus has been raised from the dead. Moreover, they are instructed to inform the male disciples that Jesus has gone before them into Galilee; it is there, in Galilee, that they will encounter him.[33] We who read Mark's Gospel today are likewise invited to the encounter in Galilee—but now, in the "Galilee" of the Gospel text.[34] That is, we can "be with" the risen Jesus by returning, again and again, to a prayerful, meditative reading of this Gospel. As individuals and (even more) as the community gathered in prayer, we can read and listen to it with eyes of faith and discerning hearts.

LISTENING TO JESUS "ON THE WAY"

The theme of listening emerges in the climactic moment of Mark's account of Jesus's transfiguration (9:2–8). From the overshadowing cloud thunders the voice of the heavenly Father to the frightened disciples, "This is my beloved Son; *listen* to him." The context of the command to listen to Jesus is crucially important to note. It is set near the beginning of the "way section" (Mark 8:22–10:52), the central part of Mark's Gospel in which Jesus journeys with his disciples to Jerusalem. The section is structured around three passion predictions (Mark 8:31; 9:31; 10:33–34) in which Jesus— the Messiah and Son of God—reveals that he must suffer and die (and be raised). Immediately following each passion prediction is a misunderstanding by the disciples, which affords Jesus the opportunity to teach about the implications of following such a messiah. The exhortation to "listen to him" thus gets to the heart of what it means for us, the family of faith, to follow the one who himself has discerned, in prayer, God's will.

Immediately following the first passion prediction, Peter rebukes Jesus, apparently because the former is not receptive to the notion of a suffering Messiah. Jesus then instructs his disciples, "If any want to follow me, let them deny themselves, take up their cross, and follow me. For whoever would save their life will lose it; and whoever would lose their life for my sake, and for the sake of the gospel, will save it" (Mark 8:34–35). The essence of discipleship is challenging. Self-denial, which is not to be equated with the negation of one's being, calls for growth in one's desire and ability to place the needs of others on a par with, or even before, one's own. It demands the type of sacrifice involved in truly loving others, the commitment to seek always what is best for them. Taking up the cross—language that would have had a particularly chilling effect for Mark's original readers—entails the willingness to endure the suffering involved in self-denial, and in the opposition and scorn that such willingness can evoke from the wider culture.[35]

After Jesus's second passion prediction, Mark recounts that the disciples were arguing among themselves about who was the greatest. This leads Jesus to teach, "If any wish to be first, let them become last of all and servant of all" (Mark 9:35). He completely reverses the prevailing standards of what constitutes greatness—both then and now. Jesus does not discourage his followers from striving to be great; but he dramatically redefines greatness as service, as taking on the mantle and demeanor of those whose role is to serve the needs of others. Moreover, Jesus embraces a child and informs his followers that such ones—the most vulnerable and least in society—have a particular claim on their loving service (Mark 9:36–37). In Mark's world, where children were regarded as tantamount to property, this symbolic gesture had all the more punch. It is not enough to be humble; true greatness calls for serving the humble.[36]

Between the second and third passion predictions, Mark narrates Jesus's response to a question concerning divorce (10:1–12) and the poignant story of a rich man who could not heed Jesus's call to sell his possessions and follow him (10:17–22). By setting these passages within the context of Jesus's teachings about following him as the suffering Messiah, Mark makes clear that those instructions are to be enacted within the nitty-gritty, day-to-day reality of our lives. Self-denial and loving service are to be practiced vis-à-vis our most significant relationships and the administration of our possessions. Fidelity to relationships and generosity with what God has given us are ways to put the principles of discipleship into practice.[37]

Jesus's third passion prediction is followed by James and John's request for special status when he comes into his glory. Jesus reminds them that the path to glory goes through suffering (Mark 10:39) and that his way of exercising authority and power is through servant love (Mark 10:42–44).[38] Jesus—who, recall, is the mystery of God's kingdom (Mark 4:11)—then summarizes his self-presentation as suffering Messiah and his teaching about discipleship in the "way section" by proclaiming: "For indeed the Son of Man has come not to be served, but to serve, and to give his life as a ransom for many" (Mark 10:45). Jesus has gone before us in the way of self-giving love—the way that reveals God's love for us. It is because Jesus has already done so that we are enabled to walk in his "way."

Returning to the notion of listening, to listen, in the biblical sense of the term, is distinct from hearing. Or better, such listening is an intensive form of hearing. Earlier, in the parables discourse, Jesus twice exhorts, "Whoever has ears to listen, let him listen" (Mark 4:9, 23). To listen to Jesus's words is to allow them to penetrate, to become part of our very being so as to transform us. It is no accident that in Greek the word "obey" is *hypakouō*, a compound form of the verb "listen," *akouō*. Thus, to listen in the sense that God commands in Mark 9:7 is to be transformed unto obedience. It is the means to do God's will as members of the family gathered around the risen Jesus. And what makes this process possible is prayer. Indeed, with his story of the deaf-mute who is healed by Jesus (Mark 7:31–37), a passage that is unique to this Gospel, Mark offers a beautiful image of such prayer. Touching the man's ears and tongue, Jesus cries, "*Ephphatha!*" ("Be opened!"). This text invites us to allow the risen Jesus to reach out and open our ears and, even more, our hearts in order to let his challenging words permeate us, to empower and encourage us to follow him in his "way."

That such transformation is an arduous and, at times, a slow process is suggested by the two stories that bracket the "way section." Both involve the healing of a blind man. In the first, the healing of a blind man from Bethsaida (another passage unique to Mark), the restoration to sight is difficult, as Jesus twice has to lay his hands upon the man's eyes (Mark 8:22–26).[39] This account intimates that what Jesus does by teaching throughout this section is tantamount to removing the spiritual blindness from his followers' hearts, the blindness that keeps us from appreciating what kind of messiah he is and what are the implications for us. At the end of the section, Jesus performs another healing. Bartimaeus, who responds to Jesus in faith, has his blindness cured. Tellingly, Mark notes that Bartimaeus then follows him "on the way" (10:46–52)—that is, in the "way" of discipleship set forth throughout 8:26—10:45. This can also be our response when, through fidelity to prayer, we allow the risen Jesus to remove from our hearts those things that keep us from following in his way.

THE NEW TEMPLE: "HOUSE OF PRAYER FOR ALL"
One of the most enigmatic passages in Mark's Gospel is 11:12–25. There, Jesus curses a leafy but fruitless fig tree, and then performs a prophetic action in the temple; the next day, the disciples discover that the cursed fig tree has "withered away to its roots," which leads Jesus to offer his most sustained teaching about prayer in this Gospel. Most commentators agree that the account of the cursing and withering of the fig tree and the story of the temple cleansing are intended to be mutually interpretive— though exactly *how* is debated. For our purposes, it is sufficient to focus on Mark's particular emphases. He has Jesus, in citing Isaiah 56:7, insist that the temple is to be "a house of prayer for all the nations."[40] Moreover, Jesus goes on to imply that his followers are to constitute a living temple, marked by faith, prayer, and the practice of forgiveness.

Jesus's invitation to join the family of faith, those who are committed to doing God's will, is open to everyone. As the temple was a place of prayer that bore witness to Israel's faith in God, so the community of Jesus's disciples is to be characterized by faith—"Have faith in God" (Mark 11:22)—and prayer. Jesus's statement about faith moving mountains (Mark 11:23) has elicited much comment. In light of what was discussed above in the previous section, I suggest that a powerful manifestation of faith, tantamount to moving mountains, is walking in the way of Jesus's self-giving servant love—especially in the face of suffering and opposition. God's kingdom gains more foothold on earth as it is in heaven when Jesus's brothers and sisters grow in our communal witness to his "way" of discipleship. Just as Jesus taught that prayer is necessary for allowing God's healing power to work through us (9:29),[41] so also is prayer the sine qua non for our moving mountains, for our being conduits of God's love.

Jesus's teaching that one's prayer, if expressed with a truly believing heart, will be answered (Mark 11:24) is easily subject to misunderstanding. We have all prayed from the depths of our hearts (e.g., for healing for sick loved ones), but our prayers have not always been answered as we hoped. Unless Jesus's words are to be regarded as mere hyperbole, they ought to be interpreted in light of his own prayer in Gethsemane: "But I ask for not what I want, but instead I ask for what *you* want" (Mark 14:36). This is the essence of prayer: aligning ourselves with God's will. It is the fruit of "an unconditional openness to the ways of God"[42] and intimate union with the One whom Jesus addressed as "Abba." It requires the type of listening that leads to transformation-unto-obedience. Indeed, to pray with integrity the petition, "Thy kingdom come, thy will be done, on earth as it is in heaven," calls forth the commitment on our part to know and enact God's will in our own lives and circumstances. And because there are many forces that attempt to pull us away from such commitment, it is necessary to heed Jesus's call to "watch and pray" (Mark 14:38).

Mark's Gospel, of course, does not include the Lord's Prayer.[43] However, he alludes to this prayer with his teaching about the importance of forgiving others (Mark 11:25). In the first place, Jesus reminds us that the one to whom we pray is our Father. Moreover, the prayer for God's forgiveness requires us who receive divine mercy to forgive others in turn. Whereas the temple was the place where sacrifice was offered for forgiveness of sins, the cross of Jesus is now the conduit of God's mercy,[44] bringing about the possibility of forgiveness of sins. We who receive God's mercy are to be instruments of that mercy vis-à-vis others. The family of faith, the living temple of prayer open to all peoples, is the place where the forgiving character of God is to be appropriated and imitated.[45] Jesus's teaching therefore makes clear that the right relationship with God also entails right relationships with others.

Conclusion

While Luke's Gospel is known as "the gospel of prayer,"[46] the theme of prayer is also central for Mark. He portrays Jesus as the model pray-er, one whose prayer allowed him to grow in intimacy with God as "Abba," as well as to discern and enact God's will. Jesus is the obedient Son whose self-giving love—manifested particularly on the cross—has brought about a new creation. Prayer is the means for disciples today to "be with" Jesus, the mystery of the kingdom of God. Mark's Gospel itself provides a privileged arena for the encounter with the risen Jesus, especially in the "way section" where he teaches the essence of discipleship. Prayerful listening to Jesus enables the transformation unto obedience that is the mark of the new family gathered around him. Our growth in self-giving love and service is, in effect, the continuation of the story Mark sets forth. The evangelist also makes clear that the family of faith is a new temple, a place of prayer, where faith is enacted in love and mutual forgiveness.

1. This first part draws in large part from Thomas D. Stegman, "Jesus as Pray-er in Mark's Gospel: 'Your Will Be Done,'" *The Pastoral Review* 5, no. 4 (2009): 10–15. I am grateful to Rev. Dr. Michael Hayes, editor, for his permission to use this material here. For the most recent and thorough treatment of prayer in Mark's Gospel, see Mathias Nygaard, *Prayer in the Gospels: A Theological Exegesis of the Ideal Pray-er* (Leiden: Brill, 2012), 74–106.

2. See, e.g., Morna D. Hooker, *Beginnings: Keys That Open the Gospels* (Harrisburg, PA: Trinity, 1997), 1–22.

3. See Joel Marcus, *Mark 1–8: A New Translation with Introduction and Commentary* (New York: Doubleday, 2000), 163–64, as well as the chart on page 161.

4. Translations of Scripture in this chapter are my own, unless indicated otherwise.

5. See Frank J. Moloney, *The Gospel of Mark: A Commentary* (Peabody, MA: Hendrickson, 2002), 38; also, Bonnie B. Thurston, *The Spiritual Landscape in Mark* (Collegeville, MN: Liturgical, 2008), 1–14.

6. As Richard Bauckham points out, Mark's use of the expression *einai meta tinos* ("to be with some/thing") normally connotes a positive, friendly association (see Mark 3:14; 5:18; 14:67). See Richard Bauckham, "Jesus and the Wild Animals (Mark 1:13): A Christological Image for an Ecological Age," in *Jesus of Nazareth: Lord and Christ: Essays on the Historical Jesus and New Testament Christology*, ed. Joel B. Green and Max Turner (Grand Rapids: Eerdmans, 1994), 5.

7. See, for example, Sharyn Echols Dowd, *Reading Mark: A Literary and Theological Commentary on the Second Gospel* (Macon, GA: Smyth & Helwys, 2000), 18.

8. For instance, the verb is employed to describe Pharaoh's pursuit of the Israelites (Exodus 14:4, 8, 9, 23).

9. See, for example, M. Eugene Boring, *Mark: A Commentary* (Louisville: Westminster John Knox, 2006), 69.

10. With the exception of a brief incursion to "the region of the Gerasenes" in 5:1–20, Jesus's ministry in chapters 1–6 is set within the confines of Galilee.

11. See Marcus, 405. Most commentators fail to make this linkage explicit.

12. Notice the foretold employment of *gegraptai* (as "it is written") in 9:12–13, pointing to how Scripture has told this.

13. See Norman Perrin and Dennis C. Duling, *The New Testament, an Introduction: Proclamation and Parenesis, Myth and History*, 2nd ed. (New York: Harcourt Brace Jovanovich, 1982), 240–241, for how Mark's Gospel is structured around pointers to Jesus's passion.

14. For more on Mark's employment of Psalms, see Timothy J. Geddert, "The Use of Psalms in Mark," *Direction* 38 (2009): 179–192. The citations of Psalms 42–43 and 22 (in the following section) use the versification in the NRSV.

15. Donald Senior, *The Passion of Jesus in the Gospel of Mark* (Wilmington, DE: Michael Glazier, 1984), 74.

16. Moloney, 293.

17. I twice supply *aiteō* ("ask for") to the elliptical Greek text. So does Robert H. Gundry, *Mark: A Commentary on His Apology for the Cross* (Grand Rapids: Eerdmans, 1993), 870.

18. Senior, 75–76 (the quoted line is from page 76).

19. Boring (*Mark*, 401) similarly remarks that, at the end of the passage (14:41–42), "it is clear that Jesus has regained his composure, that his prayer has been answered and will be answered in the ensuing events."

20. See, for example, John R. Donahue and Daniel J. Harrington, *The Gospel of Mark* (Collegeville, MN: Liturgical, 2002), 450: "Why would Mark write a 'gospel' ('good news') about a tragic figure whose life ends in total despair? Such a work might qualify as a tragedy or a pathetic biography, but hardly as a gospel."

21. See Frank J. Matera, *The Kingship of Jesus: Composition and Theology in Mark 15* (Chico, CA: Scholars, 1982), 129, for a chart that lists both explicit references and other allusions to Psalm 22 in Mark 15. See also Holly J. Carey, *Jesus's Cry from the Cross: Towards a First-Century Understanding of the Intertextual Relationship between Psalm 22 and the Narrative of Mark's Gospel* (London: Bloomsbury T&T Clark, 2009).

22. The notice of the curtain being rent apart echoes the detail at Jesus's baptism that the skies were rent open and God's Spirit descended upon Jesus (Mark 1:10). The rending in both instances (Mark uses same verb, *schizomai*) indicates God's activity and involvement.

23. This literary convention is known as the "divine passive," which reflects Jewish reverence for the divine name.

24. This second part draws in large part from Thomas D. Stegman, "'Being with' Jesus: Mark's Teaching on Prayer," *The Pastoral Review* 5, no. 5 (2009): 12–17.

25. See, for example, Sharon Echols Dowd, *Prayer, Power, and the Problem of Suffering: Mark 11:22–25 in the Context of Markan Theology* (Atlanta: Scholars, 1988), 119–121.

26. John R. Donahue, "The Revelation of God in the Gospel of Mark," in *Modern Biblical Scholarship: Its Impact on Theology and Proclamation*, ed. Francis A. Eigo (Villanova, PA: Villanova University Press, 1984), 169.

27. See Moloney, 34, for a list of (LXX) passages in which God is called "the mighty/strong one" (*ho ischyros*).

28. See also Mary Ann Beavis, "Mark's Teaching on Faith," *Biblical Theology Bulletin* 16 (1986): 140: "It is helpful to remember…the evangelist is not concerned only to recount the behavior of the historical disciples, but to address the needs of his own community, who prayed to and believed in God *and* the exalted Christ" (italics in the original).

29. Compare, e.g., Mark 6:30 with 6:35 and 6:45. As Moloney (78) points out, with the exception of 6:6b–30, Mark has disciples (along with the twelve) present to Jesus until 14:50. Indeed, it is striking that Mark employs the word *apostolos* only once, in 6:30 (the appearance of the term in 3:14 is thought to be a later insertion).

30. The reference to "disciples" in 6:35 suggests a broader group than the twelve.

31. See Luke Timothy Johnson, *The Writings of the New Testament: An Interpretation*, 3rd ed. (London: SCM, 1999), 168–169.

32. John R. Donahue, "A Neglected Factor in the Theology of Mark," *Journal of Biblical Literature* 101 (1982): 593.

33. Mark does not recount this event, however. Matthew is the evangelist who narrates the Galilean encounter (Matthew 28:16–20).

34. See Luke Timothy Johnson, *Writings of the New Testament*, 178–179.

35. See, e.g., Brendan Byrne, *A Costly Freedom: A Theological Reading of Mark's Gospel* (Collegeville, MN: Liturgical, 2008), 140–141.

36. Adela Yarbro Collins points to the background of the practice of exposing infants in the Greco-Roman world. In this context, Mark's purpose of including Jesus's teaching here may have been to mitigate this practice among Gentile converts or to advocate Christian couples to take in exposed infants and raise them as their own. See *Mark: A Commentary (Hermeneia)* (Minneapolis: Fortress, 2007), 445–446.

37. See, too, Moloney, 193: "Mark 10:1–31 is concerned with the *practice*, rather than the *theory*, of discipleship" (italics in the original).

38. Jesus "ups the ante" in 10:44 by using the term *doulos* ("slave"), after having used *diakonos* ("servant"). A slave is one who belongs to another and serves at the command of his master.

39. See, for example, Donahue and Harrington, 257: This story "is unusual because Jesus the healer is not immediately and completely successful. This may explain why both Matthew and Luke omit the episode."

40. Compare Matthew 21:13—"It is written, 'My house shall be called a house of prayer'"— and Luke 19:46: "It is written, 'My house shall be a house of prayer.'" Both omit "for all the nations."

41. In response to his disciples' queries about why they could not cast out the demon from the epileptic boy, Jesus states, "This kind cannot be driven out by anything except by prayer."

42. Moloney, 228.

43. The Our Father is found in Matthew 6:9–15 and Luke 11:2–4.

44. Recall the detail in 15:38 (in the first part above) that, upon Jesus's death, the curtain of the temple was rent in two, signaling that God's merciful presence is enacted through the cross.

45. Similarly, Nygaard, 88–89.

46. Craig G. Bartholomew and Robby Holt's assessment is typical: "As is well known, prayer is a major theme in Luke as it is not in the other gospels." See Bartholomew and Holt "Prayer in/ and the Drama of Redemption in Luke: Prayer and Exegetical Performance," in *Reading Luke: Interpretation, Reflection, Formation*, ed. Craig G. Bartholomew, Joel B. Green, and Anthony C. Thiselton (Grand Rapids: Zondervan, 2005), 351.

CHAPTER 11

Prayer and Pray-er in the Gospel of Luke

~ John R. Donahue, SJ ~

Biblical prayer can generally be described as "the act of petitioning, praising, giving thanks, or confessing to God.... Prayer can be individual or corporate, audible or silent. It is conditioned by the biblical understanding of God as a personal being who hears the prayers of his people (1 Kings 9:3; Psalms 34:15; 65:2; Matthew 7:11; 1 John 5:15)."[1] Among all the writings of the New Testament, the Gospel of Luke stands out for its emphasis on prayer.[2] In this chapter, after a brief survey of how concerns for prayer permeate the narrative of Luke-Acts, we will turn our attention to specific passages that are both challenging and nurturing with attention to the kinds of prayer found in Luke. Some final reflections will suggest how pray-ers today may engage the work of Luke, whom Dante described as *scriba mansuetudinis Christi* ("the scribe of the gentle mercy of Christ").

PRAYER THAT CHARACTERIZES JESUS AND OTHER SIGNIFICANT FIGURES IN THE GOSPEL

Elizabeth blesses Mary, and Mary offers a hymn of praise (Luke 1:46–55). Zechariah utters a canticle of blessing (Luke 1:67–79). The angels praise God (Luke 2:13). Simeon utters a prayer (Luke 2:28–32), and Anna is at prayer (Luke 2:37). Mary/Zechariah and Anna/Simeon are also female/male parallels, here at prayer. Jesus prays at his own baptism (Luke 3:21–22) and after miracles retreats to the wilderness for prayer (5:16). Disciples of John fast, as in Matthew and Mark, but in Luke they also pray (5:33). Jesus prays all night before the choice of the disciples (Luke 6:12)—a Lukan addition to Mark 3:13. Only in Luke does Jesus pray before Peter's confession (9:18). Jesus prays before the Transfiguration, which occurs when he is at prayer (Luke 9:28–29; cf. baptism, 3:20–21). In twin parables, prayer is central (Luke 18:1–14; cf. 11:5–8). Luke's eschatological discourse adds a saying on prayer (21:36). Jesus prays for Simon that his faith does not fail (Luke 22:31–34), and it does not, even though he denies Jesus. Luke's additions to the agony at Gethsemane stress the prayer of Jesus (22:44–45). Jesus prays that his Father forgive those who crucify him (Luke 23:34), and the disciples on the way to Emmaus recognize him when he blesses and breaks the bread (Luke 24:30–31). Finally, only Luke has the parables of prayer (11:5–8; 18:1–14).

In Acts

The idealized picture of the early Christian community is one of friendship and devotion to prayer (Acts 2:42). Disciples go to the temple at the hour of prayer (Acts 3:1). Stephen, the first "witness," prays for his enemies in words similar to those of Jesus before his death (Acts 7:59–60). Paul is at prayer after his conversion (Acts 9:11). While Peter is in prison, the community is at prayer (Acts 12:5). Prior to the conversion of Lydia, Paul meets the women at the place of prayer (Acts 16:13). Paul prays during his final meeting with the Ephesian elders (Acts 20:36). Paul prays before leaving Tyre (21:5). Paul takes bread, blesses it, and breaks it (Acts 27:35), and Paul prays before laying hands on the father of Publius, who is then healed (Acts 28:8).

Pivotal Events of Salvation History Occur in the Context of Prayer

This takes place in both the Gospel and in Acts. In the Gospel of Luke, we see it in the annunciation to Zechariah (1:10), at the baptism with Jesus as prayer (3:21–2), at the calling of his disciples (6:12), at the Transfiguration (9:29), in Gethsemane (22:39–46), at his crucifixion as Jesus prays for forgiveness of his executioners (23:46), in the final prayer on the cross ("Father, into your hands I commend my spirit") (23:46); and in the post-Resurrection disciples returning to temple to bless God (26:52–53). But then the same is especially true in Acts: After the Ascension, disciples with Mary and women are gathered in prayer (1:14, 24–25), the day of Pentecost takes place in the context of prayer (2:1–5), there is prayer before the choice of "deacons" (6:1–6), Peter and John pray that Samaritans receive the Holy Spirit (8:15), prayer is offered at the acceptance of Gentiles (10:2–4,9; 30–3; 11:5), Barnabas and Saul are missioned from Antioch after prayer (13:1–3), the appointment of elders in churches follow prayer and fasting (14:23), and when Paul thanks God on arrival in Rome (28:15).

Luke Offers Examples of Different Kinds of Prayer

There is thanksgiving (e.g., Luke 1:46–55; 2:29–32; 10:21–22), praise (e.g., Luke 1:67–79; 2:13–14, 20), petition and intercession (esp. Luke 11:1–4) for a variety of needs—for daily sustenance and help in the time of trial (Luke 11:3, 4), for boldness *(parrēsia)* in speaking the Word of God (Acts 4:29–30), and for Peter's release from prison (Acts 12:5–12). Especially strong in Luke is prayer for enemies (6:27; cf. Mt 5:44, but Luke adds that love of enemies will make one a child of the Most High [6:35]).

Special Texts on Prayer in Luke

The Infancy Narratives

Any reader of Luke's Gospel is greeted in the infancy narratives (Luke 1–2) by a poetic overture of prayers which echo the great prayers of the Old Testament and anticipate the major themes of the ministry of Jesus.[3] These reflect the piety and devotion of the *ánawím*, the "lowly people open to God" (anticipating the poor widow and tax collector of Luke 18:1–14). The Gospel opens with Zechariah in the temple at the hour of prayer when people were praying outside, and the first words heard in the Gospel are by an angel, "Do not be afraid, Zechariah, for your prayer has been heard," and Elizabeth is the first to speak, uttering a prayer of recognition of God's blessing. "This is what the Lord has done for me when he looked favorably on me and took away the disgrace I have endured among my people" (Luke 1:25).

The Annunciation to Mary that has spawned some of the most beautiful art in the history of humanity portrays a prayerful dialogue between Mary and the Word of God delivered by Gabriel. It also echoes the structure of calls of the prophets: (1) divine confrontation (Luke 1:26–28a), (2) introductory word (Luke 1:28b) and initial hesitation (Luke 1:29), (3) commission, (Luke 1:30–33), (4) objection (Luke 1:34), (5) reassurance (Luke 1:35–36), (6) sign (Luke 1:36–37), and (7) acceptance of commission (Luke 1:38). The final words of the angel, "For nothing will be impossible with God," and Mary's response crystallize the structure of prayer as trust in God even in the face of uncertainty: "Here am I, the servant of the Lord; let it be with me according to your word." (Luke 1:37–38). People praying with this scene might reflect on ways that God has called them in their lives and what is their mission.

The great hymns of Mary and Zechariah have been a legacy of prayer for the church, witnessed by their presence in the official liturgical morning and evening prayer sung and recited for centuries. Following immediately after the Annunciation and visit to Elizabeth, the hymn falls into two major sections. First are the words of praise and gratitude by Mary to God (Luke 1:46–50), where we learn that Mary will be called "blessed," happy, as a result of gratitude for what God has done. Prayer is always an act of gratitude, but the hymn shifts in the second part when Mary the prophet proclaims the working out of God's mercy on behalf of the *ánawím* and anticipates the ministry of the child in her womb who will preach good news to the poor (see Luke 4:18–19). She does this while heralding bringing down those who make themselves the center of their worlds and oppress others, while exalting the lowly in remembrance of his mercy, that is God's saving love of his people.

The infancy narratives are in the form of two great diptychs, stories about the annunciation, and the birth of John, paralleled by those of the annunciation and birth of Jesus, with emphasis on the superiority of the latter. Though John's birth was first announced, Mary's hymn precedes the hymn of John's father Zechariah (Luke 1:67–78). It too is a hymn of praise and gratitude that begins with a blessing and is followed by praise of God for redemption that unfolded in the history of God's people (Luke

1:67–75) described again as "mercy." The second section directly anticipates the role of John (Luke 1:76–80), who will be the prophet of the Most High, who will prepare the way of the Lord but make known God's salvation and proclaim forgiveness of sin. The theme of mercy predominates since it comes from "the tender mercy of our God, the dawn from on high will break upon us, to give light to those who sit in darkness and in the shadow of death, to guide our feet into the way of peace." These two great hymns which are sung at morning and evening prayer continue to shape the liturgical practice of the Church.

THE PRAYERS OF JESUS

Along with the texts that portray Jesus at prayer, Luke contains two significant prayers *of* Jesus. When the disciples return from a successful mission, Jesus "rejoiced in the Holy Spirit" and prayed directly to the Father, as he does so often in the Gospel of John; it has been called "a meteorite fallen from the Johannine sky."[4]

> "I thank you, Father, Lord of heaven and earth, because you have hidden these things from the wise and the intelligent and have revealed them to infants; yes, Father, for such was your gracious will. All things have been handed over to me by my Father; and no one knows who the Son is except the Father, or who the Father is except the Son and anyone to whom the Son chooses to reveal him." Then turning to the disciples, Jesus says to them privately, "Blessed are the eyes that see what you see! For I tell you that many prophets and kings desired to see what you see, but did not see it, and to hear what you hear, but did not hear it." (Luke 10:21–24)

Like so many of the psalms, it is a prayer of thanksgiving and praise for a gift of revelation, but the simple invocation—twice of God as "Father"—is unique to the Gospels. Jesus affirms that he too is gifted as Son from the Father and is both the revealer and the revealed. Then, turning to the disciples, he moves from thanksgiving to blessing (one of the most frequent prayer forms in the Bible) and declares them blessed or happy for the gift they have received, which echoes the beatitudes earlier in the Gospel (6:20–26). The importance of this prayer is highlighted by Robert Karris, who writes,

> In brief, Jesus's thanksgiving prayer in Luke 10:21–22 presents the Lukan Gospel *in nuce*. The Father is no hidden God, but has revealed himself in all that Jesus is and does. And only those truly dependent can open themselves to receive such a gracious gift. The self-sufficient find their wisdom in the boredom of living for themselves.[5]

Prayers during the Passion of Jesus

The prayers of Jesus on the Mount of Olives and on the cross are the final prayers by Jesus in Luke. After the supper when Jesus prayed for Peter, "that your own faith may not fail and you, when once you have turned back, strengthen your brothers" (22:32), when Jesus comes as "was his custom" to the Mount of Olives with the disciples, he says to them, "Pray that you may not come into the time of trial or testing," reminiscent of the Lord's Prayer (Luke 11:4). Then he prays, "Father, if you are willing, remove this cup from me; yet, not my will but yours be done," and continues to pray with such anguish that his sweat becomes drops of blood (Luke 22:42–44).

In the Old Testament, the cup is often a symbol of God's wrath (Jeremiah 25:15–17; Isaiah 51:17–22) and Jesus's prayer reflects many of the laments in the psalms where an innocent sufferer cries to God, feels God's anger, but ends with the hope of deliverance. (See especially Psalms 22, 44, and 88.) Luke's version of the Lord's Prayer contains no petition, "your will be done," as it appears in Matt 6:10, but now appears here in Luke. Jesus's short prayer combines a petition to be relieved of a horrible fate, but with deep faith in God's will however terrible this might be. No scene in the Gospels has the same poignancy and power as this picture of the total emptying of Jesus (see Philippians 2:5–11). The stark juxtaposition of anguish and hope present in the prayer of Jesus is captured in three stanzas of a poem by Dietrich Bonhoeffer written in prison as he awaited certain death:

> By kindly powers surrounded, peaceful and true,
> wonderfully protected with consolation dear,
> safely, I dwell with you this whole day through,
> and surely into another year.

> Though from the old our hearts are still in pain,
> while evil days oppress with burdens still,
> Lord, give to our frightened souls again,
> salvation and thy promises fulfill.

> And shouldst thou offer us the bitter cup, resembling
> sorrow, filled to the brim and overflowing,
> we will receive it thankfully, without trembling,
> from thy hand, so good and ever-loving.[6]

Jesus's Prayers on the Cross

Each of the Gospels hand on words from the dying Jesus on the cross, now familiar to many Catholics as "the seven last words," often liturgically celebrated on Good Friday. These distinctive sayings are themselves powerful prayers.

"Father, forgive them; for they do not know what they are doing" (Luke 23:34), are the very first words of Jesus after he was crucified between two criminals, and serve as an Introit or opening prayer for the whole narrative. Jesus's death is to offer forgiveness to all who brought it about. The prayer for forgiveness echoes Luke's Sermon on the Plain (Luke 6:27, 35) in virtually the same words found in Matthew (5:44), but concludes the exhortation with "be merciful as your heavenly Father is merciful" (Luke 6:36). Forgiveness is one of the major themes of Luke so that Jesus's words on the cross become an epitome of the gospel. Zechariah's hope for the coming of the "dawn from on high," (Luke 1:77–78), the granting of forgiveness of sin by the tender mercy of God, is fulfilled as Jesus hangs on the cross.

Final words of a dying person or a saint are often remembered as an epitome of a person's life, which is true also when Jesus prays, "Father, into your hands I commend my spirit." These words are taken from Psalm 31:5 ("Into your hand I commit my spirit; you have redeemed me, O Lord, faithful God"), where a suffering, just person manifests his faith in God and recalls also the hope of Jesus for resurrection expressed in the passion predictions (Luke 9:22; 18:31–33). This prayer also concludes a great arc that extends from Jesus's first words in the Gospel, "Did you not know that I must be about my Father's business?" (Luke 2:49). The whole Gospel was the Father's work or business; it is now complete as Jesus entrusts his spirit to the Father, a spirit which gives birth and life to the Church from Pentecost until the end of days. As he was being stoned, Stephen uttered the same prayers as Jesus: "'Lord Jesus, receive my spirit.' Then he knelt down and cried out in a loud voice, 'Lord, do not hold this sin against them'" (Acts 7:59–60). Martyrs have called out this prayer through the centuries.

Prayer, Parable, and Persistence[7]

The Lord's Prayer and a Parable of How to Pray (Luke 11:2–8)

"When you pray, say:

Father, hallowed be your name.

Your kingdom come.

Give us each day our daily bread.

And forgive us our sins,

for we ourselves forgive everyone indebted to us.

And do not bring us to the time of trial."

And he said to them, "Suppose one of you has a friend, and you go to him at midnight and say to him, 'Friend, lend me three loaves of bread; for a friend of mine has arrived, and I have nothing to set before him.' And he answers from within, 'Do not bother me; the door has already been locked, and my children are with me in bed; I cannot get up and give you anything.' I tell you, even though he will not get up and give him anything because he is his friend, at least because of his persistence he will get up and give him whatever he needs."

Luke integrates much of the teaching of Jesus found in his sources into the long journey narrative of Jesus on the way to Jerusalem. There, he will be "taken up" (Luke 9:51—19:27). Luke integrates here much of the material that is special to his Gospel and important for Christian life. After the very rich parable of the Good Samaritan and the visit with Martha and Mary (Luke 10:25–42), Jesus pauses to pray (Luke 11:1) and his disciples say, "Lord, teach us to pray, as John taught his disciples." He responds, "When you pray, say: Father, hallowed be your name. Your kingdom come. Give us each day our daily bread. And forgive us our sins, for we ourselves forgive everyone indebted to us. And do not bring us to the time of trial" (11:2–4).

This version of the Lord's Prayer is considerably shorter than the Matthean version (6:9–13), and consists of two petitions in praise of God, and three requests that should shape Christian life. Most distinctive of Luke is the petition for "daily bread" for "each day." Much discussed is the meaning of the rare Greek term *epiousios*, translated variously as "daily," "future," "necessary," "bread that we need," or "necessary for subsistence," with the latter three most current. Equally important is that the prayer is to be uttered every day, and thus intended to really shape the life of the disciple.

The Lord's Prayer is then followed by a short parable, dealing with a request for bread, "The Friend at Midnight" (Luke 11:5–8), and followed by sayings on the need for persistence in prayer and trust in the "heavenly Father's" response to prayer (Luke 11:9–13), which recalls the first words of the Lord's Prayer. On initial reading, the parable seems to be relatively simple. An unexpected visitor arrives in the middle of the night, and according to the demands of hospitality, his friend must offer a meal. Caught unawares, he then goes to "his friend" who is fast asleep with his family in the one-room house and asks for three loaves of bread. The latter, obviously perturbed (Luke 11:7, "Do not bother me") initially refuses, since he does not want to rouse his sleeping family. The narrative does not recount the granting of the request but quickly shifts to an application that the sleeping man will answer the request not out of friendship but because of "his persistence"?

Though the application of the parable seems obvious, problems of interpretation remain. Is it the parable of the "persistent friend," or is the main character the sleeping man who finally answers the request? The final verse (Luke 11:8), could be translated, "because of his shameless persistence" (i.e., of the person knocking), or "because of his 'loss of face'" (i.e., the man in bed does not himself want to be shamed because he did not want to violate the canons of hospitality by turning down the request of a friend).

The sayings of Jesus, "So I say to you, Ask, and it will be given you; search, and you will find; knock, and the door will be opened for you" (Luke 11:9–10), clearly stress the request (knock) and the persistence of the one praying. Jesus then goes on to speak of seemingly unanswered prayers (Luke 11:11–13): "Is there anyone among you who, if your child asks for a fish, will give a snake instead of a fish? Or if the child asks for an egg, will give a scorpion?" Jesus uses the familiar analogy "from the lesser to the greater," which illustrates that just as a human father (the lesser) will not give a child what is harmful, "if you then, who are evil, [the lesser] know how to give good gifts to your children, how much more will the heavenly Father [the greater] give the Holy Spirit to those who ask him!" (11:13).[8]

Prayers are answered with even a greater gift than requested. While this response hardly answers the agonizing question of people today whose prayers are not answered, it does say that ultimately the gift of the Holy Spirit is the answer to every prayer made with hope and faith. The Holy Spirit will guide and sustain not only Jesus's disciples and the early Church, but believers throughout the ages. Prayer in Luke not only looks to the prayer of Jesus on the Mount of Olives and on the cross, but to a community "gathered in prayer" (Acts 1:14) which will receive the transforming gift of the Holy Spirit (Acts 2:1–4). What Christians pray for and hope for transforms them into the kind of community they will become.[9]

The Widow and the Callous Judge (Luke 18:1–8)

Then Jesus told them a parable about their need to pray always and not to lose heart. He said, "In a certain city there was a judge who neither feared God nor had respect for people. In that city there was a widow who kept coming to him and saying, 'Grant me justice against my opponent.' For a while he refused; but later he said to himself, 'Though I have no fear of God and no respect for anyone, yet because this widow keeps bothering me, I will grant her justice, so that she may not wear me out by continually coming.'" And the Lord said, "Listen to what the unjust judge says. And will not God grant justice to his chosen ones who cry to him day and night? Will he delay long in helping them? I tell you, he will quickly grant justice to them. And yet, when the Son of Man comes, will he find faith on earth?" (my translation)

In this parable, the introduction (Luke 18:1) reflects Luke's understanding of parable as paradigm of action and, like the rich fool (12:15), begins with an application on persistency and faith in prayer (as in Luke 11:5–13). The formal narrative comprises verses 18:2–5, and verses 18:6–8 offer different applications. Perhaps those who added the verses were scandalized by the implicit comparison of God with such a judge. The final verses (Luke 18:7–8a), then, compare the vindication of the widow to the eschatological vindication of the elect and the parable concludes by asking whether the Son of man will find faith on the earth at the *parousia* (the Second Coming of Christ, which they were anticipating).

I follow the great Lukan scholar Joseph A. Fitzmyer, SJ, who argues the earliest version of the parable was verses 18:2–6, although he argues that the real focus of the parable is "the dishonest judge" rather than "the importunate widow." I contend that it is as much the "widow's story" as that of the judge. The final verse, which provides an *inclusio* to verse 18:1, is from the hand of Luke and represents his reinterpretation of the delay of the return of the Lord.[10] The original parable was surely changed in transmission by prophets in the early Church and by Luke himself.

The parable begins with a shocking picture of a judge described as one "who neither feared God nor regarded man." Both in the Old Testament (Amos 2:6–7; 5:10–13) and in New Testament times, the venal or corrupt judge appears frequently. This judge is blinded by his power, he has no fear of God, and he is not even moved by the cries of the poor, which are heard by God (e.g., Psalms 69:33; 72:12; Proverbs 22:22–23).

The next verse begins in direct parallel to the previous one: "But a widow there was in that city" (Luke 18:3a). A stark and direct confrontation is set up. In the ancient Near East and throughout the Old Testament and the New Testament, the widow is a symbol not only of powerlessness but was *de facto* a victim of injustice and exploitation. In imagining the world of this parable, we should therefore avoid thinking of the widow as aged and infirm. In a culture with short life spans where women married in their early teens, the "widow," as the subsequent narrative presumes, would most likely have been young and vigorous. The second half of the verse then describes her action. She "kept coming" and saying, "Vindicate [*ekdikēson*, or "give me justice"] me against my adversary." The shock comes here, not in the exploitation of widows, which was common, but in her public and persistent cry for justice. In the cultural context, a woman would rarely, if at all, claim her rights by appearing constantly, and presumably alone, in public, raising a public outcry. She also refuses to resort to bribery—a common recourse in a situation such as hers. The woman speaks of an "adversary," who could be an in-law, her own son, or a stepson by her husband's previous marriage. The issue is most likely a dispute over an inheritance or a dowry—that portion remaining after her husband's death. The situation of the woman could be one of life and death; she is faced with poverty and starvation if her rights are not respected.

At this point the reader expects no easy solution to the woman's plight. A judge who does not fear God would not be expected to be moved by the Old Testament exhortations on consideration of the widow. The woman's continual coming implies continual refusal, which is explicit in the next verse, "for a while" (or better, "for a long time") he refused. The change comes, as it frequently does in the parables, when the narrative moves to dialogue, in this case a soliloquy ("he said to himself"). Since this is our first inside look at the judge, we might wonder whether the characterization is fair. The answer comes quickly in the first words from his mouth, as he unabashedly says that he does not fear God, nor regard other people (Luke 18:4), but "because this widow is 'working me over' I will recognize her rights, so she doesn't give me a black eye by her unwillingness to give up" (Luke 18:5, my translation).

The language is taken from the ancient custom of boxing matches, and the original Greek better captures both the humor and the shock of the situation. A complacent and fearless judge is pummeled like a faltering boxer by a woman fighting for her rights. The parable then concludes with a summons to attend to the dialogue of the unjust judge. For those who hold that the parable in substance comes from Jesus, it is primarily an instance of the rabbinic mode of argument "from the lesser to the greater." If such a judge will vindicate perseverance, how much more will God? Jesus assures his disciples of vindication in the face of suffering and persecution.

Luke evidently adapts the parable to the situation of his community, aware now of the delay of the *parousia* and undergoing *peirasmos* ("trials" or "testing"; see Luke 11:4). Only through prayer can fidelity (faith) be assured—which Luke demonstrates by inserting the parable of the widow and the judge (18:2–7) between the exhortation to prayer (18:1) and an admonition to fidelity (18:8). By bold persistence that shatters cultural conventions, the woman's prayer is answered, and she receives justice. So the parable teaches that continual prayer is not simply passive waiting but the active quest for justice.

THE PHARISEE AND THE TAX COLLECTOR (LUKE 18:9–14)

He also told this parable to some who trusted in themselves that they were righteous and regarded others with contempt: "Two men went up to the temple to pray, one a Pharisee and the other a tax collector. The Pharisee, standing by himself, was praying thus, 'God, I thank you that I am not like other people: thieves, rogues, adulterers, or even like this tax collector. I fast twice a week; I give a tenth of all my income.' But the tax collector, standing far off, would not even look up to heaven, but was beating his breast and saying, 'God, be merciful to me, a sinner!' I tell you, this man went down to his home justified rather than the other; for all who exalt themselves will be humbled, but all who humble themselves will be exalted."

This parable concludes a diptych on prayer in the familiar Lukan pattern of juxtaposing a story in which a woman is a central character with another character, a male protagonist. The beginning of the parable seems harsh: Jesus speaks to people who are convinced of their own righteousness before God and despise everyone else. (Since the previous parable spoke of God's chosen ones, this rebuke may have in mind Christian disciples; contemporary Christians, however, hear this too often with a strong bias against the Pharisee.) The Pharisees were part of the many Jewish reform movements in the first century; they were lay, not priestly, and sought to find God's presence in all the daily routines of life. It is not surprising that a Pharisee goes to the temple to pray, and even his prayer is not as self-serving as it seems. The original hearers would not have been instantly critical. His prayer is twofold: a prayer of thanksgiving *(eucharistō)* to God for preservation from sin and an account of his fidelity in observing the prescribed fast and in giving tithes. Even the converted Pharisee, Paul, can boast of his piety and observance of the law and contrast his practices to those of others (Philippians 3:4–6), and in one of the psalms from Qumran we hear, "I praise you, O Lord, that you have not allowed my lot to fall among the worthless community" *(Hodayot* 7:34). To thank God for election and to speak of one's devotion do not of themselves make a prayer hypocritical or self-congratulatory.

What is surprising is the presence of the tax collector. These are not the publicans mentioned in the classical sources, that is, powerful people who gained the contract to collect taxes and exploitation, so much so that Julius Caesar suppressed the institution. Instead, they are rather petty bureaucrats who collected taxes for the ruling Romans or Herodian kings. They were disliked as agents of oppressive regimes, probably did engage in shady transactions, and were also thought to be unclean because of frequent contact with Gentiles at forbidden times. Throughout the Gospel, Jesus betrays a penchant for associating with them, so much so that before he is ever called Lord and Christ, his title seems to be "glutton and drunkard, a friend of tax collectors and sinners" (Luke 7:34).

The defect of the Pharisee is not that he gives thanks for what God has done for him (protecting him from evildoers), but that he harbors prideful disdain for other people. He contrasts himself with a rash of unsavory people—greedy, dishonest, adulterous—but saves the tax collector for the end. His very position of prayer betrays his pride. He steps apart from the crowd as if God could not notice him wherever he is. The tax collector simply stands at a distance and will not even raise his eyes to heaven. His bodily gesture is itself a prayer before he pleads, "O God, be merciful to me a sinner!" He goes home made just in God's eyes. The justice of God then accepts the unjust and the ungodly (see Romans 5:6–8) and is harsh on the dutiful and the respectable. The parable summons us to a prayer of love and trust in God's mercy and frees us of the need to tell God who is a sinner and who is not.

Each Pray-er and the Gospel of Luke

The above reflections are intended to aid those who raise up the Gospel of Luke in prayer. But the ways of prayer are beautiful and manifold, ranging from joyous musical renditions of Mary's Magnificat to the quiet contemplation before the cross of Jesus. Prayer is often described as *conversatio cum Deo*, or literally, "conversation with God," but the root meaning of *conversatio* is to spend time with or hang out with. Now, we will conclude by exploring some ways that this might take place.

Although any engagement with Scripture can be profitable when approaching a particular book of the Bible, it is most helpful to have some introduction which offers information on the original setting of the book, its literary narrative structure, and major themes. One fruit of the biblical renewal in Catholicism is that there are fine resources for this in terms of study Bibles, one-volume commentaries, and short volumes directed at the ordinary believer (which I have listed in a note below).[11] Since Luke is a narrative with journey as one of its principal motifs, a fine practice for any Catholic would be to prayerfully follow the Gospel, especially during the liturgical cycle when the Gospel readings are from Luke.

Prayer in the ancient world was principally oral and celebrated in public worship, much like our liturgies today. But personal and private prayer with Luke should also include reading aloud to ourselves a passage or section chosen for reflection. Memorizing the beautiful cadences of the Magnificat or Benedictus can serve to open or close a day. Since Luke so often quotes or alludes to the Old Testament, finding these texts and reading them aloud, as well, will enable us to cultivate a language of prayer, as it did for Jesus's first followers. Having heard the Word of God in Scripture can foster also quiet contemplation of its meaning.

Methods and practices of prayer used through the ages still retain great power. *Lectio divina*, long a staple of the monastic, especially Benedictine, tradition is a vehicle for all people of faith who acknowledge the power of God's word to touch their lives, and was most strongly recommended in the Post-Synodal Exhortation (*Verbum Domini*) by Pope Benedict XVI (esp. no. 87).[12] In general, a person takes up a passage of Scripture and allows the Spirit to lead them through the following steps or stages: reading (*lectio*), reflection, meditation (*meditatio*), prayer (*oratio*), and contemplation (*contemplatio*), a process that embodies the words of Psalm 37:7: "Be still before the Lord, and wait patiently for him."[13] Similar to this final stage is "centering prayer" which is quiet awareness of God's presence, which exists beyond words or even explicit thoughts.[14]

Especially helpful when engaging a Gospel in prayer are the methods described by St. Ignatius of Loyola in his *Spiritual Exercises* (first written by Ignatius after his conversion and before he became a priest).[15] In addition to highly structured meditations during a retreat which appeals to discursive reflection, in guiding people through the events of the life of Christ, Ignatius urges people to become part of the scene. For example, in the Nativity, one becomes part of the scene "by imagining the place," and later, the people and what they are doing, and to place one's self there, and "to reflect on myself to draw some profit" (*Sp. Ex.* no. 115). This is yet another way to engage with Luke.

In addition to various methods of praying over different scenes in Luke, the great tradition of Christian art can be a help. Before the printing press, Christian devotion was nurtured by art—from the primitive frescos on walls of the catacombs, the early mosaics of the Byzantine churches, through the Scripture crosses of Ireland, to the stained glass windows of the medieval cathedrals, culminating in the explosion of religious art in the early and late Renaissance—to mention but a few examples. The late Henri Nouwen's *Return of the Prodigal Son* offers profound meditations on every aspect of Rembrandt's classic painting of the same name.[16] Recently, a movement has also developed called *visio divina*, or literally, "divine watching," which shows how looking and praying with art can involve the whole person.[17] *Illuminating Luke* presents over forty examples of paintings of the public ministry of Christ during the Italian Renaissance and Baroque period.[18] With a world of art available on the web, the richness of such prayer will continually unfold.

My hope is that readers themselves may add to the ways in which the Gospel of Luke is a guide to prayer and that they might take as companion and model, Mary, who was perplexed by the Word of the Lord and pondered over its meaning (Luke 1:21). She also, when looking on her Son, "treasured all these things in her heart" (2:51).

1. Arland J. Hultgren, "Prayer," in *Harper Dictionary of the Bible*, ed. Paul J. Achtemeier (San Francisco: Harper & Row, 1985), 816; See also Oscar Cullmann, *Prayer in the New Testament* (Minneapolis: Fortress, 1995); Richard J. Longenecker, ed., *Into God's Presence: Prayer in the New Testament* (Grand Rapids: Eerdmans, 2005); Patrick D. Miller, *They Cried to the Lord: Form and Theology of Biblical Prayer* (Minneapolis: Fortress, 1994).
2. Helpful studies are Daniel J. Harrington, *Jesus and Prayer: What the New Testament Teaches Us* (Frederick, Md.: Word Among Us, 2009); Robert. J. Karris, *Prayer and the New Testament: Jesus and His Communities at Worship* (New York: Crossroad, 2000), especially chapter 2, "Prayer in Luke–Acts"; Steven. F. Plymale, *The Prayer Texts of Luke–Acts* (New York: P. Lang, 1993).
3. The major comprehensive commentary on the Infancy Narratives is Raymond E. Brown, *The Birth of the Messiah: A Commentary on the Infancy Narratives of Matthew and Luke* (New York: Doubleday, 1977); for personal and pastoral use, the major conclusions and insights are found in Raymond E. Brown, *Christ in the Gospels of the Liturgical Year*, ed. Ronald E. Witherup, SS (Collegeville, MN: Liturgical, 1988), especially 43–95, "The Coming Christ in Advent: Preparing for the Birth of Jesus, Matthew 1 and Luke 1."
4. Joseph A. Fitzmyer, *The Gospel According to Luke X–XXIV* (New York: Doubleday, 1985), 866.
5. Karris, *Prayer and the New Testament*, 63.
6. Edward H. Robinson, *Bonhoeffer's Prison Poems* (Grand Rapids: Zondervan, 1999), 121.
7. For a more complete discussion of the parables on prayer in Luke, see John R. Donahue, *The Gospel in Parable: Metaphor, Narrative and Theology in Synoptic Gospels* (Philadelphia: Fortress, 1988), 180–193.
8. See Fitzmyer, 914 on the type of argument used here.
9. An excellent treatment of the difficult problem of petitionary prayer is David Crum, *Knocking on Heaven's Door: A New Testament Theology of Petitionary Prayer* (Grand Rapids: Baker Academic, 2006).
10. Fitzmyer, 1176–1177.
11 Robert J. Karris, ed., *Collegeville Bible Commentary* (Collegeville, MN: Liturgical, 1997), published originally as a collection of individual volumes, now gathered into one volume. Michael F. Patella is the author of the commentary on Luke, available also as a single volume; Donald Senior, ed., *The Catholic Study Bible*, 2nd ed. (New York: Oxford University Press, 2006); Virginia Halpur et al., ed., *The College Study Bible* (Winona, MN: St. Mary's, 2006). Based on the Catholic translation found in *The New American Bible*.
12. Pope Benedict XVI, Post-Synodal Exhortation (*Verbum Domini*), September 30, 2010. http://w2.vatican.va/content/benedict-xvi/en/apost_exhortations/documents/hf_ben-xvi_exh_20100930_verbum-domini.html.
13. An excellent description is by Gregory J. Polan, "*Lectio Divina*: Reading and Praying the Word of God," *Liturgical Ministry* 12 (Fall, 2003): 198–206.
14. Helpful descriptions are Basil M. Pennington, *Centering Prayer: Renewing an Ancient Christian Art* (Garden City, NJ: Doubleday, 1982); and Thomas Keating, *Foundations for Centering Prayer and the Christian Contemplative Life: Open Mind, Open Heart; Invitation to Love; The Mystery of Christ* (New York: Continuum, 2002).
15. All references to the Spiritual Exercises are to the translation by George Ganss, ed., *Ignatius of Loyola: Spiritual Exercises and Selected Writings*, Classics of Western Spirituality (New York: Paulist, 1991).
16. Henri Nouwen, *Return of the Prodigal Son* (New York: Doubleday, 1992).
17. See Juliete Benner,. *Contemplative Vision: A Guide to Christian Art and Prayer* (Downers Grove, IL: Intervarsity, 2011); Karen Kuchan, *Visio Divina: A New Practice of Prayer for Healing and Growth* (New York: Crossroad, 2005); Henri Nouwen, *Behold the Beauty of the Lord: Praying with Icons* (Notre Dame, IN: Ave Maria, 1987).
18. Heidi J. Hornick and Mikeal C. Parsons, *Illuminating Luke: The Public Ministry of Christ in Italian Renaissance and Baroque Painting* (New York: T&T Clarke, 2005).

CHAPTER 12

Prayer in the Gospel of John

~ Jude Winkler, OFM Conv. ~

In the Synoptic Gospels, Jesus prays with some frequency, especially in the Gospel of Luke. In the Gospel of John, Jesus only prays three times (with a number of references to prayer in the "Last Supper Discourses" in John 14–17). He doesn't teach the apostles the Our Father as he does in Matthew and Luke. He does not present parables on prayer as he does in Luke. It almost seems as if prayer is not a high priority in his ministry in John.

That conclusion would be both an accurate read of prayer in Jesus's ministry and a mistaken impression. In the Gospel of John, prayer, in itself, is not the key point of Jesus's ministry. Relationship is. Jesus has come into this world to reveal his relationship to the Father and to invite us into that relationship. Prayer is then one means of reinforcing that relationship and inviting others into it.

PRAYER AND LIFE

The first explicit prayer that Jesus utters in John is in the passage that deals with the reanimation of Lazarus (John 11). Jesus has traveled to Bethany to perform a sign which signifies that he has come into this world to bring life. His good friend Lazarus has died and has in fact been dead for four days. Jewish people believed that the soul stayed in the body for three days, so Lazarus was considered to be irretrievably dead. Both Martha and Mary, the sisters of Lazarus, have gone out to meet Jesus, and they both greet him with a mixture of faith and frustration. They repeat the same words: "Lord, if you had been here, my brother would not have died" (John 11:21).[1] Their words could be interpreted as being a type of reproof for his tardiness (for he had remained where he was for some time even after hearing of the life-threatening illness of his friend), but both Martha and Mary also express their faith in him. Martha tells him that she believes that even at this late moment, he could ask something of God, and his request would be satisfied. Mary, on the other hand, expresses her faith by kneeling before him, a gesture that would be appropriate of one who was worshipping God.

The response that Jesus gives Martha is interesting. He promises her that her brother will rise again. She assumes he is speaking about the resurrection on the last day. Jesus assures her that he is the resurrection and the life. He does not say that he will grant her brother the resurrection; he says that he is the resurrection. Once one came to know Jesus and believed that he was the Son of God sent by the Father to invite us into the life of God, one was already in some way risen. This is a realized eschatology in which the promises of the end times were already being realized in the present. To know Jesus was to experience eternal life (here and now).

This life in God does not deny our physical reality. Although the divinity is strongly emphasized in the Gospel of John, Jesus's humanity is not ignored. The Word, after all, became flesh (a very material word). Jesus spits on the dirt to make mud, and so on. Jesus in John 11 both becomes angry and cries, very human actions. It is not even clear where his anger is directed. It could not be intended for the people who were mourning the death of Lazarus, for Jesus himself weeps a bit later. Possibly he is angry at death, which has robbed him of his beloved friend.

Jesus goes to the tomb and orders that the stone covering the entrance be rolled back. Although there is some opposition to this, for the decay process had already begun, those present obey Jesus. He then looks up into the heavens (a clear sign that he is addressing his heavenly Father) and loudly proclaims a prayer: "Father, I thank you for hearing me. I know that you always hear me; but because of the crowd here I have said this, that they may believe that you sent me" (11:41–42).

At first glance, this appears to be a rather odd prayer. It almost seems as if he is playacting for the sake of the crowd. He certainly wants them to know that what he is about to do, reanimate Lazarus, is not being done by his own authority. This is something that he has been emphasizing all throughout the Gospel. He has come into this world to reveal his relationship with the Father and to do the work that the Father sent him to do.

Yet, Jesus is not proclaiming this prayer for his own sake (that his disciples grow in their esteem of him), not even for the sake of the Father (so that everyone might know that he was performing this wondrous deed through the authority of the Father). Jesus is praying so that his followers might understand the true meaning of life. Life only has meaning if it is lived in relationship with God. He is one with the Father, and now he is inviting his followers to enter into that relationship. He is calling them to life.

The subsequent raising of Lazarus makes this clear. This was a sign. The Gospel of John does not use the word *miracle*. People often become fascinated with wondrous deeds like miracles and they focus their attention on the deed itself. Jesus in the Gospel of John performs instead "signs." A sign is a deed that points to a deeper meaning. Jesus raises Lazarus to invite him and all the disciples into life, into the same relationship which he has with the Father. The physical raising of Lazarus is the outward sign that signified a greater spiritual reality.

Interestingly enough, the life that Jesus offers proves to be dangerous. The leaders of the Jews are worried because of all the attention that both Jesus and Lazarus are receiving because of this sign. Caiaphas, the high priest, proposes that both of them should be put to death to save the nation. This, in fact, is an example of Johannine irony—for this means that they should die so that they will not inaugurate a rebellion that could bring Roman vengeance down upon their heads, but the deeper meaning of what he said was that the death of Jesus would, in fact, bring salvation to the people of Israel. Jesus gives life, and they want to put him to death because of it. The last thing that any regime which controls the lives and thoughts of a people wants is for people to be truly alive. Jesus is dangerous.

Furthermore, the life that Jesus offers is, in a sense, mixed with death. Later Jesus will insist that one has to die, like a grain of wheat, in order to have life. Physical life, while good, is not the ultimate good. Jesus, although he knew that his friend was going to die, let him die. True life is life in God which can only be attained through Jesus.

So prayer in John 11 is not proclaimed to receive a favor from God. It is an act of communication which strengthens the union between Jesus and the Father and invites us into that union. Prayer is about using words to express and reinforce our intimate union with God. We pray in a given material time and place, just as Jesus did when he raised Lazarus. We often pray for God's presence and intervention in the circumstances in which we find ourselves. But most of all, we pray to be one with the one who loves us: God, who is love. The flowers one gives or receives when one is in love is the sign, the love itself is the essence of what one wishes to communicate. The physical response to what we say to God is the sign, the loving union is the essence.

A Prayer for Glory

A second passage in which Jesus utters a prayer is found in John 12:28. Jesus has been speaking about his coming death. He tells his disciples that his hour of glory has come. Normally one would suspect that the hour of glory was the resurrection of Jesus or maybe his Transfiguration. In the Gospel of John, the hour of glory is the cross. It is that moment in the life and ministry of Jesus when we most clearly see who God is and what God wants of us: love.

Thus, the word *glory* is redefined. Glory no longer means magnificence or splendor; it now means an outpouring of love. It is surrender to the will of the Father. It is mercy and love expressed to us. In the prologue to John, we are told that grace and truth came through Jesus (John 1:17b). "Grace" is a loose translation of the Hebrew word that was applied to Yahweh in the Hebrew Bible: *hesed.* "Truth" is a loose translation of the Hebrew word *emet*. *Hesed* is covenantal love. It is the love we hear about in the book of the prophet Hosea, who forgives and forgives and forgives his wife. Hosea eventually realizes that this is what God has done toward Israel. *Emet* means fidelity. God never turns back on the covenant. Even when people sin, God remains faithful. Expressing this covenantal love, expressing this fidelity, is what glory is all about.

In chapter 12, Jesus expresses the fact that he is troubled. This is something that he does not do in the Garden of Gethsemane as he does in the Synoptics. Yet, he is ready to fulfill the will of the Father. He calls upon the Father to glorify his name. The Father responds, "I have glorified it and I will glorify it again." (John 12:28b).

When Jesus says "the name of the Father," he is simply referring to the Father. Why would Jesus's death glorify the Father?

First of all, it would be an act of obedience to the will of the Father. All throughout the Gospel of John, Jesus fulfills the Father's will first by revealing who he is (the only begotten Son of the Father) and then by revealing God's plan for humanity (to be with Jesus and the Father). This plan of salvation is that Jesus show us how much God loves us so that we might embrace that love and escape from the self-destructive works of hate and evil that are sin. John does not speak of salvation in terms of expiation (paying the price for our sins), but rather in terms of revelation (showing us quite visibly that God loves us to death). Love is the only thing that will truly bring us to conversion. Guilt and fear bring conformity, only love produced true conversion.

But this is also an act of glory because by calling upon Jesus to die for us, the Father is asking Jesus to be the most loving he could ever be. This is the ultimate destiny of the Son—to give of himself until there is nothing left to give. In John 15:13 we hear that there is no greater love than to lay down one's life for one's friends.

But how does this act glorify the Father? By calling upon his son to die for us, the Father is also pouring out his love upon us. It is not easy for a Father to ask a Son, even a divine Son, to pay the ultimate price. The Father is willing to do this for the sake of his Son (who will thus express the greatest love he ever could express) and for us (who will thus receive the greatest love). One could easily reflect upon the pain that those who lead (in families, in churches, in associations) experience when they must ask what is difficult of those for whom they have responsibility. Obviously, all of this language is allegory, for how can we speak of God's "feelings" with any accuracy? The Father is willing to embrace this pain of having to call his Son to experience suffering for our sake. The Father pours out his love, expresses his glory, in inviting his Son to live in glory. Thus, when Jesus calls upon the Father to glorify his name, he is embracing the will of the Father and his plan for us. We once again see prayer as a reinforcing of the relationship of the Father with the Son through a mutual dance of surrender and love.

How could a relationship that was already perfect grow? We receive a hint of this in the prologue to John's Gospel. There we hear that the Word was with God (John 1:1b). This is actually a bit of a mistranslation. The Greek word used in this phrase would best be translated as "toward." The Word was *toward* the Father. The Son and the Father are always drawing closer to each other without ever amalgamating and losing their individual identity. In a sense, they are eternally falling more and more in love with each other. This could easily be a useful image of what heaven would mean for us. For all eternity, we fall more and more in love with God and each other. Thus, instead of being a static image, we see heaven as a very dynamic reality.

In this prayer we also see the invitation to understand who the Son and the Father are and to join them in relationship. Prayer is an act of union and surrender.

The Last Supper Discourses

By far the longest and most important prayer proclaimed by Jesus in the Gospel of John is John 17. This is part of the long Last Supper Discourses that run from chapter 14 to 17.

The Last Supper Discourses is a bit of an artificial construction. It contains last minute instructions, allegory, exhortations and prayer. It is clear that this material was collected over time and put into the context of a last important exhortation before the Passion. At the end of chapter 14, in fact, Jesus ends the discourse with an invitation to get up and go. Yet, he continues for another three chapters, material that must have been added at a second stage of development of the discourse.

In spite of how the discourse developed and the question of whence the material came, it is best to look at it within its present context. It is the last words of Jesus and should be interpreted in light of what Jesus had just done at the Last Supper (the washing of the feet of the disciples) and what he was about to do (suffer and die on the cross).

The prayer ends the Last Supper Discourses. This type of construction, ending a long set of teachings with an extended prayer, is also found in the book of Deuteronomy. John 17 marks a solemn ending and consecration of what has been said, and it leads to that which must follow.

Most scholars have divided the prayer into three units, beginning in verses 1, 9, and 20. Each section is addressed to the Father. Each speaks of glory and of how Jesus has revealed the Father to his followers. Each speaks of those who have received that message.

Like the other two prayers that we have already examined, this prayer has a dual audience. It is clearly addressed to the Father, but it is proclaimed in the hearing of the disciples so that they might hear it and join in the dynamic presented in the prayer. In other words, they hear this prayer so that they might be one with Jesus and the Father. Thus, the primary purpose of the prayer is to intensify the relationship with Jesus and the Father and invite others into that relationship.

Yet, as with the prayer at the reanimation of Lazarus, this prayer also has physical considerations. The disciples live in the world. The world in the Gospel of John is not created reality; it is that part of reality which opposes the Son of God sent to proclaim the love of the Father. Jesus therefore asks the Father to protect the disciples from the evil designs of the world. The disciples will not be taken out of the world for that is where they will learn to share in the glory of God (the *kenosis*, "self-emptying" toward God and toward neighbor). Furthermore, this service will be for disciples in the present (among the disciples gathered around the table) as well as in the future (those who will believe because of the witness given by those first disciples).

It seems a bit odd that the Holy Spirit is not mentioned either in this prayer or in the passages where Jesus encourages his disciples to pray in his name. This is true in spite of the fact that Jesus speaks quite a bit about the Paraclete in the Last Supper Discourses (John 14:15–21, 25–26; 15:26–27; 16:7–11). It is possible that since the Paraclete is called the "other advocate" in the Last Supper Discourses (14:16), Jesus who is the first advocate might picture himself doing what the other Gospels would attribute to the Holy Spirit.

Unlike the world which is torn by division and discord, the community which belongs to Jesus and the Father will be one. This is not so much to be understood as a uniformity as a unity in love which is directed upward (toward the Father and the Son) and outward (as a witness to people of the truth of that which the disciples say and live).

Jesus asks that the disciples be consecrated in the truth. First of all, the word *truth* is a synonym for the words *name* (the Father's name) and for *word* (that Jesus preached the word that he had been given by the Father). Jesus has come into the world to reveal who the Father is. That was his work. *Consecration* means to make holy, to set aside for a particular purpose or, in this case, for a particular person. The disciples are not to belong to the world, casting their affections here and there. They are to commit themselves to the person of Jesus and the Father. This is what will fill them with joy. (The greatest joy one can experience is to give oneself without reservation to another.)

This is eternal life—for the relationship with Jesus and the Father, as we saw in the account of the reanimation of Lazarus, is so life giving that even if one were to die, one would still be alive.

Jesus speaks of already having glorified the Father. In his revelation to the disciples, he has communicated the goodness and love of God for us. Furthermore, in the Gospel of John, Jesus embraces his death on the cross from the very start of the Gospel. Two examples of this are found in chapter 2. The first is the Wedding at Cana. Jesus changes water into a great abundance of wine. This sign is a foreshadowing of his passion (as he hints when he tells his Mother that his hour had not yet come, the hour being the hour of glory, the cross). The ancient Jews spoke of there being an abundance of wine in the heavenly kingdom. Jesus is preparing his own heavenly wedding feast by transforming the water into wine. But how can we be invited to that banquet? Through the cross! Jesus knows this, and yet he performs this sign that will foreshadow his own death. He is embracing both his fate and his mission. At the end of the passage, we hear that this is the first sign (indication of a more profound reality) of glory (the outpouring of his love). The changing of water into wine is not simply a spectacular deed, it is a profound revelation of what Jesus has come into the world to reveal.

The second episode in chapter 2 which indicates that Jesus is embracing the destiny to which the Father has called him is the cleansing of the Temple (John 2:13–22). In the Synoptic Gospels, the cleansing of the Temple occurs right before the Passion and is part of the reason why the Jewish leaders put Jesus to death. In John, it occurs very, very early in the Gospel to show that Jesus is already preparing for the cross. Thus, Jesus, from the very beginning of this Gospel, and from the very beginning of his ministry, has been pouring out his love by embracing the will of the Father in his earthly ministry. He has also been pouring it out by revealing his love for his followers by being willing to die out of love for them. The culmination of that outpouring of love will be the cross, which has already been foreshadowed at the beginning of the section dealing with the Last Supper (when Jesus washed the feet of the disciples, a humble act of service).

What can we learn from this extended prayer? First, it follows the pattern already seen in the other prayer passages of being primarily unitive. Jesus speaks with the Father in a way which intensifies their loving relationship. He is not simply saying "yes" to God's will, he is saying "yes, and yes, and once again yes." Furthermore, Jesus wants his followers (present and future) to be one with him and the Father. Second, the prayer has a profoundly spiritual dimension as well as a profoundly material dimension. The two cannot really be separated in this Gospel. Like the book of

Revelation, this Gospel gives one the sense that the barrier between this world and heaven is dissolving so that the eternal life that one once expected to commence at one's death is shown to be already present. Third, the prayer is realistic. There will be problems in the world. The world which opposed Jesus will certainly oppose the disciples. Jesus does not deny this, nor does he say that this enmity will be eliminated. Rather, he prays for the sake of the disciples that they might be protected.

Fourth, the prayer is consecratory. In prayer, one sets things aside for God. This is obvious, for when one prays, one is already dedicating time to God. But it does not stop there. One's prayer must be all inclusive. One is consecrating one's joys and sorrows, one's successes and failures, one's entire being. This prayer consecrates Jesus's disciples, present and future, into the truth (and the truth is Jesus). And finally, prayer is never finished. If heaven is understood to be an eternity of growing closer and closer, then the communication of love expressed in prayer has to intensify more and more and more. One can never say, "I love you this much and no more." The glory one experiences in the outpouring of one's own love in prayer encounters the glory of a God who empties himself in order to love us more and more and more. It is almost a critical mass of mystical love whose explosion has absolutely no limits.

ASK IN MY NAME...

There are also a number of passages in the Gospel of John where Jesus tells the disciples to pray in his name to the Father for what they need. They are John 14:13–14; 15:7,16; 16:23–26. What is one to make of these instructions?

They have to be read in terms of what we have seen in Jesus's own prayers. They are profoundly unitive. One is to ask the Father for what one needs, for he is the giver of all good things. One is to ask in Jesus's name, for he is the intermediary who allows us to communicate with the Father. Thus, simply by asking for what we need, we are making ourselves one with Jesus and the Father. By doing this, we have already received what we need most—unitive love.

Yet we are to ask for things which we need. While we have already begun to live eternal life in Jesus and the Father, we are still living in this created world. We live in the here and now. Thus, the prayer which establishes and strengthens our bond with God is also one which requests particular things at a particular time and place. This does not deny the eternal dimension of what we are doing but rather consecrates the temporal and spatial dimension of our lives. Again, the rift between heaven and earth is breached by the unitive dimension of our prayer.

But our prayers can never be a simply empty repetition of words and formulas. They must be expressions of glory, of an outpouring of all we are so that we might empty ourselves to be able to receive and live in what God is pouring into us. Praying for a crust of bread is more than asking for a bite to eat. It is an act of faith and love which has a profound mystical effect upon all of reality.

CONCLUSION

The ancients believed that words were very powerful. They not only symbolized a given reality; they actually made it present. God speaks and the heavens and the earth are created. The Passover account is read, and those reading it are somehow mystically transported to participate in the events being proclaimed. This is why the phrases to speak your word, to make known your name, to perform your work, and to proclaim the truth, are all synonymous. The reality made manifest by these expressions is the presence and love of God in our midst.

When Jesus prays and teaches his disciples how to pray, he is using words to make present and intensify a profound reality: his relationship with the Father and theirs with us. When we pray, we continue to make manifest that reality. As with the Passover account which, when read, makes the event present, so also when we pray, we enter into the mystical union of the Father and the Son, proclaiming their glory and entering into their glory. We enter into a reality in which life is eternal and love unlimited. We transform a universe, consecrating it to the truth, uniting in love to God.

---

1. All quotations from Holy Scripture are taken from *The New American Bible*.

PART THREE

Praying with Different Catholic Spiritual Traditions

PRAYER IN THE FRANCISCAN TRADITION

PRAYER IN THE CARMELITE TRADITION

PRAYER IN THE DOMINICAN TRADITION

PRAYER IN THE BENEDICTINE TRADITION

PRAYER IN THE SALESIAN TRADITION

PRAYER IN THE AUGUSTINIAN TRADITION

PRAYER IN THE IGNATIAN TRADITION

PRAYING IN THE MERCY TRADITION

One of the most beautiful gifts Catholicism offers a person seeking a greater sense of divine intimacy is a breadth of spiritual traditions. In this section, eight of them will be offered to provide unique paths to a deeper life of prayer. Yet, as we shall see, in the case of any authentic Christian spirituality, they all lead to the same place: encountering the living God.

In the especially robust chapter on the Franciscan Tradition, Daniel P. Horan emphasizes diversity as the hallmark of this spirituality. To illustrate this, he presents such figures as Francis and Clare of Assisi, as well as Bonaventure, Angela of Foligno, and John Duns Scotus. Yet he also cautions us that even given this broad list of adherents, their views do not totally represent what we refer to as "Franciscan spirituality." It is even much richer than that. However, his sampling of those who represent the heart of an eight-hundred-year-old tradition brings to the fore the central contributions of this approach in a captivating way.

John Welch's discussion of prayer in the Carmelite Tradition begins by calling us back to the Rule of Carmel in the 1200s. He then discusses what he refers to as "The Land of Carmel," reviews the early documents of the Order, pathways of prayer with an emphasis on Teresa of Ávila, John of the Cross, and Thérèse of Lisieux, and closes by presenting the voices of Mary Magdalene de'Pazzi, John of St. Samson, Lawrence of the Resurrection, Elizabeth of the Trinity, Titus Brandsma, and Edith Stein. This extensive chapter is like reading a small booklet on Carmelite spirituality and, in this regard, is especially valuable for those with only a partial or tentative sense of this rich tradition.

Donald Goergen, in his discussion of prayer in the Dominican Tradition, writes about the four pillars of prayer (preaching, prayer, study, and the common life) that determine its unique character. He also points to the "Nine Ways of Prayer of St. Dominic" which some feel is formative for this tradition. Having said that, he then cautions about making such distinguishing factors too narrowly or looking for a too focused and compartmentalized Dominican method of prayer. Instead, Goergen emphasizes how the pillars, for instance, are interrelated and viewed broadly: "Prayer is shaped by the community and community shaped by its prayer.... [In addition] community is not only one's local community but a wider family." Along with St. Dominic, we are gifted with appreciation of the contributions of such spiritual giants as Meister Eckhart, John Tauler, Thomas Aquinas, Albert the Great, Catherine of Siena, Catherine de Ricci, Rose of Lima, Martin de Porres, and others. In all, we feel the unique character of contemplation in the Dominican tradition. We can also see Dominican prayer as highly integrated and balanced as well as having a pastoral dimension to it. Furthermore, we are given an appreciation that in this tradition honoring the prayer form each individual finds particularly suitable for them personally, and in communion with others, is especially valued.

Prayer in the Benedictine Tradition, presented by Laura Swan, helps us honor what St. Benedict said on prayer and to honor a rule that has been in existence for over 1,500 years. In emphasizing Benedict's call for us to be vulnerable and develop an interior serenity to truly *listen* to the voice of God in prayer and life, Swan points to a need to appreciate Benedict's hunger for God and how silence can set the stage to be free enough to attend to our own inner world. With "humility" as a watchword, liturgy of the hours and especially *lectio divina* (sacred reading) in the Benedictine tradition help us address our own hunger for God and the need for courage, curiosity, and tenacity in our spiritual journey.

Prayer in the Salesian Tradition is examined by Wendy Wright with the understanding that it "is not mainly about specific practices, although characteristically, specific practices were and are taught and advanced in order to cultivate spiritual freedom, develop a habitual sense of the divine presence, and direct all actions and surrender to the will of God." Filled with the presence of Saints Francis de Sales and Jane de Chantal, we can feel the Salesian *charism* in the discussion of prayer offered and its prompting of "affections" and "resolutions," as well as the emphasis on the importance of cultivating a true "continual sense of divine intimacy that would grow with practice." Wright also discusses the era of the Salesian renewal, the prayer of *simple remise*, which is a "more non-discursive type of prayer…a simple attentiveness or loving trustful surrender into the divine presence." The quality of the Salesian approach as seeking to approach God with a gentle and humble heart so that theonomy (God's will) and autonomy (our will or "heart") may be one comes through powerfully.

In Prayer in the Augustinian Tradition by Joseph Farrell, the theology of the *Christus totus* is presented as the key factor of St. Augustine of Hippo. By this he means "a combination of theology, ecclesiology, spirituality, and Christology woven to form an understanding of what it means to belong to Christ, but also to be Christ." With the natural inclusion of a reference to Augustine's *Confessions*, Farrell points out that this work is not simply to be considered a personal autobiographical account but, like Augustinian spirituality in general, an invitation to "discover the presence of God, who is both the initiator of [one's] spiritual pilgrimage and the treasure at its end." In other words, prayer in the Augustinian tradition is like a bridge to help us, once again as Farrell reminds us, "to rise above the distractions of life which can tempt us to lose focus on the common treasure we have in God."

The Ignatian Tradition is introduced for us by Hung Trung Pham. In it he parallels praying to falling in love, writing, "As in loving, praying does not confine itself to one particular practice, way, or method, but is open to all, and is defined by all to the extent that all serve as means to creating a space of deeper freedom, leading the person to an evermore intimate and loving encounter between the lover and the beloved." He then orients us to how Ignatius guided people to unite with the Divine. To accomplish this, he carefully reflects with the reader on Ignatius's *Spiritual Exercises* as a way of making space for both a deeper freedom and the presence of God at the heart of our lives. The call for us to be reflective, aware, grateful, and to surrender to God, remind us that the journey to God in prayer is not a linear process but a dance, a mysterious, passionate journey, to experience the ultimate encounter again and again in new ways, at different junctures, in our life.

The final chapter in this section on prayer from the vantage point of different Catholic traditions is a reflective essay on the Mercy Tradition by Rosemary Jeffries. Focusing on the inspiration offered us by the life and writings of Catherine McAuley and the Sisters of Mercy, Jeffries points out the special emphasis on "the integration of active work with prayer," which was a departure from the religious orders of Catherine's time. Catherine's sense of humor (and the need for it today!) comes through clearly, as does the gift of the mercy tradition in terms of staying spiritually connected through what I would term reflective writing and remaining in touch with others who are also on a spiritual journey. In addition, the realism of Catherine comes through in that she bore pain and dark times as all of us will need to at times. Yet, she was also inspired to find a closer connection with God during, and because of, such difficulties, as we are as well in today's anxious world.

CHAPTER 13

Prayer in the Franciscan Tradition

~ *Daniel P. Horan, OFM* ~

Diversity is the hallmark of the Franciscan tradition, which represents both its greatest blessing and greatest challenge. Unlike some other traditions within Christianity that emphasize a singular influence, whether arising from the particular vision of the respective tradition's founder or from the charism in practice, the Franciscan spiritual tradition reflects its manifold contributors in both style and form. As Franciscan theologian Timothy Johnson has explained, "There is no single, uniform Franciscan manner of prayer because there is a plurality of unique Franciscan witnesses, whose desire to live an evangelical life fostered as many individual expressions of prayer as people committed to the Poor Christ."[1] While all the major contributors and models of Franciscan prayer can, in some sense, point back to Francis and Clare of Assisi as their primary inspirations and guides, the assortment of prayers, practices, and approaches to the spiritual life present in the history of Franciscan spirituality offers the modern spiritual seeker a broad range of resources and insight.

This chapter provides an introduction to this rich, capacious, and inclusive tradition of Christian prayer. It is in no way meant to be exhaustive. Instead my aim is to present something of a sampling of the Franciscan spiritual tradition with the hope of encouraging others to explore the manifold form of prayer present in the eight-hundred-year-old movement named after the *poverello*, St. Francis of Assisi. The chapter is organized according to the key figures of the tradition so as to highlight their respective contributions to the collective enterprise we call "Franciscan prayer." Given the centrality of the model and inspiration of Francis for all who follow after him, more attention will be paid to him at the outset. The second major section focuses on the insights of Clare of Assisi and the significant contributions she made toward shaping the Franciscan tradition of prayer. Finally, the last section is devoted to a brief overview of three figures—Bonaventure, Angela of Foligno, and John Duns Scotus[2]—each selected for their distinctive approach to the diverse tradition of Franciscan prayer.

FRANCIS OF ASSISI: BECOMING A "LIVING PRAYER"

Understandably, this whole chapter could have been dedicated simply to discussing the role of prayer in the life, writings, and model of Francis of Assisi because prayer was so central to his whole experience of Christian living and religious life. To gain an appreciation for Francis's understanding of prayer, we must first recall some features of his own story.

Francesco di Bernardone (c. 1182–1226) never intended to found a religious order. His experience of Gospel conversion began with a series of events that came together in such a way as to open his eyes to a reality previously veiled from him. As the son of a wealthy cloth merchant, Francis lived a reasonably comfortable life in the thirteenth-century Umbrian town of Assisi. As a matter of birth, he did not have noble status (something Clare of Assisi did, to some degree, enjoy) though he sought to attain a greater place in society by becoming a successful knight in battle. Despite his best intentions to achieve acclaim and status for military prowess, Francis was captured in an intercity battle with the neighboring town of Perugia. It was in captivity that, according to his biographers, Francis came to an awareness of his need to change his manner of life.[3] After being ransomed from prison by his father, Francis returned home a beaten and changed man. And he was someone who began acting oddly. His interest was no longer captivated by the aspirations he once held, nor was he contented to go about living his life without fuller examination. He began taking time to be alone in prayer and reflection, and decided to begin living a new way.

It would take some time and what Francis would later identify as divine intervention to help him realize that Christian discipleship required prioritizing relationship above all else in the manner of Jesus's ministry and teaching. At first, as his first biographer Thomas of Celano put it, Francis was changed "in mind" but "not in body."[4] He was nominally committed to living a more dedicated life of Christian discipleship, but this was at first made manifest only in his personal devotional practice. Francis began living as a public penitent, donning the simple peasant clothes of one professing to live a life of personal conversion. In time he came to engage in concrete actions of charity and kindness, selling clothes from his father's storehouse and giving the proceeds to a local church or beggar. Eventually he moved outside the confines of the Assisi community he had known from birth to embrace a more precarious existence at the periphery of society.[5]

It was among the marginalized and voiceless, the poor and the lepers that Francis began to experience God in a new way. And it was the experience of breaking with his own social class to live a more permanent itinerant lifestyle that marked the most clearly recognizable moment of his bourgeoning experience of conversion to Gospel living.[6] At the end of his life, Francis dictated to the friars caring for him his *Testament*, or final recollections about his experience of this world. It begins:

This is how God inspired me, Brother Francis, to embark upon a life of penance. When I was in sin, the sight of lepers nauseated me beyond measure; but then God himself led me into their company, and I had pity on them. When I had once become acquainted with them, what had previously nauseated me became a source of spiritual and physical consolation for me. After that I delayed a while before leaving the world.[7]

As Franciscan historian Michael Cusato keenly notes, in that encounter with the experience of the marginalized—especially the "lepers outside the city of Assisi" who were "men and women whom he had always considered abhorrent and of no consequence"—"Francis had his eyes open onto a whole world of suffering humanity which, up to that time, he had been socialized by the values of Assisi to ignore, avoid, and despise as repugnant and useless blots upon social life."[8] Francis's encounter with the poor of his time radically shifted his worldview and forced him to see the inherent relational quality of Christian discipleship.

That Francis could not live an authentic Christian life alone but must always be mindful of encountering the other was further emphasized in his experience of being confronted with men and women inspired by his evangelical awakening. Just as his experience of being led by the Lord among the lepers, Francis notes in his *Testament* that it was God who gave the *poverello* brothers: "When God gave me some brothers, there was no one to tell me what I should do; but the Most High himself made it clear to me that I must live the life of the Gospel."[9] Francis did not intend to found a religious order, nor did he solicit would-be companions. Rather, as Regis Armstrong and Ingrid Peterson have said, "From [Francis's] writings, it might be concluded that he simply wanted to live the fullness of life he received at his baptism, but in a short period of time men and women began to follow his vision of a poor and simple Trinitarian life."[10] The more he surrendered to the will of God over his own initial desire to live the Gospel as something of a "lone ranger," the more relationship became the central focus of his spirituality and prayer life. It is here that the affective or praxis-oriented sense of prayer and spirituality in the Franciscan tradition meets the deeply incarnational vision that grounded Francis's own Christian worldview.

The Incarnational Vision of Francis

The heart of the Franciscan way of life (*vita evangelica*) is living after the pattern of the Holy Gospel by walking in the footprints of Jesus Christ.[11] Recognizing the central place of divine-human relationship that occasioned the eternal Word's becoming flesh in the Incarnation, Francis of Assisi was drawn to the kenotic model of humility and poverty exhibited by Christ. We see in his writings this emphasis on God's self-emptying as the emblematic mode of being in the world. Tying together this kenosis of God with the poverty of Christ, Francis writes in chapter 6 of the *Rule* for the friars minor that,

> The friars are to appropriate nothing for themselves, neither a house, nor a place, nor anything else. As strangers and pilgrims (1 Peter 2:11) in this world, who serve God in poverty and humility, they should beg alms trustingly. And there is no reason they should be ashamed, *because God made himself poor for us in this world.* This is the pinnacle of the most exalted poverty, and it is this, my dearest brothers, that has made you heirs and kings of the kingdom of heaven, poor in temporal things, but rich in virtue. This should be your portion, because it leads you to the land of the living. And to this poverty, my beloved brothers, you must cling with all your heart, and wish never to have anything else under heaven, for the sake of our Lord Jesus Christ.[12]

Poverty for Francis was not simply an end in itself but a means to becoming more like Christ in terms of entering into relationship more deeply with God, neighbor, and all creation. Evangelical poverty is always tied to the Incarnation, which for Francis most fully symbolized God's desire to draw near to humanity in creation.

This same pattern was evident in Francis's strong devotion to the Eucharist, which also occupied a particularly central place in the *poverello's* own spirituality. In a letter to the entire order, Francis wrote that the friars should not only adore the Eucharistic species or receive them with devotion. Instead, they are to recall the ongoing kenotic action of God in the celebration of the Eucharist, which should serve yet again as a model for Franciscan life and prayer. He writes:

> What wonderful majesty! What stupendous condescension! O sublime humility! O humble sublimity! That the Lord of the whole universe, God and the Son of God, should humble himself like this and hide under the form of a little piece of bread, for our salvation. Look at God's condescension, my brothers, and pour out your hearts before him (Psalm 61:9). Humble yourselves that you may be exalted by him. Keep back nothing of yourselves for yourselves, so that he who has given himself wholly to you may receive you wholly.[13]

These illustrations of Francis's writings on the significance of the Incarnation as the model for Christian living—particularly in terms of embracing humility and evangelical poverty—echo what is seen in the New Testament writings of St. Paul. Take, for example, the ancient Christological hymn in the Letter to the Philippians.

> Let each of you look not to your own interests, but to the interests of others.
> Let the same mind be in you that was in Christ Jesus,
> who, though he was in the form of God,
>> did not regard equality with God
>> as something to be exploited,
> but emptied himself,
>> taking the form of a slave,
>> being born in human likeness.
> And being found in human form,
> he humbled himself
>> and became obedient to the point of death—
>> even death on a cross.
> Therefore God also highly exalted him
>> and gave him the name
>> that is above every name,
> so that at the name of Jesus
>> every knee should bend,
>> in the heaven and on earth and under the earth,
> and every tongue should confess
>> that Jesus Christ is Lord,
>> to the glory of God the Father. (Philippians 2:4–11, *NRSV*)

One can see the resonances immediately present between the self-emptying incarnational spirituality Francis exhorted those who followed him to adopt and the Pauline theology of divine kenosis.

This sense of the importance of the Incarnation is found beyond Francis's own writings and witnessed in the early testimony of those attesting to have known Francis personally. Such is the case in an early remembrance about Francis's view of Christmas. "For blessed Francis held the Nativity of the Lord in greater reverence than any other of the Lord's solemnities. For although the Lord may have accomplished our salvation in his other solemnities, nevertheless, once He was born to us, as blessed Francis would say, it was certain that we would be saved."[14]

Francis understood the humility of the Incarnation was one-half of the two-sided coin of God's salvific action. The other side of the coin was the passion, death, and resurrection of the Lord, which also plays a key role in Francis's approach to prayer.

His early biographer, Thomas of Celano, writes that, "The humility of the incarnation and the charity of the passion occupied his memory particularly, to the extent that he wanted to think of hardly anything else."[15] Norbert Nguyên-Van-Khanh explains:

> In reality, there are not two different subjects: the incarnation and the passion. For Francis, the passion is situated along a line that leads logically from the incarnation; it is a consequence of the fact that the Son of the Father accepts the human condition to the very end. The incarnation is the movement of descent; it is not a static situation that ends in the passion and death. Therefore, in the mind of Francis, the passion is intimately linked to the birth.[16]

This incarnational vision tied to the Passion of the Lord is also never divorced from a soundly Trinitarian theological understanding of the God to whom Francis prayed. Since prayer for Francis became increasingly understood in relational terms, it is not surprising that he would name God in the triune manner of orthodox theology. For example, in so-called "earlier rule" (*Regula non bullata*) believed to have been completed around 1221, Francis includes a prayer near the end of the text in which God is addressed as Trinity: "Almighty, most high and supreme God, Father, holy and just, Lord, King of heaven and earth, we give you thanks for yourself. Of your own holy will you created all things spiritual and physical, made us in your own image and likeness, and gave us a place in paradise, through your only Son, in the Holy Spirit."[17]

Francis of Assisi's sense of prayer was an address and form of communication with his Creator, Redeemer, and Sanctifier, but also a constant return to the model of authentic human life and love. Paraphrasing the classic patristic formula *lex orandi, lex credendi* ("the law of praying is the law of believing"), which refers to the tradition of mutual influence of worship and doctrine, the Franciscan scholar Michael Blastic suggests that, "One can expand on this conviction with another formula, '*forma vivendi forma orandi*,' which suggests the mutual relationship between life and prayer, that is the pattern and meaning of one's life is articulated in the form of one's prayer, and vice versa."[18] From his writings and the early sources, we can conclude that Francis's approach to prayer extended beyond a sense of two-way dialogue to include a pattern for his way of life. What exactly that way of life looked like can be seen in his instructions to his brothers about the importance of prayer and the various modes it may take.

Francis's Instructions on Prayer

Unlike Ignatius of Loyola's concentrated, step-by-step instructions for prayer in his *Spiritual Exercises*, Francis of Assisi's guidance for those who wish to follow his example of prayer and devotion is more diffuse. It is true to think of Francis's writings as occasional and unsystematic. Nevertheless, taken in whole, they offer constructive clues for what we might describe generally as Francis's "instructions on prayer." For the sake of brevity, we will look at four such instructions: the need to prioritize prayer, reverence for the Eucharist, the importance of solitude, and the call to immerse oneself in sacred Scripture. All four of these themes are aimed at leading those inspired by Francis's pattern of life (*forma vitae*) to move from simply "saying prayers" to becoming a living prayer.

First, prayer enters early into the formal vision of the Franciscan way of life in the *Rule*. After the brief introductory section where Francis announces the pattern of life is simply the Gospel of Jesus Christ and then outlines the logistics of accepting would-be friars into the community, Francis offers a chapter on prayer, fasting, and the general way the brothers are to live in the world.[19] It should come as no surprise, given the curial hand in the formation of this officially approved *Rule* for the friars, that the Divine Office canonically required for the friar clerics would make an appearance. Yet Francis is also accommodating for those who may be uneducated or illiterate, permitting them to pray a prescribed number of Our Fathers. One may glean from this inclusion that, although not everyone could be expected to pray the Liturgy of the Hours, all the brothers in community are expected to pray in community. Unlike the monastic demarcation between so-called "choir monks" and the "lay monks" whose responsibilities largely centered on manual labor, Francis affirmed a more egalitarian vision of fraternal life and activity grounded in prayer.

The importance of grounding one's life and activity in prayer is seen especially in Francis's explicit instruction on labor in chapter 5: "The friars to whom God has given the grace of working *should work in a spirit of faith and devotion* and avoid idleness, which is the enemy of the soul, *without however extinguishing the spirit of prayer and devotion,* to which every temporal consideration must be subordinate."[20] That the work of the brothers, however conceived in terms of explicit apostolic ministry or manual labor, should always be subordinate to one's individual and collective "spirit of prayer and devotion" attests to the importance of prayer in Francis's vision of Gospel life. Francis again reiterates this prioritization when, in a now-famous letter to St. Anthony of Padua, Francis gives permission to teach theology to the brothers: "I am pleased that you teach sacred theology to the brothers providing that, as is contained in the Rule, you 'do not extinguish the Spirit of prayer and devotion' during study of this kind."[21]

In something of a departure from the Benedictine tradition's emphasis on maintaining a balanced life of *ora et labora*, prayer and work, Francis of Assisi tilts the scales toward prayer. While work is important, it is for Francis never more important than perseverance in the spiritual life. For Francis, prayer was understood as both a continual and a communal experience, even when one's activity was an effort in solitude. The sense of continual prayer—the ongoing communication with God throughout all facets of life both in the more explicit *ora* as well as during all other *labora*—is seen in Francis's "Letter to All the Faithful," in which we read: "We should praise Him and pray to Him day and night, saying, Our Father who art in heaven (Matt 6:9), because we must always pray and not lose heart (Luke 18:1)."[22] And yet this was also a deeply communal dimension of Francis's vision of Gospel life. As Blastic has observed, among Francis's authentic writings, only one is voiced in the first-person singular, that of the "Prayer before the Crucifix," which reads: "Most High, glorious God, enlighten the darkness of my heart and give me true faith, certain hope, and perfect charity, sense and knowledge, Lord, that I may carry out Your holy and true command."[23] What remains of Francis's prayers assume a collective voice, representing "the voice of the brotherhood at work."[24] Prayer is always a communal experience, one that extends beyond the individual petitioner or adorer of God to include the community gathered locally or the communion of saints more broadly.

Second, Francis frequently reflects on the Eucharist and the importance that the brothers approach the Blessed Sacrament in a spirit of prayerful reverence. Through Francis's personal devotion to the celebration of the Mass, his admiration of the office of the ministerial priesthood (in distinction to particular *priests* who, as Francis noted with realistic acquiescence, are as finite and sinful as everybody else), and his reverence for the Eucharist are commonly found throughout his writings. From the beginning of his ongoing conversion around 1206 to his death on October 3, 1226, his writings do not include extensive instruction on the role of liturgical prayer in the life of the community apart from the clerical daily office.[25] This is very likely reflective of the shift in friar demographics. In the beginning, those following Francis's nascent form of life represented a diverse mixture of backgrounds and experiences. Toward the end of Francis's short life, a larger number of ordained priests began entering the community, which shifted the availability of the sacraments within Franciscan houses. Correspondingly, the later texts of Francis tend to include references to the celebration of the Eucharist and a call for increased participation in the mass and reverence for the Blessed Sacrament on the part of his followers.

Third, the incorporation of a part-time eremitical life into the broader pattern of life was an important dimension of Francis's own spirituality and approach to prayer.[26] He believed in the need for the brothers to reconnect with God in an attentive and deliberate way, which was demonstrated in his own practice of regularly retreating to hermitages and quiet places. Though his general emphasis on relationship with others by meeting them where they are in the streets and villages of the world through a commitment to itinerant ministry is central to the Franciscan *Rule*, he nevertheless went to the trouble of composing a short "Rule for Hermitages." This unique text is worth citing at length, for it reveals at once the importance of experiencing and preserving solitude and the communal-fraternal dimension of lived Franciscan prayer.

> Not more than three or at most four friars should go together to a hermitage to lead a religious life there. Two of these should act as mothers, with the other two, or the other one, as their children. The mothers are to lead the life of Martha; the other two, the life of Mary.... The friars who are mothers must be careful to stay away from outsiders and in obedience to their minister keep their sons away from outsiders, so that no one can speak to them. The friars who are sons are not to speak to anyone except their mother or their minister, when he visits them, with God's blessing. Now and then, the sons should exchange places with the mothers, according to whatever arrangement seems best suited for the time. But they should all be careful to observe what has been laid down for them, eagerly and zealously.[27]

Striking is the freedom with which Francis invokes as instructive for the brothers the maternal imagery and the model of Martha and Mary from the Gospels. Though not often well-known or acknowledged by modern Franciscans, scholars have noted nonetheless the distinctive contribution that Francis's vision of nondominating governance within the fraternity, frequently conveyed in feminine imagery, has made to Christian spirituality.[28] Solitude was not only an important ingredient in Gospel life for Francis himself, but was intended to be a mainstay of Franciscan prayer more generally by offering an opportunity for small communities to care for one another and provide the space for ongoing, deep encounters with the divine.[29]

Fourth, Francis's way of Christian living and approach to prayer were deeply tied to sacred Scripture. Though the early sources recall Francis's self-deprecating identification as an *idiota*, or unlearned person, Francis most certainly knew how to read and write. It can be difficult for modern people who are used to mass-produced paper, living centuries after the invention of the printing press, to appreciate how important the written word was in Francis's time. Oftentimes the material needed to write a copy of a biblical book or the prayers for the Mass was difficult to acquire and expensive. Unlike our liturgical books and Bibles today, Scripture was often copied out on a variety of pages. These pages, usually unbound, had the tendency (as most loose papers do) of becoming scattered and lost. This even happened in churches. Francis was very concerned about the way these particles of Scripture were cared for (or more accurately, *not cared for*). He was almost obsessed with making sure that all pieces of Scripture were well taken care of and treated with respect and dignity. In a letter addressed to the entire Order, Francis shares his vision of the importance of caring for Scripture in a command that all friars should go out of their way to gather, protect, and venerate even the most seemingly insignificant Scriptural texts:

> He who is of God hears the words of God (John 8:47), and so we who are called to serve God in a more special way are bound not merely to listen to and carry out what he commands; in order to impress on ourselves the greatness of our Creator and of our subjection to him we must keep the liturgical books and anything else which contains his holy words with great care. I urge all my friars and I encourage them in Christ to show all possible respect for God's words wherever they may happen to find them in writing. If they are not kept properly or if they lie thrown about disrespectfully, they should pick them up and put them aside, paying honor in his words to God who spoke them. For by God's words many things are made holy and the sacrament of the altar is celebrated in the power of the words of Christ.[30]

Francis did not see in the Word of God some removed and abstract sense of God's presence but recognized the truly intimate and life-giving quality of Scripture. We see this most strongly in the assertion that Francis makes prior to instructing his brothers to collect these pieces of Scripture, when he explains that it is Scripture that allows us to "impress on ourselves the greatness of our Creator." His instruction to his followers was no mere "housekeeping" task, but a sign that he recognized God's "spirit and life" communicated through the Scripture.[31]

Though he does not outline any particular program or method of reading and meditating on Scripture (e.g., a formal process of *lectio divina*), Francis does communicate in subtler ways the necessity of living by the Word of God. This is seen in his emphasis on the daily office prayed in community as well as through the extraordinary frequency with which he cites the Scriptures in his own writings, *Rules*, and prayers. St. Bonaventure, in his *Legenda Major*, describes the unique way in which the poor man from Assisi was able to understand the meaning of Scripture such that he astounded even the most learned and wise scholars of the day.

> Unflagging zeal for prayer
> with a continual exercise of virtue
> had led the man of God to such serenity of mind that,

although he had no expertise in Sacred Scripture through learning,

his intellect, nevertheless

enlightened by the splendor of eternal light,

probed the depths of Scripture

with remarkable incisiveness.

For his genius, pure and unstained,

Penetrated hidden mysteries,

and where the knowledge of teachers stands outside,

the passion of the lover entered.

Whenever he read the Sacred Books,

and something struck his mind

he imprinted it tenaciously on his memory,

because he did not grasp in vain

what his attentive mind heard,

for he would mull over it

with affection and constant devotion.[32]

Francis's memorization of, reflection on, and constant reference to sacred Scripture led to his being imbued with the very narrative of God's self-disclosure. In turn, he was inspired to draw on passages from the Bible, especially the psalms, to compose his own psalmody and prayers. This is seen most clearly in his creative *Office of the Passion*, which was modeled on the personal devotional offices commonly found among monastic communities.[33] Here Francis weaves together various psalms from the Hebrew Bible with his own devotional interludes and psalm-like additions. The importance of Scripture in prayer was not limited to Francis's private devotional life alone, but seen by him as an essential element of evangelical life.

Becoming a "Living Prayer"

St. Augustine of Hippo famously remarks at various points in his expansive corpus that God is the one who is closer to us than we are to ourselves.[34] This experience of divine immanence, of the presence of God among and within creation, was the keystone of Francis's whole approach to prayer, though it is safe to say that he did not realize this overnight. It is always important to remember the lifelong experience of ongoing conversion when calling to mind Francis's spirituality and form of prayer. As noted earlier, he began his renewed commitment to Christian living in early young adulthood with what we might anachronistically call a "literal" approach to discipleship. His focus was on the externals of affective religiosity, such as attending Mass and physically rebuilding churches. The increasing number of relational encounters—the living among lepers, the unsolicited brothers and sisters, the reception of Clare, the protection and approval of the clerical hierarchy, the embrace of the Muslim Sultan, the increasing awakening to his part in the cosmic family of creation, and so on— shifted, over time, the *poverello's* vision of prayer. In the beginning, as Thomas of Celano notes, Francis of Assisi was one who merely "said" prayers, but over time became a "living prayer."[35]

If prayer is, as we might all agree, always a form of "communication with God," then we are in some sense always praying because God is always already present to us (again, Augustine's insight about God's immanence and proximity to us). It is, in a sense, a form of hubris to think that we can simply turn on or turn off the prayer channel, as if we had the ability to select when God is able to receive our missives. In truth, not only what we say or think, but how we act, what we prioritize, how we love, how we care for one another, and so on all combine to *communicate* something to the God who is at all times nearer to us than we are to ourselves. In commenting on Francis's *Rule*, Blastic explains, "It describes an experience of prayer and life without dichotomy, and without separating out the realms of the sacred and the secular.... This world becomes the location for prayer, the place for returning all things to God, and this is situated in the context of faith in the Trinity who acts in history as creator and savior." He continues, noting the way we must consider a summation of Francis's whole life of prayer, "Prayer is rooted firmly in the ordinary activity of life in terms of love and service, and it is expressed here in terms of praise, adoration, and glory."[36]

Long before Ignatius and his successors in the Society of Jesus popularized the expression, "finding God in all things," Francis of Assisi's understanding and experience of prayer was precisely this form of ordinary mysticism. He came to realize in time that the words said in the divine office, the community's participation in the celebration of the Eucharist, and the charitable acts of love and mercy were not as distinct as one might first assume. Instead, prayer for Francis was always a journey of growing more deeply in relationship with God and neighbor, including his nonhuman neighbors in the great family of God's creation. There is no explicit strategy or instruction manual proposed as a means to achieve this mystical awareness. And yet, Francis's own narrative of lifelong conversion and his model for how to prioritize the elements of one's life—*never extinguish the spirit of prayer and devotion*, embrace regular solitude, and so on—provides us with a pattern of life, a guide for our own journeys, a series of points for reflection. The goal of prayer (if prayer can ever be said to have a goal) in the Franciscan tradition, put simply, is nothing more than for each of us, in our own way and in our own contexts, to become more and more a living prayer.

Clare of Assisi: Poverty and Contemplation

Clare of Assisi is oftentimes portrayed as the "woman behind the man" in the hagiographical telling of the early Franciscan movement. And while it is correct to say that she was the first woman to join Francis of Assisi's nascent penitential community (she entered on Palm Sunday 1212 at around the age of seventeen), her significant role in shaping what would come to be known as the Franciscan movement and its spirituality has been largely overlooked through the centuries. This oversight is likely due in part to the patriarchal presuppositions of historiography that were commonplace until recently. Fortunately, in recent decades, scholarship has begun to catch up to reality, presenting a rich tapestry of detail about and insight into the identity, role, and legacy of Clare.[37]

Unlike Francis who was the son of a reasonably successful cloth merchant in Assisi and whose status was of common origin, Clare came from a family of some nobility and high social standing. In the regional civil war that pitted the *minores* (commoners) against the *maiores* (nobility) in the village of Assisi, Francis's family was part of the uprising of the former while Clare's family fled to the safety of a nearby town because they belonged to the latter class. This preconversion distinction between the two founders of the Franciscan movement would not be the only difference. In addition to gender identity, the importance of which should not be underestimated in medieval civil and ecclesiastical society, Francis and Clare were different in terms of how they expressed their religious convictions (Francis in itinerant mendicancy; Clare in cloistered community) and how long they lived (Francis died in 1226; Clare died almost thirty years later in 1253). Yet they shared in common a similar desire and love, which was not for each other (despite misguided romantic depictions to the contrary), but for Jesus Christ and the Gospel life. What Clare was drawn to in Francis's preaching was not a charismatic older man (Francis was about twelve years older), but the God about whom he preached.

Clare was fond of describing herself as a *plantacula* ("a little plant") of Francis of Assisi. Over the centuries this self-reference has been misunderstood according to a projected tone of subjugation and diminution. However, as the Franciscan scholar William Short explains:

> In context, however, Clare's name for herself indicates something different: she is separate but connected, rooted in the same soil of the Gospel, sharing with Francis a "form of life" she received from him as a gift from God. But the way in which she expresses her growing, intimate knowledge of "following the footsteps of our Lord Jesus Christ" is uniquely her own.

What unites Clare and Francis is not an identical experience of Christ, but
different experiences of the same Christ.[38]

To understand the Franciscan movement, and more so anything classified as
"Franciscan prayer," one must have an appreciation for Clare's place alongside Francis
as a true cofounder and long-influential shaper of the tradition. According to an
early source's account of Clare's death on August 11, 1253, among those gathered at
Clare's bedside are Leo, Rufino, and Angelo, three of the first followers of Francis.
According to the early texts of the tradition, after Francis's death the only time these
three central figures are said to have been in the same place at the same time was
when Clare embraced "Sister Bodily Death." As Short keenly observes, this scene is
important (and probably historically accurate given that all three were still alive at the
time) because of what is symbolized: "Clare at the center of the early companions,
at the core of the tradition as it is being handed over to the next generation. For this
reason, some authors today are beginning to speak of a 'Franciscan-Clarian' tradition.
More than a disciple, Clare is also a creative architect of the tradition she lived."[39]

In what ways might we locate the marks of Clare's "creative architecture" within
the tradition? Though there are surely many other characteristics of Clare's contributions to prayer in the Franciscan tradition and Franciscan spirituality more broadly,
for the sake of brevity, I suggest the two essential Clarian insights are poverty and
contemplation.

POVERTY

Like Francis, Clare had a deeply incarnational spiritual outlook. As Franciscan theologian Ilia Delio has noted, Clare "viewed the Incarnation as a coincidence of opposites, a mystery of poverty and riches. The one who is rich in mercy and love bends
low in the Incarnation to embrace us in love, and it is in accepting this gift of the poor
One that we become rich in God."[40] This incarnational theological outlook grounds
Clare's understanding of evangelical poverty, contextualizing the experience of self-
offering (*kenosis*) as a means toward an end rather than merely an ascetical end in
itself. This end is the deepening of relationship one has with God as well as increased
solidarity with the abject poor and marginalized of society. On this latter point, it is
noteworthy that Clare's religious community at the church of San Damiano was also
the site of a medieval leper hospice, which was dedicated to caring for these socially
and ecclesially disenfranchised people.

The most spiritually rich and theologically insightful writings we have from Clare
are in the form of four short letters written to Agnes of Prague (b. 1205). Agnes was
the daughter of King Premsyl Ottokar I of Bohemia and, along with seven other

noble women, left behind the status, comfort, and security of royalty to enter the newly founded "Order of Saint Damien" (modeled after Clare's Assisi community at the chapel of San Damiano) in 1234. Though Clare and Agnes never met in person, their brief correspondence conveys an intimacy and depth in light of their shared admiration of Christ and the life of evangelical poverty, which also evokes what Clare and Francis similarly shared in common. In Clare's "First Letter to Agnes of Prague," we read:

> O blessed poverty, who bestows eternal riches on those who love and embrace her! O holy poverty, God promises the kingdom of heaven and, beyond any doubt, reveals eternal glory and blessed life to those who have and desire her! O God-centered poverty, whom the Lord Jesus Christ Who ruled and still rules heaven and earth, Who spoke and things were made, came down to embrace before all else.... If so great and good a Lord, then, on coming into the Virgin's womb, wanted to appear despised, needy, and poor in this world, so that people who were very poor and needy, suffering excessive hunger of heavenly nourishment, may become rich in Him by possessing the kingdom of heaven, be very joyful and glad, filled with a remarkable happiness and a spiritual joy![41]

Here and elsewhere in the correspondence, Clare encourages Agnes and her religious sisters to continually focus on the evangelical poverty modeled by Christ in the Incarnation. The model for Christian living is the poor God who emptied himself to become like us in order to enter more deeply into relationship with all people.

Clare draws upon royal imagery familiar to Agnes and others of noble standing to illustrate the "spiritual benefits" of embracing a spirituality and praxis of evangelical poverty: precious stones, priceless pearls, sparkling gems, and a golden crown of holiness.[42] Additionally, Clare does not shy away from spousal metaphors, suggesting by way of ongoing encouragement in her "Second Letter to Agnes of Prague," that, "as someone zealous for the holiest poverty, in a spirit of great humility and the most ardent love, you have held fast to the footprints of Him to whom you merited to be joined in marriage."[43] Amid this encouragement for fidelity to the call of evangelical poverty in following Christ, Clare offers an original prayer of blessing and exhortation to Agnes, which has become itself a classic of the Franciscan tradition.

> What you hold, may you hold,
> What you do, may you do and not stop.
> But with swift pace, light step, unswerving feet,
> so that even your steps stir up no dust,

may you go forward securely, joyfully and swiftly,

on the path of prudent happiness,

believing nothing, agreeing with nothing

that would dissuade you from this commitment

or would place a stumbling block for you on the way,

so that nothing prevents you from offering

your vows to the most high in the perfection

to which the spirit of the Lord has called you.[44]

As Timothy Johnson has noted, the spousal imagery Clare uses to talk about Agnes's relation to Christ combines both the royal metaphors with the centrality of evangelical poverty. According to Clare's telling, "Agnes's spouse is like no other spouse. He is the most royal and noble of grooms, a spouse whose beauty far surpasses all others. Paradoxically, he is also the poorest of the poor, the lowest and most despicable of all men. Agnes has chosen as a spouse the poor, Crucified Christ, whom others rejected, despised, scourged and killed."[45] Through the personal relationship with Christ, one is able then to embrace a concrete model of evangelical poverty which, as Delio explains, helps create a space within one's heart to receive what we see in the divine and embrace that which is a personal, relational, loving God.[46]

Visualization and relational imagery play a key role in Clare of Assisi's style of prayer. While reflecting on the Gospel life, encouraging Agnes (and others) in their continued pursuit of evangelical perfection, and relating to Christ as spouse and divine poverty personified, Clare draws on creative descriptors, personal experience, and rich illustrations to develop a pattern of mental prayer. This is seen most fully in what we might understand as her instructions to Agnes on contemplation.

CONTEMPLATION

Although we have relatively few of Clare's writings compared to the collection that has been passed down from Francis, these texts nonetheless reveal to us profound insights into Clare's understanding and practice of prayer. As with Francis, Clare was deeply drawn to the person of Jesus Christ, and this fascination with Christ "expresses itself in unceasing prayer."[47] As we have already seen, Clare's advice to Agnes about persistence in maintaining one's commitment to evangelical poverty is deeply Christological, drawing on the Incarnate Word as both model for living and source of the call. This incarnational vision carries over into Clare's approach to prayer within the cloistered expression of the Franciscan charism of which she is the undisputed founder. The spousal language sets the context for Clare's instruction on contemplation. Clare writes:

But as a poor virgin embrace the poor Christ. Look upon Him Who became contemptible for you, and follow Him, making yourself contemptible in this world for Him. Most noble Queen, *gaze, consider, contemplate desiring to imitate your Spouse.*[48]

What Clare lays out is a fourfold process: *intuere* (gaze, focus), *considera* (consider), *contemplare* (contemplate), and *desiderans imitari* (desire to imitate). This pattern is repeated again nearly two decades later in her last letter to Agnes, written shortly before Clare's death. She expands on the fourfold formula, now drawing also on the metaphor of the mirror that she writes about in her interim third letter to Agnes.

Gaze upon that mirror each day, O Queen and Spouse of Jesus Christ, and continually study your face in it, that you may adorn yourself completely, within and without, covered and arrayed in needlework and similarly adorned with the flowers and garments of all the virtues, as is becoming, the daughter and dearest bride of the Most High King. Indeed, in that mirror, blessed poverty, holy humility, and inexpressible charity shine forth as, with the grace of God, you will be able to contemplate them throughout the entire mirror.[49]

As Armstrong has commented, "This formula, paradoxically profound in its simplicity, reflects the insights of a woman eager to awaken affection in others for the God of her heart."[50] Prayer for Clare is the experience of being in love with the God who is love (1 John 4:8). This loving relationship, though certainly a unique experience for each individual loved into existence by God, nevertheless shares something in common, which is why Clare is comfortable offering a cartographical approach to contemplation—something that Francis never attempted.

Much of the contemplative tradition of the Christian church has focused on the apophatic, according to which the dissimilarity between God and creatures leads the contemplative to negate descriptors and metaphors of the divine in an effort to be entirely open and receptive to God. And yet, within the Franciscan tradition exemplified here in Clare's pattern of prayer, contemplation takes on a decidedly kataphatic dimension, according to which, the contemplative recognizes "that there is a discernible similarity between creatures and the Creator. Consequently, it is possible to know an assent to divine realities because creatures are analogically related to the Creator."[51] Clare's incarnational worldview, like Francis's as well, placed God's embrace of the material world generally and the human person specifically at the center of her experience of and relationship to the divine. As a result, God is not some unknowable

Other far away from creation, but an immanent Creator who draws near to creation in love.

Clare's use of striking visual and humanly relational images in discussing prayer with Agnes should be seen to reflect this incarnational primacy in contemplation, which aligns well, not coincidentally, with the centrality of evangelical poverty exhibited by a God who surrenders even divinity to draw near in relationship as close as possible to creation. Johnson has observed that, "Given Clare's decidedly kataphatic spirituality, it is not by chance that she turns frequently to visual language in religious discourse, as opposed to aural language, because it is more apt to convey the sense of immanency proper to the kataphatic contemplative experience."[52] For instance, instead of "hearing God's call," which especially in our age with the advent of telephone and digital communications, can come from any location and time, the proximity necessary for visual recognition and union presupposes a profound sense of immanence. This closeness to the divine is expressed in Clare's turn toward visual language and, as Johnson notes, "Her preference for visual language underlines her conviction that Christ will be continually and intimately present to Agnes if she envisions him daily as spouse and mirror."[53]

It is in the fourth and last letter to Agnes that Clare reveals her own experience of mystical encounter with Christ through this fourfold path of contemplation. She explains that it is in praying before and opening herself to Christ on the cross that she first received the invitation to follow Christ more deeply in evangelical poverty and Gospel living. It is perhaps no mere coincidence that Clare spent forty years of her life living with her sisters at the church of San Damiano and in the regular presence of the now-famous crucifix that spoke to Francis, exhorting him to "rebuild the church."[54] It is in this first-person recounting of her prayer life so far that Clare's emphasis on spousal metaphor and visual imagery come together in a way deeply evocative of the Song of Songs. She describes her experience of prayer and relationship to Christ as an encounter with the God who pursues her, which Clare relates to Agnes by way of encouraging her fellow cloistered sister to seek similar union with God. Finally, Clare encourages Agnes to "rest" in this contemplation.[55] Clare remarks in her closing lines that one's own words begin to appear inadequate in expressing what one experiences so viscerally and proximately. Despite her otherwise kataphatic methodology of approach in contemplation, there remains a notable apophatic conclusion when left to convey the experience of divine embrace.

Among Clare's many contributions to the Franciscan tradition of prayer, too many to adequately present in this short chapter, we can include her poetic description and kataphatic instruction, both of which are lacking to some degree in Francis's own writings. Clare, inspired as she was by Francis's kindred desire for union with God, develops the Gospel exhortation to embrace Christlike poverty into a spirituality of encounter with the living God who indeed empties the divine self to draw near to humanity in the paradoxical movement of kenosis. Her use of spousal metaphor and visual imagery further concretizes the pattern and experience of contemplation as she lived it, offering Agnes and us a simple yet profound guide to respond in love to God's invitation to enter more deeply into relationship. In other words, Clare outlines a path to develop further what we generally call prayer.

THE FRANCISCAN TRADITION CONTINUES: DIVERSITY AMID SHARED INSPIRATION
In the generations that followed Francis and Clare, the rightful cofounders of what has become known as the "Franciscan movement," several women and men emerged as insightful contributors to the bourgeoning tradition that still remains today a source of attraction and inspiration for Christians and non-Christians alike.

ST. BONAVENTURE: MASTER OF ORDINARY MYSTICISM
Bonaventure of Bagnoregio (c. 1217–1274) is perhaps one of the best-known Franciscan figures of the thirteenth century after Francis and Clare of Assisi and Anthony of Padua. He was a learned man and gifted scholar whose contributions to medieval theology far exceed the ability we have here to name them. In addition to holding a chair at the University of Paris for a time, Bonaventure was also elected Minister General (that is, the successor of St. Francis who oversees the entire Order) during a particularly tumultuous time in the community's history. He is credited with holding the movement together amid disputation and efforts made toward division. His theological genius and leadership prowess caught the eye of Rome, and he was later made bishop of Albano and then named a cardinal by Pope Gregory X in 1273. Bonaventure died on July 15, 1274 during the Second Council of Lyon, for which he was an organizer appointed by the pope. He was canonized on April 14, 1482, by Pope Sixtus IV and declared a Doctor of the Church (his title: *Doctor Seraphicus*) on March 14, 1588.

Bonaventure is typically remembered for his organizational and leadership skills or his academic acumen, but not typically drawn upon as an exemplar or guide in the life of prayer outside of those within the Franciscan family who are familiar with his spiritual writings, including his best-known treatises: *The Soul's Journey Into God, The Tree of Life*, and *The Major Life of St. Francis*.[56] And yet, even in his more academic works, including lengthy treatises on Scripture or his expansive commentary on the *Sentences* of Peter Lombard, Bonaventure held prayer to be an essential component of ordinary life. Unlike the contemporary or at least commonly perceived bias against conflating "popular" or "spiritual" writing with so-called rigorous scholarly research according to scientific principles, Bonaventure's approach was one that married these ostensibly distinct worlds, claiming in fact that they were inseparable. As Charles Carpenter and Gregory LaNave have independently claimed, academic study was never an end in itself for Bonaventure, but a means toward holiness, which is the path set before all Christians.[57] Whereas practitioners of Christian prayer may today distance themselves from the "book learning" of higher studies, Bonaventure at first encouraged his university students and then the friars under his leadership to integrate the two dimensions of their intellectual and spiritual lives.

Bonaventure's own approach to prayer was, as the late Bonaventurean scholar Zachary Hayes explained, "a systematic vision deeply rooted in the spiritual experience of St. Francis."[58] Like the many women and men who followed Francis of Assisi, Bonaventure's starting point was the lived experience of the saint and founder of this peculiar penitential movement he found himself within. Hayes notes that Bonaventure

> developed key insights of St. Francis's spirituality into theological and metaphysical doctrines that greatly enrich the Christian tradition of theology. This had to do with a specific form of Christology, a distinctive form of Trinitarian theology, and a form of creation theology that moves on strongly in the direction of a contemplative sense of the world.[59]

Although there are many additional paths to pursue in gaining a deep appreciation for Bonaventure's approach to and theology of prayer, for the sake of brevity, let us look at these three aspects of his thought and writings.[60]

As with Francis and Clare before him, Bonaventure's understanding of prayer is deeply incarnational in its foundations and aim. He situates his understanding of God according to the two poles of the incarnation and the cross.[61] With these two connected, yet still distinct, bookends always in mind, Bonaventure's vision of God becomes one of a deeply humble and relational God who draws near to creation and discloses the divine self completely through the incarnate Word.[62] His understanding of prayer then was deeply shaped by this incarnational outlook, such that, as Ilia Delio explains,

> In Bonaventure's view, contemplation cannot be exclusively confined to the soul since the soul itself cannot exist apart from the body. Rather, the Word of God entered into union with the flesh to ennoble our nature by creating the object of contemplation necessary for the beatification of our nature. This object of contemplation for Bonaventure was not the transcendent

unknowable God (as it was for the Greeks) but Christ, God and man.[63]

Prayer was not something divorced from the reality of the world, from our corporeal existence, or from the quotidian moments of the ordinary. Instead, precisely because of the God who is revealed as God-for-us through the Incarnation, the object of our prayer is the incarnate Word, whose own experience of embodiment glorifies the ordinary and the everyday. Mystical experience for Bonaventure was not extraworldly, but rather intraworldly and a potential experience for all.

Next, the distinctively Trinitarian outlook Bonaventure embraced not only led to his understanding of God as humble as witnessed in the Word's kenosis to become human, but also to the realization that God is deeply relational. It pertains to God's inmost nature to be in relationship with himself and, because of Bonaventure's understanding of the nature of divine love shaped by the school of St. Victor and the mystical theology of Pseudo-Dionysius, inevitably in relationship with all creation. The fountain fullness of God's inexhaustible love, expressed primarily within the Trinity, overflows into the created world as grace, God's very presence to us. The God to whom Bonaventure prayed was no God in reserve, no distant or absent God, but a God whose very nature almost required a divine act of relationship *ad extra*. This is a vision of God who draws near out of love because his very nature and primary title is love.

Finally, the incarnational and Trinitarian aspects of Bonaventure's theological outlook lead him to assert a theology of creation in which God's presence is immanently seen and experienced. The way this is most commonly expressed in Bonaventure's writings is that all of creation has the capacity to reflect the Creator as triune. Therefore, each aspect of creation is a *speculum*, a mirror of the divine in which we can contemplate the Creator. Furthermore, all of creation also bears the *vestigium* of God—that is, literally the "footprint" or imprint of the Creator. Hayes explains: "A vestige, in Bonaventure's usage, may be compared with the footprint of a person in the sand of the beach. One who discovers the footprint may not discover a lot about the person who left it there. But something can be known about the person's size, weight, and so on. So it is with the relation of all creation to God. Every created reality can open us to some awareness of the source of this footprint."[64] At times Bonaventure's vision of creation as vestige and mirror of the divine has been described as a form of panentheism, meaning to find God *in all things*.[65] What this means in terms of an additional insight about Franciscan prayer, however, is that contemplation for Bonaventure is not something solely reserved for particular times and places in which one would merely hone her gaze (*contemplatio*) toward the divine. Rather, contemplation in Bonaventure's understanding (*speculatio*) is learning to see the world anew, recognizing God's presence always already at hand in the world around us.

In light of this, we can see how Bonaventure's depiction of Francis of Assisi as simultaneously a mystic and prophet fits well with his understanding of prayer. Francis was one whose worldview was also deeply incarnational and whose outlook increasingly awakened to the presence of God in the world around him. At first it was through the recognition of the *imago Dei* in the otherwise ignored and despised people of his age such as the lepers, but over time, this horizon of God's presence in the ordinary world included all of creation—sentient and nonsentient creatures alike. For Bonaventure, the entirety of one's life provided an opportunity for contemplation and prayer, leading to a mystical experience of the ordinary and the everyday. In the end, this increasing awareness should lead us to act differently in the world as it did for Francis in his own faith journey.

ANGELA OF FOLIGNO: FRANCISCAN CREATION MYSTIC

When on October 9, 2013, Pope Francis effectively canonized a thirteenth-century laywoman from a small town south of Assisi by extending "the liturgical cult in honor of Angela of Foligno to the Universal Church," I suspect not many of the billion-plus members of the Universal Church took notice.[66] The woman, Angela of Foligno (c. 1248–1309), was a lay follower of St. Francis of Assisi, a member of the early "brothers and sisters of penance" (what we would today call the "Secular Franciscans"). Angela was a member of the wealthy aristocratic class of Foligno who, in particularly harsh retrospection, described her youth and preconversion experiences as superficial at best and sinful at worst.[67] In many ways, Angela of Foligno was simply a woman of her time. Born around 1248, she came from a rather wealthy family and followed the pattern of life typical for a medieval woman: she married in 1270 and had several children. However, around 1288 her life took an unexpected and dramatic turn. All of her family died—her children, husband, and mother. In the years prior to the deaths of her loved ones, Angela had become increasingly more aware that the way she was living her life was not sufficient.

Darleen Pryds has described what followed as a midlife crisis of sorts, which led Angela to a profound religious conversion inspired by the life and spirituality of Francis of Assisi.[68] She felt the burden of her own sinfulness and felt a strong desire to live a more prayerful, reflective life. After the deaths of her family members, Angela was drawn to follow the example of Francis and live the rest of her life as a penitent, that is, someone who makes a public commitment to live in evangelical poverty, prayer, and service. Selling her property and using the money to help the poor in her town, Angela felt freed from the trappings of wealthy medieval life. Dedicated as she was now to follow St. Francis's way of life, her mode of prayer was that of Franciscan contemplation. She came to be close to the local community of Franciscan friars who served as her confessors, advisors, and advocates. Additionally, Angela's insights, prayerfulness, mysticism, and perceptible holiness led to her being a highly sought-after spiritual director (to use a title of our time), whom women and men would consult about faith and spiritual matters. So respected was she in her own time, despite her lack of formal or professional theological education, that she received the title *magistra theologorum* ("teacher of theologians").

Angela's contributions to the Franciscan tradition are numerous and include such topics as the Passion of Christ and the centrality of evangelical poverty.[69] And yet, another aspect of her writings, visceral and personal as they are, that makes a timely contribution to the tradition concerning prayer is her creation mysticism.[70] Like Bonaventure, Angela of Foligno believed that all of creation reflected God. Instead of describing creation as a mirror or footprint of God, though, Angela saw the world as "pregnant with God." In her famous book, *The Memorial*, Angela recounts to a friar scribe the events of her spiritual journey. At one point, Angela recalls attending Mass in Assisi, during which she had a particularly powerful experience of God's presence. She heard God say to her, "My sweet daughter, no creature can give you this consolation, only I alone." Angela shares that this experience was one of great endearment and intimacy. It was a recognition of God's closeness to and care for her. She continued:

> Afterward [God] added: "I want to show you something of my power." And immediately the eyes of my soul were opened, and in a vision I beheld the fullness of God in which I beheld and comprehended the whole of creation, that is, what is on this side and what is beyond the sea, the abyss, the sea itself, and everything else. And in everything that I saw, I could perceive nothing except the presence of the power of God, and in a manner totally indescribable. And my soul in an excess of wonder cried out: "This world is pregnant with God!" Wherefore I understood how small is the whole of creation—that is, what is on this side and what is beyond the sea, the abyss, the sea itself, and everything else—but the power of God fills it all to overflowing.[71]

For Angela, God's love and care for her were directly related to all of creation. She explicitly attributes her ability to see God in all of creation to his opening of her eyes to see the world as it *really* is—a sign of God's generous love.

Angela provides us with another model of Franciscan contemplation, one that is also described as mysticism. Theologian Richard McBrien explains that mysticism is that graced transformation of our awareness or consciousness that "follows upon a direct or immediate experience of the presence of God leading to a deeper union with God." He goes on to explain, "that union, however, does not isolate the individual from others or from the world. The deep union achieved by Bernard of Clairvaux, Francis of Assisi, and Catherine of Siena, for example, led them into greater apostolic activity and into service of others."[72] Such was the case with Angela.

As we read in the passage above, Angela's personal outlook and worldview were dramatically impacted by her decision to live a life of prayer and poverty after the example of Francis. She began to see the world as it really was. She increasingly came to view creation and others as God views them. Her life of contemplation led to a deeper experience of God and that, in turn, shaped her relationship with others. Angela's experience of God in creation, in the world around her, is not something that is of her *doing*, but instead something about her *being*.

JOHN DUNS SCOTUS: PRAYING WITH THE SUBTLE DOCTOR[73]

For many, to read and study the work of John Duns Scotus (c. 1265–1308) can be a burdensome endeavor. Scotus, though he died young in his early forties, left behind a significant body of influential work that is admittedly dense and technical. Yet, those who are interested in exploring the Franciscan approach to prayer in its fullest detail must endure the difficulties of his writing. As a Franciscan friar, Scotus is an inheritor of and a contributor to a rich and dynamic spiritual tradition beginning with the lived example of Francis of Assisi. So often, as philosopher Mary Beth Ingham reminds us, Scotus is seen as a participant and leader in the equally rich Franciscan intellectual tradition, without due regard for his role in the spiritual life of the same community.[74]

Love is the foundational lens through which Scotus views his relationship to God, to others and to creation.[75] But *love* is an amorphous term. The confusion surrounding its meaning is complicated further by the English language's lack of specificity and our unfortunate tendency to overuse the word. When used in its proper context, *love* is perhaps one of the most powerful words in the English lexicon. Its authentic use connotes sacrifice, care, concern, selflessness, affection, self-gift, passion, tenderness, consideration for, loyalty, respect, attraction, fidelity, and other feelings or experiences that transcend language all together. This powerful word is at the core of Scotus's worldview. His entire system evolves from and revolves around love.

In his *Tractatus De Primo Principio* ("Treatise On God as First Principle"), Scotus begins with a prayer,

O Lord our God, true teacher that you are, when Moses your servant asked you for your name that he might proclaim it to the children of Israel, you, knowing what the mind of mortals could grasp of you, replied: 'I am who am,' thus disclosing your blessed name. *You are truly what it means to be, you are the whole of what it means to exist.* This, if it be possible for me, I should like to know by way of demonstration. Help me then, O Lord, as I investigate how much our natural reason can learn about that true being which you are if we begin with the being which you have predicated of yourself.[76]

This text presents Scotus as someone beyond simply an inquiring mind. He shows himself to be a thinker that is deeply connected to his subject—God—in a personal relationship. He connects his proceeding endeavor with the source of its origin. And he acknowledges that God is the definition of what it means to be, and it is only with God's assistance that he might come to understand anything correctly. The late Scotist scholar Allan Wolter, in his commentary on this text, tells us that this prayer, while repugnant to modern philosophers as being superfluous to the task at hand, was extracted from the original text and showcased in a condensed form in a collection of ascetical writings devoid of the philosophical argumentation.[77] At some time, the prayers of Scotus were considered to be of value enough to be rewritten.[78]

Clearly a man whose scholarly work began with prayer and centered on prayer as a way of life, Scotus's theological contributions also shed light on a Franciscan perspective of what it means to talk about God and what it means to talk about us. And the thread that knits both of these themes together is Scotus's maintenance of the absolute primacy of love.

Concerning God, we see this importance of Scotus's hermeneutic of love surface in his theological reflection on the reason for the Incarnation. Scotus asserts God's unconditional love in Christ, stating that Jesus would have been born regardless of human sinfulness. Even if humanity had never sinned, the Word would still have become flesh. Scotus radically shifts the focus from us to God, from debt to gift, from sin to love. According to this hermeneutic of love, the response we have to the Incarnation is not a debt based in human sin, but an obligation anchored in love.[79] Scotus summarizes this position himself:

Neither is it likely that the highest good in the whole of creation is something that merely chanced to take place, and that only because of some lesser good. Nor is it probable that God predestined Adam to such a good before he predestined Christ. Yet all of this would follow, yes, and even something more absurd. If the predestination of Christ's soul was for the sole purpose of redeeming others, it would follow that in foreordaining Adam to glory, God would have had to foresee him as having fallen into sin before he could have predestined Christ to glory.[80]

There is no doubt that the Incarnation played a significant role in the spirituality of Scotus. One attuned to recognize God's love, Scotus's personal prayer almost certainly involved meditation on the immense generosity and limitless care God has for his own creation. And if the Incarnation serves as the most explicit and concrete sign of God's love while also glorifying humanity through God's physical entry into our world, then the creation of humanity must reflect the love of God in tremendous ways and to unfathomable degrees. Put simply, Scotus believed that God loved each individual aspect of creation—human and nonhuman alike—into existence and celebrates the particular character of that creature before anything shared in common with others.

The technical philosophical term developed to express this is *haecceitas* (literally "this-ness" in Latin). If we look closely at the meaning of *haecceitas*, we see the inherent dignity that is ascribed to humanity—and later to all of creation—that arises from the principle that individuation is the result of God's direct creative work. In his early lecture at Oxford, *De Principio Individuationis* ("The Principle of Individuation"),[81] Scotus rejects a number of previously held theories about the nature of individuation. Ranging from the assertion of Aristotelian causes and quantity to negation and matter, Scotus found these proposals inadequate.[82] It seemed to Scotus that these views were beneath the obvious dignity of God's creative work. Instead, he insisted, individuation is rooted in the very substance of a thing or person and not simply its accidents (shape, color, number, etc.).[83]

Allan Wolter explains the significance of Scotus's development of the notion of *haecceity*:

> [Scotus] makes an important claim, that where rational beings are concerned it is the person rather than the nature that God primarily desired to create. His remark is in answer to an objection that individuals do not pertain to the order of the universe, for order is based on priority and posteriority, and individuals are all on par with one another. Not only do individuals pertain to the order of God's universe, Scotus retorts, but, in communicating "his goodness as something befitting his beauty, in each species" he delights in producing a multiplicity of individuals. "And in those beings which are the highest and most important, it is the individual that is primarily intended by God" (*Ordinatio* II, d. 3, n. 251).[84]

This principle has dramatic implications for our lived experience of community, society, and faith. Scotus argues for the primacy of God's creative intent in the creation of every single person. Therefore, we cannot limit the reading of Genesis 1:31 to suggest that humanity in general was created "very good," but that each and every person was created very good. Wolter goes on to explain that this notion of *haecceity*, when applied to the human person, "would seem to invest each with a unique value as one singularly wanted and loved by God, quite apart from any trait that person shares with others or any contribution he or she might make to society."[85] In other words, it is not what we do, what we have, or how we act that makes us loved by God and worthy of love from others. Rather, it is *who we are*—individually created, willed and loved into being by God—that is the source of our dignity and value.

Though it is not always easy to see, given its delivery amidst technical and nuanced philosophical argumentation, Scotus's spirituality and understanding of prayer follows from and contributes to what began with Francis and Clare of Assisi. The centrality of the Incarnation is the first notable point of continuity, which reminds us of the deeply relational perspective of the Franciscan view of God. Grounding one's activity, that of scholarship or praxis, with an awareness of the inherent dignity and value of all individuals and creation further reflects Francis's own attitudinal conversion and disposition toward solidarity in prayer. The Scotist notion of *haecceitas* gives the relational sense of Franciscan "lived prayer" a theological and philosophical foundation.

Scotus has much to teach us today about living in a grace-filled world. Retrieval of his spiritual insight shaped by Franciscan influence can help guide us in our contemporary world. While some will insist that the fear, greed, and violence of today has replaced the goodness in our world, Scotus's work is founded on and supported by faith and hope that transcends the challenges of the present time to recall the source of our being—God's love. As we pause to reflect and pray, may we look to Scotus's prayerful philosophical insight to find God's presence in our world and to work for the well-being of our brothers and sisters. Such prayer should lead us from our place of contemplation back into the world with a response of loving action.

CONCLUSION

While the collective Christian imagination tends to associate "Franciscan prayer" or "Franciscan spirituality" with Francis of Assisi, and understandably so, there are many essential voices that contribute to the rich harmony of prayerful diversity within the tradition. Following Francis, it was Clare of Assisi, Bonaventure, Angela of Foligno, and John Duns Scotus, among others, who were inspired by what began as one man's individual quest to live the Gospel more authentically and became a radical example of profound Gospel living. Though expressed in different ways, the manifold vision of Franciscan prayer nevertheless holds evangelical poverty, the Incarnation, and the importance of relationship at its center. The challenge of discussing Franciscan prayer is its complexity. And yet, the many distinctive voices of the tradition provide a seemingly endless collection of resources for contemporary women and men interested exploring Christian spirituality and prayer in a deeper way. The tradition of Franciscan prayer lives on today in those communities of women and men who have professed to follow closely the lived example of Francis and Clare as religious sisters, friars, and laypeople. Their own experiences of Gospel living in our own time adds yet another layer to the living heritage of what we call Franciscan prayer, providing contributions to a living tradition that continues to grow in as inclusive and diverse a manner as it once began centuries ago.

1. Timothy J. Johnson, introduction to *Franciscans at Prayer*, ed. Timothy J. Johnson (Leiden: Brill, 2007), vii.

2. As indicated above, this list is hardly exhaustive. There are many Franciscan women and men, both those contemporaneous with those selected here as well as those who come later in history, who could also be added to this list. Yet, for the purposes of brevity and comprehensiveness, I have limited the list to these five foundational figures according to their importance, originality, and representation of Franciscan diversity in voice.

3. Recently, two excellent biographies were published: Augustine Thompson, *Francis of Assisi: A New Biography* (Ithaca, NY: Cornell University Press, 2011); and André Vauchez, *Francis of Assisi: The Life and Afterlife of a Medieval Saint*, trans. Michael Cusato (New Haven, CT: Yale University Press, 2012).

4. Thomas of Celano, "The Life of Saint Francis," book 1, 3:6, in *Saint Francis of Assisi, Omnibus of Sources*, ed. Marion A. Habig, 2 vols. (Cincinnati: Franciscan Media, 2008), 1:233. All references to the early sources are from this translation unless otherwise noted. Future page references will include volume number and page number cited parenthetically. When necessary, this translation has been modified by the author for accuracy according to the latest critical edition, which is *Francesco D'Assisi: Scritti*, ed. Carlo Paolazzi (Rome: Collegio San Bonaventura, 2009).

5. For more on this, see Jacques Dalarun, *Francis of Assisi and Power* (St. Bonaventure, NY: Franciscan Institute, 2007).

6. For more on this theme of ongoing conversion and the stages of moving toward solidarity in Francis's life, see Daniel P. Horan, "Profit or Prophet? A Franciscan Challenge to Millennials in Higher Education," *The AFCU Journal* 8 (2011): 59–73.

7. Francis of Assisi, "Testament" (1:67).

8. Michael Cusato, "The Renunciation of Power as a Foundational Theme in Early Franciscan History," in *The Early Franciscan Movement (1205–1239): History, Sources, and Hermeneutics* (Spoleto, Italy: Centro Italiano di Studi Sull'alto Medioevo, 2009), 37. Also, see Michael Cusato, *La renunciation au pouvoir chez les Frères Mineurs au 13e siècle*, PhD dissertation (Université de Paris IV–Sorbonne, 1991).

9. Francis of Assisi, "Testament" (1:68).

10. Regis J. Armstrong and Ingrid J. Peterson, *The Franciscan Tradition* (Collegeville, MN: Liturgical, 2010), xvii.

11. See the opening of the *Regula bullata* (1:57).

12. Francis of Assisi, *Regula bullata*, chap. 6 (1:61); emphasis added.

13. Francis of Assisi, "A Letter to the Entire Order" (1:105–106); adapted by author.

14. "The Assisi Compilation," no. 14, in *Francis of Assisi: Early Documents*, ed. Regis J. Armstrong, J. A. Wayne Hellmann, and William J. Short, vol. 2 (New York: New City, 2000), 130.

15. Thomas of Celano, "The Life of Saint Francis," book 1, 30:84 (1:299).

16. Norbert Nguyên-Van-Khanh, *The Teacher of His Heart: Jesus Christ in the Thought and Writings of St. Francis* (St. Bonaventure, NY: Franciscan Institute 1994), 109–110. Also, see Daniel P. Horan, "Revisiting the Incarnation: What Is (and Is Not) the 'Franciscan Approach to Christ,'" in *Francis of Assisi and the Future of Faith: Exploring Franciscan Spirituality and Theology in the Modern World* (Phoenix: Tau, 2012), 115–130.

17. Francis of Assisi, *Regula non bullata*, chap. 23 (1:50).

18. Michael W. Blastic, "Prayer in the Writings of Francis of Assisi and the Early Brothers," in *Franciscans at Prayer*, 3.

19. For a good, detailed commentary on this chapter and the whole *Regula bullata*, see William J. Short, "The Rules of the Lesser Brothers," in *The Writings of Francis of Assisi: Rules, Testament, and Admonitions*, ed. Michael W. Blastic, Jay M. Hammond, and J. A. Wayne Hellmann (St. Bonaventure, NY: Franciscan Institute, 2011), especially 161–204.

20. Francis of Assisi, *Regula bullata*, chap. 5 (1:61); emphasis added. This is also seen in the *Regula non bullata*.

21. Francis of Assisi, "A Letter to Brother Anthony of Padua," in *Francis of Assisi: Early Documents*, ed. Regis J. Armstrong, J. A. Wayne Hellmann, and William J. Short, vol. 1 (New York: New City, 1999), 107.

22. Francis of Assisi, "Letter to All the Faithful" (1:94).

23. Francis of Assisi, "The Prayer before the Crucifix," in *Francis of Assisi: Early Documents*, vol. 1, 40.

24. Blastic, 5.

25. Blastic, 9.

26. See André Cirino and Josef Raischl, eds., *Franciscan Solitude* (St. Bonaventure, NY: Franciscan Institute, 1995).

27. Francis of Assisi, "Religious Life in Hermitages" (1:72–73); adapted.

28. See Jacques Dalarun, *Francis of Assisi and the Feminine* (St. Bonaventure, NY: Franciscan Institute, 2006), especially 56–58.

29. See Grado G. Merlo, "Eremitismo nel francescanesimo medievale," in *Eremitismo nel Francescanesimo Medievale* (Perugia, Italy: Universitá degli Sudi di Perugia, 1991), 27–50.

30. Francis of Assisi, "Letter to the Entire Order" (1:107); adapted.

31. See Daniel P. Horan, *Dating God: Live and Love in the Way of St. Francis* (Cincinnati: Franciscan Media, 2012), 82–83.

32. Bonaventure, *The Major Legend of Saint Francis*, 11:1, in in *Francis of Assisi: Early Documents*, vol. 2, 612.

33. This was recently published in a form more accessible to a general audience for prayer and study. See Francis of Assisi, *The Geste of the Great King: Office of the Passion of Francis of Assisi*, ed. Laurent Gallant and André Cirino (St. Bonaventure, NY: Franciscan Institute, 2001).

34. For example, see Augustine, "The Literal Meaning of Genesis," 5.16.34, in *On Genesis*, trans. Edmund Hill (New York: New City, 2002), 293; and Augustine, *Confessions*, 3.6.11, trans. Henry Chadwick (New York: Oxford University Press, 1991), 43.

35. See Thomas of Celano, "The Second Life of Francis of Assisi," chap. 61, no. 95 (1:440): "When he prayed in the woods and in solitary places, he would fill the woods with signs, water the places with his tears, strike his breast with his hand; and discovering there a kind of secret hiding place, he would often speak with his Lord with words. There he would give answer to his judge; there he would offer his petitions to his father; there he would talk to his friend; there he would rejoice with the bridegroom. Indeed, that *he might make his whole being a holocaust in many ways,* he would set before his eyes in many ways him who is simple to the greatest degree. Often, without moving his lips, he would mediate within himself and drawing external things within himself, he would lift his spirit to higher things. *All his attention and affection he directed with his whole being to the one thing which he was asking of the Lord, not so much praying as becoming himself a prayer"* (emphasis added). Also, see Thomas of Celano, "The First Life of Francis of Assisi," chap. 4, no. 97 (1:311).

36. Blastic, 13.

37. There have been several important studies about Clare and the early Poor Clare Sisters published in recent years. For example, see Margaret Carney, *The First Franciscan Women: Clare of Assisi and Her Form of Life* (Quincy, IL: Franciscan Press, 1993); Maria Pia Alberzoni, *Clare of Assisi and the Poor Sisters in the Thirteenth Century* (St. Bonaventure, NY: Franciscan Institute, 2004); Joan Mueller, *The Privilege of Poverty: Clare of Assisi, Agnes of Prague, and the Struggle for the Franciscan Rule for Women* (University Park, PA: Penn State Press, 2006); and Lezlie S. Knox, *Creating Clare of Assisi: Female Franciscan Identities in Later Medieval Italy* (Leiden: Brill, 2008).

38. William J. Short, *Poverty and Joy: The Franciscan Tradition* (Maryknoll, NY: Orbis, 1999), 32.

39. Short, 33.

40. Ilia Delio, "Clare of Assisi and The Mysticism of Motherhood," in *Franciscans at Prayer,* 40.

41. Clare of Assisi, "The First Letter to Agnes of Prague," v. 15–21, in *Clare of Assisi: Early Documents,* ed. Regis J. Armstrong (New York: New City, 2006), 45. Unless otherwise noted, all references to Clare's writings come from this edition. Future references will be cited as *CA:ED* followed by page number.

42. For more on this subject, see Ingrid Peterson, "Clare of Assisi's Letters to Agnes of Prague: Testaments of Fidelity," in *The Writings of Clare of Assisi: Letters, Form of Life, Testament, and Blessing,* ed. Michael W. Blastic, Jay M. Hammond, and J. A. Wayne Hellmann (St. Bonaventure, NY: Franciscan Institute, 2011), 43–44.

43. Clare of Assisi, "The Second Letter to Agnes of Prague," v. 7, in *CA:ED,* 47.

44. Clare of Assisi, "The Second Letter to Agnes of Prague," v. 11–14, in *CA:ED,* 48.

45. Timothy J. Johnson, "Visual Imagery and Contemplation in Clare of Assisi's 'Letters to Agnes of Prague,'" *Mystics Quarterly* 19 (December 1993): 163.

46. Delio, "Clare of Assisi and The Mysticism of Motherhood," 46.

47. Regis J. Armstrong, introduction to *CA:ED,* 20.

48. Clare of Assisi, "The Second Letter to Agnes of Prague," v. 18–20, in *CA:ED,* 49.

49. Clare of Assisi, "The Fourth Letter to Agnes of Prague," v. 15–18, in *CA:ED,* 55.

50. Armstrong, 21.

51. Johnson, "Visual Imagery and Contemplation," 166.

52. Johnson, "Visual Imagery and Contemplation," 167.

53. Johnson, "Visual Imagery and Contemplation," 168.

54. Peterson, 49.

55. Clare of Assisi, "The Fourth Letter to Agnes of Prague," v. 33, in *CA:ED,* 57.

56. Thanks to a somewhat recent and accessible translation of these titles, all contained in one volume, a broader audience can approach Bonaventure's texts. See Ewert Cousins, ed., *Bonaventure: The Soul's Journey into God, The Tree of Life, and The Life of St. Francis* (New York: Paulist, 1978).

57. See Charles Carpenter, *Theology as the Road to Holiness in St. Bonaventure* (New York: Paulist, 1999); and Gregory LaNave, *Through Holiness to Wisdom: The Nature of Theology according to St. Bonaventure* (Rome: Instituto Storico dei Cappuccini, 2005).

58. Zachary Hayes, *Bonaventure: Mystical Writings* (Phoneix: Tau, 1999), 19.

59. Zachary Hayes, *Bonaventure*, 19.

60. For another, excellent and alternative outline of Bonaventure's approach to prayer, see Timothy J. Johnson, *The Soul in Ascent: Bonaventure on Poverty, Prayer, and Union with God* (Quincy, IL: Franciscan Press, 2000), 97–131.

61. See Zachary Hayes, *The Hidden Center: Spirituality and Speculative Christology in St. Bonaventure* (St. Bonaventure, NY: Franciscan Institute, 1992); and Ilia Delio, *Crucified Love: Bonaventure's Mysticism of the Crucified Christ* (Quincy, IL: Franciscan Press, 1998).

62. See Ilia Delio, *The Humility of God: A Franciscan Perspective* (Cincinnati: Franciscan Media, 2005).

63. Ilia Delio, *Simply Bonaventure: An Introduction to His Life, Thought, and Writings* (New York: New City, 2001), 130.

64. Zachary Hayes, *Bonaventure*, 59.

65. Despite the "finding God in all things" expression's popularity associated with the Society of Jesus and Ignatius Loyola, this concept can be traced through the Ignatian tradition back to at least Bonaventure and the Franciscan tradition. See Ewert Cousins, "Franciscan Roots of Ignatian Meditation," in *Ignatian Spirituality in a Secular Age*, ed. George P. Schner (Waterloo, Ontario: Wilfred Laurier University Press, 1984), 53–63.

66. Vatican Radio, "Pope Declares New Saint, Advances Seven Causes," October 10, 2013. http://www.news.va/en/news/pope-declares-new-saint-advances-seven-causes.

67. See Short, 46; and Darleen Pryds, *Women of the Streets: Early Franciscan Women and their Mendicant Vocation* (St. Bonaventure, NY: Franciscan Institute, 2010), 34–36.

68. Pryds, 35.

69. For a sampling of recent secondary literature on Angela's contributions to prayer and Franciscan spirituality, see Diane V. Tomkinson, "Angela of Foligno's Spiral Pattern of Prayer," in *Franciscans at Prayer*, 195–220; and Katherine Wrisley Shelby, "A Performative Christ and the Performing Penitent: Exploring the Possibility of a Feminine Franciscan Christology in Angela of Foligno's *Liber*," *Cult/ure: The Graduate Journal of Harvard Divinity School* 8 (Fall 2012). What follows in this section is based on research originally presented in Daniel P. Horan, *Dating God: Live and Love in the Way of St. Francis* (Cincinnati: Franciscan Media, 2012).

70. This is particularly timely given the substantive nod to the Franciscan intellectual and spiritual tradition by Pope Francis in his encyclical letter *Laudato Si* ("On Care of Our Common Home"). While Bonaventure is cited extensively and Angela makes no direct appearance, I believe Angela's "creation mysticism" as I call it helps develop Bonaventure's theological contributions for a robust understanding of the Franciscan relationship between prayer and creation, especially today.

71. Angela of Foligno, "The *Memorial*: The Stages of Angela's Inner Journey," in *Angela of Foligno: Complete Works*, ed. Paul Lachance (New York: Paulist, 1993), 169–170.

72. Richard McBrien, *Catholicism*, new edition (San Francisco: HarperCollins, 1994), 1052.

73. This section is based on a condensed presentation of material published earlier and in more detail. See Daniel P. Horan, *Francis of Assisi and the Future of Faith: Exploring Franciscan Spirituality and Theology in the Modern World* (Phoenix: Tau, 2012), 159–173.

74. See Mary Beth Ingham, "*Fides Quaerens Intellectum*: John Duns Scotus, Philosophy and Prayer," in *Franciscans at Prayer*, 167–191.

75. See Daniel P. Horan, "Light and Love: Robert Grosseteste and John Duns Scotus on the How and Why of Creation," *The Cord*, 57 (2007): 252–253.

76. John Duns Scotus, *Tractatus De Primo Principio* 1.2, in *John Duns Scotus: A Treatise on God as First Principle*, trans. Allan Wolter (Chicago: Franciscan Herald, 1982), 2; emphasis added.

77. Allan Wolter, "Commentary on the *De Primo Principio* of Duns Scotus," in *John Duns Scotus: A Treatise on God as First Principle*, ed. Allan Wolter (Chicago: Franciscan Herald, 1982), 160–161.

78. Wolter makes reference to the Berlin manuscript (Codex B) and the proximity of the condensed form of Scotus's *De Primo Principio*, minus the philosophical argumentation, to Bonaventure's *Itinerarium Mentis in Deum*. The compiler(s) of the manuscript obviously found Scotus's prayers of great spiritual value to be included alongside Bonaventure's most acclaimed spiritual work.

79. Mary Beth Ingham, "Duns Scotus, Divine Delight and Franciscan Evangelical Life," *Franciscan Studies* 64 (2006): 343.

80. John Duns Scotus, *Ordinatio* III, dist. 7, q. 3, trans. Allan Wolter, "John Duns Scotus on the Primacy and Personality of Christ," in *Franciscan Christology*, ed. Damian McElrath (St. Bonaventure, NY: Franciscan Institute, 1994), 148–151.

81. The English translation is found in Allan Wolter, *John Duns Scotus: Early Oxford Lecture on Individuation* (St. Bonaventure, NY: Franciscan Institute, 2005).

82. Kenan Osborne, "Incarnation, Individuality and Diversity: How does Christ reveal the unique value of each person and thing?" *The Cord*, 45 (1995): 25.

83. Osborne, "Incarnation, Individuality and Diversity," 25.

84. Wolter, *John Duns Scotus*, xxi.

85. Wolter, *John Duns Scotus*, xxi.

CHAPTER 14

Prayer in the Carmelite Tradition

~ John Welch, OCarm. ~

Carmelites have served the Church in numerous ministries and in diverse lifestyles, but the one constant preoccupation over the centuries has been attentiveness to God in prayer. In April 2009, Pope Benedict XVI declared that "Carmel teaches the Church how to pray."

The Carmelite tradition began around 1200 with a small group of men, mostly from the West, who traveled to the Holy Land as pilgrims. They formed a community of hermits taking up residence in the *wadi-ain-es-Siah*, a valley on the slopes of Mount Carmel. The mountain is the ancestral home of the Carmelites.

THE RULE OF CARMEL (1206–1214)

The Rule of Carmel is the first document produced by the original Carmelites living in the *wadi-ain-es-Siah*. Albert, the patriarch of Jerusalem, is honored as the law-giver, but the men in the valley certainly drew up their pattern of living for Albert's review and final editing. The Rule of Carmel is more exhortatory than precisely prescriptive. Laced with Scripture, it provided a life-structure for these hermits and helped the Carmelites to live in a way whereby God could find them. In following the Rule's light-handed guidance, the Carmelite becomes more available to God.

The Rule provides conditions for prayer. Each Carmelite is to have a "cell," staying in or near the cell "meditating on the law of the Lord day and night." Most likely these early Carmelites had memorized passages of Scripture and would at times recite them aloud in the cell and its environs. This ruminating on Scripture is known as *lectio divina*, a way of seeking to know God's guidance through the sacred Word. This pondering of the Word is a way of encountering God in the Bible.

The Rule requires silence at night, but also recommends quiet in the valley during the day. The Carmelite is to interiorize the silence and become an expectancy, keeping vigil for the approach of the Lord. The Rule forbids exchanging cells. In other words, the Carmelite is encouraged to be unblinking in his reflection and not run away from himself.

The Carmelite tradition from the very beginning included celebration of the Eucharist. The community gathered each morning in an oratory in the center of the cells. Together they celebrated the Paschal Mystery, the life, death, and resurrection of the Lord, which would be their pattern of living. And they eventually incorporated the Divine Office. Someone reading the Rule today might easily assume that the community is living in quiet solitude keeping vigil for the first faint rays of dawn, the Lord on whose land they lived. Later reforms of Carmel required a rereading of this Rule and a creative following of its blueprint, giving the tradition ever new expressions.

THE LAND OF CARMEL

Mount Carmel was a place of attentiveness to the Lord, whether in the cell, or at Eucharist, in the refectory or in fraternal gatherings. The original site on the mountain is now in ruins. But for the Carmelite, the mountain is carried in memory and imagination. It is part of a geography of soul, an interior landscape for the Carmelite's encounter with the Lord. Carmelites thus speak of "entering Carmel."

This Carmelite paracosm, this landscape of the imagination, is populated by the saints of Carmel, as well as the twin icons of Elijah the prophet who fought the prophets of Baal on Mount Carmel, and Mary, Mother of the Lord, to whom the Carmelites dedicated their first chapel in the valley. The blesseds and saints inhabiting the land of Carmel also include Andrew Corsini, Peter Thomas, Mary Magdalene de' Pazzi, Teresa of Ávila, John of the Cross, John of St. Samson, Lawrence of the Resurrection, Thérèse of Lisieux, Zelie and Louis Martin, Elizabeth of the Trinity, Titus Brandsma, and Edith Stein. These men and women represent both the Carmelite Order and its sixteenth century reform, the Discalced Carmelites.

EARLY DOCUMENTS

THE FLAMING ARROW (C. 1270)

Within the first century of their existence as an order, the Carmelites all migrated to Europe. They joined the other mendicant orders, living less in isolated solitude and more in contact with the populations in the newly emerging cities. A retired general of the order, Nicholas the Frenchman, in a passionate letter, *Ignea Sagitta* (*Flaming Arrow*) bemoaned the changes.

Nicholas maintained that the Carmelites, nurtured in part with a desert spirituality, would not be equal to spiritual combat in the cities. He urged a retreat back to the slopes of Mount Carmel, if not literally, then wherever those original conditions could be reestablished. In the city, the separate cells had given way to contiguous rooms in a single building. In his letter to the order, Nicholas asked, "When do you ponder God's Law and watch at your prayers?... Cells are of no use to those whose thoughts and pastimes are vain. They are for those who make prayer their business."

He reminisced about life on the mountain: "Every creature we see or hear in the desert gives us friendly refreshment and comfort; indeed, for all their silence they tell forth wonders, and move the interior man to give praise to the Creator—so much more wonderful than themselves.... But in the city..." A disappointed Nicholas resigned as general of the order in 1271.

THE BOOK OF THE INSTITUTION OF THE FIRST MONKS (C. 1380)

A Carmelite provincial from Catalonia, Philip Ribot, wove various strands of the tradition together to provide a foundational story for Carmel. In particular, Ribot brought together Elijan and Marian traditions that made a more coherent myth for the order.

The *Book of the Institution* presents a twofold goal for Carmel:

> One part we acquire with the help of divine grace, through our efforts and virtuous works. This is to offer God a holy heart, free from all stain of actual sin.... The other part of the goal of this life is granted us as the free gift of God; namely, to taste somewhat in the heart and to experience in the soul, not only after death but even in this mortal life, the intensity of the divine presence and the sweetness of the glory of heaven.

The ascetical ideal, offering to God a pure and holy heart, opens to the mystical ideal, experiencing in mind and heart the presence of God which is pure gift. The *Institution* is considered the second most important document for Carmelite spirituality after the Rule.

PATHWAYS OF PRAYER

The Church has declared three of Carmel's saints Doctors of the Universal Church: St. Teresa of Ávila, St. John of the Cross, and St. Thérèse of Lisieux. These saints were chosen because of their "eminent doctrine." They tell the story of prayer as a journey into an "interior castle," through a "dark night," along a "little way." The following discussions provide a path through the spirituality of each saint.

ST. TERESA OF ÁVILA (1515–1582)[1]

Teresa understood prayer to be conversation with a friend. In *The Book of Her Life*, Teresa defined prayer to be "nothing else than an intimate sharing between friends; it means taking time frequently to be alone with Him who we know loves us" (chap. 8, no. 5). When the Carmelite mystics looked for a story which captured their experience of God, they pointed to the Song of Songs, a story of the Lover and the Beloved.

The purpose of prayer, said Teresa, is conformity with God's will. She did not mean that prayer is a contest of wills, with God's stronger will winning. What the saints report is that in the prayer relationship, their will changed. More and more their will was in accord with God's will. "And now I want what You want," reported Teresa.

In *The Way of Perfection* Teresa identified three foundations for a life of prayer: charity, detachment, and humility. The members of her communities were to be friends with Christ, and friends with one another. Teresa set a high standard: "all must be friends, all must be loved, all must be held dear, all must be helped" (chap. 4, no. 7). Nothing should undermine the spirit of charity in the house. Detachment was not the absence of relationships or possessions, but a freedom of the individual to be able to respond to God. Humility is a bedrock virtue for Teresa. It counters our tendency to be self-centered, setting ourselves apart from others. Humility allows us to admit we are poor and to accept our situation as sinners. But it also helps us acknowledge that we are rich in God's mercy.

For example, Teresa warned about living in the past. She said the only reason to dwell on the past is to learn to tell our story correctly. Our past is not simply a story of our sinfulness, nor is it a story of our achievements and goodness. Our life is always a story of God's mercy, a mercy that can forgive and heal our past, a mercy that gives us strength.

Teresa said she could not think much. She was obviously very intelligent, but she did not think in an orderly, systematic way. Nor, she said, could she imagine in a controlled way. So, she practiced what she called the "prayer of recollection," a prayer which helped quiet and focus her mind.

Initial efforts at prayer were helped by reading a book. Later, simply opening the book assisted her prayer. She said she pictured Jesus alongside her. Or she imagined Jesus within her in one of the scenes of the gospel where he is alone and would not mind her company. She also said she looked at fields, and flowers, and water, and said that she probably looked at water more than anything else in life.

The common thread in all these practices is that each brought about an awareness of God's presence in her life. Awareness of presence was the key. Before we can have conversation with a friend, we have to be aware of our friend's presence. The only terminal problem is to stop praying.

THE INTERIOR CASTLE

At the age of sixty-two, Teresa of Ávila presented a summary of her life of prayer in *The Interior Castle*. She imaged her spiritual journey as the journey from the outside of a crystal, global castle to the center room where the King lived. Outside it was dark, cold, and noisy. The King at the center of the castle invites the soul, the individual, into a deep union. As the soul moves through the castle, the dark gives way to light, the cold to warmth, and the noisy creatures become less distracting.

The journey to the center of the castle moves through seven suites of rooms or seven mansions or seven dwelling places. These are seven stages in the soul's relationship with God. All the rooms on the outer surface of the castle, perhaps a "million" or so, constitute the first dwelling places. The next layer of rooms represents the second dwelling places and so forth, until the soul reaches the center. Teresa said it is like a palmetto with its enfolding leaves.

This work responds to four questions: (1) What is Teresa's basic image for our spiritual journey? (2) What is the problem we encounter on the way? (3) What is the solution proposed by Teresa? (4) What is the goal of the journey?

Teresa's basic image for our spiritual journey pictures a journey from the periphery of our life to its center. In this image God is not somewhere else but God is always already there. St. Augustine prayed, "You were inside, but I was outside. You were with me, but I was not with you." One of the most difficult transitions for Christians is to move from moralism to Christian morality. Moralism holds that if I am good, I am rewarded; if I am bad, I am punished. It is the morality of a child, but then applied to God. I believe that if I am good, I earn God's love. If I sin, God then withdraws love.

Christian morality holds that I am loved before I do anything good or bad. I cannot earn God's love. I cannot win it. I cannot barter for it. I do not have to appease God to be loved. I am loved into life and God continues to love me throughout my life. I cannot turn the love away. I may not believe it, I may turn my back on it, but God does not walk away. God is always already there.

The problem we encounter along the way, said St. Teresa, is that we "lack self-knowledge." She said, "I cannot know you, God, unless I know myself, but I cannot know myself unless I know you." We believe God is mediated through his creation. We are the first part of God's creation we meet. Theologian Karl Rahner once asked if we knew what God says to us in prayer. We know what we say in prayer, but what does God say to us? Rahner's answer was, *we* are what God says to us in prayer. In hearing the word that we are, we begin to hear more clearly the God who speaks us. However, Teresa taught, we cannot know ourselves unless we know God. Only in a relationship with God do we come to see ourselves, and the world, with clarity.

Teresa said she was at sea the first eighteen years of her life in the convent of the Incarnation. When she was with the things of God, she wanted to be with the things of the world. When she was with the things of the world, she wanted to be with the things of God. By the "world," perhaps Teresa meant she was continuing to be involved in the news of Ávila through conversations in the parlor and other means of communication. By "things of God" she meant she was working hard to be seen as an observant religious in the convent.

One day when a statue of the beaten Christ, the *Ecce Homo*, was brought into the convent, Teresa fell to her knees and said she would not get up until she was healed. The encounter with the beaten Lord did heal her. She got up free from her ambivalence and, not long after, began to plan a reform of Carmel. Teresa does not say what exactly was healed, but we may guess what happened from knowing our own needs. Perhaps our deepest question is, are we loved? Are we essentially good? Do we have worth? What is our value? Teresa realized she had been asking society around her, and religious life, to validate her, to give her worth. She had been trying to be a valued member of society, as well as being seen as a very good religious. She sought her worth outside. At this time, Teresa also read about St. Augustine's conversion in his *Confessions*, and she identified with his struggle.

In encountering the beaten Christ, Teresa realized that this suffering was borne out of love for her. She did not have to ask the world around if she were loveable and of worth. She learned that she had immense worth and dignity because she was already loved by God. Her worth came from the God who was at the core of her life.

The solution proposed by Teresa is summarized in her writing, "The door of entry to this castle is prayer and reflection" (I, chap. 1, no. 7). What keeps us on the periphery of life are many preoccupations and concerns. She mentions "pastimes, business affairs, pleasures and worldly buying and selling." In other words, rather than having one center in our life, we have many centers, each calling for our attention. The many concerns, the many centers, fragment us. What frees us from our dissipated and fragmented life outside the castle, on the periphery of our life, is prayer.

In Teresa's castle story, the call is coming from the King at the center. In prayer, it is God who speaks first and initiates the relationship. God called us into life, and continues to call us more deeply into our lives. We, on our part, are essentially *listeners* for God's call. The Rule of Carmel stresses the silence needed to hear God's call. All our words in prayer are an effort to say the one word, which is God's. In this engagement with the mystery at the core of our lives, all other lesser loves are put into order. The many centers keeping us on the margins of our life are now oriented around the one center. Identity and validation now come from the center of our life. Other loves and interests find their proper place in our lives. The invitation from the center of the castle disengages us from the periphery and allows us to continue to journey.

The only terminal problem, in Teresa's estimation, is to stop praying. When we stop praying, we stop listening, and when we stop listening it is very hard to hear the gentle whistle of the shepherd. One theologian summarized Teresa's message: a faithful and perduring attentiveness to our depths and center is the best cooperation we can give to God who is reorienting our life.[2]

The goal of the journey, according to Teresa, is union with God in love. As the soul listens more deeply and responds more generously, the relationship with the mystery at the core of our life deepens. We believe God is always calling us into a fuller humanity, a wider freedom, and a more intimate union. On this journey to the center of one's life, the self is born as God is met. The more Teresa could say "God" in her life, the more she could say "Teresa."

Carmelite understanding of the journey speaks about transformation. In the Rule of Carmel, the Carmelite is obliged to put on the armor of God, or rather to be available so that God can clothe the Carmelite in virtue. And the Constitutions of the Carmelite Order state, "Contemplation is the inner journey of Carmelites, arising out of the free initiative of God who touches and transforms us leading us towards unity in love with him."

The dwelling places in *The Interior Castle* represent stages in prayer. The first dwelling place refers to a person who occasionally stops and prays, perhaps a few times a month. But the basic concerns of one's life take place on the periphery. Teresa is positive about this apparently minimal effort. To have an interior life, she says, to stop and pray, requires courage. The enemies of this interior life are fear and faint-heartedness.

Teresa describes the condition of the person at this time: "Even though it may not be in a bad state it is so involved in worldly things and so absorbed with its possessions, honor, or business affairs, as I have said, that even though as a matter of fact it would want to see and enjoy its beauty, these things do not allow it to, nor does it seem that it can slip free from so many impediments" (I, chap. 2, no. 14).

In the second dwelling place, the one who prays is beginning to have a sense of a personal call and a need to respond to God's communication. At this time, God communicates with the individual through the ordinary experiences of reading books, hearing sermons, meeting good people, experiencing illnesses, undergoing trials, and having moments in prayer. However, Teresa warns, "hearing His voice is a greater trial than not hearing it." She said she had assumed that while she had many problems to deal with, she thought that going "within" in prayer would be like going home. But, she said, she found the problems inside herself much more difficult than the problems outside. She said she went within and, instead of peace, she found she was "at war" with herself. The inner journey forces us to face the unacknowledged life we have been living. Prayer throws light on the false selves and false gods in our life.

In the third dwelling place, Teresa describes the good, adult Christian, the one who prays regularly, is generous with his possessions, has a well-disciplined household, and is viewed by others as someone to be consulted. It is a good situation, the result of a faithful attempt to have an interior life. But it is not the final destination, and the temptation is to conclude that one has arrived. Teresa hints at the problem when she says these lives are well-ordered. And they have such control that there is no danger that they will go to any extremes. The danger here is contentment, self-satisfaction, and a life-structure impervious to change. Teresa's analysis is that individuals in the third dwelling place lack freedom. They have responded generously to God and now have secure patterns in their life.

But Teresa keenly observes that something comes into these lives and begins to undermine their control. They become anxious and sensitive. Teresa comments that they begin to dramatize every little thing. The situation is reminiscent of theologian Karl Rahner's observation that in life "every symphony is unfinished." In every relationship, every possession, every situation, there is an incompleteness. Teresa's analysis is that God continues to call this individual beyond where he or she wants to go. Teresa encourages a letting go, adopting a listening posture, rather than continuing to word one's life in an effort to maintain control. It is time for a more contemplative prayer.

In the fourth dwelling place, Teresa describes a transitional situation. Prayer takes on a different quality. The relationship with God is experienced in a different way. In the early stages of the first three dwelling places, Teresa likens the experience to filling a fountain from a distant source; it requires effort to draw the water and convey it to the fountain. But in the remaining dwelling places, the fountain appears to be over the source of water, and it is filling up from within. Is it God who steps in and out of a life depending upon the individual's response? Or do the two halves of the castle journey express more the pilgrim's growing awareness of God's activity? In the early dwelling places, the individual is much more aware of the effort she is making to establish a life of prayer. In the later dwelling places, the pilgrim is much more sensitive to the graced dimension of the journey. The pilgrim has become more available to God's work.

In describing the fifth dwelling place in her relationship with God, Teresa gives an important instruction. She experienced what she called the "prayer of union," momentary experiences of being stilled by God, usually no more than a half hour.

She was convinced of the authenticity of the experience because it left with her the conviction, "Now not I live, but Christ lives in me." However, in commenting on this experience of union with God, Teresa makes an important distinction: true union with God is a union of wills, to want what God wants. If a life is more and more cooperative with God's reign, God's will, then the journey through the castle is going well, whether or not there are extraordinary experiences to report. She says she knows individuals who are very close to God, and have no special experiences to report.

Teresa's experiences were great graces for her, and confirmed her path. But, she taught, such extraordinary religious experiences are not essential to the journey.

Nor are they ever the goal of the journey. Her companion in the reform, John of the Cross, was even stronger in his comments on extraordinary religious experiences: renounce and reject them all, he advised. If they are truly from God, God will bring about what he wants.

In the rooms of the sixth dwelling place, Teresa lists the difficulties she experienced. Both criticism and praise initially disturbed her. Illness was a constant companion. And perhaps the most difficult experience was that her confessors told her that her experiences in prayer were not from God. In this sixth dwelling place, Teresa gives a lengthy account of her extraordinary religious experiences, such as voices and visions. These are almost completely absent in the seventh dwelling place. Also in the sixth dwelling place, Teresa reports the experience of doubting if she had ever done any good. Had she made the whole thing up? Her doubt and the interior oppression was so great that she could not do anything about it. Her only remedy was to do external acts of charity.

Evelyn Underhill in 1911 called the mystics "pioneers of humanity." They are not an elite group traveling a special road on their pilgrimage of faith. They are traveling the same road with us. They are at the head of the column reporting back the impact of God's love on their humanity. In seeing them, we are seeing our potential.

In the seventh dwelling place, as Teresa describes a soul deeply in love with God, she is describing herself toward the end of her life. She is telling us how things turned out, up to that point, from her pilgrimage through life. And in this description, we see a Teresa who is humble, free, loving, and generous. She knows that life deepens and matures when we give it away. She has work to do. She will expend her energies and give of her giftedness in service of God's kingdom. Neither she nor her sisters joined religious life to serve themselves. The outcome of the life well lived, the purpose of the spiritual marriage, she says, is "Good works! Good works!"

Her energies are focused on the task at hand. "Don't build castles in the air," she told her sisters. It is too easy to dream about possible endeavors and miss what is in front of us and calls for our attention. The goal was never to have a spiritual life or be a saint; the goal was always to do God's will, to live in a way that promotes the reign of God in this world. She and her communities would serve this kingdom through the witness of their life together and their prayer for the world.

St. John of the Cross (1542–1591)[3]

St. John of the Cross said that his experiences of God were ineffable, unwordable. All he could do was stammer in the similes and metaphors of his poetry. His prose commentaries were only one way of understanding what was more completely contained in the poetry.

It was during his imprisonment, the result of his efforts to reform the order, that John of the Cross began to write his major poems. In the dark of his cell he composed the first thirty-one stanzas of *The Spiritual Canticle*, a poem based on the Song of Songs in the Old Testament. After his escape he became prior of El Calvario, and there he wrote the poem *The Dark Night*, and he began a commentary, *The Ascent of Mount Carmel*.

Later, John was elected prior of the monastery in Granada. There, on the hill near the Moorish palace of the Alhambra, John was inspired to complete the final stanzas of *The Spiritual Canticle* and write a commentary on it at the request of Ana de Jesus. He also completed his commentaries on the poem *The Dark Night*. These two commentaries, *The Ascent of Mount Carmel* and *The Dark Night*, discuss the active and passive dimensions of the dark night. It was during this time, too, that he wrote *The Living Flame of Love* and its commentary at the request of a friend and benefactress, Ana de Peñalosa.

John used the best psychology of his day to describe the process of divinization. It was an Aristotelian faculty psychology which understood the soul (person) to have certain powers or faculties. The faculties were in two groups, sensory and spiritual. The sensory, or lower, more exterior faculties are touch, taste, sight, smell, and hearing. The spiritual, or higher, more interior faculties are intellect, memory, and will. Each faculty seeks its own fulfillment. Together, the faculties express the soul's desire for God, who is the soul's center.

But the faculties confuse God's creation for God and form idols. John uses the image of night to write about the purification of the faculties. The spiritual journey is like a journey through the night. The beginning, the healing of the sensory faculties, is like twilight. The middle, the healing of the spiritual faculties, is like midnight. And the end, union with God is like dawn, which still partakes of the night. All of our faith journey is a night, with occasional sightings.

When our saints looked for a story which captured their experience of God, they often referred to the Song of Songs of the Hebrew Bible. This ancient love story of the lover seeking the beloved provided a narrative which gave expression to the love story being lived by the saints. John's poem, *The Spiritual Canticle*, uses the story of the lover and the beloved from the Song of Songs.

> Where have you hidden, Beloved,
> And left me moaning?
> You fled like the stag
> After wounding me;

I went out calling you,

But you were gone. (stanza 1)

John of the Cross says that God is the first contemplative. God's gaze on us makes us irresistibly attractive to him. So it is not we who first loved God, but God who first loved us. We wake up in the middle of a love story. We did not begin it. Someone has wounded our heart with love, and we ache for fulfillment. We do not know who wounded our heart, but we seek the one who did it and ask that one to complete this love story.

But the desires of the heart form attachments, relationships, with God's creation which ask too much of that creation. The heart, restlessly seeking God, settles down with other gods, asking them to be the fulfillment of its deepest desires. The heart takes a good in God's creation and asks it to be a god. The heart asks something created to be uncreated, to be the fulfillment which only God can be. The issue is not being *related* to something or someone. We have to be related to our world and the people in it. An *attachment* is an inordinate relationship. It ties the heart to an insubstantial food for its deepest hungers. The heart is now no longer free to follow its desires; the heart is enslaved.

The heart cannot form attachments without a penalty. In John's analysis, when the heart gives itself to a false god, two deaths begin to occur. Whatever or whomever the heart is asking to be, its god cannot bear the expectation. The heart begins to hurt the very thing or person it has loved inordinately. Its expectations begin to crush the idol. And, because we cannot grow past our god, the individual begins to die. I can find some nourishment from my idol for the hungers of the heart; I can grow up to my god. But, because the idol is not sufficient food for the hungers of the heart, the person no longer grows. And the desires, which only God can fulfill, emerge again and undermine an apparently stable situation. An attachment is destructive to the idol, shrinks the self to the size of its god, and marginalizes others.

In *Ascent of Mount Carmel* (bk. 1, chap. 13) John offers counsels for freeing the heart from its attachments. He refers to the efforts as the "active night." And he claims if these counsels are put into practice, they will be an effective remedy. Among the suggested remedies are:

1. Imitate Christ by bringing your life into conformity with his. This counsel is not too jarring because we are used to hearing it. But, the implication is challenging.

2. Renounce and remain empty of any sensory satisfaction that is not for the honor and glory of God. At first, this counsel seems psychologically unhealthy. But, when the senses are functioning according to their created purpose, then they do give honor and glory to God.

3. Endeavor to be inclined always, not to the easiest, but to the most difficult, not to the most delightful, but to the most distasteful. John seems to suspect we are *inclined* the other way; we are inclined to the easiest and the most restful. He is probably correct. But often, the loving way is a way that costs. John seems to be saying, "Don't immediately reject the path that brings suffering; it may be the way to life."

4. Act, speak, and think with contempt for yourself. John is not encouraging self-hatred. He is recommending an attitude which counters egocentrism and self-aggrandizement. The purpose is to have a proper perspective on oneself and to make space for God.

5. To reach satisfaction in all, desire satisfaction in nothing; to come to possess all, desire the possession of nothing. Notice that John agrees that we are meant to be fully satisfied, to possess all. In order to have this happen, we cannot ask anything to be our all except the One who is no thing (*nada*). On the stylized mountain John drew for Carmelite nuns, there are three paths. Two of the paths, those of material possessions and spiritual practices, do not reach the top. Only the path of the *nadas* reaches the top where God is *nada y todo*. John is not recommending a total renunciation of material and spiritual possessions. He is simply saying, don't ask any of them to be god, and then they can be used appropriately.

After recommending these counsels as an effective way of detaching from our idols, John says that the attraction of idols is too strong to be overcome by asceticism and willpower alone (*Ascent*, bk. 1, chap. 14). The heart cannot tear itself away from an idol which gives some nourishment, and go into an affective vacuum. The heart has to have someplace to go. It is only when God enters a life and kindles a deeper, stronger love that the soul can let go of the lesser loves. In *The Dark Night* (bk. 1, chap. 2–7), John describes how this deeper love may be enkindled in an experience of God which is dark to us. But first, he further explains the necessity of this night by analyzing the deeper faults of a person through the prism of the seven capital sins.

First, is pride. Beginners can become vain about their spiritual life. They become competitive with others and want to be acknowledged as holy. They want spiritual directors to agree with them and congratulate them. They downplay their faults. But if they become aware of faults, they are sad because they are not a saint. John observes that "their motive is personal peace rather than God."

Second is avarice. These individuals seek more consolation through religious reading, spiritual discussions and devotional objects. "Many never have enough of hearing counsels, or of learning spiritual maxims, or of keeping them and reading books about them." John is critical when individuals focus too much on the beauty or workmanship of a devotional object. Some individuals find security in the mere possession of an object. John relates this incident: "I knew a person who for more than ten years profited by a cross roughly made out of a blessed palm and held together by a pin twisted around it. He carried it about and never would part with it until I took it from him." John urges an interior poverty which frees the heart from its possessiveness.

Third, there is what is called "spiritual lust." The lust itself is not spiritual, but accompanies spiritual activities. John writes about impure feelings which accompany prayers or the reception of sacraments. The spiritual and sensory parts of the person form a whole and resonate with one another. The very fear of such thinking may stir up impure thoughts. The thoughts may involve people who have been helpful to the soul. John worries that the fear of such thoughts may cause someone to abandon prayer. Here, John offers a guideline for friendships that may begin in lust but then become spiritual: when the love of God increases as a result of affection for another person, this friendship is good and spiritual. A person loving another with an inordinate love will experience a coldness in the love for God.

Fourth, comes anger. Individuals may be angry with themselves because of their imperfections. John is critical of people who are impatient and wish to become "saints in a day." He does not encourage the other extreme either: "Some, however, are so patient about their desire for advancement that God would prefer to see them a little less so." These individuals may also be quite critical of others whose behavior is sinful. They act righteously, "setting themselves up as lords of virtue."

Fifth is spiritual gluttony. These people may impose extreme penances upon themselves, even against others' advice. They are spiritually proud and do only what they want to do. John's focus is not on the possession of devotional objects or on devotional practice but on the individual's relationship to them. The challenge is to go about one's spiritual life with a heart free to be submissive to God.

Sixth and seventh are envy and sloth, which can occur when others are praised for their goodness. A person can be sad or annoyed when others seem to be farther down the road of holiness. A truly "holy envy" would rejoice at the goodness of others. At times souls give up prayer because of a lack of satisfaction. John says they have substituted their own will for God's. What is not their will, is not God's will either. "They measure God by themselves and not themselves by God."

In reviewing the seven capital sins in their more subtle form, John is pointing to the shadow side of the good person, a side unknown to, or at least not admitted by, the person. True detachment, then, requires a "passive night," an activity of God drawing us beyond our attachments. John testifies that there is nothing in the night experience that is negative. The night is a positive experience of God's love freeing our hearts. It is initially experienced by us as negative because of our condition. And because this experience of God's love can be confusing and mistaken for other issues, John gives three signs for when God is coming into a life to liberate the heart from its attachments (*Dark Night*, bk. l, chap. 9):

1. No satisfaction or consolation from the things of God, nor from creatures either. It would be one thing if religion were no longer of interest and something else in life is taking on great meaning and passion. But that is not the case here. One's whole life is being wrung out.

2. A wish for the former sense of well-being, but an awareness of a distaste for the things of God and a feeling of not serving God but turning back. If a person did not care about what was happening, that would not be this sign. Here, a person still cares and wishes to have his former sense of well-being restored, but he admits he cannot make it happen. This sign indicates a person may blame himself for the situation. Has he been indifferent? Has he been lax? So built into the experience is the suspicion that it is not a positive experience, such as the dark night, but is the outcome of a tepid spirituality.

3. A powerlessness to meditate or use the imagination as before. John understands meditation as discursive analysis and synthesis of ideas, such that one can no longer think one's way through the problem. The normal way of analyzing a problem and deducing a solution does not work now. One is literally not able to "word" one's life as before.

Because a person experiences a loss of control in the dark night, the temptation is to restore control by redoubling efforts. John says that would be like finding something and then looking for it again. This outcome of a dark night is the right outcome.

John recommends staying with the experience. In other words, unable to understand what is happening, and also unable then to solve the problem, John encourages the individual to accept the situation. Rather than wording and controlling one's life, it is time for listening and surrendering one's life in trust. As far as possible, John says, have a "loving attentiveness" in the night for the approach of God. He recommends entering the night with patience, trust, and perseverance. The work of the night may take a while. John says God knows how much light and how much dark a person needs. But the person needs to trust that this apparently negative experience is actually a loving activity of God meant to free our hearts.

An experience in one's life, such as an illness, may contribute to the experience of the dark night. When John recommends entering the night with trust, he is not advising an individual to be passive in the face of something that may have triggered the night. In other words, remain in the night in trust, but at the same time, seek treatment for health issues. John maintains that the night is a spiritual condition not fundamentally a psychological problem. However, the night could be accompanied by some "melancholia."

OUTCOMES OF THE DARK NIGHT

John lists three outcomes of the dark night experience. They are experienced in our three fundamental relationships: with ourselves, God, and others. First, the experience of the night exposes the "lowliness and misery" of the individual, "which was not apparent in the time of its prosperity." The subtle seven capital sins are revealed. The shadow side of the soul becomes apparent.

Second, the night also produces a reverence in the individual. The presumption that was the condition of the soul before the night now has turned to reverence. We are immersed in mystery and need to proceed with faith. Life's journey is over sacred ground.

Third, John said that before the night, he had judged his brothers and sisters and was negative about them. As a result of the night and the experience of seeing his own brokenness, he now esteems his brothers and sisters, believing they are better than he is. In this night, a love is kindled deep in the soul, and it is lured past its attachments. The liberated heart is now free *for* desire. And the love story continues.

NIGHT OF THE SPIRIT

Following the night of the senses in which a person's loves are brought into harmony, John understands that the soul will attempt to live a life of faith, hope, and love. It is the active night of the spirit (*Ascent*, bk. 2, chap. 3). This period of time he understands to be the way of the proficient or the illuminative way.

This night, too, requires a passive experience of God freeing the spiritual faculties of their attachments, their idols. John says that the night of the spirit completes the purgation begun in the night of the senses. The first night is like cutting off a branch; this night of the spirit is like taking up roots. The first night is like removing a new stain; the second night rubs out an old deeply embedded stain. In Jesus's life, the first night is like "The Son of Man has no place to lay his head"; the second night is reminiscent of "My God, why have you forsaken me."

In John's framework, the passive night of the spirit (*Dark Night*, bk. 2) empties the intellect, memory, and will of their content and replaces it with truly theological faith, hope, and love. John understands this night to be an inflow of God into the soul that "contemplatives call infused contemplation or mystical theology." Nothing can be done to alleviate this midnight experience in our spiritual journey. The most difficult part of the experience is the sense that God has rejected the soul, that it is losing God. No doctrine or director can help. "Indeed, this is not the time to speak with God but the time to put one's mouth in the dust," suffering patiently, waiting in hope.

A Carmelite nun once wrote about this condition from her personal experience:

> The process that seeks to free us from false images of ourselves and from our limited ideas of God has periods of particular intensity.... When the action of God usually again through life's circumstances, exposes the self-protecting self-serving motivation that has always lurked behind the best that we have done then this is stripping indeed.... Ultimately we are help-less before this dismantling of our ego.
>
> ...While the night is still blinding us along the darkest stretch of the way, it may be that God no longer answers to any of the names we give him, to our familiar way of relating to him: "and even on the mountain nothing." Here, we can easily interchange "Where have you hidden?" (SC, st. 1) and "Why have you abandoned me?" (Matthew 27:46).
>
> ...Where there is no longer any barrier between my essential self and the essence of God, there is union.... In fact, the union was always there.[4]

This experience led to a freedom in her prayer, and she became conscious of a simple oneness with God and God's creation.

John of the Cross maintains that this difficult experience is actually the result of God's love in which nothing is dark or negative. But "the brighter the light the more the owl is blinded." He maintains that this deep healing allows the soul to "reach out divinely to the enjoyment of all earthly and heavenly things with a general freedom of spirit in them all."

St. John Paul II, a student of St. John's spirituality, expanded our understanding of the dark night beyond the experience of the individual:

> Our age has known times of anguish which have made us understand this expression better and which have furthermore given it a kind of collective character. Our age speaks of the silence or absence of God. It has known so many calamities, so much suffering inflicted by wars, and by the destruc-tion of so many innocent beings. The term dark night is now used of all of life and not just of a phase of the spiritual journey. The Saint's doctrine is now invoked in response to this unfathomable mystery of human suffering.[5]

"The soul's center is God," writes John of the Cross. With one degree of love, we are in the center, in God. What is the journey then? Just as a stone is in its center when in the earth, a stone can always go deeper in the earth. So a soul residing in God can always go deeper in God. Carmel tells the story of a continuing exploration into the mystery of God.

The result of this deep purgation of the soul is a profound union with God. The first commandment is realized: have one God, and love the one God with your whole being. John uses the language of divinization. The intellect, memory, and will now function in a *divine* manner. "And thus this soul will be a soul of heaven, heavenly and more divine than human." Again, "it has become God through participation in God."

John charts a remarkable transformation. When we love at the sense level, we may love in a disordered way, seeking our own fulfillment. Through the night of the senses, order is brought back into the soul, and the senses are now in harmony with the spiritual faculties. But through the night of the spirit, the motivation for our love seems to pass from the soul into God. John writes, "The soul here loves God, not through itself, but through [God]."

The goal of the spiritual journey was never to be a saint, or a contemplative. The goal was always to unite one's deepest desire with God's desire, to want what God wants. Or as Teresa said, the goal of prayer is conformity with God's will.

The human faculties of the soul so participate in God's knowing and loving that John cannot tell who is acting in his actions, his spirit or God's Spirit. John's spirituality is about the transformation of desire so there is a consonance of desire: "What you desire me to ask for I ask for; and what you do not desire, I do not desire, nor can I, nor does it even enter my mind to desire it."

John celebrates this union in his poem, "The Living Flame of Love":

> How gently and lovingly
> You wake in my heart,
> Where in secret You dwell alone;
> And in Your sweet breathing,
> Filled with good and glory,
> How tenderly You swell my heart with love.
> (st. 4)

The image of an awakening is one of the better images for the spiritual journey. The awakening is to what has been there all along. The soul did not have to find or achieve God or bring God back into one's life. God was always already there. The journey is actually a realization, an awareness, an awakening to the reality of being embraced by God.

St. Thérèse of Lisieux (1873–1897)

"For me, prayer is an aspiration of the heart, it is a simple glance directed to heaven."[6]

Ordered by her sister Pauline, the superior of the Lisieux convent, to write down her memories of their family, Thérèse Martin began writing *The Story of a Soul.* Thérèse did not have the intention of simply writing an autobiography. "I shall begin to sing what I must sing eternally: *The Mercies of the Lord.*" She explained: "It is not, then, my life properly so called that I am going to write; it is my thoughts on the graces God deigned to grant me." Again, on this first page of her book, Thérèse quoted St. Paul: "So then there is question not of the one who wills or the one who runs, but of God showing mercy" (Romans 9:15).

Thérèse was born in Alencon, France, in 1873. Her parents were Louis Martin and Zelie Guerin (canonized as a couple in 2015). She was the youngest of nine children, five of whom lived. At her birth, Thérèse was entrusted to a woman in the countryside who would nurse her. She lived on a farm for over a year. She was then returned to her mother. When Thérèse was four and a half, her mother died. Thérèse viewed her life in three phases: she was a happy child until her mother's death; after her mother's death, she then entered the saddest period of her life; and she only emerged from this time when she was thirteen years old.

Thérèse became very self-involved and hypersensitive. Writing about her mother's death, she said she learned not to trust the world. She confessed that she cried easily, and then cried because she cried. After the mother died, Pauline said she would be Thérèse's mother. But then, when Pauline decided to enter the Lisieux Carmel, Thérèse had a psychosomatic reaction that lasted for over two months. Thérèse experienced a "cure" when she saw "the ravishing smile of the Blessed Virgin." Commentators point to the loss of mothers as potentially having an impact on her spirituality.

Thérèse recounts an incident in her early years when she and her sisters were given an opportunity to each take an item of doll clothing. But Thérèse reacted to this sharing, saying, "I choose all!" And she wrote, "This little incident of my childhood is a summary of my whole life" (*SS*, 27).

In May, 1884 she made her First Communion. She said she experienced a union with Christ in love, "as a drop of water is lost in the immensity of the ocean." Her sister Marie, who had been advising Thérèse in her struggle with scruples, then entered Carmel. Thérèse was still timid and overly sensitive. "I was really unbearable because of my extreme touchiness." She turned to her siblings in heaven for help. She reasoned that if they had loved her while they were living, they would still love her when in heaven.

Thérèse describes events at Christmas 1886, which set her on a new phase of her life. Thérèse, her sister Celine, and her father were returning from Midnight Mass. The girls were going upstairs to remove their hats. The family tradition then would be for the girls to come to the living room and find candy in shoes placed by the fire. As they were going up the stairs, Thérèse heard her father say, "Well fortunately this will be the last year!" Celine knew that Thérèse had heard the father, and thought that Thérèse would dissolve in tears.

It did not happen. In that instant Thérèse had the strength to take a stand against her emotions, pretend not to have heard the father, and continue up the stairs. And when she came down to find the shoes filled with candy, she expressed such delight that she knew that she had made her father very happy.

This quite domestic experience was important for Thérèse going forward in life. Until this point, and since her mother's death, Thérèse had been very self-preoccupied and sensitive. She knew she had this problem and worked hard to change, but to no avail.

Thérèse described what happened in words recognizable by many who have been caught in obsessive or addictive situations: "God was able in a very short time to extricate me from the very narrow circle in which I was turning without knowing how to come out" (SS, 101).

Events around Thérèse entering the convent at age fifteen were dramas in themselves. Her initial request at age fourteen was supported by her father but discouraged by Canon Delatroette, the religious superior of the convent. She and her father then approached Msgr. Hugonin, the bishop of Bayeau, who also thought Thérèse too young to enter such a strict life. Not dissuaded, Thérèse and her father joined a pilgrimage to Rome with the intention of asking the pope for his permission. Thérèse's descriptions of her travels, of the arrival in Rome, are engaging.

The pilgrims were given an audience with Pope Leo XIII. Each pilgrim would be introduced to the pope, and they were instructed not to speak to him. Thérèse, far too brazen and encouraged by her sister, asked the pope's permission to enter Carmel. The pope eventually answered, "You will enter if God wills it." Swiss guards had to lead Thérèse away. Wearing down all opposition, Thérèse received permission to enter Carmel at age fifteen. At the time, twenty-six nuns formed the Carmel of Lisieux.

The superior, Mother Marie de Gonzague, refused to baby Thérèse. Thérèse was unskilled in household chores. The convent was cold, the food was poor, and her prayer was arid. Soon after she entered the convent, her father began to experience mental deterioration, and some blamed the condition on Thérèse's departure from home. Only Celine was left to take care of the father.

Thérèse took the name "Thérèse of the Child Jesus," adding "and of the Holy Face" when she received the habit January 19, 1889. The child Jesus reminded her to have a childlike abandonment to the Father. The Holy Face reminded her of Christ's love for humanity. These two names linked the nativity and the cross. Thérèse would live in the convent of Lisieux for nine years. In the year following her profession, she wrote of "the great graces" received during her retreat.

The retreat was conducted by a Franciscan, Fr. Alexis Prou. He would seem an unlikely candidate for a cloistered Carmel since he ordinarily conducted retreats for factory workers. But the community liked him. Thérèse was very private about her interior dispositions, but she experienced this priest reading her like a book.

Fr. Prou's words greatly consoled and assured Thérèse. She had a deep desire that her sister, Celine, would also join the Carmel of Lisieux. She even prayed that Celine would not be able to dance at a party! When her father died, Celine's mission to stay with him was finished. She joined her sisters. It was Celine who took the photographs of Thérèse we now prize.

In the Lisieux convent were sisters who offered their lives to God's justice. They asked to be victim souls who would take on themselves the punishment that sinners deserved but were not experiencing. Thérèse did not know such a God. The faces of God in her life did not demand appeasement, not her mother, nor her father, not her sisters, nor Jesus who called little ones to him. Thérèse recalled praying in bed and declared, "Contrary to the Bride in the Canticles, I always found my beloved there."

Thérèse decided to make an act of oblation, not to God's justice, but to God's merciful love. She certainly believed that God was just, but that God's justice would take into account our poverty. "He was perfectly aware of our fragile nature." Thérèse made her "Act of Oblation to Merciful Love" in 1895: "I desire, in a word, to be a saint, but I feel my helplessness and I beg you, O my God! To be Yourself my Sanctity.... I OFFER MYSELF AS A VICTIM OF HOLOCAUST TO YOUR MERCIFUL LOVE, asking you to consume me incessantly, allowing the waves of infinite tenderness shut up within You to overflow into my soul, and that thus I may become a martyr of Your love, O my God!" (*SS*, 276–277).

She understood God's love to be overflowing, not able to be contained, and needing someplace to go. Thérèse concluded that God was not looking for people to punish, but for people who would open their lives to his transforming love. We love God back with the love with which he has loved us. One commentator concluded that the most profound way of loving God is to allow him to love us.

Thérèse found words for her experience of God in the poetry of "our holy father," St. John of the Cross. She quotes from John's *Spiritual Canticle:*

In the inner wine cellar
I drank of my Beloved, and, when I went abroad
Through all this valley
I no longer knew anything,
And lost the herd that I was following.
Now I occupy my soul
And all my energy in his service;
I no longer tend the herd,
Nor have I any other work
Now that my every act is LOVE.
(stanzas 26, 28)

THE "LITTLE WAY"

Thérèse had infinite desires, desires which ultimately were for heaven. But she only had very finite possibilities for achieving them. She knew she would never lead armies such as her heroine, Joan of Arc, did. She knew she would not be a foundress of a religious community such as Teresa of Ávila. Thérèse sought "a means of going to heaven by a little way, a way that is very straight, very short, and totally new." Her conviction was that God "cannot inspire unrealizable desires." In other words, we are not a useless passion.

When Thérèse's sister, Celine, finally entered the convent in Lisieux, she brought with her quotes from the Old Testament. They spoke to Thérèse's desire for a new, little way to get to heaven. "Whoever is a little one let him come to me" (Proverbs 9:4). "As one whom a mother caresses, so will I comfort you; you shall be carried at the breasts, and upon the knees they shall caress you" (Isaiah 66:13, 12). Reflecting upon these words from Scripture, Thérèse concluded, "The elevator which must raise me to heaven is Your arms Jesus! And for this I had no need to grow up, but rather I had to remain *little* and become this more and more" (*SS*, 208).

Her sister Marie had asked Thérèse to further explain her "little doctrine." On September 7, 1896, Thérèse responded to Marie, and her response would form part of Manuscript B in *The Story of a Soul*.[7] These dozen pages are considered a gem in spiritual literature. They are made up of two documents: her letter to Marie and a soliloquy written to Jesus at the beginning of her retreat.

In this manuscript, Thérèse expresses a desire to be all the vocations in the church: an apostle, a priest, a missionary, a Doctor of the Church, and a martyr who would suffer all the martyrdoms to prove her love for God. She wanted to proclaim the gospel to all the corners of the world. She concluded that her vocation was "to be love in the heart of the church."

After Thérèse answered Marie, Marie responded that Thérèse's explanation left her sad because she did not have the great desires that Thérèse had. Marie wrote, "I have read your pages burning with love for Jesus, but a certain feeling of sadness came over me in view of your extraordinary desires for martyrdom. They are proof of *your* love. Yes, you possess love, but I myself! No!"

At the end of her retreat, on September 17, 1896, Thérèse attempted a further explanation: "My desires of martyrdom are nothing; they are not what give me the unlimited confidence that I feel in my heart.... I really feel that it is not this at all that pleases God in my little soul; what pleases Him is that He sees me loving my littleness and my poverty, the blind hope that I have in His mercy.... The weaker one is, without desires or virtues, the more suited one is for the workings of this consuming and transforming Love.... It is confidence and nothing but confidence that must lead us to love."[8] This letter is considered by some to be the clearest expression of St Thérèse's little way. It has also been described as revolutionary. Unfortunately, the letter is not included in *The Story of a Soul*.

The little way has been a great contribution to Christian spirituality. Bishop Patrick Ahern, a lifelong devotee of St. Thérèse, admitted that it is difficult to define. Thérèse never put things in a formula; she lived them. Bishop Ahern summarized his understanding: "The Little Way finds joy in the present moment, in being pleased to be the person you are, whoever you are. It is a school of self-acceptance which goes beyond *accepting* who you are to *wanting* to be who you are."[9] Similar to Pope Francis, Thérèse testifies that God is "nothing but Mercy and Love." We are at the heart of the Gospel.

Thérèse is also remembered for capturing her gospel insight in a charming story of a little bird who realizes it cannot fly to the sun. It can only stand on the earth and bask in the light and warmth radiating from the sun. Even when clouds come between the bird and the sun, the bird trusts the sun is still there, but not seen or felt. Sometimes the bird gets distracted and starts looking for worms. It may step in puddles and get its wings wet. But eventually it comes back to its place, holds its wings out, and once again experiences warmth and light.

THÉRÈSE'S TRIAL OF FAITH

On Good Friday, 1896, Thérèse experienced her first symptoms of the tuberculosis which would take her life. And at Easter she entered into her dark night of faith. This trial would last eighteen months until her death, September 30, 1897.

In this trial, the certainty of heaven evaporated. One of the first words the little Thérèse could recognize was *heaven*. She pointed to a cluster of stars and told her father they formed a T for Thérèse, so her name was written in heaven. Heaven would be like the good things on earth, but unending. For example, on Sundays Thérèse would sleep late, and the family would bring her chocolate in bed. They then curled her hair. She would walk to church hand in hand with her father, the "King of Navarre" and the handsomest man in church! Heaven would be like Sunday, but unending, without the melancholy which may attend Sunday afternoon with Monday looming.

In her trial of faith, Thérèse could no longer say there was a heaven. She wrote in *Story of a Soul*:

> Then suddenly the fog that surrounds me becomes more dense; it penetrates my soul and envelops it in such a way that it is impossible to discover within it the sweet image of my Fatherland; everything has disappeared! (213).

It appears the fog did not lift before Thérèse died. John of the Cross might say, "Thérèse, you are finally living with faith, the only proximate means of union with God." Her experience would seem to be an example of John's dark night of the spirit, when intellect, memory, and will are emptied of their content (such as "heaven") and replaced by faith, hope, and charity. Thérèse was living with a truly biblical faith and trust.

Amazingly, most of her writing occurred while she was in this condition.

She wrote manuscripts B and C of *The Story of a Soul*, eighteen letters to two missionaries, eighty other letters, and about twenty-four poems while experiencing her trial of faith. In this writing, there is no sign of depression or even discouragement. She is buoyant and faith-filled. She said to Mother Agnes, her sister Pauline, "Ah! What darkness! But I am at peace." (*SS*, 188–189).

It was Thérèse's conviction that God was not looking for people to punish; God was looking for people who would open their lives to his transforming love.

She concluded *Story of a Soul* saying,

> Yes, I feel it; even though I had on my conscience all the sins that can be committed, I would go, my heart broken with sorrow, and throw myself into Jesus' arms, for I know how much He loves the prodigal child who returns to Him. It is not because God, in His anticipating Mercy, has preserved my soul from mortal sin that I go to Him with confidence and love. (259)

It is her little way and her example of living by faith in difficult times that draws people to Thérèse.

The Doctor

In a letter issued October 19, 1997, Pope John Paul II proclaimed St. Thérèse of Lisieux Doctor of the Universal Church. The letter, *Divini Amoris Scientia*, is a surprisingly thorough account of her life and contribution to Christian living. It was issued on the one-hundredth anniversary of Thérèse's death in 1897. The pope proclaimed that Thérèse's spirituality contains eminent doctrine, the major criterion for declaring someone a Doctor of the Church.

The letter recounts Thérèse's early life and then her entry into Carmel. It describes her writings, which interestingly form a corpus of literature greater than that of St. John of the Cross. The pope testifies that Thérèse's teaching "conforms to Scripture and the Catholic faith, but excels (*eminet*) for the depth and wise synthesis it achieved.... Therese offers a mature synthesis of Christian spirituality: she combines theology and the spiritual life." The letter identifies Scripture, Old and New Testaments, as the primary source for Thérèse's spiritual doctrine. "Her writings contain over 1,000 biblical quotations; more than 400 from the Old Testament and over 600 from the New."

The document points out the reception of her teaching by the people of God and its widespread dissemination. "She helped to heal souls of the rigors and fears of Jansenism, which tended to stress God's justice rather than his divine mercy." The pope mentions special elements that make Thérèse a significant teacher of the church in our time: she is a woman whose "feminine genius" grasped the gospels in a manner that was practical, experienced, and wise. Her hidden life, which was fruitful for the church and the world, testified to the "beauty of the contemplative life as the total dedication to Christ"; she is the youngest Doctor of the Church and closest to us in time.

This letter ends with the formal proclamation:

> Fulfilling the wishes of many brothers in the episcopate and of a great number of the faithful throughout the world, after consulting the Congregation for Saints' Causes and hearing the opinion of the Congregation for the Doctrine of the Faith regarding her eminent doctrine, with a certain knowledge and after lengthy reflection with the fullness of our apostolic authority we declare St. Thérèse of the Child Jesus and the Holy Face, virgin, to be a doctor of the universal church. In the name of the Father, and of the Son and of the Holy Spirit.

OTHER VOICES OF CARMEL

MARY MAGDALENE DE' PAZZI (1566–1607)

Keep me, O Lord, in that innocence that you gave me from the beginning! Keep the pact that You made with Yourself for me! Keep me, I beseech you, so that I can pour You into my neighbor. I mean, Your love Your light, into the creatures that You love.[10]

JOHN OF ST. SAMSON (1571–1636)

[Aspirative prayer] is a loving and inflamed thrust of the heart and of the spirit, by which the soul surpasses itself and all created things and unites itself intimately with God in the liveliness of its loving expression.[11]

LAWRENCE OF THE RESURRECTION (1614–1691)

I have given up all my non-obligatory devotions and prayers and concentrate on being always in His holy presence; I keep myself in His presence by a simple attentiveness and a loving gaze upon God which I can call the actual presence of God or to put it more clearly, an habitual, silent and secret conversation of the soul with God.[12]

ELIZABETH OF THE TRINITY (1880–1906)

O my God, Trinity whom I adore; help me to forget myself entirely that I may be established in You as still and as peaceful as if my soul were already in eternity.[13]

TITUS BRANDSMA (1881–1942)

Nothing is accomplished without effort, without struggle. In our better moments, we no longer shed tears over our own weaknesses or over those of others, but we recall what was interiorly said to St Paul: My grace is sufficient for you; in union with me you can do all things.[14]

EDITH STEIN, ALSO KNOWN AS SR. TERESA BENEDICTA OF THE CROSS (1891–1942)

Our daily schedule ensures us of hours for solitary dialogue with the Lord, and these are the foundation of our life.... No human eye can see what God does in the soul during hours of inner prayer. It is grace upon grace. And all of life's other hours are our thanks for them.[15]

The last chapter of the Rule of Carmel states:

We have written these things briefly for you,
establishing a formula for your way of life,
according to which you are bound to live.
But if anyone will have expended more,
The Lord himself when he returns,
will repay him.
Use discernment, however,

which is the guide of the virtues.

(chap. 24)

For over eight hundred years the Carmelite tradition has inspired men and women to live in "allegiance to Jesus Christ" (Rule of Carmel, chap. 2). With the Rule of Carmel as a foundation and Carmel's saints as companions, the pilgrim in the land of Carmel is invited into the mystery of God, expending more in surrender and trust.

1. Translations from *The Collected Works of St. Teresa of* Ávila, trans. Kieran Kavanaugh, OCD, and Otilio Rodriguez, OCD, 3 vols. (Washington, DC: ICS, 1976–1985).
2. Monica Hellwig, "St. Teresa's Inspiration for Our Times," in *Carmelite Studies* 3, 214, 215.
3. Translations from *The Collected Works of St. John of the Cross*, trans. Kieran Kavanaugh, OCD, and Otilio Rodriguez, OCD, rev. ed. (Washington, DC: ICS, 1991).
4. Mary McCormack, OCD, *Upon This Mountain* (Oxford, UK: Teresian, 2009), 39, 40.
5. Master in Faith, Apostolic Letter of John Paul II, in *Walking Side by Side with All Men and Women* (Rome: Institutum Carmelitanum, 1991), 22.
6. Thérèse of Lisieux, *Story of a Soul: The Autobiography of Saint Thérèse of Lisieux*, trans. John Clarke, 3rd ed. (Washington, DC: ICS, 1996), 242. Hereafter, all quotations from this work are taken from this edition and abbreviated "SS," followed by page number, in the text.
7. *The Story of a Soul* is composed of three manuscripts. Manuscript A was written at the request of Therese's sister Pauline when she was prioress. Manuscript C was requested by Mother Marie de Gonzague at the urging of Pauline.
8. Thérèse of Lisieux, *General Correspondence*, trans. John Clarke, vol 2. (Washington, DC: ICS, 1988), 999, 1000.
9. Patrick Ahern, *Maurice & Therese: The Story of a Love* (New York: Doubleday, 1998), 114.
10. Stephen Payne, OCD, *The Carmelite Tradition* (Collegeville, MN: Liturgical, 2011), 77.
11. Redemptus Maria Valabek, *Prayer Life in Carmel: Historical Sketches* (Rome: Carmel in the World, 1982), 98.
12. Lawrence of the Resurrection, *The Practice of the Presence of God* (New York: Doubleday, 1977), 55.
13. Prayer quoted from Elizabeth of the Trinity, *I Have Found God, Complete Works*, vol. 1: *Major Spiritual Writings*, trans. Aletheia Kane (Washington, DC: ICS, 1984), 183.
14. Payne, 145.
15. Payne, 157.

CHAPTER 15

Prayer in the Dominican Tradition

~ Donald J. Goergen, OP ~

Prayer in any tradition, but particularly in the Dominican tradition, is difficult to describe. Dominicans, including Dominic himself, never had an authorized or methodical approach to prayer, other than the prayer that the Church itself prescribed, namely the Liturgy of the Hours, the sacraments, and time for personal prayer. Forms of prayer have varied widely apart from those inscribed in the life of the Church. However, Dominicans today do speak about their spirituality in terms of four pillars: preaching, prayer, study, and the common life, all deeply interconnected. These pillars give Dominican prayer its particular character. Then there are other qualities that emerge, qualities that one finds in the prayer of St. Dominic himself, such as were later reported in the so-called "Nine Ways of Prayer of St. Dominic,"[1] to which we will refer later. So what begins as a not very highly regulated approach to prayer emerges as having a Dominican flavor after all. The way a preacher celebrates the Eucharist is affected by his appreciation of the Liturgy of the Word. His or her spirituality and ministry focuses on the Word around which one's prayer and study take shape. And as is the life, so is the prayer, always flowing from and into the communal.

So Dominican prayer and praise may be more Dominican than one at first might think. Nevertheless, it still remains diverse, unprescribed in detail, and pastorally shaped. One can speak about prayer in the Dominican tradition as liturgical, as contemplative, and as integrative of both head and heart. These are three general overarching ways of taking a look at Dominicans at prayer. From there, we can go to other emphases within Dominican prayer, concluding with a look at St. Dominic himself as a man of prayer.

A Life Grounded in Liturgy

The Eucharist, confession or reconciliation, and a communal celebration of the Hours form the heart and soul of a Dominican's prayer. Personal prayer flows from and into them. They manifest both a sacramental as well as biblical spirit. The Office of Readings puts one in touch with biblical and patristic sources for a meditative life. Morning Prayer and Evening Prayer, or Lauds and Vespers, preferably celebrated communally, are the hinges on which one's life in Christ and relationship with God depend. Compline, or Night Prayer, closes one's day. And even if an individual is not always able to pray each of the Hours daily, they still shape the life of the wider community within which context one's own prayer arises. Two things are to be noted here. First, liturgical prayer is common prayer, communal prayer, the community at prayer. Thus one cannot compartmentalize the so-called four pillars. Prayer and community are not two different things. The prayer is shaped by the community, and community shaped by its prayer.

Second, the community is not only one's local community but a wider family. Dominican life comprises friars, nuns, active sisters, laity, and associates. Each is called to pray in his or her own way, from within his or her own distinctive branch of the family. Each is also called to a deep liturgical life. At the center of this liturgical life is the Eucharist itself. It is the source and summit of the Christian life in general[2] and of every baptized member of the body of Christ. It is particularly so for Dominicans in every branch of the family. From Jesus's own instruction to "do this in memory of me" to St. Dominic's own devotion to the Eucharist to the centrality given to the Mass in the various constitutions of the Order, the Dominican meets Christ not only in the Word, not only in one's ministry, but at Mass, from which one's ministry flows. The Mass is where it all begins, and the Mass is directed to our being sent forth. "Go, the Mass is ended." And the Eucharistic celebration is not accidental to contemplative prayer or devotional practices.

But we must come back to the awareness that Dominican prayer is not only, not even predominantly, individual. It is personal, yes, but liturgical, praying with the Church, whether that be in its Liturgy of the Hours or in its gathering for the proclamation of the Word and the breaking of the bread and the sharing of the cup or in one's celebration of the rite of reconciliation. At the core of Christian life, and certainly at the core of the life of a religious community, lies the need for reconciliation celebrated sacramentally. Dominican friars through the centuries wrote manuals for confessors, exhorted people to the practice of confession, and studied deeply moral theology. One cannot preach what one does not practice. Living what one teaches was central to the vision that St. Dominic had as he allowed the Lord to guide him from his earliest preaching to the founding of an Order of Preachers. Thus one sees and preaches the value of confession for others while realizing its need in one's own life. Deeply personal, it is also liturgical in that it is celebrated in and with the Church, of which we are reminded as the celebrant reminds us that "God is a God of mercy," and that forgiveness is proclaimed and given "through the ministry of the Church."

To see a Dominican at prayer is to see her seeking reconciliation with God, neighbor, and brothers and sisters; to see him participating wholeheartedly in the celebration of the Eucharist, and as a hearer or proclaimer of the Word, whether at

Mass or elsewhere; and to see them joining the Church in sanctifying the hours of the day with their personal and communal praying the long honored Psalter. Praying for others, intercessory prayer, is also very Dominican. Dominic himself is reported as often having asked with urgency the question: What will become of sinners? His was a life poured out for others.[3] Intercession is deeply liturgical, even if not exclusively so. Space is provided for pleading on others' behalf within the Liturgy of the Hours as well as following the Liturgy of the Word in the celebration of the Mass. In the Eucharistic epicleses, we ask the Holy Spirit to intercede not only to transform the bread and wine into the Body and Blood of Christ, but to continue to transform us into his Body as well. We offer the sacrifice of praise for ourselves and intercede for those dear to us.

Mass has been described by some as a continuation of the Incarnation. Christ is really present among us once again. The awareness of Christ, our remembrance of him, is at the heart of Dominican contemplation. Liturgy and contemplation both have an incarnational dimension for Dominicans. We celebrate the Word as incarnate, enfleshed, and enfleshed in preaching as well. Both Meister Eckhart and John Tauler, two significant fourteenth-century Dominican preachers, spoke about the threefold birth of Christ: eternally within the Triune Godhead as the only begotten Son, historically within the womb of Mary as the incarnate one, but also as born again in us, which they maintained even for the Blessed Mother was the most significant of the three, for of what value is the birth of the Word in history if he is not born again among us today?[4]

There is a worldly orientation in Dominican theology which flows into Dominican prayer as well. We are attentive to God's presence in the world, grace building on nature, God's omnipresence in things. Thomas Aquinas outlined his most matured and tripartite Summa to a great degree along the lines of God's presence in all of creation, his special presence in the human person through grace, and his most intimate and unique presence in the humanity of Christ.[5] Dominican prayer is creation-centered, humanistic, and appreciative of the human Christ—all anti-Manichean as was the Order in its origins.[6]

The reality of Christ present in the Eucharistic celebration, the matter of each sacrament as having saving significance, as well as the Aristotelian emphasis in Aquinas's theology all contributed to the defeat of the Manichean tendency in Christian theology. Theology itself was a form of prayer. Doing theology and being at prayer were not two disparate acts but two sides of the same coin. Thinking about God was as essential as talking to God. You can't have one without the other. But this leads us to another form of prayer in the Dominican tradition, that of contemplation.

In some ways, the communal celebration of the Mass is a Dominican community at its most powerful. But that celebration emerges out of a deeply contemplative life which it also nourishes. For a Dominican, liturgy and contemplation are not in opposition to each other. They not only complement but complete each other. One participates in the liturgical life of the Church contemplatively, and one contemplates the sacred mysteries that liturgy celebrates. No either/or here. If liturgy is the community at its most powerful, contemplation is the individual at his or her deepest.

A Life Lived Contemplatively

To be Dominican is to be a contemplative. One of the mottos of the Order, based on a text from Thomas Aquinas,[7] is *"contemplari et contemplata aliis tradere"* ("to contemplate and to hand on to others the fruits of one's contemplation"). The text indicates that a Dominican's life is grounded in contemplation, but also that Dominican contemplation is a distinct kind of thing. One is not either contemplative or active in ministry but both, an active contemplative. And contemplation is a way of life, not only a form of prayer. Living contemplatively and praying contemplatively are intimately connected. But what does it mean to say that contemplation is foundational in Dominican life? Is the mission of the Order, preaching, not an active ministry? Are there different kinds of contemplation? And what makes contemplation to be Dominican contemplation? But first, what does *contemplative* mean?

Etymologically, it simply means living within the temple. Its Latin root is *templum*, or "temple." *Con* or *cum* suggests "together" or "with." Thus a contemplative is someone who abides in a temple. But that temple is not necessarily a church, synagogue, mosque, or temple as such. St. Paul instructs us that we are God's temple because the Holy Spirit dwells within us.

"Do you not know that you are God's temple and that God's Spirit dwells in you?... God's temple is holy and that temple you are" (1 Corinthians 3:16–17).[8] Thus abiding in the temple, for a Christian, suggests an interior life. It is an awareness of the Spirit who lives within. It calls us to be mindful of who or whose we are, living out of that supernatural life, namely sanctifying grace. It challenges us to accept both the gift of the Spirit and the gifts of the Spirit. The purpose of this is to live a life of faith, hope, and love. Being contemplative is akin to the practice of supernatural charity. But supernatural here suggests another aspect of contemplation, a passive or receptive aspect, the life of grace. Contemplation, in other words, is not something *we* do, but something God does within us, something we receive in the innermost recesses of our hearts that transforms our way of being in the world. Contemplative prayer then is pure passivity, receptivity, and openness. At the same time, it is a mindfulness, a focused awareness, an active attentiveness, and a concentrated consciousness. It is letting God be God in us.

To be contemplative then, whether in life or at prayer, is to be grounded, centered, and single-minded. Meister Eckhart used the metaphor of the "ground of one's soul" to denote that deepest, innermost facet of ourselves.[9] Catherine of Siena, another Dominican mystic of the fourteenth century, wrote about the "cell of self-knowledge."[10] This is an interior dwelling place, in contrast to an external space, within which one lives. Here we are aware of God in us and our being in God, as a fish is in the sea and the sea in the fish. To borrow an expression from a contemporary Dominican sister, it is to find one's self "drenched in God."[11] This is contemplation. In and of itself it says nothing about being in the world or out of the world, but rather living from within God rather than apart from God. Contemplation is a conscious and graced receptivity to the divine life, allowing oneself to partake of the divine nature, letting the deifying God transform us into deified gods.[12] And it has both an individual as well as corporate dimension. *Contemplative* can describe one's personal life as well as communal life. It can describe prayer as well as study. It can also define ministry.

What does it mean to say that contemplation is foundational in Dominican life? In contrast to monastic life, Dominic inaugurated a form of religious life that was itinerant, mendicant, and associated with how one serves the Gospel in the life of the Church, in this case through preaching.[13] Is this not active in contrast to contemplative? This common misperception is to misunderstand the nature of contemplation and to identify it only with its historic monastic expressions. Dominican life is indeed an active life. All the great Dominican mystics were engaged in the world in a wide variety of ways. Thomas Aquinas himself did not so much see the Preachers as a contemplative order but as mixed. That mix comprises both a contemplative life and a life of ministry. The *vita apostolica* is a mix, or better, an integration, of both Martha and Mary, which awareness led Eckhart to interpret Martha as more spiritually mature than Mary, in contrast to the centuries of interpretation of the text from St. Luke to the contrary.[14] It is that same mix that led Jesus in his apparition to Catherine of Siena following upon her being called from three years of solitude back into the world to say to her, "On two feet you must walk my way; on two wings you must fly to heaven."[15] Each foot is important, one not more so than the other—again not so much a mix but a balance.

Dominican contemplative life is a balanced life, but at its foundation are its contemplative roots. The motto is to contemplate *and* to hand on the fruits of contemplation, or to be contemplative and to allow that to bear fruit in the lives of others, to be receptive to divine graces and to share what one has received. The charism of the Order, in line with the freely given graces of which St. Paul spoke (1 Corinthians 12:4–31), is to be at one and the same time contemplative and engaged in the world, to be grounded in God and, from that grounding, to allow oneself to be God's instrument. But being Dominican does mean being so grounded, in contemplative as well as liturgical prayer, not emphasizing one at the expense of the other. and in *living* contemplatively.

But there are different kinds or degrees of contemplation.[16] There is natural contemplation, or the contemplation of nature, its beauty, its vastness, the ocean, the wilderness, the desert, the mountains, the sunrise, a full moon, a rose garden, wildlife, a soaring eagle, a butterfly, a hopping bunny, even a festive meal. There is also a more reflective, philosophical contemplation, what Aristotle would have seen as the epitome of a life well lived, the contemplation of first causes,[17] of being itself, which understanding has made its imprint on the Christian traditions of contemplation and Dominican contemplation to be sure. Then there is contemplation proper, mystical contemplation if you will, that pure gift of mindful wordless awareness of God and one's oneness with that Source of All Being. As purgative and illuminative as the spiritual path may be, in contemplation one is held by God in union with himself. There is only the one. To speak of living contemplatively is to empty oneself to a gracious receptivity to a full life. It all begins and ends with God. Or as Dominic himself encouraged his brothers, "to speak only to God or with God"[18]—again the twofold mix that Lacordaire, the nineteenth-century French Dominican who reestablished the Order in France would put it, both *présence à Dieu* and *présence au monde*.[19] We are called to an obedience that responds to a potentiality that is part of our created natures.

What makes this contemplation specifically Dominican? For there are many ways of being contemplative. "In my Father's house there are many dwelling places" (John 14:2, NRSV). Contemplation for a preacher is not an end in itself, but more of a beginning, or both a beginning and an end. Unlike how it may be understood in more Platonic traditions, contemplation is intended to bear fruit. Eckhart used the words *boiling* and *boiling over* to talk about the divine life within itself and its overflow into creation. The same two words (*bullitio, ebullitio*) could be used here.

Both Eckhart and Catherine spoke about giving birth, for Eckhart in particular the birth of the Word in the ground of one's soul and that birth also in the world. For Catherine the whole raison d'être of becoming pregnant is to give birth, and one cannot give birth without becoming pregnant.[20] Dominican contemplation is becoming pregnant with the Word and then, through preaching, giving birth to it in the world.

We come back to the highly integrated, balanced character of contemplation. Prayer in the Dominican tradition has a pastoral dimension to it. It is also for others. It does not end with one's own personal interior journey. There is something ultimately extroverted about it. But again, one must be careful lest we put the cart before the horse. It is an easy temptation to see the overflow into ministry and the salvation of souls as what it is all about, without undertaking the arduous work of allowing transforming grace to do its work in us. Neither hyperactivity nor withdrawal from the world is that to which an active contemplative is called. Albert the Great was a profound mystic, but also a naturalist, philosopher, theologian, provincial, and bishop.

There had emerged in the medieval tradition in the century prior to Dominic the awareness of a rhythm to prayer as it moved from *lectio* (the prayerful reading of a sacred text) to *meditatio* (pondering reflectively or meditation on the text) to *oratio* proper (prayer itself, intercessory, talking to God, not yet wordless so to speak) to *contemplatio*. Dominic was reported to have been transferred from *lectio* to *contemplatio*. His was a contemplative life but a life lived in complete service of others as a "servant of the Preaching."[21] While Dominican contemplation is not monastic, it has its roots in the monastic traditions. Dominic himself, as a canon early in his life in Osma, Spain, kept by his bedside the *Conferences* of John Cassian. They undoubtedly helped to shape the character of his contemplative life. One does not jump to contemplative prayer immediately but neither ought one hesitate to be taken there.

A DEVOUT LIFE

Dominicans often affirm and are recognized for an emphasis on the intellectual life. It is indeed a significant dimension of their tradition, and it has an impact on their prayer as well. Intellectual contemplation plays as important a role in our spirituality as does mystical contemplation. Yet our mystical tradition stands out as prominently as our intellectual tradition. Nevertheless, study, and even study as a form of prayer, received strong emphasis. It is not surprising that a Dominican doing his doctoral dissertation in New Testament studies wrote on "Study as Worship."[22] Although prayer and study are spoken of as two distinguishable pillars of our life, they are not always separable in the concrete. What one studies morphs into one's prayer, and what one prays is often brought to study for further intellectual clarification. Doing theology itself can become a way of praying. Thomas Aquinas was not only a notable scholastic but also a mystic and poet.[23] The integral relationship between prayer and theology goes back as far as Evagrius of Pontus (fourth century), who wrote, "If you are a theologian, you pray in truth; if you pray in truth, you are a theologian."[24]

So there is also the other side to Dominican life and prayer, a recognition of the importance of the affective dimension in life, acknowledged in the value placed on friendship in the tradition, already so present in the life of Dominic, and later Jordan of Saxony and Catherine of Siena, as well as others.[25] There are not only the to-be-held-in-balance four pillars but the need to balance head and heart. Thus liturgical prayer and contemplative prayer are also integrated with one's personal prayer and devotions. Aquinas gave a significant account of the emotions, or passions, in his theology and recognized their positive role in the Christian life.

This is nowhere more apparent than in the Marian emphasis in its spirituality, as well as appreciation of devotion to the Blessed Sacrament, along with that of the Passion of Jesus Christ. Mary, of course, plays a prominent role in the spirituality of most religious Orders as well as of the Church at large. That does not make her less important to the Order of Preachers, for whom she is one of its patrons. Whether it be the practice of singing the *Salve Regina* after Compline or their celebration of Marian liturgical feasts or praying with the rosary, Mary is central. And the Marian devotion with which Dominicans are most identified is the rosary. The tradition that Mary herself entrusted the rosary to St. Dominic is not historically reliable, but that the rosary became a particularly Dominican practice and something they preached is assured. The rosary has an interesting history.[26] The association between it and the Order of Preachers goes back at least to the fifteenth century, although Dominican devotion to Mary goes back to Dominic himself.

Praying the rosary is an encounter with the life of Christ—its joyful, sorrowful, and glorious moments—and is one more manifestation of the incarnational character of Dominican prayer. In its own way, it is a mantric or repetitive kind of prayer that leads to contemplation. It can be prayed personally or communally. It can be intercessory in character, prayed for others, or a meditative practice, with greater attentiveness to the words of the prayers and the mysteries, or simply a petition to Mary herself to act on one's behalf. It expresses confidence in her intercessory power but does not replace the Christocentric character of prayer. It rather includes Mary in the circle of those who most powerfully intercede for us before God. She is the queen of all the saints. Devotion to other saints, of course, is also part of Dominican practice, especially to the members of its Dominican family, most noteworthy being Dominic himself, but Albert, Thomas, Catherine of Siena, Catherine de Ricci, Rose of Lima, Martin de Porrés, as well as others. Dominican prayer happens within the context of the community of saints, at whose core is Mary herself, whose favored devotion for Dominicans is the rosary. The Hail Mary became and remains the preeminent prayer acknowledging Mary's role in the story of salvation.

But right alongside an appreciation of Marian piety is devotion to the Blessed Sacrament.[27] Dominic himself was known to have spent hours in prayer before the Blessed Sacrament, frequently all-night vigils. On the road, when arriving at his destination, he would go immediately to the chapel of the brethren or to a church to pay a visit to the Blessed Sacrament. At Santa Sabina in Rome, which became eventually the headquarters for the friar preachers, Dominic's cell was situated as close to the church as possible so that he might easily slip over there for prayer.

Thomas Aquinas was invited by Pope Urban to compose the liturgy for Corpus Christi which led to some of his best known poetry, such as the *Pange Lingua*, which to this day is considered central to Eucharistic devotion. The final two stanzas (*Tantum ergo sacramentum*) have been part of Benediction of the Blessed Sacrament since the fifteenth century. Many monasteries of cloistered Dominican nuns, who trace their roots back to the first foundation that Dominic established at Prouilhe in southern France in 1206, of converted Cathar women, even before the founding of the Order itself, are dedicated to perpetual adoration. Most monasteries have been devoted either to perpetual adoration or to the perpetual recitation of the rosary. Even today there are over two hundred monasteries of cloistered Dominican nuns who share in the preaching mission of the Order with their apostolate of prayer. The Eucharist, the Liturgy of the Hours, the rosary, adoration, meditation, and personal prayer all help shape the rhythm of Dominican life, as do life in common, study, and mission, the latter being that toward which all the others point.

Although it is not always so readily recognized, given the particularly speculative or contemplative character of Dominican theology, at the heart of Dominican devotion is an attentiveness to the Passion of Christ. Dominic was also known to have spent time in prayer at the foot of the cross. Some of the most memorable of the frescoes painted by Fra Angelico (John of Fiesole), a fifteenth-century Dominican artist, depict Dominic praying before the crucifix. The same would be true of Thomas Aquinas and the crucifix from which Jesus spoke to him, saying, "You have written well of me, Thomas, what do you seek?" Thomas replied, *"Non nisi Te"* (Nothing except you, O Lord).[28] He made great efforts in his theology to do justice to the full humanity of Christ, which he saw as the instrumental cause of our salvation and the source of the grace we receive through the sacraments.

Catherine de Ricci, whose life as a Dominican nun is less well known to us than that of her namesake, Catherine of Siena, had an intense devotion to the cross and Passion of Christ, such that it led to her having been given the gift of the stigmata. Henry Suso too, one of the disciples of Eckhart, had a profound devotion to the cross. But for Eckhart himself, as for saints and scholars and ordinary friars, nuns, and sisters, both before and after him, balance was always important. Eckhart's was "a middle way," indeed even a "wayless way," not emphasizing to any excess ascetic practices. The cross was the source of salvation and the Order was founded for the sake of preaching *and* the salvation of souls.

Mercy is a theme in Dominican prayer. I have mentioned Dominic's own prayer, "What shall become of sinners?" Mercy is at the heart of why Thomas Aquinas saw redemption so intimately linked to the Incarnation. Why did God become incarnate? Because God is mercy. It ought not be a surprise that, in a significant text from one of his German sermons, Eckhart makes mercy the hallmark of God, cutting through previous Dominican and Franciscan disputes about whether intellect or will or truth or love is more foundational or more apt. He preached:

> A master says the highest work that God ever performed in all creatures is mercy. The most secret and hidden work that He performed even in regard to the angels is borne up in mercy: it is the work of mercy as it is in itself and as it is in God. Whatever God performs, its first breaking-forth is mercy, not in the sense of His forgiving man's sins or of one man showing mercy to another, but he means that the highest work that God performs is mercy. A master says the work of mercy is so akin to God that, though truth, riches and goodness are names for God, one of them names Him better than the other. God's highest work is mercy, and this means that God places the soul in the highest and purest place that she can attain to, into space, into the sea, into a bottomless ocean, and there God works mercy.... The best masters declare that intellect strips everything off and grasps God bare, as He is in Himself, pure being. Knowledge breaks through truth and goodness and, striking on our being, takes God bare, as He is, without name. I say that neither knowledge nor love unites. Love takes God Himself, insofar as He is good, and if God were to lose the name of goodness, love could go no further. Love takes God under a veil, under a garment. Understanding does not do this: understanding takes God as He is known to it: it can never grasp Him in the ocean of His unfathomableness. I say that above these two, understanding and love, there is mercy: there God works mercy in the highest and purest acts that God is capable of.[29]

And St. Catherine of Siena is just as insistent as becomes evident in her prayers that have been bequeathed to us, as well as in her *Dialogue*, in which she writes:

> Your mercy is life-giving.... Your mercy shines forth in your saints in the height of heaven. And if I turn to the earth, your mercy is everywhere....

You temper your justice with mercy. In mercy you cleansed us in the blood; in mercy you kept company with your creatures. O mad lover! It was not enough for you to take on our humanity: You had to die as well!... O mercy! My heart is engulfed with the thought of you! For wherever I turn my thoughts I find nothing but mercy! O eternal Father, forgive my foolish presumption in babbling on so before you—but your merciful love is my excuse in the presence of your kindness.[30]

Just as doing theology is for a Dominican a form of prayer, even if not a devotional practice, so preaching too is a way of praying. In many ways, a Dominican friar is most himself when preaching. That is when he is who he is. That is why today, among Dominican women as well as throughout the Order, there has been a strong move toward women preaching. They too are Preachers.

The cross was at the heart of Dominican preaching, the message of salvation, good news for hearers of the Word. "How beautiful...are the feet of the one who brings good news" (Isaiah 52:7, NAB). This Isaian text is often the first reading for a Dominican feast, such as that of St. Dominic himself. Thomas Aquinas, like Catherine of Siena and Augustine before him, saw the cross as the pulpit from which Christ preached or the professorial chair from which he taught.[31] The mystery of salvation is central to Dominican preaching, theology, the rosary prayer, and the liturgical and contemplative life of the Church. The Eucharist itself is a commemoration of the death of Christ until he comes again. We return to it as the source of our salvation.

I have mentioned before that there is no Dominican method of prayer, no prescribed way of praying, no particular approach to meditation that is characteristically Dominican. Dominicans pray with the Church in its liturgy and in their devotional practices. And Dominicans have bequeathed their theology as well as prayers such as the *Adoro Te Devote* to the Church. But there is no straightjacket, one might say, into which Dominicans at prayer can be put. Dominican prayer is organic, not methodical. It is whatever fits. This is to say as well that there are as many forms of Dominican prayer as there are Dominicans. Dominican prayer, therefore, is intensely personal. No two pray alike and yet all together pray in common. Prayer may vary with the branch of the Order or the region of the world, always remaining of course liturgical and contemplative with its favored Marian and Eucharistic devotions. In contemporary times, there has even been an Eastern or Asian influence among Dominicans. Shigeto Oshida was a Japanese Dominican of Buddhist origins who saw Zen not as a philosophy but as a way of being, as capable of being integrated into Dominican life.[32] He was highly respected by Japanese Buddhists as well as being a

Dominican priest. Dominican prayer is open to whatever deepens one's contemplative life. What is most important is "to pray always," as St. Paul's instruction put it (1 Thessalonians 5:17). Prayer, doing theology, celebrating the sacred mysteries, what is most important is to remain grounded in God in the midst of the Church for the sake of the preaching. The nine ways of prayer of St. Dominic exemplify Dominican prayer in varied forms, and that prayer fits both a person and an occasion.[33]

THE NINE WAYS OF PRAYER

The so-called *Nine Ways of Prayer* of St. Dominic is a little book or manuscript in which Dominic's ways of praying became depicted both in drawings and descriptive words. What it makes apparent is that Dominican prayer is also embodied. At prayer, Dominic was not living in some disembodied world, as one sometimes caricatures Dominicans at study. The *modi orandi* were particularly distinct by the bodily postures they assumed. It is difficult to date the treatise precisely, but it is generally considered to have been composed somewhere between 1274 and 1280, and is considered to reflect fairly accurately Dominic at prayer. In fact, at times it refers to testimony from an eyewitness. Dominic died in 1221. The text depicts Dominic bowing humbly before the altar, lying prostrate on the ground, taking the discipline with an iron chain, kneeling or genuflecting with his gaze fixed on the crucifix, standing with his arms out in front of him or with hands stretched out wide in the form of a cross or raised high, sitting in a mode of reading or recollection, and while walking or traveling on a journey.

The descriptions, as well as the pictures, are vital to the text. The images give a precise appreciation of what is described. The text elaborates the reverential as well as deeply felt dimension of a particular mode of prayer. Dominic is portrayed as filled with devotion, even with outbursts of emotion at times, often with tears, shaping the prayer or being shaped by the prayer. Dominic is seen as praying with humility, compunction, radiant with joy, wiping away tears, sometimes shouting out loud, now talking, now listening, now thinking, fixed on the presence of God, calling to mind or meditating on a text from Scripture, praying with his body. One could not describe Dominic as James Joyce once described a character in one of his short stories: "Mr. Duffy lived a short distance from his body."[34] Dominic was completely engaged in his prayer: body, soul, and spirit. The *Nine Ways of Prayer* is a text worth reading and pondering in its own right.

These modalities of prayer are not bodily techniques but manifestations of the spirit within, aids to prayer, expressions of a kind of prayer, whether of praise, of remorse, of intercession, begging for a miracle, or giving thanks. These holy gestures are exterior manifestations of an interior disposition. They reveal a congruence between the world without and the within in the life of a person. One's interiority is not to be concealed. Neither of course is it to be publicly dramatized. One ought not be self-conscious about one's prayer, nor showy. These were ways that Dominic prayed in private but not in private settings. They were in a chapel or before the crucifix, often at night or while on the road. They could be seen but not used for the sake of seeing. As Eckhart had put it in the expressions I referred to above, they were prayer's bubbling over into the body in a non-self-conscious and spontaneous way, while at the same time allowing a movement or the body to be receptive to a grace to be given, a *gratia gratis data*.

The pictorial representations embody the words they describe. Each is integral to the other and show how art itself can be an expression of prayer, praying with one's gifts, whether that be mind or voice or hands. Dominican art was itself a form of preaching and gave witness to a form of praise congruent with a talent given. Just as the body plays a role in prayer, so it can in preaching. Prayer can take place everywhere. Although Dominic is most often depicted at prayer in the chapel, before the crucifix or altar or Blessed Sacrament, so he is depicted praying while at study or studying while praying or while on the road. He lifts both his mind and his heart to the Lord. There is less emphasis on kneeling (present in the fourth way) than on various ways of standing distinguished by the use of the arms as the expression of the prayer.

This little text is also not the only early Dominican reference to the value of bodily gestures in prayer. Humbert of Romans, the fifth master general of the Order, had previously written of two kinds of bodily inclinations, two kinds of genuflections, and two kinds of prostrations, the second form of prostration being the *venia*, with the body stretched out on the ground, a posture friars also take during the singing of the litany of the saints during the profession of vows. Some of these bodily modes of Dominican prayer were also later portrayed in the fifteenth century by Fra Angelico in frescoes in the cells at San Marco in Florence. They are part of Dominican tradition.

The pictorial depictions accompanying the nine ways are not static but show movement. Dominic as a saint was on the move, itinerant, and so likewise there is movement in his prayer, even when he is standing in one place. A meditation on the nine ways indicates once again that liturgical, contemplative, and devotional prayer are all of a whole—not three distinct kinds of prayer. As with an icon, these portraits of Dominic at prayer, or one might suggest of a Dominican at prayer (for to some degree the intent of the treatise on the nine ways was pedagogical for the brethren), deserve meditation. They are not only intended to draw what is described but to invite a reflection on the nature of prayer itself.

If Dominican prayer is embodied, so likewise is it drawn upwards toward its transcendent source. If its intercessions come from below, its praise is directed up above. Just as its depths lie within, so its expressions flow without. The deeper one goes within, the more one finds oneself above. It is to the Trinity that one prays; it is the Trinity that prays. Dominican prayer is Trinitarian. Its source is the Trinity; so is its goal. As the ancient theme of *exitus* and *reditus* are woven into the theology of Aquinas's *Summa Theologiae*, so they are part and parcel of prayer. All comes from God; all goes back to God. It is now not I who pray, but the Spirit who prays within me. And it is the Spirit who knows the mind and heart of God (1 Corinthians 2:10–11) and draws us ever closer here on earth to the divine life predestined for us from the foundation of the world (Ephesians 1:4). In prayer we see God even if only dimly. It is God whom we seek, whether in prayer, in study, in ministry, or in community. It is all about God—a theocentric and Trinitarian life embodied in the cross of Jesus Christ. Dominican prayer, as I have said in various ways, is not confined to one way of praying.

St. Dominic: Man of Prayer

There are many saints, scholars, mystics, missionaries, artists in Dominican history, most of whom are not known to us by name. We also recognize that we are sinners, for we are fragile women and men. The inspiration for the prayer of the Preacher remains that of Dominic, our brother, friend, and founder whose life and prayer manifest a simplicity that comes from life in the Spirit. There was a graciousness about him, a cheerfulness, that drew others to him. He belonged to God but poured himself out for the sake of the gospel. He lived what he preached. He begged for his daily bread and trusted in divine providence. Prayer is shaped by life and gives one's life its shape. Dominic's indomitable spirit in the face of adversity, his love of learning and desire for God, his care for the salvation of souls, his capacity to read the signs of the times, and his gift for friendship all came together in praying the Psalter, in his prayer before the crucifix, in the tears that flowed while celebrating Mass, in the depths of his contemplative and apostolic heart, and in his singing the *Salve Regina*.

How does one plumb the depths of another's relationship with the divine? That love for God came through in his preaching. The gospel he proclaimed and his innate integrity made him sensitive to the poor, as on the occasion as a student in Palencia when he sold his books in order to provide for the hungry during a time of famine, saying, "How can I keep these dead skins when living skins are dying of hunger?" and in his frequent prayer "What shall become of sinners?" Dominic was no extraordinary man, but he was extraordinarily graced. What can be said about his *modus orandi*? Simply, that he prayed. Unceasingly. Not self-conscious about a right way to pray. Whether with the brethren, the nuns, the Bible, or on the road, he prayed. He let God be God and let himself be God's instrument. What is prayer in the Dominican tradition? It is receptivity to grace. It is surrender to God, conforming one's life to that of Christ's in faith, hope, and love. Prayer is bred in our bones. Not rapture. But, like preaching, it is who we are. We cannot not pray even when we are not conscious of praying.

> Likewise, the Spirit helps us in our weakness, for we do not know how to pray as we ought, but the Spirit himself intercedes for us with sighs too deep for words. And he who searches the hearts of men knows what is the mind of the Spirit, because the Spirit intercedes for the saints according to the will of God. (Romans 8:26–27)

The text comes from Dominic's beloved St. Paul, whose epistles and the Gospel of Matthew he carried with him wherever he went. That and the *Conferences* of John Cassian deeply influenced his life. They were at his bedside. A Dominican prays the Scriptures, studies the Scriptures, preaches the Scripture. One's prayer and one's ministry are shaped by the Word.

CONCLUSION

Prayer in the Dominican tradition is opening oneself to the gifts the Spirit gives. Thomas Aquinas's theology emphasized heavily the role of the Spirit in the spiritual life.[35] If the Spirit dwells in our hearts, or as Eckhart would put it, in the ground of our soul, then prayer is in our bones. I am reminded here of a poem, "Bone Ecstasy / Prayer on Bones" by Elisabeth Dearborn.

> We arrive small seed at first
> in soil plowed by disappointment
> and by longing. Humbly
> we submit to the power of your will
> and watch the loosening husk
> which encloses us peel off.
> The belly holds a burning fire
> ready to consume us. Visions
> rise and keep us waking in the night.

We stand in the coursing light
of your intensely penetrating love,
agape at being known and opened
and alive beyond all reach of time.
This holiness makes us a little crazy.
We wander, burning with desire.
Is it then the choice arrives?
To burn alive or bank the embers
for a long, slow warmth?
The one arises from a fire in the belly,
the other from a fire in the bones.
Because, dear One, it is our task
to care for you, our living body
becomes prayer-on-bones and
ecstasy takes root.[36]

If I were to give advice to a Dominican novice who already had some experience with prayer, I would say, there is no one particular way to pray, no Dominican method. Pray as you pray best. Pray as God prays in you. Let God be God. Let the Spirit in you pray. Pray always. Keep it simple: Thank you, Lord. I'm sorry. I love you. Help me, God, come to my assistance. Let your prayer be deeply personal, deeply communal. Let it flow. Let it become pure awareness. Let it be grace.

In the end, it is not I who pray, but the Spirit who prays within us. It is not I who pray, but the community that prays with me, within me, through me. Prayer can be praise, intercession, or contrition, offered through the body, the voice, the hands, the heart, the mind. It is the whole person, the whole of the person, all of the person, the person with his or her relational network, our mystical body, cosmic body. It is the Church at prayer celebrating on earth that sacrifice of praise which models the heavenly liturgy. Dominic begged for God's mercy, prayed with tears, trusted in God's benevolent providence. To be at prayer is to be at one with God, in season and out, living simultaneously in this world and the other, speaking to God and about God.

There is no final way to say what prayer is. Each person is a distinct prayer and a distinct pray-er. Yet when the community comes together, God is there. Having found one's home in the Word, one places one's trust in God, whom we celebrate liturgically, contemplate personally, and to whom with devotion and reverence we offer our lives as we once again recall whom we are called to be: contemplative preachers.

1. See "The Nine Ways of Prayer," in *Early Dominicans, Selected Writings*, ed. Simon Tugwell, OP, Classics of Western Spirituality (New York: Paulist, 1982), 94–103.

2. *Lumen Gentium*, 11; *CCC* 1324.

3. Jean-Jacques Pérennès, *A Life Poured Out* (Maryknoll, NY: Orbis, 2007), the story of Pierre Claverie of Algeria, Dominican bishop of Oran, and his assassination.

4. See among other references, Johannes Tauler, *Sermons*, trans. Maria Shrady, Classics of Western Spirituality (New York: Paulist, 1985), 35–40, a sermon for Christmas Day.

5. See Thomas Aquinas, *Summa Theologiae*, I, q 8, a 3, especially ad 4.

6. The Order of Preachers was established in the midst of the Albigensian or Cathar heresy which flourished in the south of France, an extreme dualism manifesting the ancient Manichean philosophy that denied the goodness of matter. Anything connected with the material world was the work of a second ultimate principle or evil God.

7. Thomas Aquinas, *Summa Theologiae*, II–II, q 188, a 6.

8. Quotations from Holy Scripture are from the *Revised Standard Version*.

9. For example, see Meister Eckhart, *Sermons and Treatises*, trans. M. O'C. Walshe, vol. 1 (London: Watkins, 1979), sermons 1 and 2, 1–23, among many others. Also see Richard Woods, OP, *Eckhart's Way* (Wilmington, DE: Michael Glazier, 1986).

10. See Catherine of Siena, *The Dialogue*, trans. Suzanne Noffke, Classics of Western Spirituality (New York: Paulist, 1980), 25, 27, 118, 120, 125, 135, 158. Also see Thomas McDermott, OP, *Catherine of Siena, Spiritual Development in Her Life and Teaching* (New York: Paulist, 2008).

11. See Linda Gibler, OP, *From the Beginning to Baptism* (Collegeville, MN: Liturgical, 2010), xv.

12. See *Partakers of the Divine Nature, The History and Development of Deification in the Christian Traditions*, ed. Christensen and Wittung (Grand Rapids: Baker Academic, 2008). Also see Juan Arintero, OP, *The Mystical Evolution in the Development and Vitality of the Church*, trans. Jordan Aumann, OP, 2 vols. (St. Louis: B. Herder, 1949).

13. For an updated account of the life of Dominic, see Donald Goergen, OP, *St. Dominic: The Story of a Preaching Friar* (New York: Paulist, 2016).

14. *Meister Eckhart, Teacher and Preacher*, ed. Bernard McGinn, Classics of Western Spirituality (New York: Paulist, 1986), sermon 86, 338–345.

15. Raymond of Capua, *The Life of Catherine of Siena*, trans. Conleth Kearns, OP (Wilmington, DE: Michael Glazier, 1980), section 121, 116.

16. Jacques Maritain, *The Degrees of Knowledge*, trans. Gerald Phelan (New York: Charles Scribner's Sons, 1959), 247–290.

17. Aristotle, *Metaphysics*, bk. 12, chaps. 7, 9; and *Nichomachean Ethics*, bk. 10, chaps. 6–8.

18. Speaking *cum Deo vel de Deo* ("with God or of God") is an expression contained in the Primitive Constitutions of the Order (no. 31). The same expression is also ascribed to Stephen of Muret (1045–1124), the founder of the Abbey of Grandmont. The canonization process for St. Dominic interprets the phrase as an admonition or instruction of Dominic's for his brethren.

19. See Donald Goergen, "Spirituality," in *The Praxis of the Reign of God: An Introduction to the Theology of Edward Schillibeeckx*, 2nd ed., ed. Mary Catherine Hilkert, OP, and Robert Schreiter (New York: Fordham University Press, 2002), 117–131.

20. Catherine of Siena, chap. 11, 45.

21. That was the way Dominic often signed something, "*humilis minister predicationis*."

22. Benedict Thomas Viviano, OP, *Study as Worship, Aboth and the New Testament* (Leiden: E.J. Brill, 1978).

23. Paul Murray, OP, *Aquinas at Prayer: The Bible, Mysticism, and Poetry* (London: Bloomsbury, 2013).

24. Andrew Louth, *The Origins of the Christian Mystical Tradition* (New York: Oxford University Press, 2007), 108.

25. Consider, e.g., the relationship between Jordan of Saxony and Henry of Cologne (see Jordan of Saxony, *On the Beginnings of the Order of Preachers*, trans. Simon Tugwell, OP [Dublin: Dominican, 1982], chaps. 7–8); or between Jordan of Saxony and Diana d'Andalò (*To Heaven with Diana*, ed. Gerald Vann, OP [New York: iUniverse, 2006]); or between Catherine of Siena and Raymond of Capua. See Paul Hinnebusch, OP, *Friendship in the Lord* (Notre Dame, IN: Ave Maria, 1974); and Christopher Kiesling, OP, *Celibacy, Prayer, and Friendship* (New York: Alba House, 1978).

26. Anne Winston-Allen, *Stories of the Rose: The Making of the Rosary in the Middle Ages* (University Park, PA: Pennsylvania State University Press, 2005).

27. See Joan Ridley, OSB, *The Spirituality of Eucharistic Devotion* (Ligouri, MO: Liguori, 2010). Joan is a Benedictine sister of Perpetual Adoration and was previously a Dominican sister with the Eucharistic Missionaries of St. Dominic.

28. Jean-Pierre Torrell, OP, *Saint Thomas Aquinas*, vol. 1, *The Person and His Work*, trans. Robert Royal (Washington, DC: The Catholic University of America Press, 1996), 285.

29. Meister Eckhart, *Sermons and Treatises*, trans. M. O'C. Walshe, vol. 2 (London: Watkins, 1981), sermon 72, 188–189.

30 Catherine of Siena, chap. 30, 72. Also see *The Prayers of Catherine of Siena*, 2nd ed., trans. Suzanne Noffke (New York: Authors Choice, 2001).

31. Thomas Aquinas, *Summa Theologiae*, III, q 46, a 4. Catherine of Siena, *The Letters of Catherine of Siena*, vol. 3, trans. Suzanne Noffke (Tempe, AZ: Arizona Centre for Medieval and Renaissance Studies, 2007), Letter T316, 330.

32. *Takamori Sōan, Teachings of Shigeto Oshida, a Zen Master* (Buenos Aires: Ediciones Continente, 2007). Also see Paul Philibert, OP, "Zen Spirit in Christian Contemplation," *Spirituality Today* 33 (June, 1981): 159–171.

33. Although there are several excellent articles on the nine ways of prayer, the best by far is that by Paul Philibert, OP, "Roman Catholic Prayer: The *Novem modi orandi sancti Dominici*, in *Contemplative Literature, A Comparative Sourcebook on Meditation and Contemplative Prayer*, ed. Louis Komjathy (Albany, NY: State University of New York Press, 2015), 503–545.

34. James Joyce, "A Painful Case," in *Dubliners* (Clayton, DE: Prestwick House, 2006), 85–92.

35. See among other references, Charles Bouchard, OP, "Recovering the Gifts of the Holy Spirit in Moral Theology," in *Theological Studies* 63(2002): 539–558; Donald Goergen, OP, *Fire of Love, Encountering the Holy Spirit* (New York: Paulist, 2006), 128–147; Christopher Kiesling, OP, "The Seven Quiet Gifts of the Holy Spirit" in *Living Light* 23 (1986): 137–146; Thomas McDermott, OP, *Filled with All the Fullness of God* (London: Bloomsbury, 2013), 53–58.

36. This previously unpublished poem is used here by permission of the author.

CHAPTER 16

Prayer in the Benedictine Tradition

~ *Laura Swan, OSB* ~

"Let us prefer absolutely nothing to Christ, and may he lead us all together to ever-lasting life."[1]

St. Benedict (480–547), along with his twin sister Scholastica, was born in the small town of Nursia, an administrative center for the Roman Empire, situated in the Apennine Mountains of Italy. Enticed away from his hermitage, now known as *Sacro Speco*, near Subiaco, he set out to reform some rather lax monasteries. Benedict culled the best wisdom from the desert and early monastic traditions to guide his small group of monasteries of men.[2] What we now know as the *Rule of Benedict*, a spiritual and not legal document, was written and rewritten over many years of trial and error, prayer, and hard work with his diverse group of monks.

St. Benedict had accepted anyone who came knocking at his door expressing a desire to know and serve God. The entrance process culled out those who were not serious about their calling and, because of his growing fame, those who just sought the attention of a spiritual master. He was serious about the pastoral care of his monks, and yet gentle and loving as well. One of Benedict's challenges was that he was welcoming men from disparate cultures and languages, differing social and educational backgrounds—from the illiterate to the well-educated—and trying to shape them into "one in Christ."[3] As community was central to Benedict's vision of the Christian journey, he worked arduously to create and protect the integrity of each of his communities. Community is where conversion of life happens. While he never wrote a particularly brilliant tome on prayer (as many of the saints since his time had), he knew that the spiritual journey, lived out through community living, required some degree of structure. Benedict provided structure, flexible and sensitive and strong.

Thus Benedict organized and pastored his communities with the intent of creating the space where each monk might deepen in his relationship with God, suggesting ways to organize their observance of the Liturgy of the Hours, as well as time for personal prayer. He protected times and places of silence so his monks could get away from distracting noise in order to nurture their spiritual journey. Benedict under-stood that spiritual growth happens in a life structured around prayer and in the daily context of living in community.

For over 1,500 years Benedictines have tried to follow Benedict's *Rule*. The Benedictine world includes nuns and monks of the Benedictine, Cistercian,

Camaldolese, and Trappist traditions. We are also blessed with the presence of Oblates who commit themselves to live the Benedictine way of life attached to a particular monastery and within the context of their lives. We have quietly gone about our business of searching for God through prayer within the context of community. We seek honest and peaceful relationships with a colorful, surprising, and at times, challenging group of fellow members. We attempt to weave a healthy sense of community among ourselves and with our immediate environs. Friends and other seekers may join us for prayer and ministry for shorter or longer periods of time.

Community may be your families, your faith community, or those to whom you share a commitment to the work of social justice. It is the people God has placed in your life—for a period of time or for a very long time. Many seekers with a commitment to prayer express a sense of connectedness to others, even those they do not know.

BENEDICT ON PRAYER

Obsculta! "Listen!" The first word in the *Rule of Benedict* embodies the heart of the Benedictine way of life. Benedict calls his followers to "listen with the ear of their hearts."[4] The most radical thing we humans can do is to stop and truly listen. Do we hear what our children are saying? Do we listen to our spouse, our best friend, our neighbor? What might happen if we listened to a coworker, especially one we struggle to be around? Do we listen to ourselves? Listening requires a stance of vulnerability. To what or to whom do we resist listening? What within might frighten us? Listening may challenge our stereotypes and expose our prejudices. Listening may enliven a part of us long dormant that, in turn, may require a change or expansion of our self-image. We may find ourselves changing, and change evokes fear in many of us. Listening requires courage. Yet listening can be liberating, and freedom is what Jesus came to proclaim.

Benedict wanted his followers to cultivate an interior serenity that allowed them to develop an intimate awareness of God's voice in their lives. In this stillness we learn to recognize the voice of God and become familiar with how God chooses to interact with each of us. In intimate friendship, we learn to trust the leading of the Holy Spirit in our lives. We cultivate an inner simplicity and interior freedom that empowers us to act on the leading of the Holy Spirit. Father William Shannon taught that "*awareness of God*, at its deepest level, is not so much something we *do* as something we *are*."[5]

What does listening have to do with prayer? While the words we speak, which embody the concerns, fears, anxiety, hopes, and aspirations held within our heart are important, we deepen to a new level of prayer when we silence our mind and hearts and mouths to hear what the divine presence, God, might desire to whisper back to us. Our spiritual journey is about relationship, and God longs for an intimate relationship with each of us. Authentic relationship requires two-way communication as well as time spent in each other's company.

To intensely listen is the beginning of contemplative prayer. We stand in the presence of God and listen with a radically open heart. We behold God's love for us. We are listening for the heart and mind of Christ (1 Corinthians 2:16). Slowly we are given a new vision, a new perspective on our place in the world, our connection to our extended family or community, and our relationship to creation.[6]

As we listen deep within for the Holy Spirit's promptings, we become aware of our internal contradictions and motivations. We peel back the layers of meaning to unpack and discover God's call in our life at this time. We come to a deeper self-knowledge of both our strengths and foibles. We come to hunger for a deepened interior freedom, detaching from all that keeps us from God and from a richer relationship with family, friends, and faith community.

This journey of contemplative listening teaches us a life of discernment, listening for how and where the Holy Spirit may be leading us. While discernment is essential for making the best possible life choices (whom to marry, which religious community to join, which university or training program to attend, and so on), it is also important for the smaller choices in life. God cares about the details of our lives. God is found in the details of our lives.

Benedict hungered for God. His desire for a deep and mature relationship with God was impelled by desire. He wanted this for his followers. We are created with a basic inner yearning and drive toward our most whole self and union with the divine. For his monasteries, Benedict set up times and places for silence. Silence deepens our awareness of God and allows us to truly listen within.

It is a good practice for you to establish places of silence in your parishes. Most do. But also consider times or places of silence in your home. Children love quiet time before going to bed, even when they verbally squawk at it. Find times for silence in your own life and commit to this. Listen to a quiet chant in your car while you are commuting to work or running errands. Go for long walks and listen to the birds and the sound of the wind through the trees. Bike without listening to music and instead listen to the wind and the birds singing. Go behold a sunrise or sunset and marvel at God's beauty. Gardening can be an intentional time of cultivating inner and outer silence. Physical activity, the burning off of excess physical and emotional energy, frees us to attend to our inner world. We live noisily. Benedict challenges us to disconnect for a while and be with our inner selves and with the Divine.

When Benedictines pray, and particularly when we gather together for prayer, we are holding all the people of God, their needs and yearnings and aspirations, in our hearts. We feel deeply connected to every person and to creation. I am reminded of a story from the *Life of Benedict*.

> When the brothers were still asleep, the man of God, Benedict, got up to watch in prayer before the time for the Night Office. Standing at the window and praying to almighty God in the middle of the night, he suddenly saw a light pour down that routed all the shadows. It shone with such splendor that it surpassed daylight, even though it was shining in the darkness. A wonderful thing followed in this vision, for as Benedict reported later, the whole world was brought before his eyes as if collected in a single ray of sunlight.[7]

We humans live with a basic hunger for the divine presence. Once we awaken to this yearning, our spiritual journey has begun. We seek connection. We long for some sense of understanding. We desire to embrace wisdom. This spiritual journey is not linear, rather—like the famous labyrinths that have become popular tools for prayerful pondering and meditation—it is more a complex and beautiful helix. We encounter twists and turns, what might feel like a folding back on itself (those times when we feel like we are regressing), and yet full of rich mystery and possibility. But our *holy discontent* will motivate us to seek further and deeper within ourselves.[8]

The spiritual journey requires courage, curiosity, and tenacity. While we may delight in our rich Catholic tradition, discovering inspiring voices from the past, developing a rich relationship with the Holy Spirit, and embracing a more mature understanding of God, we also come crashing into ourselves. All that I do not want to see within myself becomes, once I begin this journey of hard work, the rich soil of a more mature spiritual life. In a difficult interpersonal relationship, I might learn to get curious rather than angry. I may learn to listen to the wisdom of my fear but no longer allow it to be a tyrant. The Holy Spirit places in our lives the very people and encounters we need to learn the spiritual lessons we are ready to learn.[9] We frail humans create elaborate walls, detours, and delusions in order to avoid facing God. We fear our emotional and spiritual nakedness, forgetting that we cannot surprise God. Prayer empowers us to face into ourselves where we will meet God. Prayer becomes the impetus for the removal of all hindrances within ourselves that keep us from fully experiencing God's presence. God does not withdraw from us. We withdraw from God.

With our Catholic understanding of the mystical body of Christ and of the communion of saints, our journey may be one of remembrance of those who have gone before us and those among us that we have not yet met. This is a rich and complex connectedness that we may behold and savor. Our spiritual hunger entices us to learn from those who have gone before us as well as those around us. The Holy Spirit places in our lives those people and sacred texts[10] that we need for this present moment to grow and mature, both spiritually and in our humanity.

With this hard work, we deepen in self-awareness as well as God-awareness. God is everywhere,[11] and as we become truly aware of this, we mature spiritually. We become more grounded in ourselves before God, warts and foibles and all. Father William Shannon called that mistaken belief that we are somehow apart from God, except for special moments and in special places, "spiritual apartheid."[12] This authentic sense of awareness reduces the distance between ourselves and the one of whom we are aware, God. We invite the Holy Spirit to deepen our awareness, our attentiveness, of the divine presence who is everywhere.

In his *Rule*, Benedict included a chapter on humility, which is essentially about the steps taken to remove all barriers between ourselves and God. While he uses the image of a ladder (echoing Jacob's dream at Bethel [Genesis 28:10–17]), today we might understand this better as a helix. While, in one sense, we might progress from step one to step twelve in a linear sense, we are always again at step one as we work out the stuff of our lives.

Humility should never be confused with humiliation. Authentic humility means that we are deepening in self-awareness and self-knowledge. We are growing in awareness of our gifts and strengths along with our weaknesses and growing edges. We become aware of our internal contradictions and motivations, but also our deepest desires and joys. Humility is getting really real, accepting with gratitude who God created us to be, and accepting that as OK.

Benedict understood that growth in humility is a journey from that public persona we have built up in our early adult years toward that true *self* made in the image and likeness of Christ. Humility is the fruit of letting go of all the interior stuff that weighs us down, distracts us from our life's passions and goals, and keeps us from a simple and empowering relationship with God. With the fruit of humility, there is a growing congruence between our inner and outer world. Our behavior more closely matches our words; we walk the talk. We are becoming whole. With the helix of humility, we are ever growing nearer to our real selves while remembering our spiritual childhood. We return to our beginnings with a greater awareness of our internalized self-hatred: the insidiously subtle ways that we cooperate with the evil one in undermining our coming home to our truest, most authentic selves.

This journey begins to unpack our awareness of who God is and who God is not. We begin to question narrow, exhausted God images. The language we have inherited from our tradition begins to take on new possibilities and meaning, especially when we bring this language to our prayer through Liturgy of the Hours and *lectio divina*.

LITURGY OF THE HOURS: PONDERING THE WORD

> "Let us open our eyes to the light, and let us listen with astonished ears to
> the warning of the divine voice, which daily cries out to us."[13]

The Liturgy of the Hours, or Divine Office, provides a framework for a life of prayer. Benedictines pause during the day to remember our foundational relationship with the divine. However, this is hopefully not merely inserting prayer into a life otherwise devoid of prayer. It is not one more thing we do in a daily schedule cramped with to-dos. The Liturgy of the Hours frames our day and supports our saner choices around work and commitments.

While all are called to this prayer, it is the monastics who are tasked with praying these hours of the day on behalf of the people of God, joined by their guests and oblates.[14] Celebration of the Liturgy of the Hours was not unique to St. Benedict as this practice dates back to the earliest years of the Christian movement. Benedict dedicated twelve chapters in his *Rule* to the possible organization of the celebration of the psalms and canticles and then encouraged his followers to make adjustments if something else worked better in their community. While there has been a Roman (or Cathedral) Office for centuries, Benedictines have long taken to heart Benedict's admonition to create a Liturgy of the Hours that works best for each community.

The Liturgy of the Hours consists of the 150 psalms (which are poetry) of the Old Testament along with canticles taken from the Old and New Testament. With the morning office, or Lauds, the Benedictus is chanted as part of the closing prayers. With evening office, or Vespers, the Magnificat is chanted. Each Office typically includes a reading, often reflecting the liturgical season.

When some begin to pray the Liturgy of the Hours consistently, the content of some of the psalms can become quite disturbing. "This is contemplative prayer?" you may ask. Good question, if we are paying attention. Communities of faith have been singing and chanting and praying these Psalms for more than three millennia. They have the capacity to challenge us, to encourage us, and to help us celebrate important events of our lives. There are psalms of praise of God, psalms that express our trust and confidence in God's care for us. There are psalms of wisdom, reminding us of how to live a righteous life, and psalms of lamentation, teaching us how to grieve. Cursing psalms confront us with our own anger and capacity to wish (and do) harm to others. And the royal psalms remind us that God is God and we are not.

Biblical scholar Walter Brueggemann speaks of the psalms' capacity to move us from a place of orientation, where we are essentially satisfied with our life, through disorientation, where we have been thrust into seeming chaos, and returning to yet a new space, a stance of new orientation. Our lives—our beloved *shoulds* and *oughts*— are disrupted in order to experience a more authentic and meaningful relationship with the divine. How the world ought to be and the way my life should be gets challenged, when we truly pay attention to the movement of these words, and the movement that the Holy Spirit works in us as we wrestle in our prayer.

Our sense of who God is, our images for God, have an opportunity to expand and deepen and mature. Our heart connections to our fellow seekers, for all God's children, grow as well. I bring the grief of families torn apart by addictions and violence and civil war to the psalms, praying for those who cannot pray for themselves at this time.

My Dominican professor of liturgy referred to faithfully praying the Liturgy of the Hours as "holy monotony," coming back again, day in and day out, to old and familiar words that slowly shape my attitude, my heart, and my spirit. This is a slow-drip method method of quiet transformation. Rarely do I leave chapel feeling the exhilaration of an encounter with God, but I do notice when life's circumstances keep me from chapel for a few days. Something is missing. And yet I feel the connection to my community to continue to enter the chapel three times daily, faithfully praying the Office.

Research and select the volume of the Liturgy of the Hours[15] that seems most welcoming and easy to use. While there are many complete Office books that contain a four-week cycle with the full 150 psalms, there are also abbreviated forms of the Office that works well for people. Note that some Liturgy of the Hours books are not user-friendly: the headache of trying to flip pages around to locate hymns, antiphons, the day's psalms, and prayers can be quite (unnecessarily) distracting to the work of prayer. Choose one whose translation of the psalms resonates for you, and where locating the appropriate day's Office is clear. These can be purchased in bulk for use in parishes and prayer groups, and increasingly some Offices are available online.

If you have the opportunity to join a monastic community for Liturgy of the Hours, notice that attention is paid to seemingly unimportant matters. Light is sufficient to read the text without being glaring and harsh. Chairs and pews are comfortable. Candles are lit. Monastics sit with relaxed knees and feet squarely on the ground. Our backs are straight without being rigid—this allows our lungs to fill with air—and our heads are held squarely on our shoulders. Bodily postures are important as we attend to the divine in our midst and give fully bodily attention to our prayer.

Frequently the beginning of the Liturgy of the Hours is signaled by a bell or gong. Monastics, like good Catholics, have times for standing (when we begin the Liturgy of the Hours, during the Benedictus or Magnificat, and the closing of the Office). We bow for the doxology (Father, Son, and Holy Spirit), and in some communities, for the blessing by the abbot or prioress. Otherwise we sit while we chant or recite the Office. We bring our mind and body to this prayer as a fully embodied and all-encompassing act of devotion.

While hymns can be belted out a full throttle, chant is soft and airy, what Hildegard of Bingen[16] referred to as "a feather on the breath of God." Monastics strive to make their voices as one choir. Benedict stated, "And let us stand to sing in such a way that our mind is in harmony with our voice."[17] This becomes something of an ascetical practice when I strive attend to what I am singing or chanting, and to be one with my neighbor and not stand out. You may be wise to bring in your parish choir director or another professional to train your core group of leaders and dedicated pray-ers to find this balance.

As any accomplished poet or spoken word artist will tell us, the space between the words is as important as the speaking or chanting of the words. Pauses affect us in important ways. Maintain a peaceful pace. Pay attention to each word, allowing it to permeate your being. Pray each word as if that word is the totality of your prayer. If praying in a group, a leader may be needed to work with members, as some tend to rush as if this were merely one more task to be accomplished. An easy, gentle pace is the goal.

Some parishes do make their churches or side chapels available for parishioners to gather to celebrate the Liturgy of the Hours. Inquire as to the possibilities. You will seek a balance in welcoming all to join you in prayer while minimizing distractions from doors slamming, hallway conversations, and normal parish activities.

Increasingly, seekers have committed themselves to a practice of praying the Liturgy of the Hours in their home. Many people have created a sacred space within their home for prayer. This should be a relatively quiet space with a comfortable chair. Many have found it helpful to create a small prayer altar with an icon or other images that speak to them of the divine or remind them of particular prayer intentions. Some will have a candle that they light as they prepare themselves for this time with God. If it is helpful, have a device nearby that plays soft music that drowns out any distractions—choose a soft piece of chant or nature sounds, anything that stills your spirit. Do not let this space be too warm or you might fall asleep.

Place yourself in a comfortable position. Many of us find that our posture is important to this attentive listening. While your spine does not need to be rigid, you want to sit so that your lungs can fully function. Rest your prayer book on your lap, take a moment of silence and touch in with those around the world who are also praying the Liturgy of the Hours, possibly begin by listening to a hymn, and then gently move through the experience of praying the Office. Do not be in a hurry. Many conclude praying the Office with silent intercessory prayer for needs and intentions.

Some seekers have found that, as part of their long commute to and from work, they can integrate listening to an Office in their car while driving or riding the bus. Others found a favored spot on the way home from work, such as a park or church parking lot, turned off their engine and prayed their Office there. Refreshed, they return home ready for the evening.

LECTIO DIVINA: SACRED READING

"I will now allure her, and bring her into the wilderness, and speak tenderly to her." —Hosea 2:14

Lectio divina is an ancient form of prayer that the earliest followers of Jesus inherited from the Jewish tradition and then made their own. The practice deepened in the early Christian desert with the *ammas* and *abbas*, spiritual elders. A word was given and the disciple went away to meditate, to chew upon this word or phrase, and returned to the spiritual elder a changed person. After holy conversation (today our practice of spiritual direction), another word was given and the disciple yet again departed to ponder and wrestle with this word. Engaging, embracing, wrestling with, and savoring one word holds the potential to shape our hearts and minds, to nudge us toward maturity, and to deepen our capacity for compassion.

This is not the reading done for leisure (something Benedict valued and called holy), nor for professional development, nor for seeking information or data. We are wise to avail ourselves of opportunities to study the Bible in order to unpack its meaning, to place the sacred stories in historical context, and to engage what the prophets, the histories and the Jesus event might mean for us. But during *lectio divina*, we are not approaching these same texts to learn something, but rather to be shaped by the words. This is a shaping at a deeper, heart and gut level.

By the early Middle Ages, Carthusian monk Guigo II taught *lectio divina* as having four stages: *lectio, meditatio, oratio*, and *contemplatio*. Benedictines continue this tradition while also maintaining fluidity around the movements of *lectio divina*. There is no rigid one way of entering into *lectio divina*; rather, follow the leading of the Holy Spirit through your own intuition.

Benedict set up structures in his monastery to ensure that his monks' commitment to *lectio divina* would be protected. A certain spaciousness of time is necessary. We cannot be rushed. This cannot become another to-do on our long list of to-dos. But there is the spaciousness of heart and affect that is important. *Lectio divina* does not have a goal except that of allowing the Holy Spirit to shape our inner world according to God's design—in God's timing. Too often this time set aside for *lectio divina* can feel like a waste of time. Do not be deceived.

As with praying the Liturgy of the Hours, find that quiet place with minimal noise and few disruptions. Some reserve time and space in their homes, and some prefer to do their *lectio divina* in the Eucharistic or meditation chapel at their parish. Many people find that a certain routine supports their commitment to this sacred time. Sit comfortably upright with good but not stiff posture. Set your Bible comfortably on your lap so that you can read the text before you with ease. Be sure the lighting is soft but still allows you to see the text with ease. Breathe deeply and invite the Holy Spirit to be with you.

Some people like to stay with one book of the Bible through to the end, others simply open the book and see where their eyes land, some people literally go from Genesis through, over the many years, to Revelation. Then some have a means of choosing a section of the Bible that, for them, corresponds to a particular liturgical season. Your method of choosing texts is not what is important. Just stay with the Holy Spirit, who may well speak to you through your intuition. Let your eyes gently rest upon the page and begin to slowly read. Some people find it helpful to begin by reading softly aloud. This slows them down until they move into and through the text. A word or a phrase will stand out. Stop there and rest with it, repeating the word or phrase slowly. If the energy has passed or your intuition tells you to proceed, just continue to read the words slowly. You are not engaging the text with your mind so much as with your heart and spirit. Let an attitude of quiet receptivity permeate this time of prayer.

You will find yourself drawn toward quiet meditation on a word or phrase. Stay there and do not be in a hurry to move on. Linger on the experience of this word or phrase upon your heart, and even deep in your gut. Bask in the present moment. Allow your senses to evoke possible images, feelings, and memories. Do not force this. Just accept any gift from the Holy Spirit that might be present. Listen for how your body responds to savoring this text. Notice any questions (not of the intellectual kind) or insights or challenges that emerge. What awakens in your imagination? Be attentive with all that is stirred within. You are cultivating an attitude of quiet receptivity that will permeate your being. This interaction with your memories, feelings, and images is the place of meditation. Benedictine Sister Macrina Wiederkehr says of meditation:

> A touched heart means that God has, in some way, come. God has entered that heart. Begin your meditation. Meditation is a process in which you struggle with the Word of God that has entered your heart. If this word wants to be a guest in your heart, go forth to meet it. Welcome it in and try to understand it. Walk with it. Wrestle with it. Ask it questions. Tell it stories about yourself. Allow it to nourish you. Receive its blessing. To do this you must sink your heart into it as you would sink your teeth into food. You must chew it with your heart.[18]

When our hearts have been touched by the Holy Spirit through our wrestling with the word, we have in some small or deeper way been changed. We give voice to that hope, to that expectation, or to that new awareness. Be aware of any prayer that rises up within you that expresses what you are experiencing. What implication might this word or phrase have for you today? What gratitude or hope is arising within you? This is where our time of *lectio divina* begins to connect with the rest of our lives. Pray as if speaking with a close friend—no pretenses or formalities as this is someone who knows you. Allow for spiritual intimacy. Again do not be in a hurry.

The natural movement from spoken prayer is into contemplation. Contemplation is far more ingrained in our DNA than most of us realize. We may hold the mistaken notion that contemplation is something limited to hermits and cloistered contemplatives. Quite the contrary: we were created for a contemplative relationship with God. It is only natural for the beloved (us) to draw close, in silence, with the lover (God). Trappist Thomas Merton described contemplation as "life itself, fully awake, fully active, fully aware that it is alive. It is spiritual wonder. It is spontaneous awe at the sacredness of life, of being."[19] Contemplation is simply attentive awareness of the divine presence.

Take time, dwell in your quiet space, move your attention deep within, breathe deeply, and savor the silence. While you may receive a word or an image, this is mostly about beholding God's love for you and allowing the divine presence to deepen and expand your heart. Over time, that slow-drip method will deepen your capacity to love. You may find yourself becoming a far more compassionate person. Your spirit will be touched by the pain and aspirations of the world around you. People who deepen in their contemplative life are also deeply committed to social justice issues.

Pope St. Gregory the Great preserved the story of the last yearly visit between Benedict and his twin, Scholastica. They had met for a day's visit in a house on the side of Monte Cassino. The hours passed by quickly, and as dusk began to approach, they shared a meal. While the visit continued, Benedict began to grow concerned as darkness was encroaching and he had quite the hike back up the steep mountain. While Benedict was enjoying his visit with his sister, he also felt pressed to return to his monastery before total darkness.

Scholastica begged him to stay the night so that they could continue their visit, but her brother was something of a stickler for the letter of the law. Rarely were monks permitted to stay away overnight from the monastery unless the distance of their necessary travel required them to do so. When Benedict refused her request and stood to depart, Scholastica put her clasped hands on the table and bent in prayer. She prayed earnestly to God. Soon the clear night sky was filled with dark, angry, foreboding clouds. As she raised her head heavenward, thunder and lightning erupted, then a heavy downpour of rain. Benedict turned toward his sister and asked her what she had done. Scholastica reminded him that she had requested he stay for the night (it was his monastery's house after all) and he had refused her request. So she petitioned a higher authority (God) who listened and responded. Pope Gregory the Great then reflected that, of course a woman's prayer was deemed more powerful than her famous brother as she who loved more should accomplish more. The power of love.

Throughout this chapter, I have made the presumption that the source of your *lectio divina* would be the Bible. While Benedict assumed his monks had consumed the Word of God through years of *lectio divina*, he also encouraged them to make use of the writings of other early Church Fathers and Mothers, to seek Wisdom where she is to be found.[20] As your spiritual hunger leads you, explore the writings of spiritual masters who have gone before us as well as contemporary writers. These, as well as poetry, might be sources for your own spiritual reading and *lectio divina*.

CONCLUSION

The Benedictine way is immensely practical and mixed up in daily life. The invitation is to find, claim, protect, and savor moments and places of the contemplative so that we might grow in a deeper sense of God's presence and more fully into our own humanity. Benedictine prayer will always be about strengthening our connection to others and embodied in service to others. Benedictine prayer is never just about ourselves. That is the meaning of community as the context of our prayer.

> Nothing is more practical than finding God, that is, than *Falling in Love* in a quite absolute, final way. What you are in love with, what seizes your imagination, will affect everything. It will decide what will get you out of bed in the morning, what you do with your evenings, how you spend your

weekends, what you read, who you know, what breaks your heart, and what amazes you with joy and gratitude. Fall in love, stay in love, and it will decide everything.[21]

Fall in love.

1. *Benedict's Rule*, 72: 11–12, trans. Terrence Kardong, OSB (Collegeville, MN: Liturgical, 1996).
2. St. Benedict established twelve monasteries for men, preferably numbering twelve men in each monastery, with Monte Cassino, the most famous, being the last, which is also where he died. Benedict did not have women in mind as monastic women already had their own monastic tradition.
3. From Galatians 3:28, which reads: "There is no such thing as Jew and Greek, slave and free, male and female; for all of you are one in Christ Jesus." All Scripture quotations are from the NRSV.
4. *Benedict's Rule*, prologue: 1.
5. William Shannon, *Silence on Fire: Prayer of Awareness* (New York: Crossroad, 2000), 32.
6. Hence Pope Francis issued his encyclical, *Laudato Si'*. Pray with this document with a stance of openness: How am I called to respond? What does the Holy Spirit want me to learn from this?
7. *The Life of St. Benedict by Gregory the Great*, trans. Terence Kardong (Collegeville, MN: Liturgical, 2009), 131–132.
8. To loosely paraphrase the desert ascetics, the spiritual journey is one inch long and many miles deep.
9. I do not believe that God sends evil our way to teach us something—that would be a rather cruel and wicked god—but when (as Rabbi Harold Kushner reminded us) bad things happen to good people, we can learn and grow as well as heal.
10. The standard sacred text for Roman Catholics, of course, is the Bible. However, we also reverence the writings of those who have explored, shaped, embodied, and passed on a rich spiritual tradition to us (such as the Doctors of the Church). Benedictines are generally comfortable with the idea that poetry or literature or other rich writings can be acknowledged as sacred text for us as individuals, thus fodder for *lectio divina*.
11. The best definition of hell that I have encountered is that hell is the complete absence of God.
12. Shannon, *Silence on Fire*, 32.
13. *Benedict's Rule*, prologue: 9.
14. Oblates are people connected to a monastery, making their oblation (meaning offering) to live out the Benedictine way of life in their particular circumstances. Oblates may be married or not, Roman Catholic or as a member of another Christian tradition, but they work to integrate Benedictine values and live the monastic way as they are able.
15. Most of you probably already realize that there are electronic editions of the Liturgy of the Hours as well as websites dedicated to downloading today's Office.
16. Hildegard of Bingen (1089–1179) was a Benedictine abbess and Doctor of the Church whose writings are still being studied, whose chant is still being used (those with strong lungs), and whose medicine is undergoing revival.

17. *Benedict's Rule*, 19:7.
18. Macrina Wiederkehr, *A Tree Full of Angels: Seeing the Holy in the Ordinary* (San Francisco: HarperSanFrancisco, 1990), 54.
19. Thomas Merton, *New Seeds of Contemplation* (New York: New Directions, 1961), 1.
20. *Benedict's Rule*, 73.
21. This quote is attributed to Pedro Arrupe, now deceased leader of the Society of Jesus. It resonates with his life story.

CHAPTER 17

Prayer in the Salesian Tradition

~ Wendy M. Wright ~

Jane de Chantal (1572–1641), early modern French cofounder of the women's religious congregation the Visitation of Holy Mary, is quoted as claiming that "the best method of prayer is to have no method at all."[1] In retrospect, her claim appears somewhat ironic in that Jane, along with her cofounder Francis de Sales (1567–1622), Bishop of Geneva and popular spiritual author from the duchy of Savoy, both promoted a wide variety of prayer practices.[2] These two spiritual friends are at the fountainhead of the larger spiritual family known as Salesian. While it was mainly the bishop's writings, especially the *Introduction to the Devout Life* and the *Treatise of the Love of God*, through which the Salesian perspective originally was, and still continues to be, disseminated, the congregation of the Visitation that the two founded in 1610 was, for several centuries, the chief institutional bearer of the Salesian charism.[3]

In the nineteenth century a pan-European revival of interest in Salesian spirituality produced several religious congregations and lay organizations explicitly dedicated to practicing the Christian life or engaging in ministry in the Salesian spirit. These religious communities and organizations include, among others, (1) the Salesians of Don Bosco, Daughters of Mary Help of Christians, and the Salesian Cooperators, (2) the Oblates of Saint Francis de Sales and the Oblate Sisters of Saint Francis de Sales, (3) the Daughters of Saint Francis de Sales, and (4) the Missionaries of Saint Francis de Sales (Fransalians). These groups, as well as lay associates connected to them or the educational institutions they have founded, can be viewed as sharing the Salesian charism. From these branches of the spiritual family come varied teachings on prayer.

Despite this, Jane's claim about the significance of methodless prayer is not an empty one. For the basic spiritual orientation of the Salesian tradition is toward what might be termed "the freedom of the children of God," a suppleness of heart, mind, and will that allows the divine Spirit ample room to inhabit and thus animate a woman or man.[4] This freedom or liberty of spirit may be facilitated by any number of prayer practices. The primary imagery with which this deep interior liberty is cast in the Salesian lexicon is profoundly affective and focuses on the heart (understood as the core of the human person not simply as feeling but also as intellect and will). It focuses specifically on an "exchange of hearts."[5]

For Francis and Jane and those who follow in their footsteps, the universe is best conceptualized as an interconnected world of hearts, the heart of the God and human hearts conjoined together through the heart of Jesus. That human-divine heart as revealed in Matthew 11:28–30 is gentle and humble. Thus women and men, whose hearts are created by and for God who is love itself, are invited to embrace the fullness of life promised in Scripture and to live Jesus. This is realized through the practice of the little virtues, chiefly gentleness and humility, the receptive, relational virtues of Jesus's own heart. A radical reorientation of agency, this living Jesus, or cultivation of a generous interior liberty that allows for divine initiative to become the guide and animator of all thought and action is, in the Salesian view, the vocation of *all* Christians no matter their situation in life. Persons whose life circumstances are varied—laity, religious, priests, wives and mothers, shopkeepers, governors, and servants, whether wealthy, powerful, powerless, or poor, those with leisure and those who are thrust into constant activity—all are called to the devout life through an exchange of hearts. And as there are different personal dispositions and persons with differing levels of spiritual maturity (who can be male or female, educated or not, young or old) there will be different approaches, practices, and methods of cultivating the liberty of spirit that can allow for an exchange of hearts so that a woman or man might echo St. Paul, in saying "I no longer live but Christ lives in me" (Galations 2:20).[6]

Introduction to the Devout Life

Until the mid-twentieth century, de Sales's *Introduction to the Devout Life* was the most frequently read spiritual guide in the Catholic world. It continues in the present day to be frequently reprinted and adapted for contemporary Christian readers. As a man prompted by early modern Catholic reforming zeal, the Savoyard believed that God desired intimacy with ordinary men and women as well as with those in professed religious life. The *Devout Life* was written for such as these with the assumption that they, who had long been assumed to be less spiritually capable than their vowed peers, long to learn how to respond to the divine desire that stirs deep in the human heart. Prayer is one of the chief avenues of response to the divine initiative.

The *Devout Life* assumes that its reader, Philothea, (Lover of God),[7] comes to personal prayer in the larger context of Christian sacramental practice. The bishop describes prayer as necessary for anyone who longs to grow in God's love as prayer clarifies the mind and draws the will by exposing it to the warmth of divine ardor. In his typically imaginative and image-rich rhetorical style, Francis writes,

> [Prayer] is the water of blessing which by its watering causes the plants of our good desires to become green and to flower, washes our souls clean from their imperfections, and quenches the passions of our hearts.[8]

All types of prayer de Sales deems important. Vocal prayers such as the Hail Mary and the Our Father are lauded. The bishop himself prayed the rosary with his episcopal household daily.[9] But more importantly, he prompts Philothea to move gradually into interior mental prayer focused especially on the Passion of Jesus and offers a detailed method for the aspirant who longs for a deeper awareness of the divine. This brief method of interior meditation is recommended after Philothea has given serious attention to purifying the soul from attachment to sin and consideration of God's love and the true end toward which human life is appropriately directed. First, she is encouraged as she begins to pray to place herself in God's presence, becoming aware that God is everywhere in everything, including the depths of the human heart. Humbled by the majesty of the divine, she should ask for the grace to serve well. Then, a particular mystery (for example Jesus on the cross) is proposed to the imagination, and Philothea is encouraged to enter the scene imaginatively in order to draw insight from it, pausing when a meditation elicits edifying response.

> And if your mind finds enough flavor, light, and fruit in one of the reflections, you should stop yourself there without going any further—doing as bees do who do not leave the flower until they have gathered all the honey. [10]

Finally, these meditative reflections should prompt affections and resolutions. The will should be moved toward salutary impulses such as trust, zeal for heaven, compassion, or joy that then should be turned into resolutions that seek to transform affections into actions that can amend faults or encourage growth. Prayer in the Salesian tradition, even in this fairly elementary method, never remains notional but always draws the one praying toward active growth and alignment of the will with the divine prompting. The final movements of this interior process include thanksgiving, the offering of one's affections and resolutions, and supplication. Then, with his typically encouraging spiritual pedagogy, Francis assures that the fruits of the meditation will not fade by proposing that Philothea collect a souvenir or "spiritual bouquet."

> To all of this I add the need to gather a little souvenir of devotion, and here I mean those who have walked in a garden do not leave willingly without taking in their hands four or five flowers for the scent and to keep for the length of the day: so that when our minds have thought about some mystery through meditation, we ought to choose one or two points that we found most to our liking...for us to recall for the rest of the day and for the spiritual scent.[11]

For those familiar with Ignatian spirituality, the influence of that earlier tradition in this advice book for lay Christians is easily detectable. With their Christian humanist orientation toward liberty of spirit, self-examination, their positive view of human capability and God-directedness, and their promotion of imaginative scriptural meditation, which is in itself a modality of classic *lectio divina*,[12] Ignatian and Salesian spiritual traditions aim toward the surrender and commitment of the whole person to the purposes of God. As a youth, Francis was a student of the Jesuits at the Paris college of Clermont, and throughout his life, he chose Jesuits as his personal spiritual guides: their influence is evident in his teachings.

But Salesian spirituality is not merely a version of the Ignatian way. Its tonality is original, beautiful, optimistic, even rhapsodic, and it is saturated with the affective language of the Song of Songs. While in Paris with the Jesuits, Francis also studied with a Benedictine Scripture scholar who uncovered for his pupil the spiritual meaning of the song. The deepest assumptions of Salesian spirituality are thus rooted in a vision of a God of immeasurable outflowing love who creates human beings with hearts designed to beat in rhythm with the divine heartbeat, even though human hearts are wounded by sin and need to be realigned. Thus the importance of the revelation of Jesus, who invites, "come to me…and learn from me for I am gentle and humble in heart" (Matthew 11:30).[13]

The end toward which human beings are created is understood to be intimate union, an exchange of hearts, with the divine lover. The brief method that de Sales taught in the *Devout Life* was directed toward cultivating a continual sense of divine intimacy which would grow with practice. When, after his death, his spiritual friend Jane de Chantal wrote of Francis's prayer method in her deposition for his canonization, she attested to his deep trust and familiarity with God as the fruit of his prayer:

> God had indeed given him a great gift of prayer, and he used to talk to our Lord in a very familiar and simple way with a love of perfect trust. One day when talking to me, he used an image about his prayer and compared it to oil poured out on a smoothly polished table and spreading even further on this shining surface; in the same way, from a few words or thoughts of prayer remembered, a feeling of love spread through his soul and was sweetly maintained there. He told me he woke to the thought of God and fell asleep in the same way if he could. [14]

This intimate interior relationship that Jane recounted seems to have shifted to a more nondiscursive experience in the last years of de Sales's life, although the shift was met with characteristic indifference:

Some five or six years before his death he told me when talking to me about prayer that he now felt nothing, and that only the highest point of his soul had any share in the light and feeling God sent him, and that all the rest was a blank...he took little notice of his state of mind at prayer, and whether it brought comfort or desolation; when our Lord sent him good thoughts he took them quite simply, and when none were forthcoming, he left it at that.[15]

The point of prayer was not for the Savoyard to gain any particular experience or perceived level of union but the cultivation of profound availability, spiritual liberty, so that God might use one as God willed. Jane testified that:

Neither I myself nor anyone else as far as I know, ever saw him attached to any devotional occupation, or indeed to anything else; he kept his mind supple in a spirit of holy liberty to do whatever providence offered. One often saw him about to say Mass, or to pray, and then put this off or even give it up altogether when his neighbor needed him or some other rightful claim presented itself.... And this was why he was always praying, because he always kept his heart wide open to everything God chose to send him... he often said that if we wanted to serve God perfectly we must cleave to him alone, long for him ardently and always, and yet not cling to the ways and means by which we reach out to him, but keep quite free and poised to go where charity and obedience call us, and when we have heard the call, go cheerfully and in peace.[16]

THE DIRECTION OF INTENTION

If de Sales encouraged Philothea to become immersed in a sense of divine promise and presence through imaginative mental prayer and meditative entry into Scripture and to learn to live Jesus, cultivating a free response to the divine will, he had other explicit suggestions for prayer for those who were in religious life. Along with their *Constitutions*, he created a *Spiritual Directory for Daily Actions* for youthful members of the Visitation of Holy Mary that provided suggestions for ways in which God's presence might be cultivated in the midst of everyday activities. When he was a university student at Padua, the Savoyard had drawn up a similar guide for daily living for himself and considered it foundational to his own spiritual growth. Although most of the Visitation communities over the centuries interpreted the *Spiritual Directory* as advice primarily for novices, in the nineteenth century, two religious congregations—the Oblates of Saint Francis de Sales and the Oblate Sisters of Saint Francis de Sales—were founded in France to engage in apostolic work in the Salesian spirit. They adopted the *Directory* as a formative document for members throughout the life-span.

Chief among the figures of this era's Salesian revival as expressed in these communities are Marie de Sales Chappuis (1793–1875), the superior of the Visitation in the city of Troyes and known as "the Good Mother"; the Visitation convent chaplain, Father Louis Brisson (1817–1908); and former student in the convent boarding school, Leonie Aviat (1844–1914). The Oblate Sisters, founded by Brisson and Aviat, ministered to young working class women crowding into France's newly industrialized cities seeking employment. The Oblates, a men's congregation, was founded by Brisson at the urging of the Good Mother to educate and catechize young men in post-revolutionary France.

The *Constitutions* of the Oblates of Saint Francis de Sales reveals how crucial Louis Brisson felt the *Directory* was for formation in the Salesian spirit by claiming that it was crucial for "retracing" or "reprinting" in themselves the image of St. Francis de Sales, who was himself an image of the Lord.[17]

> As the Good Mother said, the aim of St. Francis de Sales and the effect of all his spiritual doctrine is to have the Savior seen once more on earth. Not only should our intellect and will be drawn away from evil and directed toward God but the whole man should be led to God. His heart, his intellect, his soul, his body, his entire being should be brought to the divine likeness, to the likeness of the Son of God made man.[18]

At the heart of this transformative process was the habitual practice of the "Direction of Intention" outlined in the *Directory*. This is the practice of asking for grace and offering to God all the good that may come from any action one is about to undertake. It is about the *attitude* with which every daily action is approached, an intention. Thus Brisson enjoined his confreres,

> The purpose of the Direction of Intention is not to have us practice a given exercise of devotion or piety, but to have us take our whole life and bind it to God.... It precedes each act of our life whether great or small. It helps us overcome and renounce ourselves. It is no longer our life, our nature, our way of thinking that matters most. It is the will of God and our inclination towards God that matters most, as the Good Mother used to say.[19]

A contemporary recasting of this seminal Oblate prayer in light of the teachings of the Second Vatican Council was crafted by in Oblate Anthony Ceresko in 2001. The new version moves beyond personal metanoia to concerns for social justice and the need for awareness of the communal and social dimension of all actions: "My God give me your grace. I offer you all the good that I shall do in this action and all the pain and suffering to be found in it. Stay close to me and help me to see how what I am doing can advance Christ's blessed hold upon the universe. Amen."[20]

"Simple Remise"

As suggested, Salesian prayer is not mainly about specific practices, although characteristically specific practices were and are taught and advanced in order to cultivate spiritual freedom, develop a habitual sense of the divine presence, and direct all actions toward and surrender to the will of God. The Salesian tradition also has encoded in it a classically contemplative tradition of prayer that is associated primarily with Jane de Chantal and the sisters of the Visitation. Jane's own spiritual itinerary might serve as an example of this type of prayer.

Before she was founding superior of the Visitation of Holy Mary, Jane was a baroness and widow with four young children who came under Francis de Sales's spiritual direction. At first he directed her as he would other lay directees in practices that allowed her to honor the demands and responsibilities of her state in life, which in her case meant overseeing her household, her late husband's estate, and her children's educations. Meditative reflection on the mysteries of the life of Christ carried out in the gentle Salesian mode formed the backbone of her personal prayer. But always, freedom of spirit was paramount in the exercise of prayer as her director Francis underscored in a letter written in 1604:

> [I]f you really like the prayers you are used to saying, please don't drop them; and if you happen to leave out some of what I am telling you to do, have no scruples about it, for here is the rule of our general obedience written in capital letters
> "DO ALL THROUGH LOVE, NOTHING THROUGH CONSTRAINT; LOVE OBEDIENCE MORE THAN YOU FEAR DISOBEDIENCE."
> I want you to have the liberty of spirit…that excludes constraint, scruples and anxiety. If you really love obedience and docility, I'd like to think that when some legitimate or charitable cause takes you away from your religious exercises, this would be for you another form of obedience and that your love would make up for whatever you have to omit in your religious practice.[21]

As Jane matured and the relationship between her and the bishop ripened into a deep spiritual friendship, the spiritual suppleness toward which Jane had been directed yielded a more nondiscursive type of prayer. She would later refer to this as the prayer of "simple remise," a simple attentiveness or loving trustful surrender into the divine presence. Advising a group of novices after the Visitation was established, Jane drew on her own experience of this maturing prayer and suggested that, "Resting in the spirit of God is the most important vocation for the daughters of the Visitation to have. They must not be at all concerned about formal reflections, ideas, notions or speculation about other matters, although they should honor these as gifts capable of leading to God himself."[22]

Elsewhere she was more explicit about exactly what this prayer of *simple remise* entailed:

> Those who are led by this path are obligated to a great purity of heart, humility, submission and total dependence on God. They must greatly simplify their spirit in every way, suppressing each reflection on the past, the present and the future. And instead of looking to what they are doing or will do, they must look to God, forgetting themselves as much as possible in all things in favor of this continual remembrance, uniting their spirit with his goodness, in everything that happens to them from moment to moment. This should be done very simply.[23]

What Mother de Chantal, by this time an adept spiritual guide, described here mirrors the dynamics of classic contemplative prayer.[24] She was also able to advise her sisters in religion about the sometimes disconcerting passage into this resting in the divine presence.

> What often happens to souls on this path is that they are troubled by many distractions and that they continue without any support from the senses. Our Lord withdraws the feeling of his sweet presence from them as well as all sort of interior consolations and lights so that they remain in total impotence and insensitivity, although sometimes this is more true than others.
>
> This somewhat surprises souls who are as yet inexperienced. But they must remain firm and rest in God above every thought and feeling, suffering, receiving and cherishing equally all the ways and works God is pleased to perform in them, sacrificing themselves and unreservedly abandoning any of these works to the discretion of his love and every holy will, without seeing or wishing to see what they are doing or should do. But completely above their own sight and self-knowledge they must be joined to God in the supreme point of their spirit and be utterly lost in him. They will find, by this means, peace in the midst of war and rest in the midst of work. Simply

put, we must remain in the state where God puts us: in pain we must have patience, in suffering, we must endure.[24]

As Jane was to report later in her life, this type of nondiscursive, imageless gazing toward God was to become the characteristic prayer of the Visitation community:

> I have recognized that the almost universal attraction of the daughters of the Visitation is to a very simple practice of the presence of God effected by a total abandonment of themselves to Holy Providence.... [S]everal are attracted this way from the beginning and it seems as though God avails himself of this one means to cause us to achieve our end, and the perfect union of our soul with him. In short, I believe that this manner of prayer is essential to our little congregation, that it is a great gift of God which requires infinite gratitude.[25]

MARTYRDOM OF LOVE

The Visitation of Holy Mary order spread rapidly across Europe. By the time of Jane de Chantal's death in 1641, a mere thirty years after its initial foundation, there were approximately eighty houses. The prayer of simple remise remained the order's characteristic spiritual orientation. Despite this popularity, the order's contemplative teaching was not confined to the monastic world. Not only was Francis de Sales the chief spiritual confidant of Jane until his death, he was also the privileged confessor and guide for the founding Visitation house in Annecy, and his writings were staples of the Visitandine formation across Europe. In 1616 the Savoyard bishop published the *Treatise on the Love of God*, his most ambitious work that proposed to chart the "birth, progress, decay, operations, properties, benefits and excellences of divine love."[26] The inner chapters of that tome, which treat of advanced states of prayer, were, as he admitted, shaped by the conversations and personal knowledge he accrued from his friendship with Jane and his familiarity with the daughters of the Visitation. One striking descriptive passage likens the one who prays this way to a deaf court musician playing before his prince. While working on the text Francis corresponded with his friend about how her experience shaped his composition of the section in his *Treatise* on mystical prayer:

> I am working on your book number nine of *The Love of God*, and today, praying before the crucifix, God showed me your soul and your [inner] state by the metaphor of an accomplished musician, born subject to a prince who loved him perfectly and who had expressed to him how wonderfully pleasing the sweet melody of his lute and voice were. This unfortunate singer, like

you, became deaf and could no longer hear his own music but he did not
cease to sing because he knew that his master retained him to sing. [27]

The metaphor of the deaf musician suggests the deep levels of contemplative prayer
that in the present age we tend to associate with the teachings of Carmelite John of
the Cross about dark nights: that cruciform *kenotic* (self-emptying) process of detachment from all mental, sensual, intellectual and spiritual ways of knowing and relating
in order to be in union with the transcendent God. Neither Jane de Chantal nor
Francis de Sales knew John's works, as the Spaniard's writing had not been translated
into French and was not available to them. But they were familiar with the long tradition of Christian nondiscursive or apophatic prayer.

Salesian ideas about prayer, whether for beginners or those more mature, and for
all their gentle graciousness and emphasis on the love that God bears human beings,
are steeped in a spirit of sacrifice and surrender. They assume that as a practitioner
matures in the Christian life and begins to live Jesus that the image they "reprint," to
use Louis Brisson's language, is the image of Christ crucified. It is not surprising then
that de Sales's great *Treatise on the Love of God* closes with the insight that "Calvary
is the mount of lovers. All love which does not spring from the Savior's passion is a
perilous plaything.... In our Lord's passion love and death blend so inextricably that
no heart can contain one without the other."[28]

The modality through which the crucifixion is most explicitly experienced in the
Salesian tradition is in the cultivation of a supple spirit of availability, the achievement of an interior freedom that allows for the surrender of self-will and a radical
openness to the divine will. This hidden, profoundly interior process of openness
came over time in the Visitation world to be characterized as a type of martyrdom.
Jane was the one to first name it in this manner. In 1632, on the feast of St. Basil,
ten years after Francis's death, she was at recreation with her sisters in religion when
she fell into a reverie. Asked what she was considering, she evoked the language of
martyrdom to describe her own sense of the truly detached person, the one who had
taken on the heart of Jesus. The sisters recorded her thoughts, knowing that she was
speaking both autobiographically and about the sort of lives to which the women in
the Visitation were called, those women who carried in their hearts and expressed in
all their words and actions the heart of the gentle, humble, crucified Savior:

> My dear daughters, Saint Basil and most of the fathers and pillars of the
> church were not martyred. Why do you think this was so?... For myself,
> I believe that there is a martyrdom of love in which God preserves the
> lives all of his servants so that they might work for his glory. This makes

them martyrs and confessors at the same time. I know...that this is the martyrdom to which the daughters of the Visitation are called in which God will allow them to suffer if they are fortunate enough to wish for it.... What happens is that divine love thrusts its sword into the most intimate and secret parts of the soul and separates us from our very selves. I know one soul whom love had severed in this way who felt it more keenly than if a tyrant with a sword had separated her body from her soul.[29]

Later in the seventeenth century, a young Visitandine at the French monastery of Paray-le-Monial, Margaret Mary Alacoque (1647–1690), would give expression to this theme of martyrdom in a very different modality. Beginning in 1693 Margaret Mary was the recipient of a series of visions of Jesus revealing his Sacred Heart and asking for hers, which, like his, would become marked with the suffering and blood of the cross. Jesus then entreated her to promote a series of devotional practices that included reception of Holy Communion on the first Friday of each month, Eucharistic Adoration during a "Holy Hour" on Thursdays (during which meditation on Jesus's agony in the garden of Gethsemane would take place), and a celebration of the Feast of the Sacred Heart (to be held in the week following the Eucharistic Feast of the Body and Blood of Christ). Adoration of Jesus's heart and reparation for sins committed against that Eucharistic heart were central to this sort of prayer. Eventually these practices spread beyond the Visitation, were promoted by the Catholic magisterium and became a popular form of prayer for Catholics across the globe. As they became more universally adopted, their specifically Salesian character was profoundly muted.[30]

THE PRAYER OF THE SALESIAN FAMILY

Much else could be said about prayer in the varied branches of the Salesian tradition as it has expressed itself over the centuries: the vibrant, joyful spirit Don Bosco and his followers brought and continue to bring to their global ministry with marginalized youth, as well as the processions, festivals, and playfulness that accompany their method of pedagogy; the adaptation of the *Introduction to the Devout Life* that the lay association, the Daughters of Saint Francis de Sales, follow for their formation as ordinary women of faith; and the inviting, gentle spirit the Fransalians bring to their missionary work on the Indian subcontinent. Each of these modalities of the Salesian way has its own history and ways of prayer. The methods are many. It may even be said that the best method of Salesian prayer is to have no method at all. But all of the varied approaches are joined together by a common quality of heart taught by the two friends, Francis de Sales and Jane de Chantal, who are at the taproot of this spiritual family. The quality of the Salesian heart is gentle and humble. It is a heart, like the crucified heart of Jesus, radically open to the promptings of divine love and abandoned to the divine will. The exchange of the heart of the Savior for one's own heart, this is, quite simply, what characterizes Salesian prayer.

1. Ste. Jeanne François Frémyot de Chantal, *Sa Vie et ses oeuvres*, édition publiée par les soins des Religieuses du Premiere Monasère de la Visitation Sainte Marie d'Annecy (Paris: Plon, 1874–1879), 3: 260.

2. Francis de Sales, a native of the duchy of Savoy, located in what is now southwest France and northern Italy, was bishop in exile of Geneva thus his episcopal seat was in Annecy in Savoy. The canton of Geneva during his lifetime was a stronghold of the Calvinist reform, and Catholic observance was outlawed there.

3. The Visitation was originally a simple diocesan congregation. In 1616 it received canonical recognition as a formal enclosed religious order.

4. For a detailed exploration of this fundamental theme consult Eunan McDonnell, *The Concept of Freedom in the Writings of St. Francis de Sales* (Bern: Peter Lang Academic, 2007). A briefer treatment along with treatments of five other central Salesian themes is found in *Francis de Sales, Jane de Chantal: Letters of Spiritual Direction*, ed. Wendy M. Wright and Joseph F. Power, trans. Péronne Marie Thibert (New York: Paulist, 1988), 34–69.

5. On the heart in Salesian spirituality, see Wendy M. Wright, "That Is What It Is Made For: Image of the Heart in the Spirituality of Francis de Sales and Jane de Chantal," *Spiritualities of the Heart*, ed. Annice Callahan (New York: Paulist, 1990), 143–158.

6. All Scripture quotations are taken from the *New International Version* (NIV).

7. The majority of de Sales's directees and spiritual correspondents were women: hence the feminine Philothea. The *Devout Life* was, in fact, created using letters the bishop had written to a number of women, including Louise de Châtel, Madame de Charmoisy, a young woman who consulted him about how to live a Christian life while her husband was serving at the courts of Europe where Christian virtue was notoriously absent. His longer and more systematic *Treatise on the Love of God* is addressed to the masculine "Theotimus."

8. Francis de Sales, *The Complete Introduction to the Devout Life*, trans. Father John-Julian, OJN (Brewster, MA: Paraclete, 2013), 77.

9. Daily rosary in the episcopal household was a result of a vow Francis made as a young man. During his era, Marian devotion was very much a focus of reformed Catholic faith. See Wendy M. Wright, "Saint Francis de Sales (1567–1622) and the Conception of the Virgin Mary," *Marian Studies* 55 (2008): 135–158.

10. Francis de Sales, *Complete Introduction*, 87.

11. Francis de Sales, *Complete Introduction*, 89.

12. The Ignatian version of *lectio divina* that Francis de Sales would have practiced was somewhat distinctive in that it consisted of an intertwined rumination blending together the four "phases" of *lectio* (*lectio, meditatio, oratio, contemplatio*). The *Exercises* as the Basque saint developed them were heavily reliant upon the particular manner in which scripture reading was outlined in Ludolf of Saxony's *Vita Christi*. Based on a harmony of the four Gospels both Ludolf and Ignatius each made his own selection of New Testament scenes and arranged them according to his own intention. The Gospel text did not need to be read directly but might

be summarized for the retreatant doing the *Exercises*. The location of each Gospel scene was considered. However, Ludolf's approach was to indicate the significance of the scene while Ignatius left the one praying free to appropriate the scene in a personal way.

13. De Sales was Scotist, not Anselmian, in his theological orientation, teaching that the Incarnation was not a result of human sin but was planned from before the creation itself as God innately desires intimacy with the created order.

14. *St. Francis de Sales: A Testimony by St. Chantal*, ed. and trans. Elisabeth Stopp (Hyattsville, MD: Institute of Salesian Studies, 1967), 97.

15. *St. Francis de Sales: A Testimony*, 98.

16. *St. Francis de Sales: A Testimony*, 99.

17. On the ongoing significance of the Directory and the Direction of Intention among the Oblates of Saint Francis de Sales, consult Anthony R. Ceresko, "St. Francis de Sales' 'Spiritual Directory' for a New Century: Reinterpreting the Direction of Intention," *Indian Journal of Spirituality* 14, no. 4 (October–December 2001): 377–391.

18. *Cor ad Cor: Meditations for Every Day of the Year from the Teachings of Father Louis Brisson*, trans. Joseph E. Woods (Philadelphia: William Cooke, 1955), 14.

19. *Cor ad Cor*, 138–139.

20. Ceresko, 91.

21. *Francis de Sales, Jane de Chantal: Letters of Spiritual Direction*, 134.

22. Quoted in Wendy M. Wright, *Bond of Perfection: Jeanne de Chantal and François de Sales*, enhanced ed. (Stella Niagara, NY: De Sales Resource Center, 2001), 142.

23. Wright, *Bond of Perfection*, 142–143.

24. Jane knew about Teresa of Ávila's reforming work, as did Francis de Sales, and before she founded the Visitation, she used to consult with the Carmelites in Dijon about prayer. The Carmelite way was newly imported from Spain into France (Dijon was founded in 1605) and was a contemplative sort of prayer influenced by the tradition of Rhineland mysticism. It seems to have been popular in the Dijon Carmel. The writings of John of the Cross were not yet translated and available in France and thus could not have influenced Jane.

25. Wright, *Bond of Perfection*, 143.

26. Francis de Sales, *Treatise on the Love of God*, vol. 1, trans. John K. Ryan (Stella Niagara, NY: De Sales Resource Center, 2007), 40.

27. Wright, *Bond of Perfection*, 144.

28. Wendy M. Wright, *Francis de Sales: Introduction to the Devout Life and Treatise on the Love of God*, 2nd ed. (Stella Niagara, NY: De Sales Resource Center, 2005) 160.

29. Wright, *Francis de Sales: Introduction*, 154.

30. This sort of devotion to the Sacred Heart inaugurated by Margaret Mary has complex origins and a history wedded to political and ecclesial issues during the seventeenth through twentieth centuries. It tended to be associated with Roman Catholic identity, symbolized in the Eucharist, during periods when that church was on the defensive against the non-Catholic or secularizing modern world. On this, see Raymond Jonas, *France and the Cult of the Sacred Heart; An Epic Tale for Modern Times* (Berkeley, CA: University of California Press, 2000).

CHAPTER 18

Prayer in the Augustinian Tradition

~ Joseph L. Farrell, OSA ~

Chapel walls echo with psalms, canticles, scriptural readings, and intercessions. Morning, daytime, evening, and night are guided by the rhythm of prayers said aloud, followed by silent listening, of voices antiphonally praying millennia-old psalms and canticles proclaiming the magnificence and saving power of the Lord while also listening to what God is saying in the voices of those with whom one prays. The Augustinian tradition of prayer, like the tradition of many of our sisters and brothers whose daily ritual includes the Divine Office, values the ever ancient and yet ever new treasure we have in uniting together in sacred spaces to pray the rhythm of Christian prayer. This tradition also includes the beauty of exercising an intimate relationship with God by building into one's day a personal or individual rapport with the one in whose image we are created.

Augustinian prayer is realized in both word and deed, in contemplation and in action, in praise and in supplication, which has, as its goal, unity of both mind and heart in God. The roots of the Augustinian tradition of prayer are grounded in the writings, preaching, and life of St. Augustine of Hippo, and it continues to flourish in the lives of those who find value in this rich tradition.

St. Augustine of Hippo

Aurelius Augustine was born on November 13, 354, into a family of mixed religious beliefs and into a society comprised of both Roman and African cultures. The nuclear family in which Augustine was raised consisted of his father Patricius, his mother Monica, a brother Navigius, and at least one sister. Individually and collectively they played no small part in contributing to the development of the young Augustine. Later in life, Augustine's family extended to include his son Adeodatus and also the unnamed woman who was his faithful concubine for fifteen years and his son's mother. Through their word and example, their presence and their absence, their beliefs and disbeliefs, each member, in his or her own unique way, helped to form Augustine in the most impressionable years of his life. What we find in Augustine's family is that he never forgot the influences which helped to shape him, led him to his conversion, and aided him in his understanding of prayer.

Many of the details of Augustine's early life have been preserved in his *Confessions*.[1] We know from the *Confessions* how much influence Monica had on Augustine, especially on his understanding of prayer. Augustine makes mention of the frequency with which his mother brought her intentions before God. Her prayers often focused on the salvation of her son. Augustine describes his mother's prayer life in book 5 of *Confessions*[2] and admits that her tearful intercessions are what taught Augustine how to nourish his relationship with God through prayer.

Monica taught Augustine by prayer and by an example which spoke volumes in his formative years and was then reflected in his own life when he began to form his communities. Beginning with the gathering of his friends and family in Cassiciacum[3] and continuing on to the formation of lay and clerical communities in Thagaste and eventually Hippo, Augustine placed a great emphasis on the importance of communal prayer and developing one's personal relationship with God.

We can see how Monica's devotion and passion for prayer influenced her son. Prayer was a part of her daily experiences. It was a natural part of her routine, and Augustine eventually adapted this appreciation for prayer into his own life.[4] For Augustine, prayer, in fact, is what unites Christ to the Church, his body. Indeed, it is Christ who prays for us, in us, and is prayed to by us. The one whole Christ is completely encompassed in this act of conversing with God.[5]

Christus Totus

A key factor for understanding how Augustine called his community into prayer is found in his theology of the *Christus totus*. It is a combination of theology, ecclesiology, spirituality, and Christology woven to form an understanding of what it means not only to belong to Christ but also to be Christ,[6] relying primarily on the Pauline teaching of *Corpus Christi*. If we take St. Paul's First letter to the Corinthians as a foundation of this aspect of Augustine's spirituality, we see the scriptural basis supporting his idea:

> As a body is one though it has many parts, and all the parts of the body, though many, are one body, so also Christ. For in one Spirit we were all baptized into one body.... Now the body is not a single part, but many.... If they were all one part, where would the body be? But as it is, there are many parts, yet one body.... Now you are Christ's body, and individually parts of it. (1 Corinthians 12:12–27)[7]

Augustine insisted on recognizing Christ's presence in the community as a whole and in each individual member.[8] He reinforced the message of St. Paul with the Gospel message of Jesus, "Whatever you did for one of these least brothers of mine, you did for me" (Matthew 25:40)[9] The bishop called his community to prayer and to action to remind them that although their head is already in heaven, he is also present among them on earth. He preached, "Christ is hungry here, thirsty here, he's naked, he's a migrant, he's sick, he's in prison. You see, whatever the body suffers here, he said he suffers too."[10]

Those who were regular members of his congregation were witnesses to the number of times Augustine referred to the community as *Christus totus*.[11] Jesus Christ, for Augustine, is made manifest in our world in three ways: (1) as God, coeternal and coequal to the Father; (2) as the incarnate Word, mediator and head of the Church; and (3) as the whole Christ in the fullness of the Church.[12] Augustine's spirituality of prayer teaches that "formal prayer can never be separated from ordinary daily occupations; it cannot be a sacred interval in an otherwise profane day. Rather, it is meant to inform all our time and activity by sustaining and increasing our desire for God so that all we do may tend toward the rest and peace of God's Sabbath."[13] *Christus totus*, then, prays in words and action in a corporate and in an individual way. As *Christus totus*, the Church is made real in the way it recognizes its responsibility to be Christ for and with each other. The central core of this responsibility is the love which animates the community in responding to the two-fold commandment of loving God and one's neighbor. The love which exists among the members of the community is a relationship in Christ which nourishes the members as a whole.[14] It is the way Christ is made real in all of his members. Instead of focusing solely on the individual, Augustine's thought is basically corporate, with the whole present in the parts as much as the parts are present in the whole.

Tarsisius Van Bavel, OSA, draws attention to Augustine's emphasis on the whole Christ when he states:

> Consequently, Christ is for him not only an "I", but also a "We." Christ incorporates us into Himself.... Just as our personality is constituted by hundreds of relationships, the person of Christ is to be seen as having a relationship with every human being, because his love is universal.[15]

Christus totus is made completely present in the union of each of the members in community and is just as completely present in each of the members separately. The Body of Christ is whole and complete in each person as well as in community. Each member individually, and collectively, makes up the whole Christ.[16]

With this understanding we come to a fuller appreciation of Augustine's *Sermon* 272 on the Eucharist. Here, he recognizes the presence of the whole Christ in the sacrifice which is celebrated in the Eucharistic meal. He encourages his congregation to recognize themselves in that sacrifice; to accept their responsibility to be the body of Christ that they receive and celebrate at the table. He quotes 1 Corinthians

12:27, "Now you are Christ's body, and individually parts of it," and he encourages his congregation to recognize themselves in the mystery which is placed upon the altar and the mystery which they receive:

> It is to what you are that you reply "Amen," and by so replying you express your assent. What you hear, you see, is "The body of Christ," and you answer, "Amen." So be a member of the body of Christ, in order to make that "Amen" true.[17]

In reaching an understanding of what it means in Augustine's thought for the praying Church actually to be Christ, *Christus totus*, Head and members, it is necessary to be aware of the distinction which he recognizes as existing between Christ and humanity. As much as Augustine identifies each person with Christ, he does not mean that there is no distinction at all between the two. What Christ is by nature, we as the body of Christ are by grace. We as the members of the body of Christ are the saved, our Head is the Savior.[18]

RESTING IN THE LORD

Augustine's *Confessions* is not simply an autobiographical account of the spiritual pilgrimage of a north African bishop; it also provides the modern reader with an opportunity to discover the presence of God who is both the initiator of that spiritual pilgrimage and the treasure at its end. In the first chapter, he made this point perfectly clear when he penned those famous words that develop the core of Augustinian spirituality: "You have made us for yourself O Lord, and our heart is restless until it rests in you."[19] Augustine recognized in himself a truth which informed his understanding of Christian anthropology and will inform his understanding and practice of prayer. The restless search to return to the God who created him is prompted by the desire to find rest in the One in whom there is the only possibility of true peace. Eternal rest or Sabbath is our ultimate goal. Augustine concludes his *Confessions* with a prayer which revisits the theme of rest that he introduced in the opening chapter. He prays, "Give us peace, Lord God, for you have given us all else, give us the peace that is repose, the peace of the Sabbath, and the peace that knows no evening."[20]

Possidius, Augustine's friend and biographer, describes the first community which Augustine formed in *Thagaste*. He states that the members "lived for God in fasting, prayer and good works and in meditating day and night on the law of the Lord."[21] However, even before the establishment of the monastic communities in Africa, Augustine and Monica were living a life of community and prayer. They spent the first few months after Augustine's conversion living in Cassiciacum, just north of Milan, in community with friends, former students, and family members. There they found the opportunity to include in their daily discussions essential themes such as the search for the happy life, beauty, order, and truth. These themes, whose seeds were planted at Cassiciacum, bear fruit throughout Augustine's writings and also his preaching in the Basilica of Peace in Hippo. These are themes which shape Augustine's prayer life and which he shared with those whom he lived his life in community.

It was when he took the time to retreat to Cassiciacum that Augustine discovered the beauty of rest (*otium*)[22] in the Lord and in the company of friends and family. Soon, he was baptized by St. Ambrose in Milan. He then soon began his journey back to north Africa by way of Rome. Not long before Monica's death in the Roman port city of Ostia, Augustine and his mother shared an intense experience of contemplative prayer which he describes in his *Confessions* as a journey transcending mind, body, and spirit in order to reach the "land of never failing plenty." He recounts that they both were able to "just touch the edge of it by the utmost leap of our hearts."[23] This was a taste of the eternal rest, Sabbath or peace which is key to understanding Augustinian prayer. In a paradoxical way the journey to that eternal rest is a journey deep within in order to transcend all that is outside. Augustinian prayer seeks detachment from those things that distract us from the eternal rest for which we were created. Even though they may be good and beautiful, these objects or things can distract us from complete peace and rest.

While Augustine was bishop of Hippo, finding time for prayer, which nourished his soul, was not always easy to achieve. We know that the bishop's desire for leisure— *otio*—and contemplation in enjoying the company of friends was something which was a cherished treasure and a desire he never completely abandoned.[24] He, however, was also one to recognize the necessity of activity—*negotio*—in fulfilling the demands of the day. Augustine acknowledged that these demands had taken the place of the life of that Neoplatonic ascent which he enjoyed in Ostia with his mother. On many occasions, he reminded himself and his congregation of the need to search for a balance between the two aspects of a Christian's prayer life. *Otium sanctum* was a gift of grace allowing one to anticipate and participate in the peace and beauty of God's heavenly kingdom to come, while *negotium iustum* required one's active participation in constructing that kingdom here on earth.[25]

In the *City of God* he wrote:

> For no one ought to be so leisured as to take no thought in that leisure for the interest of his neighbor, nor so active as to feel no need for the contemplation of God. The attraction of a life of leisure ought not to be the prospect of lazy inactivity, but the chance for the investigation and discovery of

truth, on the understanding that each person makes some progress in this, and does not grudgingly withhold his discoveries from another.[26]

And in his *Confessions*, he expresses a wish to have everyone know of the necessity for inner prayer—a desire for God within. In speaking of this gift and his desire to share it with those around him, Augustine declares, "Ah, if only they could see the eternal reality within! I had tasted it, and was frantic at my inability to show it to them."[27]

After his search for success, happiness, contentment, fame, and fortune, Augustine came to the awareness that his search outside of himself came up empty. It was when he searched within that he was able to discover the God who created him and called him. The master of interiority learned from experience that the search for knowing God accompanies the search for self-knowledge. Thus, he prays in his *Soliloquies*, "Lord let me know myself, let me know you."[28]

In one of the most beautiful prayers from the *Confessions*, Augustine puts into words his spiritual journey in discovering God. His prayer is an honest assessment of what he experienced in life and can be an example of how to incorporate the reality of one's life into prayer. His testimony gives witness to a relationship of love which surpasses the bodily senses affected by sound, sight, smell, taste, and touch. He invites the reader of this prayer to discover with him where he was able to find God. It is deep within his very being. Not someplace outside, but only deep within the core of his being. Prayer in the Augustinian tradition, then, always affirms this interior journey in order to arrive at the true fulfillment of our desires.

> Late have I loved you, Beauty so ancient and so new, late have I loved you!
> Lo, you were within, but I outside, seeking there for you, and upon the
> shapely things you have made I rushed headlong, I, misshapen. You were
> with me, but I was not with you. They held me back far from you, those
> things which would have no being were they not in you. You called, shouted,
> broke through my deafness; you flared, blazed, banished my blindness; you
> lavished your fragrance, I gasped, and now I pant for you; I tasted you, and I
> hunger and thirst; you touched me, and I burned for your peace.[29]

In this prayer and in other prayers that Augustine left us in the *Confessions*, we are given the opportunity to peer into his mind and heart and to journey through some of his deepest theological thoughts, his most personal struggles, and the highs and lows of the relationships he had with the people so dear to him. These prayers form part of the tradition of Augustinian spirituality which took shape during Augustine's life and which, centuries later, would bear fruit and quickly spread throughout the world.

From Augustine to Augustinian

At the time of his death in the year 430, Augustine finally reached that eternal peace and self-knowledge for which he searched his entire life, and from that time on, small groups of individuals continued to benefit from his letters, sermons, and other writings, especially the *Rule of Life*, which he left the members of his community. Although the Order of St. Augustine was not established as a religious order within the Church until the middle of the thirteenth century, the gift of Augustine's thought on living and praying together in community continued to be present and manifest itself in the lives of individuals and in small groups searching for God together.

Eight centuries after Augustine's death, in the Tuscan hillside of Italy, the seeds of community life with "one mind and heart intent upon God,"[30] planted during the north African bishop's ministry, took on a new life. That was when the Catholic Church, in the person of Pope Innocent IV, called for a unification of various groups of Tuscan hermits who were all following the *Rule of Life* originally composed by Augustine for those who were living together with him in community. From the thirteenth century forward, the Order of St. Augustine, developed and spread throughout the world, and its members continue to pray and minister, now in over fifty countries.

The Augustinian prayer tradition includes many women and men who are highlighted as saints. They include the Italian contemplative women Rita of Cascia and Clare of Montefalco; the bishop of Valencia, Spain, Thomas of Villanova; pastors Stephen Bellesini and Nicholas of Tolentino; martyrs such as John Stone of England and Thomas of St. Augustine and his Japanese companions. These men and women, who valued Augustinian community life and sought to journey together with their sisters and brothers on their way to God, all contribute to the tapestry of Augustinian prayer tradition. Particular devotions to Mary as Our Mother of Good Counsel and Our Mother of Consolation, the Marian Corona prayer which invites one to meditate upon the twelve articles of belief in the Apostles' Creed while reciting the Our Father, Hail Mary, and Glory Be, and Eucharistic adoration as the "Sacrament of Love,"[31] also contribute to the treasures of this rich tradition.

The influence of Augustine's Rule, preaching, and writing reaches a far wider audience than the professed members of the Order of Saint Augustine (OSA). Many religious communities of men and women, for example the Norbertines (OPraem), Dominicans (OP), School Sisters of Notre Dame (SSND), Augustinians of the Assumptions (AA), Augustinian Recollects (OAR), and Discalced Augustinians (OAD), along with a variety of contemplative religious communities, all follow the Rule of Augustine as their fundamental guide to the common life. There is also a large group of lay men and women who form Associations and Fraternities as

Secular Augustinians throughout the world. All of these communities benefit from and contribute to the rich treasure of the wisdom of Augustine and the Augustinian tradition.

Prayer in Common

Augustine of Hippo placed utmost value on living together as one in community. The opening lines of his *Rule* urge those who are living together in community to live the way the first community in Jerusalem strove to live, "one in mind and heart, sharing all things in common."[32] The emphasis he placed on sharing, which takes place in the common life, brings the greatest value to the Augustinian tradition of prayer and is one which Augustine made manifest in his ministry and preaching. This aspect is the unifying thread woven throughout community life and is that which brings it priceless value. Augustinian community life takes its unique shape when members come together having one soul and heart, possessing nothing on their own, but sharing all things in common. When this is done, one soon discovers that the greatest of treasures the community holds in common is nothing less than God. When one becomes detached from all of the external distractions of life, the core that remains is God.

In one of Augustine's sermons, *Sermon* 355, he explains this beauty of having God as a common treasure. In describing to his congregation what his community was like, he explained that he and all the other members distributed what personal property they had to the poor, "so that we might live on what we had in common. But what would be our really great and profitable common estate was God himself."[33] The pursuit of the common sharing of God is, in fact, at the very heart of Augustine's *Rule*. Using the passage from Acts 4, he writes at the beginning of his *Rule*, "The chief motivation for your sharing life together is to live harmoniously in the house and to have one heart and one soul seeking God."[34] God is not only the common goal and treasure of living together, but also the condition for the possibility of living together. This common treasure of God is then made real in the love that is shared as a community and distributed in good works from the community. Fraternal love uniting the members is one of the three main characteristics of Augustinian monastic life listed by John Gavigan, OSA, in his study of the monastic life in north Africa.[35] Fraternal love reaches out not only in one's relationship with God, but also with one's neighbor. God, made manifest in love, is not only the motivation to love but also the motivator as love. When the life of fraternal love in God is accomplished, it makes real the ideal which Augustine set out to establish. Love, or God, as the common possession becomes verbalized in prayer and in action.

In his *Exposition on Psalm* 133, Augustine goes into greater detail of just how precious this ideal is for him. He cites, "How good and pleasant it is when brothers dwell together as one" (Psalm 133:1)[36] and finds scriptural support for not only his monastic ideal but also encourages this ideal as a goal for which all people should strive. He recognized in this psalm the seeds for the common life. This is why Augustine declared and described with such delight, the beauty and sweetness he found in this psalm.[37] It is what sparked the flame of that initial desire to live together in God and is that which fanned that flame in his life as he developed the various communities in which he lived. It is also that which continues to give life to the fire of love today in Augustinian communities and in the lives of all who participate in the tradition of Augustinian prayer.

Sharing the treasure of God within the common life is displayed in the love that compels its members to live in unity. For Christians, it is the sharing of Jesus Christ, his life, passion, death, and resurrection which makes that love a reality. As much as one participates in Jesus Christ, that one has no need of the material goods the world offers. Once again, Augustine makes this point clear in *The Work of Monks*, this time by writing that a member of his monastery is one who is "no longer seeking what things are of his own but rather those of Jesus Christ, he has devoted himself to the charity of common life, intending to live in companionship with those who have one heart and one soul in God, so that no one calls anything his own but all things are held in common."[38]

When one recognizes God as a common estate in the monastery, or in any community, one is able to recognize more clearly the place of love and self-sacrifice within that community. It is an altruistic love. It is a love of God made real in the love of neighbor. This love of neighbor takes priority for Augustine over the love of God, not necessarily in theory but in practice.[39] It is in the love of neighbor where all that is good, sweet, and beautiful that comes from living together becomes actualized.

In recognizing the value of community, Augustine also acknowledges the necessary work involved in inviting others to share the value of community life. When someone discovers the goodness and beauty of a harmonious common life based on prayer and praising God, then one should be compelled to invite others into that community. All those who, as the body of Christ, find happiness and peace in living with one heart and mind intent upon God, respond to this gift by inviting others to share that life. With an Augustinian spirituality to guide it in prayer, the Church is not a closed society for the select few, but rather seeks to welcome others to share in the beauty it has to offer. Augustine preached:

Magnify the Lord along with me. Who is the speaker, who is encouraging us to join him in magnifying the Lord? My brothers and sisters, every one of us who is in the body of Christ should bend his or her efforts to encourage others to magnify the Lord with us.... Let this love burn in you. Why else are these verses of the psalm recited to you, and expounded? If you love God, seize all your kinsfolk and drag them along to the love of God, and all your household. If the body of Christ is dear to you, if you love the unity of the Church, seize them all and bring them along to enjoy it; say to them, Magnify the Lord with me![40]

When the community of believers recognizes that its greatest treasure is the common sharing of God, then the realization of Augustine's ideal happens within history. An authentic community which has love at its core brings to the world in which it participates, love itself. Love becomes the realization of what is shared at the core of community life. God, as the greatest common treasure, is best revealed when shared in mutual love among the members. A community is destined to grow when its members invite others to share in the common treasure. When this is actualized, all of the other common treasures find their proper places.

An Exercise of Desire

Since we have established that community, living together with "one mind and heart intent upon God," is the foundation for Augustinian spirituality, we can now focus on how prayer in community is a critical part of that common life. In Psalm 34, we pray, "I will bless the Lord at all times, his praise shall be always in my mouth." How can the Lord be praised at all times? An answer to this question comes from a letter that Augustine wrote to a wealthy widow in North Africa.[41] Her name was Proba, and she asked Augustine to assist her as a kind of spiritual director. Her request focused on prayer and its purpose. In his response, Augustine describes prayer as an "exercise of desire." He wanted her to realize that the more this desire is conditioned, the stronger it becomes. The more this desire is exercised, the more the heart becomes open to pray as one ought to pray and to be open to receive the response of our prayers. The theological virtues of faith, hope, and love condition the flame of the desire to remain ablaze. Our bodies will not physically be able to offer constant praise to God, but the desire can always remain strong. Our mouths would eventually tire out from a constant outpouring of words of prayer and praise, but the desire continues to be lit and give life to the growing and never tiring desire for prayer.

Augustine insists on the need to reflect on what one asks for in prayer. He uses the Our Father as the perfect example of how one should pray and points out in that prayer the need to strip away any desire for possessions, or power and to aim at asking only to be able to live in true happiness.

The theme of the happy life is one that Augustine investigates throughout his writing and his preaching. He began this theme with *On the Happy Life*,[42] one of the dialogues he had written while with his family and friends in Cassiciacum, and he often revisits this topic in sermons, letters, and other writings. The happy life is one that is complete peace. There is no want, nor is there too much. The happy life consists of perfect measure, and an Augustinian spirituality of prayer takes this desire for perfect measure into account when one reflects on how one should pray.

Augustine reminded Proba that the prayers that we use to communicate to God do not tell God anything new or inform or change God. Prayer changes the one praying. If one is open to this conversion, then in the act of praying, one needs to be constantly ready for change so that God's will becomes the only desire of our prayer. Without this openness to conversion, we can quickly develop into experts on how to direct God instead of letting God direct us. When we bring our prayers before God, we formulate the words so that we can be open to what God has to offer us. God does not need to be informed of our will, even when that will is to pray. Augustine states:

> The Lord our God does not want our will, which he cannot fail to know, to become known to him, but our desire, by which we can receive what he prepares to give, to be exercised in prayers.[43]

The verbalization of words is for the one praying.

He continued in his letter advising Proba that we

> always pray with a continuous desire filled with faith, hope, and love. But at certain hours and moments we also pray to God in words so that by those signs of things we may admonish ourselves, realize how much we have advanced in this desire, and arouse ourselves more intensely to increase it.[44]

This direction for prayer at certain times is also present in Augustine's *Rule*. In a few sentences, in fact, in the shortest chapter in the *Rule*, Augustine advises those living in community of the essential elements of prayer. He reminds them to be assiduous at the times and hours for prayer, to keep the space dedicated to prayer sacred, and to be sure that the words being sung or spoken in prayer are also being pondered in the heart.[45]

In whatever moment we find ourselves, we are reminded that prayer is always for the pray-er. The benefits of prayer come from understanding why we pray in the first place. It is not to change God, but to open ourselves to the possibility of change and conversion. This openness allows one to be led by the Spirit to strip away all of the external distractions of possession, loss, fear, sadness, power, or prestige. Those external realities that draw our attention and energy away from the peace that we truly desire. Augustine advises those who are ordained for the ministry of preaching, that before uttering a word, the speaker should always pray, not only for himself, but also for those who are about to hear what he has to say.[46]

PRAYER IN ACTION

In a sermon on Psalm 47, Augustine preached on the importance of action to go along with words of praise. At times, he found it necessary to remind his congregation that prayer in action is an important aspect of responding to our call to be Christian. As he sought the balance between prayer and contemplation in his community life, he also encouraged the members of his congregation in Hippo to reflect on praising God in both words and in deed. He preached:

> All nations, clap your hands, because God's grace has come to you. Clap your hands: what does clap suggest? Rejoice. Yes, but why with your hands? Because you must express your joy in good actions. You must not make merry with your voices and leave your hands idle. If you are happy, clap your hands.... All nations, clap your hands, raise a shout of joy to God with exultant voices. So you must use both voice and hands. It is not a good thing to employ your voice alone, because then your hands are lazy, but neither is it good to use only your hands, because then your tongue is dumb. Hands and tongue should be in harmony: the tongue confessing, the hands at work.[47]

And so Augustinian prayer exists in both word and in deed. As the words of our prayers come from our mouths, so too should the action of our prayer come from our hands. That is how one can best respond to God's presence in our lives. Our response should continuously seek to find ways which include the two-fold commandment of the love of God and the love of neighbor. Our world calls us to respond to the various needs of our sisters and brothers. When those who are poor, hungry, homeless, sick, in prison, or seeking refuge from violent situations in their home countries call out to us in their need, we are called to respond in prayer and in action. As Christ's body, we respond to the suffering Body of Christ in the person of our neighbors most in need.

In a number of Augustine's sermons and writings, he uses the image of the ten-stringed harp, which we find in various psalms, to reflect on the necessity of responding in prayer with both words and deeds. The harp represents the ten commandments, he says, and the first three strings direct us to the love of God, and the remaining seven strings direct us to the love of neighbor. The harp is played with the fingers, which indicates that not only is the voice used in living these commandments, but that also the hands must take an active role in how one lives in loving response to the vocation to follow those commandments.[48]

PRAYER AS RESPONSE TO LOVE RECEIVED

As we continue with the theme of Augustinian prayer, we must remember that as Augustine was preaching in fifth-century north Africa, the Pelagian controversy was in full bloom. It was a complicated heresy growing in the Church and, simply put, denied the necessity for the salvific work of Christ for all people. Pelagius and his followers insisted that it was possible for a person to live a virtuous life on one's own. If one had a strong enough will, one could resist the evil temptations of the world and earn one's way to salvation. At almost every chance he found, Augustine was sure to remind his listeners that they are completely dependent on God's grace. He quotes Romans 5:5 many times as he developed the theology of grace which informed his spirituality. The doctor of Grace insists that all that we have we have received from God is pure gift. It is God's love, God's gift of God's very self, that has been given to us in complete freedom. "Because the love of God has been poured out into our hearts though the holy Spirit that has been given to us" (Romans 5:5). Augustine acknowledges the goodness that exists in the desire to thirst for the virtuous life, but also reminds his congregation, "you can't pour yourself a drink of virtue."[49] Augustine views the person as creature, as the *imago Dei*, but we are infected by sin and require God's grace for redemption.

This anthropological view of the human person informs the way Augustine sees every act in which we, as humans, participate. There is nothing that we can do which we do on our own. Our very being depends upon our openness to God's love poured into our hearts. Our lives, then, should reflect the love that we have already received. It is a response to that love received that enables us to act. This influences even our ability to pray. True prayer is only made possible because of God's grace. God's loving act of grace in our lives is the stimulus for our response in prayer. In accepting God's grace, we are best prepared to be open to understanding the desire of the heart that leads to the happy life. This, then, compels the direction of that desire to be pointed toward the origin of our very selves, which, as we have seen, is also the goal of resting eternally with God. It is by God's grace and only God's grace, that we are even able to exercise the desire of our heart in communicating with both our origin and our destination in prayer.

The following homily, which is based on the dialogue that takes place in the liturgy as an introduction to the preface of the Eucharistic Prayer, is a fine example of Augustine's theology of prayer. He reminds his congregation of the necessity of prayer, but also of how it is done only with divine assistance:

> So our head is in heaven. That's why, after the words "Lift up your hearts," you reply, "We have lifted them up to the Lord." And you mustn't attribute it to your own powers, your own merits, your own efforts, this lifting up of your hearts to the Lord, because it's God's gift that you should have your heart up above. That's why the bishop, or the presbyter who's offering, goes on to say,… "Let us give thanks to the Lord our God," because we have lifted up our hearts. Let us give thanks, because unless he had enabled us to lift them up, we would still have our hearts down here on earth. And you signify your agreement by saying, "It is right and just" to give thanks to the one who caused us to lift up our hearts to our head.[50]

LOVE, AND DO WHAT YOU WILL

All people are called to recognize the importance of developing a relationship with God through prayer. In answer to the vocation that one has received, whether married, single, ordained or religious, we live our lives in recognition of the One who has called us into a loving covenant of holiness.[51] This covenant is best nourished through the regular practice of prayer, of exercising the "desire of our heart" to be one with God. In whatever situation we find ourselves, whatever our age, whatever our vocation or avocation, we answer our call from God by recognizing the relationship to which we have been invited and our acceptance of that invitation includes the prayerful response of "Amen."

The options are many for just how this response is made real in our daily lives. For some it may be through ten minutes of quiet meditation, for others it may be realized in a Eucharistic celebration or adoration. Reading and praying through Scriptures, alone or with a group, is another way of developing a prayerful relationship with the God who inspired those Scriptures. For others, prayer takes the form of actively serving at a school, hospital, soup kitchen, or homeless shelter. Developing the habit of prayer is what is important. It is what Augustine learned from the example of his mother and it is what he taught through his ministry. He found great comfort in creating time for meditation and contemplation, but realized that with his busy schedule it was not always possible. The many demands on his time, however, did not stop him from freeing himself for that precious time. He wrote in the *Confessions*:

> It is still my constant delight to reflect like this; in such meditation I take refuge from the demands of necessary business, insofar as I can free myself. Nowhere amid all these things which I survey under your guidance do I find

a safe haven for my soul except in you; only there are the scattered elements of my being collected, so that no part of me may escape from you. From time to time you lead me into an inward experience quite unlike any other, a sweetness beyond understanding.[52]

These words remind us that making that time to free ourselves from the duties of life in order to spend time in prayer is possible even for a person as busy as the Bishop of Hippo. Therefore, we should not let the difficulty of a busy schedule discourage us from trying to find and create that sacred time. Augustine had many opportunities to remind his congregation of their duty as members of Christ's body. The duty to prayer is no exception. We are called to a prayerful relationship in response to the freedom we have received as sons and daughters of God and brothers and sisters in Christ. Our prayer, in whatever form it takes, should be offered as a loving response to what has been given to us.

Love is what the bishop wanted to teach as the motivation behind his instructions to God's faithful. In fact, we have seen that it is the root of what we have been exploring in the Augustinian prayer tradition. It is a tradition which grew from Augustine's experience in living in community, developed in the growth of the professed members of Augustinian religious communities and continues to manifest itself in the everyday experiences of all God's faithful. Without the presence of love in all that we have explored with regard to Augustine and his message of prayer, there is nothing on which to base his identification of the Church being the body of Christ on earth. That body, the *Christus totus*, authentically responds only when it is animated by love.

In one of the oft-quoted sections of Augustine's *Tractates on the First Epistle of St. John,* we hear the bishop imploring parents and all member of the community to respond to their call to action with love as *the* motivating condition behind every choice. It is what unites the members into one, the *Christus totus*, and animates its every move.

Once for all, therefore, a short precept is presented to you: Love and do what you will. If you should be silent, be silent out of love; if you should cry out, cry out out of love. If you should correct, correct out of love; if you should spare, spare out of love. Let the root of love be within; from this root only good can emerge.[53]

We have seen how for Augustine every Christian act requires the necessary ingredient of love. Here he emphasizes that in all that is accomplished, love must be what motivates. It is love, the sacrifice from a humble heart, which enables the human response of prayer. When rooted and motivated by love, every action becomes the sacred sign of God's presence among us. Instead of his sermon being a declaration giving free reign to moral anarchy, Augustine reminds us that from love, *only good can emerge*. This love is rooted in a love of Christ which binds the family and unites each member as Christ's body.

CONCLUSION

Augustinian prayer, then, participates in the rich history of prayer in the Christian tradition. Its distinctiveness comes from having its roots planted in the foundation of Augustine of Hippo's writings, teaching, and preaching. The emphasis it places on the common life and journey to God shapes the context in which this prayer is developed. We have seen how prayer in the Augustinian tradition is a response to "the Love that has been poured into our hearts" by the one who created us and calls us to rest peacefully in his eternal love.

As Augustine was drawn to value the beauty found in the common life, he sought to share it by inviting others to participate in that beauty. His teaching that the one praying is doing so as a member of the *Christus totus* brings each participating individual to an acceptance of his or her role as the body of Christ. Christ, then, through contemplation and action, through word and deed, is not only the one prayed to, but as *Christus totus*, is also the one praying.

Prayer is an exercise of desire. God already knows what is in our hearts before we utter a word, making a multiplication of words unnecessary: "For to speak much in praying is to do something necessary with superfluous words, but to petition him much to whom we pray is to knock with a long and pious stirring of the heart."[54] It is the desiring heart which springs from an understanding of knowing what should be the purpose of our prayer that shapes and informs an authentic longing for the eternal peace for which we were created. That pure desire is not influenced by possessions, power, and pleasure, but rather is guided by a complete openness to God's will.

Prayer in the Augustinian tradition, in summary, is like a bridge, but not one that connects two separate entities over an unsurpassable chasm. Augustine revealed that the God for whom he searched was always already deep within. The bridge of Augustinian prayer is one that assists the one praying to arrive at a higher level in one's relationship with God. In other words, it is a way to rise above the distractions of life which can tempt us to lose focus on the common treasure we have in God. It brings the one praying in contact with the one who is already closer to us than we are to our very selves.[55]

Prayer in the Augustinian tradition is a bridge that expands as more and more people are invited to participate in the experience of praying together in communion of mind and heart. It is built by love made real in word and in action. The initiative for the construction of that bridge comes first from the one who is both the origin and the goal of prayer. It carries the one praying as the body of Christ into a communion of love with Christ. A love which has no other desire than to live in a perfect measure of peaceful rest in the happy life. "There we shall rest and see, see and *love, love* and praise."[56]

1. Augustine, *Confessions*, trans. Maria Boulding, OSB (Hyde Park, NY: New City, 1997).

2. See *Confessions*, V, 9, (17). Never a day would pass but she was careful to make her offering at your altar. Twice a day, at morning and evening, she was unfailingly present in your church, not for gossip or old wives' tales but so that she might harken to your words, as you to her prayers.

3. Augustine describes his experience in *Cassiciacum* in *Confessions*. IX, 4, (7)–5, (13). Peter Brown offers a comprehensive study of the months between Augustine's conversion and baptism; see *Augustine of Hippo*, (Berkeley, CA: University of California Press, 2000), chapter 11, "*Christianae Vitae Otium: Cassiciacum.*"

4. For a further study of prayer on St. Augustine, see G. Corcoran, "Saint Augustine on Prayer," *Augustinian Heritage* 34:2 (1988); M. Vincent, "*Le vocabularie de la prière chez saint Augustin,*" *Augustiniana* 41 (1991), 783–804.

5. See Augustine, Exposition of Psalm 85.1. "When we speak to God in prayer we do not separate the Son from God, and when the body of the Son prays it does not separate its head from itself. The one sole savior of his body is our Lord Jesus Christ, the Son of God, who prays for us, prays in us, and is prayed to by us. He prays for us as our priest, he prays in us as our head, and he is prayed to by us as our God. Accordingly we must recognize our voices in him, and his accents in ourselves." Psalm 85:1.

6. See Tractate on the Gospel of John, 21.8. "Let us rejoice, then, and give thanks that we are made not only Christians, but Christ. Do you understand this grace of God upon us? Marvel, be glad, we are made Christ!" *Io. eu. tr.* 21.8.

7. All Scripture texts in this chapter are taken from the *New American Bible.*

8. *Sermon* 46.37.

9. T. van Bavel, "The Double Face of Love in St. Augustine. The Daring Inversion: Love is God," *Atti del Congresso internazionale su S. Agostino nel XVI Centenario della Conversione, Roma 15–20 settembre 1986, Studia Ephemeridis Augustinianum* 24–6 (Rome: Institutum Patristicum Augustinianum, 1987), 3:69–80. Van Bavel attests to over 275 references to Matthew 25 in the works of St. Augustine, 80.

10. Augustine, *Sermon* 137.2.

11. H. Marrou makes note that in Augustine's preaching, especially in his *Enarrationes in Psalmos*, he uses the expression *Christus totus* at least two hundred times, not to mention the dozens of allusions to the topic and his use of *corpus Christi*. See H. Marrou, *Théologie de l'histoire*, (Paris: Éditions du Seuil, 1968), 43. Cf. *en.* Psalm 17:2; 26:2; 30:2-3; 54:3; 56:1, 6; 74:5; 100:3; 132:7; 138:2.

12. Augustine, *Sermon* 341.1.

13. G. Corcoran, "Saint Augustine on Prayer," 210.

14. *Tractates on the First Epistle of John,* 10, 3.

15. T. van Bavel, "The Double Face of Love," 73.

16. Augustine, *Sermon* 133.8.

17. Augustine, *Sermon* 272.1.

18. Augustine, *Sermon* 246.5.

19. Augustine, *Confessions* I, 1.

20. Augustine, *Confessions* XIII, 35, 50.

21 Possidius, *Life of Augustine,* ed. John Rotelle (Villanova, PA: Augustinian, 1988), 3:2.

22. See B. Bruning, "*Otium* and *Negotium* within the One Church," *Augustiniana* 51 (2001), 105–149.

23. Augustine, *Confessions,* IX, 10, 24.

24. We know from our reading of *Letter* 21 that Augustine soon after his return from Africa had set out to create this time for *otio* with his friends immediately before his impromptu ordination to the priesthood in Hippo in the year 391. Cf. *ep.* 21.3.

25. G. Moioli, "Sulla spiritualità sacerdotale ed episcopale in S. Agostino," *La Scuola Cattolica* 93 (1965), 218.

26. Augustine, *City of God,* XIX, 19.

27. Augustine, *Confessions,* IX, 4, (10).

28. Augustine, *Soliloquies,* II, 1.

29. Augustine, *Confessions,* X, 27, 38.

30. *Rule of St. Augustine* 1,1.

31. *Tractates on the Gospel of John,* 26, 13.

32. Acts 4:32, *Rule of St. Augustine* 1.

33. Augustine, *Sermon* 355. 2.

34. *Rule* 1, 1.

35. J. Gavigan, OSA, *De Vita Monastica: in Africa Septentrionali inde a temporibus S. Augustini usque ad invasiones Arabum* (Rome: Augustae Taurinorum, 1962), 51–52. Along with *Fraternal love in God,* Gavigan lists *apostolic work* and *discernment* as the notable characteristics of the Augustinian monastic life.

36. The modern reader should keep in mind that the text of the psalms which Augustine would have used as the basis for his preaching was the Latin text from the Septuagint, which makes for the numbering of Psalms 9–147 to be one behind the Hebrew numbering used now in most contemporary Bibles.

37. *Exposition of Psalm* 133:2.

38. Augustine, *The Work of Monks,* trans. Sr. M.S. Muldowney, RSM. *FOTC* 14, *Treatises on Various Subjects,* (Washington, DC: Catholic University of America Press, 1965), 323–394.

39. T. J. van Bavel, *La communauté selon Augustin: Une grâce pour notre temps* (Bruxelles: Éditions Lessius, 2003), 76–77.

40. Augustine, *Exposition of Psalm* 33.2.

41. Augustine, *Letter* 130.

42. Augustine, *De beata vita.*

43. Augustine, *Letter* 130.17.

44. Augustine, *Letter* 130.18.

45. Augustine, *Rule,* chapter 2.

46. Augustine, *Teaching Christianity,* IV, 32.

47. Augustine, *Exposition of Psalm* 46.2.

48. Augustine, *Exposition of Psalm* 92.5; *Confessions* III, 16.

49. Augustine, *Sermon* 150.9.

50. Augustine, *Sermon* 227.

51. *Lumen Gentium*, 11. "Fortified by so many and such powerful means of salvation, all the faithful, whatever their condition or state, are called by the Lord, each in his own way, to that perfect holiness whereby the Father Himself is perfect."
52. Augustine, *Confessions* X. 40. 65.
53. Augustine, *Tractates on the First Epistle of John, ep. Io. tr.* 7.8.
54. Augustine, *Letter* 130, 20.
55. Augustine, *Confessions* III. 6. 11.
56. Augustine, *City of God*, XXII, 30.

CHAPTER 19

Prayer in the Ignatian Tradition

~ Hung Trung Pham, SJ ~

Praying in the Ignatian tradition can be compared to falling in love. Neither of them pinpoints one specific moment or one simple experience, but they both reveal an ongoing process involving diverse and dynamic movements that embrace and embody all the moments and experiences of encounter between the lover and the beloved, including times of deep silence or even the seeming absence felt by one or the other. As in loving, praying does not confine itself to one particular practice, way, or method, but is open to all and is defined by all to the extent that all serve as means to creating a space of deeper freedom leading the person to an evermore intimate and loving encounter between the lover and the beloved. Thus, the ultimate goal of praying lies not in formulating one magical method, nor in searching for the correct acts and practices of devotion, nor in developing some perfect religious rituals and ceremonies, though all remain helpful and necessary. Ultimately, prayer orients, leads, and unites the individual person with the Divine.

Metaphorically, praying could also be compared to a courting dance where God—the lover—constantly and continually woos the person who prays—the beloved. Being madly in love, God attracts, inspires, and draws the individual to respond in love and freedom. Thus, while the lover who initiates the dance waits attentively, lovingly anticipates, and readily accompanies the beloved onto the next step of the dance, the beloved engages in prayer by remaining open and ready to be led by God—the lover. Thus, prayer does not end but continues progressing toward greater integration and deeper intimacy with the divine. Like dancing, the more frequently prayer is practiced, the more graceful and integrated its movement and rhythm become. The intimacy and the love shared between the lover and the beloved, radiating from each and every moment of the dance, illuminate the relationship in its beauty. Such a beauty in turn inspires, attracts, and draws others to join in the dance. Therefore, prayer proceeding from the individual naturally flows out to touch and to enliven the community.

The Method and Weeks of the Spiritual Exercises

Such emphasis on an intimate and interactive encounter with a personal God remains at the heart of prayer in Ignatian tradition. In fact, one of the preliminary notes that prefaces the *Spiritual Exercises*—one of the foundational texts of the Ignatian tradition—explicitly points out that these spiritual exercises facilitate the process of the Creator acting immediately with the creature, and the creature with its Creator and Lord.[1] Consequently, such a personal and direct interaction and communication between God and the individual are emphasized throughout the *Spiritual Exercises*, thus in prayers in the Ignatian tradition. In fact, a colloquy is one of the most common forms of prayer, which the individual retreatant is often instructed to make. Accordingly, making a colloquy is understood to be "speaking as one friend speaks with another, or a servant with a master, at times asking for some favor, at other times accusing oneself of something badly done, or telling the other about one's concerns and asking for advice about them" (55). However, just as in any type of relationship, how direct and intimate the interaction and communication are depend on where the individual is in terms of his understanding of who God is and the direction in which his relationship with God is moving. Before entering in the discussion of various weeks of the Exercises that correspond to different manners of communication or prayer, it is important to address the attitudes or qualities that are presupposed and necessary from each partner in the encounter.

The final preparatory notes that preface the *Spiritual Exercises* not only direct the individual's attention to the desired condition that would yield greater contact between the individual and the Lord both in terms of frequency and intensity, but indicates the type of God whom the individual is encountering. "As a general rule in making the Exercises," the twentieth annotation instructs, "the more one disengages oneself from all friends and acquaintances, and from all worldly preoccupations, the more profit will there be" (20). In other words, as is important in other relationships, to pray well one must take a break or withdrawal from one's daily activities or routine to create space for the encounter with the other, in this case, God. Three principal advantages, which are explicitly stated in the Exercises as results from such a break or withdrawal, merit a full citation:

> First, by withdrawing from friends and acquaintances and likewise from various activities in order to serve and praise God Our Lord, one gains small merit before the Divine Majesty. Second, in the state of withdrawal, when one's mind is not divided among many matters, but by concentrating instead all our attention on one alone, namely, the service of our Creator and our own spiritual progress, we enjoy a freer use of our natural faculties for seeking diligently what we so ardently desire. Third, the more we keep ourselves alone and withdrawn from others, the more capable we become of drawing near to and reaching our Creator and Lord, and the more we reach

Him, the more we make ourselves ready to receive graces and gifts from His divine and supreme Goodness. (20)

Thus, the God with whom the individual is communicating and encountering in prayers is the Divine Supreme Goodness. In short, God remains the God of Supreme Goodness who continually and unconditionally graces the individual with good gifts. This God of goodness remains the main goal and objective, which the retreatants as well as their directors are seeking after and aiming for in their prayers and spiritual exercises as indicated in the presupposition in the beginning of the *Spiritual Exercises* (22). However, such a loving gift is given and manifested differently in different stages in the individual's relationship with God, hence, corresponding to different forms of communication or prayers.

On the part of the individual person who prays, two qualities or attitudes are recommended for their interaction with the Divine, one negative, the other more positive. On what seems to be a negative quality, the individual is advised basically to withdraw into a state of seclusion or solitude disposing oneself to the divine Goodness (20). Here, the individual works to have her mind and her natural faculties free from friends, acquaintances, and other preoccupations and to focus only the Lord. Thus, prayer means being involved in a process of letting go, of doing nothing, of surrendering. However, letting go or doing nothing or surrendering does not mean being passive or inert in prayer. Positively, the individual is instructed to actively engage and encounter the Lord in a "magnanimous spirit and with great liberality" (*grande ánimo y liberalidad*) (5).[2] In other words, the person is actively working, exercising, and praying so that she would become more in tune, open, and ready to be led by God.

Using the Exercises to fine-tune the individual's spiritual condition to where he would become more open and ready to respond to the unconditional love of God serves as the main goal of the First Week of the *Spiritual Exercises*. Consequently, at the end of the First Exercise of the First Week, each retreatant is given three questions to reflect upon during his speaking one-on-one with Christ suspended on the cross: "What have I done for Christ? What am I doing for Christ? What ought I to do for Christ?" (53). On a first glance, these questions seem to place an emphasis on the individual as the one who first takes the initiative to act or to do something *for* Christ in the past, present, and future. However, a more thorough examination of the preposition *for* in the original Spanish within the dynamic of the first week reveals what the individual is moved to do in the past, present, or future remains only as a response to what Christ first has done, is doing, and will do for him or her. Two Spanish prepositions, namely *para* or *por*, are often translated to the English word "for." *Para* indicates the end goal of the action; *por* points to the cause for such an act. In each of the three questions mentioned above, Ignatius used the preposition *por*. Thus, the three questions should be literally translated as follows: Because of what Christ has done for me, what have I done? What am I doing? And what will I do? These questions themselves are responses in consideration of what one was/is/will be given. In other words, God in Christ remains the initiator of the encounter.

Given what the God of Supreme Goodness has done in Christ, the individual's prayer or speaking one-on-one with Christ in the First Week remains as a way to examine and to meditate on God's unconditional love first, and only after steeping herself in God's unconditional love can the retreatant look to her sins. The order is important. Only after being convinced and grounded in such a love of God, may the individual begin to engage in prayers and spiritual exercises reflecting and raising her self-awareness, regarding not only her shortcomings and brokenness, but also toward the disordered social network that she inherits and is a part of. Thus, prayers of the first week most often evoke a heart-to-heart conversation between the loving God and the remorseful and grateful individual.

It is essential that prayers of the First Week begin with the recognition and conviction of the unconditional love of God. We are told that Ignatius had kept Pierre Favre, one of his close early companions, from making the *Spiritual Exercises* for four years due to Favre's scrupulosity. Underneath the deep scrupulosity, Ignatius had recognized Favre's real doubt about God's unconditional love. Subsequently, for four years, Ignatius accompanied Favre on his journey to recover the true image of the loving God. After having been healed, Favre not only was able to make the Spiritual Exercises, but also, according to Ignatius, "had the first place in giving the Exercises."[3]

Like Favre, people may come with an operative image of God different from that of a loving God. As in the case of how Ignatius had dealt with the younger Favre, it is essential for the director to take as much time as needed to heal or to "remove those false images or at least to set the stage for their removal by enabling the retreatant to reach a degree of freedom and openness."[4] Most often these false images are rooted in the individual's past social upbringing and religious formation. Moreover, whether true or false, any human image of God must undergo constant reexamination and renewal in order to avoid risking idolatry. As we are reminded in the Hebrew Bible, those who are chosen are also those who "are wrestling with God and with humans and have overcome" (Genesis 32:28).[5] Without going into any further spiritual and psychological analysis, any emotions or thoughts that arise from the individual's struggles in the process of reconciling himself and his image of God with that of the loving God, ought to be the very matters spoken about or discussed with God in colloquy or prayers. However, Ignatius instructed the director to remain especially "gentle and kind" toward the individual retreatant during this challenging yet grace-filled time. And it is a good practice for the individual to apply the same instruction toward himself in his prayers (7).

In summary, prayers in the First Week involve interactions or conversation between the individual person who, with various degrees of openness and freedom, disorder and brokenness, is on his journey, moving to discover God's unconditional love that has been operative all along in his life, and the God of Supreme Goodness who loves unceasingly and who constantly reaches out to the beloved individual in patience and kindness. Consequently, toward the end of the First Week, prayers are expressed in words that flow from the grateful heart of one who has recognized himself as sinner, yet constantly and continually loved and called by God.

After having recognized God's unconditional love and having recognized herself as a loved sinner, the tone of the prayer moves toward companionship, from one companion to the other. For the Second Week, the God who has been moved by the severe brokenness of creation and who loves the sinner and pardons sins, has thus decided to become human in Jesus Christ, subsequently, calling, inspiring, and attracting others to collaborate and to labor with God in the divine plan to save the human race (102). Consequently, at the beginning of the Second Week, a retreatant hears the call of Christ, our Lord, the eternal King announcing, "my will is to conquer the whole world and all my enemies, and thus to enter into the glory of my Father. Therefore, whoever wishes to come with me must labor with me, so that through following me in the pain he or she may follow me also in the glory" (95). As God has adopted a more inviting and collaborative approach in God's way of communication, he or she too is moved to adjust the tone of his/her prayer in responding to the divine call.

Prior to entering into contemplation of the life of the incarnate God in Jesus Christ, the individual is asked to pray both for "the grace of not being deaf to his call, but ready and diligent to accomplish his most holy will" (91), and also for "an interior knowledge of Our Lord, who became human for me, that I may love him more intensely and follow him more closely" (104). While the former focuses on self-emptying that prepares and creates better interior space to hear the call, the latter underscores the dynamic process and its direction of how such a companionship with the Lord could be developed, cultivated, and grown. For Ignatius, order is important. Only after having known the Lord more intimately, can the individual then love him more intensely, and finally, follow him more closely. Looking in the opposite direction, the act of following presupposes a certain degree of loving. Similarly, loving necessitates knowing. However, the knowledge presumed here springs up from the heartfelt knowledge that results from a personal encounter with the Lord.

One's love for the Lord must be grounded in the deep felt knowledge of "how Our Lord became human *for me*," not for the creation *en masse*, not for some abstract idea, but *for me*, a unique individual human person both living in and bounded by a particular historical, cultural, and religious context. Similarly, the act of following necessitates that the individual fall in love with a personal and human Christ. Thus, praying or contemplating during the Second Week of the *Exercises* means "seeing, hearing, smelling, tasting, and touching" (121–125)—the living Jesus Christ—the human God—in detail, so as to be drawn deeper into the divine life. In short, praying or contemplating means imitating and becoming more and more identified with the one whom the individual prays to or contemplates.[6] Therefore, contemplating and praying in the Second Week means taking time to gaze and to engage, to watch and to ponder, to interact and to converse, to reflect and to discern, and so on. both at the intellectual level and, more importantly, at the level of the heart.

The contemplations of the Second Week of the *Exercises* takes retreatants on a journey that begins with Christ who first appears as an ideal and mighty King with heroic plans to stand tall and speak to "all the world assembled" (95), and concludes with a rather surprising—even puzzling—image of Jesus quietly on his way to a humiliating death. The purpose of these contemplations is not to develop a doctrine about, or to do a systematic study of, suffering and salvation, though both might be fruits that flow from these contemplations. What these contemplations are most interested in is the enfolding intimacy taking place and deepening within the interpersonal relationship between Christ and the individual on the journey.

Through creatively composing the biblical scenes found in the Scriptures and imaginatively placing oneself in them, the individual intimately engages with the historical Jesus and other characters as if she were actually present in Palestine more than two thousand years ago. Simultaneously, during these contemplations, Jesus enters and interacts with the individual in her present historical, cultural, and religious milieu. Thus, through active contemplation, the individual is becoming more at home and alive with Jesus. And prayers along the journey that consist of watching, seeing, hearing, smelling, tasting, and touching the Lord arouse a personal expression of growing interior affection that gradually deepens to love.

Those praying must include the time to construct in imagination those sacred spaces and the conversation that will be taking place in them. Within those sacred spaces, the mystery of the Incarnation no longer remains as an abstract idea or intellectual doctrine, but takes form in a baby boy born in a manger of Bethlehem. There,

I have witnessed his birth, even held his tiny fingers. I have watched and spoken with him struggling through adolescence, rebelling against his parents while remaining obedient. I have sat by his side during his many restless nights figuring out what it means to be a man. "I've seen his struggle and loved his laughter. I've gazed at him and found him gazing back; I've heard my name on his lips. I've been drawn into his friendship; I've watched him work, suffered his hardship, wrestled with his self-discovery. I've discovered I need him, and been sweetly shocked that he needs me too."[7] No longer a distant and impersonal King, Christ has become a personal friend and companion whom I know and love in human details and particulars. Most important, I have fallen in love with him and desired to follow him. Hence, praying— like falling in love—is made up of personal exchanges, impressions, and affections in each of those particular moments of the journey and in the experience of discipleship as a whole.

The journey of discipleship continues into the Third Week of the *Exercises*. However, there is a monumental shift in how one prays, since the Christ being contemplated and encountered is no longer the one who is filled with zeal and creativity miraculously and triumphantly demonstrating the glorious power of God over sins and illnesses as depicted in the second week. Moving to the Third Week, the individual contemplates the same Christ, who is passively enduring great pain and suffering, being led to condemnation and death. Though our contemplations are focused on a Christ who suffers passively, the divine choice to be passive is intentional. In the "passion according to Saint Ignatius," Christ "desires to suffer" (195). And Christ who, being divine, could destroy his enemies "goes into hiding" and "allows himself in his sacred humanity to suffer most cruelly" (196). Moreover, Christ suffers all this "for my sins" (196). The only reason that could explain this "stumbling block" and "foolishness" (1 Corinthians 1:23) is love. "So if God suffers, it is because of His boundless love from the beginning; it is because He remains faithful to His love for us, even when this love entails the sufferings of His only Son...the love from above."[8]

As in the dynamic of the Second Week, the individual does not contemplate the passion as an historical event, nor a theological interpretation, or even Christ's very real sufferings. Rather, he comes face-to-face with the person of Christ on his Paschal journey here and now, being drawn into the mystery that Christ has suffered all this *for me, for my sins*. Even more stunning, in continuing with the intimate companionship that had been developed, cultivated, and deepened, it is no longer a distant and impersonal Christ who suffers, but it is the one I love that suffers and is crucified. Accordingly, prayers or communications with the suffering Christ must be the responses from that profound anguish and pain felt and expressed from the heart of the beloved, who has stood and watched helplessly the love of his life being tortured, has been baffled at the utter agony and humiliation endured, and has been reduced to silence. In other words, encounter with the suffering Christ and any form of communication or prayers taking place in that encounter would not be authentic without "sorrow with Christ in sorrow, anguish with Christ in anguish" (203). It is important to make sure that the focus of prayers remains *not* on the sufferings of Christ but on the Christ—the one I have known intimately, loved intensely, and followed closely— who suffers.

As in the previous weeks of the *Exercises*, prayers are elicited responses from the individual's heart, after having journeyed side-by-side with Jesus into the paschal mystery. Consequently, inspired by Christ who is suffering and ultimately "hanging on the cross," the individual is moved from pondering the general question, "What ought I to do for Christ?" as found in the First Week to asking a question that leads to a more specific emphasis and direction, namely, "What ought I to do *and suffer* for him?" Like the dynamic in the First Week, praying for "what I ought to do and suffer for Christ" involves a response that comes from the heart to Christ, who has *first* suffered for me. Thus, the crucified Christ remains the one who stirs up the heart and inflames the soul of the individual making the retreat.

Moreover, the individual's response is rooted in a deeper sense of "suffering with" the Lord, in other words, compassion. However, the emerging compassion is neither a kind of pure sentimentality nor a sort of comforting pity often used to console oneself or others over misfortune or misery, nor "aesthetically tolerable for us by means of some happy turn." Rather, prayers in the third week are grounded in the compassion revealed in the mystery of how Christ has endured and suffered for me out of love. If by Ignatian contemplation the individual imitates and becomes whom she contemplates, then through prayers of the Third Week, she is to ask for graces seeking to be "poor" and to be "accounted as fool" for the greater glory of God, "not some carbon-copy imitation of the passion of Christ" (71).

After having walked, danced, and wept through all the stages of the interactive and intimate encounter with the personal Lord as portrayed through the first three weeks of the *Exercises*, the individual's eyes, enabled by the divine grace, are opened to a fuller vision of creation that is saturated and permeated with the overwhelmingly loving presence of God. Consequently, the contemplations in the Fourth Week elicit responses from the heart of the individual, who is won over by, is completely in awe of, and surrenders to the endless unconditional love of his lover—God. Thus, the dynamic of the Fourth Week inculcates God's loving presence, no longer as something that the retreatant's ear has heard about, but something that his eyes have witnessed in contemplation and now sees with deeper understanding.

Such is love that manifests itself and is expressed "more in deeds than in words" (230). This love is considered, felt, and understood through the various points Ignatius proposes in the Contemplation to Attain Love. The contemplation first encourages the retreatant to recall and ponder with deep affection all the gifts—that is, her own creation, which the God of Supreme Goodness has lovingly bestowed on her thus far. The second point of the contemplation moves beyond the individual and contemplates God's loving presence as infusing all forms of creation from the lowliest to highest, sustaining them and giving them life. In all, God does not stand outside and simply observe as a spectator, but actively and meticulously "labors" and "is working" *everywhere* "in the heavens, elements, plants, fruits, cattle and all the rest" (236), giving all their existence, maintaining and supporting them, breathing in them the divine life. Being deeply moved by such an overwhelming and pervasive love, prayer conveys a deliberate act of surrendering and submitting the whole self to God: "Take, Lord, and receive all my liberty, my memory, my understanding, and all my entire will.... Give me only the love of you, together with your grace for that is enough for me" (234). Beyond falling in love, the individual has begun to love.

EXAMINATION OF CONSCIENCE (EXAMEN)

I have spoken so far about Prayer in the Ignatian tradition as a linear trajectory moving in a sequential order through the *Spiritual Exercises* of St. Ignatius of Loyola, for the sake of locating and clarifying the unique spiritual movement, and the prescribed prayers found in each of the weeks. However, as in any human relationship, the prayers of the *Spiritual Exercises* offer many surprising twists and unexpected turns, all of which are intertwined, interwoven, and integrated into the rhythm and fabric of life. One could find oneself in prayers moving from the first week to the third, or from the fourth to the second, or even two weeks in the same prayer period. Therefore, the ultimate focus of prayer is neither about identifying what week one is in, nor on determining where one should move next, but rather attending to the divine loving presence in one's life in order to deepen our relationship with God here and now.

Examination of conscience or the examen, which is highly recommended and practiced in variety of ways during all weeks of the *Spiritual Exercises*, captures the essentials of prayer in Ignatian tradition. First, it is a reflective act, during which the individual looks back and reviews the activities of a day under the divine light. Such a reflection presupposes a certain degree of solitude or withdrawal from people or any other preoccupations that might interfere with the space needed for looking back and reviewing. Practically, the examen is meant to be more a moment of quiet done in the midst of daily activities.

Second, it is an act of awareness in which the individual is able to listen to and differentiate the various movements of his or her interior life and learning where those movements lead, subsequently, accepting the good and rejecting the bad (313). Such awareness assumes a certain level of knowledge of God's unconditional love and of self-knowledge as a loved sinner continually being called and drawn into companionship with God.

Third, it is an act of gratitude in which the individual comes to a realization that all God has done and suffered is simply for him or for her. Such gratitude would move the individual to some kind of heartfelt response.

Finally, it is an act of surrendering, neither giving up nor handing one's life over in despair, but "falling in love in a quite absolute and final way,"[9] thus being led into a deep union with the living God in an evermore intimate and loving dance of cocreating. Shall we then dance with God?

1. George E. Ganss, SJ, trans., *The Spiritual Exercises of Saint Ignatius* (St. Louis: The Institute of Jesuit Sources, 1992), 15. Reference to the *Exercises* will be taken from this translation throughout this work unless otherwise noted.

2. Michael Ivens, SJ, trans., *Understanding the Spiritual Exercises* (Herefordshire, UK: Gracewing, 1998).

3. *Fontes Narrativi* I, 658.

4. Philip Sheldrake, "The Principle and Foundation and Images of God," *The Way Supplement* 48 (1983): 90–96, 92.

5. All scriptural quotations are taken from the New International Version unless otherwise noted.

6. George Aschenbrenner, "Becoming Whom We Contemplate," *The Way Supplement* 52 (1985): 30–42.

7. Robert R. Marsh, "*Id quod volo*: The Erotic Grace of the Second Week," *The Way* 45, no. 4 (2006) 7–19, 8.

8. Peter H. Kolvenbach, "The Passion According to Saint Ignatius," *Centrum Ignatianum Spiritualitatis* (Rome, 1989), 63–91, 70.

9. A popular prayer credited to Pedro Arrupe.

CHAPTER 20

Praying in the Mercy Tradition

~ Rosemary Jeffries, RSM ~

The tradition of Mercy requires integrating action with prayer in such a way that there is wholeness to life. This is much easier said than done.

During my own path of Mercy life in ministry for nearly a half century, I have tried numbers of prayer styles, types of retreat, and methods of meditation all aimed at having my relationship with God become more integrated in daily life. Reading and pondering the Mercy resources available, in particular, the words of its foundress Catherine McAuley (1778–1841), helps me to identify important insights to pursue that goal of integration despite the business and noise of life that surrounds us all.

Like many, I have lost myself in the activity of ministry to the point of having no time for quiet or reflection along the way. But the tradition of Mercy established by Catherine and her early followers shed some light for me on how she managed to integrate her deep desire for God with her equally deep desire to serve those in need. It is exemplified in the real life stories of the early days establishing the foundation of Mercy and is complemented by the numerous writings and documents of Catherine McAuley as she puts words to the deeds. Here I will share some examples of the stories and writing that reveal, for me, very clear characteristics of a Mercy tradition. I will then share some of my own methods of incorporating those characteristics into my own journey.

INSPIRATION OF CATHERINE AND HER FOLLOWERS

One of the richest resources of the Mercy tradition is surely the numerous letters and original documents written by Catherine McAuley during the early days of founding the order in Ireland. Her very personal and down to earth letters to her companions and acquaintances reveal how she so aptly integrated her burning desire to serve the poor of her time while still pursuing an intimate relationship with God. Her writings, missives, and instructions along with her writing of the original rule are a treasure preserved and analyzed by numerous writers over these 180 plus years since the founding of the first foundation of Mercy in 1831.[1]

For example scholars found in the *Foundation Circulars* written by Catherine to inform sisters working in the various mission sites of the mundane happenings in one place, helped the sisters living and working in sites throughout Ireland to have a "sense of belonging to the same tradition." These letters included news about the entrance of new members, health of each other, challenges facing the local work, and good advice often mixed with scriptural references. This simple practice managed to create a tradition in the short ten years that Catherine lived after the founding of the order.[2]

Taking the time to write letters seems very simple but it is a practice that eludes us in our modern era where a quick text with abbreviations takes the place of a longer note that elaborates on the stuff of life. Catherine took time to write about the stuff of life and seemed to personally reflect in this process of writing. Maybe the sheer act of writing and reflecting increased Catherine's ability to see God in all aspects of daily life both the mundane and the profound.

The Mercy tradition lived—by thousands of sisters, associates, and millions of colleagues throughout the world over the past nearly two centuries—has a spirit marked by some definite characteristics that still offer great insight to us in the twenty-first century. At the heart of Catherine's vision for mercy in her community was the deliberate insistence on the integration of prayer and active life to the point there should be no dichotomy between the two. As her retreat instructions advised,

> Prayer, retirement and recollection are not sufficient for those called to labor for the salvation of souls [They should be like] the compass that goes round its circle without stirring from its center. Now our center is God from Whom all our action should spring as from their source and no exterior action should separate us from him…the function of Martha should be done for Him as well as the duties of Mary.[3]

Integration of active work with prayer is a long-held goal of many seeking deeper holiness, but in Catherine's time religious orders were much more slanted toward the contemplative practice of enclosure rather than active ministry.

The final exhortation in the passage above to be both like Martha and Mary reminds me of my novitiate days when doing a million assigned chores with my sister companions, we would say to one another, "Be a Martha, not a Mary!" Doing work tasks evokes a sense in all of us to do our part and expect others will do their part. We easily begrudge anyone spending the time in a more reflective way while we and others toil. In the Mercy tradition, the work is prayer. All parts of a full day are to be prayer with no separation. So being both a Martha and Mary is not an either or, as we thought in novitiate, but rather a wholeness of being constantly aware of the holy in the quiet as well as in the business of each day.

We all have a great example of being constantly aware of the holy in our Holy Father, Pope Francis, as he visits many people of the world. He is a contemporary example of living wholeness of life which makes all activity a prayer. In his recent trip to the United States we could observe firsthand no dichotomy between his natural greeting of each person as an encounter with Christ and the deeply spiritual person whose words and deeds inspired us. We are so blessed to have this very powerful example among us. His universal call to us to be a church of mercy encourages a real embrace of the Mercy tradition, which seeks to erase all dichotomies and calls for wholeness in life. Much like Catherine McAuley, he exemplifies in this century a deep love of people regardless of their station, and he continues to ask us to pray and be aware of God in our midst at all times. He also manages to exude a lighthearted way that immediately puts people at ease.

Catherine's insistence on integrating work and prayer met with some resistance which caused her some challenges throughout the early days of establishing the order and setting up new foundations where the work of the sisters was so needed. As one reads about the challenges that the pull between action and contemplation naturally created in the new community, a second characteristic of the Mercy tradition is slowly revealed in the good humor and lightheartedness of Catherine's response. Likewise, the lighthearted spirit I observed in the sisters who taught me in high school was very attractive to me as a young person. Now, I find this light grasp on life and good humor a great gift for the good times and the hard times.

A good example of her humor and her model of lightheartedness is found in exchanges between Catherine and her earliest companion, Mary Ann Doyle. They highlight Catherine's desire for her followers to be out among the people and not overly burdened with long prayers or customs that sap energy that is needed in ministry.

Mary Ann Doyle, Catherine's first companion, was a woman whose training in convent schools encouraged in her a love of traditional and ascetical practices of women religious of the nineteenth century. She held on to her love of the traditional but was clearly attracted to the very active work of Catherine McAuley and joined her as a founding member of the first House of Mercy in Dublin on Baggot Street. She even accompanied Catherine to make a novitiate with the Presentation Sisters as a prelude to the founding of the Mercy Order. Catherine subsequently asked Mary Ann to become the leader of the first convent outside of Dublin. Naturally, Mary Ann as the leader of a new foundation in Tullamore began to include more and more devotions and ascetical practices. Catherine was not in agreement here, probably because of her own past. Catherine's life by contrast to Mary Ann was not dominated by encounters with Catholics and certainly not Catholic nuns of the time. As one author reports, "She found convent customs particularly distasteful."

In her playful and humorous way, she referred to Mary Ann Doyle as "Her Reverence" or "the Divine Mother" and teased her and the other sisters to help them understand her insistence on not allowing ascetical practices to infringe on the active work of helping the poor. She had a new vision of religious life that challenged her followers to integrate prayer and work. In other words, while Catherine's style was to entrust the development of a new foundation to her chosen leader, she was not without her opinion and assessment, which she readily shared often with lighthearted humor. Another good example is her description of the convent rooms designed by Mary Ann Doyle for the Convent in Tullamore. "Mother Mary Ann has met with her 'beau ideal' of a conventual building at last, for our rooms are so small, that two cats could scarcely dance in them."

The ongoing tension between the desire of some of her followers wanting more of the trappings of cloister and others realizing the new vision of this Mercy Order was often dissipated with good humor and fun loving ways. In establishing her tradition, she surely held that good humor and the ability to laugh at one's self and laugh with others amidst the seriousness of ministry were holy too.

Another of my favorite examples of good humor includes Catherine's preparation to visit Tullamore and once again to encounter "the Divine Mother," Mary Ann Doyle. "We must banish all these visionary matters with laughing notes.... We will set up what I will call a Nonsensical Club. I will be president, you Vice-President and Catherine can give lectures as Professor of Folly," she writes!

In all of these stories and words depicting Catherine's humor, there is an underlying insistence on being joyful and intimately engaged with those whom we share our journey. There is too a deep belief that rigid practices of rituals and formal prayers might not lead to holiness but rather stiffness and seclusion, which would not achieve the wholeness of life Catherine sought to teach by her deeds and her words.

While meeting the challenges with humor there is a third more profound characteristic of the Mercy tradition, as I understand it, that is acceptance and trust in the "bitter and sweet" of life. This characteristic reveals a reverence for the joys and disappointments of life as God's plan. A good example is found in Catherine's letter to the Limerick community who were ready to experience the first death of a young sister. To them, she writes:

> This has not been done in anger. Some circumstance will soon prove that God is watching over your concerns, which are all His own, but without the Cross the real Crown cannot come. Some great thing which He designs to accomplish would have been too much without a little bitter in the cup.

Bless and love the fatherly Hand which hurt you. He will soon come with both Hands filled with favors and blessings.

Catherine had many encounters of trial throughout her life before founding the order which deepened her faith and prepared her for the challenges she encountered as a foundress with a new vision for religious life. First, she lost both of her parents as a young woman leaving her to care for her younger siblings with meager resources. Her orphaned state rendered her virtually homeless at times. Providentially, she found herself depending on the charity of a Quaker couple, the Callaghans. Though they did not approve of her Catholic beliefs, they tolerated her commitment to the practice of her faith and her practice of reaching out to serve the needs of the poor. As time went on, the Callaghans grew to admire her commitments to first her faith and equally her commitment to serve the poor. Through the darkness of these days of being without home or family, Catherine remained faithful and accepted her circumstances with grace.[4]

An unexpected inheritance from the Callaghans to Catherine offered her a security she never experienced, but she chose to use this fortune to forward her vision of helping the poor, especially women. The project to build the first House of Mercy to serve poor women in Dublin was met with much ridicule from her family, friends, neighbors, and even her church. Many referred to it as "Kitty's Folly." Amidst the joy of having resources to realize her dream of helping others, she encountered ugly resistance. There is in this dark and light story of the early founding of the Mercy Order a repeating pattern of "the bitter and sweet" that Catherine met throughout her life with trust and acceptance.

The sickness of young sisters early on in the history of the order was a great cross to Catherine, as were other controversies associated with doing something new with religious life in the Church, but she exhibited great acceptance of these crosses and trusted in God's providence. As she wrote to her good friend Frances Warde, "Thus we go on…flourishing in the very midst of the Cross, more than a common share of which has lately fallen to my lot, thanks be to God. I humbly trust it is the cross of Christ." The deep immersion into the pattern of death and resurrection in the Mercy tradition, as in all spiritual traditions, is a cornerstone to daily prayer and a help in sorting through the stuff of life.

How can we embrace the Mercy tradition?
The goals of Catherine McAuley and her followers to integrate prayer and work, hold a light grasp on life, and to trust in the providence of God amidst joys and sorrows holds out a challenge that transcends time. I believe the daily practices of

Catherine and her early followers offer insight on how these goals took root in their lives. For example, Catherine wrote often about her day-to-day life with others as well as writing other manuscripts that captured her desire for wholeness in her life and in the lives of her followers. Her retreat instructions, as well as her essay, "The Spirit of the Institute," offer clear testimony of her conviction to integrate prayer and work. Her discipline to write and to write often provided a great treasure for future generations, but it also crystallized her own intentions for herself and her companions. Early followers of Catherine also wrote letters that captured the challenges of the everyday as well as writing about their experience of Catherine herself.

Making an effort to stay connected to friends with notes or taking time to write important thoughts down, or just simply embracing a discipline to write and reflect consistently might aid anyone in reaching the goal of integrating work and prayer as it did for Catherine. For me, journaling every day gives me a concrete way to sort through the events of my days and see the hand of God in the simplest and often mundane occurrences. It took me many years and many attempts to become disciplined to do this daily, but the practice has helped prepare me for events of the day and absorb challenges along the way. Writing also helps me to see the providence of God's plan in both the light and dark times. As I got better at this daily journaling practice, I also found myself taking more time to write to friends and colleagues to say thanks or just let them know I am thinking of them.

The Mercy tradition is rooted in Catherine's attention to writing letters to friends and thoughtful documents to preserve important instruction for the community. In all of it, she aimed at integrating work and prayer. This very available discipline of writing increases awareness of God in daily life for anyone who strives for wholeness and balance in work and prayer. Very simply, writing is a big part of this Mercy tradition as I see it and try to practice it.

Adapting a lighthearted approach to life comes easier to some than others, as we saw in the stories of Catherine and her companions. Some, like me, with a more reserved manner, are lucky to have the gift of community. There is always someone who can see humor in the moment or add some lighthearted perspective even at challenging times. The tradition of Mercy is surely a shared reality that requires good companions for the journey. The "lighter grasp on life" also presents a wider perspective that can be helpful, less urgent, and more thoughtful. I have been blessed with a community that both challenges me in this Mercy tradition and helps me not to take myself too seriously in the process.

The third characteristic of the Mercy tradition, learning to trust in God's providence, is surely a lifetime pursuit. There is no magically quick way to develop faith as deep as Catherine McAuley exhibited. A longer view lets me see that lightness even presents challenges, just as gaining some perspective through writing leaves space for God's providence to be felt. In all of this, making the space to let God be and act in my life seems to honor the tradition of Catherine, who waited on God's design for her life for many years. She patiently remained faithful through homeless times, challenging times, and disappointments. For anyone pursuing a spiritual life amidst an active life, there are always challenges and times of waiting on God for solutions and answers. Waiting is not easy and at times seems endless, but writing at least keeps the dialogue with God ongoing and sometimes provides a little insight and perspective along the way.

Challenging and uncertain times brought Catherine closer to her God. She gave herself in trust to God as she met difficulties or as she waited on God's plan. In the Mercy tradition, the path to a deeper prayer life requires being faithful and open to a call to come closer to God in good times and hard times with unwavering confidence in God's providence. The call to come closer and trust does not always feel wonderful, but it is an opportunity to practice integrating prayer and work, find lightness in the joys and sorrows of everyday and accept "the bitter and the sweet" with faith along the path of mercy, which as Catherine McAuley would say, is the real "business of our lives."

The Suscipe of Catherine McAuley

The Mercy tradition of prayer is best summed up in the simple and beautiful words of Catherine's prayer:[5]

> My God, I am yours for time and eternity. Teach me to cast myself entirely into the arms of your loving providence with a most lively, unlimited confidence in your compassionate, tender pity. Grant me, O most merciful Redeemer, that whatever you ordain or permit may be acceptable to me. Take from my heart all painful anxiety; suffer nothing to sadden me but sin; nothing to delight me but the hope of coming to the possession of you, my God and my all, in your everlasting kingdom. Amen.

This prayer captures the deep faith of Catherine as she strove to integrate prayer and work, accept the challenges with a lightness that comes from confidence in God, and embrace "the bitter and the sweet" of life as her way to come ever closer to God. The Mercy tradition of prayer at its core is a personal suscipe lived and prayed every day.

1. *The Correspondence of Catherine McAuley 1827–1841*, ed. Angela Bolster, RSM, 1989; other references available through Mercy International Center, mercyinternational.org.
2. Joanna Regan, RSM and Isabelle Keiss, RSM, *Tender Courage: A Reflection on the Life and Spirit of Catherine McAuley, the First Sister of Mercy*, a biography and analysis of the charism of mercy as revealed in Catherine's writing commissioned the Federation of the Sisters of Mercy in the late 1970s and finally published in 1988. The Federation predates the founding of the Institute of the Sisters of Mercy of the Americas in 1991.
3. Catherine McAuley, *Retreat Instructions*. Conferences given by the Foundress to her first novices (1832–1835). Noted and collected by the first Sisters. Collected by Sister M. Teresa Purcell (1834–1853), Dublin and Tullamore convents of Mercy. Edited by the Sisters of Mercy, Albany, New York, 1952. This document is often quoted in biographies and other volumes about the Sisters of Mercy.
4. There are many biographies of Catherine McAuley and collections of her letters. Among the most recent biographies is *The Path of Mercy: The Life of Catherine McAuley* by Mary C. Sullivan (2012). An earlier work by Sullivan, *Catherine McAuley and the Tradition of Mercy* (1995), provides insightful analysis of Catherine's sayings and writing as well as the text of letters and documents written by the early Sisters of Mercy, which offers first-person accounts about Cathreine McAuley from her contemporaries. Both of these volumes and the many articles by Sullivan are a great source for understanding the Mercy tradition.
5. The online collection of articles, prayers (including the mobile app for Morning and Evening Prayer of the Sisters of Mercy) is available on the website of the Institute of the Sisters of Mercy of the Americas, sistersofmercy.org, and other resources are available from the Sisters of Mercy International website, mercyworld.org.

PART FOUR

Praying with Classic and Contemporary Spiritual Guides

TERESA OF ÁVILA

JOHN OF THE CROSS

THÉRÈSE OF LISIEUX

BROTHER LAWRENCE OF THE RESURRECTION

THOMAS MERTON

HENRI NOUWEN

JOHN MAIN

In this section, we begin by receiving guidance on prayer from four Carmelites. In Teresa of Ávila: Prayer Is an Adventure in Love, the opening chapter, Keith J. Egan guides us to appreciate "one of the outstanding teachers of Christian prayer, [a] saint and first woman doctor of the Church." He does this by helping us see, through Teresa's eyes, prayer as the greatest of human adventures. Beginning with a fine historical background to set the stage for his later comments, he then addresses such topics as "Prayer of (Active) Recollection," "Real Presence to Christ," and "Prayer of Four Waters." He then closes by discussing Teresa's "mysticism of love"—not as a "dreamy state" but in Teresa's words, a "strong determination to please God in everything."

Constance FitzGerald's John of the Cross and Prayer is also both scholarly and worthy of prayerful reflection. In it she writes about this Carmelite poet and saint in a way that impels us to both ponder and pray over her words. What comes through in this treatment of John's spirituality is, in FitzGerald's words, that "for John prayer is a life path to transformation by and in love, not simply a method, a practice, a time set aside each day for God." Central to John's spirit and her discussion of it is his poetry that is filled with the "image of human love and the beauty of creation." In addition, the author addresses three areas to especially note when considering prayer in John of the Cross: "the centrality of Jesus Christ," "the experience of dark night or purification," and what she terms "the fullness of Christ's consciousness."

The brief, inspirational, and compelling chapter that follows is by Barbara Jean LaRochester, entitled Praying with St. Thèrése of Lisieux. Beginning with a historical introduction, LaRochester addresses the intriguing topic of "How Jesus Taught Thérèse," followed by a discussion of meditation, contemplative prayer, desires, surrender, and gratitude in light of this important saint's life. She closes by pointing out an unpleasant reality of our modern culture as well as a challenging question for all of us to address in our own prayer and reflection.

The fourth Carmelite to be highlighted in this section on praying with spiritual guides is Praying with Brother Lawrence of the Resurrection by Leopold Glueckert. In the beginning of this treatment of Brother Lawrence's approach to prayer, we are provided with a fascinating historical overview of his life. This then seamlessly moves into a presentation of his struggle and journey in prayer that is instructive to all of us wishing to be closer to God. As Glueckert notes, "Lawrence took the prayer of recollection and made it attractive to anyone. He was blessed with a clear, no-nonsense way of speaking, and gave lucid advice to help others follow his process." After reading this chapter, a desire will be raised in many of us to read or reread Brother Lawrence's *Practice of the Presence of God*, which is a true spiritual classic.

In Thomas Merton: Monk, Mystic, and Missionary (the most extensive chapter in this section as well as one of the most thorough in the book), Anthony Ciorra proposes that three vocations of monk, mystic, and missionary were blended into one by Merton. Starting out by providing an in-depth historical background, along with helpful insights on the import each turn in Merton's history had on his spiritual life, Ciorra partially draws upon the work of Anthony Padovano in structuring it into three phases:

1. The Monastic Period (Traditional Prayer): 1941–1951
2. The Church Period (Prayer and Social Justice): 1951–1960
3. The World Period (Contemplation and Solitude): 1960–1968

Ciorra then asks us to look at the goals of our own spiritual journeys by learning from Merton's modeling, as well as by what is reflected in writings of his such as *Seeds of Contemplation*. He closes with themes of "guideposts for the journey," "the journey from head to heart," and by offering quotes from Merton on them. This chapter is worth a weekend retreat to be able to absorb and pray over its contents.

Lisa Cataldo's Praying with Henri Nouwen: A Journey toward Home is a natural follow-up to the one on Merton since many of their themes resonated. Cataldo begins by relating her personal connection with Nouwen, which brings the material to life in a special way. One of the key themes she presents with respect to Nouwen is "praying our uniqueness." She writes, "Henri used to say that his middle initials, 'J.M.' stood for 'just me.'" This little joke reminded him that no matter how many books he wrote, no matter how many talks he gave, and no matter how famous he became, he was still "just Henri," a person who struggled, as all of us do, to become the person he felt God was calling him to be. As Cataldo addresses the paradoxes that Nouwen embodied in his own life and spiritual journey, she sees him calling us to pray our own vulnerabilities, fears, and contradictions. As in the chapter on Merton, this one will ignite or reignite the desire to fathom Nouwen's numerous works which are notable by their accessibility no matter where we are in our spiritual journey.

The final chapter in this section, Praying with John Main, is unique in that it offers us the voices of two leading spiritual guides in one sitting: John Main and the noted proponent of his spiritual tenets (and respected spiritual guide himself), Laurence Freeman. We are given access to John Main via stories of Freeman's early and evolving relationship with him. Freeman then speaks to questions and topics such as "What does praying with your teacher mean?" "Who Is John Main?" "John Main as Teacher," and closes by offering nine key aspects of John Main's teaching, each of which can serve as a reflective theme when in prayer alone or with others.

CHAPTER 21

Teresa of Ávila:
Prayer Is an Adventure in Love
~ Keith J. Egan, TOC ~

Sewn deep in the human heart is a desire for God that expresses itself in prayer. One of the outstanding teachers of Christian prayer is the Spanish Carmelite Teresa of Ávila, saint and first woman Doctor of the Church. This essay explores Teresa, who clearly saw prayer as an adventure in love.

Teresa would heartily agree with Thomas Aquinas: "When we pray we ought to ask to be united to God,"[1] and Thomas adds that union with God is an effect of love.[2] Teresa's colleague, John of the Cross was convinced that the love of deepening prayer transforms one into the person God created her to be.[3] Moreover, for Teresa, prayer is the greatest of all human adventures.

Doña Teresa Sánchez de Ahumada y Cepeda: The Adventuress

Cervantes writes that Don Quixote "spent his times of leisure...reading books of chivalry."[4] Quixote was not the only Spaniard addicted to books of romance. Teresa and her mother, Doña Beatriz, avidly read these romances, but they did so clandestinely because Teresa's father, Alonso, disapproved of this harlequinesque literature. Teresa eventually considered this reading of romantic literature as a waste of time (*The Book of Her Life*, BL 2.1). But I differ with Teresa. This romantic literature not only appealed to her adventuresome spirit, it enlarged her imagination and provided her with vivid imagery that to this day delights her readers. Teresa became a voracious reader of spiritual books: "My fondness for good books was my salvation" (BL 3.7). The romances helped to make Teresa a gifted storyteller of the adventure that is prayer and contemplation. She was gifted with what Thomas Aquinas calls *gratia sermonis* (a gift of speech), the gift of sharing with others what one has received from God.[5] My own experience when I read Teresa, is to feel Teresa's fondness for me the reader; others tell me that they share the same experience.

Teresa of Ávila was not, in her time and is not now in ours, easy to forget. Five centuries since her birth have not diminished the widespread fascination with this intriguing mystic. The Church on March 12, 1622, recognized Teresa's holiness when it canonized her forty years after her death. In 1970 Pope Paul VI named Teresa the first woman Doctor of the Church. The latter title means that Teresa of Jesus, as she called herself once she began her reform of Carmelite life, has wisdom about prayer for the whole Church.[6]

FROM BIRTH TO MONASTERY

Teresa's father made a laconic entry in his notebook: "On Wednesday, March 28, 1515, my daughter Teresa was born about five thirty just as dawn was breaking."[7] That day in March is a truly notable day in the history of Christian spirituality. Professor Bernard McGinn calls Teresa "the premier Catholic mystic of the Counter-Reformation period."[8]

In the *Book of Her Life*, Teresa shares with her readers only a few incidents from her childhood.[9] One story is about the seven-year-old Teresa and her brother Rodrigo leaving home so that the Moors could "cut off our heads." Vigilant parents scuttled that adventure (BL 1. 4). George Eliot in her novel *Middlemarch* admired the pluckiness of the child Teresa.[10] Teresa came by her adventuresome spirit naturally. Her half-brother Juan joined an Italian regiment and disappeared in Africa or Italy.[11] All seven of her brothers became conquistadors in the New World.[12] Imagine what life was like in this large rambunctious family where obviously Teresa was the ringleader.

Teresa describes her parents, Alonso and Beatriz, as "virtuous and God-fearing." Teresa was impressed that her father refused to have slaves. When an uncle's slave girl spent time in Alonso's household, the latter treated her "as though she was one of his children" (BL 1.1–2). Beatriz saw to it that prayer was a regular part of the family regimen. As a young girl, Teresa "sought out solitude to pray [her] devotions, and they were many," and she recalls that she and her girlfriends liked to play at being nuns (BL 1.1,6). This vigorous Catholic piety was a hallmark of the home of Alonso and Beatriz. The family's *converso* status may have been an added incentive for this conspicuous piety. Teresa's paternal grandfather Juan Sánchez, a Jewish *converso*, reverted to Jewish practice, and for his lapse he performed public penance.[13] Ironically Teresa, a Catholic nun with Jewish blood—that she never mentions—discovered that her key relationship is with the Jewish Jesus.

Love flourished in this family. Teresa tells us that she "was the most loved of [her] father" (BL 1.3) and that her father's love for her was "excessive" (BL 2.7). Her mother died when Teresa was only about fourteen, a devastating loss for an adolescent girl who had an especially close relationship with her mother. Teresa sums up her experience: "Everywhere I was always loved" (BL 3.3).[14]

Teresa's father did not approve of certain companions with whom Teresa spent time; one companion was a possible marriage partner. A widower twice over, Alonso whisked Teresa off to Our Lady of Grace monastery in Ávila where one of the nuns,

Doña María de Briceña shared with Teresa her love of religious life and prayer. This saintly nun helped Teresa moderate her antagonism to a religious vocation, and she awakened in Teresa a renewed appreciation of prayer. But Teresa "asked God not to give her this vocation" (BL 2.10, 3.1–2). God was not going to entice Teresa into a monastery without a battle. After about eighteen months, Teresa, for reasons of health, left Our Lady of Grace. She says that she then "began to recite many vocal prayers" (BL 3.2).

After battling with herself over whether she was called to religious life and much against her father's resistance to her becoming a nun, Teresa early one morning, at age twenty, secretly made her way to the Carmelite monastery of the Incarnation,[15] located just beyond the majestic walls of Ávila. Teresa's departure from home was a wrenching experience: "It seemed that every bone in my body was being sundered" (BL 4.1).

Teresa often writes about the need for *determinación determinada* (determined determination) and for the need to have courage as adventurers must. Teresa needed this determination and courage especially when she later encountered opposition to her reforms and to the endless difficulties that plagued the making of new foundations. The papal nuncio Felipe Sega famously called Teresa a "vagabond of a woman, disobedient and contumacious." In 1982 St. John Paul II put Sega in his place when he called Teresa "God's vagabond."[16]

Adventurer that she was, Teresa knew that in life, risk is necessary: "Whoever in fact risks all for God will find that he has lost all and gained all. I don't say that I am like this, but I wish I were" (BL 16.7). Risk is especially at play in matters of love. "Be certain [Teresa says] that the Lord will never fail His lovers, when they take a risk for Him alone" (MSg 3.7). Teresa's greatest adventure in life was her journey to God through prayer that led her deep within herself, where she ultimately encountered the Triune God in spiritual marriage (IC 7.1.6).

PRAYER AS ADVENTURE IN LOVE

Bishop Christopher Butler wrote, "Prayer is an adventure into unplumbed depths of the love of God, the depths of God who is love."[17] Teresa of Jesus, in and through prayer, discovered that the God who is love loved her and loves us lavishly. Everything about Teresa is about prayer, prayer as the journey to become like God's self, a lavishly loving person. She wrote, "In this life there could be no greater good than the practice of prayer" (BL 7.10), and for Teresa, prayer is always about love. Dom David Knowles, the director of my dissertation and a devotee of Teresa in his last letter to me wrote, "As I get older, I discover that prayer is about love."[18]

Teresa has left us a snapshot of the role of prayer in her young life:

> Most nights, for many years before going to bed when I commended myself
> to God in preparation for sleep, I always pondered for a little while this
> episode of the prayer in the garden [Gethsemane].... I believe my soul
> gained a great deal through this custom because I began to practice prayer
> without knowing what it was; and the custom became so habitual that I
> did not abandon it, just as I did not fail to make the sign of the cross before
> sleeping. (BL 9.4)

This is the prayer of a mystic in the making who prayed the prayers of ordinary
Christians.

Teresa personifies the principle made famous by Thomas Aquinas: grace perfects
nature.[19] With a healthy sense of her self-worth and God's gifts, Teresa wrote, "As I
grew older, I began to know of the natural attractive qualities the Lord had bestowed
on me (which others said were many)" (BL 1.8). As Teresa matured, a vibrant personality emerged; indeed, her personality is full of paradoxes, which make her a hugely
interesting person: eminently practical yet intensely contemplative, an able bargainer
in business matters yet deeply spiritual, manly (*varonil*) according to some contemporaries, yet Teresa was feminine to her finger tips, "wholly a woman" says Raïssa
Maritain,[20] demanding yet utterly humane, outgoing and warm but with a willingness to venture deeply within herself to meet her friend, her spouse, her Lord.[21]
Teresa was no one-dimensional woman. Christ found in her an abundant humanity
to work with. Teresa's rich personality is a mixture of nature and grace which honed
her capacity to become an utterly charming saint and a wise doctor of the church, a
reformer of the Carmelite tradition—all the while she was still Teresa, an unschooled
female who composed globally acclaimed spiritual classics.

From the Incarnation to San José

Teresa was drawn to the Incarnation because she had a friend there, Doña Juana de
Suárez; in addition, Teresa wanted to be near her father (BL 4.1). These quite human
motivations began an adventure that would impact the practice of prayer and the
shape of Christian mysticism for more than four centuries and beyond.

Teresa's two decades at the overly crowded Incarnation were no picnic. A few
years after her entry into Carmel, Teresa became quite ill; she nearly died. Her father
arranged for her to visit a healer (think *quack*) who caused Teresa more harm than
good. On her way to the quack, Teresa visited her pious Uncle Pedro, who gave his
niece a copy of Francisco de Osuna's *Third Spiritual Alphabet*, which introduced

Teresa to the prayer of recollection, that is, a going within to encounter Christ. Teresa embraced this form of prayer enthusiastically, because she confessed that at this time she "did not know how to proceed in prayer or how to be recollected." She adds: "I was very happy with this book and resolved to follow that path with all my strength.... Taking this book for my master (*maestro*)," and "I tried as hard as I could to keep Jesus Christ, our God and our Lord, present within me, and that was my way of prayer" (BL 4.7), the prayer of recollection. The Franciscan Osuna was much influenced by the affective character (will and love) of the medieval interpretation of the Pseudo-Dionysius's *téologia mystica*,[22] an affective orientation that fit well with Teresa's own warm personality.

Teresa the young nun was still struggling to find her footing in the spiritual life. Four years after she entered the Incarnation, Teresa, out of a sense of false humility, alleged that she was not good enough for mental prayer and so abandoned it (BL 19. 10). For the rest of her life Teresa regretted this lapse that lasted a "year or more" (BL 7.11). In the almost two decades that Teresa spent at the Incarnation, her life of prayer was a mixture of ups and downs, growth and hesitations, even a restlessness not unlike Augustine's restless soul. She did not yet "surrender...into the arms of love" (IC 4.3.8), something she bids her readers to do.

Teresa says of her spiritual life at this time: "I wanted to live (for I well understood that I was not living but was struggling with a shadow of death), but I had no one to give me life" (BL 8.12). But, help was on the way. Now thirty-nine years old, Teresa had lived at the Incarnation for nearly twenty years when one day during Lent she took notice of a borrowed image of the wounded Christ that brought her to her knees and caused her to weep uncontrollably. With her distinctive boldness, Teresa declared to the Lord that she would "not rise from there [that spot] until He granted what [she] was begging Him for" (BL 9.1–3). Teresa, not to be forestalled, was fearless before the Lord.[23] She realized that one lives as well as one prays, and one prays as well as one lives. Teresa's life and prayer were undergoing integration. Love of God weaves the disparate fragments of life into a tapestry of wholeness and holiness.

Teresa read a translation of Augustine's *Confessions* that appeared in 1554, the very year of her conversion.[24] As he did for others, Augustine led Teresa within herself to find God (BL 40.6; cf. IC 4.3.3). Teresa did so with a remarkable trust in her own experience: "I shall say nothing about things of which I don't have much experience" (BL 18.8). Experience here is not only emotional experience but the whole gambit of her rich personality,[25] especially the mystical consciousness that Bernard McGinn says is the lens through which one can understand the mystical life.[26]

Teresa made much of her lack of learning. To compensate for that lack, Teresa consulted the *letrados* (learned). Then Teresa, with her native intelligence and aided by grace, shared her wisdom about prayer and contemplation with her daughters and with posterity. Teresa's naturally warm personality made her an effective reformer, gifted foundress, and an extraordinary teacher of prayer. Teresa's description of mental prayer is a gem of conciseness and precision: "For mental prayer, in my opinion is nothing else than an intimate sharing between friends; it means taking time frequently to be alone with Him whom we know loves us" (BL 8.5). For Teresa, mental prayer is an authentic intimacy with a friend, prayed constantly, and with a firm trust in the Lord, a friend who loves her unrestrictedly.

Prayer of (Active) Recollection—A Form of Mental Prayer

In her early years as a Carmelite, Teresa began to practice the prayer of recollection that she read about in Osuna's *Third Spiritual Alphabet*. Teresa describes this prayer in several chapters in *The Way of Perfection* (26, 28–29) in *The Book of Her Life* (12.2–4) and in *The Interior Castle* (4.1.7). Teresa suggests to close your eyes, go within to be with Christ, for example, at Gethsemane or with Christ conversing with the Samaritan woman. Do so lovingly! Teresa's prayer of recollection[27] is part of the evolution leading to modern contemplative prayer forms like centering prayer and Christian meditation. Teresa does not, however, recommend the use of a mantra as these modern forms of prayer do. The equivalent of the mantra for Teresa is to turn with love, when one's mind wanders, to events in the gospel like Christ conversing with the Samaritan woman. Here, she says, one "can make many acts to awaken love" (BL 12.2).[28] Loving attention to the living Christ within is an anthem that runs through Teresa's life and prayer with an emphasis on love: "the important thing is not to think much but to love much; and so do that which stirs you to love" (BL 4.1.7; cf. BF 5.2). For those who doubt their capacity for love, Teresa wants readers to know that "all souls are capable of loving" (BF 5.2). Teresa also wants one to remember that "prayer is an exercise of love" (BL 7.12). Teresa uses various Spanish words for love, for example, *amor* 479 times; *caridad*, "love/charity," 269 times; and *querer* 3,352 times. For Teresa *querer* often means to love. Teresa heartily agrees with Aquinas that "true perfection consists in love of God and neighbor" (IC 1.2.17).[29]

Real Presence to Christ

Teresa in her description of mental prayer uses the phrase *re-presentar Cristo*, which can be and is translated as to "represent Christ," but I suggest that Teresa is here emphasizing prayer in which one becomes really, truly, and lovingly present to Christ—real presence to Christ. I make this suggestion because the prefix *re* in Spanish can be, and

I think here is, an intensifier so that in this case *representar* means to be really present with Christ—to be really present is to love. Prayer, like Eucharist, is an exchange of gifts. Despite the risk in giving and receiving gifts, that exchange of gifts brings about mutual presence. Mutual presence makes commitment possible. Love is the commitment, the gift of giving one's self to another, to the Christ to whom one becomes really present.[30] Real presence is not only about Eucharist but is as well about the presence that comes with ever deepening prayer.

As Aquinas says: to love another is to inhere or to exist in the other.[31] To love Christ is to exist more consciously, more deeply in Christ as we hear in the New Testament that Christ is in us and we are in Christ.[32] Some in Teresa's time thought that it was more spiritual in prayer to go beyond the humanity of Christ. For a short time, Teresa attempted to imitate this practice. However, she soon discovered how crucial it was for her to pray with, in, and through the humanity of Christ. In fact, she famously insisted on keeping "this most sacred humanity always present" in prayer (BL 22 and IC 6.7).[33]

When she discovered the inadequacy and mistakenness of this approach, she insisted that we pray with, in, and through the "sacred humanity of Christ." Teresa's eyes are always on Christ. Ever the mystagogue, Teresa reminds her readers that even in spiritual marriage, one is to "[fix] one's eyes on Christ and all will be as it should be" (IC 7.4.8).[34]

Unlike St. Ignatius, Teresa does not emphasize detailed imagining of scenes in the gospels. Rather her emphasis is on loving Christ, whom she encounters when she situates herself before Christ in various Gospel scenes. Teresa no doubt has herself in mind when she writes: "There are some souls and minds so scattered they are like wild horses no one can stop" (WP 19.2).

Teresa acknowledges that the active prayer of recollection is not mystical (WP 29.4); rather, this prayer does not transform the human person to the extent that mystical prayer does. Rather, this prayer of active recollection enables one by ordinary grace to pray and to live lovingly in the presence of Christ. Teresa urged her daughters to learn to pray this prayer of active recollection. She suggests that if they are humble and liberated from whatever keeps them from growing in love, they will become candidates for the gift of mystical prayer which she often calls *sobrenatural*, which means "work that only God can perform." John of the Cross could have told Teresa that Christ had been birthed within her at baptism and that the grace of baptism is the very same grace as the grace of contemplation (CB 23.6).[35] To be contemplative is to become fully human.

Prayer of the Four Waters

No one has ever accused La Madre of being a disciplined writer. As she writes, she often breaks into prayer. At other times, she repeats herself, and not infrequently, she digresses. Her best known digression is the treatise known as "The Prayer of the Four Waters," which Teresa inserted into a redaction of the *Book of Her Life* after her account of her midlife conversion (BL 11–22). When Teresa resumes her text after a digression of twelve chapters, she says: "This is another, new book from here on—I mean another, new life" (BL 23.1). In infused prayer, in any prayer, one is always a beginner and always a learner. In "The Prayer of the Four Waters," Teresa takes one from nonmystical prayer through ever deeper stages of mystical prayer but not as far as spiritual marriage because, when she wrote this treatise, she had not yet received that gift. Those who set out on this journey of the prayer of (active) recollection are, says Teresa, "beginning to be servants of love" (BL 11.1). The "Four Waters" describes the prayer of active recollection as fetching water by hand from a well. The next three waters describe stages of mystical prayer in which God's loving presence is evermore evident, such as obtaining water by means of a waterwheel and aqueducts, then by water coming from a river or a stream. Each step forward finds God more deeply in evidence. Finally, in the fourth stage, water comes as a downpour of rain: *mucho llover*. The Spanish *llover* and equivalent words in other romance languages are the source of the English word *lavish*. What Teresa discovered in the prayer of the fourth water is that God is the God of lavish love. For Teresa, prayer is just that: an ongoing discovery of God's love until one finds the lavishness of God's love.

From San José to Alba de Tormes[36]

In 1562, at age forty-seven, Teresa's adventure in reforming Carmel got underway when she made her first foundation of San José in Ávila. The Lord informed Teresa that this new monastery would be "a star shining with great splendor." (BL 32.11) Teresa wanted her foundations for the sake of solitude to have a limited number of nuns.[37] From 1562 until her death in 1582 Teresa was often on the road making new foundations. She made or oversaw seventeen new monasteries for women and was involved in the establishment of two convents for Carmelite friars.[38] The making of foundations kept this contemplative nun very busy. Yet, her mystical encounters continued and deepened with the reception of spiritual marriage in 1572, when John of the Cross acted as her spiritual guide (IC 7, ST 31). Teresa is a prime example of the integration of action and contemplation, the Martha-Mary life wherein, says Teresa, "Mary and Martha walk together" (WP 31.5; cf. IC 7.4.12).

The nuns of Teresa's first monastery asked her to share with them her wisdom about prayer (WP 2.4). Her response was to compose *The Way of Perfection*. She wanted all her foundations to be houses "where all must be friends, all must be loved, all must be held dear, all must be helped" (WP 4.7). Teresa's ideal dovecote is a community of praying friends who discover God's lavish love and who love God and one another.

TERESA'S MYSTICISM OF LOVE

Teresa often asked why she, "a wretched"[39] (*ruin*) woman was the recipient of mystical gifts. Teresa received not only the grace that makes one holy but also the grace that is a blessing for others.[40] Through nature and grace Teresa became a magnanimously loving woman on whom God showered mystical gifts. Teresa is a mystic's mystic whose writings along with those of John of the Cross, shaped the contours of modern Christian mysticism in the West. Yet, she uses the phrase "mystical theology" only four times, always in the sense used by Pseudo-Dionysius, that is: mystical theology describes not the study of mysticism but a transforming encounter with the divine. To know and to love are what make Christian mystics possible. In Christian mysticism in the West, knowing gives way to loving. St. Bonaventure put it this way: "In this passing over, if it is to be perfect, all intellectual activities must be left behind and the height of our affection must be totally transferred and transformed into God."[41] Teresa would agree with Bonaventure but would add that for her, from the beginning, love in prayer is more important than thinking in prayer. The mystic is one who undergoes "inner transformation," one who becomes like God through love. Though she does not use the language of deification that is what Teresa describes in her mystical texts. Through nature and grace, Teresa became a magnanimously loving person on whom God showered mystical gifts for the sake of her daughters and all who seek wisdom from her.

Teresa offers a test for the authenticity of one's love for God. She says, "The most certain sign, in my opinion, as to whether or not we are observing these two laws [love of God and love of neighbor] is whether we observe well the love of neighbor.... The more advanced you see you are in love for your neighbor the more advanced you will be in the love of God.... I cannot doubt this" (IC 5.3.8).

Teresa wants her readers to know that mystical love is not some "dreamy state" (IC 5.1.4–5; see 4.3.11), some set of soft, fuzzy feelings. For Teresa, love "doesn't consist in great delight but in desiring with strong determination to please God in everything, in striving, insofar as possible, not to offend Him, and in asking Him for the advancement of the honor and glory of His Son and the increase of the Catholic Church. These are the signs of love" (IC 4.1.7). Teresa asks herself what is "the reason for prayer…the purpose of this spiritual marriage: [the reason is, she says,] the birth always of good works, good works." (IC 7.4.6)

Until the time of Teresa, the primary influence on Carmelite spirituality, after Scripture, was John Cassian, where the Song of Songs is not a central theme. I contend that Teresa is responsible for bringing bridal mysticism into the Carmelite tradition, a bridal mysticism that John of the Cross refined theologically. The argument for this contention would take too long to share here. So only a few comments on the bridal mysticism that Teresa gradually developed. She wrote: "God espouses souls spiritually. …even though the comparison may be a coarse one (*grosera*) I cannot find another.… For it is all a matter of love united with love, and the actions of love are most pure and so extremely delicate and gentle that there is no way of explaining them" (IC 5.4.3). Benedict XVI, in his first encyclical, God Is Love, writes that "marriage…becomes the icon of the relationship between God and his people and vice versa." Teresa found, I think, endorsement for the use of bridal mysticism in the likes of Gregory the Great[42] and Bernard of Clairvaux. The latter's *Sermons on the Song of Songs* were everywhere including Spain.[43]

Teresa has a word for readers of her mystical texts who may be tantalized by the reports of mystical phenomena rather than in the growth of love. She wrote that "there are many holy persons who have never received one of these favors (*mercedes*); and others who receive them but are not holy" (IC 6.9.16),[44] and, "Do not think, even if the locutions are from God, that you are better for them" (IC 6.3.4).

Briefly, prayer for Teresa is a journey in love, love which is kept alive by fidelity to prayer, a prayer nourished by frequent intimacy with the living Christ who laid down his life for her. I shall let Teresa have the last word: "Love begets love., [so].…let us strive to keep this divine love always before our eyes and to waken ourselves to love.… Amen." (BL 22.14)

1. Aquinas, *Summa Theologiae* 2.2.83.1 ad 2.
2. Aquinas *Summa Theologiae* 1.2.28, ad 2.
3. Aquinas, *The Spiritual Canticle* B 29.3.
4. Míguel de Cervantes, *Don Quixote*, trans. Edith Grossman (New York: Ecco, 2003), 20.
5. *Summa Theologiae* 2.2.177.1, resp.
6. Bernard McGinn, *The Doctors of the Church* (New York: Crossroad, 1999), 138–142. Keith J. Egan, "The Significance for Theology of the Doctor of the Church: Teresa of Ávila," *The Pedagogy of God's Image: Essays on Symbol and Religious Imagination*, ed. Robert Masson, "Annual Publication of the College Theology Society," (Chico, CA: Scholars, 1982), 153–171.

7. Efrén de la Madre de Dios and Otger Steggink, *Tiempo y Vida de Santa Teresa*, 2nd ed. (Madrid: Biblioteca de Autores Cristianos, 1977), I, n. 26. Henceforth: *Tiempo y Vida*.

8. Bernard McGinn, *The Essential Writings of Christian Mysticism* (New York: Modern Library, 2006), 357.

9. *The Collected Works of St. Teresa of Ávila*, translated by Kieran Kavanaugh, OCD, and Otilio Rodriguez, OCD (Washington, DC: ICS, 1976, 1980, 1985). Volume 1: *The Book of Her Life* (Hereafter, cited in text as BL); *Spiritual Testimonies* (ST); Volume 2: *The Way of Perfection* (WP); *Meditations on the Song of Songs* (MSg); *The Interior Castle* (IC); Volume 3: *The Book of Her Foundations* (BF). The Spanish edition of Teresa's writings used in this chapter are from Santa Teresa de Jesús, *Obras Completas*, 5th ed., ed. Enrique Llamas et al. (Madrid: Editorial de Espiritualidad, 2000).

10. George Eliot, *Middlemarch: A Study of Provincial Life* (New York: Knopf, 1991), Prelude and 888.

11. Tomás Alvarez, *St Teresa of Ávila: 100 Themes on Her Life and Work*, trans. Kieran Kavanaugh, OCD (Washington, DC: ICS, 2011), 59; and see Daniel de Pablo Maroto, *Santa Teresa de Jesús, Nueva Biografía* (Madrid: Editorial de Espiritualidad, 2014), 66.

12. These brothers were the children of Alonso Cepeda and Beatriz de Ahumada. Teresa had seven, not eight, brothers as in Alvarez, 59, probably only one half-brother.

13. *Tiempo y Vida*, I, chap. 1.

14. Teresa reminds readers that her elder half-sister and substitute mother, María "loved [her] so deeply." The Kavanaugh-Rodriguez translation says that María's husband "also *liked* [her] very much" (BL 3.3). The Spanish original, however, is *"también me amaba mucho."*

15. The full name of the monastery is "María de la Encarnación."

16. *The Collected Letters of St. Teresa of Ávila*, vol. 2, trans. Kieran Kavanaugh, OCD (Washington, DC: ICS, 2007), Letter 269.3, n. 5 and 6. See John Paul II, "Teresa of Ávila: God's Vagabond," *Origins* 12 (November 11, 1982), n. 10.

17. B.C. Butler, *Prayer: An Adventure in Living* (London: Darton, Longman and Todd, 1961), 41.

18. Letter of July 1974, cf. David Knowles, "Contemplative Prayer in St. Teresa," *Downside Review* 51, 201–230, 406–430, 611–633.

19. For example, *Summa Theologiae* 1.1.8 and 2.

20. Raïssa Maritain, *Raïssa's Journal*, ed. Jacques Maritain (Albany: Magi, 1974), 88.

21. The paradoxes are mine, but they were inspired by Louis Cognet, *Historire de la Spiritualité* (Paris: Aubier, 1966), 81–82.

22. Peter Tyler, *The Return to the Mystical: Ludwig Wittgenstein and the Christian Mystical Tradition* (New York: Continuum, 2011), especially chap. 5.

23. See for example, BL 21.4; WP 3.7. See the Spanish *atrevido* and its various forms. *Concordancias de los Escritos de Santa Teresa de Jesús*, eds. Juan Luis Astigarraga with collaboratrion of Agustí Borrell (Rome: Editoriales O.C.D., 2000).

24. Daniel de Pablo Maroto, *Lecturas y Maestros de Santa Teresa* (Madrid: Editorial de Espiritualidad, 2009), 97.

25. See Edward Howells, *John of the Cross and Teresa of Ávila: Mystical Knowing and Selfhood* (New York: Crossroad, 2002), 94.

26. Bernard McGinn, "Mystical Consciousness: A Modest Proposal," *Spiritus* 8 (Spring 2008): 44–63.

27. Teresa is not clear about a distinction between Active Recollection and Passive Recollection. See Marie-Eugene, *I Am a Daughter of the Church*, trans. M. Verda Clare (Chicago: Fides, 1955), 7–9.

28. See brief description of Teresa's Prayer of Recollection in Ernest Larkin, *Contemplative Prayer Today: Christian Meditation* (Singapore: MedioMedia, 2007), 65–68.

29. Aquinas, *Summa theologiae* 2.2.184.1 and 2.2.25.1.

30. My comments here on gift have been inspired by Kenneth L. Schmitz, "Aquinas Lecture, 1982," in *The Gift of Creation*, (Milwaukee: Marquette University Press, 1982), 44ff.

31. Aquinas, *Summa theologiae* 1–2.28.2. I owe this point to Walter Principe, "Loving Friendship according to Thomas Aquinas," Lecture at Brock University, February 1991.

32. For example, Romans 6:3; Galatians 2:20; Ephesians 3:17, Colossians1:27; 1 John 2:24.

33. Daniel de Pablo Maroto, *Santa Teresa de Jesús: Nueva Biografía* (Madrid: Espiritualidad, 2014), 334–337.

34. My translation.

35. *The Collected Works of Saint John of the Cross*, trans. Kieran Kavanaugh, OCD, and Otilio Rodriguez, OCD, rev. ed. (Washington, DC: ICS). CB=*The Spiritual Canticle*.

36. From 1562, the founding of San José in Ávila until 1582, when Teresa died at Alba de Tormes.

37. *Collected Works of St. Teresa of* Ávila, vol. 2, 458, n. 5.

38. On the founding of the monastery of San José in Ávila, see BL 32–36; for all the other foundations see BF.

39. Teresa uses the Spanish *ruin*, "wretched," 209 times.

40. The first in traditional theological terminology: *gratia gratum faciens*, the second *gratia gratis data*.

41. Bonaventure, *The Soul's Journey into God*, trans. Ewert Cousins, Classics of Western Spirituality (New York: Paulist, 1978), chap. 7, 113.

42. Daniel de Pablo Maroto, *Lecturas*, 104–109.

43. Teresa mentions Saint Bernard only once, BL 22.7, where Teresa refers to Bernard and others as "great contemplatives."

44. See also IC 6.3.2; 6.8.10; BF 8.3.

CHAPTER 22

John of the Cross and Prayer

~ Constance FitzGerald, OCD ~

Through the years, I have looked at John of the Cross through various heuristic lenses: the transformation of desire, impasse and dark night, purification of memory in the dark night, perplexing prayer experiences, the primacy of Christ and the central function of incarnate wisdom—Sophia—in human transformation and communion with God, mutuality and equality, beauty, feminism, creation and ecology, evolution and emergence. Each manner of breaking open his teaching provides guidance in prayer because for John prayer is a life path to transformation by and in love, not simply a method, a practice, a time set aside each day for God.

John of the Cross's teaching is so rich that one single chapter can hardly capture his understanding of prayer. Whether the great Carmelite poet is singing of the wonders of union with God that he has experienced, or the quintessential spiritual guide is describing the searing purifications of the dark nights, in him one encounters magnificent passion bordering on excess. The way he guides and educates is by showing us how passion for God grows, that is, how desire matures in focus and ardor, how one's relational identity changes as intimacy with Christ takes over one's life, how transformation of consciousness and being God's partner in love—Lover and Beloved— comes about in our lives. John beckons us toward the frontiers of human consciousness and addresses us from the farthest edges of the human spirit. I want, therefore, to contextualize all that follows with the enticingly affective language and cosmic intensity he uses to describe this communion in his final work, the *Living Flame of Love:*

> The soul feels its ardor strengthen and increase and its love becomes so refined in this ardor that seemingly there flow seas of loving fire within it, reaching to the heights and depths of all earthly and heavenly spheres, imbuing all with love. It seems to it that the entire universe is a sea of love in which it is engulfed, for conscious of the living point or center of love within itself, it is unable to catch sight of the boundaries of this love…. For the soul beholds itself converted into an immense fire of love that emanates from that enkindled point in the heart of the spirit. (2.10–11)

Inasmuch as John is one of the greatest poets in the Spanish language, one will only grasp his spirit and understand his teaching on prayer by always looking at it through the prism of his poetry. What we see in this primary expression of his own mystical experience is divine desire coming to meet human desire and kindling in human hearts an unquenchable desire.

> Where have you hidden
> Beloved, and left me to my moaning?
> You fled like the stag
> after wounding me;
> I went out calling you, but you
> were gone. (SC 1)[1]

> My Beloved, the mountains
> and lonely wooded valleys, strange islands,
> and resounding rivers,
> the whistling of love stirring
> breezes.
> The tranquil night
> at the time of the rising dawn,
> silent music,
> sounding solitude,
> the supper that refreshes and
> deepens love. (SC 14–15)

In this interpretive environment, dense with images of human love and the beauty of creation in all its diverse, magnificent forms, three areas stand out when considering prayer in St. John of the Cross: the centrality of Jesus Christ, the experiences of dark night or purification, and what I would express in a summary way as the fullness of Christ consciousness. In the third area I will reflect on the breathtaking mutuality, equality, beauty, and transformative possibilities, marking union with God, with the Trinity, what John calls the spiritual marriage.

In view of John Welch's contribution to this volume which surveys thoroughly John's teaching in the framework of the wider Carmelite tradition, I am choosing to highlight these three key elements in hopes of complementing Welch's work. Furthermore, I am offering my contribution within the contemporary context of evolution and emergence, specifically the emergence of Christ consciousness in the life of prayer. John of the Cross is a pioneer in the evolution of Christ consciousness.

The Centrality of Jesus Christ

For John, desire has a central and defining role in our lives. He assumes, first of all, that we are propelled by our insatiable desire (focus of the First Book of the Ascent); second, the desire for Jesus Christ, as *the* Beloved One, has to grow greater than all other desires and loves that give us pleasure (A 1.14.2); third, this is not achieved by pulling us away from our deepest longings, but by educating them by the love of Christ. What is indicated here is a priority that does not exclude other loves but situates them firmly and securely within the great embrace of Christ's love. In the development, purification, and transformation of desire, the critical influence is Jesus Christ. We cannot get away from this: one begins with Jesus, he is the pattern of the dark night even when he recedes from our conscious awareness and seems hidden, and one ends with transformation in Jesus Christ, the Beloved, incarnate Wisdom.

This means only one thing: desire to know Jesus, understanding that human desire is educated, first of all, by immersion in the Jesus of the Gospels, whereby one builds up more and more conscious references to him. This is how the risen Jesus becomes the focus of meaning in one's life (A 1.13.3; LF 3.32). The accent here is on the humanity of Jesus because desire needs something—someone—concrete to motivate it (SC 1.21). If you channel your affective energy toward knowing Jesus Christ, his love and companionship will slowly claim your desire, redirect your motivation, and subvert your egoic self and life. This dynamic underlies John's whole philosophy of prayer and indicates how a conscious decision of the heart for Christ takes place (active night of sense), how a shift in the focus of desire and meaning develops in one's prayer life (A 1.14.2; A 2.7.2–3).

He delineates a movement from a possessive, entangled, confining, unfree desire for pleasure, safety, and reassurance to a love that transcends the consuming concern for one's egoic self and is fulfilled in a deep communion with Christ where God's desire becomes our desire! In this prayer process of growing intimacy with Jesus, consciousness is gradually changed by who one knows and loves. Who one is in one's autonomous selfhood gradually morphs, over a lifetime, into a new relational identity characteristic of a profoundly pervasive union with Jesus Christ and all that he loves. One's consciousness becomes so deeply aligned with the consciousness of the one who is, for John of the Cross, divine wisdom, that the Word spoken ceaselessly in the depths of Trinitarian life is heard, actually experienced, in the soul in the silence of their embrace.

Initial Dark Night

Initially, intimacy with Christ is a consoling process: it moves one's desire, reorients one's will toward God, and in that same movement, in that sweet companionship, desire is satisfied. The deepening presence of Jesus is a strength and spiritual support motivating one toward a generous, self-giving life influenced by the Jesus of the Gospels and sensitizing one to this Christic presence in the world energizing and connecting all reality—the presence within recognizing and catching the reflection of the presence without. In fact, this presence in human relationships, throughout the beauty and wonder of the entire cosmos, in human culture and creativity, causes desire for Christ to grow by leaps and bounds in the person of prayer. We need this expansive spiritual consolation to persevere in prayer and, for some, it may last a long time.

But insofar as individuals choose to open their lives to increasing intimacy with Christ, they will inevitably be led by God's choosing, to a prayer that is increasingly God's initiative. Evolution in Christ consciousness, or Christ union, will show itself in the experiences of the dark nights where human desire is progressively purified and transformed. Ironically, it is the withdrawal of spiritual pleasure, the advent of dryness and ambiguity in prayer, and the muting of other sources of satisfaction or consolation in our lives that signal growing depth in prayer and herald the purification of the dark night.

The dark nights have two faces: purification and union. Insofar as the dark night is about purification, it is a transition; insofar as it is about union and identity, it is a new stage of growth. Purification is always about emergence, about preparing us for something: deeper interiority, union with God, new love knowledge, closer relational identity with Christ, a new stage of Christ consciousness. Ordinarily, we are painfully aware of the forces of purification in our lives; the emerging union is far less available to our conscious awareness. However, there are signs in our prayer and in our lives to indicate both the authenticity of the purification and the emerging new stage of intimacy (A 2.13.3; DN 1.9.2; LF 3.32–42).[2]

Dryness in prayer and in life, the inability to pray and love as one formerly did with spiritual consolation and peace or illuminating thoughts and consoling affections, coupled with anxiety about one's faithfulness and one's inability to regain the reassuring sense of God's or Christ's presence, are all marks of a painful transition, or purification. They cry out confusion, disappointment, boredom, anger, disillusionment, even loss of meaning. John of the Cross calls them signs for the discernment of the dark night of sense. They point to egocentric dependencies and destructive limitations and neuroticisms that must be left behind if a person is to appropriate, or live into, a new stage of faithfulness and freer, stronger, more committed love. For the egoic self, there is a sense of "I" in every desire, every thought, every memory, every interpretation, opinion, viewpoint, reaction, emotion. Dark night is the place where egoism dies, where desire is gradually purified and transformed, and true unselfish love for the other is set free.

The temptation to quit prayer and a deeper, more demanding relationship, to attempt to turn back to a more consoling, familiar way of praying, to reject a path devoid of accustomed satisfaction and thereby refuse purification of the egoic self can be overwhelming. Such an inclination to turn away from trust in God in the face of the seeming disintegration and real losses being experienced is the deepest challenge of this night. It does not come from the good spirit but from the false self and its unredeemed desire, and one must not succumb to it. The dryness and limitation of creation I am tasting, the sadness seeping from my prayer into my relationships, ministry, and work is a religious experience and is a sign of the dark night's purifying transition, according to John, but insofar as the feeling includes a temptation to move away from Christ, to resist God's deeper claim on me, and quit prayer, it is a backlash of the egoic self, "one of the most burdensome goads and horrors of this night," says John in the last, often overlooked, chapter of book 1 of *The Dark Night* (14). This is a fine distinction between an important marker of the dark night—dryness, boredom, "nothing happening" in prayer—and the often accompanying, strong temptation to turn one's back on God and seek satisfaction in the pleasures and idols of former days.[3]

A person has to be alert and responsive to the last and absolutely essential sign of the dark night: the inner drawing to remain alone in quiet, loving awareness and openness to a deeper kind of Christ presence that is largely hidden from our explicit consciousness. It is a sensitivity to this intuition, this deceptively quiet inner claim, that assures a newly emerging stage of Christ consciousness or union. It is imperative that spiritual directors know how to detect the still obscure, secret, divine wisdom welling up within the soul so as to validate and encourage the inner impulse toward silent attentiveness and quiet, unpretentious surrender. When the person feels herself *placed* in solitude and spiritual listening, a director dare not make the inexcusable mistake of urging her to forsake this "inner idleness" by returning to the discipline of more discursive or active prayer (LF 3.35, 42–46).

It is critical to realize that the dark night is the time in prayer development to seek not the escape of other experiences or practices but the living presence of Christ within and remain silently open to the purifying, transforming presence of this divine wisdom, who is actually experienced as *no one* and *nothing*. This soul experience is not easy to grasp because to all appearances Christ recedes from consciousness and loses significance, God seems beyond reach, belief is threatened, and even atheism seems logical (A 2.12.3–8). In an effort to control their experience and rescue their God from oblivion, it is not uncommon for individuals to turn to a kind of "cosmic presence" that transcends Christ. Such an inclination is almost understandable if one considers the hidden mystery operative in this prayer, but John cautions against such a temptation (A 2.22).

God *is* drawing the individual more and more into God's life and love so that all that is not God becomes unsatisfying and painful to stay with. Liturgy, prayer forms, ministry, community, the routines of everyday life, even our most cherished human friendships and especially the friendship with Christ we have known up until now, are drained of meaning and become sources of disappointment, disillusionment, and self-doubt. A deeper intimacy with Christ, a secret wisdom, is taking hold of the person and silently prying loose the grasp of the unfree heart from all that is not God, from all the idolatries of one's self-centered attachments—consoling and accustomed ways of praying, human achievements and ambitions, spiritual consolations, images of the loved one(s), images of self laboriously and often unconsciously fashioned from childhood, lifelong images of God and of Christ. While the heart's deepest longings are being realized at some profound level and a new relational identity, transformative of human desire, is being forged, this is beyond the reach of explicit consciousness.

John of the Cross knows by experience that purification is tailor made for each one of us. It invades our lives in diverse ways, for different durations, spasmodically or in huge doses, at different times in life. How it is experienced and understood—the shape it takes, its severity—will depend on the stage of a person's Christ consciousness or union. The dark nights are not stair steps but episodic states of purification that come to the fore as the limited boundaries of one's present level of Christ consciousness begin to show themselves, precisely because a new stage of intimacy or relational identity is emerging within us. The pain of transition and emergence to deeper love and life in God go hand in hand and the darkness we have been describing does ordinarily open into a time (or times) of peaceful contemplative prayer, committed dedication to others, and relative spiritual maturity. A person may live and grow for years imbedded in this comparatively stable God/Christ environment, only occasionally receiving hints of the more intense purifications and more profound transformations yet to come.

Deeper Experiences of Night

In the second book of the *Dark Night*, John of the Cross does go on to describe even more acute experiences of darkness in prayer when Christ's action takes on new depth and urgency. His action, within the framework of intimate relationship, involves both the divinization and humanization of the person, and John is strikingly clear about this. Moreover, he is more astutely aware than most of the obstacles to this transformative Christic action. First of all, we are impeded by the false self, that is, all the remnants of the unredeemed self that remain even after the purifications of earlier times and that become all too evident in this more severe refining of the soul (DN

2.13.10). The second obstacle is human finitude, the familiar boundaries of the soul which are not evil, just limited. They must be stretched and stretched if one is to become more and more *capax Christi*, capable of holding within oneself as one's own inmost center, the *full* relational life of Christ. The soul must be broken wide open, must surrender more and more of the self, to contain all with which Christ stands in relationship. This stretching and opening up one experiences is both much desired and harrowing. It is both blessing and agony. It is blessing because the soul recognizes, out of a certain depth of spiritual maturity, that this is the action of the one who loves the soul exquisitely and supremely. But it is agony because of the pain involved.[4]

Now, John explains, God blinds one with divine light and oppresses and dries one up with divine fire. Always the interplay between purification and deeper union, transition and emergence. Inasmuch as the dark night of the spirit is experienced as an extreme sense of deprivation that invades the total personality—body, psyche, spirit—it seems to dispossess one of one's very selfhood (DN 2.3.3). John does not minimize the anguish of this undoing of one's sense of self which undermines the identity one has been imbedded in and strips one of what one has to leave behind in order to live into the fullness of Christ consciousness, for John the spiritual marriage and ultimate transformation.

Such a drastic subversion of all the powers of the human person—John names them intellect, memory, and will—can best be understood within the context of his anthropology. As long as the great "caverns" of the mind, heart, memory, and imagination are filled with human knowledge, loves, dreams, and memories that seem to promise absolute assurance and complete fulfillment, or at least more than they can ever deliver, a person will never realize the depths of the capacity that is there. Only when we actually experience their emptiness and darkness, in the face of the breakdown of what we have staked our lives on, do we thirst and hunger and yearn for these "caverns" to be filled with God (LF 3.18–22).

John dwells at some length on the night of blindness and emptiness in the intellect when meaning fades and reason can no longer satisfy. What steadily and stealthily moves into the empty space when meaning disappears is authentic theological faith, a grasping for God that reaches beyond the horizon of natural, human understanding. Paradoxically, faith dispossesses one of any ability to construct, from a lifetime of accumulated knowledge, a meaningful world or a meaningful God. In fact, the light of faith causes darkness in our very power to understand and is at cross purposes with our struggle to make logical sense out of life or death or eternity. Insofar as this kind of theological faith is imparted, it is nothing else than a blind surrender to a hidden, loving knowledge, the incarnate wisdom of God, who is deeply present and is actively transforming and divinizing the intellect (DN 2.5.2–3; 8.4, 9; 13.10).

John explains, as well, the heartbreaking experience of profound abandonment, loss, and weariness that marks this deeper night. The vast recesses of selfishness and falseness in the self are overwhelming. Not only does one feel rejected by God but frequently isolated by misunderstandings and even persecutions. It is when the human soul is broken wide open that the purification of the will by theological love unfolds, first of all, in the difficult handing over of the shattered self to the never failing love of God, and second, in the courageous decision to reject violence and refuse hatred, to love faithfully and serve others—often with great effectiveness and daring—regardless of the cost and in spite of intense affective deprivation, loss, or betrayal. Such intimacy with and assimilation to the self-giving death and glorification of Jesus are all in service of a person's Christification, her becoming humanized and divinized by the human and divine Christ (DN 2.13.9).

Last and most important, John puts a refined emphasis on the purification of the memory (DN 2.8.2). Looked at through the contemporary prism of identity and emergence, dark nights are always about my memory of myself and God's future for me. I believe it is in the mysterious unravelling of the memory that we find *the key* to the deepest dimensions of the dark night transition.[5] Our memories have made us who we are, spiritually and humanly. What we remember, what others remember with us and for us, how we remember, how we weave our memories together into a fabric of meaning, matters decisively in shaping our identities. But in this dark transition time, I find no refuge in my memory of past graces or past pleasures, past relationships, or past achievements of mind and heart. Least of all does the memory of my cherished relationship with God, with Christ, console me. The spiritual gifts that marked deeper intimacy seem like a faraway dream. Memory of all this constitutes my identity, but now I find no resting place in my accustomed sense of my self, *my* identity. There is a sense in which I do not know who I am. I become a stranger to myself—undone, silenced. I am no longer at home in my own house.

So much I have learned and achieved intellectually or treasured affectively loses its cogency, as has been said. My deeply held beliefs blow in the winds of doubt and my most cherished relationships tell of abandonment and loss. My life projects, to which I had selflessly (I thought!) committed myself, appear to fail. Everything I have done seems tainted. My goodness, my fidelity, my motivation, my story to myself, seem to be an illusion, a lie. So much that has given me assurance and meaning fades into insignificance and this is keenly felt as a loss of authenticity, of identity. On a very fundamental level, my selfhood—who I am—is radically undermined. The slide into depression, a kind of backlash from this dark spiritual experience, can loom large in the face of such inexplicable disorientation. God is purifying me in my conscious self and even more in my unconscious, a place to which God/Christ alone has entry.

I am being thrown into the fire of God's love, but it can only be described as suffocation and destruction because of the extreme dryness I am experiencing in my prayer *and in my life.*

Still, the fire that now oppresses, wounds, and dries up my soul in its deepest center is the same flame that is wounding me with love. The Spirit is uniting me with Christ so intimately that God is taking over my selfhood. I am being drawn right into his life. I am growing into Christ's own relational identity. But none of this is occurring in my daily "daylight" consciousness, and so I derive no support, in the ordinary sense of the term, from what God is doing. On the other hand, I sense I must forfeit the identity in which I am imbedded. I must freely yield to this process that is breaking down the boundaries of my soul. There is no real alternative that promises me what I am so deeply longing for at this point. This is the darkness that is to be trusted, hoped into, in faith and surrendered to in love.[6]

I am being taught in the outpouring of a secret, inner wisdom that the memory of all I have been can hold me back from God's future for me. What God wants to do for me—me becoming Christ, his life becoming mine, his knowing and loving becoming mine—is far greater than what I have been. I need only let my life go into the memory of God. A terrifying, dispossession of identity! This is true theological hope which comes into play when I am really radically at the end, unable to find any further resources to connect the memories, feelings, and experiences of life into a meaningful pattern, an independent identity of my own.[7] Hope then frees the memory not only of its life burdens but of all that must be left behind. Purified and emptied by such hope, freed from the snares of all calculation, memory is open to the God of infinite transformative possibilities who is always coming from the future and constantly fostering emergence to the full relational life of Christ, the deepest level of Christ consciousness.

THE FULLNESS OF CHRIST CONSCIOUSNESS

Now it is not a matter of my becoming increasingly conscious of Christ *in* my life but of my becoming conscious *with* Christ's consciousness, becoming Christ's equal, Christ's self, by graced participation. It is important to realize that Christ's identity is fashioning our graced identity. Christ, incarnate wisdom, is the fullness of humanity and divinity in one person. As we grow in Christlikeness we are being drawn into this twofold fullness. John believes that during the time of dark purification, when limitation looms large and deadly silence envelopes the soul, Christ is bringing us to the fullness of humanity which mediates the fullness of divinity, two fullnesses as totally united, not separate but distinct, not forming a third reality. And it is not the humanity of Christ alone that is crucial for our growing union with God. We are being drawn into the human *and* divine reality of Christ so that Christ's human and divine reality are becoming our reality (SC 38.1). Whether John writes of divine wisdom or the incarnate Word or the Son, of lover or beloved or bridegroom or spouse, of secret, solitary, purifying contemplation or hidden loving knowledge, it is Jesus Christ, truly human and truly divine, as one's own inmost center, who is bringing us into his own selfhood and his relationships in a focal way. So what slowly emerges from the dark transition of purifying unknowing and surrender to become exceedingly explicit is a profound loving identification with Christ, the union of lover and beloved in the spiritual marriage, "a total transformation in the Beloved in which each surrenders the entire possession of self to the other" (SC 22.3).

> O guiding night!
> O night more lovely than the dawn!
> O night that has united
> The Lover with his beloved,
> Transforming the beloved in her Lover. (DN 6)

According to Edward Howells, the union attained by the radical process of stretching and emptying the soul gives a new structure of relationality, that is, a new relational identity, to the deep level of the soul that was not there before. The transformation is a real change of selfhood, moving the soul beyond the bounds of the self that was and into God.[8]

We can only wonder at the beautifully extravagant language John uses to describe the emergence into the fullness of union in the spiritual marriage, knowing he sings of the unspeakable from his own profound experience. Sharing in Christ's own relational identity now means for him that the relationships that constitute Christ have become John's in an explicit way. Completely united with Jesus Christ in his humanity and divinity, he, like Teresa of Jesus, his companion in the reform of Carmel, is profoundly drawn into the mutual dynamic relationships of Trinitarian life. Like her, he is explicitly conscious of the Father with Jesus Christ's consciousness and is bonded to the Father by the Holy Spirit. John knows Abba as Christ knows Abba and experiences being under the influence of the Holy Spirit. He is drawn into the interflow of life and love, the communion, in the Trinity, "capable of breathing in God the same spiration of love that the Father breathes in the Son and the Son in the Father. This spiration of love is the Holy Spirit, who in the Father and the Son breathes out to her in this transformation in order to unite her to God's self. There would not be a true and total transformation if the soul were not transformed in the three persons of the Most Holy Trinity in an open and manifest degree" (SC 39.3).

Now he understands, knows and loves *in* the Trinity, as one membered into the communion of Trinitarian life (SC 39.4; see SC 39.3–6; 37.6; LF 2.1–20; 1.6). This inclusion of the transformed self in the life of the Trinity has reached its high point where everything the soul does is itself an act of relation to God within the mutuality of the Trinity, as Howells indicates (126). This is why John can tell us with shockingly bold language the degree to which human consciousness is transformed and the human person "made like God":

> Finally, all the movements, operations and inclinations the soul had previously from the principle and strength of its natural life are now in this union...changed into divine movements, and alive to God.... Accordingly, the intellect of this soul is God's intellect; its will is God's will; its memory is the eternal memory of God; and its delight is God's delight;... It has become God though participation in God, being united to and absorbed in God. (LF 2.34)

Mutuality, Equality, Beauty of Union

Yet entry into Trinitarian life does not mean that our knowing and loving cease to be human when divinized. Rather the soul attains a relational identity in Christ that is capable of mediating the self-knowing and self-loving of the Trinity.[9] God's intensifying presence in the transformed self always means the enhancement, not the reduction, of the human person in her or his authentic reality, as John explains:

> If anything pleases God it is the exaltation of the soul. Since there is no way by which he can exalt her more than by making her equal to himself, he is pleased only with her love. For the property of love is to make the lover equal to the one loved. Since the soul in this state possesses perfect love, she is called the Bride of the Son of God, which signifiers equality with him. In this equality of friendship, the possessions of both are held in common, as the Bridegroom himself said to his disciples: "I have called you my friends, because all I have heard from my Father I have made known to you." (SC 28.1)

The latter part of the *Spiritual Canticle* (as well as the poetry of John and parts of *The Living Flame*) abounds with iconic, artistic images expressive of the mutuality, equality and shared beauty of deep communion. Dominant among them is the symbol of bride/bridegroom or lover/beloved, which allows John to unfold a plethora of soul experiences. In their plenitude and extravagance these experiences push all the boundaries of our imagination and our hope. Yet for this very reason, we cannot fail to examine for direction, encouragement and meaning the myriad, interlacing nuances of divine/human indwelling and reciprocal belongingness they reveal.

I intended reflecting at some length on these soul experiences, but no word of mine striving to break open the meaning of these passionate, mysterious texts can compare with the revelatory, transformative experience of immersing oneself in them. This kind of deep engagement with such exquisite, prodigal texts and images plunges the person of prayer right into the experiences of mutuality and equality with God and stokes, even inflames, one's desire for the depth and boundlessness of intimate communion there portrayed. I am indicating here a profound prayer process whereby one moves around in these texts, allows them to seep into one's soul until one slowly participates in some way in the total mutuality and self-gift of lover and beloved, the incredible equality God desires and gives, the breathtaking beauty and giftedness the lover and beloved share with each other, the true mutuality of desire that blossoms, the resulting partnership with God/Christ in love and service to the totality of creation the divinized person lives out.

Such surrender to John's unitive writings, in the latter part of the *Spiritual Canticle* particularly, is transformative of the self. It involves the pray-er in a powerful appropriation of her own experience and deepest desire and one understands to the extent that one has been there in some way. Most of us do not lay claim to the overwhelming, explicit experiences of loving union with Christ and the Trinity of which John of the Cross sings, but conscious immersion in the extravagant language of divine love can illuminate the hidden, tranquil, even dark, presence of Christ in one's prayer and life, the quiet often unpretentious prayer of union, the silent, mysterious working of holy mystery day by day. Living in these texts of mutuality and beauty can give meaning to the darkest night and hope when the boundaries of the soul are stretched and broken open and the self we have known seems threatened on every side. To participate in these texts as a pray-er is to be brought, at least for a short time, into Christ's own selfhood, Christ's own consciousness.

One may think that the fullness of Christ consciousness, the communication of God's own self in Trinitarian love, in such intimate relationship and fulfillment of desire, is static or self-contained. John makes clear, however, that the fruit of total mutuality and equality is availability for others in prophetic hope and loving service. God, by giving the loved one his own love, shows her how to love as she is loved by

God. God teaches her how to love purely, freely, totally, and disinterestedly, as God loves us. "As if [God] were to put an instrument in her hands and show her how it works by operating it jointly with her, [God] shows her how to love and gives her the ability to do so" (SC 38.4). She becomes, John says, "the shadow of God" in the world, rejoicing not only in the sweetness of love she possesses in a habitual union, but also in that which spills over into the effective and actual practice of love in works directed to the service of all those God loves (LF 3.78; SC 36.4). Because her experience overflows outside of herself into the world around her and others actually recognize it, she becomes a prophet of communion and mutuality, one who bears witness to the inseparable connectedness of all life and everyone (SC 17.7).

No matter where we are in our spiritual development, John's mystical descriptions of the spiritual marriage have an important role to play in our lives of prayer. They inspire us to breathe, by the energy of our desire, mutual, selfless love into our world and onto the currents of human consciousness. They impel us to live, with intentional dedication, as prophets of the mutuality and communion and equality in which God always embraces us even while we are still on the way.

Continuing Emergence and Transformation

Finally, John places a significant accent on the progressive character of transformation. At the end of the *Spiritual Canticle*, he insists that such a communion of love and knowledge opens into continuous yet to be realized possibilities of emergence to new depths of consciousness, a vast and ever unfolding future. Moreover, this potential for emerging transformations is always essentially Christocentric, that is, rooted in Jesus Christ, divine wisdom, the incarnate Word of God. John's commentary on stanza 37 of the Canticle is both audacious and unequivocal testimony of this truth:

> And then we will go
> to the high caverns in the rock
> which are so well concealed;
> there we shall enter
> and taste the fresh juice of the pomegranates.

> The rock mentioned here is Christ.... The high caverns of this rock are the sublime, exalted, and deep mysteries of God's wisdom in Christ, in the hypostatic union of the human nature and the divine Word, and in the corresponding union of human beings with God.... As caverns are deep and have many recesses, so each of the mysteries of Christ is singularly deep in Wisdom and contains many recesses.... There is so much to fathom in

Christ, for he is like an abundant mine with many recesses of treasures so that however deep individuals may go, they never reach the end or bottom, but at every recess find new veins with new riches everywhere (SC.B 37.3–4).

There we shall enter and be transformed in the transformations of new knowledge and new acts and communications of love. For although it is true that the soul, when she says this, is already transformed...in this Wisdom... it does not therefore follow that she cannot in this estate have new enlightenments and transformations of new kinds of knowledge and divine light. Indeed, she has very frequent illuminations of new mysteries communicated to her by God in the communication that is ever made between God and the soul. And this communication God makes to her in himself, and she enters into him as it were afresh, according to the knowledge of those mysteries which she knows in him; and in that knowledge she loves him afresh, most intimately and sublimely, being transformed in him according to those new kinds of knowledge; and the sweetness and delight, which at that time, she receives once more are altogether ineffable (SC.A 37.5).

Most remarkable of all, John suggests this continuing transformation is open to us in this life. John wrote two redactions of the *Spiritual Canticle*, and in the last stanzas we find a surprising and pervasive difference between the two. In the freer, more passionate and daring first redaction, Canticle A (1584), John situates his marvelous expectations for unending transformation this side of death with only a minor gesturing to life after death. In the second, more theologically refined redaction, Canticle B, written a year or two later (1585–1586) with an eye on the Inquisition, his great hope sees these same emerging consequences taking place over the horizon of death in the environment of resurrected life. Inconsistency? I think not. John of the Cross could place his experiences in both the time and space of the present age and the time and space of the age to come, without equivocation, because he had somehow experienced their intersection in his own life. (Worthy of note, in Canticle A, is his theological witness, conscious or not, to the presence of the reign of God, here and now, in the Risen Christ.)

It makes a considerable difference in our prayer life whether we think of the deepest reaches of Christ consciousness and Trinitarian life as evolving in this earthly life or only in an afterlife, in the age to come. What these experiences of communion might mean is greatly enlarged by how this world, this age, interprets Canticle A. This is very important for our hope, our fidelity to prayer, and our sense of responsibility for the continuing evolution of higher stages of human consciousness.

On the one hand, there is little doubt that the Inquisition's suspicion of contemplative prayer influenced the changes John made in the second redaction of the *Spiritual Canticle*. On the other hand, it seems significant that at one time John can describe experiences of union and transformation as happening during this earthly life and at another time taking place in the age to come. If "what makes a person immortal is his/her relationship or communion with God," and if "our bodies, our whole materiality, our earth, and our universe, are not to be replaced but transformed in death," then mutuality, communion, and equality are on a continuum, and where the present age ends and the age to come begins is not so clear cut, nor is the movement between them strictly linear. John, the mystic, knows both the now and not-yet of the reign of God in a way we do not; he experiences a bridging or intersection of time and eternity and sees beyond the boundaries of faith and consciousness that confine most of us.

Physicist and theologian John Polkinghorne throws a contemporary light on John's prophetic intuition by offering a perspective for appreciating the relationship between the time and space of "this creation" and the time and space of the "new creation:"

> Although the new creation is the transformation of the old creation, it is not necessarily the case that [our] time and "time" [of the new creation] should be in a strictly sequential relationship, with the new "time" beginning "after" the ending of the old…. [And therefore] what we would naturally think of as the spaces of the old and new creations could be "alongside" each other, with the continuity of resurrection being the result of a structure-preserving mapping (patterning) from one space into the other. From this point of view, it would be conceivable that all persons arrive at the general resurrection at the same "time," irrespective of the time of their deaths in this world. The "clock" of the world to come need not be synchronized with the clocks of the old creation. If Christ's resurrection is the seminal event from which the new creation stems, then something like this must be so. The resurrection appearances are then intersections between these two spaces.[10]

This would mean that the continuity of and participation in resurrection is brought about by the Christ consciousness (the structure preserving pattern or relational identity or soul) alive in each space and time. And John's marvelous experiences can be understood as intersections between the two times or spaces—an alongsidedness.

What I want to accent in John's bold testimony is that profound contemplative union—the fullness of Christ consciousness—changes individuals radically; it transforms the character and effectiveness of their presence in the world. In them humanity is opened to new possibilities, new vision, a vast unimaginable future toward which deep theological hope must continue to reach even during life on this earth. And John is a pioneer of that hope. He has carved out a pathway and crossed a threshold for humanity.

With John we give over our bodies, our spirits, our psyches to Christ, daring to trust where the transformations and stretching of deepening Christ consciousness may lead us—not only in the deeper life of the age to come but *now* in this earthly life. Following John of the Cross, persons of prayer must sing, not only for themselves, but for the entire earth community:

> Let us rejoice, Beloved,
>
> and let us go forth to behold ourselves in your beauty
>
> to the mountains and to the hill,
>
> to where the pure water flows
>
> and further, deep into the thicket (SC 36).

1. Abbreviations in references: A = Ascent of Mount Carmel; DN = Dark Night; SC = Spiritual Canticle; LF = Living Flame. The levels of division of a work (book, chapter, paragraph number or stanza, paragraph number) are separated by periods; succession of references on the same level are separated by commas. In most instances John of the Cross citations are from *The Collected Works of John of the Cross*, trans. Kieran Kavanaugh, OCD, and Otilio Rodriguez, OCD (Washington, DC: ICS, 1991). Where quotations are referenced as SC.A (Canticle A) I am using *The Collected Works of St. John of the Cross*, vol. 2, trans. E. Alison Peers (Westminster, MD: 1945). Peers translated both redactions of the Spiritual Canticle.

2. For a more complete description of the signs and experience of the dark night, see Constance FitzGerald, *Impasse and Dark Night* in *Living with Apocalypse*, ed. Tilden Edwards (San Francisco: Harper and Row, 1984), 93–115.

3. St. Ignatius of Loyola in his teaching on discernment of spirits would call this experience spiritual desolation.

4. I want to acknowledge the work of Brian McDermott, SJ, in this paragraph. For the fifth centenary of Teresa of Ávila's birth, we collaborated in the study of Teresa and also of John of the Cross in terms of the dark night. We developed, among other areas, the growth of Christ consciousness in Teresa, including her experience of the Trinity. I am including important insights from our research, collaboration, and writing in this chapter.

5. For a more thorough treatment of the purification of the memory, see Constance FitzGerald, "From Impasse to Prophetic Hope," Proceedings of the Sixty-fourth Annual Convention, ed. Jonathan Y. Tan (n.p.: Catholic Theological Society of America, 2009), 21–42.

6. See Brian McDermott, "Contemplativeness and Spiritual Direction," in *Presence: An International Journal of Spiritual Direction* 21, no. 4 (December 2015), 6–13.

7. For more detailed interpretation of the purification of the memory by hope, see Constance FitzGerald, "Transformation in Wisdom," in *Carmel and Contemplation, Transforming Human Consciousness*, ed. Kevin Culligan and Regis Jordan (Washington, DC: ICS, 2000) 323; see also Karl Rahner, "On the Theology of Hope," *Theological Investigations*, vol. 10 (New York: Herder

and Herder, 1973), 242–253, and "Theology of Death," *Theological Investigations*, vol. 13 (New York: Crossroad, 1983) 169–186. Karl Rahner has helped me interpret John's thought on theological hope.

8. See Edward Howells, *John of the Cross and Teresa of* Ávila: *Mystical Knowing and Selfhood* (New York: Crossroad, 2002), 127.

9. Gillian Alhgren has developed the understanding of "a new relational identity" in her work *Entering Teresa of Ávila's Interior Castle* (New York: Paulist, 2005).

10. John Polkinghorne, "Eschatology: Some Questions and Some Insights from Science" in *The End of the World and the Ends of God*, eds. John Polkinghorne and Michael Welker (Harrisburg, PA: Trinity, 2000), 40.

CHAPTER 23

Praying with St. Thérèse of Lisieux: The Nineteenth-Century World and the French Church

~ *Barbara Jean LaRochester, OCD* ~

At the canonization of St. Thérèse of Lisieux on May 17, 1925, Pope Pius X proclaimed Thérèse "the greatest Saint of Modern Times."[1] What is it about her that continues to capture the imagination of the world in this twenty-first century? Why do people still entrust their cares and concerns, their pain and anxieties to Thérèse who lived a cloistered life and was virtually unknown? If we look at the Church and world in which she lived, we might better understand how her thoughts developed and perhaps, see things as she did.

History tells us that Thérèse of Lisieux was born in 1873, entered Carmel in 1888, and died in 1897. These years were structured by political unrest and disputes between the Church and state. By reading the daily paper or speaking with someone who did, Thérèse grew up knowing every detail about what was going on in France. This is how she learned about the criminal Henri Pranzini, who was sentenced to death because of his crimes. The missions were also a big part of Thérèse's thought and prayer. The knowledge that French colonies were being founded in distant places increased Thérèse's desire and zeal to preach the gospel to the people of these lands.

During Thérèse's time, there was little cooperation between the Church and state. Catholics torn between the Church-centered life and the pull of moral corruption in the culture arranged their lives accordingly. On the one hand was the tendency to turn inward and settle for a purified world of home, family, and church with minimal outside contact. Or one could opt to make reparation for the horrors committed against God and the Church through one's own personal suffering. The Martin girls were raised within this social construct.

THÉRÈSE: LIFE AND TIMES

Thérèse Martin was the youngest of nine children born to Louis and Zelie Martin on January 2, 1873. Because they lost three infants and a five year-old, Thérèse was especially welcomed into life. Due to a physical condition Thérèse had, or her mother who would later die of breast cancer, two-month-old Thérèse was unable to nurse. Zelie, fearing the child would starve, gave her to a wet nurse, Rose Taille, who took Thérèse away to her farm, where she thrived and grew. Thérèse was fifteen months old when she rejoined the Martin household. The Martins were a prosperous middle-class bourgeois family who lived a largely insular life, creating a comfortable and pious world within the confines of the home. With family members having few opportunities for serious interaction with outsiders, relationships tended to be super invested with emotional freight. The lifestyle provided a safe environment for the expression of a rich and delicate affective development, but it could also be subtly manipulative or oppressive. Thérèse's early development was shaped by both the positive and negative aspects of this insular way of life.

All five of the Martin girls became nuns. Leonie entered the Visitation Sisters; the other four sisters entered Lisieux Carmel. This may have been the fruit of their particular family lifestyle, in which an intense quest for holiness was woven into every aspect of daily life. The larger context was the Catholic culture with its strengths and weaknesses which shaped Thérèse and her spiritual quest for authentic holiness.

In 1877 when Thérèse was four years old, her mother died of breast cancer. This loss changed Thérèse, who was so full of life and exuberance, to a timid, retiring, sensitive child. She chose her sister Pauline to be her second mother. It was from her that Thérèse learned her catechism, prayers, and reverence for God. In October 1882, Thérèse was hit with another loss. Her sister Pauline entered the Lisieux Carmel. Thérèse, who was only nine years old, had already experienced three traumatic experiences. It should not surprise us that Pauline's entrance left Thérèse distraught. Entrance into Carmel in those days meant that the nun would never again leave the cloister, and family visits were a group affair with a barrier separating the religious from her lay family. Pauline's departure so affected Thérèse that she came down with a mysterious illness and would have died had it not been for the intervention of the Virgin Mary who worked a miracle in her behalf. Thérèse describes how "The Blessed Virgin appeared to [her] and her ravishing smile penetrated the very depths of [her] soul. In an instant, all [her] pain disappeared."[2] Thérèse continued to mature in grace, interacting with her sisters, her cousins, and her father, for whom she had a profound affection.

After Pauline left for Carmel, Marie took on the role of mother for young Thérèse. Four years later, in 1886, Marie joined Pauline at the Carmel of Lisieux. With this third departure, we can understand that Thérèse, in spite of her many advantages, suffered from a very early age.

THÉRÈSE'S CHRISTMAS GRACE

It was customary for young children to leave their slippers by the chimney to be filled with gifts at Christmas. Since Thérèse was the youngest in the family, her sister Celine wanted to continue the custom. After midnight Mass in 1886, her tired father saw the shoes and said, "Well, fortunately, this will be the last year!" Thérèse heard the remark as she was going up the stairs. Forcing back tears, she quickly descended the stairs, took the slippers and placed them in front of her father, withdrawing all the gifts joyfully. She said, "I had the happy appearance of a Queen."[3] Having regained his own cheerfulness, her father laughed. Seeing all this, Celine believed she was dreaming. Thérèse had discovered once again the strength of soul which she had lost at the age of four and a half. She was to preserve it forever.

What was this strength of soul? It was the grace to move away from self-centeredness and focus more generously on being a child of God. As Thérèse continued to grow, her one desire was to offer her life totally to God as a Carmelite nun. At the age of fourteen when a group of people from the diocese of Bayeux-Lisieux visited Rome, Thérèse and her father were among them. The group had an audience with Pope Leo XIII and Thérèse took the opportunity to ask the pope for the grace of entering Carmel by the age of fifteen. This was an unheard of gesture, but very courageous of Thérèse. The pope did not give her direct permission, but told her to "abide by the decisions of the Bishop of Lisieux."[4] Although Thérèse was made to wait for some months, her prayer, persistence in asking, and the support of her father provided the context for this unusual request to be granted. On April 9, 1888, at the age of fifteen, Thérèse joined her sisters Pauline and Marie in the Carmel of Lisieux.

THÉRÈSE IN CARMEL

When Thérèse entered Carmel, she took the name Thérèse of the Child Jesus and the Holy Face. She spent six years in Carmel before her father got sick and passed away in 1894. During these years, Thérèse had extraordinary spiritual insight and creativity. She wrote three manuscripts that formed her autobiography *Story of a Soul*. In June of 1895, Thérèse wrote her *Act of Oblation to Merciful Love*. This is perhaps the richest and most significant testament of her spirituality. In this *Oblation*, Thérèse offers herself as a victim of merciful love transforming the spirituality of reparation which was common within her cultural environment. While others offered themselves as victims of divine justice and prayed to suffer, Thérèse offered herself as a sacrifice to be consumed by love. This meant that she would work for God's love alone and save souls who would love him eternally. For Thérèse, Christian martyrdom was total committed love that would stop at nothing to manifest and fulfill that love.

There are many things that can be said of Thérèse during her relatively short time in Carmel. What she has taught us through her confidence, unconditional love, her experience of littleness, of suffering, her trial of faith, all remain her legacy to us. In her correspondence, in her autobiography, Thérèse speaks only of God's mercy and love. Her way of spiritual childhood was simple and spoke to her experience. It is my belief that people are still attracted to Thérèse today because she lived everyday life in an extraordinary way. With her help, we can do the same.

How Jesus Taught Thérèse

Jesus set before Thérèse the reality of a garden and helped her understand that all flowers made by God are beautiful. She learned how the splendor of the rose and the whiteness of the lily do not take away from the perfume of the little violet or the simplicity of the daisy. Thérèse considered herself a wild flower. Wild flowers are hidden in the woods, very few people see or even notice them, yet they give glory to God by being there and blooming. Today, Thérèse is best known as the "Little Flower." She is an example of unhistorical significance because of her great sanctity. Why? She places herself as an equal among simple people who will never be especially noticed or acclaimed and affirms the capability for each one of us to follow in her little way of sanctity.

We live in a society today where most of us want to be noticed, acclaimed, soar like eagles, and do great things. Thérèse, however, saw herself as a little bird with an eagle's heart. From her, we can learn true humility, the ability to accept life, to recognize our limits and see ourselves as part of a larger picture. God will use our strengths and weaknesses, our dreams and disillusionments, to create the garden of his delight in Carmel, in families, in the world. We need to understand why we are planted in that garden, and blossom into what God is creating in us. The variety and the richness of the garden will be compromised and limited if we try to become something we are not. If we live from the truth in our heart that is transformed by the love of God growing in us, God is glorified. This is the lesson of Thérèse. We are invited to live ordinary life with extraordinary love. Thérèse, with her protected, privileged environment, was and is a wild flower that still captures our souls and inspires our hearts today.

Meditation and Contemplative Prayer

Thérèse was fond of the countryside, the flowers, and the birds. She preferred to be alone, to sit on the grass filled with flowers, and to be carried away with deep thoughts. Without knowing what it was to meditate, her soul was absorbed in real prayer. She was aware of the sounds of music from far away, the murmuring and movement of the wind through the trees, and for her this was heaven. Like Thérèse, we can also grow in prayer by taking every opportunity to please God, by being aware of all that is around us. We can allow our spirits to touch the Holy as we contemplate a beautiful sunset, look on the face of a newborn baby, or watch children at play. Prayer is as simple as raising our hearts and minds to God. Thérèse used the ordinary things of daily life to help her grow in love and prayer. We can do the same.

Someone may ask, what about the desert times? What were they like for Thérèse? How did she handle dryness in prayer? Thérèse didn't force herself or allow herself to become discouraged when her prayer was dry. She simply recited a prayer such as the Our Father very slowly or spoke the simple words "Draw me" and knew that everyone she loved would be drawn into her prayer. She says, "I say very simply to God what I wish to say...and God always understands me."[5] For Thérèse, prayer was an aspiration of the heart, a simple glance directed to heaven, a cry of gratitude and love in the midst of trials or joys. Notice the words: a glance, a cry, a movement of the heart. These simple acts are open to all of us and can direct the inner attention of our soul and our prayer to God. They are the kindling that keeps the fire burning when times seem hard.

DESIRES

Thérèse had a great desire to become a saint, but in her autobiography, she writes, "To be your Spouse, to be a Carmelite, and by my union with You to be the Mother of souls."[6] While these three privileges sum up her vocation—Carmelite, Spouse, Mother—Thérèse also felt called to be a priest, a missionary, and martyr. Though none of these things happened in her lifetime, it never disillusioned her spirit. She believed that God's grace was refining her in surrender in marvelous and powerful ways through love, and not just through her deeds. We need faith like Thérèse because we all get trapped in betrayal, unanswered questions, and unfulfilled longings. Thérèse invites us to trust God's work in our lives.

Very early in her religious life Thérèse understood that the Church had a heart burning with love and that it was love alone that made members of the Church act. She understood that love comprised all vocations, that love was everything, that love embraced all times and places. In short, love is eternal. Thérèse had found her vocation. In the heart of the Church, she would be love. From that moment on, Thérèse knew how her life would be lived. She would prove her love for God by doing the smallest things with great love and would not allow one little sacrifice to escape her attention. Jesus taught Thérèse perfection in and through hiddenness, humility, surrender, and gratitude. She learned that happiness would consist in hiding herself and remaining unconcerned about created things. Her one desire was "to love Jesus to folly."[7] It was love alone that drew her and abandonment that guided her. What mattered most to Thérèse was the accomplishment of God's will. She often exclaimed, "O how sweet is the way of Love! How I want to apply myself to do the will of God always with great self surrender."[8] Thérèse reminds us that Jesus does not demand great actions from us. All God wants is our love, our surrender, and our gratitude.

Because Thérèse was an open and willing learner, God was able to teach her in many different ways, and she used this to her advantage. Her Little Way is a way of love that is straight and very short. It doesn't provide for detours or side trips for relaxation. It guarantees that *anyone* can walk this route at any time. Thérèse wrote, "My way is all confidence and love."[9] The only prerequisite for the journey is trust and a willingness to take the first step from wherever we are, knowing that Jesus will accept us, just as we are.

Thérèse's Spiritual Childhood and little way are an echo of the gospel message, "Come to me all you who labor and are heavily burdened."[10] Thérèse had faith in a God of love, mercy, kindness, and compassion, in a God who communicates grace and new life. She believed in her littleness that she knew her limitations and believed that we can give God glory by being who we are. Who among us does not feel at times the labor and heavy burden of human existence? Who among us does not need loving kindness to make the journey of life not only bearable but worth celebrating? To be human is to take on the ups and downs of everyday life, to rejoice and to live in wonder. Thérèse believed in living ordinary, daily life selflessly.

Because Thérèse lived in community, her context for union with God was living with others in community. She once remarked, "You live with some people in community who are difficult to get along with, who make life hard for you."[11] They may be people who are uneducated, stubborn, naïve, or emotionally or physically challenged. With God's grace, Thérèse accepted the limited character of her environment by her affirming and loving presence within the community. By forgiveness, understanding, and loving outreach, she became the mediator of new life. This is how grace worked for Thérèse in community. This is how grace can work in us, with our sisters and brothers, with family and friends, at any moment or circumstance in life. We are to be the instruments of God's love in the world because God is present in us. Thérèse understood this and lived it well.

Today, St. Thérèse of Lisieux is a perfect complement for our twenty-first century's obsession with power. She uncovers the tremendous intensity of energy in daily life and shows that this energy residing within each of us is so powerful that it can spill over into relationships with others. We can no longer say, "I cannot love like that," or,

"I am not a member of a religious community," or, "I know nothing of that kind of power," or, "I do not have Thérèse's genius or her power to love." Thérèse has closed all escape routes. She demonstrates that we can love at any moment, any day, any place, anywhere, here and now. Whatever the circumstances, if we open ourselves, we will find the way that God chooses for our journey of growth and relationship with him. This is how Thérèse lived. She is an example of how God's grace, a family's love, a community's support, honest work, loyal friends, a smile, and an attitude of acceptance can help all people to live with faith, hope, and love. Her overwhelming desire for communion with God, her enduring spirit, and her intercession for others still affect and continue to draw people to love, blossom, grow, pray, and serve as she did. Her spirit may draw you to extraordinary self-sacrifice. Will you be ready to answer the call to serve as she did and, at times, to live at odds with the direction of the world as you know it?

1. Bernard Bro, OP, *The Little Way: The Spirituality of Thérèse of Lisieux* (London: Darton, Longman & Todd, 1997), 3.
2. *Story of A Soul: The Autobiography of St. Thérèse of Lisieux*, 3rd ed., trans. John Clarke, OCD (Washington, DC: ICS, 1996), 66.
3. SS, Manuscript A. See *Story of A Soul*, 98.
4. SS, Manuscript A. See *Story of A Soul*, 134.
5. Christopher O'Donnell, OCarm, *Prayer: Insights from St. Thérèse of Lisieux* (Dublin: Veritas Publications, 2009), 14.
6. SS, Manuscript B. See *Story of A Soul*, 192.
7. SS, Manuscript A. See *Story of A Soul*, 178.
8. SS, Manuscript A. See *Story of A Soul*, 181.
9. SS, Manuscript A. See See *Story of A Soul*, 174, 178.
10. The New American Bible, Matthew 11:28.
11. *Experiencing St. Therese Today*, ed. John Sullivan, OCD (Washington, DC: ICS, 1990), 134.

CHAPTER 24

Praying with Brother Lawrence of the Resurrection: The Practice of the Presence of God

~ Leopold Glueckert, OCarm. ~

While many experts and teachers of prayer and devotion are often gentle men and women with a decent education and a flair for good writing, Brother Lawrence is an odd variant on that pattern. A rough-cut commoner who worked with his hands, he walked a simple path alongside his loving God. He serves as a vivid reminder that even the little guy is not an alien in God's mansions. Through his writings, Lawrence continues to teach and inspire countless readers with his good sense and simple encouragement.

Although he died three centuries ago, Brother Lawrence seems to be surprisingly at home in any age, including our own. Because of the seemingly endless wars in our time, most of us have seen soldiers return from battle with their bodies intact but their souls virtually destroyed. What we call PTSD is finally receiving attention from medical and psychological researchers. The traumatic horrors of what these men and women have seen and done in war continue to disturb their sense of balance and well-being. Traditional values of right and wrong sometimes don't seem to apply anymore. Our faith in the essential fairness of God and the universe gets blown to smithereens, and a permanent sense of discouragement and pessimism takes control of even our most cherished activities. Lawrence lived in that gloomy realm.

But in some rare cases, these disturbing events can become a blessing in disguise, as individuals struggle to cope with their own tragedy and suffering, and that of others. Lawrence's odyssey began when he was Nicholas Herman, a young soldier from the Duchy of Lorraine. In the seventeenth century, Lorraine was not yet a part of France, but an independent state of the Holy Roman Empire, where people spoke either German and French or a jumble of both. He was born around 1614 and raised near Lunéville, a medium-sized market town in what is now the easternmost part of France. We know that his parents were respected people who raised him to be a religiously inclined young man and that he could read and write. But that's about all. We would certainly like to know more about his personal background and education, but the information is simply not there.

As fortune would have it, young Nicholas grew up during the calamitous Thirty Years' War, which devastated all of central Europe between 1618 and 1648. This dramatic clash is sometimes passed off as a simple conflict between Catholics and Protestants in Germany, but it was far more complex than that. There were actually about fifteen separate conflicts with distinct political, economic, and social causes which started and stopped during the same period and then sometimes burst into flame all over again. But each separate war managed to influence and aggravate many of the others, and each seemed to carry its own toxic blend of religious hatred and intolerance, to say nothing of horrid atrocities. It was certainly not a good time for gentle idealists.

Since war pervaded all of Europe, it may have seemed that fighting for some ambitious prince or religious faction was a fairly normal existence. Possibly at the age of twenty, Nicholas enlisted in the Duke of Lorraine's army. He may have done so out of religious zeal as a loyal Catholic or simply because poverty left him few other opportunities. It was a horrid experience. The chaotic nature of seventeenth-century warfare was something that affected his mind deeply. At that time, there were a few units of disciplined, professional soldiers, but most military contingents of the age were simply bands of heavily armed thugs who were not paid but were expected to support themselves at the expense of the civilian population.

Bitter hatred among Lutheran, Calvinist, and Catholic factions during this period was further complicated by the shifting alliances of private armies and small mercenary units who made and unmade coalitions among themselves for the most dissolute motives. Soldiers' primary loyalty was to their commanders, rather than any religious or regional ideals. And those commanders generally saw their purpose as getting rich at the expense of everyone else, regardless of what means they used. It was all but expected that marauding armies would plunder villages, murder civilians, and shoot or dismember their prisoners. Since the officers had no interest in disciplining their troops, the path of any army usually left devastation, with the pitifully injured and beggars in its wake. Even two centuries later, vast areas of Germany had not recovered from the War's desolation.

At the time when Nicholas served, there were six distinct armies fighting in Lorraine battling civilians and one another. In 1635, he fought with the Lorraine militia against Swedish infantry and French cavalry at Rambervillers, not far from his home village. (Rambervillers had 2,660 inhabitants at the time; eight years later there were only 400 survivors.) He received a serious wound which caused him to limp for the rest of his life. He was later captured by German Protestant soldiers who accused him of spying and threatened to hang him. But then they released him because his manner was so nonviolent. Because of his serious injury, he was discharged from his regiment as no longer fit to fight. Once again he was a civilian and very much on his own. He had survived the war, but his chance of returning to a normal life was virtually destroyed.

The ghastly experience of battle seared his mind to such a degree that the specters of those atrocities never left him. We have no way of knowing if Nicholas had killed others or had just seen killing, looting, and pillage. He never spoke of the horrors he had experienced, but the effects remained with him for the rest of his life. One thing which also remained with him after his military career was the need to turn away from the violent conduct of his past. He remained obsessed with his quest for redemption. He had experienced too much horror to ever be free again.

He drifted through civilian life for several years without any real success. He saw a life with God as his refuge and attempted to become a hermit, but with no proper direction or mentorship. Being an authentic hermit is not a prospect for beginners, and this endeavor failed miserably. Then he attempted to serve as a footman to William de Fieubet, treasurer to the king of France. But he was so clumsy, so awkward, that he "broke everything" as he later recounted.[1] There was no future for him as a gentleman's servant either.

It seemed that the only positive thing that he was able to cling to in his life was a religious conversion event. He remembered that at age eighteen, he had experienced a powerful insight when he saw a stark, ghostly tree stripped of its leaves and all signs of life during a particularly severe winter. And yet he knew through the eyes of faith that in the early spring, God would restore life to that tree, with a profusion of leaves and fruit. Buoyed by this shred of hope, he decided to take a bold step toward restoring spiritual health to his own devastated life.

So finally, in 1640, he went to Paris, where he asked for admission to the Discalced Carmelites as a working brother. His uncle, Jean Majeur, had also been a Carmelite brother and a significant spiritual influence in his life. His uncle helped him to see the dangers of the secular world, which would never allow him to leave his past behind. Nicholas was twenty-six years old, still awkward and lacking in most practical skills. He fully expected to do badly in the monastery and to be ridiculed. But he was welcomed and accepted by the other friars, treated kindly, and fit well into the community. He later addressed God in an upbeat mood, "You tricked me!" In those days, religious brothers were the practical work force for the monastery, doing manual labor, begging for alms, and praying as they worked. Nicholas remained there for the next fifty years with the religious name of Brother Lawrence of the Resurrection. For much of that period, he worked as a cook for a community of nearly a hundred friars and later also served as a sandal maker and a wine buyer.

His first ten years in the monastery were a time of difficult inner struggle, when he still felt he had no hope of salvation. He had a private nook near his pantry where he would go to pray in desperation, as if he had nothing left except his stubborn trust that God would not allow him to be lost. He had a small picture of Jesus tied to the pillar, covered with wounds. It served to remind him that he was not the only one who had suffered. But this desperation led him to a point of resignation to the mercy of God, which helped him find peace. He was afraid of self-deception, so he simply placed all his trust in God without any conditions.

The hope Lawrence had learned from the resilience of the barren tree stayed with him as he purged the lingering wartime demons. If life could flood back into that dead trunk, then maybe God's love and forgiveness could restore love and courage to him as well. He decided to reject the love of anything which was not God, and thus grew in the active recognition of God's presence in every detail of his life. He discovered that he was able to pray at all times, even if it was no more dramatic than just repeating the Lord's Prayer. Even in distractions, God's help was there.

"I have very often experienced the ready help of divine grace upon all occasions. When I have business to do, I do not [worry] about it beforehand. When the time comes to do it, I see in God, as clearly as in a mirror, all that is needed for me to do."

It surprised him that even when he was peeling potatoes, seasoning soup, or scrubbing kettles, he was able to make his tasks an integral part of his prayer, the actual vehicle of the process. Using his "methodless method," he was able to carry on a running exchange with the loving God of the universe. His anxiety and fear gradually turned to gentleness toward everyone. Instead of apprehension, he began to radiate gratitude and quiet joy.

He was later able to say, "The time of business does not differ with me from the time of prayer; and in the noise and clatter of my kitchen, while several persons are at the same time calling for different things, I possess God in as great a tranquility as if I were upon my knees at the blessed sacrament."

He had plenty of spiritual stimulation to help him formulate his prayers. Lawrence had joined a community of other men who were also dedicated to silence, solitude, and reflective prayer. Other friars in his community helped with devout conversations, spiritual reading in the refectory, and good preaching in the chapel. There was the regular rhythm of liturgical prayer every day, as well as a continuous stream of teaching from the Holy Scriptures and the classic writings of Carmelite authors. There were many outsiders who came to visit the community or worship in the

Carmelite church. Conversations with accomplished professors or humble seekers raised questions and formulated answers about God's walk with the individual. He learned eagerly from all of it.

Once he had come through the turmoil of those first ten years, Brother Lawrence was able to help others to be comfortable with their own prayer in the most ordinary circumstances. In his contact with beggars and working people, he encouraged them in simple conversations with God. His kitchen became a sort of chapel where cart drivers, grocers, or fishmongers could hear practical advice on how God cared for their concerns. He was fond of telling people that God had so much treasure to share with each of them, but that we so often tend to be satisfied with small bits of private devotion that block us from going further.

His personal prayer life developed by simply being aware of the presence of God in his kitchen, and carrying on a loving conversation with one who loved him dearly. In the early years, he had been obsessed with his sinfulness. He thought a lot about death, judgment, heaven, and hell. But then he gave up all the devotions, helps, and props that were not strictly required. He fell back on the simple awareness of God's presence under all circumstances. Speaking was not required. If he lost the awareness for a moment, he tried to get it back without delay. After a while, his work and other activities were no longer distractions, but springboards to more creative conversation with the Lord.

On one occasion, he wrote, "I flip my little omelette in the frying pan for the love of God, and when it's done, if I have nothing to do, I prostrate myself on the floor and adore my God who gave me the grace to do it. After that I get up happier than a king! When I can do nothing else, it is enough for me to pick up straw from the ground for the love of God."

Lawrence took the prayer of recollection and made it attractive to anyone. He was blessed with a clear and no-nonsense way of speaking and gave lucid advice to help others follow his process. Countless people of every social class learned to begin, continue, and end every action by lifting themselves to God. He actually wrote very little himself, but his conversations and personal letters served as a lasting record of his simple technique. A priest friend, Joseph de Beaufort, engaged in a series of instructive dialogues with Lawrence between 1666 and 1667. He made it a point to write down everything he remembered from their conversations immediately afterward. These notes provided the framework for the "writings" of Brother Lawrence in later years.

In his time, there were many methods, rules, and structures for mental prayer and formal meditation. Lawrence disliked all of them as too artificial and mechanical. He said,

We look for methods to learn how to love God. We want to get there by I don't know how many practices. A multitude of methods makes it more difficult for us to remain in God's presence. Isn't it much shorter and more direct to just do everything for the love of God?

Brother Lawrence lived in a state of constant awareness of his dearest friend, and that recognition colored the quality of his work, as well as his kind treatment of whomever he met.

After about fifteen years in the kitchen, Brother Lawrence began to have difficulty moving around because of his old war wound. It seems to have been a variety of sciatic gout that made him limp painfully. Although he was not a complainer, it became evident that he was no longer able to stay on his feet for long hours without intense suffering. The prior reassigned him to the sandal shop, where he could sit down while repairing the worn soles and broken straps of his brothers' footwear. The new task also had the advantage of him being able to work in a quieter atmosphere with fewer urgent deadlines to worry about. Obviously, the prayerful atmosphere could only increase.

Another occasional task which he received was the unwelcome responsibility of selecting and purchasing the year's supply of wine for the community. In 1665, this meant a round trip of about five hundred miles to the wild and beautiful Auvergne region. The following year, he made a similar trip to Burgundy, about 375 miles both ways. For a brother with a crippled leg, this was certainly a hardship, although he would have been able to ride in a cart or a river barge for much of the journey. Since walking was out of the question, he joked about having to get around by rolling over the barrels aboard the boat. But then too, there was the blessing of enjoying beautiful scenery and of meeting new and interesting people. In any case, he had fresh things to discuss with the Lord, and the wine was certainly delivered successfully to his community.

He never lost his awareness that most ordinary people did not have the advantages of a supportive religious family, as he did. But he never tired of encouraging prayer and recollection in the most ordinary circumstances. Each tiny flower could bloom where it was planted. On one occasion, he fell back on his own memories, as he advised soldiers who were in danger of losing their lives or their souls to remain conscious of God's concern, even as they advanced at a run with sword in hand. No one falls outside God's realm of love.

Although Lawrence's process of praying under all circumstances took many years to develop, the majority of what we may call his teaching came together during the last ten years of his life. Most of his letters which have survived were written between 1682 and 1691. By that time, there were many people who asked for his advice about their own prayer. He shared advice and sympathy with men and women, nuns and spiritual directors. He always hastened to remind them that there was nothing unusual in his activity. Anyone who wants to pray can pray. It is enough to renounce whatever is not God.

Perhaps the best of his commentary was distilled from his conversations and writings in the final three years, as he consciously approached his increasing weakness and the time of his own death. He matter-of-factly expected pain and suffering in his declining days, since he had already known so much joy and happiness. Like Job, he was prepared to accept whatever the Lord sent him and then praise his name for that privilege. He fondly remembered that Teresa of Ávila taught that God does not care so much for the greatness of our deeds as for the love with which they are offered.

After Lawrence's death in 1691 at seventy-seven years of age, his friend and biographer Joseph de Beaufort assembled his notes and published them in book form as *The Practice of the Presence of God*. The practical simplicity of his style of prayer immediately touched the hearts of readers from every stratum of society. His personal letters were also published, demonstrating how much serenity had come in his later years. The badly damaged young soldier had finally come to peace and tranquility in company with a loving God who cures all ills.

His published thoughts and maxims went through many editions and translations. Protestant publishers also found his prayer methodology simple and direct, in harmony with their own preferences. They were also quick to circulate his simple insights, and Brother Lawrence quickly became well known in most parts of the Christian world. Like the later writings of Thérèse of Lisieux, his thoughts gained an intense popularity with ordinary people, and they remain a popular source of spiritual wisdom today. Anyone who can think and feel can also pray. Brother Lawrence showed how easy it really is.

---

1. All quotations from the writings of Brother Lawrence of the Resurrection are taken from *The Practice of the Presence of God: Critical Edition*, trans. by Salvatore Sciurba (Washington, DC: ICS, 1994).

CHAPTER 25

Thomas Merton:
Monk, Mystic, and Missionary

~ Anthony J. Ciorra ~

Thomas Merton is a religious and literary figure who will transform the minds and hearts of people for generations to come. I believe that he is the most significant Christian writer of the twentieth century.

Dom Jean LeClerq placed Merton among the early and medieval fathers of the Church. He is someone whose life, writings and influence deeply touch the human psyche. In *The Seven Storey Mountain*, Merton has given to modern Christians what St. Augustine gave to the ancient and medieval Church; his spiritual autobiography provides a template for the spiritual life that speaks to the contemporary human experience. And like Augustine, Merton's influence is not limited to autobiography. His theological, spiritual, and literary impact is demonstrated in over sixty published books; hundreds of articles, journals, and letters published since his death; poetry, photography, and over seven hundred hours of taped conferences that he gave to novices, scholastics, and religious women. Brother Patrick Hart, OCSO, Merton's secretary at the Abbey of Gethsemani, once told me that he thought Merton was addicted to writing, that writing was the most important tool of his spiritual growth.

Fr. John Eudes Bamberger, the former Abbot of Genesee Abbey in Piffard, New York, and a student monk under Merton's guidance often says that Merton had the energy of three people. Fr. Irenaeus Herscher, OFM, who was the librarian at St. Bonaventure University during the years that Merton taught there, told me that he believed the way people walk is an indication of what is going on in their inner life. He said that Merton was somewhat awkward and had a bounce in his gait that reflected his energy was bubbling over. We are fortunate that he channeled much of that energy into his writings, conferences, photography, and art. We are the beneficiaries of his theological and spiritual wisdom.

Merton concludes *The Seven Storey Mountain* with the Latin phrase, *Sit Finis Libri, Non Finis Quaerendi* ("Here ends the book but not the searching").[1] His masterpiece was only a beginning since Merton experienced multiple conversions that brought about endless transitions in his life. When he later looked back at the things he wrote in *Seven Storey Mountain*, he had second thoughts because he'd grown into a different person. Once again, he was not unlike Augustine, who wrote retractions at the end of his life, negating some of his earlier works. As we will see, the Merton of *The Asian Journal* (published just after his death) was a very different monk from the man who wrote *Seven Storey Mountain.*

Merton has been a spiritual guide and mentor for me for many years. I have studied him, read most of his books, listened to his many conferences, and taught courses about him. I am still getting to know him. I have passed over from being a student of Merton's thought to a disciple who is learning about the spiritual life from this spiritual master. The Japanese have an expression, "Do not mistake the finger that points to the moon for the moon." Merton points beyond himself to the mystery of God. I think this is the reason why there is always freshness to his writings, because he leads the attentive reader into the experience of God, who is always calling us to go deeper into the mystery.

I am proposing that Merton is monk, mystic, and missionary. I believe that key to understanding Merton's spiritual teaching is appreciating how he blended these three vocations into one. Nicholas of Cusa coined the phrase "coincidence of opposites." Merton brings together a coincidence of opposites as a monk who evolved into a mystic and a missionary. He was clearly rooted in his monastic vocation. There are those who wonder if Merton was on his way out of the monastery after the affair he had with a nurse whom we know simply as M, twenty years his junior, in 1967. This suspicion was compounded when he journeyed outside the monastery to the Far East in 1968. I would argue that both of these events gave him the opportunity to say a second and deeper "Yes" to his vocation as a Trappist. His love poems about M reflect the reality of a man who was transformed by a love relationship. His journey outside the monastery made him realize how much he loved the Abbey of Our Lady of Gethsemani. The monks became his only family. They were all that he had in this world, having lost both of his parents, Owen and Ruth, in his youth and his brother John Paul only one year after he entered the monastery. As with any family, his monastic family wasn't perfect, and Merton wasn't shy in voicing complaints about his brother monks. Nonetheless, it was home for him and he loved the community. A letter that arrived at the monastery after his death on December 10, 1968, confirmed the deep affection he had for the monks and his monastic home.

Merton was not the typical, everyday monk. His monastic vocation was an ever-evolving process. He was a monk who became a missionary, not in the classical sense but in the manner of St. Thérèse of Lisieux. She never left her Carmel but was named the patron of the missions because she had a heart that melted cloister walls in her concern and prayers for the needs of the world. In this sense, Merton of the 1950s and '60s also went beyond the monastery walls that he came to know in the 1940s. He moved in his heart from the monastic cell to the streets where human beings suffered. He was a spiritual missionary who transformed the world through contemplation and an asceticism that embraced the pain of the world.

What was the one variable that held monk and missionary together in a creative, dynamic tension? The mystical path and its related experience gave Merton a framework. He lived constant transition in the context of monastic stability. He thought as a mystic and saw the world through mystical eyes. A mystic is one who sees the connection between things, who has found wisdom in the journey from the head to the heart. A mystic is one who has the ability to frame the moment and stay there until he absorbs the one who lives there as the one, the good, the true, and the beautiful. Merton's evolving experience of God made him into a twentieth-century monk and twenty-first–century missionary. His was the journey into inner space. He was a solitary explorer.

MERTON'S JOURNEY AND PRAYER

Merton is the teacher of prayer par excellence. Pope Francis acknowledged this recently in his address before a joint session of Congress when he said that Merton was one of the great American spiritual teachers. Merton's teachings about prayer only make sense in the context of his life. Indeed, the medium is the message. His theology of prayer evolved as he grew and changed. Pope Francis, in that address to Congress, quoted the beginning of Merton's journey from the opening of *Seven Storey Mountain*:

> On the last day of January 1915, under the sign of the Water Beaver, in a year of war, and down in the shadow of some French mountains on the borders of Spain, I came into the world. Free by nature, in the image of God, I was the prisoner of my own violence and my own selfishness, in the image of the world in which I was born. That world was the picture of hell, full of men like myself, loving God and yet hating Him; born to love him, living instead in fear and hopeless self-contradictory hungers.[2]

Merton believed that he was living out the deepest human crises of the twentieth century. His story was embodied in the drama of several wars (World Wars I and II, Korea, and Vietnam). He acknowledges that his whole life was consumed, hopefully not meaninglessly, in crisis.

The uncertainties of the larger world were made more complex for him in the lack of stability within the family structure. His parents were both artists who met in Paris and, when married, moved to the south of France, where Merton was born. They moved to Long Island later because of World War I. It was there that Merton's only sibling, John Paul, was born. His mother died of cancer in 1921 when Merton was only six years old. She never shared with Merton the fact that she was dying. She left him a note saying good-bye, which his father handed to him after her death and left him to read alone. His loneliness was then deepened when his father often traveled, leaving Tom behind with relatives. He was separated from his brother in 1925 when his father sent him at the age of three to live with his American grandparents. Later, Tom and his father settled again in France for a time before he was sent to live with an aunt in England to study at Ockham. While there in France, his father died, leaving Tom an orphan at the age of sixteen. The trauma of these changes and losses left its mark on the young Merton.

He roamed around Europe for a time after his father's death before going to Clare College in Cambridge in 1932 at the age of eighteen. He had two experiences before going to Cambridge that he understood only late in life. The first happened when he made a trip to Rome and was drawn into the beauty of the mosaics of Christ depicted in the churches. The second took place when he was praying in his room one night and had a vision of his father that filled the room with his presence. It was only later on in the monastery that he became aware of the fact that these were moments of grace where God was trying to break into the darkness of his life.

It is not hard to understand why he acted out in Cambridge with womanizing and drinking, and as a result, his legal guardian sent him to New York to finish his studies at Columbia University. Merton had a sense of shame, guilt, and worthlessness for betraying his father's expectations and squandering his time at Cambridge. Despite this, he continued his reckless behavior at Columbia, which led to a minor breakdown that would be the beginning of a change in the direction of his life.

He began to form friendships that would support him and give him a sense of direction and order to his chaotic life. Among these new friends was Daniel Walsh, a philosopher who eventually was ordained a priest. Walsh became a spiritual guide for Merton and introduced him to philosophy. At about this same time, it was by coincidence that as he was passing a bookstore and saw the newly published book *The Spirit of Medieval Philosophy* by Etienne Gilson. Merton was appalled when he realized after buying the book that it was written from a Catholic perspective and had official ecclesiastical approval. But he read it. He also started to read and was influenced by the works of William Blake, Dante, Jacques Maritain, and the poetry of Gerard Manley Hopkins. All of these events and authors were eventually among the factors that led him to the Catholic Church. Merton was baptized on November 16, 1938, at Corpus Christi Church, just a few blocks from Columbia. His life now had a religious cohesiveness, and he began to experience a sense of peace and rootedness that he never knew before.

He received his master's degree in literature in 1939. Since his deepest passion was the study of literature and writing, he was planning on pursuing a doctorate in literature as well. However, he started to think about a possible vocation to the priesthood and religious life. His first impulse was to apply to the Franciscans, and he was accepted by the friars. But they later rescinded the acceptance when they discovered his past history of promiscuous behavior. Many speculate that Merton had fathered a child during his Cambridge years, and this was the reason why he was rejected.

He then went to St. Bonaventure University in Olean, New York, where he taught English from 1939 to 1941. During this time, he became more settled into his recently discovered Catholic faith and continued to nurture the friendships that would support his faith journey and eventual call to religious life. After making a retreat at the Abbey of Gethsemani, he decided to join the Order of the Cistercians of the Strict Observance, also called the Trappists, one of the strictest orders in the Church noted for its ascetical practices, fasting, long periods of time at prayer, and total silence and solitude. At the same time, he heard the Baroness Catherine de Hueck lecture about her work with the poor in Harlem. Merton's visits to Friendship House in Harlem deepened his attraction to finding God in the poor, needy, and outcasts. Now he was faced with a tough decision: Friendship House in Harlem or the Trappist monastery in Kentucky? On December 9, 1941—just two days after the bombing of Pearl Harbor that led America into World War II—he headed for the monastery. He describes the trip:

> Mile after mile my desire to be in the monastery increased beyond belief.... What if they did not receive me? Then I would go to the army. But surely that would be a disaster? Not at all. If, after all this, I was rejected by the monastery and had to be drafted, it would be quite clear that it was God's will. I had done everything that was in my power; the rest was in his hands. I was free. I had recovered my liberty. I belonged to God, not to myself; and to belong to Him is to be free.[3]

Some speculate that Merton was on the verge of a breakdown before entering Gethsemani and that it was the regimen of the monastery that saved him by finally giving him a home and a spiritual family. The Thomas Merton of the 1940s, the recent convert to Catholicism, certainly did enthusiastically follow their strict regimen on prayer, fasting, and penance, and it probably held him together and gave him a sense of security.

Merton's life in the monastery is a biographical template for building a structure of prayer that was ever evolving. The structure is a triptych for the spiritual journey:
- The Monastic Period (Traditional Prayer): 1941–1951
- The Church Period (Prayer and Social Justice): 1951–1960
- The World Period (Contemplation and Solitude): 1960–1968[4]

THE MONASTIC PERIOD: TRADITIONAL PRAYER

Merton found peace and a home at Gethsemani. He found security and new life in the horarium and structure of the monastery. The monastic community gave him a home and a stability that he had never known before. The only family he had left in this world was his brother, John Paul, who came to visit him once before joining the Royal Canadian Air Force. The joy of this reunion was short-lived as his brother's plane was shot down in the North Sea several days after his visit with Merton. Merton's deep sense of loss and sorrow was expressed in his poem "For My Brother: Reported Missing in Action, 1943":

> Sweet brother, if I do not sleep
> My eyes are flowers for your tomb;
> And if I cannot eat my bread,
> My fasts shall live like willows where you died.[5]

Another loss that Merton experienced was letting go of his love of writing in the monastery. Could he be a monk and also continue to write? Early on, he demonstrated that in the midst of personal questions and struggles he would submit to the will of God as manifested through his superiors. Fortunately (at least for us), the abbot, Dom Frederic Dunne, recognized Merton's gift for writing and gave him permission and encouragement to write. He initially wrote poems and reflections on Cistercian life and continued his practice of journal writing. In 1946 he started to write *The Seven Storey Mountain*.

But new struggles and questions emerged as he started to feel the need for even more solitude. He started to discern a possible call to join the Carthusian Order, an austere community that would offer more opportunities for solitude than the Trappists could offer. In his discernment process, he identified with the prophet Jonas, who also was very conflicted as to where God was leading. Journal entries written during his formation period as a monk, some of which reflect this tension, were later published in 1956 as *The Sign of Jonas*.

James Fox, who was now the abbot, recognized Merton's great need for solitude and allowed him to spend time in a vault in the monastery and eventually in a tool shed in the woods. Despite these concessions, Merton's struggles continued. In fact, in the months prior to his ordination to the priesthood on May 26, 1949, he was going through such internal turmoil that he couldn't pray or write. On the very night before ordination he wrote in his journal:

> My life is a great mess and tangle of half-conscious subterfuges to evade grace and duty.... My infidelity to Christ, instead of making me sick with despair, drives me to throw myself all the more blindly into the arms of His mercy.[6]

His deep desire for solitude only intensified after his ordination to the priesthood. In fact, the call to solitude was even deeper and stronger than the desire for ordination. He says it clearly in *The Sign of Jonas*: "I have only one desire and that is the desire for solitude—to disappear into God.... It is clear to me that solitude is my vocation, not as a flight from the world, but as my place in the world."[7]

He also struggled during this time with exhaustion and poor health driven by the austerity of the lifestyle and the demands he placed on himself. Writing continued to be not only his passion but also his medicine. In the midst of physical and personal struggles he produced some of his finest works, such as *New Seeds of Contemplation*, *No Man Is an Island*, and *Thoughts in Solitude*. He became Master of Scholastics in 1951, and this begins a new chapter in his writing career and spiritual journey.

The Church Period: Prayer and Social Justice

As you examine his writings from 1951–1958 and listen to his taped conferences to the scholastics, you will discover that in teaching the scholastics Merton was continuing his own monastic formation and developing his own understanding of solitude and contemplation. What gradually emerges is a breaking away from the closed monastic structure to a wider understanding that would shape his monastic vision to embrace the world that existed outside the cloistered wall. Merton was gradually evolving into a different person, maturing and becoming his true self.

He began to pay attention to the social issues of the '50s and '60s in America. Initially, it was the civil rights movement, inspired by the preaching and teaching of Martin Luther King Jr. that captivated his attention. He also started to read and study Gandhi. He was now primed to move out of the mode that he describes so well in *Seven Storey Mountain* into a whole new world. He no longer needed a strict external structure to hold him together. The strength he found in the relationships in and outside the monastery helped him to grow and change once again. He actually could pinpoint the date, time, and place when this shift occurred. It was on March 18, 1958, on a trip outside the monastery for a doctor's appointment. He describes what happened on that day in his book *Conjectures of a Guilty Bystander*:

> In Louisville, at the corner of Fourth and Walnut, in the center of the shop-
> ping district, I was suddenly overwhelmed with the realization that I loved
> all those people, that they were mine and I theirs, that we could not be alien
> to one another even though we were total strangers. It was like waking from
> a dream of separateness, of spurious self-isolation in a special world, the
> world of renunciation and supposed holiness. The whole illusion of a sepa-
> rate holy existence is a dream. Not that I question the reality of my voca-
> tion, or of my monastic life: but the conception of "separation" from the
> world that we have in the monastery too easily presents itself as a complete
> illusion: the illusion that by making vows we become a different species
> of being, pseudo-angels, "spiritual men,"... It is a glorious destiny to be a
> member of the human race.[8]

This moment of grace placed Merton on a new path on his spiritual journey. He came to a new awareness of God's presence in other people. "If only they could see them-selves as they really are. If only we could see each other that way all the time.... I suppose the big problem would be that we would fall down and worship each other."[9]

He intuited what the Second Vatican Council would later affirm in its universal call to holiness. The Council began its discussion on holiness in the Decree on Religious Life and then moved the discussion into the Document on the Church (*Lumen Gentium*). This was the watershed moment at the Council where the centrality of baptism was claimed as the call of all Christians to holiness. This gave theological language and ecclesiastical sanction to what Merton experienced at the corner of Fourth and Walnut.

This realization and new insight would lead Merton to pay attention to the social issues of his day. He began to reach out to those who were on the ground working for social justice. As he wrote to Dorothy Day:

> You people are among the few that still have an eye open. I am more and
> more convinced that the real people in this country are the Indians—and
> Negroes etc. The reason I mention the Hopis is that (this is in confidence) I
> think more and more that the only final solution to my desires will be some-
> thing like getting permission to go off and live among the Indians or some
> such group, as a kind of hermit-missionary."[10]

The World Period: Contemplation and Solitude

Merton now had to grapple with integrating his awareness of social issues with his life of contemplation. His vow of silence would now evolve into a vow of contem-plative conversation with the painful struggles of the world. He would integrate and model the polarities of social justice and contemplation. Because of his writing and personal experience, these were no longer polarities but a unified goal for the spiritual life.

The pain and conflict of the Vietnam War became the primary focus of the American people during this time. Given Merton's life trajectory and his new awareness of God's presence in the midst of contemporary issues, he became preoccupied with the theme of peace. He was in conflict with the superiors of the Trappist Order about his writings on peace. He wrote a collection of "Cold War Letters" that the superiors censored. They told him that he should stop writing on this controversial topic. When Pope John XXIII wrote his encyclical letter *Pacem in Terris*, Merton said that it was a good thing that his encyclical did not have to first be approved by the censors of the Trappists. Although he was angered by the stance that the superiors took, it is to his credit that he accepted their decision in obedience.

Merton became the center of gravity for an emerging peace movement in America. Fr. Daniel Berrigan and other like-minded peace activists started to go to Gethsemani to meet with Merton to pray and discuss strategies for peacemaking. The turmoil of the 1960s continued to unfold with the assassination of President John F. Kennedy, then-presidential candidate Robert Kennedy, Dr. Martin Luther King Jr., and the race riots that consumed major American cities.

What is important is that Merton's social activism was integrated with monastic prayer, silence, contemplation, and penance. The spiritual genius of Merton was that he was able to integrate the concerns of social activists with the vision of the Gospel. For him it was not social activism that ruled the day but the social vision of the Gospel of Jesus Christ. Merton considered himself a "guilty bystander" as he observed the world falling into chaos. However, he wrote, "The Monastery is not an escape from the world. On the contrary, by being in the monastery I take my true part in all the struggles and sufferings of the world."[11] Other books that Merton wrote during this time, such as *Seeds of Destruction* and *Gandhi on Non-Violence*, exhibit his mature reflections on the place of social issues in the spiritual life. He becomes increasingly clear that contemplation must be at the root of all of our social justice activities.

It is fascinating that Merton's passion for the social issues of the day deepened his craving for solitude, the source of his inner peace, and joy. Br. Patrick Hart, Merton's secretary, told me that he felt that Merton's love for solitude would always win out at the end. This was his deepest vocation, where he found his true self. His dream for the solitary life was fulfilled when Abbot James Fox gave him permission to be a full-time hermit. In 1965, Merton gave a beautiful conference to the scholastics that is entitled "A Carefree Life." In this conference, he said good-bye, as this would be his last conference as Master of Scholastics. When you listen to it, you find that he exudes a great deal of peace and joy. A lightness of spirit comes through as he takes off for the hermitage in the woods that he called St. Ann's Hermitage. He concludes that there is nothing left for him except to live fully and completely in the present, praying when he prays, writing and praying when he writes, and worrying about nothing by living in the sacrament of the present moment.

The hermitage did not isolate him from the world. Instead it brought him closer to the social issues of his day as theologians, social activists, and ecumenical visitors came to pray and reflect with him in the solitude of the woods. It was there that his passion for peace became rooted in the Gospel and where Merton became known as the father of the peace movement. The title of one of the books that he wrote in the hermitage, *Contemplation in a World of Action*, illustrates the new depth and vision for peace that emerged from his prayer in the hermitage.

Merton was hospitalized in 1967. It was then that he met the nurse we call M, who was twenty years younger than Merton. A love affair began in the hospital that spilled over into encounters with one another in the hermitage. When Abbot James Fox found out about this, he told Merton that he would leave it up to him to resolve the situation, since it placed him in conflict with his monastic vows. In an interview many years later, James Fox acknowledged that Merton fell in love, and that there was nothing you can do to make people fall out of love. Merton wrote beautiful love poems to M. These poems are a testimony to Merton's growth in understanding the true meaning of love and his struggle to make a choice between M and his monastic vocation. He did remain in the monastery chastened by this experience of transition to a reaffirmation of his monastic vows of stability, obedience, and chastity.

The next event that would be life-altering for him was the Second Vatican Council (1962–1965). Merton was consulted on several Council documents, especially the documents on interreligious dialogue and the liturgy. When you listen to the lectures that he gave to the monks about the Council, it is clear that he not only understood the Council but also had a passion for the new direction that it was bringing to the Church. The larger transition that the universal Church was experiencing coincided with Merton's inner journey. The Council opened the doors to the reform of religious life, dialogue with the world, and interaction with other religious traditions. This new openness to other religions most deeply resonated with Merton's vision for the spiritual life.

For many years, Merton had a strong interest in other religious traditions. For example, he wrote about the Sufi mystics in the 1950s, when most people knew nothing about the Islamic mystical tradition. He had close ties with the Jewish community, especially with his friends Rabbi Abraham Joshua Heschel and Rabbi Zalman Schachter. He had a strong interest in Zen Buddhism and its prayer forms, as demonstrated in his books *Zen and the Birds of Appetite* and *Mystics and Zen Masters*.

One can only imagine the excitement Merton felt when he was invited to speak at a conference in the Far East on monastic experience and East-West dialogue. Fr. Flavian Burns, who was a student-monk under Merton and who was now his abbot, gave him permission to take a long trip out of the monastery to cities in various countries of the Far East in 1968. Merton's spiritual doctrine integrated Eastern and Western prayer practices. His trip and speeches on this journey are a clear indication of the new levels of prayer that he was experiencing. These are recorded in *The Asian Journal of Thomas Merton*.

On December 10, 1968, Merton delivered a paper at the Conference in Bangkok entitled "Marxism and Monastic Perspectives." In it, he proposed that there was a synergy between Marxism and monasticism. Both called for transformation, the first of economic systems, the second of human consciousness. After the conference, Merton went to his room to rest. At 4:00 PM a monk went to his room and found him dead, electrocuted by a fan. The irony is that his body was flown back to Gethsemani on the same plane with corpses of American soldiers who were killed in the Vietnam War—a conflict that Merton vehemently protested.

He was laid to rest in the cemetery of the Abbey of Gethsemani. At his grave, the abbot read the words from the conclusion of *Seven Storey Mountain*:

> But you shall taste the true solitude of my anguish and my poverty and I shall lead you into the high places of my joy and you shall die in Me and find all things in My mercy which has created you for this end and brought you from Prades to Bermuda to St. Anonin to Oakham to London to Cambridge to Rome to New York to Columbia to Corpus Christ to St. Bonaventure to the Cistercian Abbey of the poor men who labor in Gethsemani: That you may become the brother of God and learn to know the Christ of the burnt men.[12]

MERTON'S JOURNEY AND YOUR PRAYER

Merton's life story can be summed up in two words: paschal mystery. In fact, he could have subtitled *The Seven Storey Mountain*, "Living the Paschal Mystery." The paschal mystery is the theological term that we would use to describe the inner workings of Merton's transformation. He imitated Christ in the many deaths and risings of his life, constantly entering into the cross and resurrection. Merton's whole life was the paschal mystery over and over again. It is in dying to the self that the doors of contemplative prayer are gradually opened. This was at the core of the teachings of the desert fathers and mothers. If we do not die to self, prayer is an exercise where we are not communing with God but rather are talking to ourselves. It is here that we find constant evolution in Merton's thought. I would go so far as to say that it was his ultimate revolution and legacy that he opened the way of contemplation to not only every Christian but to all men and women on this planet.

His letter on the contemplative life, written on August 21, 1967, only a few months before he died, shows his profound experience of the paschal mystery that led him to die to former certainties of authentic religious experience:

> Can I tell you that I have found answers to the questions that torment the man of our tie? I do not know if I have found answers. When I first became a monk, yes, I was more sure of "answers." But as I grow old in the monastic life and advance further into solitude, I become aware that I have only begun to seek the questions.... [I]f you dare to penetrate your own silence and risk the sharing of that solitude with the lonely other who seeks God through you, then you will truly recover the light and the capacity to understand what is beyond words: it is the intimate union in the depths of your own heart, of God's spirit and your own secret inmost self, so that you and He are all in truth One Spirit.[13]

Merton's life is spiritual autobiography. He models for us what it means to become a person of prayer. It would be presumptuous to claim that these pages have captured the depth of all of Merton's teachings on prayer, but I would like to conclude by sharing what I believe are the main tenets of his teachings about prayer. I will cite some quotations from Merton that I suggest you use for your meditation and prayer. Each set of quotations is prefaced with a heading phrased in the imperative. This is because, most of all, Merton was practical: he taught that we should stop talking and reading about prayer and just do it.

Learn to Be Alone

> When my tongue is silent, I can rest in the silence of the forest. When my imagination is silent, the forest speaks to me, tells me of its unreality and of the Reality of God. But when my mind is silent, then the forest suddenly becomes magnificently real and blazes transparently with the Reality of God. For now, I know that the Creation, which first seems to reveal Him in concepts, then seems to hide Him by the same concepts, finally is revealed in Him, in the Holy Spirit. And we who are in God find ourselves united in Him with all that springs from Him. This is prayer, and this is the glory![14]

BECOME AN EVERYDAY CONTEMPLATIVE

The first chirps of the waking birds mark the "point vierge" of the dawn under a sky as yet without real light, a moment of awe and inexpressible innocence, when the Father in perfect silence opens their eyes. They speak to Him, not with fluent song, but with an awakening question. That is their dawn state, their state at the "pointe verge." Their condition asks if it is time for them to "be"? He answers, "Yes." Then, they one by one wake up, and become birds. They manifest themselves as birds beginning to sing. Presently they will be fully themselves and will even fly.[15]

I beg you to keep me in this silence so that I may learn from it the word of your peace and the word of your mercy and the word of your gentleness to the world.[16]

BECOME YOUR TRUE SELF

My false and private self is the one who wants to exist outside the reach of God's will and God's love—outside of reality and outside of life. And such a self cannot help but be an illusion.[17]

The inner self is as secret as God and, like Him, it evades every concept that tries to seize hold of it with full possession.... It is not reached and coaxed forth from hiding by any process under the sun, including meditation.[18]

Keep me, above all things, from sin. Stanch me in the rank wound of covetousness and the hungers that exhaust my nature with their bleeding. Stamp out the serpent envy that stings love with poison and kills joy. Untie my hand and deliver my heart from sloth. Set me free from the laziness that about disguised as activity when activity is not required of me, and from cowardice that does what it is not demanded, in order to escape sacrifice. And then to wait in peace and emptiness and oblivion of all things.[19]

PRAY WITH THE OTHER

I will be a better Catholic, not if I can refute every shade of Protestantism, but if I can affirm the truth in it and still go further. So, too, with Muslims, the Hindus, the Buddhists.... If I affirm myself as a Catholic merely by denying all that is Muslim, Jewish, Protestant, Hindu, Buddhist, etc., in the end I will find that there is not much left for me to affirm as a Catholic and certainly no breath of the Spirit with which to affirm it.[20]

Thus with all due deference to the vast doctrinal differences between Buddhism and Christianity, and preserving intact all respect for the claims of the different religions: in no way mixing up the Christian "vision of God" with Buddhist "enlightenment," we can nevertheless say that the two have this psychic "limitlessness" in common. And that they tend to describe it in much the same language. It is now "emptiness," now "dark night," now "perfect freedom," now "no mind" now "poverty."[21]

Contemplate and Do Justice

If we really understood the meaning of Christianity in social life we would see it as part of the redemptive work of Christ, liberating man from misery, squalor, subhuman living conditions, economic or political slavery, ignorance, alienation.[22]

At the root of all war is fear: not so much the fear men have of one another as much as fear they have of everything. It is not merely that they do not trust one another; they do not even trust themselves.... They cannot trust anything, because they have ceased to believe in God. It is also not only our hatred of others that is dangerous but also and above all our hatred of ourselves: particularly that hatred of ourselves which is too deep and too powerful to be consciously faced. For it is this, which makes us, see our own evil in others and unable to see it in ourselves.[23]

No matter what happens, I feel myself more and more closely united with those who, everywhere, devote themselves to the glory of God's truth, to the search for divine values hidden among the poor and the outcast.... The air of the world is foul with lies, hypocrisy, falsity, and life is short, death approaches. We must devote ourselves with generosity and integrity to the real values: there is no time for falsity and compromise.... What we do that is pure in His sight will avail for the liberty, the enlightenment, and the salvation of His children everywhere.[24]

Conclusion

At the end of his life, St. Francis of Assisi said, "Let us begin for up until now we have done nothing." We have read about Merton, and we have prayed with Merton. So now, let us begin. We are invited to become monks in the world through the mystical path that makes us missionaries of mercy. We enter into the paschal mystery as we take the next step into our journey. As Merton writes,

My Lord God, I have no idea where I am going. I do not see the road ahead of me. I cannot know for certain where it will end. Nor do I really know myself, and the fact that I think I am following your will does not mean that

I am actually doing so. But I believe that the desire to please you does in fact please you. And I hope that I have that desire in all that I am doing. I hope that I will never do anything apart from that desire. And I know that if I do this you will lead me by the right road, though I may know nothing about it. Therefore, I will trust you always though I may seem to be lost and in the shadow of death. I will not fear, for you are ever with me, and you will never leave me to face my perils alone.[25]

1. Thomas Merton, *The Seven Storey Mountain* (New York: Harcourt Brace and Company, 1948), 423.
2. Merton, *The Seven Storey Mountain*, 1.
3. Merton, *The Seven Storey Mountain*, 370.
4. Anthony T. Padavano, *A Retreat with Thomas Merton* (Cincinnati: St. Anthony Messenger Press, 1995), 36.
5. Merton, *The Seven Storey Mountain*, 404.
6. Merton, *The Sign of Jonas* (New York: Image, 1956), 190–191.
7. Merton, *The Sign of Jonas*, 238.
8. Merton, *Conjectures of a Guilty Bystander*, (New York: Doubleday, 1966), 140–141.
9. Merton, *Conjectures of a Guilty Bystander*, 142.
10. Merton, *The Hidden Ground of Love: The Letters of Thomas Merton on Religious Experience and Social Concerns*, ed. William H. Shannon (New York: Farrar, Straus & Giroux, 1993), 136.
11. Thomas Merton, *Honorable Reader: Reflections on My Work*, (New York: Crossroad, 1991), 65.
12. Merton, *The Seven Storey Mountain*, 422–423.
13. Merton, *The Hidden Ground of Love*, 156-158.
14. Thomas Merton, *Entering the Silence: The Journals of Thomas Merton*, vol. 2, *Becoming a Monk and a Writer*, ed. Jonathan Montaldo (New York: HarperOne, 1997), 471.
15. Merton, *Conjectures of a Guilty Bystander*, 177.
16. Merton, *Conjectures of a Guilty Bystander*, 178.
17. Thomas Merton, *New Seeds of Contemplation* (Norfolk, CT: New Directions, 1972), 34.
18. Thomas Merton, *The Inner Experience: Notes on Contemplation*, ed. William H. Shannon (San Francisco: HarperSanFrancisco, 2004), 296.
19. Merton, *New Seeds of Contemplation*, 44–46.
20. Merton, *Conjectures of A Guilty Bystander*, 128–129.
21. Thomas Merton, *Zen and the Bird of Appetite* (Norfolk, CT: New Directions, 1968), 8.
22. Merton, *Conjectures of A Guilty Bystander*, 81–82.
23. Merton, *New Seeds of Contemplation*, 112.
24. Thomas Merton, *The Courage for Truth: Letters to Writers*, ed. Christine M. Bochen (New York: Farrar, Straus & Giroux, 1993), 188.
25. Thomas Merton, *Thoughts in Solitude* (New York: Farrar, Straus & Giroux, 1999), 79.

CHAPTER 26

Praying with Henri Nouwen:
A Journey toward Home

~ *Lisa M. Cataldo* ~

To pray, I think, does not mean to think about God in contrast to thinking about other things, or to spend time with God instead of spending time with other people. Rather, it means to think and live in the presence of God.[1]

—*Clowning in Rome*

In prayer, I am constantly on the way, on pilgrimage.[2]

—*With Open Hands*

THE HUMAN HENRI

We can only love each other because you have loved us first. Let us know that first love so that we can see all human love as a reflection of a greater love, a love without conditions and limitations.[3]

—*A Cry for Mercy: Prayers from the Genesee*

Henri Nouwen is among the most prolific and revered spiritual writers in the Christian tradition, and his work has touched thousands of people around the world, from all walks of life, and from many different spiritual traditions. I first met Henri in 1993, when I was at a crossroads in my life. Just the day before, I had quit my job as a real estate banker, with little idea of what to do next, except that I felt called to live a more meaningful and spiritual life. Because of that encounter with Henri, I ended up visiting and later becoming a summer assistant at L'Arche Daybreak, the community for people with intellectual disabilities where Henri served as the pastor after leaving his own career as an academic. I entered into spiritual direction with Henri for what turned out to be the last two years of his life, and this experience has shaped my understanding of prayer in more ways than I can count. I hope to share some of what I learned from Henri in these pages, to help you find the prayer of your own heart.

Both before and after his move to Daybreak, Henri wrote about the spiritual life and the human longing for love, acceptance, and care. His famous empathy arose from an ongoing prayerful engagement with his own emotional suffering, particularly

the weaknesses and flaws that continually challenged him and troubled his relationships. His time at Daybreak served to bring him closer than he had ever been to a
sense of home, of being cared for and loved for just being Henri. It also allowed him
to become more clear that his own restless longing for intimacy could never be fully
satisfied by anyone but God, and that for all of us, God is the ultimate home and
resting place for our hearts' desires. From all his experiences, Henri was convinced
that each of us is called to acknowledge and celebrate our belovedness, and it was
from this place that he approached the life of prayer.

Despite the fact that Henri had an incredibly powerful intellect, his writing about
prayer and the spiritual life always used simple, direct language that everyone could
understand. That's not just because Henri wanted to communicate with as many
people as possible (although I think he did), but because he believed that true spiritual connection was always made from the heart, not from the head. Even before
Henri went to live with people with intellectual disabilities at Daybreak, he taught,
gave workshops, and wrote in this simple, accessible way. He spoke directly to our
most familiar experiences, cutting through any desire to hide, obscure, or gloss over
either the painful or joyful aspects of the human condition. This was one of Henri's
greatest gifts, and formed the foundation for his understanding of prayer and its place
in Christian life—Henri insisted on being absolutely and imperfectly human, and
encouraged all of us do to the same. It was from this humanness that Henri teaches
us about prayer.

PRAYING WITH HENRI

> Every day I see again that only you can teach me to pray, only you can set my
> heart at rest, only you can let me dwell in your presence.[4]
>
> —*A Cry for Mercy*

When Bob Wicks asked me to write something about praying with Henri Nouwen,
I laughed a little to myself, because what first came to mind was a completely literal
interpretation of the task. That is, I remembered what it was like to actually pray *with*
Henri, to sit next to him during the very early morning silent prayer sessions in the
small chapel in the basement of the Dayspring house at Daybreak. Let's just say that
praying with Henri Nouwen in the flesh, at least in the context of silent meditation,
was quite a different experience than I'd expected after having listened to him speak
and having read several of his books. I thought that this great spiritual writer, this
teacher about prayer, this man who was a spiritual giant in my eyes, would be a model
meditator. How wrong I was! It brings a smile to my face now, all these years later,
to say—very respectfully—that meditating with Henri was a bit like praying with a

small child or a puppy who knows he is supposed to be quiet and still, but just can't manage it.

He looked painfully uncomfortable on a floor cushion. There was fidgeting, shifting, sighing, and more fidgeting. It seemed that Henri, the person who wrote so beautifully about prayer and the spiritual life, could not sit still for more than ten seconds! But that really shouldn't have surprised me, given the intensity of Henri's personality and the speed at which he seemed to conduct his day. What Henri was actually doing in that chapel was something that I very much needed to learn, and that I think all of us on the spiritual journey need to learn: he was, quite simply, being himself. And while he could be fidgety in meditation, in other occasions of group prayer, especially when saying Mass, Henri prayed openly, passionately, and with a profound spirit of welcome that inspired everyone in the room. Henri's prayer seemed to be always on the move, gathering in anyone who sought a place of welcome and acceptance. It is in that spirit of humanness that was Henri's, that I offer these thoughts about Henri and prayer.

The quote from *With Open Hands* at the top of this chapter sets us on our course: "In prayer, I am constantly on the way, on pilgrimage." Praying with Henri means going on a journey. In describing the spiritual life, Henri not surprisingly often uses metaphors of motion—from here to there, from this to that. Through our prayer, as through our whole life, we are on the move, traveling from one state of mind, one disposition, to another. Henri encourages us to move from loneliness to solitude, from greed to gratitude, from hostility to hospitality. This journey starts wherever we are right now, and leads us through an honest engagement with ourselves to a deep relationship with God where "heart speaks to heart." It is a journey toward relationship that takes us into the midst of our own imperfect selves, into the depths of our own suffering, and through it to the fullness of joy that God created as our true dwelling place.

PRAYING OUR UNIQUENESS: THE JOURNEY TOWARD OUR HEART

> From the moment we claim the truth of being the Beloved, we are faced with the call to become who we are.[5]
>
> —*Life of the Beloved*

Henri used to say that his middle initials, J. M., stood for "just me." This little joke reminded him that no matter how many books he wrote, no matter how many talks he gave, and no matter how famous he became, he was still "just Henri," a person who struggled, as all of us do, to become the person he felt God was calling him to be. And if he ever forgot this, his friends in the Daybreak community would readily remind him, whether by gently teasing him about his quirks and imperfections or by simply living honestly and well their own vulnerabilities.

This sense of simplicity and humanness is one of the fundamental things that Henri teaches us about prayer. I pray as "just me," you pray as "just you," and we all pray as "just us." What this means is that we can only approach God as ourselves. We may try to hide the parts of ourselves we don't like or try to keep them out of our prayer because we fear God's disapproval. We may attempt to put on the guise of holiness, righteousness, or superiority, but this only gets in the way of our prayer. Instead, Henri reminds us that we can only begin our journey toward God exactly where we are, with all our pain and all our faults, insecurities, worries, and flaws. The journey of prayer starts, then, with a deep and honest look at our own lives.

Henri calls us to examine our lives honestly, so that the person we bring to God is our whole self, not a mask or a disguise constructed by fear. In *Can You Drink the Cup?*, he writes,

> Holding the cup of life means looking critically at what we are living. This requires great courage, because when we start looking, we might be terrified of what we see. Questions may arise that we don't know how to answer. Doubts may come up about things we thought we were sure about. Fear may emerge from unexpected places. We are tempted to say: "Let's just live life. All this thinking about it only makes things harder." Still, we intuitively know that without looking at life critically we lose our vision and our direction. When we drink the cup without holding it first, we may simply get drunk and wander around aimlessly.[6]

These words hold forth a challenge to face ourselves, to get real about our lives and all that they present to us: the joys and the sorrows, the victories and the defeats, the loves and the losses. When we get real in this way, we might not like everything we find in ourselves, but the search is the beginning of an honest prayer life.

What is so powerful about Henri's approach to prayer is that it refuses to jump over sorrow, grief, pain, and suffering to what we might call a "premature joy." The passage above presents this challenge so clearly: the cup that we are given to drink is the cup of our life, and so it must be filled with all that comprises life. There is no life without suffering, but it is through embracing and befriending our suffering that we will find our joy.

Anyone who has read Henri's books knows that he suffered a lot. He writes about his suffering in almost every volume, sharing with his readers his courageous confrontation with those personal weaknesses and flaws that plagued him in his relationships with others and created blocks in his path to spiritual growth. Over the many years of his writing, Henri identified and explored his neediness, resentment, jealousy, envy, and rage, his sense of emptiness and his sometimes overwhelming sense of longing for intimacy and a heart-to-heart connection. His courage in facing these less than nice discoveries about himself, and his willingness to share them with countless readers is what makes Henri such an inspiration for those who want to practice prayer. He models for us an openness to self-critique that is grounded in hopefulness and faith that our reflection is held in the embrace of a love that is large enough to hold all our faults, weaknesses, and failings.

I have sometimes thought that Henri is too hard on himself, that he overemphasizes the negative and underplays the positive in his own humanness. He reveals himself as often guilty, angry, and worried. He is saddened by his own neediness and resentment, and judgmental toward his own longings. But if we remember that Henri is praying and writing as "just me," then we can also realize that these are his honest reflections about his experience. Henri knew how easy it is to feel big when being praised for his writing, his teaching, and his public speaking. It was exactly the conflict between this external success and his internal feeling of brokenness that led Henri to discover the many fears and weaknesses in himself and to incorporate those into his approach to prayer. He reminds us that the life of prayer is not about pretending that our flaws aren't so big, our weaknesses aren't so weak, or our failings are not sometimes damaging to us and those around us. Rather it is about bringing all those things, along with our gifts and joys, into our engagement with the God who loves us from all eternity.

In the end, self-examination is not the same as prayer, but it can lead us into an honest prayer when we bring the reality of our inner life to God. Prayer leads "all our thoughts out of their fearful isolation into a fearless conversation with God."[7] Praying with Henri lets us embark on the journey to "just-me-ness." This kind of prayer embraces all of our humanness, including its glorious and broken aspects. And we can engage in this fearless conversation, Henri says, because we are each one of us, beloved of God. "Being the Beloved," Henri insists, "is the core truth of our existence."[8] Because we are the Beloved, we can also allow ourselves to be "just us."

Being ourselves before God leads us home to ourselves, to what Henri always refers to as the heart, that place within us where we truly *live*, where we are at home. The heart is the truth at the center of ourselves where we can relate most authentically and deeply to God, others, and the world, and it is the place where our prayer arises. Prayer "launches us on an inward journey to the heart, that intimate home, where an unceasing conversation of love can take place."[9] So prayer leads us to our own heart, a place of intimacy and vulnerability.

Praying Our Vulnerability: The Journey toward Intimacy

> Do you know where the word "vulnerability" comes from? It comes from a Latin word for "wound." Jesus's way is the way of woundedness.[10]
>
> —*The Vulnerable Journey*

Henri writes about prayer as an experience of intimacy, where we are deeply vulnerable to and with the other who addresses us in the very heart of ourselves. The ability to be vulnerable implies the risk of getting hurt; that's the connection between vulnerability and woundedness. If we want to have a truly intimate relationship with someone, we are offering our heart to them and risking its breaking. Being vulnerable is frightening, as Henri well knows:

> The tragedy is that we are so possessed by fear that we do not trust our innermost self as an intimate place but anxiously wander around hoping to find it where we are not. We try to find that intimate place in knowledge, competence, notoriety, success, friends, sensations, pleasure dreams, or artificially induced states of consciousness. Thus we become strangers to ourselves, people who have an address but are never home and hence can never be addressed by the true voice of love.[11]

When we act like people who have an address but are never home, we have created a dwelling where no visitors are welcome, and so no intimate communication can take place.

When we live this way, the call, Henri says, is to be "converted"—we need to convert or change our ways so that we move from the "house of fear" to the "house of love." "Conversion," he writes, "means coming home, and prayer is seeking our home where the Lord has built a home—in the intimacy of our own hearts. Prayer is the most concrete way to make our home in God."[12] In prayer, we are coming home to ourselves and finding that God is already there waiting for us.

This experience of at-homeness with God is how Henri envisions the intimacy of prayer. Getting to this is a process of extending ourselves. Henri often uses metaphors that evoke a feeling of expansion—we expand in order to connect. So when we pray "from the heart," we are "reaching out," to God "with open hands." In this expansive kind of prayer, Henri says, we are not just asking for God to conform our circumstances to our desire, to give us things we want, or even to save our lives. Those kinds of prayers of asking for what we want are more like a Christmas list for Santa

Claus rather than a true reaching out to God. In mature and expansive prayer, we are extending ourselves toward God so that we might feel God extending toward us. We are reaching out with our hearts, putting our hearts out there for God to touch. Think of the kind of vulnerability implied in this image. To let someone actually touch your heart would be an act of the greatest trust.

This vulnerability is not easy. It is risky. I would even say very risky. When we make ourselves vulnerable to another person, we risk being hurt, being rejected, or being left. In my therapy practice, I find that the fear of intimacy and the vulnerability it requires is deep and strong. Although in order to find healing, we must expose our wounds. To do so feels like great danger to that part of us that seeks certainty and control. It might seem that making ourselves vulnerable to God would be different. After all, God is good, and faithful, and loves us through everything. If it is true that God is all of these things, then there wouldn't be much risk in opening ourselves up in prayer. It would seem, anyway, that there is no risk, that we are guaranteed to be rewarded for our vulnerability to God.

But somehow that's not the way faith works. If we were able to embrace God's promise of unconditional love with complete certainty, then faith would not be necessary. Faith without doubt, as the theologian Paul Tillich says, is not faith. Without doubt, what need would we have to risk trusting God? How could our prayer then be vulnerable or truly intimate? Part of the intimacy of prayer is embracing the paradox of faith—in order to be truly vulnerable in prayer, we have to include our doubt as well as our faith. And for Henri, paradox lies at the heart of prayer itself.

PRAYING OUR CONTRADICTIONS: THE JOURNEY TOWARD PARADOX

> When God dwells in us…we can wait while we have already arrived and ask while we have already received.[13]
>
> *—Reaching Out*

To understand prayer, we have to understand that prayer itself is a paradox. Countless treatises have been written about prayer. This book itself is full of many reflections on prayer that come from different traditions and spiritual perspectives within the Catholic framework, and we know there are many other traditions that have something valuable to say about prayer and how to pray. Henri observes this tendency to teach prayer as residing in what he calls the "paradox of prayer." The paradox is that "we have to learn how to pray while we can only receive it as a gift."[14] He notes that when we focus too much on the concrete details of any prayer technique, we can become convinced (erroneously) that we can "reach any level of prayer by just hard work and stern perseverance."[15] While learning and perseverance in prayer is necessary, reliance on our own effort will ultimately leave us frustrated and maybe even further from God than before we started.

The paradox of prayer is that while we need to be intentional about prayer, to learn and practice, it is actually the Spirit of God who is praying within us.

Even our seeking for God in prayer is actually a sign that we have already found God. Henri writes, "You can only seek God when you have already found God. The desire for God's unconditional love is the fruit of having been touched by that love."[16] So we might say that we can only pray to God when God is already praying in us—we are praying and "being prayed" at the same time. By our prayer, we dispose ourselves to receive the gift of prayer. We pray so that God can pray in us.

There is also another paradox that Henri identifies in relation to prayer. Above I proposed that a prayer that is truly vulnerable is prayer with no guarantees, prayer in which we embrace our doubt as well as our faith. Henri addresses a related idea when he proposes that the experience of God's presence in prayer is not enough—we must also experience fully God's absence. Paradoxically, in prayer the two are inseparable:

> [God's] presence is so much beyond the human experience of being together that it quite easily is perceived as absence. [God's] absence, on the other hand, is often so deeply felt that it leads to a new sense of [God's] presence.[17]

The prayer life that is based only in an experience of God's presence is incomplete, Henri says. It allows us to become complacent in a false or illusory certainty, when the mature life of faith leads us to a mysterious and numinous uncertainty. That is, in a mature spiritual life, we pray into a space of surrender, an experience of vulnerability where we cannot control the other, nor can we know what will happen next.

The prayer of God's absence also puts us in touch with our spiritual longing, because "it is in the center of our longing for the absent God that we discover [God's] footprints."[18] Finally, it teaches us to befriend our own losses and to have compassion for the suffering of others. Without entering into that place of loss and absence within ourselves, how could we really understand and bring a healing touch to the pain of the world? For Henri, presence without absence is like faith without doubt—it is an illusion that we must move beyond on our journey toward a full and creative spiritual life that can be a sign of healing in the world.

True intimacy with God in prayer is impossible without a willingness to enter into vulnerability and risk our hearts. We have to make this movement toward vulnerability over and over again. The conversion of prayer is not a onetime thing, but an ongoing commitment to engage with ourselves and our pain, to once again connect with ourselves and to be at home for God. From this place, full of the experience of both the presence and the absence of God, our whole engagement with others and the world can be a prayer.

A PAUSE ON THE JOURNEY: HOW TO PRAY

> May the Lord guide you with his tender care as you search for your deepest call.[19]

As I mentioned previously, many spiritual teachers develop or transmit methods of prayer, specific practices, or techniques that they believe are helpful in cultivating spiritual growth and the life of faith. Some, like John Main or Thomas Keating, recommend particular methods of meditation; others might advocate a deep engagement with the Lord's Prayer or some other verbal prayer. Henri doesn't do that. He doesn't have one prayer method or practice that he advises us to follow. Henri believed that many methods of prayer could facilitate the kind of intimacy with God that is the goal of spiritual life. What is important, he says, is for each of us to ask the question, "What is *my* way to pray? What is the prayer of my heart?"[20]

When I met Henri, I was wandering around in several different methods of prayer: a form of yoga meditation, discursive prayer, journaling, saying the rosary, centering prayer. I found something helpful and important in each of these practices, but I was also concerned that perhaps I wasn't praying the right way. A famous charismatic preacher came to my church and told the crowd, "If you're not praying in tongues, you're not really praying." Some spiritual books I read said that you must only pray without words. Others extolled the power of words in prayer. Some embraced the body as integral to prayer, while others saw the body as a distraction or deterrent to good praying. Certainly, I thought, Henri would help me weed through all these messages and practices and advise me on the right way to pray. But again, I was surprised—Henri advised me only to persevere in an intentional journey inward, where I would discover the prayer of my heart. This prayer, he said, would feel real and true to me because it would lead me to an experience of the heart of God. Perhaps the most liberating message was his affirmation that a rigid, intellectualized, or anxiety-driven prayer practice was surely not about praying from the heart!

The right way to pray is going to be different for each of us, but it is going to be a way. Henri writes, "The fact is that no one who seriously wants to live a life of prayer can persevere in that desire and realize it to some degree without a very concrete way. It may be necessary to make many changes in direction and to explore new ways as life develops, but without any way we won't arrive anywhere."[21] So on our prayer journey, we may try many different ways to pray. But if we make the commitment to discover and stay true to the prayer of the heart, this is exactly what will lead us home to God.

Praying with Henri: The Journey toward Life

> Prayer, therefore, is God's breathing in us, by which we become part of the intimacy of God's inner life, and by which we are born anew.[22]

—Reaching Out

It is easy, when we read the work of the great spiritual teachers, to believe that they have found the way, that through their prayer they have attained a permanent state of enlightenment or holiness that makes them very different from you and me. We imagine that their success at prayer has allowed them to transcend or leave behind their anxiety or depression, their personality problems or inner anguish. I don't think this is true for most of them, and for Henri it certainly wasn't. Henri let us all know that even with his years and years of praying and attempting to pray, he still struggled at least sometimes with the same issues that had always plagued him. Throughout his life, he wrote about his neediness, his fear of rejection and abandonment, his longing for intimacy, and his tendency toward envy and resentment. Even in the last years of his life, with a lot of prayer under his belt, these issues were still present for him.

So should we assume then that prayer just didn't work for Henri? That if he had either prayed better (or read his own books, as a friend once advised him), he would have been able to become completely free of the emotional pain and the relational challenges he had struggled with for so long? Not at all. Henri persevered in prayer and in the spiritual life, and he grew immensely in the process as his writing attests. But in his frankness and openness, Henri reveals that while prayer brings a tremendous sense of liberation and freedom, it does not turn us into different people. Life will challenge us, and we may—even after many years of prayer—find ourselves, as Henri did, still wrestling with the old demons of resentment, envy, self-doubt, or fear. But those struggles are now different because of our prayer. They are different because a life of prayer allows us to more easily access that sense of belovedness that connects us to who we really are, and whose we really are. This doesn't make our weaknesses and failings disappear, but it allows them to be held in the all-embracing arms of the one who loved us before we were born.

In teaching us about prayer, Henri gives us an immense gift. He shows us time and again his humanness, his brokenness, and his persisting imperfection. He doesn't pretend that his prayer life or his commitment to seeking intimacy with God has made him a different person, one without fear or inner pain. He is still that "just me" Henri, the one who sometimes still worries whether people will like him, who can feel deeply hurt, and who can even hurt others. By revealing all of this to us, his readers, Henri gives us a gift that is tremendously liberating. We do not have to feel pressure to somehow be cured of ourselves through prayer, to become someone other than ourselves, to become perfect people. This is so freeing! Prayer is not about transforming ourselves into perfect beings. It is rather to pray so that God can pray in us, to experience God's absence so that we can rejoice in God's presence, and to trust hopefully in the power of God to work in us and transform us into living witnesses to God's love and justice in the world.

1. Henri J. M. Nouwen, *Clowning in Rome: Reflections on Solitude, Celibacy, Prayer, and Contemplation* (Westminster, MD: Christian Classics, 1992), 70.
2. Henri J. M. Nouwen, *With Open Hands* (Notre Dame, IN: Ave Maria, 1972), 69.
3. Henri J. M. Nouwen, *A Cry for Mercy: Prayers from the Genesee* (Maryknoll, NY: Orbis, 2002), 52.
4. Nouwen, *A Cry for Mercy*, 13.
5. Henri J. M. Nouwen, *Life of the Beloved: Spiritual Living in a Secular World* (New York: Crossroad, 1996), 37.
6. Henri J. M. Nouwen, *Can You Drink the Cup?* (Notre Dame, IN: Ave Maria, n.d.), 27.
7. Nouwen, *Clowning in Rome*, 71.
8. Nouwen, *Life of the Beloved*, 28.
9. Henri J. M. Nouwen, *Lifesigns: Intimacy, Fecundity, and Ecstasy in Christian Perspective* (New York: Doubleday, 1998), 40.
10. From "Henri Nouwen's The Vulnerable Journey," YouTube video, 15:30, posted by PathwaysAwareness, May 3, 2013. https://www.youtube.com/watch?v=Idze_Mg3P2U.
11. Nouwen, *Lifesigns*, 38.
12. Nouwen, *Lifesigns*, 39.
13. Henri J. M. Nouwen, *Reaching Out: The Three Movements of the Spiritual Life* (New York: Doubleday, 1979), 148.
14. Nouwen, *Reaching Out*, 124.
15. Nouwen, *Reaching Out*, 124.
16. Henri J. M. Nouwen, *The Inner Voice of Love: A Journey through Anguish to Freedom* (New York: Doubleday, 1996), 16.
17. Nouwen, *Reaching Out*, 127.
18. Nouwen, *Reaching Out*, 128.
19. This is the inscription Henri wrote to me on the flyleaf of *The Road to Daybreak* in 1994.
20. Nouwen, *Reaching Out*, 134. Although Henri does not advocate for one kind of prayer, and explored several methods of prayer himself, he does recommend that whatever approach we take, it should include reading of scripture, quiet time or silence, and the companionship of a spiritual guide or community. See *Reaching Out* for his most developed discussion of this.
21. Nouwen, *Reaching Out*, 136.
22. Nouwen, *Reaching Out*, 125.

CHAPTER 27

Praying with John Main

~ Laurence Freeman, OSB ~

In my first year of university, I was facing some hard personal challenges, and I went to spend Easter with John Main, who was then headmaster at the Benedictine school of St. Anselm's Abbey in Washington, DC. Our paths had first crossed nearly ten years earlier when I was a boy at another Benedictine school in London. To me and my fellow students then, Dom John stood out with a distinctive quality from all the other teachers and monks working in the school. He was not soft on rules, but he openly disagreed with corporal punishment and challenged the students of all ages by treating them as intelligent beings who had a right to express their opinion. This was before John Main became my spiritual teacher, but in later years as my guide in the monastic life, this quality of detachment and respect always characterized him. He helped you to see what you should do but left the choice—sometimes painfully— to you.

When I went to see him that Easter, I was not aware either of what personal suffering he had gone through in being sent there—a conflict in the London monastery over school policy had divided the community—nor that he had begun to meditate again after many years. In our conversations during Holy Week, he listened skillfully and compassionately. He expanded the frame of meaning in which I could deal with my issues. Without any kind of indoctrination, I felt I was picking up valuable knowledge and seeing the paths of wisdom. They felt vaguely familiar and strikingly new at the same time.

Then, at the end of a long conversation, he introduced me to meditation. I cannot remember his exact words. He spoke quietly and briefly and, I imagine, restricted what he was saying to practical advice. Despite the low-key quality of what he was saying, I felt an immense impact. This hit me at two levels which were clearly not in harmony as I felt very conflicted listening to what he said. At one level, the intellectual, I was totally bewildered. How could one let go of thoughts? Surely, I think therefore I am? Meditation as he described it seemed nihilistic and abstract. At that time, I would have probably agreed with an English abbot some years later who dismissed John Main's teaching as platonic, by which he probably meant idealistic and nonincarnate. I didn't have this theological response, but the kind of prayer he was describing seemed incomprehensible on the level that I was thinking about it. I was on an intellectual search for truth. I had begun to read widely in other spiritual traditions. I must have read about meditation, but I had never before tried it or been given a clear instruction of how to do so.

Yet at another level—one that had clearly been touched awake by his words and presence but that was quite new to me—I knew that I was extraordinarily blessed by hearing what I was being told. It had the crystal clear tone of an absolute integrity and truth. I did not understand it, but I trusted it completely. More than that, or because of it perhaps, I felt a new hunger or spiritual desire surge. Where before I had felt confusion and doubt, I now experienced a clear longing. For what, I was not sure. But I knew I wanted and needed to meditate to find out.

That same evening, I tried to meditate alone in my room in the monastery guest house. I floundered and failed. My mind, as if driving under the influence, skidded and crashed into every thought, feeling, anxiety, and fantasy that it produced. But I also felt that I was beginning. I would be beginning for a long time. Indeed, I feel I still am, but in another sense of beginning.

Over the next few years, whenever I met Fr. John, I would often ask if we could meditate together, which we often did. But he never checked on my performance or gave any intrusive impression of wanting me to or being disappointed that I didn't. Perhaps because it was clear to me that he was my teacher in this journey of false starts, I never looked elsewhere for support. I knew what I should do, and I didn't do it. I was impatient but he seemed quite prepared to wait for as long as necessary until the penny of wisdom he had dropped hit the ground.

One Sense of "Praying With"

The next turning point occurred when, some years after finishing university, I was in a career transition. John Main had returned to his London monastery and was setting up a small lay community for a six-month retreat opportunity in which meditation and the monastic experience were the essential elements. I asked him if I could join, and to my humbling surprise, he seemed unconvinced that I should. I kept applying and eventually he agreed.

In the community house on the monastery grounds, we would all meditate together three times a day. We would then walk over to the church for the Office with the monks and meals. The first few weeks were hard going, but I felt deeply sure it was what I should be doing. Again I was conflicted—I was convinced, but I did not understand what I was convinced about. In my conversations with Fr. John, my reading in the contemplative tradition, and discussion with those with me on this inner pilgrimage, I began to put together a language and system of symbols that helped me understand what I was doing. Fr. John watched and listened carefully and intervened occasionally but did not interfere with the experience that was unfolding. It was then that I heard and understood for the first time the words of the desert fathers and one of their great sayings, *magistra experientia,* "experience is the teacher." It was the wisdom at the heart of John Main's way of teaching prayer.

Sitting with him and the other community members, also occasionally with a monk from the monastery who was interested, I began to develop the practice as a discipline. It was not easy, but I felt that something was growing, and I began to see the obvious explanation. Meditation was making me more aware. It was not solving all my problems. But it was leading me to self-knowledge. I began to understand John Main's talks and daily comments much better when I saw this happening in me.

Suddenly I had a crisis in my eyes and almost lost my sight through detached retinas. Thanks to John Main's worldly wisdom and contacts, I was examined immediately and operated on just in time to save my sight. This took my attention off other matters for the time being and plunged me into a deeper level of attention and of meditation. It was then that I realized that meditating with Father John was a unique kind of gift and that it made an inestimable difference to my practice and to the transformation—whatever that might be—that was now happening.

The title Praying with John Main has a number of meanings, some of which I will look at in the following sections. But I wanted to start with the obvious, literal meaning: praying in the physical and spiritual presence of a master of prayer, one's teacher, someone who has something in his or her own experience to communicate.

This is a more familiar idea in Eastern Christian spirituality than it is in the Western church because of its more mystical, monastic dimension. The *staretz* in Orthodox Christianity is a living sacrament of the presence of Christ, a tangible Word of God. Of course there are such figures in Latin Christianity, but they have a lower profile, more often suspect or feared because of the personal authority they radiate in their personality and way of communicating. The desert tradition was built on this personal relationship between disciple, *abba* and *amma.* It is still possible, but it is rare and delicate.

What the East calls the grace of the guru (*gurukrupayoga*) has often been faked in the popular orientalism of Western spirituality in recent times. The spiritual vacuum left in western culture by the collapse of the Church and traditional religious authority has often led to abuse of this precious gift of finding and praying with one's teacher. But the marks of a true teacher are clear—authority based on personal experience, a renunciation of power, complete detachment and a desire only for the well-being and maturing of the student. These are the marks, one might almost say the wounds, of the root guru of the Christian lineage, Jesus himself. Jesus prayed with his disciples.

And he continues to do so—as any true Christian teacher-disciple, as John Main was, does not fail to explain to those he is teaching.

What does praying with your teacher mean? Many meditators in the World Community for Christian Meditation, which John Main inspired, meditate in weekly groups or together on retreat or on special teaching sessions. Meditating together is an element of all our events. Most people find that meditating in a group like this is beneficial and upbuilding and also makes the daily, personal work of the meditation much easier. Some, however, do not and complain that they find it distracting to meditate with fidgety people sniffing and clearing their throats. But the great majority find an additional source of inspiration and inner stability in this sacrament of Christ's presence which is formed when, as he said, "two or three are gathered in my name" (Matthew 18:20).[1]

His mentioning these small numbers should give those anxious over the Church's demographic problems today pause for thought. Many Church leaders bewail—and many journalists mock—the falling numbers of church attendance. But placed beside the extraordinary experience and meaning of a very few people praying together, what do numbers really matter? Perhaps the numbers will only begin to rise again when Christians stop counting them.

John Main certainly did not worry about numbers. He felt impelled to communicate widely and to make it as easy as possible for people to begin to meditate, but he was not at all compulsively into scaling up. Soon after we opened up the lay community to anyone who wanted to come and meditate at regular groups that were started, the rooms were filled. But they were not huge rooms. Soon, groups began to form around London, the country, and now the world. But the numbers in the groups are modest. A contemplative mean seems about eight.

I certainly learned this by praying with John Main. On those occasions— sometimes the midday meditations or when we were traveling together—when we meditated alone I was even rather possessively pleased to have that privilege. But if for some reason the group one evening was diminished, Fr. John showed no concern.

I have said that he did not take over or control those he was teaching. Like a desert father, he would listen, pray with and then send you back to the cell of solitude and personal responsibility that would "teach you everything." Nevertheless, he did have, at times, a subtle but palpable influence on my inner state when we were meditating together. This by definition is hard to describe; one cannot easily externalize what is within. By this, I mean that at times of great difficulty or struggle he would subtly help from within to make it easier, to pull you through that hard phase into the next one. It would be similar to a stronger hiker giving a weaker one struggling uphill a helping hand. It would have been nice to have had that boost all the time, but then, as he said, that's not how you learn to stand on your own feet.

In the last days of his life, when I meditated with him or just sat beside his bed, I realized that he had already effectively passed over into the state of continuous prayer which he said is the goal of the discipline and discipleship of all prayer. On some of these last occasions, when I prayed with him, in the sense I have been using so far, I was convinced, if I had not been before, of the existence of this deeper, non-dual dimension of consciousness. Here, in full silence and stillness, perfectly devoid of desire or fear, a great communication can be effected, a transmission that is real and actual but that, even as it happens, in time and out of time, does not disturb the stillness or break the silence.

One other and most important aspect of praying with John Main for me was to learn to recognize Jesus. I had been raised in Christian faith, but as I entered a questioning, self-discovering phase, the belief system around this faith began to dissolve. Jesus became an ever-more distant enigma. Fr. John's emphasis on delving into the experience which meditation opens up through stillness and silence allowed me, for the time being, to put the self-identifying question of Jesus—"Who do you say that I am?" (Matthew 16:15)—to one side. It would return later. Praying with Fr. John, however, eventually reawakened this question of faith at a much deeper level of self-knowledge than I had ever been at before. In John Main's vitalizing free spirit and in his deep faith in and love for Jesus, I began to see what that great question might mean.

Just as Jesus did not point to himself but to the Father and thereby expressed his true authority, so John Main also both taught and practiced taking the attention off one's self. There were potent moments when I glimpsed, through the way he lived and responded to situations, Jesus in him. This was usually a brief transfiguration moment that made visible what was always present but very rarely seen. When he later spoke about Jesus or opened the Scriptures, the meaning of the words flowed out of him in a direct transmission which led many to say they had never heard the Scriptures or the key elements of faith expressed in this clear and self-authenticating way before.

It became clear to me over time that, at the heart of my experience of praying with John Main, there was a personal validation of the truths of our common faith. In particular, I heard his insistence that in deep prayer we move beyond my own prayer altogether and indeed beyond everything on which we can slap a possessive pronoun. For him, in theology and in practice, we enter into the prayer of Jesus himself and thus move with him within the stream of love that flows between the Father and the Son, through him, with him, in him.

This is the point now to look at the other meaning of "Praying with John Main." How does his teaching on prayer—that continues to enrich and inspire more and more people around the world in all walks of life—help them to pray more deeply and in more radical conformity with the teaching of Jesus on prayer? It may help to give context to this teaching to look briefly at the life-journey of one of the major spiritual teachers of our era.

WHO IS JOHN MAIN?

His grandfather was a Scottish engineer who came to the small town of Ballinskelligs in County Kerry in the South of Ireland to complete the laying of the first trans-atlantic cable. Perhaps this symbolizes John Main's wish to connect traditions and cultures and find common ground for communication. His grandfather met and married a local girl and thus prepared the ground for John Main's later local and ancestral relationship with Kerry which he felt gave him a physical place the universe. John (originally Douglas) Main was born in London in 1926 and was educated (by the Jesuits) and grew up there. But he looked to this part of Kerry as his "insertion point in the cosmos" as he playfully called it. Maybe with an Irishman's sense of exile he also felt the common need to be rooted, and in a world of change and separation to find one's home within one's self. His childhood in a family of six boisterous children gave him this in loving and lively ways.

He was called into the army in the last year of the war and worked behind enemy lines identifying their radio locations. This work was facilitated by the introduction of the quartz crystal which increased the accuracy of the radio search systems. He once used this as an example of the mantra—putting us on the wavelength of Christ. Long after he had died, I had to defend his teaching from the charge leveled by a ferocious defender of orthodoxy that his teaching was New Age. Puzzled by this in the light of John Main's Trinitarian theology and personal Christ-centeredness, I asked the prosecution why he said this. "Because he advocates the use of crystals in prayer," the fast-reader replied.

After the war, he entered religious life for two years, the Canons Regular of the Lateran. During his studies in Rome with them, he understood it was not his time for this or his right place, and he decisively left. He studied law at Trinity College Dublin, and was later called to the Bar at Grays Inn in London and joined the British Foreign Service. He studied Chinese and continued to learn the language when he was posted to Kuala Lumpur to the staff of the British Governor General. One day he was sent to visit a Tamil monk who had been made a justice of the peace and was respected for his reconciliatory work among the conflicting ethnic and religious groups. John Main went to the Pure Life Society, then on the outskirts of the city to deliver a diplomatic message of thanks and encouragement. The monk, Swami Satyananda, struck the young diplomat as a man of profound interiority as well as possessing a powerful social conscience. Their conversation turned to religious and then spiritual themes and finally to prayer. John Main learned to meditate on that occasion and returned weekly to meditate with his teacher. When he asked the swami if he could teach him, as a Christian, to mediate, the monk smiled and said of course it would make him a better Christian.

The teaching on the mantra, on the heart, silence, and stillness and daily practice all struck deep chords in John Main's own religious and spiritual training and became essential elements of his later mature teaching of Christian meditation.

When he returned from Asia he became the youngest professor of international law at Trinity College, Dublin. He rose early and worked hard in the early part of the day and, with the time he gained, enjoyed music, racing, and literature. He was disappointed in love when an offer of marriage to a young woman he had known for many years was declined. Not for the last time in his life, he achieved what those around him saw as brilliant success and the conditions of happiness without feeling satisfied by it.

He described in his talks to the monks of Gethsemani in 1976 that the wheel of his true vocation turned again when he accompanied his sister in the slow and painful death of her young son from a brain tumor. Soon after, to the surprise of even those who knew him well, he became a monk at the Benedictine monastery of Ealing Abbey in London. After he had sold his red sports car and donated his wine cellar to the monastery, the novice master predicted he would last three months.

It was a dramatic change of life from that of a brilliant young and popular intellectual around town to shaving with the discarded blades of your novice master and being monitored in the most menial tasks of the monastery. But he thrived and prospered except for one shocking and demanding renunciation demanded of him. He had continued meditating after he returned from Asia. No one he knew understood it, so he kept his practice to himself. On entering the monastery, he looked forward to meeting monks who would understand this prayer of the heart that had quietly become so central to his life. When his novice master listened to what he had to say of the influence of the Indian monk, he told the new monk to stop meditating—and return to more discursive forms of prayer—Brother John was deeply challenged. But he complied even though, as he was to say at Merton's monastery twenty years later, he was now to enter a long spiritual desert.

After study in Rome, profession, and ordination, John Main was appointed to teach in the school at Ealing, where he remained until he was sent to Washington and became headmaster of its school. There he was asked to help a young student who had just returned from a tour of Eastern spiritual centers and was asking if anything comparable existed in the Christian mystical tradition. In helping this young seeker, so typical of his generation, John Main recognized how far the Church was failing to connect people to its own rich tradition. He put the student on a reading program which led him also to a rediscovery of the teaching on meditation that he found in the desert tradition and in particular the Conferences of John Cassian. He recognized the method of the mantra in the monologistic teaching of Cassian's Tenth Conference and then in the affinity between the hesychast tradition and what he had learned twenty years before in Malaysia. He was back on his path of meditation, now convinced of its Christian identity.

In 1975 he returned to his London monastery to establish what was to become the first Christian Meditation Centre. Although welcomed by the monastic community, he realized that the vocation of this new mission would not be fulfilled in this setting. New wine, new wineskins. Accepting the invitation of the Archbishop of Montreal he, on behalf of the London community, established a Benedictine Priory there specifically focused on the practice and teaching of Christian meditation.

The early days of the new foundation brought us back to the radical simplicity, the essentials of the monastic life. But as the community grew in numbers and his own teaching began to receive wider recognition and acclaim, his health declined and he died from cancer in Montreal at the age of fifty-six. Many believed that his work, thus tragically cut short as it was about to flourish, would inevitably dissolve. In fact, as he had realized, it was greater than him individually and it continued to grow. Today, the World Community for Christian Meditation is present in more than a hundred countries.

Bede Griffiths called John Main "in my experience the best spiritual guide in the church today." Ramon Pannikar said he possessed the "genius of simplicity." We will now look what it means to so many around the world today, more than thirty years after his death, to pray with John Main.

John Main as Teacher

Unlike other spiritual teachers who describe their own experience and the circumstances of their lives in some detail, John Main was not autobiographical. His most explicit description of his spiritual journey is in the talks he gave to the monks of Gethsemani in 1976, significantly a more intimate and familiar audience than usual.

Nevertheless, his appeal to experience is fundamental. "In your own experience" is one of his characteristic phrases. Rather than describing what he had experienced he used the authority of what he knew firsthand to urge others to discover the experience for themselves. This was possible because he had a very particular and simple teaching on how to enter it; simple enough, he said, to write on the back of a postage stamp. Well not quite, but near enough:

> Sit down with your back straight. Relaxed but alert. Close your eyes lightly, Breathe normally. Begin to repeat, silently, interiorly, a single word or short phrase—a "mantra." The word recommended is "maranatha." Say the word gently and continuously. Return to it when you become distracted. Meditate twice a day for between twenty and thirty minutes, morning and evening.

He would sometimes add, "I am not saying this is the only way to pray or the only way to heaven," but it was the way he knew and practiced, and it belonged to the mainstream of the Christian prayer tradition. Some found this too simple or too radical or too demanding. Others, however, embraced it enthusiastically knowing that it was, as he warned, simple but not easy. He insisted that beginning to meditate in this way was more than just starting a new method or technique. It was and would become a way of life. But it did not replace or exclude other ways of prayer. On the contrary, meditation could rehabilitate forms of prayer that for many in our time, in and outside the Church, had lost their meaning.

To pray with John Main, then, meant (and still means) to find in his teaching a powerful, liberating encouragement to one's own practice of meditation. He advised patience and fidelity and warned that most people stop and start many times. The important thing, he would say, is to begin and to keep on beginning. He discouraged self-evaluation and self-conscious analysis of the experience. "Do not try to experience the experience. Enter the experience." Anyone who embarks on this practice soon discovers why it is a discipline. His own role, John Main saw, was encouraging by word and example those who are learning the discipline. In doing this, he returns frequently to the core simplicity of the message which he summed up as the instruction to "say your mantra." To those who are not learning the discipline this may seem repetitious, overly simple. But to those who are learning in their own experience and with a beginner's mind, his teaching and companionship is fresh and reassuring.

Not surprisingly, then, John Main was, in his lifetime, a personal teacher specializing in the oral transmission of this wisdom tradition. He convened regular meditation groups at his monasteries, gave retreats and conferences and personal direction to those who came to him. He also wrote, and his talks were recorded. Today his *Collected Talks*—about 250 of them—represent a unique corpus of the oral teaching of a master in this ancient tradition.

For various reasons, including that of institutional suspicion of contemplation, many of the classical Western Church teachers of the past did not write down their specific teaching on prayer. Many perhaps believed that it was a surer way of communicating it to keep the transmission personal. *The Cloud of Unknowing* is an exception to this, but the author clearly feels uncomfortable writing it down.

John Main did both. His primary way of teaching was personal, direct. So, for that matter, was the style of Jesus and the Buddha and many of their followers. But John Main also wrote—essays, newsletters, published talks, many published posthumously. His books and his *Collected Talks* represent a style of teaching that engages many today who seek a deeper path of prayer, who eagerly embrace a discipline and who are thankful for continuous encouragement.

For John Main, the teacher's role is not to substitute his or her experience for that of the student. Nor is it to make the student unduly dependent on them or their authority. Father John's detachment in all things was very pronounced. It could be felt psychologically by those he was guiding as it can be seen today spiritually in those influenced by the teaching he left behind. The teacher's job, he would say "is to say don't give up" and then to get out of the way as soon as possible.

How did John Main see the role of Jesus as teacher? The meditation group and the "community that meditation creates" are manifestations of the activity of Jesus as the one true teacher of those who are his disciples. The manifestation in a person, in the Abba-disciple relationship, is also occasionally to be found but it is based directly on the reality of Jesus as the teacher within.

The Spirit of John Main's Teaching

His teaching on prayer is simple and direct and focused on the discipline of the mantra that he found in Cassian and the Christian tradition generally. But in teaching it, John Main also developed a context for his teaching that enriches all who read it today, but especially those who follow the practice. I will highlight a few of the aspects of his teaching in this context.

The Indwelling Christ

After he began to meditate again, Fr. John reread the New Testament in the light of his renewed experience of the prayer of the heart. It burned itself into his thought and imagination. He draws greatly on the Gospels and letters to explain and illustrate the reasons for meditating and the meaning of the experience.

This meaning is grounded in the reality of the risen Christ present within the human person. As important as the gospel accounts of the historical Jesus, it is the risen Christ we meet in reading them, and this encounter prepares us to meet him in full personal force within ourselves as our self-knowledge grows.

The modern lack of interiority and the failure of Christian spirituality to give due account to it have led to a crisis in both religion and society. The first step, for John Main, back to the heart of Christian faith, is to rediscover one's own authentic inwardness and then to find the Christ within us, the "hope of a glory to come."

THE PRAYER OF JESUS

The consequence of this discovery is the experience of the theological truth that, as St. Paul said, "we do not know how to pray as we ought, but that very Spirit intercedes with sighs too deep for words" (Romans 8:26). It is challenging but also extraordinarily liberating to many seeking this deeper level of prayer to be told, as John Main says, that in meditation we give up "[our] prayer" and enter instead into the "prayer of Jesus." For him, this is a Trinitarian mystery. By entering into union with his prayer, we go with him, in him, through him, in the Spirit to the Father. For Fr. John, the experience of this transcendence of self-attachment in the spirit of Jesus releases the transformative fruits of the Holy Spirit—love, joy, peace, patience, kindness, goodness, fidelity, and self-control. Meditation is simply a way into this essential Christian experience of becoming fully human and so sharing fully in the divine mystery of love.

INTERIORITY OR EGOCENTRICITY

This interiority is not to be confused with the ego, the narcissism of modern culture, its consumerism, degradation, self-centeredness, and enslavement to fantasy and desire. On the contrary, meditation recenters one's consciousness away from the ego. This is the essential asceticism of all prayer, and prayer is the essential asceticism of the Christian life. In saying the mantra, we are following the radical call of the gospel to leave self behind.

DEATH AND RESURRECTION

Every time we meditate, according to John Main, we enter into a great living tradition. We also enter into the dying and rising of Christ. By taking the attention off oneself, by leaving thoughts, words, and images behind, we are truly dying to our false image of self and all attachment to that image. So much so, that meditation becomes a preparation for our physical death. By then, through the practice of meditation, we will have become familiar with the death process, and we will have experienced for ourselves why, to the degree that we die, we rise to fuller life.

In the last phase of his life and especially in his last community letter, Fr. John addressed the mystery of death, and his writings have become especially useful to those facing their own end and to those caring for the terminally ill or the bereaved. In *Death: The Inner Journey* he invites us to face our own mortality head on and to discover how deep prayer dissolves the deep fear and resistance we all feel when mortality is no longer denied but fully accepted.

COMMUNITY OF LOVE

Contemplation is the work of love—it is about turning attention from self to the other. But in this experience, relationship at a deeper level is uncovered and community is thereby formed. "Meditation creates community," which has many forms. Such a community, small or large, temporary or long-term, will be subject to all the normal pressures and foibles of human nature, including conflict and misunderstanding, but as its conception is love, it will be a community of love, meaning one whose primary currency is love refreshed and continuously renewed by a return to its source. John Main believed that the most energized forms of monastic and religious life in the Church of the future would develop by recovering the contemplative experience and placing it at the center of the common life of prayer together in daily life.

THE PRIMACY OF LOVE

Because he saw meditation itself as the work of love, opening us to the primal, creating love at the source of our being, and thus empowering us to love in return, John Main's theology and psychology was centered on the primacy of love. "All morality is a morality of love," he said. He believed that meditation becomes a way of life that becomes an expanding openness to the power of love. Forgiveness, inner healing, compassionate action, the passion for justice are all more or less inevitable manifestations of this irrepressible power.

He advised people not to measure their progress in meditation day by day but to be alert to the changes in their relationships through the slow release of love. The experience of love transforms all relationships beginning with our relationship with ourselves, extending outwards to those close to us, to our wider community, to acquaintances and to strangers (now seen without fear because love casts out fear), to the environment of our common home, and to the mystery of the expanding universe itself.

The Church

Although fully aware of and often frustrated by the hierarchical institution, John Main had and communicated a contemplative vision of the Church, indeed a mystical one. This enabled him to see at least some of the foibles of the institution with humor. He was convinced that the failures of the Church to connect with the spiritual hunger of the times was due to a tragic underestimation of the richness and power of the Christian mystery. Some people who are hurt by their upbringing in the Church needed a debriefing period away from it, and some would inevitably find their support and insertion point elsewhere.

But by reversing the long marginalization of contemplation in the Church and by restoring the contemplative dimension of faith to the heart of the Church's common life, the whole Church would become a truly evangelizing—not just moralizing— witness to the Gospel as it is called to be. Discipleship is the fruit of this.

John Main liked to connect the meanings of discipline and discipleship by relating them to the Latin root *discere*, "to learn." Meditation for him was a learning process, not a technique to be mastered but a discipline to be loved because it makes us disciples. In the spiritually maturing process of the journey of meditation, we feel ourselves empowered, with self-confidence and a zeal for service and mission precisely because we are set free from the isolated sense of self to which the ego clings and set free for the selfless witness to Christ.

Other Faiths

Although personally and theologically centered in the person of Jesus, John Main felt a reverence for "all that is true and holy in other traditions." He frequently quoted from their Scriptures, the Upanishads, Buddhist texts, and the Chinese wisdom he had encountered earlier in his life. Seeing meditation as the common ground among all faiths enabled him to feel at home with them in this contemplative dimension. His friendship with the Dalai Lama, whom he met shortly before he died, illustrated the fraternity felt by monks of all traditions and the commitment they both shared to bringing spiritual wisdom to bear upon the crises of the modern world.

A Spiritual Family

Many are helped to pray better simply by the spiritual breadth and inclusiveness of John Main's wisdom. But those who most could be said to pray with him would be those who follow his teaching on meditation which he passed on, faithful to the tradition in which he had discovered it. Over the years, they have formed a worldwide community of weekly meditation groups, communities gathered around Christian meditation centers, a Benedictine Oblate community, and a digital network of meditators inspired by his teaching.

John Main loved community and saw it as the place in which the human being is called by love out of isolation into fullness of being. Now, as in his lifetime when he formed small monastic families around the experience of silence, he would see his role simply to pray with those who were learning that we all pray with the one whose prayer is the Spirit.

---

1. All biblical quotations are taken from the *New Revised Standard Version*.

PART FIVE

Praying through Life's Challenges

PRAYING THROUGH DIFFICULT TRANSITIONS

LOSING THOMAS...FINDING GOD: PRAYING WITH OUR SACRED STRUGGLES

In this section on praying during challenging times, Joyce Rupp, in Praying through Difficult Transitions, reminds us that during important changes the spiritual fog doesn't often lift as quickly as we'd like. The transitions may be positive as well as unwanted but are significant in how they are in a position to alter our situation in ways that our security is undermined—including our connection to God. Not knowing can truly throw us into upheaval for even longer periods than we might expect. Yet, even though, in her words, "there is nothing that will chase the bleakness of spiritual angst out of our spirit" during those times, Rupp reminds us that we are called to "wrap our faith around the love of the Holy One and stand on the threshold of ambiguity with confidence in what is yet to be revealed." By employing a wide array of sources (John of the Cross and Teresa of Ávila, Joseph Campbell, Gerald May, Pema Chodron, Lawrence Kushner, Steven Levine, and others) as well as her own personal experiences, Rupp helps us be willing to face ambiguity, fear, uncertainty, as well as to embrace the necessity of surrender and trust. In addition, one other essential topic, the need for us to appreciate the spirituality of waiting, is included in this simple yet powerful treatment of the challenge and potential treasures inherent in change.

In Losing Thomas...Finding God: Praying with Our Sacred Struggles by Mary Beth Werdel, we are asked to be open to recognize that extreme trauma, loss, and serious stress need not be the final word in our spiritual journey. Instead, to the contrary and in line with the previous chapter, it may be the opening to a new sense of spiritual depth and awakening. Through sharing a profound experience from her own life, Werdel relates to us in a poignant, clear way how loss can totally rearrange your life—not only in an exterior manner but potentially for the better in an interior way. To accomplish this, she begins by posing several questions: Why is it that some people experience growth after stress and trauma and others do not? Why do some people find deeper relationships with God after stress and trauma, and why do others lose God and faith completely? And how does one who has faith find an accessible God in times of stress? In other words, how does one locate the sacred in struggle? Following this, she gives us three understandings worth noting and draws from the recent posttraumatic growth literature in psychology to offer some key helpful reflections on incorporating certain elements in one's prayerful meditations when negative events happen in life.

Both chapters should provide nourishment both to those who are going through certain difficulties or serious challenges in their lives and to those who are in a position to minister to them in such situations as well.

CHAPTER 28

Praying through Difficult Transitions

~ Joyce Rupp, OSM ~

The fog loomed so thick I could barely detect the street signs when I left for my weekly morning retreat of solitude and prayer by the Des Moines river. In spite of the blurred visibility, I kept on driving, confident the heavy mist would soon lift. It didn't. By the time I arrived and parked my car facing the water, I could only see a white blanket of film in front of me. From past experience I knew the thick woods existed on the opposite bank and the attentive blue herons would be sitting on the branches waiting to snatch their breakfast. And so I sat there, enveloped in a world of indistinguishable reality, knowing I could do nothing to alter the landscape. I could only enter into it and wait silently for the obscure view to change.

Ever so slowly the dense fog dissipated. Gradually the objects of the Cottonwood Recreation area took on shape and color. First, I dimly glimpsed the rapidly moving water, then the blurry outline of the trees on the opposite bank, and finally the herons patiently perched on the branches. As the air cleared, white terns flying low over the water and an eagle sitting on a rock surprised me with their presence.

When I drove away several hours later, I left with a new awareness of the dense fog being a powerful portrayal for the spiritual experience of losing a sense of relationship with the Holy One during difficult times of transition. As with physical fog, when our inner world is clouded, we can only perceive what we know of that relationship from past experience and wait with hope for what will be revealed. Like the unanticipated terns over the water and the eagle on the rock, positive surprises often reveal themselves when our inner sky finally clears.

Our prayer life is bound to be affected by what happens in our outer life. Events such as medical emergencies, divorce and other relationship breakages, death of a loved one, loss of home or work, accidents resulting in ongoing disability, serious mistakes that harm self or others, clinical depression, illnesses that refuse a diagnosis, debilitating aging, and many other unwanted experiences all affect our inner world in some way. Even events that seem positive can shift our inner landscape significantly, such as retirement, the last child leaving home, a new position at work, or a move to another city. Loss of any kind pulls us inward and often takes away our secure history of relating to the Holy One.

Undesired transitions elicit all sorts of unexpected emotional and mental responses. *Anxious, uncertain, angry, bleak, boring, blaming, resentful, confused, doubtful, questioning, hopeless*—these and a multitude of similar words describe the undesired developments that take over the sacred space we once regarded as a tender joining of our heart to the one heart.

If we do not resist the process, these transitional occurrences that conceal our mental vision and block our emotional connection with the Holy One serve to release our inner world of its egoic security and lessen our tight grasp on our supposed treasures.

Not-Knowing

During my thirty-five years as a spiritual director, one of the most challenging and rewarding aspects of this ministry has been to witness the profound movement of spiritual growth that takes place when a person openly enters an uncomfortable period of uncertainty, a stage that leads eventually to discovering and accepting a deeper, broader, and oftentimes, quite different way of being in relationship with self, God, others, and the larger world.

Not being able to identify where we are or how we are interiorly is particularly disconcerting to the person who embraces a daily spiritual practice and yearns for union with the beloved. When foggy times arrive, instead of sensing this former state of consolation, an inability to do so emerges and with it a certain powerless-ness to sense anything but an inaudible void. No striving, pushing, shoving, enticing, coercing, promising, crying out, resisting, insisting—nothing a person attempts—changes the dulled landscape of the heart.

I first came across the phrase "don't know" and the necessity of this experience for spiritual growth in Stephen Levine's *Healing into Life and Death*. Levine quotes a Korean Zen master telling students to "trust that don't know." Levine then develops the significance of this teaching:

> It is the space in which all wisdom arises, in which alternatives are to be discovered. "Don't know" is without all previous opinion; it does not perceive from old points of view, it is open to the many possibilities inherent in the moment. It doesn't force conclusions, it allows the healing in…the differ-ence between confusion and "don't know" is that confusion can only see one way out and that way is blocked, while "don't know" is open to miracles and insights.[1]

This "not knowing" period finds its way into most everyone's experience during diffi-cult changes. It has been given a variety of names and metaphors. *Liminality* is one of the terms psychology uses to designate this transitional "don't know" phase of personal growth. A "limen" consists of the threshold or in-between space in a doorway, thus liminality suggests the place where one is neither in nor out. It contains the ambiguity that develops when we are standing in the middle of a juncture of significant change. Liminality implies a disoriented vagueness in which we wander about, searching for what seems out of reach. We lose a sense of clear identity, question what seems to be a dissolving relationship with what we once believed or experienced, and doubt the nearness of divine presence. All of which leads to a painful or uncomfortable review of the values and beliefs that have given our life meaning and direction.[2]

My liminal times have been many and varied. Usually some unexpected and unwanted development shoves me on the threshold of uncertainty. Something as devastating as the sudden death of my twenty-three-year-old brother sucked me into a bleak cave of sorrow where I could neither pray nor find any sort of consolation. Something as deliberate as moving from a beloved home where I lived for twenty years took my spiritual breath away and left me weary with the reality of impermanence. In each of my liminal times, I have rarely lost a belief that what I was going through was necessary for my ongoing spiritual transformation even though I could not find my way spiritually.

One of my experiences of this foggy spiritual realm occurred when I entered my early fifties. I had meditated with Scripture for thirty years, usually taking as my source the liturgical readings of the day. This form of meditation provided both insight and inspiration. Gradually, Scripture no longer worked as a source for meditation. I felt more and more distant and disjointed in prayer. No matter how persistent I was, I could not force even a remnant of satisfaction.

Over a year later my restless fog lifted when an intuitive spiritual director suggested I stop struggling to pray as I did in the past and be open to another way. With some fear and trepidation, I stepped across the threshold and went toward the unknown. Gradually, I discovered contemplative prayer, a silent meditation without words or deliberate thoughts. Slowly the fog lifted, and I began to sense again the one I trusted to always be with me, albeit now in a quieter way.

Zen teacher Adyashanti writes,

> We must leave what we know and enter that mysterious reality of the unknown. The unknown is a very intimate place. You may feel very exposed when you open yourself to this inner space of unknowing, but really, the unknown is our only doorway. It's by allowing ourselves to not know that we can become truly sensitive, open and available. It's the most humbling thing in the world to admit that we don't know.... As the great mystic Saint John of the Cross said, "In order to come to the knowledge you have not, you must go by a way you know not."[3]

Metaphors describing this experience abound in literature, science, the Scriptures, and spiritual teachings of major religions. Some of these include the gestation period in a pregnant womb, the inert tomb of Jesus on Holy Saturday (Luke 23:50–55), the metamorphosis of the monarch butterfly in the tightly enclosed chrysalis, the waiting seed beneath the soil, the move through a dark tunnel before reaching the light, the space between the takeoff and landing of the trapeze artist, the dormant season of a plant in winter, the Exodus journey of the Israelites (Exodus 14:1–40:38), Joseph discarded in the cistern by his brothers (Genesis 37:18–36), and the forty days of Jesus in the desert (Matthew 4:1–11).

Mythologist Joseph Campbell refers to this passageway of growth as "the night sea journey" when Jonah spends three days in the belly of a whale—"swallowed into the unknown" (Jonah 1:1–16; 2:1–3). In the scriptural story, Jonah looks back on his experience with this terrifying depiction: "The waters swirled about me, threatening my life; the abyss enveloped me; seaweed clung about my head. Down I went to the roots of the mountains; the bars of the nether world were closing behind me forever" (Jonah 2:6–7).[4]

When depression, especially clinical depression, accompanies or leads to liminality, hope is not easily maintained, if at all. In a profound and keenly vulnerable talk, author, educator, and spiritual leader Parker Palmer spoke openly and with great vulnerability of how a severe depression affected him. "I not only was *in* darkness," he explained, "I *became* darkness."[5] I heard the pain in Palmer's voice as he revisited those excruciating periods. I recognized, too, that it was this very pain and Palmer's willingness to enter into it that led to the visionary and wise man he is, respected by countless readers and participants in his *Circle of Trust* programs.

I have never "become darkness," but I have known others who have. This kind of darkness can seep in slowly or crash in like a lightless thunderbolt, shattering belief systems, destroying foundations of love that lead one to feel like darkness itself: boredom that slides slowly into a priest's ministry, the instant destruction of a woman's self-esteem when her supposedly faithful spouse announces divorce when it's never been so much as a whisper, a phone call with the dreaded news of a child killed in an automobile accident, a longtime friend gradually slipping away without so much as giving a reason for the ultimate break, a church decision regarding dogma that cuts the strong rope tethering one's faith since childhood, a determined desolation that grinds itself into every corner of a person's existence.

Joseph Campbell explains that in this liminal journey we are pulled inward. During these metaphorical "regions of the unknown (desert, jungle, deep sea, alien land, etc.)," the content of our unconscious or our deeper self finds the freedom to float to the surface of our awareness.[6]

This vulnerability allows the Spirit to draw forth what we held at bay when we felt stronger and more in control. When we have little to hang on to we move toward the possibility of mining both the gold of our goodness and the rusted metal of our shadowy self. All of this is essential for us to bring to the surface of our awareness if we are to become a whole human being

My mid-forties felt like being in the belly of the whale. During that era, I struggled with what I deemed to be significant injustices in the Church regarding women, found release from my overly managed approach to ministry, and gradually healed from the wounds of past hurts that I had refused to tend. I learned much about my shadowy self during those dark Jonah episodes and shed some armor around my soul that kept me imprisoned. The clarity I gained regarding both my gold and my rust gave me increased freedom to draw forth and express the best of my deeper self.

The myth of Inanna, one of the earliest recorded pieces of literature regarding transitions and transformation (3,500 BC or earlier), graphically describes this dark corridor of growth. While there are various stories about Inanna, a Babylonian queen of the Upperworld, the myth about her descent to the Underworld most relates to the necessity of liminality for personal growth. When Inanna makes this journey, the guards at seven different gates stop her and demand she shed a piece of her persona: first her crown, then her jewels, her robe, and so on, until she is completely naked at the final gate before entering the Underworld (totally stripped of her power and her persona). Then she steps into this dark domain where she dies and remains for three days and nights before being brought back to life by the god Enki. He escorts Inanna to the Upperworld, where she rules with a different view of her leadership and those she serves.[7]

Much like the stripping of Inanna's persona, Jesus insists that we must lose our self to find our self (Matthew 16:24–25), that we let go of the person we think we are— the one we have shown on the outside—let go of the God we think we know, and the undesirable cultural influences holding sway over us or keeping us from giving ourselves wholeheartedly to genuine, generous love. Like a chick in an incubating egg or a seed in the soil, we enter a period of not knowing so we can gain a clearer, more perceptive way of living, perhaps with fewer answers but more satisfaction regarding questions that might never find an ultimate response.

When losing the self to find the self leads to consequent liminality, Christians tend to name this as the dark night of the soul, a term from the insightful writings and lived experience of St. John of the Cross and St. Teresa of Ávila regarding their own encounters with inner fog. The public, in general, uses this term quite loosely, without rendering its deep impact and full reality. Spiritual guide and psychologist Gerald May notes, "When people speak of going through a dark night of the soul, they usually mean they're experiencing bad things."[8] The term *dark night of the soul* actually has a specific meaning: a turning away from the familiar, known, secure sanctuary of who we think we are and toward a significant change of mind and heart, a transition holding the possibility of drawing us evermore fully into relationship with the Holy One by becoming the best of who we are at the core of our being.

In Jewish thought, Rabbi Lawrence Kushner takes his reader into the transformative Exodus story to describe this stage of in-between: "In Kabbalistic thought this is called 'entering the *ayin*,' or the 'Holy Nothingness.' In order for something to change from what it is into whatever it hopes to become, there must be a moment when it has stopped being what it was yet before it has become what it hopes to become." Kushner then goes on to describe the parting of the Sea of Reeds with the strong metaphor of "passing through the sea (of amniotic waters)." Kushner continues: "Indeed, it has always seemed to me that the miracle was not that the waters parted for the Israelites but that they all walked into the midst of the sea, drowned, and were reborn free men and women on the other side." Kushner emphasizes: "You have to let go of the old you. You must be willing to walk into the midst of the sea on dry ground and risk it all."[9]

Indeed, risk it all. In a Western, capitalistic culture that seeks financial security above all else, small wonder that feelings of inadequacy or uncertainty receive little applause. Add to this an easy access to instant knowledge and quick answers via web browsers. Knowledge is at our fingertips, so the conclusion would seem to be that we do not need to wait for what is unfolding slowly in our inner world. And yet, without this element of unknowing, our inner life would be incomplete and stunted.

FACING FEAR

Whatever metaphors we use to identify this transitional experience, ambiguity and uncertainty remain. In the midst of this discomforting vagueness, we gradually become ill at ease with our spiritual life, sometimes to the point of believing our faith has left us forever. Like Jonah, we sink into the depths so deep it feels like we are joining Jonah in "the roots of the mountains," a powerful metaphor to describe the depth of spiritual darkness. It is not unusual for fear to manifest when our inner world of transitioning swallows us with its persistent haze.

During our Jonah-like experiences, we may be tempted to give up, to allow ourselves to be submerged in a downhearted state instead of staying open and continuing to be faithful to prayer while we intentionally entrust ourselves to the one who is forever faithful to us no matter how dull our senses might be. When we face our fears, they loosen their power over our emotional response. Wendell Berry points this out clearly in a poem that begins with "I go among the trees and sit still." In that essential still-ness, (where fear is allowed to show its face) Berry not only meets what he fears in himself, he eventually experiences that fear leaving him. As the fear departs, "It sings." Berry "hears its song."[10] In other words, when we draw on our courage and turn toward our fears to see what they are and how they pursue and press on us, they not only loosen their grip, we find relief and freedom from believing we have to be strong and in control all the time. When we face our fear, we acknowledge our vulnerability and allow the music of our soul to resound in us. We open up to the movement of divine grace flowing in and through us.

In *Comfortable with Uncertainty*, Pema Chödrön writes, "Openness doesn't come from resisting our fears but from getting to know them well. We can't cultivate fear-lessness without compassionate inquiry into the workings of the ego. So we ask ourselves, 'What happens when I feel I can't handle what's going on? What are the stories I tell myself? What repels me and what attracts me? Where do I look for strength and in what do I place my trust?'"[11] These and other questions—What does holding on to this fear do to my spirit and approach to life? How does this fear keep me from opening myself in trust to the Holy One? How would my spiritual prac-tice change if I allowed myself to be vulnerable with the divine beloved?—move us toward fear instead of running from it.

One of the most graphic renderings of facing one's fear can be found in the film *Beasts of the Southern Wild*. A young girl, Hush Puppy, lives in a wretchedly poor bayou community cut off from everyone by a huge levee. The motherless child survives amid dirt and rubble, sometimes eating cat food for her meals. Tremendous fear arises when she realizes her father is dying. This fear is depicted in the film as enormous wild beasts. These massive, buffalo-like creatures terrify her. Hush Puppy runs and runs and runs from them. Finally, she stops and slowly turns around to face what has terrified her. The snorting beasts instantly stop, stomp and drool, and approach her with their fierce eyes. Hush Puppy bravely makes contact, looking directly back into those wild eyes and whispers, "Sometimes I like you." Such a powerful turning toward what one fears! Then the wild beasts do an amazing thing. They bend their hairy front legs to the earth and bow their heads to this small girl. After this, Hush Puppy's fear leaves her, and she is finally able to accept that her father is dying. She goes back to him and lays her head on his chest. They cry together, finding comfort in the love they have never verbally expressed to one another. Facing her fear, Hush Puppy can now be consoled by her father and release the terrifying fear of loss that has consumed her.

Our fears can act like the savage beasts that pursued Hush Puppy. They will terrorize us with emotional and mental imaginings until we turn around and face them. In turning towards them, we ask, "What is it that scares me so much?" Then we call on our loving source of strength to help us be with what frightens us, whether that fear is named loneliness, depression, vulnerability, illness, failure, dying, joblessness, lack of identity, rejection, loss of faith, or any other thing that frightens our heart and mind. I have learned that when I turn around and look at my fear, it never carries the immense power it first had over me. I might shudder and shake when I acknowledge it, but I also know fear does not have to conquer me unless I allow it to do so. The more I believe in the presence of the Holy One and the possibility of liminality to activate my personal growth, the less influence fear will have over me.[12]

The Necessity of Surrender and Trust

If anyone had to face her fear, it was Mary of Nazareth. When the angelic messenger approached Mary and asked her to consent to being the mother of Jesus, that request moved through her like dense fog on a river. Scripture tells us that Mary "was greatly troubled." We know she was frightened because the messenger offered assurance with the words, "Do not be afraid." How Mary must have struggled with uncertainty, with not knowing what that invitation meant. Although Luke's Gospel presents this story in a neat package as a onetime event, it seems to me that Mary must have pondered this inner stirring for quite some time before she gave her consent. She searched deep within herself, pondered her life, reviewed her beliefs, and drew on her faith. Only after experiencing this liminality, this threshold of not knowing, did Mary then give her answer: "Yes, may it be done to me according to your word" (Luke 1:26–38). Mary's trust in what she did not yet perceive led her to surrender her desire for control. With faith in the Holy One, she could give her consent to live with the fog that currently kept her from seeing clearly what lay ahead of her.

I have come to believe what the mystic Andrew Harvey asserts as essential for a truer and fuller relationship with the Holy One: "The great secret of the mystic life is trust absolute. If you trust absolutely, you will always be receptive enough to the signals that life and God and yourself—your deep self—will be giving you."[13] Harvey bases his insights on the poetry of Jalaluddin Rumi, from whom he derives essential wisdom for spiritual growth. Harvey writes,

> If you want transformation in God, surrender and you will be given all the
> information necessary and all the insights in their right time, but there can

never be complete understanding. That desire to understand is the ego's desire to control; to imperialize the highest kind of knowledge for its own ends. That desire to understand is the ego's desperate attempt to pretend that it is doing the initiation.... Many seekers on the Path really think they know the Divine Truth and it is just this concept that traps them and stifles their growth.... God is always transcending any concept that we can have of God.[14]

Ah, yes, that pesky ego. We cannot live without our ego, our consciousness, but we also cannot let this ego rule and take over our ability to be open to what is yet to be revealed and to what must be left behind. Cynthia Bourgeault refers to the image of an acorn when she teaches the necessity of surrendering to the don't-know dimension of our spiritual growth:

This "I" whom I take to be myself, this individual who moves about on the planet making choices and doing her thing, is not who I am at all. It's only the acorn. Coiled within this acorn is a vastly more majestic destiny and a true self who lives in it. But this oak tree of myself can come into being only if it lets go of its acorn.[15]

Mary of Nazareth's faith was large enough to lead her to trust in the great surrender asked of her. Little did she know at the time of her initial assent that the beloved child of her womb would become the teacher who insisted that none of us can grow spiritually unless we become like the seed falling into the ground and dying in order for new growth to emerge (John 12:24–25). And, of course, Mary could not perceive that this same child of her womb would experience the enormous liminality of the darkened tomb before being raised to new life.

Maintaining our trust in the unseen presence of the Holy One requires constancy in prayer. When Jonah reviewed his days in the dark world of uncertainty, he recalled his desperate plea: "Out of my distress I called to the Lord, and he answered me; From the womb of Sheol I cried for help, and you heard my voice" (Jonah 2:3). Our prayer in foggy, disconcerting times will contain our own pleas and cries for release. Whatever words or silence we choose, it is the intentionality of our heart that counts. We choose to maintain contact with our faithful companion, be it ever so unsatisfying.

Sometimes the most helpful prayer during extended liminal periods consists of rituals to keep us from collapsing into despair. Finding images or symbols that carry messages of hope and creating some gesture of expression, some significant movement, can keep us trusting that we will eventually grow beyond the darkness and immobility of our spiritual stalemate. Rituals such as planting a seed and tending its growth, lighting a candle every day as a reminder of the inner light, selecting an outdoor tree and observing it through the seasons of the year, holding a cross to remember the liminal experience of the crucified one, opening our hands to receive the Eucharist like a vulnerable baby bird needing to receive nourishment, gazing upon an empty seed pod when trying to find the courage to let go—any meaningful ritual—can serve to sustain our hope during difficult transitions.[16]

Spiritual Transformation

I value the transformative process of spiritual growth. When I find myself on the threshold of uncertainty, I am conscious of how much my past experiences of transition stretched me beyond ego satisfaction to a humbler and ever richer life based on gratitude and compassion. Being in the place of not knowing where the mental and emotional tone of prayer slips into gray monotony or sharp agony does not seem like the place anyone would want to be. We do not have to like this place of growth, but we do need to go through it if we are to become more fully one with the divine one.

In liminal times, we cannot see ahead, do not know for sure where we are going, and cannot force or make clarity happen. Nor can we push our way into a more complete union with the Holy One. We simply have to go with a thread of hope that something positive and valuable will come out of the fog that engulfs us. James Finley, author of *Christian Meditation*, quotes from the *Cloud of Unknowing* as he reflects on how to be in relationship with the source of love when we are in a state of not knowing:

> If you ask me precisely how one is to go about doing the contemplative work of love, I am at a complete loss. All I can say is I pray that Almighty God in [God's] great goodness and kindness will teach you.... For in all honesty I must admit I do not know. And no wonder, for it is a divine activity and God will do it in whomever [God] chooses.

Finley then continues with his own reflection:

> To hear this great mystic admit he did not know gave me permission to admit I did not know. More significantly still, his humble admission helped me to begin to understand that I was being led by God along a path in which I had to be willing not to understand, on my own terms, what was happening to me. Nor could I know just where my self-metamorphosing path would end. For how could my finite mind understand the infinite ways of God into which I was being led?[17]

A time does not come when we can definitely say, "Liminality won't happen again for me." In his metaphor of the hero passing through the night sea journey into a new state of being where he comes to eventually know his mission and true endeavor, Joseph Campbell describes the hero crossing several thresholds before discovering what lies on the path he is to take.[18]

Our thresholds and times of not knowing continue periodically throughout our lifetimes. The last transition of our earthly life may well bring with it a phase where we once again find ourselves on the threshold of not knowing. I recall standing at the bedside of one of our holiest community members as she lay dying. I was in my early thirties. It never occurred to me that her connection to the divine might be in flux. How startling to hear her speak about the bleakness she felt. She begged us to pray for and with her because her union with the Holy One seemed to have turned to stone. She who at one time felt a deep bond now experienced a vast chasm between herself and her beloved.

Kathleen Dowling Singh comments on this kind of liminality in *The Grace of Dying:* "The mental suffering of terminal illness is a crucible of transformation. It is here that the imagined walls of our separateness begin to crack. Both Eastern and Western wisdom traditions recognize that *the deepest reason we are afraid of death is that we do not know who we are.*"[19] Even in our final stage of life, we are still being encouraged to grow, still discovering further regions of our own being, as well as the measureless expanse of the Holy One.

WAITING FOR THE FOG TO LIFT

Our relationship with the Holy One, if it is healthy, involves much more than seeking to maintain a comfortable, satisfying consolation. If we are willing to be with the natural flow of spiritual growth then we will be gracious and open when the cloud of uncertainty arrives on the doorsill of our prayer. We will learn how much patience and attentiveness we need to have. We will keep opening our mind and heart to the beloved's call to stretch toward more than we now believe ourselves to be.

Fog rarely lifts instantly. We do not zoom quickly through the liminal effects of significant transitions. If we watch fog closely, we observe a gradual shift from the nonvisible to the visible. If, however we close our eyes, deny, avoid, or run from inner cloudiness, we may not realize the fog is dissipating. If we lack quiet and deliberate spaces of silence, the move from not knowing to knowing will seem to take much longer because of our nonawareness.

The day I sat in the fog, it took almost three hours for it to slip aside and reveal nature's treasures. Just like my inner life during transitions, I thought the air ought to clear quickly. Instead, the fog enveloped everything more fully. There was absolutely nothing I could do to hurry the thick cloud of white away. Similarly, there is nothing that will chase the bleakness of spiritual angst out of our spirit.

One day when we have spent sufficient time on the threshold of not knowing, we will step across that boundary of uncertainty and rejoice in what awaits us. Until then, we wrap our faith around the love of the Holy One and stand on the threshold of ambiguity with confidence in what is yet to be revealed.

1. Stephen Levine, *Healing into Life and Death* (New York: Doubleday, 1987), 39–40.
2. Joyce Rupp, *Open the Door* (Notre Dame, IN: Sorin, 2008), 92–94, 97–99.
3. Adyashanti, *Falling into Grace* (Louisville, CO: Sounds True, 2011), 88–89.
4. Scripture quotations are taken from the *New American Bible.*
5. Parker J. Palmer, *An Undivided Life* (Louisville, CO: Sounds True, 2009), compact discs.
6. Joseph Campbell, *The Hero with A Thousand Faces* (Princeton, NJ: Princeton University Press, 1949), 79.
7. Betty DeShong Meador, *Uncursing the Dark: Treasures from the Underworld* (Wilmette, Ill.: Chiron, 1992), 17–31.
8. Gerald May, *The Dark Night of the Soul* (San Francisco: HarperSanFrancisco, 2004), 1.
9. Lawrence Kushner, *Eyes Remade for Wonder* (Woodstock, VT: Jewish Lights, 1998), 25.
10. Wendell Berry, *This Day* (Berkeley, CA: Counterpoint, 2013), 7.
11. Pema Chödrön, *Comfortable with Uncertainty* (Boston: Shambhala, 2008), 47.
12. Joyce Rupp, *Little Pieces of Light* (New York: Paulist, 1994), 19–28.
13. Andrew Harvey, *The Way of Passion* (Berkeley, CA: North Atlantic, 1994), 146.
14. Harvey, *The Way of Passion*, 48.
15. Cynthia Bourgeault, *The Wisdom Way of Knowing: Reclaiming an Ancient Tradition to Awaken the Heart* (San Francisco: Jossey–Bass, 2003), 65–66.
16. Joyce Rupp, *Praying Our Goodbyes* (Notre Dame, IN: Ave Maria, 1988), 87.
17. James Finley, *Christian Meditation* (San Francisco: HarperSanFrancisco, 2004), 134.
18. Campbell, 77–89.
19. Kathleen D. Singh, *The Grace of Dying: How We Are Transformed Spiritually As We Are Dying* (New York: HarperOne, 2000), 104.

CHAPTER 29

Losing Thomas…Finding God:
Praying with Our Sacred Struggles

~ Mary Beth Werdel ~

While many of us avoid extreme trauma, stress and the challenges of a life lived fully are universal experiences. Every one of us will experience some level of stress in life: illnesses, separation, divorce, loss of a job, the sudden absence of a support system, death of a loved one. When this happens, trauma and stress can come with a number of expected and obvious negative psychological and physical consequences, such as increased anxiety, the onset of depression, unexpected social isolation, decreased physical health, and even death.

Yet even though stress and trauma are fundamentally negative, recent psychological research provides evidence of the paradoxical result of enduring stress that echoes the longstanding claims of the literature on the spirituality of suffering. By living through experiences of loss and pain, *sometimes* a person may discover a piece within the self (such as, "I realize I am stronger than I thought"), a perspective of others ("I value my time with my family more deeply"), or an understanding of God ("I have a deeper more mature relationship with the Lord") that turns out to be intrinsically positive. In psychology, now highlighting what various religious traditions have long before suggested, we realize that suffering does not have the final word. Rather, through prayer and self-reflection, what we may discover as we move through the experience of suffering is something truly sacred. I know this has certainly been true in my own life.

Losing Thomas…Finding God

For all of us, life is full of small epiphanies—brief awakenings to the presence of God that signify meaning and hope. These entryways to the sacred may be something as simple as a conversation with a child, recovery from illness, or the gentle embrace of a close friend. But as some of us can attest, epiphanies can, and do, come in large ways, as well.

Roughly twenty years ago, I received a phone call that my youngest brother, seventeen years old at the time, had disappeared. Thomas, my brother, was participating in a group glacier expedition in Alaska. I was told that he had broken into a small group with two other young men. They had completed a strenuous eight-hour hike, one of many over the previous twenty-nine days that had taken place on a glacier. The group was tired, thirsty, and in need of setting up camp and cooking dinner. This was to be their last night on the glacier before group members were to return to their respective homes. Thomas offered to collect water while the other two young men set up tents. Thomas removed his hiking pack, picked up two tin buckets, and walked off in search of water. He was never to be seen again.

One bucket was recovered near a drainage hole in the glacier known as a crevasse. It is believed that, while attempting to fill one bucket from a small stream of water near the top of the crevasse, Thomas slipped, falling thousands of feet into the interior of the glacier. Many attempts were made to recover his body. All proved unsuccessful. Faced with a reality too far removed from what I had previously constructed as real, into the depths of the crevasse, too, fell my understanding of life.

I remember traveling to Alaska, each family member coming from different parts of the United States at different times within a twenty-four hour period. I left when there was still hope that Thomas would be found. My eldest brother left at a time when hope was slipping away. My mother, my father, another brother, and my sister boarded a plane to Alaska when prayers of remaining hope turned to prayers for the remains of the dead. It was upon word of this reality, in a field outside the base camp of the glacier expedition, that I literally fell to my knees. I placed my head in my hands. For the first time in my life, I felt completely empty. I see now how for the first time in my life, I felt like I had an honest prayer to pray: "God, please greet Thomas in heaven."

I remember, too, traveling home from Alaska. My sister and I had been given the task of carrying Thomas's hiking pack back home. For purposes of the plane, the pack was placed in a large black bag. The pack was heavy, weighing around fifty pounds. It took the strength of both my sister and I together to move the pack across the Anchorage airport. Perhaps because of the shape of the bag or the color or the weight or for the reason that the bag possessed all that was materially left of Thomas, I felt as if I was carrying my brother's body. I carried this image in my heart, returning home. I read the journal he kept while on the glacier, my one-way conversation with him from the grave. I looked through the pictures from the film that was developed, trying to piece together images of his final days. Each step I took with his bag brought the weight of his loss. As I read each page of his journal, as I flipped through each picture from his trip, I felt myself losing more and more of my belief in a comprehensible world.

With Thomas's body never recovered, my spirituality risked the same disappearance. I questioned everything around my brother's death, from the possibility of Thomas still being alive to the possibility of him never really having existed. I asked the same spectrum of questions about the reality of God: "Is God still alive?" "Did he ever really exist?" Spiritually, I see how I was broken. I was encountering God at this time in a very raw way. No more time for politely dialing some metaphorical prayer phone, the way I learned to talk to God in grammar school and was still using in my life as a young adult at that point. In the wake of Thomas's death, out of a type of necessity, I learned to encounter God each second of the day. We had conversations nearly every instant of the day on nearly every subject. Nothing was too big or too small to bring to God. While I was not aware of it at the time, I see now how it was at this point in my life that I began to truly own my spiritual identity. I took God out of the box I had previously placed him in and began to encounter him everywhere. For how else could I come to truly comprehend the incomprehensible event of my brother's death but enveloped in the embrace of God?

Without restricting encounters with God to formal prayer, I see how I started to encounter God in many places. I did not purposefully attempt to reconstruct my spirituality. Yet, upon reflection, I see all this was happening. The God of my child-hood had died with Thomas. I began the process of experiencing and deepening my relationship with the sacred as my young-adult self. While the death of my brother still is the most painful loss of my life, enduring the experience, moving through the experience, has allowed me to experience profound growth. Such growth I would characterize as *nothing less than sacred*. Yet, experiences like this not only leave us with a potential portal to a greater relationship with God and life, they also leave us with some questions and an opportunity to examine our openness to the holy and what this might offer. For instance,

- Why is it that some people experience growth after stress and trauma and others do not?
- Why do some people find deeper relationships with God after stress and trauma, and why do others lose God and faith completely?
- How does one who has a faith find an accessible God in times of stress? How does one locate the sacred in struggle?

Three Understandings Worth Noting

From my work as a faculty member in the pastoral care and counseling areas as a researcher on the intersection of spirituality and stress, in my clinical work as a licensed mental health therapist working with abused and neglected children, as well as through my journeys to Central America, primarily Honduras, and from my own personal experiences as a woman, mother, and person journeying in faith, I have noted three understandings. These have helped me to frame life in a way that I believe allows not only me, but persons in general, to engage God in times of struggle and to experience moments of close connection to the sacred, leading to an embrace of both God-given grace and growth. These three understandings are

1. Whether we realize it or not, we are each telling a story with our life.
2. We belong to each other.
3. We need to nurture our relationship with God in the small struggles, or we will miss an opportunity to engage God in the big struggles.

By incorporating such understandings into one's prayerful meditations when negative events happen in a person's life, I believe we may be more likely to find the connections to the sacred that we seek or need.

To begin, in reflection upon experiences with stress in my life and in others' lives, I have noted that some people hold a belief that they are telling a story with their lives and others simply do not. Yet a vital Christian faith is told in stories. Given this, one might assume that if one has a faith life, there is a natural inclination to see one's life as a story being told and so reap the positive consequences when stress presents itself. However, this is certainly not what I have found to be true, and an experience made this idea especially clear to me.

I was giving a presentation at a minister's retreat that focused on the topic "Telling Your Faith Story." The participants of the retreat were predominately parishioners from one local parish who had volunteered for the various ministries over the year as catechists, lectors, Eucharistic ministers, and bereavement ministers. In preparation for the talk, I met with the leaders of the retreat. The major theme of the discussion focused on the idea that in the minds of the retreat leaders, from their experience, most persons in volunteer ministry did not believe they had a faith story. I listened empathically and indicated I would prepare a talk accordingly. However, at some level, I must confess that I doubted that this could be true. While cognizant that I was asked to present on the topic because of my own faith story and not naïve enough to think everyone in the pew who claims a faith holds a belief that they have a faith story, I thought everyone who was actively ministering to the parish community on some level believed they were living out a story of their faith.

Rather than take either extreme of the idea (everyone would claim a faith story; no one frames their life as having a faith story) as truth, at the start of my presentation I began with a question: How many people believe they have a faith story? Of the fifty people present, only five raised their hands. I was astounded.

Curious, I asked follow-up questions. How do you know you do not have a faith story? What makes you feel you do not have a faith story? Is it because you do not have an aha moment? No angelic choir singing at the second of recognition that you are a beloved child of God? Do other people's stories feel "bigger" or louder? Or, is it that the type of self-reflection that is necessary to process a faith story is an odd or foreign concept?

To some degree, it seems that the answer to all of the aforementioned questions was yes. However, the most disconcerting feedback I received, echoed by almost everyone I spoke to was this: People did not believe they had a faith story because they did not experience major trauma in their lives. No violent deaths, no cancer scares, no injured or dead children, no domestic abuse, no parental divorce. People seemed to equate the presence of a major life struggle with having a faith story. If there was no big struggle, no massive pain, one had no faith story to tell. People were focusing on a major negative life event as testimony of the presence of faith. After I understood the general sense of what people were thinking, I offered a perspective: If you feel as though you have had no big struggles in your life, say a prayer of thanksgiving to God...and wait.

The participants and I shared chuckle. In part, the idea of waiting was a joke. It was a way to release anxiety in the room that was building over people's fears that they lacked something significant (a faith story) and their self-judgment proceeded from this belief affecting their spiritual outlook. This of course was the exact opposite of the intention of the retreat. However, in part, the perspective that I offered them was not a joke but meant as a wake-up call—one all of us need at times.

By suggesting that we wait for what might come to a person in life, my intention was to suggest two ideas. First, we do not need to go looking for struggle. The reality is that we all experience struggle. We all experience stress. Some of us intentionally carve space in our prayer lives for reflection on the stress present in our lives and the ways that God is speaking to us in the process of living through the space. Second, perhaps the most useful stance to take if we seek a deep relationship with God is to intentionally be in the present moment with a perspective of gratitude. Gratitude makes an optimist out of a pessimist. It gives us eyes and ears to see and hear the blessings that are born from brokenness.

In his book *What Doesn't Kill Us: The New Psychology of Posttraumatic Growth*, psychologist Stephen Joseph writes about growing after times of stress and trauma. He suggests the idea of stress and trauma as breaking a mirror into hundreds of small pieces that can never be restored to the original mirror again. Growth, he suggests, is being able to take the broken pieces and create a new mosaic. The mirror shattering is negative. The mosaic, born from the negative, is beautiful and positive. The same can be said with our relationship with God and a deepening of our faith.

A sense of optimism (or what as persons of faith we might refer to as trust in God) helps a person see the broken glass as something useful to the creation process. A sense of gratitude helps a person honor the Creator who gave them eyes to see.

In considering the retreat again, I recognized that I was asked to share about the experience of the death of my brother. I was asked to highlight a major negative life event. However, for myself, the important piece that I have come to recognize as essential is actually not related to having a negative life experience and reflecting on it. It is not that I have broken glass to build a mosaic. Rather the key piece for me and everyone else encountering life's challenges is that we need to envision our life as a story in which we are engaging a God who engaged us first. If not for this piece, building from my broken glass may be beautiful, but it may not become sacred. The key to a faith story is not the bad turned good; the key to a faith story is the encounters with God that are recognized and honored as part of facing life's challenges.

And so, the idea of framing our life as a story being told can be essential as we pray because it helps us to live in a more immediate space. Whatever the experience, good or bad, when it is presented in the immediate, it can also be acknowledged for its temporariness. When life is honored in the immediate space, relationship and gratitude are more naturally invited into prayer. Additionally, the idea of framing life as a story that we are telling helps us to honor the responsibility that our actions have. As Gandhi simply and powerfully proclaimed, "My life is my message." The same can be said of us when we don't divorce our beliefs from our actions.

When we begin to see life as a story, a good way to begin to create more space in our prayer life can be by considering a number of questions. In periods of silence, and possibly solitude, we can gently ask ourselves:

- How am I telling the story of my life?
- In doing this, what type of story am I telling?
- Who am I telling it to?
- How do I experience God in my story?
- Where do I hear God?
- Where do I see God?
- In what chapters or experiences in my life does God feel close to me?
- In what chapters or experiences in my life does God feel far from me?
- What would the title of my story be at this moment?
- What message am I sharing with others?

Times of quiet meditation and prayer, seeing oneself gently but honestly, can illuminate how close or far we feel we are from living a message of divine mystery. When we consider that we are telling, in active tense, the story of our lives, the focus moves from product (I am a Catholic; I prayed) to process, (I am living a Catholic life in this moment; I am praying in this moment). Our perspective shifts from future to the immediate. We stop waiting for grand revelation in the days ahead or only scrutinizing the past for signs and signals of what could have been present. Instead, we are becoming ourselves in the moment. Rather than waiting for God, we are actually opening ourselves in daily life to experience the Spirit. And so, we are not merely waiting for faith to show itself in new ways. We are experiencing faith in the common and profound. We are embracing the reality that faith, like struggle, demands immediacy. In this sense, we are persons on a pilgrimage. We are living our relationship with God.

When we are ever journeying in this way, we can experience the movement of life in more dynamic ways. We are not static or still—even if it feels this way at times. In this light, we seek to frame our experiences of loss and judgment in a softer voice that includes forgiveness and relationship. This can then allow some of the suffering normally associated with the pain to lessen. Also, in a similar vein, we can frame experiences of joy, surprise, excitement, in a voice that includes gratitude and communion. When this occurs, it can enhance our pleasant experiences.

In my own experience, it is when I noted my life as a story unfolding that I was able to tap into a sense of mystery around me because I had first tapped into the mystery within me and within the story of me that God and I were writing together. This sense of mystery within and around is nothing less than the true spiritual self, designed, called, and created by God to be in relationship with him. As Brennan Manning has suggested, you should "define yourself radically as one beloved by God. This is the true self; every other identity is illusion."[1]

We Belong to Each Other

The second belief that I have noted as integral to being able to find the sacred in times of stress is the understanding that we belong to each other. We do not merely exist near each other. We are by God's design relational beings. We are born in relationship, we die in relationship, we are hurt in relationship, and we are healed in relationship. We grow in relationships. We become our true self in relationships. We are, simply put, deeply connected with each other.

When we consider we are telling the story of our life, the idea of being deeply related to each other follows logically. Our stories are not monologues. They are a series of dialogues with our parents, friends, children and communities. Perhaps most deeply and honestly, they are a series of dialogues with God. We need each other to tell the story of our lives. By this I mean we need each other to enrich and deepen our stories. We need each other to comprehend and make sense of our stories. We need people to help us understand more deeply the story we are telling.

This is why separation is so challenging and why death is usually experienced as such a loss. We must confront and consider a painful question: "How am I to become me without you?" I certainly faced this question when my brother Thomas died. I also felt I needed to address the questions

- Why do bad things happen to good people?
- Why do young people die?
- How can there be suffering if God is all-powerful and all loving?

In stress and trauma work, psychologists and counselors talk about what they refer to as "cognitive processing." This is an approach to understanding how we think and feel about an event. Sometimes we can process information out loud, in telling our stories to another who can help us identify thoughts and feelings that we are not aware of or that are irrational. It is through cognitive processing that we can uncover, discover, and create new meaning. Sometimes we may do this alone though mental reflection, journal writing, or through conversation with God in prayer. When we take a more universal, communal perspective of our lives and of life by doing this, we see the call, the true invitation, to a life of encounter with both God and ourselves amidst life's struggles, and joys can be nothing less than sacred. What a gift to us...*if* it is opened this way.

In my own case, in times of suffering when I sought in prayer a loud, clear, articulate answer to questions, I struggled to hear God's voice. During this time, I noticed that when in prayer I sought relationship with God in each instance, I felt comfort. I could feel my prayer life dramatically altering in such instances. With such an experience as a beacon toward what would truly make my encounter with the divine real and compelling, I stopped looking for the one right answer to the infinite existential questions that I carried in my heart and mind. Instead, I started seeking relationship with God in prayer in all ways. When this happened, I started to realize how deeply we belong to each other and to God. I started to realize how it is the grace of deepening our relationships—including *the* relationship—not answers, that heals.

This idea of relationship as an essential piece to healing, and growth feels particularly true when I consider raising my oldest son, Peter, who has developmental concerns centered on sensory integration, social relationships, and speech. In a reflection on my relationship with him, I wrote an article published in *America* entitled "Raising Peter."[2] Its central thesis was that God is present to us in relationship, especially the close, possibly initially puzzling, or in some way challenging ones. I suggested this by sharing how a phrase that Peter uttered in church helped me to reconsider the entire way I had been framing church. An example of this is when Peter shared with me in church that he wanted to "blow out people prayers," a phrase that spoke to me by rattling in my mind and heart for a long time. What I came to realize and still encounter in raising Peter is that he has and continues to blow out my prayers of normalcy and replace them with prayers of relationship. He erased the idea of disability and replaced it with the idea of openness. He expunged the idea of inclusion versus exclusion and imprinted the idea of communion. By being present in a relationship with Peter and allowing his relationship with me to enter into my prayer life, I found myself growing in awareness, in communion, and in love.

Once the article was published, I received e-mails from many people: parents who had similar stories to mine in the experience of raising children; academics and clergy who shared their experiences of loved ones in their lives who had difficulties in accepting them for their disabilities. Almost unfailingly, the emails expressed gratitude for the words that resonated with them, that helped them find a new or renewed sense of understanding. The experience of writing about my son was powerful for me. It helped me to process raising him, helped me to become a better mother and more open person. In addition, the experience of other's reading my words, and being moved by them helped me understand even more deeply the idea that we require each other's stories to become whole. I realized once again that my life is intensely personal, but it is also deeply universal when it is shared and received in the right light.

The idea that we belong to each other is in line with Mark 4:21: "Is a lamp brought in to be put under the bushel basket, or under the bed, and not on the lampstand?" (NRSV)

Our stories, our lives, are communal. We were designed to share ourselves. We belong to each other by God's design. So then, just as parents have a responsibly to be in relationship to raise their children, we have a responsibility to help others see how they are also beloved sons and daughters. This is right not only at times of struggle, but in times of struggle this idea is particularly true. As I wrote in *As Faith Matures: Beyond the Sunday God*,

> Living a spiritual life, we dare to consider questions that the secular world may not necessarily encourage or support. And we come to live those answers with our very lives. Why would you volunteer at a soup kitchen on a Friday night, not make much money working for social-justice-minded

volunteer programs, not sleep in on Sunday mornings? Why would you? In my own life, and through meeting the lives of others in various walks of life, I have noticed that they would just as well not, if not for the fact they can't "not." When you see a hungry person, you can close your eyes and they are forgotten; when you come to see, on any level, that hungry person is connected to your sense of freedom, you no longer have your own eyes to close. Now you share them.

Nurturing God in the Small and the Big

I can never answer with personal certitude what my faith life would be like without the death of my brother. Would I have remained engaged with a childlike image of God? Would my God image have ever matured?

I do, however, recognize that my relationship with God and the sacred existed before the death of my brother. My mother had helped me to create and nurture a relationship with God long before I even had a younger brother. As I matured, I slowly started to claim my own relationship with God through engaging God in the small stresses in life: middle school and high school friendships, college applications, romantic relationships, moving, career plans. To some degree, I engaged God in each of these minor stresses. To some degree, I also felt the presence and the absence of God. I recognize now that we can certainly experience struggle and not grow. We can also grow but miss an opportunity to deepen further a relationship with the sacred.

For example, I am reminded of a neighbor and a friend of mine. We lived near each other in the same small town. Our oldest children played together and attended the same school. Our children went to the same birthday parties and music classes. We went to the same doctors and dentist. So when we discovered we were both pregnant with our second child and due at the same time, it was exciting. We were ships passing in the night at the hospital as I went home with my new baby boy, and she arrived to birth her new baby girl. When she returned home we exchanged our admiration for each other's new little blessings. It was a time of little sleep but great joy. Within a few weeks, however, my friend had to confront a serious health concern of her child. It took many months to confirm a debilitating and life-altering diagnosis. Her assumptions about how the world is supposed to work and how life is supposed to be were shattered. The map that she was following told her the direction of her life seemed to be worthless. She was scared. She was tired. She was angry. She was lost.

She told me that when she had learned the news that she went to talk to a rabbi as she struggled to find justice in the diagnosis and in the world. She shared that she didn't worship except on major Jewish holidays and had no prayer life to speak of;

however, she knew nowhere else to turn. For some reason at that point, speaking with a religious leader somehow felt right.

The diagnosis of a child's health condition is certainly a major life stress. It calls into question the basic assumption most of us live with: young people aren't supposed to get sick or die. And so, turning to God with the question of why children are born sick and seeking religious guidance at such a time felt natural to her. Yet as quickly as she sought God's presence and voice, she seemed to turn away from it. The medical diagnosis certainly changed her perspective of life. However, it did not change her relationship with God.

If we are to engage God in the big life stressors, it is a wonderful help if we have a faith life before the life stressor exists. The work of God is slow and reveals itself over time. My experience is that it doesn't happen in grand encounters, even though I am grateful to have had them. To feel God's embrace in the big stress, we need to know what being held like that feels like first. In essence, it is imperative to find God everywhere in the day-to-day if we are to find him anywhere in major stress, which is my central message; namely, we need not wait for great spiritual tragedy to experience great spiritual growth. For even the large epiphanies risk being missed if we do not learn to foster the small ones. And we cannot foster spiritual encounter even the small ones if we do not find a way to orient our days to God in prayer. As Mother Teresa so wisely preached: "Be faithful in the small things because it is in them that your strength lies."

CONCLUSION

In *A Farewell to Arms*, Ernest Hemingway wrote, "You learn a few things as you go along and one of them is the world breaks everyone and many are strong in those broken places."[3]

As was noted in the beginning of this reflection, psychological research has now documented the need we have to make sense of stress and trauma. For some, the sense that is made includes new experiences of the self, others, and their relationship with a God that allows a person to grow stronger in the broken places. An important caveat to keep in mind though that could too easily go overlooked is that the struggle alone is not that which is sacred. The sacred is the God who lives within and among us during our challenges and sadness. Make no mistake about it: stress and trauma are intrinsically negative; they can have devastating effects on our psychological and physical well-being. However, when we can remain in conversation with God through the struggles all of us must face at times, some of the results of such encounters can have unequivocally positive and deeply sacred elements to them.

In addition, struggle can feel deeply isolating. My point here is that maintaining an active prayer life may help to frame our lives to the three understandings that we are telling a story with our lives, we belong to each other, and that we need to nurture God in all things, big and small. Specifically, such church and communal prayer experiences can have a timely positive impact by

1. aiding to decrease our sense of psychological and physical isolation,

2. helping us frame our life in a way that allows for gratitude so we can appreciate the little things as supports while we face the big challenges, and

3. encouraging us to discover new strength to both endure suffering while maintaining a hope that will increase the possibility of the development of new meaning.

Stress and trauma often cause multiple losses. We feel as though so much has been taken away from us during a crisis. Yet a loving God image need not be one. What is necessary to prevent this is a maturing and nurturing of our prayer life so that the God who loves us, who holds us, who weeps with us, who dies with us on his cross, can be accessible in our life from the very first breath we take to the very last and all the many we are gifted in between each day.

Allowing our wounds to break us open so we can be filled with the messages and mysteries of God's love and connection is a true way of transformation where our struggles can become sacred. This is the way that life's down moments become conversations with God, palpable and accessible at every moment.

Relationship with God and openness as a way of being in the world hold our hope that the suffering experienced in struggle not hold the final word, that through prayer and reflection our suffering can be redemptive in part by deepening our relationship with our self, with others, and with God. Such growth begins when we gently begin to notice ourselves in this world, draw our attention inwards to our thoughts and feelings, make sense of them, and share the story of us with others, including, and especially, God.

When we do this, we discover that all of our selves, not simply pieces, are beloved by God. All of our joys and all of our sadness, as well as all of our strengths and all of our weaknesses, in essence, *all* that feels blessed and all that feels broken holds the possibility of a way to grow in love and faith and so unearth the sacred in our struggle.

---

1. Brennan Manning, *Abba's Child: The Cry of the Heart for Intimate Belonging* (Carol Stream, IL: NavPress, 2002), 44.

2. M. B. Werdel, "Raising Peter: What My Son Taught Me About My Faith," *America*, February 23, 2015.

3. Ernest Hemingway, *A Farewell to Arms* (New York: Scribners, 1995), 315.

PART SIX

Praying with the Old Testament

PRAYING WITH THE PSALMS

PRAYING WITH JOB

A PLACE FOR PRAYER: SOLOMON'S PRAYER AT THE
DEDICATION OF THE TEMPLE (1 KINGS 8)

Praying with the Old Testament is a natural part of a rich prayer life. In this section, three chapters illustrate this. The first of them is one that should be expected in a book on prayer for Catholics: Praying with the Psalms. In this reflective piece, Maribeth Howell reminds us that in the Psalter "we find prayers that speak of despair (perhaps none so poignantly as Psalm 88), hope, longing, trust, anger, frustration, and resentment...[and] that they bring every human feeling before God." She also points out that in reflecting on the psalms we must recognize that they are prayers and poems that can evoke emotions in us, and, of course, songs as well. Following this, Howell provides helpful information on how the psalms can be used in such private and communal prayer as praise, lament, thanksgiving, and trust or confidence. She closes by offering suggestions on praying the psalms (Liturgy of the Hours, Christian Prayer, and *lectio divina*). This chapter, indeed, encourages us to more deeply appreciate how we, in Howell's words, "might pray with these outpourings of our ancestors in faith."

In the second offering, Praying with Job, Dianne Bergant breaks open in a scholarly and intriguing way a story all of us are familiar with but are now given a greater sense of. Only someone with both extensive scriptural and pastoral wisdom could accomplish this on our behalf. We see Job shift in his way of prayer as his dilemma develops in the story. Beyond that, we also are able to remove our distance from him and see how, in Bergant's words, the "four examples of Job's prayers mirror ways we pray as well."

The third and final chapter is designed to encourage us to see once again how wonderfully relevant the Old Testament is for us as Catholics to read, pray over, and examine further commentaries so as to increase our depth of knowledge, so essential to our faith and spiritual life. Leslie Hoppe's A Place for Prayer: Solomon's Prayer at the Dedication of the Temple (1 Kings 8) shows how this passage can come alive in amazing ways. We can begin to appreciate the background, paradox, and import of this event not simply for the people of the day but how and why, in Hoppe's words, "Believers today can embrace the values affirmed in Solomon's prayer." In this chapter, we begin to see, in particular, that even when "institutions die, prayer still offers a pathway to God. When all else fails, there is prayer—and that is enough." This is an important message for us to know more about and embrace, especially in contemporary society when so much of what we may have depended upon is under such (probably needed) question today.

CHAPTER 30

Praying with the Psalms

~ *Maribeth Howell, OP* ~

What can be said about praying the psalms that has not already been said? With that question in mind, we begin this essay. What follows is not likely to be terribly original. After all, these texts have been prayed by Christians of every imaginable denomination for well over two millennia and by Jews for hundreds of years before that! And the material written on the psalms within the past thirty years alone is enough to fill a small library. What you will find in these pages is the offering of a Dominican sister who loves the psalms, who has prayed them, studied them, translated them, and taught them in a variety of settings for several decades.[1]

INTRODUCTION AND THREE POINTS TO KEEP IN MIND

The 150 prayers that make up the Psalter are extremely varied in tone. They are expressions of the human heart that cover every imaginable emotion, from pure delight to utter despair, and possibly every other feeling that the human heart and soul has experienced. It may come as a surprise to readers that expressions of delight open and close this book of prayers. The very first Hebrew word of Psalm 1 is *'ashrei*, a word that is most often translated "happy"; the final word of the Psalter, which appears at the close of Psalm 150 is a word that needs no translation, *halleluia!* Thus, it does indeed seem fitting that the Hebrew title of this book is *Sefer Tehillim*, "Book of Praises." Between the opening and closing words of the Psalter we find prayers that speak of despair (perhaps none so poignantly as Psalm 88), hope, longing, trust, anger, frustration, and resentment.[2]

It would seem that this vast array of feelings brought directly to God by our early ancestors in faith is what has made these prayers so appealing to countless generations of women and men who recognize that their lives too are intimately entwined with their Creator. If we take the time to engage with the Psalter, we will discover that everything is placed before God in these prayers. Nothing is held back. Nothing. No thing is too good or too evil, too weighty or too trivial that it is unworthy of being brought to God's attention by the psalmists. The psalms teach us that our foremothers and forefathers in faith were bold in their prayer, daring to bring to God every aspect of life.[3]

Before considering various ways we might pray the psalms, there are three points that require recognition. First, the psalms are prayers. Second, they are poems. And third, they are songs. It is quite easy to recognize that the psalms are prayers, since in the vast majority of texts God is either called upon directly or we hear the voice of the psalmist inviting others to call upon God for the purpose of either giving praise or requesting help.

The second point of which we need be aware is that the psalms are poems. Poetry, as we know, is language of the heart. It is certainly not necessary that we be scholars of either Hebrew or English poetry to recognize this fact. We know that poetry is emotive and evocative. It both expresses emotion and evokes emotion. Thus, while the psalms express the emotions of the psalmist, they also have the power to elicit from us our own feelings of yearning, hope, trust, anger, and so on. When reading or praying the psalms, we can readily recognize that the psalmists' feelings are anything but hidden. These varied sentiments are expressed in these few examples:

- Why so downcast my soul? Why do you weep? 42:6 (yearning)
- My soul waits quietly for God, who alone is my hope. 62:5–6 (hope)
- My soul is at peace, content as a child in a mother's arms, so is my soul within me. 131:2 (trust or confidence)
- Oh God, I hate them with a perfect hate. 139:21 (anger)
- Why, O Lord, do you stand far off? Why do you hide yourself in times of trouble? 10:1 (NRSV) (frustration)
- The heavens declare the glory of God; the skies proclaim God's handiwork. 19:1 (delight)
- It is you who deprive me of friend and neighbor, my only companion is darkness. 88:18 (despair)

If our hearts are attuned to what we hear in the psalms, something within us will be stirred. Good poetry does that.

Since the psalms are translated poetry, the reader or pray-er will not be able to appreciate all of the poetic characteristics of the texts. Yet every good translation provides us with the ability to appreciate many of the poetic features of these prayers.[4] As observed in the lines cited above, a variety of feelings are expressed quite clearly. Similarly, a careful reader will note the use of metaphors, a figure of speech that suggests that one thing is another (e.g., "Your word is a lamp for my feet," Psalm 119:105, and, "God alone is my rock and my haven," Psalm 62:2). Other poetic devices found frequently in the psalms are word pairs, sets of words that frequently appear together and are often considered an aspect of parallelism (e.g., "The ends of the earth are in awe as morning and evening rejoice in your might," Psalm 65:9, and "The sun shall not strike you by day, nor the moon by night," Psalm 121:6); the repetition of key words or themes (consider the frequent references used in Psalm 139 that speak of God's intimate knowledge of the psalmist: "You search me, you know me, you know when I sit and when I stand, you understand my desires from afar, you observe when I walk and when I rest, you enfold me," Psalm 139); and refrains, lines, and variations of lines that appear at the beginning and end and possibly in other places of a psalm (for example, "O Lord, our God, how great is your name through all the earth!" Psalm 139:1,9), while Psalm 80 provides an example of a varied refrain that appears in four verses, 3, 7, 14, and 19. Each occurrence of the refrain opens with the words "Restore us," followed by a reference to God and a request that the people be saved). While numerous other poetic devices can be found in the psalms, the above mentioned are the most easily identified.

Finally, it is helpful for us to know that the psalms were sung. This should not be difficult for us to grasp. Since the liturgical renewal of the 1960s, countless musicians have composed many memorable melodies to accompany psalms. The popularity of some of these melodies sung regularly during the Sunday eucharistic liturgy has served to familiarize the faithful with psalmody. More will be said about psalms set to music later in this chapter.

TYPES OF PRAYER

As mentioned above, the psalms are prayers that bring every human feeling before God. Since the time of Hermann Gunkel (1862–1932), whose critical approach to the Psalter identified psalms according to their literary forms, types, or, genre, the psalms have been recognized as particular kinds of expressions to God. Essentially, this has led to a greater emphasis on the psalms as different types of prayer. While Gunkel identified five main types of psalms and four smaller and mixed types,[5] these categories have been revised and simplified by any number of scholars, particularly Walter Brueggemann, whose work on the psalms is nothing less than monumental.[6] Since the main purpose of this chapter is to explore ways of praying with the psalms, we will focus upon four primary types of psalms: praise, lament, thanksgiving, and trust or confidence. Let us now take a brief look at the disposition of each of these expressions of prayer. We will then turn to how we might use these psalms in private and communal prayer.

PRAISE

The tone or sentiment of these psalms is that of delight, joy, and happiness. As soon as one begins to read a psalm of praise, one knows the disposition of the psalmist.[7] Historically, psalms of praise have been divided into three categories, with the divisions being a result of their specific focus: (1) God the Creator and Lord of history; (2) celebration of God's earthly dwelling, the holy mountain of Zion/Jerusalem;

and (3) celebration of God's kingship, also referred to as enthronement psalms. Two examples of each form of praise will demonstrate the unique character or focus in these three types of praise.

> Beauty and majesty crown your works;
> everlasting is your faithfulness.
> We remember your holy deeds,
> God of mercy and compassion.
> Psalm 111:3-4 (God as Creator and Lord of history)

> The Lord rebuilds Jerusalem,
> gathers Israel's exiles,
> heals the brokenhearted,
> binds up every wound,
> appoints every star, and calls each one by name.
> Psalm 147:2–4 (God as Creator and Lord of history)

> Mount Zion, summit of the north,
> city of the great king.
> God resides within its walls,
> a sure defense against the foe.
> Psalm 48:2b–3 (in praise of Zion/Jerusalem)

> Pray for the peace of Jerusalem:
> "May those who love you abide in peace.
> May peace be within your walls,
> and may peace abide within your homes."
> Psalm 122:6–7 (in praise of Zion/Jerusalem)

> God reigns over all the earth;
> Let us sing our hymns of praise.
> God rules over every nation
> and sits on the heavenly throne.
> Psalm 47:7–8 (God reigns)

> Strong ruler who loves justice,
> it is you who established what is right,
> who created justice and equity in Israel.
> We exalt you, O Lord, our God, and worship before you,
> for you, O God, are holy.
> Psalm 99:4–5 (God reigns)

These excerpts all demonstrate how the psalmists express praise to God. Some texts do this within the broad context of God as Creator and Lord of history, while other texts refer to God's dwelling within Zion/Jerusalem, and still others declare God as sovereign over all the earth. Regardless of the specificity of these texts, their tone is definitely that of praise.

LAMENT

Psalms identified as laments make up over one-third of the Psalter! Recalling that one of the names for this book is the "book of praises," we might think this statistic remarkable. But let us keep in mind that regardless of the nature or tone of prayer, the fact that the psalmist brings these prayers directly to God is indeed a way of giving God praise. The psalmist is well aware that the only one who can do anything about the current situation is God.

In the laments, the psalmist pours out pain, frustration, sadness, anger, and despair. Within these prayers we recognize that God is often identified as the source and reason for the psalmist's current state. Therefore, God often becomes the target at which the psalmist takes aim. Within these bold prayers, the utter desperation of the psalmist is palpable. A few excerpts will show the extreme anguish that the psalmist is experiencing.

> Turn your ear to me, O Lord;
> consider my cries for help.
> Listen to my pleas,
> my king and my God.
> At dawn you hear my voice;
> at dawn I watch and wait for you. (Psalm 5:1–3)

> Have mercy on me, O God,
> have mercy on me.
> I seek refuge in the shadow of your wings,
> where I am safe through every storm. (Psalm 57:1)

> Restore us again, O God our savior;
> Be pleased with us once more.
> Will your anger never cease?
> Will your anger last forever? (Psalm 85:4–5)

> Be merciful, O God, be merciful;
> we are disgraced.
> Scorned by the vain and the arrogant,
> we can bear no more. (Psalm 123:3–4)

The first two examples are laments of an individual, while the latter two examples are laments of the community. What these psalms have in common is that both individual and communal laments plead for God's compassionate love.

THANKSGIVING

It may be best to think of these psalms as words of an individual or a community who has recently experienced deliverance from some type of tragedy. The relief is recent, and so the psalmist, though rejoicing in God's goodness, remembers well what life had been like prior to deliverance. Often these psalms seem to tell a story. It is as if the psalmist, now on the other side of pain, cannot help but express gratitude for the action of God in his or her life. Once again, we will demonstrate the tone of these psalms with two examples. The first is from an individual psalm of thanksgiving; the second from a communal thanksgiving.

> I praise you, O Lord,
>
> for you have lifted me up
>
> and did not let my enemies rejoice over me.
>
> O Lord, my God,
>
> you heard my cry and healed me.
>
> You delivered me from death,
>
> brought me back from the land of darkness.
>
> Sing to the Lord, all you faithful;
>
> to God's holy name give thanks. (Psalm 30:1–4)

> Had our God not been with us,
>
> declare this, O Israel,
>
> had our God not been with us
>
> when the enemy attacked,
>
> they would have swallowed us alive
>
> as their anger burned against us…
>
> Blessed be God who saved us,
>
> spared us from the wrath of the foe. (Psalm 124:1–3, 6)

TRUST OR CONFIDENCE

We now turn to the fourth and final type of prayer that we have identified, psalms of trust or confidence. This is a small collection of psalms that might easily be overlooked. We have chosen to identify them and lift them up for consideration because we believe that they speak quite beautifully to a season of the soul. This is a season or disposition of contentment. Two examples of such psalms are found below.

I bless my God, who guides me,
who speaks to my heart in the night.
I keep you ever before me;
with you, O God, at my side,
I shall not be moved. (Psalm 16:7–8)

My soul is at peace,
content as a child in a mother's arms,
so is my soul within me.
O Israel, hope in the Lord,
both now and forever. (Psalm 131:2–3)

Having identified four significant types of prayer found within the Psalter—praise, lament, thanksgiving, and trust or confidence—we will now consider some ways in which we might pray these prayers privately and in common.[8]

Suggestions for Praying the Psalms

It may be helpful to recognize that unless one has established the habit of praying the Liturgy of the Hours or has intentionally studied the psalms either privately or within a study group, it is not likely that one will be familiar with much of the Psalter. Still, most churchgoers are likely to have some degree of familiarity with psalms that have been set to music for use as the responsorial psalm within liturgical worship. As a matter of fact, it sometimes comes as a surprise to people when they learn that some of their favorite songs from church are actually adaptions of psalms.

Liturgy of the Hours

When we speak of praying the Liturgy of the Hours or Christian Prayer, it is most important that we keep in mind that even when prayed privately, the nature of this prayer is ecclesial. This is expressed well in the introduction to *Dominican Praise* where it states:

> When Dominicans pray the Liturgy of the Hours, we pray as ecclesial people for the life of the world. This form of prayer is an integral expression of our common life. For this prayer we leave our private places to be in one another's presence. For this prayer we leave our individual devotional styles and preferences to rely on forms and language that we hold in common. For this prayer, our individual needs and concerns are stretched by common purpose and mission. Whether we pray in a large or small community, or in the solitude of our room, we know that *we are a people praying for the whole world....* These prayers help us to praise and to remember our solidarity with

all humanity. As the *Pastoral Constitution on the Church in the Modern World* proclaims: "The joys and hopes, the griefs and anxieties of people of this age, especially those who are poor or in any way afflicted, these too are the joys and hopes, the griefs and anxieties of the followers of Christ."[9]

The Liturgy of the Hours, whose deepest roots are in the synagogue, has a very complex history that we need not explore here.[10] However, it is appropriate that we offer some suggestions as to how we might provide some variety to this prayer. Carmelite Roland E. Murphy has noted that the practice of praying the psalms "choir to choir" or "side to side," a practice found in both Catholic and Protestant traditions, seems to have originated in the monastery.[11] Further, anyone who has had much experience in praying the Hours in this manner, knows that it can be deadly.

Participants will often find the pace too fast or too slow, particularly if the psalms are recited and not chanted. Each community must regularly examine how well they are praying these texts, since the practice of recitation can lead to boredom. Murphy offers a concrete suggestion that would require that the presider plan well and take seriously his or her responsibility of leading the congregation in prayer. Drawing our attention to Psalm 46:10, which reads: "Be still and know that I am God," Murphy writes,

> Such a verse calls for a solo voice, as the structure suggests. It should not be swallowed up by the rush of the opposite side of the choir. It is ironic that the (liturgical) voice of God is dimmed in this and other instances. It is easy to surmise that in Israel's liturgy such key verses were pronounced by one of the Temple personnel in the name of the Lord. So should it be today in the sense that the divine voice is not simply to be bandied back and forth by the choir. This destroys the power in such psalms as 50:5, 16; 81:7; 82:2, 6; 91:14; 95:8. In other instances a solo voice is appropriate even when it does not represent a divinity, especially where a leader seems to be giving instructions to a group (e.g. Ps. 33:1–3). In some instances, the possibilities of several "voices," solo and choral, are many, as in Psalm 32.[12]

The full composition of Morning and Evening Prayer includes: Invitation to prayer, Psalmody (two psalms and a canticle from either the Old Testament or New Testament), Scripture reading, Gospel Canticle, Intercessions, and Sign of Peace. In some congregations the psalmody is simplified, with only one psalm or canticle being prayed. This format can provide the community with a lovely opportunity to add some new or different practices in their common prayer. First, the community may consider incorporating ten minutes of contemplative sitting immediately after the psalm or canticle. A second variation might be to have the psalm sung to a contemporary setting, rather than have it recited or chanted.

On more formal occasions, say Morning or Evening Prayer on a special feast (e.g., the parish feast day or that of a community's founder or foundress), the psalmody could be varied considerably, with one psalm sung to a contemporary setting, another led by a cantor, and the canticle chanted by the congregation or sung solo. The Benedictus or Magnificat could also be sung to one of the many contemporary melodies that have appeared in recent years.

When the Hours are prepared with care, the community can experience very powerful communal prayer events. On any number of such occasions I recall members of the community remaining seated and quiet in the chapel for some time after the stipulated prayer period had come to an end. Later I heard different individuals say that they did not want the time to end because they had felt such a strong sense of communion with God and with one another. Wouldn't it be wonderful if such experiences were not uncommon?

Although the above suggestions are specifically geared toward praying the Hours in common, similar variations can be made when praying the Hours in private. A few simple adaptations that one might try on occasion are these:

- Use a CD with a recording of one of the psalms.
- Pray the psalms aloud. It is amazing how much better we hear and identify with the psalms when we say them aloud, even when alone.
- Chant or sing one or more of the psalms; use a familiar melody or a simple one that you make up. No one other than God need hear you. While you may feel uncomfortable at first, after a few experiences of this kind of singing, you may surprise yourself with how natural this feels.
- Consider using gestures that help you express the mood of the psalm and of your soul. These can be very simple, such as a lifting up of your hands or arms, or a gentle bow. Whatever feels natural to you and helps reinforce the words of the prayer. You needn't gesture through the entire psalm, but only when it feels right.
- If you do not already light a candle or use incense when you pray, this might be a good way to begin experimenting with the use of your senses in prayer.

You will note that in each of the suggestions mentioned above you are invited to use at least one of your senses. By doing this, you will be bringing more of yourself to prayer. Experiment with these few suggestions. There are many other ways in which to add variety and richness to praying of the Liturgy of the Hours. These suggestions are intended to help you feel more comfortable in exploring ways in which this rich tradition can continue to be a meaningful experience of prayer.

Lectio Divina

The practice of *lectio divina* has a very long and rich tradition in the Church. Volumes of materials are available both in written and video format that elaborate upon this method of prayer.[13] Literally, *lectio divina* means "divine" or "sacred reading." This practice consists of four movements that we will elaborate upon below. The purpose of *lectio*, and therefore its goal, is encounter with God. While *lectio* can be and often is practiced in community settings, we will focus upon how *lectio* might be used in personal prayer with the psalms.

Let's consider two possible ways in which you might use *lectio* with the psalms. The first is the traditional practice of using a single psalm in prayer; the second will flow from a growing familiarity with the psalms that have been prayed in this way. To begin, choose to either move through the Psalter systematically, beginning with Psalm 1 and proceeding through the Psalter with each practice of *lectio*, or use a chart that identifies the various types of prayer discussed earlier in this article (praise, lament, thanksgiving, and trust or confidence,).[14] If following the second suggestion, then you might choose to pray a psalm that expresses the disposition of your soul on that occasion.

The overall method of *lectio* will be the same in whichever procedure you choose to follow. The four movements of *lectio* are read (*lectio*), reflect (*meditatio*), respond (*oratio*), and rest (*contemplatio*), and will be spoken of briefly. But before entering into these movements, it is important to prepare yourself for this encounter.

Most of us live hectic lives, moving from one task to next. Our prayer can become on occasion one more thing that we know we need or want to do. And while none of us want to have this disposition, sadly it is a common experience. So when you sit down to engage in *lectio*, please, follow these suggestions.

Find a comfortable and quiet place to sit. The simpler the environment, the more likely you will be able to engage in this practice. Settle yourself. Consciously let go of all that is on your agenda. Slowly, very slowly take a deep breath. Consciously and slowly release that breath, freeing yourself of tension and anxiety. Repeat this step about four times. You are likely to be surprised at the change you feel within your body. Continue to breath slowly (not quite so deeply), mindful that you are in God's presence and that your deepest desire is to know and love God.

Now that you are settled, you are ready to pick up your Scripture and begin the sacred reading of your psalm. The first movement, that of reading (*lectio*), should be done slowly and preferably aloud. Listen to the words of the psalm. Breath with the psalm. After a pause of five to ten minutes, read the psalm again, slowly. This process is similar to letting the ingredients of a fine recipe blend together. There is no rushing the process. With several such readings of the text, words or verses will speak to you. Notice them. Don't force them to have any special significance or meaning. They will do what they will do within you. Simply notice these words or lines.

The second movement of *lectio* is reflecting (*meditatio*). As you can see, this movement flows naturally from reading. This is when you begin to return to the words or lines that spoke to you in your reading. Begin to savor these lines as they begin to feel at home within you. Eventually these words will elicit a response within you (*oratio*).

In this third movement you now speak to God of what you are experiencing in this prayer. Whatever the psalm has stirred within you, be it delight, anger, longing, or something else, share this with God. Tell God what this Word means to you and listen for God's response.

After responding to God's Word, you will come to a place of quiet (*contemplatio*). This is a period of simply resting in God's presence, it is contemplation. It is peacefully being with the one you love.

Following your period of *lectio*, it can be helpful to make notes in a journal. Particularly helpful would be identifying lines that spoke to your heart and the type of prayer they evoked. If feelings of praise arose within you, write the lines that spoke to you under the category of praise; if feelings of hurt arose, identify these under this listing. By collecting verses under different categories, eventually you will have a wonderful resource for prayer, to which you can turn when you desire to more spontaneously express to God what is in your heart. This prayer resource can be a tremendous aid if you are a spiritual director who desires both to become more at home with Scripture yourself and to offer directees suggested Scripture texts for their prayer.

Conclusion

Having looked at some of the many types of prayer found within the Psalter and having considered a few ways in which we might pray with these outpourings of our ancestors in faith, I would offer one more suggestion. Consider composing your own psalm or psalms. Retreat can be the ideal time for such a composition. While a lengthy retreat might be impossible, even a weekend away, a weekend in which the intention is to nurture your relationship with the God you love and who loves you more deeply than you can imagine is a perfect time to become a psalmist.

Let your psalm be the words of your heart. If your heart is heavy, pour out your lament. If your heart is joyful, sing of God's glory. If grateful, extol how God has

brought you to this place of giving thanks. And if your heart is content, express your
confidence and trust in God's designs.

Let the words of my mouth and the meditation of my heart

be acceptable to you,

O Lord, my rock and my redeemer.

1. Unless otherwise indicated, all psalm translations found within this article are those of the
   author.
2. The titles of John F. Craghan's two books on the psalms appropriately capture the content
   of the Psalter. His earlier work, published by Michael Glazier in 1984 was titled *The Psalms:
   Prayers for the Ups, Downs, and In-Betweens of Life*. His revised and expanded work published
   by Liturgical Press in 1993 is titled *Psalms for all Seasons*. Both titles, I believe, capture what is
   found within the Psalter. For some wonderful insights into the rich vocabulary of the psalms
   see Jean-Pierre Prévost's *A Short Dictionary of the Psalms* (Collegeville, MN: Liturgical, 1997).
   In this compact text, Prévost identifies and elaborates upon forty key words that are used
   throughout the Hebrew Scriptures but are especially significant in the Psalter. Having a better
   understanding of this vocabulary and its use in the psalms can enrich our appreciation of these
   texts.
3. Walter Brueggemann has written extensively on this topic. One of his groundbreaking articles
   that has appeared in multiple publications, "The Psalms and the Life of Faith: A Suggested
   Typology of Function," *JSOT* 17 (1980): 3–32, remains a work of tremendous import.
4. Among the very fine psalm translations available today are the following: *The New Revised
   Standard Bible* (NRSV, 1989); *The New American Bible* (NAB or NABRE, 2014); *The Jewish
   Study Bible* (JPS, 1999); *The New International Version* (NIV, 1984); and *The New Grail
   Translation* (2014). While the *New Jerusalem Bible* (NJB) is a lovely translation, we choose
   not to recommend this work because of its use of the divine name. The four consonants that
   represent the Hebrew name of God revealed to Moses in Exodus 3 (YHWH) and which
   Judaism holds to be most sacred, and thus not to be uttered, appear as "Yahweh" in the NJB.
   To our knowledge, every other contemporary Bible translation renders the divine name
   "Lord," following the Jewish tradition that the Hebrew word *Adonai*, "Lord," be substituted
   whenever the tetragrammaton occurs. See the letter of Cardinal Francis Arinze, Prefect of
   the Congregation for Divine Worship and the Discipline of the Sacraments, written to the
   Bishops' Conferences, in which he gives specific directives on the use of the divine name. This
   letter of June 29, 2008, is available online at http://www.usccb.org/liturgy/NameOfGod.pdf.
5. Hermann Gunkel, *Introduction to the Psalms: The Genres of the Religious Lyric of Israel*, trans.
   James D. Nogalski (Macon, GA: Macon University Press, 1998).
6. Brueggemann's work on the psalms is prolific. For an excellent summary of his contributions
   to psalm study, see Strawn's bibliography in Walter Brueggemann, *From Whom No Secrets Are
   Hid: Introducing the Psalms*, ed. Brent A. Strawn (Louisville: Westminster John Knox, 2015),
   178–188.
7. On rare occasions, one will discover that a psalm will have a change of direction or tone. A
   clear example can be found in Psalm 89. The first portion of this lengthy psalm, 89:1–37, celebrates the Davidic monarchy; the second portion, 89:38–51, laments the end of that monarchy.

8. The 150 psalms that comprise the Psalter cannot all be easily classified as one of the four types of psalms we have just examined. However, since the nature of Christian prayer tends to fall into praise, lament or petition, thanksgiving, and trust or confidence, we believe that this division will be helpful to our readers.

9. *Dominican Praise: A Provisional Book of Prayer for Dominican Women*, 2005.

10. See Robert Taft, *The Liturgy of the Hours in the East and West: The Origins of the Divine Office and Its Meaning for Today*, 2nd ed. (Collegeville, MN: Liturgical, 1985).

11. Roland E. Murphy, *The Psalms Are Yours* (New York: Paulist, 1993), 72.

12. Murphy, *The Psalms Are Yours*, 71–72.

13. Many of the videos available online are excellent. See for example the video by Trappist monk Thomas Keating, OCSO, a renowned and prolific writer on the spiritual life, particularly the practice of "Centering Prayer": http://www.contemplativeoutreach.org/category/category/lectio-divina. See also the videos of Cardinal Thomas Collins of Toronto: "Lectio Divina with Cardinal Thomas Collins," https://www.archtoronto.org/lectio.

14. While there are numerous works that identify different types of psalms, here we will offer a condensed selection of psalms that can serve as an introduction to the four types of prayer. Keep in mind that this is not a listing of all 150 psalms. Praise: 8, 15, 19, 29, 33, 46, 47, 76, 84, 87, 93, 95, 97, 98, 99, 100, 103, 104, 119, 122, 145, 146, 147, 148, 149, 150. Lament: 3, 4, 5, 22, 27, 42, 43, 51, 88, 130. Thanksgiving: 30, 34, 66, 67, 92, 116, 138. Trust or confidence: 11, 16, 23, 62, 91, 121, 125, 131, 139.

CHAPTER 31

Praying with Job

~ *Dianne Bergant, CSA* ~

Even those who have little or no knowledge of the Bible are acquainted with the phrase "the patience of Job." They may know nothing of the biblical character or of the book that bears his name, but they are familiar with his trademark virtue. They may not realize that Job's patience was a religious virtue that sprang from deep spiritual fervor, and not simply a particular strength of character. Consequently, they cannot be expected to know that there are really three very different Jobs in that book, three very different virtues that characterize him, and three very different ways that he prayed.

"BLESSED BE THE NAME OF THE LORD" (JOB 1:21)

As the story unfolds in the biblical book, Job is described by God as one who was "blameless and upright, one who feared God and turned away from evil" (Job 1:1, 8; 2:3).[1] It is one thing to be known by other human beings as being righteous. It is quite another thing when God describes you in this way. In fact, whenever God refers to Job, it is with this remarkable description. This is important, because people often believe that there is a direct correspondence between one's goodness and the circumstances of one's life. This correspondence is actually the basis of the theory of retribution, which maintains that goodness is rewarded with success and happiness while evil is punished with failure and unhappiness. Since Job is described by God as "blameless and upright, one who feared God and turned away from evil," we would expect him to be an exceptionally successful and happy man. The first chapter of the book describes him in precisely this way.

Given the prevailing understanding of the dynamics of retribution, the tragic reversal of Job's fortunes appears to be not only inexplicable but unjust. However, while the characters within the story might be thrown into confusion, the reader is made privy to an extraordinary exchange that took place in the heavenly council. There the satan[2] appeared with the members of that heavenly court. When God pointed to the righteous Job, the satan challenged the steadfastness of Job's integrity and dared God to test it: "Does Job fear God for nothing?... But stretch out your hand now and touch all that he has, and he will curse you to your face" (Job 1:9, 11).

The satan's challenge is based on a reversal of the dynamics of retribution. The theory states that blessing follows righteousness. The satan claims Job is righteous because he has been blessed. Take away his blessings, and he will relinquish his righteousness. God accedes to the test and allows misfortune to overwhelm Job.

In immediate succession, Job loses his flocks, his servants, even his children. But he does not curse God. A second meeting in heaven transpires. Once again God points out Job's righteousness, the depths of which have now been demonstrated. However, the satan is not yet satisfied. Job may have lost possessions and the people in his life, but he has retained his physical integrity. A second challenge is posed: "But stretch out your hand now and touch his bone and his flesh, and he will curse you to your face" (Job 2:5). Once again God allows this to happen. And still Job does not curse God. Instead, after each trial, Job responds with prayer:

> Then Job arose, tore his robe, shaved his head, and fell on the ground and worshiped. He said, "Naked I came from my mother's womb, and naked shall I return there; the LORD gave, and the LORD has taken away; blessed be the name of the LORD." (Job 1:20–21)

Job's response to his afflictions reflects the traditional practices of mourning; he tears his garments and he cuts his hair. By prostrating himself, he adds the customary gesture of obeisance, a sign of abasement and acceptance. His words consist of three distinct and independent sayings. With the first proverbial saying, he acknowledges that the possessions he has lost belong to human life. He came into life with none and he will leave this life with none. Job assumes no inherent right to his possessions. This is a realistic acknowledgment of human vulnerability. While he might be referring to his human mother's womb, the fact that he actually would not return to it at death has led many to conclude that the reference here is to 'Mother Earth,' a reference that coincides with a theme found in an earlier creation story: "For...you are dust [dry earth], and to dust [dry earth] you shall return" (Genesis 3:19). Job's prayer in the face of heart-wrenching loss is one of humble acceptance.

The second proverbial saying is similar to one that was frequently recited by Arab tribesmen at the death of a kinsman: "His Lord has given him; his Lord has taken him." Whether Job is referring to the giving and taking of his possessions or of his life, with this second saying he acknowledges that everything is in God's hands, subject to God's plans. He is merely the recipient of God's good pleasure. Job's prayer is a trusting admission of human finitude and a declaration of divine sovereign control.

The third saying is a benediction that is also found in Psalm 113:2. There is a euphemistic play on words here. The satan claimed that, if stripped of his good fortune, Job would curse God (Job 1:11). However, the Hebrew word used in that verse is really the word for "bless," which is meant to be understood there euphemistically. Here

Job does indeed bless God, but not in the inverted way the satan claimed he would. In traditional societies like ancient Israel, a person's name was thought to contain a degree of that person's identity or character. Thus, to bless God's name is to praise God's character. Job does this in the face of great bereavement.

The simple prayer that brought these three sayings together produces a progressive reflection on life. It begins with an admission of human vulnerability, especially at birth and at death. It then attests to the sovereignty of God. This is a humble prayer; one that leads to trust in God's providence; one that ends in devout praise.

Though Job does not utter another payer after he is stricken with a loathsome physical ailment, his sentiments remain the same. Speaking to his wife, he says: "Shall we receive the good at the hand of God, and not receive the bad?" (Job 2:10). Unknown to himself, Job has passed the test decided upon by God and the satan. He has shown that his commitment is authentic and beyond question. He is not merely motivated by the promise of reward. The satan has been confounded.

Other than humble acceptance, we know nothing of Job's other sentiments. Was he in shock? Was he too startled to realize what might lie ahead of him? Had he any sense of how long he might have to endure such devastation? Did he presume that he had the inner strength to persevere and carry on? Each one of these matters and all of them together would certainly influence anyone's state of mind. Such devout acceptance of hardship is the kind of prayer for which most believing people long and, perhaps, even initially offer to God. However, it is very difficult to sustain. The drive for survival and comfort, the need to be assured that life has meaning, and the impetus to overcome obstacles can too easily be thwarted by unrelenting misfortune. When this happens, humble acceptance often requires heroic effort. This form of prayer might stand as a goal toward which we strive, but how realistic is it?

This is probably the version of the story of Job known to most people. As inspirational as it may be, it is not the whole story. In fact, it is not the principal biblical story. This book consists of a prose folktale framework found in the first two chapters of the book and the last ten verses of chapter 42. It is in this very brief framework that Job meekly accepts his lot, declares his devotion to God, and proclaims his prayer of praise. In the last verses of this prose framework, his fortunes are reinstated and he lives happily ever after. The other thirty-nine and a half chapters are written in poetry. Thirty-five of them, comprising the main body of the book, portray an entirely different Job, one who laments his lot and cries out to God in defiance. When God finally appears toward the end of the book, we meet yet a third Job, a chastened man whose piety has been proven, whose commitment is unshakable, and whose prayer is simple yet heartfelt. One might say that the book of Job is made up of two dissimilar literary compositions, which together offer us three distinct sketches of the main character. But which one is the real Job? And whose prayer stands as a model of prayer for the rest of us?

"LET THE DAY PERISH" (JOB 3:3)

The main body of the book, the poetry section, opens with Job cursing (3:1–10) and lamenting (3:11–26). It is chapter 3 that sets the stage for the dialogues between Job and his visitors that unfold in the following thirty-four chapters. Here Job is far from the docile, accepting devotee that we met in the prose framework, and his prayer is angry and demanding. One wonders if it can even be called prayer. It is more like a malediction, a plea that harm might befall someone of something. The light and darkness imagery that Job employs here contains strong mythological significance. It suggests that the contrast between light and darkness really reflects a battle between order and chaos. Unlike the creation narrative in Genesis 1, which describes the victory of light over darkness, order over chaos, Job cries out here for a reversal of that victory, a counter-cosmic upheaval. He would have darkness victorious over light, chaos conquering order:

> Let the day perish in which I was born,
>> and the night that said,
>> "A man-child is conceived."
> Let that day be darkness!
>> May God above not seek it,
>> or light shine on it.
> Let gloom and deep darkness claim it.
>> Let clouds settle upon it;
>> let the blackness of the day terrify it.
> That night—let thick darkness seize it!
>> let it not rejoice among the days of the year;
>> let it not come into the number of the months.
> Yes, let that night be barren;
>> let no joyful cry be heard in it.
> Let those curse it who curse the Sea,
>> those who are skilled to rouse up Leviathan.
> Let the stars of its dawn be dark;
>> let it hope for light, but have none;
>> may it not see the eyelids of the morning—
> because it did not shut the doors of my mother's womb,
>> and hide trouble from my eyes. (Job 3:2–10)

Job pleads that his birthday might perish, that darkness and deep gloom would come over it rather than light. This is more than merely poetic embellishment. He is asking for more than a mere reversal of nature, for that would mean that the night would then be light, and this is not what he wants. Even night, specifically the night of his conception, would be consumed by darkness and emptiness if he could have his way. That night would then never again be a time of conception and fertility. He wants both the day of his birth and the night of his conception to be condemned to the absolute darkness of chaos. He further calls upon those who, by means of incantation, are able to conjure up Leviathan, the mythical monster of chaos. Many ancient people believed that an eclipse was a return to the utter darkness of chaos caused by a monster of darkness swallowing up the light of day. This is the reversal of creation for which Job pleads. He wants the powers of darkness and destruction to overcome the powers of light and harmony; he wants the creator-God to be vanquished by the god of chaos. Is this blasphemy? Has Job finally cursed God?

Why does Job cry out for such total disorder? Why should he blame the day of his birth or the night of his conception? Might it be that the misery he experiences appears to him to be a violation of the basic harmony of life? He is, after all, a righteous man, and yet he is assaulted again and again. He has reached that point in his suffering where he bemoans the fact that he was ever born, and he curses that day. He maintains that if the present day has fallen victim to the terrors of chaos, the first day of his life should know the same fate, for it is his birthday that is responsible for his coming forth from the womb.

The satan had predicted that Job would curse God. This did not actually happen. Instead, his life and the time of its beginning are the subject of his imprecations. Jeremiah expresses the same sentiments in almost identical language:

Cursed be the day
on which I was born!
The day when my mother bore me,
let it not be blessed!
Cursed be the man
who brought the news to my father, saying,
"A child is born to you, a son,"
making him very glad.
Let that man be like the cities
that the LORD overthrew without pity;
let him hear a cry in the morning
and an alarm at noon,

because he did not kill me in the womb;

> so my mother would have been my grave,

> and her womb forever great.

Why did I come forth from the womb

> to see toil and sorrow,

> and spend my days in shame? (Jeremiah 20:14–18)

The prophet even cursed the man who brought the news of his birth to his father. Suffering has brought both Jeremiah and Job to the point of wishing that their lives had never begun.

Job goes even further. He realizes that if one can no longer trust regularity in life, it makes little sense to trust the rhythms in nature or in the universe. Why trust anything? Might this be Job's blasphemy? Is he really cursing God by denying God's providence and universal power? Is he accusing God of having lost control? Because he is dealing with cosmic matters, is he really suggesting that the all-powerful God has been defeated by the monster of chaos? Or is it possible to consider his words as prayer?

Job is not yet finished. His malediction is followed by lament. Having cursed his conception and birth, he now bemoans having survived after birth:

Why did I not die at birth,

> come forth from the womb and expire?

Why were there knees to receive me,

> or breasts for me to suck?

Now I would be lying down and quiet;

> I would be asleep; then I would be at rest

with kings and counselors of the earth

> who rebuild ruins for themselves,

or with princes who have gold,

> who fill their houses with silver.

Or why was I not buried like a stillborn child,

> like an infant that never sees the light?

There the wicked cease from troubling,

> and there the weary are at rest.

There the prisoners are at ease together;

> they do not hear the voice of the taskmaster.

The small and the great are there,

> and the slaves are free from their masters. (Job 3:11–19)

He wonders why he was cherished, received on the knees by his father or at his mother's breasts during his first days of life. He believes that to be treated in this way at the beginning of life instills false hopes for continued security. His present life belies that hope. Had he met with an early death, he would have been spared the trouble and weariness that he now experiences. Even a stillbirth would have been better than his present predicament. There is no thought here of a life of peace after death. The focus is on death as the end of his present affliction and suffering, of his trouble and weariness, his imprisonment and hard labor, his enslavement. Each of these characterizations symbolizes life as Job encounters it. Being born into a life like this is certainly not a blessing. It is a calamity, a tragedy. Death would be a relief. One can only curse the day of such a birth and look to death for an escape from such a life.

Job was conceived; he was born; and he survived. Now, having been torn from a life of harmony and security, he must find a new way. However, this is precisely the crux of his quandary. The way that he must travel is hidden from him. He is expected to live a life in accord with the underlying principles of order, but the way of these principles and their comprehension are kept from him. Once again he challenges the value in enduring such an existence. No wonder he tastes bitterness and questions why he should have ever seen the light of the day of birth. For him, the search for wisdom has turned into a frantic search for death as if it were a treasure beyond value. The satan accused God of hedging Job in, protecting him (Job 1:10). Now it is Job who accuses God of fencing him in, confining him, imprisoning him (3:23).

The scope of Job's outbursts seems to change its focus as his complaints progress. In the beginning he attacked the cosmic order itself. He then challenged the purpose of his own birth. Here he wonders about the sufferings endured by anyone. Each of the three sections of this chapter consists of a challenge from Job and a reason for that challenge. He curses the day of his birth because it did not shut his mother's womb; he demands to know why he did not die at birth, for then he would be at rest from struggle; he wants to know why he continues to live, for he fears that his suffering will never end. Job is trapped, hedged in, with no end in sight. There is no theological questioning here, no demand for an explanation for his suffering. This is an unabashed outpouring of raw emotion, emotion that tears at the very sinews of one's being.

Who has not known suffering like that of Job? Who has not stood, as he stands, in darkness and gloom and confusion? Who has not cried out to heaven in desperation and anger in the face of suffering that sears and cripples and beats down the human spirit, suffering that catapults one into a chasm where the universe itself seems to be an enemy, and life has lost its meaning? While the Job of the prose framework is better known, it is the Job of maledictions and lament with whom people can more easily identify, and it is more likely that words such as these will be found on the lips of suffering believers. It is no wonder that the largest category of biblical psalms is lament. The prayer of humble acceptance might well be the ideal toward which we strive, but most people experience the dread and anger before they can place everything in the hands of God. This does not necessarily mean that they have lost faith. It means, instead, that life itself is crying out from the depths of pain. Lament is an honest and heartfelt prayer.

"I LOATHE MY LIFE!" (JOB 7:16)

Most cultures have devised protocols for mourning, words and practices that enable members of that culture to express the sentiments provoked by suffering. We have already seen that Job tears his garments and shaves his head. Another custom dictates silence in the face of mourning. This silence should only be broken when the chief mourner speaks. We see this custom in the book of Job. Three men came to console and comfort Job:

> They raised their voices and wept aloud; they tore their robes and threw dust in the air upon their heads. They sat with him on the ground seven days and seven nights, and no one spoke a word to him, for they saw that his suffering was very great. (Job 2:12b–13)

Job finally broke the silence with his maledictions and laments, giving his visitors permission to respond. And respond they did, with criticism rather than understanding, with unwanted advice rather than support. Their injunctions along with Job's rejoinders make up three cycles of speeches. In responding to them, Job defends his righteousness and names God as the perpetrator of his troubles. Job both defends himself to his visitors and, at times, speaks directly to God. One example of this latter type of response will give us insight into the character of Job's prayer at this point in his struggle:

> I will not restrain my mouth;
>> I will speak in the anguish of my spirit;
>> I will complain in the bitterness of my soul.
> Am I the Sea, or the Dragon,
>> that you set a guard over me?
> When I say, "My bed will comfort me,
>> my couch will ease my complaint,"
> then you scare me with dreams

and terrify me with visions,

so that I would choose strangling

and death rather than this body.

I loathe my life; I would not live forever.

Let me alone, for my days are a breath.

What are human beings, that you make so much of them,

that you set your mind on them,

visit them every morning,

test them every moment?

Will you not look away from me for a while,

let me alone until I swallow my spittle?

If I sin, what do I do to you, you watcher of humanity?

Why have you made me your target?

Why have I become a burden to you?

Why do you not pardon my transgression

and take away my iniquity?

For now I shall lie in the earth;

you will seek me, but I shall not be." (Job 7:11–21)

Job's initial lament found in chapter three has now turned to accusation. He insists that God alone is responsible for his afflictions, and he will not be slow to make this known. Reverence for the majesty of God does not temper Job's outburst. His desperate situation has brought him to the point of disregard for religious conventions. We should not think that these are the outpourings of an irreligious man. On the contrary, it is his faith in God as the architect and guardian of world order that motivates his allegations. Job never questions God's sovereign control of all things. Thus, it stands to reason that God is the one behind all of his misfortunes, or God has allowed them to happen. Therefore, God is the one to whom his vituperations should be directed.

Job reverts again to the ancient Near Eastern mythological imagery of creation (7:12). It is in such a myth that one finds the god of chaos, characterized as the sea or a sea dragon, engaged in mortal battle with the mighty god responsible for order. This was no mean battle; it was a cosmic conflict, one upon which the future of the universe depended. Job claims that God is treating him as if he were that cosmic deity, a threat to the order of the universe, an enemy that compelled God to constrain him. But this is not the case; Job does not jeopardize cosmic order. Even if he was an opponent, he is no match for the mighty creator. This is an unfair contest, for if the cosmic forces of chaos were defeated by the creator, what chance could a broken pathetic human being stand?

There is no escape for Job. He thinks that perhaps he will find comfort in sleep, but this is not to be. Even there he is terrified by dreams and nightmares (7:13–14). God will afford him no respite, but attacks him even when he is most vulnerable. It seems to him that his only recourse is death (7:15). Persecuted day and night by God, Job looks to death as a release. Still, even his death is determined by God, for Job never even considers the possibility of taking matters into his own hands. In the face of it all, his words are searing: "I loathe my life!" (7:16).

I loathe my life; it is intolerable! Nothing else need be said. It is no wonder that Job prefers death. He is harassed by God, and so he cries out to that tormentor: "Let me alone!" Speaking of the brevity of life, he employs the Hebrew word *hebel*, which means "breathe" or "vapor." However, the word also means vain, empty of meaning, pointless, as it is used in the book of Ecclesiastes: "Vanity of vanities!" (Ecclesiastes 1:2). While Job is stating that his life is brief, he is also declaring that it is meaningless. Why does God even bother? After all, he is not a threat to God as the sea or the dragon might be. Job's predicament simply underscores God's apparent brutality in terrorizing a lowly creature who has no place to hide from unrelenting divine scrutiny.

Once again Job refers to human insignificance. Earlier he focused on his standing. Here he asks about the importance of humankind generally, and he does so by parodying a famous verse from Psalm 8:

What are human beings	What are human beings
that you are mindful of them,	that you make so much of them;
mortals that you care for them?	that you set your mind on them?
(Psalm 8:4)	(Job 7:17)

In both passages, the Hebrew word for human beings is *ĕnôsh*, a word that emphasizes human frailty. Psalm 8 is a hymn that praises God for the marvels of creation, as in the midst of all these marvels, God lifts up humankind. The psalmist goes on describing human dignity demonstrated in the responsibility placed on women and men by God for the care and prospering of the rest of natural creation. Job maintains that rather than raising this human insignificance to the dignity of being representative of God and steward of creation, God has exploited it in Job, making human beings the prey of divine ruthlessness, day in and day out. Once again an embittered Job cries out: "Let me alone" (7:19).

Job's final questioning of God addresses divine reaction to sin (7:20–21). He mentions three different kinds of sin, which in sequence indicate a progression of wickedness: *sin*, which simply means missing the mark; *transgression*, which is a breach of relationship; and *iniquity*, which refers to perversion. This is not an admission of sin, for throughout his speeches, Job maintains his innocence. Rather, he is arguing that even if he is guilty of sin, God's assaults are out of proportion. However, if by chance Job is actually guilty of some offense of which he is unaware, why does God not simply forgive him? How might any supposed infraction of Job's affect God in such a way as to necessitate such a merciless response? Job calls God "watcher of humanity," a well-known designation that refers to God's providential care. However, Job reverses its meaning, characterizing God as an indefatigable scrutinizer rather than a benevolent protector. Rather than the object of God's care, Job has become the target of God's aggression.

Job claims that he is ready to die. Should God seek him, he would then be beyond God's reach. Since ancient Israel did not have a clear idea about life after death, Job would not in any way be alluding to such a concept here. At issue is the reason for God seeking Job. The word *seek* is usually used positively, "to seek in order to help and care for." Thus, Job is suggesting that if God does nothing now to relieve his anguish, when God finally does relent, it will be too late. Job ends his words, open to the possibility that God will yield to Job's cries and grant him some measure of comfort.

What is one to make of Job's words? Are they blasphemous? Or might they be a form of prayer? While those who later visit Job will criticize him, finding fault with both his condemnatory words and the abrasive attitudes out of which his words emerge, Job is never censored by the author of the book. Furthermore, the readers all know that Job is correct in what he says. God is indeed responsible for his hardships. Finally, in the prose ending of the book, God actually defends Job to one of the visitors: "You have not spoken of me what is right, as my servant Job has" (Job 42:7). This means that Job's blistering critique of God is certainly bold, but it is also well founded. Job's lament is a genuine prayer, not unlike the prayer of another innocent sufferer who cries out on agony, feeling abandoned by God: "My God, my God! Why have you forsaken me?" (Mark 15:34; Matthew 27:46).

A lament directed to God is grounded in at least three very profound religious sentiments. First, it is an honest admission of human inadequacy, and human inadequacy is very difficult for self-directed people to admit. By means of a lament, we complain about matters over which we have no control. Second, it is an acknowledgment of divine power, even though sometimes a negative acknowledgment. As we lament we often criticize God for either misusing that power against us or for not using it to relieve us of suffering. Third, when we complain to God, we are presuming that God not only can remedy the distressing situation within which we find ourselves, but that God actually will remedy it. If we did not think this, we probably would not turn to God. Finally, even the most desperate laments contain a glimmer of hope. Once again we see that lament is a heartfelt prayer.

"I UTTERED WHAT I DID NOT UNDERSTAND" (JOB 42:3)

In his last impassioned effort to defend his uprightness, Job challenges God to respond, and God does—but not in the way Job had hoped. God breaks the cosmic silence and thunders through the heavens, but never answers Job's questions, nor responds to his accusations. Instead, God asks questions, and these questions never even allude to the miserable circumstances of Job's life. God poses question after question regarding the marvels of the cosmos and the wonders of the animal world. God's questions focus on the broader scope of natural creation rather than the narrow focus of Job's personal history. The use of elements of nature as a means of instructing is a well-established feature of the wisdom tradition, and the manner of God's questioning follows the pedagogical style of the traditional wisdom teacher. In responding to Job in this way, the creator has assumed the role of the wisdom teacher.

Just what does this Creator-God intend to teach? Is the display of cosmic wonders meant to dazzle Job with the magnitude of God's creative ability? Is the parade of rare animals aimed at confounding him with their grace and agility or their awesome dimensions? Is God merely concerned with forcing a confession of weakness and surrender from this man who is already reduced to almost nothing? Will this show of unquestioned divine superiority be enough to quell Job's turmoil, end his pleading, and satisfy his demand for an explanation?

Question after question is put to Job, each one challenging his knowledge of some aspect of the universe or his control over it. What does he know about the purpose or scheme of God in the creation, control, and maintenance of the world? Questions put to Job challenge his power over the world and the creatures in it. God's questioning lays bare the limitations of Job's insight and knowledge. Through queries about nature, Job comes to see that just as there are mysteries in nature that are far beyond his comprehension, so there are mysteries in human existence that he will never be able to grasp or control. By means of this analogy of nature, Job is brought to a new horizon of insight and trust. If he cannot imagine the ways that God continues to sustain creation, how can he possibly fathom God's mysterious care in his own life? Job's ability to comprehend can no longer be the standard he uses to measure God's providence.

Job gradually gains insight into the lesson that God is teaching. The magnitude of the universe forces Job to admit his inferiority. He was certainly wrong to expect that he could understand the ways of God. He has now come to realize this and so he desists in his demands:

> I lay my hand on my mouth. (Job 40:4b)

> I have uttered what I did not understand,
>> things too wonderful for me, which I did not know. (Job 42:3b)

> I had heard of you by the hearing of the ear,
>> but now my eye sees you;
> therefore I despise myself,
>> and repent in dust and ashes. (Job 42:5–6)

Formerly, Job had known of God through the testimony of the ancients as well as the teaching of the sages. According to this teaching, God exercises dominion over the world and all contained within that world. Job never questioned this, nor has his experience of God bought him to question it now. What Job criticized was the way he thought God was using that power. This unexpected breathtaking encounter with the God of creation through aspects of that creation has now given him new insight. Previously, he expected to understand just how God exercised that dominion. Now he realizes that such will never be the case. Job actually entertained the possibility that chaos now enjoyed the upper hand. His new cosmic experience reassured him that God was undeniably in control, even though Job might not comprehend how this control is accomplished.

The ironic questioning of God's speeches exposed Job's restricted knowledge of the universe and power over it. Job is indeed rebuked by God's questioning, but it is for his lack of vision, not for any lack of integrity. Although Job had never intended to usurp any divine privilege or status, his anthropological presuppositions were exaggerated. He expected, even demanded, an insight into reality far beyond what can be expected for humans. God's questioning sought to correct this by pointing out time and again: God is God and Job is not. Job does not repent of sinfulness but of the foolish speech that sprang from his mistaken presuppositions. "Dust and ashes" refer to his humble condition as a mortal human being with limitations. God's questioning forced him to ponder these limitations. The purpose of this experience was not to silence Job, but to reassure him of divine control over the universe and to inspire him to confidence in this wondrous yet incomprehensible God. Job's questions may not have been answered as they had been asked, nor were his demands met, but his fears were dissipated, and his trust in God has been restored. He has come to see that, as important as human well-being might be, it is only a part of the vast cosmic reality over which God reigns. At issue is whether or not he can trust, without understanding.

The splendor of creation transcends Job's comprehension and he can only stand in wonder. The man whose misfortunes wrested from him cries of lament and outbursts of recrimination now very meekly admits that he was wrong. After the theophany, Job's attitude toward God takes on a completely different quality. His confidence now rests totally in God and not merely in some specific discernible act of God, past or future. His mystical encounter with the mighty, provident, and incomprehensible Creator has left him humbled, yet assured. Realizing that he stands in the presence of "things too wonderful for me," he is filled with awe. In a sense, he has come full circle. The prayer of this chastened Job could well be the prayer of the Job found in the prose prologue: "Blessed be the name of the LORD" (1:21). However, now Job's devotion has been tried in the fires of adversity, fires that have refined that devotion, not consumed it. Job is now wise, no longer naïve; he does not presume his strength, but accepts his weakness. Job's dark night has given way to the dawn of mystical insight.

PRAYING WITH JOB

The four examples of Job's prayers mirror ways we pray as well. For most of us, we might begin with a prayer of selfless devotion. When first struck with tragedy, we might turn to God with acceptance and surrender. However, when suffering endures and increases, it is very difficult to sustain such piety. We easily cry out in anguish and near despair, as Job did when he lamented his birth and miserable life. Even religious people find themselves, like Job, blaming God for their hardships. They should remember that those around Job criticized him for his lament and complaint, but God did not. In fact, God said that Job had spoken what was right. Still, the story of Job encourages us to move beyond lament and complaint, back to acceptance and surrender. However, Job's final prayer of acceptance is very different than his initial one. This is the prayer of one who knows from experience that suffering can come unexpectedly and remain indefinitely. It is the prayer of one who trusts in God's care without knowing how that care will manifest itself. It is the prayer of the religious person we are all called to be.

---

1. All scripture quotations are taken from the *New Revised Standard Version*.
2. This Hebrew word means "adversary." The concept has not yet developed into the contemporary notion of devil. Furthermore, in the Hebrew text, the word is always found with the definite article (*the* satan), designating a function, not a proper name.

CHAPTER 32

A Place for Prayer:
Solomon's Prayer at the Dedication
of the Temple (1 Kings 8)

~ *Leslie J. Hoppe, OFM* ~

The cleansing of the Temple by Jesus is one of the few incidents of Jesus's life to be recounted by all four evangelists (Matthew 21:12–13; Mark 11:15–17; Luke 19:45–46; John 2:13–22). In the Synoptic versions of the cleansing, Jesus justifies his action by asserting that the Temple was to be a "house of prayer," though it had become a setting for petty commercial activities. Commentators usually see Jesus's description of the Temple as a "house of prayer" as an allusion to Isaiah 56:7, which is the only time this expression appears in the Hebrew Bible.[1] This should not be surprising since the principal activity in the Temple was the offering of sacrifice. While prayer was certainly a component of the worship, no prayer formularies from the Temple have been preserved in the Bible except the prayer of the Israelite farmer who brings his first fruits to the Temple (Deuteronomy 26:5–10).[2] Despite this, it is obvious that the Temple was an important setting for both personal and communal encounters with God.

While the expression "house of prayer" is Isaian, this notion also finds expression in the Deuteronomic tradition—specifically in 1 Kings 8, which is a prayer ascribed to Solomon on the occasion of the Temple's dedication. The prayer underplays the Temple's role in the political sphere and undercuts its significance as a setting for sacrificial worship, focusing instead on the Temple as a setting for prayers offered by Israelites and gentiles in their time of need.

Scholarly study of 1 Kings 8 has focused on the history of its composition. At one time, Martin Noth regarded the entire chapter, except for Kings 8:27 and 34b, as the work of the Deuteronomistic Historian.[3] He later reversed himself, suggesting that vv. 38–39, 44–51, 52–53, 59–60 were later additions to the prayer.[4] Other commentators have also seen the text of 1 Kings 8 as the product of a complex editorial process.[5] The very length of 1 Kings 8 has led scholars to assume the composite character of Solomon's prayer. Gary Knoppers, on the other hand, has argued for the literary unity of Solomon's Prayer by describing a chiastic structure for this text, suggesting that the text is the product of a single hand.[6] Though I agree with Knoppers's basic insight, what follows differs from his arrangement of the text's structure, though it also points to the literary unity of Solomon's prayer. This prayer, then, is the composition of a Deuteronomistic author who wished to underscore the Temple's function as a place of prayer and downplay its function as the dwelling place of God on earth to which people bring sacrificial offerings.

A. *A narrative introduction* (vv. 1–13): a description of a festival during which a very large number of animal sacrifices were offered (v. 5).

    B. *A prayer of blessing* (vv. 14–21) in gratitude for the fulfillment of God's promises to David.

        C. *A prayer of assurance* (vv. 22–30) based on God's fidelity to David.

            D. *The seven petitions* (vv. 31–51) which define the temple as a place of prayer.

        C. *A prayer of assurance* (vv. 52–53) based on Israel's uniqueness.

    B. *A prayer of blessing* (v. 54–61) in gratitude for the fulfillment of God's promise of rest for Israel.

A. *A narrative conclusion* (vv. 62–66) a description of a festival during which a very large number of "sacrifices of well-being" were offered.

The chiastic structure of 1 Kings 8 provides a literary framework highlighting the central section of the chiasm: the seven petitions of vv. 31–51. These verses serve to transform the idea of the Temple as the house of God to a house of prayer, thus resolving the tension between Solomon's assertions in vv. 13 and 27. In v. 13, Solomon addresses the Lord: "I have built you an exalted house, a place for you to dwell in forever" while in v. 27 the king has second thoughts about significance of the Temple he had built: "But will God indeed dwell on the earth? Even heaven and the highest heaven cannot contain you, much less this house that I have built!" The tension between the belief that the Temple is the dwelling place of God on earth and the belief that no Temple could actually serve such a purpose is woven throughout 1 Kings 8. The function of Solomon's prayer is to demythologize and humanize the Temple. It is not a place for God to reside—rather it has an entirely different function: It is the setting for people to ask for divine help in times of great need.

THE PRAYERS OF BLESSING

Another significant step in transforming the idea of a temple is taken in the two prayers of blessing (A: vv. 1–13 and A: vv. 62–66). In the ancient Near East, the building of temples was considered a royal prerogative.[7] Such a project served to legitimate the rule of the king responsible for the temple building project. The prayer of blessing in vv. 14–21 begins with a recapitulation of Nathan's oracle (2 Samuel

7:8–17), which serves to provide divine warrant not merely for David's accession to kingship but also for the legitimacy of his Davidic dynasty as a whole. In the course of this recapitulation, the Deuteronomic characterization of the Temple as the place for God's name to dwell if repeated four times in vv. 17–20,[8] effectively shifting the focus of the prayer from the promise to David of an eternal dynasty to the promise that David's successor (Solomon) would build the Temple (2 Samuel 7:13; 1 Kings 8:20). The Deuteronomist exploits the association of Temple and dynasty to subvert the status of Jerusalem and its Temple. Verse 16 asserts that the choice of Jerusalem was not made by God and verse 17 affirms that the construction of the Temple was David's idea, implying that the decision to build a Temple in Jerusalem was the result of human initiative.[9] In 2 Kings 25, the Deuteronomist tells of the Temple and city sharing the fate of the Davidic dynasty. All this serves to demythologize the Temple and its function in ancient Israelite religious thought.

Verse 21 of the first prayer of blessing (B: vv. 14–21) shifts attention away from the promises made to David to the exodus from Egypt and the Sinai covenant that constitute Israel as God's people. The ark, which symbolizes that relationship, is to be placed in the Temple. This redirects the focus of the prayer from the interests of the dynasty to those of the people as a whole. The Deuteronomist, then, transforms the idea of the Temple from an expression of the legitimacy of the Davidic dynasty and royal prerogatives to an expression of the covenant between God and Israel as a whole. This movement away from dynastic concerns with which the prayer begins also appears in the seven petitions (vv. 31–51) and the narrative conclusion (vv. 62–66).

The second prayer of blessing (B: vv. 54–61) does not even mention the dynasty but praises God for fulfilling the promises made through Moses by giving Israel "rest" (v. 56).[10] This prayer speaks of the nearness of God to Israel but makes that nearness the result of Israel's obedience (vv. 57–58) rather than to the presence of God in the Temple. In fact, the content of the prayer bears no explicit relationship to the dedication of the Temple.[11] It reflects the core affirmation of the Deuteronomic tradition: obedience to the "statutes" and "commandments" is the key to maintaining a right relationship with God (v. 61). This is a principal Deuteronomic concern since this tradition sees Israel's future as dependent upon its obedience to the Mosaic Torah as articulated in the book of Deuteronomy (see Deuteronomy 30:15–18).

THE PRAYERS OF ASSURANCE

The two prayers of assurance (C: vv. 22–30 and C: vv. 52–53) also reflect the shift from concern for the dynasty to a concern for the people as a whole. The first prayer of assurance is the last time that 1 Kings 8 concerns itself with the dynasty. The assurance that this prayer offers to worshipers is based on the uniqueness of Israel's God (vv. 23, 27). The horizon of the second prayer is not the dynasty and Temple but Moses and the exodus. Israel is God's people and its uniqueness among the nations provides the assurance that Israel's prayers will be heard.

The Prayers of Petition

The seven petitions found in vv. 31–51 are the heart of Solomon's prayer. These petitions imagine the Temple to be a place for Israelites and gentiles alike to offer their prayers to God. This portion of Solomon's prayer asserts eight times that God's dwelling place is "in heaven" (vv. 30, 32, 34, 36, 39, 43, 45, 49). This stands in tension with the idea expressed in verse 13—namely, that the Temple is God's "exalted house"—a place for God to dwell. The Temple, then, is not the divine abode on earth but a place for prayer. In fact, it is not necessary that the one who prays be present in the Temple. It suffices that the one who prays face in the direction of the Temple while at prayer (vv. 44–45).

The first petition (vv. 31–32), unlike the others, is not occasioned by a difficult circumstance that leads the worshiper to call upon God for help. It is a prayer that asks God to ensure that justice is done when a person accused of a crime takes an oath of innocence before the altar (see Exodus 22:7–12; Numbers 5:11–31). The prayer asks God to judge between the two parties in the dispute. While the oath-taking is made before the altar of the Temple, the passing of judgment takes place in heaven, where God dwells (v. 32). This is another instance of the Deuteronomistic distinction between the Temple and God's actual dwelling place, which is in heaven.

The second (vv. 33–34) and third (vv. 35–36) petitions are communal prayers, begging for forgiveness and restoration for the people of Israel. The second petition asks that a repentant people be spared the effects of military defeat and continue their presence in their ancestral homeland. The third petition assumes that the droughts that threaten Israel's survival were punishment for the people's infidelity. It prays that God give rain upon Israel's repentance and obedience, thus ensuring the nation's survival.

The fourth (vv. 37–40) and fifth (vv. 41–43) petitions end with a clause introduced by the Hebrew conjunction לְמַעַן, "so that" (vv. 40 and 43). The clause in verse 40 suggests that the goal of prayer is not simply the amelioration of conditions brought about by famine and disease; rather, it is to lead people to a right relationship with God. The fifth petition is extraordinary given the usual Deuteronomic attitude toward gentiles (see Deuteronomy 23:3–6). It envisions Gentiles coming to the Temple to pray and asks God to grant their requests so that they will experience God's goodness for themselves and will also have a right relationship with God.

The final two petitions (vv. 44–45 and vv. 46–51) return to the themes of the second petition: war and loss of the land. While the second petition assumes that the people of Israel will still have access to the Temple (v. 33), petitions six and seven assume that the opposite since they will be taken off as exiles to the land of their enemies. Both petitions pray for relief after military defeat and forced migration; however, petition six does this with brevity, while petition seven is more than a brief prayer for deliverance. It also includes the motifs of repentance (vv. 47–48) and forgiveness (vv. 49–50). Though the petitions do not explicitly ask for an end to the people's exile from their homeland, the allusion to the exodus from Egypt in v. 51 makes it clear that this is the point of the prayers of the people in exile.

There are differences among the seven petitions, for example, the first deals with a situation faced by an individual Israelite while the others deal with circumstances that affect all the people. Some assume that the people will have access to the Temple, while others do not. Some mention the repentance of the people, while others do not contain this detail. One motif common to all seven petitions is the request that God hear these petitions from heaven where he dwells (vv. 32, 34, 36, 39, 43, 45, and 49). This request then undercuts the notion that the Temple is God's dwelling place. While the first two petitions assume that those who pray are present in the Temple (v. 31, 33), the other five petitions affirm that prayers need only be offered while the petitioner is facing in the direction of the Temple—actual presence in the Temple is not necessary for the prayer to be heard by God (vv. 35, 38, 42, 44, 48). It is the disposition of the petitioners—their readiness to repent and ask forgiveness—that will lead to their prayers being heard.

The Transformation of the Temple Idea

The prayer of 1 Kings 8 stands in contrast to the priestly code, which assumes that God is actually present in the Temple to receive the sacrifices and prayers of those who come to the sanctuary that Israel is to erect for its patron deity (Exodus 25:8; 29:45–46). The Deuteronomic tradition appears to reject the attempt to conceive of God as dwelling in heaven and on earth simultaneously. The Deuteronomic formula which speaks of the place where God will make his name dwell there (Deuteronomy 12:5 *et passim*; see also 1 Kings 8:29) marks a significant departure from the ancient Near East and ancient Israelite belief that a Temple was the dwelling place of the divine on earth. There, God is present to receive the sacrifices that are an essential component of divine service. The prayers of petition in 1 Kings 8:31–51 modify that belief by speaking of the Temple as a place for prayer while ignoring its function as a place for sacrifice. This does suggest that Deuteronomy and the Deuteronomic tradition reject sacrificial worship (see for example, Deuteronomy 12:6, 11, 27; and 1 Kings 8:5, 62–64). But it serves to relativize the actual Temple structure: while it is necessary for sacrificial worship, it is not necessary for prayer since one can pray everywhere—even in lands of exile.

A second feature of the Deuteronomic tradition's transformation of Temple worship is to humanize the divine-human relationship. Consider the verbs of which God is the subject in the petitions. They ask God to listen, forgive, send rain, send the people forth, take action, pass judgment, and teach people the right way. They indicate that the appropriate action for the people who pray includes repentance, acknowledgment of God's name, and prayer. All God's activity takes place in heaven. That of the people takes place outside the Temple except in the cases mentioned in the first two petitions. In every other instance the Temple serves simply to provide an orientation for the worshiper to pray. The Temple and the dynasty slip into the background, and God and Israel take center stage—with the interaction between God and worshipers taking place independently of the Temple.

Jon D. Levenson argues that Solomon's prayer is about the function of the Temple as a place that enables worshipers to escape mundane reality. The Temple, according to Levenson, was a vehicle for self-transcendence.[12] Levenson begins his article by criticizing scholars who denigrate the theological significance of the Temple by creating a negative stereotype of Temple-centered worship in the ancient world and in ancient Israel in particular.[13] Levenson is correct when he rejects the views of those scholars who characterize the Deuteronomic tradition as anti-Temple. The Deuteronomic tradition sees the Temple as the focus of interaction between God and human beings—both Israelite and gentile. But that tradition underscores the significance of the Temple as a place for prayer in addition to sacrifice. The "escape from mundane reality," then, comes by means of a prayerful encounter with God, who responds to the people's repentance with forgiveness.

The final form of both Deuteronomy and the Deuteronomistic History (Joshua—2 Kings) view ancient religious and political institutions through the lens of the fall of the two Israelite national states of Israel and Judah and the forced migration of some of their citizens. Despite these disasters, this literature reflects a belief in the future of the people of Israel without, however, providing a sketch of the contours of that future except to insist that it depends upon the people's obedience to the written, authoritative law as found in the book of Deuteronomy. All Israel's institutions are subordinated to that law. The Temple is one of those institutions.

Jerusalem and its Temple occupied a central position in the Judahite national state. The psalms celebrated the city and its Temple (see Psalm 48). The problem was the reality did not match the ideology and its rhetorical expression. In fact, prophets such as Micah (3:9–12), Jeremiah (7:1–4), and Ezekiel (8:1–18) maintained that what went on in the Temple actually hastened the day of Judah's judgment. The actual fall of Jerusalem and the destruction of its Temple had their effects on the Deuteronomic treatment of the Temple. The two principal Deuteronomic attempts to salvage the Temple as a religious institution were, first, its notion of a Temple without a divine resident (a demythologizing of the Temple) and second, the related notion of the Temple as a place of prayer (a humanizing of the Temple). The Deuteronomic tradition does not reject a Temple-centered religion. The Temple has a legitimate role to play in facilitating Judah's relationship with God, but that role is, nonetheless, subordinate to obedience to the Torah as the prayer of 1 Kings 8 suggests:

> The LORD our God be with us…may he not leave us or abandon us, but incline our hearts to him, to walk in all his ways, and to keep his commandments, his statutes, and his ordinances. (vv. 57–58)

The Afterlife of Solomon's Prayer

Some forty years after Jesus characterized the Temple as "a house of prayer" as he disrupted commercial activities taking place there, the Temple was destroyed by the Romans in the course of putting down a revolt against their rule. Despite this devastating loss, Judaism was able to survive the loss of the Temple. Sacrificial worship did have a place in early Judaism, but prayer, study, and Torah observance were becoming increasingly important as religious expression central to Judaism because of the growing significance of Deuteronomy and the Deuteronomic tradition. A most influential expression of that tradition was Solomon's prayer at the dedication of the Temple as found in 1 Kings 8.

The fundamental thrust of 1 Kings 8 is toward the future. Absent from the prayer is any allusion to ancient Israel's obligation to serve God alone as found in other Deuteronomistic texts, for example, Joshua 23, Judges 2, and 2 Kings 17. The struggle with idolatry was part of Israel's past. Similarly, the prayer does not offer any explanation for Israel's tragic history. First Kings 8 looks to the future as it suggests that the future begins with repentance and prayer that will bring God's forgiveness (vv. 46–51). Forms of the Hebrew verb חלס (forgive) with God as the subject occur five times in Solomon's prayer (1 Kings 8:30, 34, 36, 39, 50). This represents 15 percent of the thirty-three times the verb appears in the Hebrew Bible. Such concentration in a single chapter is noteworthy. First Kings 8, then, suggests that the basis for

Judah's future is God's forgiveness that responds to the people's repentance. The goal of Solomon's prayer is to provide assurance that God will forgive in answer to prayer that gives expression to the authenticity of their repentance. Hope for the future, then, resides in God's readiness to hear the prayers of God's people.

The way that the Deuteronomist relativizes the Temple in 1 Kings 8 made it possible for early Judaism to survive the destruction of the Temple by the Romans.[14] Judaism had to reconstitute itself in a world without a Temple. First Kings 8 helped to facilitate the transformation of Judaism by affirming that prayers for forgiveness need not be offered in the Temple but merely by facing in the direction of the Temple. Forgiveness, after all, opened the way for the people to reclaim their future.

CONCLUSION

Solomon's prayer that is the core of the story of the dedication of the Temple in 1 Kings 8 is almost completely at odds with the tenor of the event that is depicted in that chapter. One expects the story of the Temple's dedication to be described as a most joyous event. After all, it was the concrete expression of God's fidelity to the promises made to David (1 Kings 8:17–21, see 2 Samuel 7). The narrative of 1 Kings 8 presents the completion of the Temple as a triumph of the political and organizational skills of Solomon, David's son and successor. But the bulk of the prayer centers on what Israel should do in the face of natural disaster, military defeat, and forced migration. What the prayer of dedication achieves is the reinterpretation of the Temple idea in Judaism. The Temple is not God's dwelling place on earth, for even the highest of heavens cannot contain Israel's God (1 Kings 8:27), but it is a place for prayer. This reinterpretation contributed to the continuation of the Temple idea in Judaism despite the building destruction by the Romans since one need only pray in the direction of the Temple. The Deuteronomic tradition paves the way for the rabbinic declaration that prayer is the one form of sacrifice still available to Judaism in this world which is without a Temple.

As worshipers walked up the hill on which the Temple was built and its monumental architecture gradually revealed itself, they must have been in awe. Most folk lived in simple four-room houses with earthen floors. As they drew closer to the Temple itself, they could hear the Levites singing and smell the fat burning on the altar attended to by the priests. The feeling of God's power and majesty must have been overwhelming. But all this would be gone one day. Jesus himself wept at the prospect of the destruction of Jerusalem and its Temple (Luke 19:41–44). What remained to sustain believers was prayer. When their religious world appeared to be collapsing, there remained prayer. They learned that they did not have to depend upon a monumental structure and glorious rituals to have an authentic encounter with the divine. They had prayer—and that was enough.

Believers today can embrace the values affirmed in Solomon's prayer. Above all, it underscores the personal dynamic of the divine-human relationship. Although that prayer does not ignore the role religious rituals have in the public, institutional domain, it highlights the personal, individual plane. Prayer transcends barriers that institutional religion erects for God will hear the prayers of those who are denied access to the Temple because they are foreigners (1 Kings 8:41). Prayer is the way that ordinary folk can approach God with their ordinary concerns with the confidence of being heard (1 Kings 8:37–40). Prayer is the way to connect with God when the structures that support religious belief and practice are collapsing. Prayer still offers a way when there appears to be no other way. Above all, prayer offers believers the means to deal with their own moral frailty (1 Kings 8:46). It offers a path to forgiveness and reconciliation. When all else fails, prayer is the pathway leading to God's compassionate love. When institutions die, prayer still offers a pathway to God. When all else fails, there is prayer—and that is enough.

---

1. This phrase also appears in 1 Maccabees 7:37. This book is not included in the Hebrew Bible. It has been preserved in the Septuagint, the Greek version of the Old Testament, and is considered canonical by Catholic and Orthodox Christians. All quotations from the Bible in this chapter are taken from the *New Revised Standard Version*.

2. The psalter has been described as the "hymn book of the temple." But it is not clear how and when these hymns were used in temple worship. See especially Sigmund Mowinckel's *The Psalms in Israel's Worship*, 2 vols., trans. D. R. Ap-Thomas (New York: Abingdon, 1962). Mowinckel suggested a cultic setting for the psalms, suggesting that these poetic prayers were a component of ancient Israel worship in the temple.

3. Martin Noth, *Überlieferungsgeschichtliche Studien* (Halle: M. Niemeyer, 1943), 7 n. 6. In this essay, Noth offers the hypothesis of a Deuteronomistic history, comprising the books of Joshua, Judges, Samuel, and Kings and reflects on the theology of Deuteronomy. He claims that the history was the work of an individual writing sometime after 560 BC to explain the reasons for the fall of the two Israelite kingdoms.

4. *Könige*, Biblischer Kommentar des Altes Testament (Neukirchen-Vluyn: Neukirchener Verlag des Erziehungsvereins 1964, 1968), 174, 184–186, 188–190, 193.

5. See L. J. Hoppe, "The Afterlife of a Text: The Case of Solomon's Prayer in 1 Kings 8," *Liber Annuus* 51 (2001) 9–30, here 12–13.

6. Gary Knoppers, "Prayer and Propaganda: Solomon's Dedication of the Temple and the Deuteronomist's Program," *Catholic Biblical Quarterly* 57, no. 2 (April 1995): 229–254.

7. Gary Beckman, "Temple Building among the Hittites," *From Foundations to Crenellations: Essays on Temple Building in the Ancient Near East and the Hebrew Bible*, ed. Mark Bodney and Jamie Novatny, Alter Orient und Altes Testament, 366 (Münster: Ugarit-Verlag, 2010), 71;

Joseph Blenkinsopp, *David Remembered: Kingship and National Identity in Ancient Israel* (Grand Rapids: Eerdmans, 2013), 75.

8. The notion that the Temple is a place for God's name to dwell is motif that is characteristic of the Deuteronomic tradition. Moshe Weinfeld has calculated that this motif is expressed in several forms in Deuteronomy and the Deuteronomistic History more than fifty times. See his *Deuteronomy and the Deuteronomic Tradition* (Oxford, UK: Clarendon, 1972), 324–325. The origin of this expression is still a matter of scholarly investigation, but it is clear that Deuteronomic tradition sees God's abode in heaven. The Temple has a humanistic function as a place for people to pray.

9. The Septuagint version of 8:16, however, states explicitly that God did chose Jerusalem as the place where his name was to dwell. This is probably the result of the transfer of the temple's holiness to the entire city of Jerusalem that took place in the exilic and post-exilic periods, e.g., Isaiah 52:1; Nehemiah 11:1; Tobit 13:9.

10. In the Deuteronomic tradition, *rest* usually refers to the settlement of the tribes in Canaan (e.g., Joshua 23:1) or the "rest" from his enemies that David enjoyed (2 Samuel 7:1, 11). Here, it refers to God's accessibility to Israel through prayer and obedience. See Wolfgang M. W. Roth, "Deuteronomistic Rest Theology: A Redaction-Critical Study," *Biblical Research* 21 (1976): 11–12.

11. This second prayer of blessing has no parallel in the chronicler's version of Solomon's Prayer in 2 Chronicles 6. This omission by the chronicler is not surprising given that tradition's focus is on David and his dynasty.

12. Jon D. Levenson, "The Temple and the World," *Journal of Religion* 64, no. 3 (July 1984): 297–298.

13. Levenson, "The Temple and the World," 275–277.

14. Jon D. Levenson asserets that the most remarkable feature of Jewish history is the survival of Judaism after the destruction of the Second Temple. See his *Sinai and Zion* (Philadelphia: Fortress, 1985), 181.

PART SEVEN

Prayer among Different Types of Groups

PRAYER AND MARRIAGE

MILITARY POSTURES IN PRAYER

IN SEARCH OF COMMUNION WITH CHRIST

Each group of people has varying needs when it comes to prayer. In this section, to illustrate how we can be sensitive to such groups, either as a member or someone seeking to support someone in it, three different populations have been chosen.

The first chapter is Prayer and Marriage by Paul Giblin. He provides wonderful information based on his work with couples and a survey of one hundred spouses asking such questions as: What motivates your prayer? Do you pray more in times of crises or celebratory times? How does prayer connect to your daily loving, communicating, struggling, committing, and recommitting? From such questions, he provides fascinating and helpful information on such areas as major prayer "learnings," benefits of prayer in daily marital interactions, communication, managing conflict, prayer and marital development, and family life. He closes by offering reflective questions for spouses as well as prayer activities that will be helpful not only for couples themselves but possibly even more for those who are called to guide them on their spiritual journey.

The next chapter is entitled Military Postures in Prayer: Moments of Spiritual Intimacy by F. Richard Spencer. In it, he frames prayer creatively in terms of the postures of kneeling, time out, family engagements, lying face down, sitting, walking in a daze, the sword, running, emptiness, forgiveness, water, simplicity, beach ministry, and gratitude. Anyone presently serving or having served in the military, as well as those who have supported military personnel (family, friends, employers, veterans' groups), can identify with the imagery in this chapter. Spencer's extensive military chaplaincy experience adds authority to his insights.

The third and final chapter is In Search of Communion with Christ: Praying as a Seminarian by Michael Rubeling. He reflects on the roles sacred Scripture, Liturgy of the Hours, Mass, adoration, penance, solitude, and Marian devotion can play in a seminarian's life. Concerned with the place prayer plays in the formation of not only the seminarian but the priest he is to become, Rubeling aptly emphasizes a spirituality that centers itself on the threefold path of encountering Christ in "sacred Scripture, in God's holy mysteries, and in those he will serve in his ministry."

CHAPTER 33

Prayer and Marriage

~ Paul Giblin ~

I have long been interested in strong marriages, marital well-being, and the role that spirituality, religion, and in particular, prayer, can play in marriage. Why do couples pray? What motivates their prayer? Do they pray more in times of crises or celebration? Do crises prevent them from praying? How does prayer connect to their daily loving, communicating, struggling, committing, and recommitting? Do they pray with and for each other, with and for their children? Has prayer changed for them over time? Has their image of and relationship with God changed over time? How much has prayer influenced their marriage and vice versa? Is it helpful to think of spouses' relationships with God as a dynamic triangle? What does it mean to speak of praying unceasingly in the context of marriage? Do husbands and wives typically pray differently? Has prayer been a negative influence in some marriages?

I set out to answer many of these questions in several ways. I surveyed one hundred spouses for whom faith was important. Responses were solicited from couples in Catholic and Protestant parishes, Jewish congregations, and university contexts. In a second study, I interviewed spiritual directors and asked about their experience with married individuals and on rare occasion with married couples. I have explored the place of prayer and meditation in couples' lives with whom I have worked in marital counseling. And finally, I bring my own experience as a married person. What follows is a summary of learning from these multiple sources.

Let me begin by saying this is not an easy area to explore. Couples (perhaps laypeople in general) seem to suffer from low prayer esteem. That is, they assess themselves as poor to fair prayers. They prefer to defer to holy people. They seem to hold an ideal image or expectation of prayer that they feel they do not live up to. Yet, very interestingly, in the next breath, when asked about their relationship with God, they quickly and assuredly indicate they feel very close to God. A paradox. Let me summarize a number of my prayer learnings.

Major Prayer Learnings

- Marriage influences prayer as much as prayer influences marriage.
- Prayer and marriage are about relationship, friendship, honesty, trust, vulnerability, coming to know and be known.

- Prayer supports increasing intimacy in marriage and cycles through similar periods of closeness and distance.
- Prayer and marriage are designed to bring about growth and healing, typically through encounter with depth of self, spouse, and God.
- Marital life is dangerous without some form of prayer or meditation.
- Prayer clarifies, calms, encourages, and empowers spouses.
- Prayer expands couples' consciousness, making them more empathic and socially conscious.
- Gratefulness and forgiveness are at the heart of marital prayer.
- Prayer serves as a marital compass, providing vision, direction, and meaning.
- Spouses use many different forms of prayer, each making sense at specific times.
- Prayer in marriage changes over time, seemingly in accord with how marriage changes, spouses change, and experience of God changes.
- Spouses encounter many obstacles to prayer, beginning with busyness, fatigue, and less than loving images of God.
- Almost all spouses of faith pray regularly for their partner and children. Few spouses pray with each other outside of mealtime grace and church liturgy.
- Remembering and imagining are important to marital and family prayer. Sin is about forgetting we are loved by and present to God.
- Couples can benefit from a regular practice of reflection on and sharing about their prayer experience.
- Couples are hungry for assistance in making connections between their prayer and marital lives.

Benefits of Prayer in Daily Marital Interactions

Marital well-being is often described in terms of three Cs: good communication, effective conflict management, and strong commitment. Sometimes a fourth C, a sense of community, is also highlighted. When couples were surveyed about connections they make between prayer and their daily interactions, they had many observations.

Communicating

The creation of a cooperative, collaborative team requires self-awareness, responsible sharing, dedicated listening, the ability to convey respect and caring, to make and respond to clear requests, and to negotiate roles and expectations, among numerous other skills. Good communication is the foundation of an effective marriage. Couples offered the following connections:

- "Prayer helps me understand my feelings, thoughts, wants, and needs."
- "Prayer helps me be more authentic, to connect with my deeper self."
- "Prayer helps me communicate better with my spouse."
- "Prayer helps me listen to and appreciate my spouse."
- "Prayer helps in making marital and family decisions."
- "Prayer holds me accountable, and connects us to a deeper level and bonds us."
- "Prayer helps me be more reflective, open to healing, and to change my behavior."
- "Prayer helps me be more accepting of my spouse as a child of God."

Managing Conflict

Couples need to be able to negotiate differences, be aware of and constructively express anger, articulate and not act out fears, learn to give and take, and balance different needs for closeness and independence. Partners need trust, tolerance, patience, and compassion. The psychologist Rollo May once said that true freedom is the ability to pause and in the pause choose. However, we are hardwired to react, to defend, to scan for danger and the negative instead of pausing and freely responding, instead of focusing on strengths. Prayer helps couples pause and choose, and build on strengths. Effective conflict management skills are essential to marital well-being. Couples offered the following connections:

- "Prayer helps me be more compassionate and less judgmental."
- "Prayer helps me slow down and not say things I will later regret."
- "Prayer helps me blame less and take more responsibility."
- "Prayer helps me surrender or let go of things I need to let go."
- "Prayer helps me accept my limitations and faults."
- "Prayer helps me see things through God's eyes."
- "Prayer helps me be more accepting and forgiving of my partner."
- "Prayer helps me to manage my fears."
- "Prayer changes my single-mindedness when we are in conflict."
- "Prayer helps me prioritize what is important when we are struggling."
- "It is prayer that leads us back to each other, to transformation and reconciliation."

While prayer is most often a support in managing marital conflict, it is actually a source of conflict for a small number of couples. Spouses cited differences in prayer styles and expectations of when, how, and why to pray. They spoke of their partner's unwillingness to pray with them or being envious of the spouse's closer relationship with God or of feeling ganged up on by the spouse and God. Interestingly, interfaith differences were not cited as generating conflict.

Committing

Commitment is the backbone of a marriage, providing vision, direction, and purpose. In the absence of efforts to express their own life-giving vision, spouses unconsciously adopt the vision of the culture. This cultural vision or narrative for marriage is typically short-sighted, individualistic, egocentric, limiting, and not life-giving. It is the couple's commitment that carries them through difficult times. Commitment creates healthy boundaries. It is about making the choice to give up choices that paradoxically is freeing. Couples made the following connections between prayer and commitment:

- "Prayer helps me sustain my marital and family commitments."
- "Prayer contributes to my vision of marital and family life."
- "Prayer gives meaning to the silent sacrifices of marriage."
- "Prayer reminds me God is in control, there is more than me guiding us."
- "Prayer helps us live our values."
- "Prayer keeps me open to life in new ways and helps me look to the future."
- "Prayer helps me appreciate the mystery dimension of life."

Prayer and Marital Development

Marriages change and develop. So does prayer. I suggest there is a synchronicity between these changes. Marriages are hypothesized to evolve through a number of stages, typically three to five.[1] For example, marriages begin in a honeymoon stage with partners very attuned to each other, eliciting their best selves in each other, minimizing differences, and most accepting of each other. They have to ask for little and it is as if they can read each other's minds. As couples settle into a routine of shared roles and responsibilities, as they come to know each other more fully, their awareness of differences arises, disappointments begin, and now they have to know what they want and ask for it. In an effort to return to status quo they seek to change the partner, change this unpleasant and unexpected situation. Differences can become disagreements and power struggles. This is a critical time when couples either come apart or grow individually and together in new and deeper ways. They either separate or reconcile and recommit. Couples learn to negotiate differences, and focus on changing self as opposed to changing partner. Marriages cycle through these stages not just one time but multiple times, each time with greater awareness and sensitivity.

We might guess what prayer looks like across these various stages. For example: In the beginning, a couple's prayer might emphasize praise and thanksgiving. This partner is an answer to prayer, marriage is gift and grace. Feelings of joy, excitement, wonder, happiness, and hope abound. They pray their own Song of Songs and psalms of thanksgiving and praise. Further into the relationship, as struggles increase, prayer might shift to petition: "God, help me to change." "God, please help him or her to see the light." Psalms of petition and lament come to mind. Feelings of hurt, disappointment, fear, sadness, loneliness, and anger prevail. As partners work through their differences, experience struggles as normal and an invitation to grow, they pray for forgiveness, offer forgiveness, and again gratitude and praise and wonder.

SPIRITUAL DIRECTION AND MARRIAGE

Spiritual formation and direction is typically offered to individuals and rarely for couples. Cursillo and Marriage Encounter are two exceptions. Yet another exception offers a design for couple spiritual direction in which spouses are invited to consider the marriage as their director.[2] The assumption is that God speaks not only through spouses but through the marriage itself. Thus, partners consider: How and in what ways is your marriage asking you to grow, heal, and change? What would be best for your marriage? Where and how is your marriage calling you to be free, whole, more fully yourselves?

PRAYER AND FAMILY LIFE

In the survey study, all spouses prayed regularly for each other and for their children. However, beyond family meals and liturgical contexts, almost no spouses prayed with each other. Some indicated they had never considered it and appreciated the question. Those few spouses who did pray together offered the following:

- "Prayer together is satisfying, it increases our intimacy, it creates unity, healing, and accountability."
- "It's how I learn what's really important, what's on his mind."
- "It's where we share what we believe God is asking of us."

PRAYER: AN EVOLVING REALITY

If prayer is about relationship, then we can expect change, growth, and development to follow. While most surveyed spouses learned to pray from their parents, the strong majority indicated their current form of prayer was different. Likewise, their image of and relationship to God had changed.

- "Prayer as a child was focused on necessity; now it is on relationship."
- "Prayer has become more personal, conversational, spontaneous, informal."
- "Prayer has become more contemplative."
- "Prayer used to be rote and formal; now it is simpler and shorter."
- "As life got more complicated, prayer has changed and deepened. It has become more reflective and less petitionary, more for others and less for myself."
- "I didn't pray before marriage. Now I do."
- "I've changed, so my prayer has changed."

- "I used to see God as distant and judgmental. Marriage has taught me about God's intimacy and love."
- "Through marriage, I understand God better and the fullness of God's attributes."

A necessary qualifier: For a quarter of survey participants, discussion of a change or development in prayer and image of God made no sense. Their prayer had not changed. Their relationship with God had not changed. And that was fine.

Prayer Practice and Marriage

I was curious about when and how spouses pray, what praying unceasingly looks like in marriage, whether they talk with each other about prayer, and whether they had communities of prayer to support them. The majority of spouses indicated they prayed from three to four times a week to daily. They opted less for a dedicated time and space than "praying throughout the day," "always and everywhere," more often in the morning and night, but also traveling to and from work, when doing the dishes, and when showering each day.

"Do you pay attention to your body in prayer?" Very few responded affirmatively. It is interesting to contrast this with older traditions of prayer often characterized by postures of head down, eyes closed, and hands folded! It is also interesting to contrast this with Eastern forms of meditation that pay particular attention to meditation postures. When spouses were asked if they had strategies for calming and quieting themselves in preparation for or during prayer, a good number responded affirmatively. Strategies included paying attention to breath, sitting quietly and still, doing relaxation exercises, and using some form of letting go, unburdening, or surrendering exercises. The large majority of spouses reported encountering resistance or obstacles to prayer. Few reported using spiritual or religious objects for support, and few reported having a dedicated space in the home for prayer.

Pastoral Strategies

Those who work with couples in adult faith formation, spiritual direction, marriage enrichment, pastoral counseling, and other forms of ministry are here offered two sets of practical strategies: reflective questions and prayer activities. As mentioned previously, many couples suffer from low prayer esteem and are hungry for assistance in deepening their prayer lives. Many have never thought of praying together outside the context of liturgy, grace at meals, or more formal prayers. The following strategies could be offered in the context of work with individual couples, couples groups, or a couples retreat.

REFLECTIVE QUESTIONS

Spouses are encouraged to reflect on the following questions.

1. What is the *purpose* of prayer for you?
2. What have you learned about God's love, acceptance, and forgiveness in your marriage?
3. What have you come to recognize as *signs* of God's presence in our midst?
4. How do *moments* of beauty, surprise, gratitude, surrender, forgiveness, and mystery or unknowing speak to you of God's presence?
5. What *benefits* from prayer do you experience?
6. When is prayer a *joyful* experience for you?
7. How does prayer help *desire* come alive for you?
8. Has prayer changed for you over time? *How* has prayer changed you?
9. (How) Have your marital differences ultimately become a source of unity through prayer?
10. How would you answer, "I knew my marriage was a sacrament when…"
11. What *obstacles* to prayer do you encounter? How do you deal with them?
12. Is prayer easier or more difficult during crisis times versus good times?

PRAYER ACTIVITIES

Reflect on your *prayer histories*: Who first taught you to pray? What do you remember about prayer back then? What were your earliest images of God? Who have been your prayer mentors since? Who and what experiences have continued to influence your prayer life?

Invite couples to draw a marital timeline indicating significant moments, highs and lows, of their life together. Encourage them to take considerable time to do this and discuss the result. Next, have them examine the timeline in terms of where, when and how God was present to them. When were they on holy ground? What were sacred moments? Finally, what was prayer like across the timeline? Suggest they repeat this exercise annually, reflecting on God's action in their midst, perhaps putting it in writing each year. For many of us, God's presence is revealed only upon reflection.

Encourage couples to regularly revisit and perhaps rewrite their marriage vows. This keeps their vision fresh and their intentionality dynamic.

A popular exercise in Marriage Encounter is the end-of-the-day practice of writing about one's feelings, exchanging journals, and discussing them with the partner. Husbands especially find this helpful; it gives them time to access their feelings and seems to level the conversation field. Spouses are invited to bless each other at the close of this process, in light of what each knows the other is celebrating or struggling with.

Invite spouses to reflect on and share their moments of consolation or joy and desolation or sadness with each other at the end of each day. Through this process they attune to the activity of God in and through the people and events of their day. See this resource for an excellent application of the examen to marital and family life.[3]

Explore with couples how ritual practices of honoring the Sabbath and spiritual mindfulness might enhance their lives. Developing Sabbath practices can help couples and families step out of the one speed, fast-paced, multitasking culture to better enjoy each other, meals together, nature, God, and the broader world.[4] Robert J. Wicks offers excellent suggestions for "praying always" called practicing "spiritual mindfulness."[5] Likewise, Ron DelBene offers the "breath prayer" in which a person responds to God's question, "What do you want?" with their name for God and their answer as a mantra or brief prayer spoken throughout the day.[6] Henri Nouwen suggests we convert our unceasing, nonreflective thinking to a God-centered dialogue, that we think and live in the presence of God and turn our thoughts into conversation.[7]

Explore ways in which body awareness, breath, posture, and movement might enhance prayer.

Explore ways in which space in the home might enhance prayer, for example, through the use of icons, pictures, prayer cushions, or an altar.

Receive a daily e-mail meditation from sources such as Sacred Space, Pray As You Go, or the Center for Action and Contemplation.

Read spiritual poetry to each other (see Daniel Ladinsky, Gerard Manley Hopkins, Denise Levertov, Mary Oliver, Jessica Powers). Read and discuss books on prayer and spirituality together (see William Barry, Margaret Silf, Anthony Bloom, Joyce Rupp, Robert Wicks, Joseph Schmidt).

Read the psalms together and write your own psalms of praise, petition, lament, and thanksgiving. Write and share your own prayers.

CONCLUSION

Bill Barry, Jesuit priest, psychologist, spiritual director, and author, wrote a 2001 article in *America*, "Why Do You Pray?"[8] He chronicled the evolution of his motivations for prayer. He got me thinking about how this article would read if it were written by a married person. At the same time, I read Joseph Schmidt's lovely book on prayer, *Praying Our Experiences.*[9] He, like Barry, advocates honest sharing of feelings and experiences with God. Again, I wondered about sharing marital and family experiences, joys and struggles, hopes and fears, and intimacy and sexuality in prayer. And so began my curiosity and exploration of prayer and marriage. Throughout this process, I have come to believe that far more spouses are more deeply prayerful than they take credit for, that they pray spontaneously and unceasingly throughout the day, connecting their lives with God. They suffer from low prayer esteem. I also believe that many spouses are hungry to learn more about prayer and can benefit from discussion of and teaching about prayer. They are hungry to explore the reciprocal relationship between prayer and marriage.

1. See Sari Harrar and Rita DeMaria, *The Seven Stages of Marriage: Laughter, Intimacy and Passion Today, Tomorrow and Forever* (New York: Reader's Digest, 2007); and B. Dym and M. Glenn, *Couples: Exploring and Understanding the Cycles of Intimate Relationships* (New York: HarperColllins, 1993).
2. Paul Giblin, "Spiritual Direction with Couples," *Presence*, 11, no. 4 (2005): 48–53.
3. Dennis Linn, Sheila Fabricant Linn, and Matthew Linn, *Sleeping with Bread: Holding What Gives You Life* (New York: Paulist,1995).
4. See Marva Dawn, *Keeping the Sabbath Wholly: Ceasing, Resting, Embracing, Feasting* (Grand Rapids: Eerdmans, 1989) and Wayne Muller, *Sabbath: Finding Rest, Renewal and Delight in Our Busy Days* (New York: Bantam, 1999).
5. Robert J. Wicks, *Prayerfulness: Awakening to the Fullness of Life* (South Bend, IN: Sorin, 2011).
6. Ron DelBene, *The Breath of Life: A Simple Way to Pray* (Eugene: Wipf & Stock, 2005).
7. Henri J. M. Nouwen, "Unceasing prayer," *America*, August 5, 1978, 46–51.
8. William Barry, SJ, "Why Do You Pray?" *America*, June 4–11, 2001, 7–9.
9. Joseph Schmidt, *Praying Our Experiences* (Winona, MN: St. Mary's, 2000).

CHAPTER 34

Military Postures in Prayer: Moments of Spiritual Intimacy

~ F. Richard Spencer ~

Paratroopers for the U.S. Army Airborne are taught that, for a successful and safe landing, a parachutist must make five points of contact (postures) when landing: the feet, the leg muscles, the hip, one side of your body, and the shoulder, all in sequence and all the while keeping your head tucked into your chest. I vividly recall my first jump and the profound reliance and trust upon God and the silence and the beauty of God's presence surrounding me as I safely returned to the earth and landed. As I prepared to depart the plane I hesitated, made the Sign of the Cross, exited, and suddenly—there was God! I trusted and enjoyed this moment of beauty, everything in its place, harmony, contentment, deep peace, bliss. The stillness and peace made me think of the silence of God. I found myself wondering if this was what heaven is like, a perfect bliss.

As an airborne paratrooper for almost forty-five years, I have targeted and experienced many and various postures of prayer while living my life as a *soul*-dier priest in the US Army through word and action, all the while keeping my head and heart focused on Jesus. I have experienced many postures in prayer and would like to share with you thirteen of those moments trusting in God's presence, intimacy, and grace that enabled me to experience safe and secure landings through some difficult and some very heartwarming, joy-filled experiences as a Christian who trusts that the Lord truly has me in the palm of his hands!

The Posture of Kneeling

My earliest recollection of a kneeling prayer posture came from my mother. Yes, my mom wore combat boots! As a sergeant in the US Marine Corps, she knew and taught us kids how important it was to bring body and soul together in prayer. Mom taught us that being on your knees is a growth in humility.

During family prayer, with all five of us kids kneeling as a group at our assigned worship spaces in the living room of our home, we would pray the rosary together. Those early childhood experiences helped to shape my humility and my prayer life. All the people, places, and things that God has put in my life are ways that God makes me aware of his presence and love. All the love that God sends my way through relatives, friends, and even those who regard me as an enemy touches my heart and makes me more loving, forgiving, and humble.

The Posture during "Time Out"

Wednesdays in my hometown of Sylacauga, Alabama, during the '50s and '60s were declared midweek church days. Everything closed at noon. The public schools were dismissed at noon (and without any homework assignments for the night), gas stations, food stores, department stores, everything was closed from noon Wednesday until the next morning in order to allow church people to attend worship services. For us Catholic kids, this was time for our *Baltimore Catechism* classes followed by novenas, benediction, and adoration. Meanwhile across town, our Southern Baptist friends, and other Protestant denominations, were also at prayer on Wednesday evenings during this time-out from daily routines. I learned early in these experiences that surrounding myself with good people, neighbors, friends, and relatives put me in touch with the divine.

The Posture of Family Engagements

After working for the paper mill for forty consecutive years, my father had earned his first four-week period of paid vacation. It was a family decision to venture out to California from our home in Alabama to visit my mom's sister and her family (and of course Mickey and Minnie) and then travel up to Wisconsin to visit the rest of our relatives before the eventual return home. Having minimal financial resources for such an adventure required us to camp in tents throughout the experience. In preparation for such an event, my parents conducted practice sessions in our backyard. These were timed events, and each of us kids had tasks to perform in setting up base camp. Of course, before we even unpacked the contents of the car to set up, a prayer was offered, and then there was the excitement of competition to perform each task correctly and timely. My task was to set up the gas stove, obtain water, and begin to boil the water that would be used for the meal and for washing dishes. The neighbors watched from a distance at the events and then also watched the award ceremony for the kid who performed his or her task most efficiently. As a family, we experienced our graciously loving God as brother and sister, who saves us, reconciles us with one another, and shows us how to grow up and become responsible to others. We experienced God also as friend, lover, and companion who lives within us in the most intimate relationship as a family and makes us eager to tell others about Jesus and share his love with them.

THE POSTURE OF LYING FACE DOWN

Not once but three times, my face and nose have pushed against the marble floor of two cathedrals during ordination ceremonies. The first was my diaconate ordination, and the second, my priesthood ordination, both at Cathedral of Mary Our Queen, Baltimore. The third moment, lying prostrate before the altar while the Litany of Saints was being recited was ordination as a bishop at the Basilica of the National Shrine of the Immaculate Conception, Washington, DC. During all three liturgical moments, I vividly recall thinking to myself, "No turning back, now!" and, "What have I said 'yes' to, once again, in responding to the call by the Lord to serve God's people?" Very humbling, it was, lying face down as I was giving my life for the Church, God's people, and to the Lord, just as the Lord laid down his life for me.

THE POSTURE OF SITTING

I was sharing First Eucharist with a young cancer patient, a seven-year-old girl dressed in a new white dress made by the hands of her own dear mother. While in her home, moments before she died, sitting with her on the sofa in the family living room is a posture of prayer that I will never forget. Moments following the sacramental exchange, I witnessed her transition from this earthly life into eternal life. Her smile after receiving the Eucharist for the very first time and then the closing of her eyes as she stopped breathing were both holy moments. It will remain with me for the rest of my days. I marvel at God's timing and loving embrace. What also came to my mind were the final lyrics of *Les Miserables*, as Valjean was dying and as the sacred words were being voiced, "To love another person is to see the Face of God." On this day with this First Eucharistic moment for this young child, I saw the face of God.

THE POSTURE OF WALKING IN A DAZE

Teams were quickly formed to go into the smoldering five-sided building to remove bodies. Protestant chaplain Robert Jenkins and I, the Roman Catholic chaplain, were the first team selected to enter the Pentagon on 9/11. After the FBI photographed and tagged the remains and indicate the location found, soldiers put them into body bags, and then we prayed a blessing over the remains before they were carried out of the building to a refrigeration truck waiting with a medical team and another chaplain. Respect for the dead and a chain of custody of the remains were of paramount importance. Both Chaplain Jenkins and I could feel the weight of the responsibility, but both of us also found relief and strength through prayer and the knowledge that what we were doing for the living and the dead was necessary and a sacred honor. Neither of us knew what we were getting into, nor just how much we would need God's grace and strength in order to provide meaningful and effective ministry to those assembled around us. We walked among the soldiers listening, offering words of encouragement and hope, praying with some, and silently praying for all and for each other. Many of the soldiers were simply walking in a daze—confused, angry, hurting. The fire continued to consume the Pentagon, and nightfall was upon us when we were told there would be no further entering the building that night.

The following day, on September 12, 2001, we were initially stopped from going into the Pentagon because of renewed fire concerns and additional structural damage on the left side of the building. Chaplain Jenkins and I moved among the troops waiting to continue the removal of remains. Many were anxious and nervous. Most had never done this before. Some were not sure they could. Soon permission and orders were given to enter once again. We entered a long, dark hall through four inches of standing water and debris to where remains were tagged and ready for removal. One soldier returned; he could not handle the confinement or the darkness. As each stretcher came and stopped, Chaplain Jenkins and I would simultaneously bless the deceased; each body removed from the disaster would have a Protestant and a Catholic prayer offered. If anyone knew that someone was Jewish or Muslim, we were prepared for that as well. We did with deep respect what our consciences and duty as chaplains called for: We comforted the living and honored the dead.

THE POSTURE OF THE SWORD

We were just two days from celebrating Palm Sunday at the US military base in Taji, Iraq, and my chaplain assistant came to me worried that the Army supply system would not deliver the requested supply of palms on time for our services. "No worry," I said, as there were many palm trees on the military compound. That same day, while exploring one of Saddam Hussein's abandoned palaces, I found on the wall a sword. With permission, I borrowed the sword, and off we went to cut palms for Palm Sunday Masses and services and to decorate our makeshift chapel. We were pretty successful even though the dullness of the sword made cutting the palms difficult, resulting in both of us having plenty of blisters on our hands. As I used the sword, I reflected on the Bible verse: "They shall beat their swords into plowshares and their spears into pruning hooks. One nation shall not raise the sword against another, / nor shall they train for war again" (Isaiah 2:4). These verses from the prophet Isaiah are on a plaque in the gardens of the United Nations building in New York. *The Jewish Study Bible* has this note regarding this passage:

> The prophet does not imagine a future without borders or distinct nationali-
> ties. International conflicts will still occur, but nations will no longer resolve
> them through warfare. Instead, nations will submit to arbitration at Mount

Zion. The Temple will become the headquarters of a divine Security Council with a membership of one and unsurpassed ability to ensure compliance.[1]

An interesting image: God as arbitrator among nations, helping us to settle our differences without resorting to war.

THE POSTURE OF RUNNING

Good Friday 2004 in Iraq was one of the bloodiest days of the war; several of our military convoys, mostly fuel tankers, were attacked. We lost 134 soldiers that day. Our convoy was quickly diverted to a nearby forward-operating base. Our vehicle, a Humvee with soft-sided doors and cover, was very vulnerable to the multiple rockets. Luckily, we arrived after the chaplain driver raced across the open fields, driving at ridiculous but necessary high speeds. Immediately upon gaining access to the compound, we became further engaged carrying the stretchers of the wounded and the dead to the medical tent and to the back room, which became the morgue. We had US casualties as well as our Iraq friendly forces and also Iraq enemy soldiers. So, how were we initially able to tell who was who in our medical tent? Who was the Iraq friendly soldier working with us as our interpreter and who was the Iraq enemy? A simple look at their underwear was our first clue as to who was who, as many of our Iraq friendly forces at this location had been given, just the week before, standard US military brown underwear.

That night, exhausted and in need of fresh air, I climbed to the top of one of the buildings in our compound and spent most of the night on the rooftop with a sniper, while we used night-vision goggles to watch the enemy try to infiltrate our perimeter. The perimeter wire eliminated the threat.

It is easy to see the divine shining in the people I love: family, relatives, friends. It is not so easy to recognize God in the people who regard me as enemy. God is not in the bad things or in the evil that people do, but God is in the people who do them. I pray that as I become more aware of God in me and in the beauty and goodness around me, I will find it easier to recognize the Divine shining in those I find unattractive.

THE POSTURE OF EMPTINESS

I had just returned to the US from a second tour in Iraq and was completing my clinical pastoral education graduate program at Walter Reed Army Hospital. For a residence, I was renting a rectory from the archdiocese of Baltimore. One Sunday morning in the midst of a snow and lightning storm, the rectory exploded and burned to the ground. Luckily, I was not inside on that Saturday night and Sunday morning; I had weekend duty in the hospital. I received a phone call around 6:30 AM from the pastor of the parish, who lived at another location, telling me that the rectory was gone. He further shared that there was an explosion and the fire truck never made it there. It was one block away from the fire when it slid on the snow-covered roads and tipped into a ditch! All the firefighters could do was watch the home burn and crumple into the basement. All that remained above ground were the two chimneys.

I arrived to view the scene around noon that Sunday. The fire was still burning in various locations of the basement. There I was, standing on the edge of this big hole in the ground looking at all my stuff, and I began to realize that I needed a place to spend the night. I also needed to go to the store and make some purchases, such as a toothbrush, razor, some clothing items. I arrived at a big retail store and secured a large cart and started walking the aisles. My mind was racing, and I was simply overwhelmed at all the choices on the shelves. I also felt angry, inconvenienced, and challenged, but trusted that God had a plan for me. I knew I wanted toothpaste, but to look at row after row of choices became overpowering to my senses. Just months earlier in Iraq, where the local PX store often had one variety of toothpaste, and now looking at dozens of options, I felt stressed out. I left the empty cart and went out to my car and cried. Was I sad? Angry? Abandoned? Yes.

About ten minutes later, I thought I was composed enough to enter the store a second time. Again, I was overwhelmed with the decisions and choices and quickly ran out of the store and to the sanctuary of my car. Finally, a third attempt, and this time I was quickly grabbing items off the clothing racks and pharmacy shelves, not really concentrating on what I was putting into my cart but knowing I had to keep moving. I will never forget the empty feeling of that day as the sun had already set and a dark winter evening began. It looked like darkness had won. But I knew that was not so. In my mind and heart, I reflected on the reading from Isaiah 9:1, from Christmas Midnight Mass: "The people who walked in darkness have seen a great light; / Upon those who dwelt in the land of gloom a light has shone."[2] I chose that day not to live in gloom but to trust. I further reflected on the lives of St. Paul and St. Francis of Assisi. They expressed and lived very well their total dependence on God, their full awareness that in everything God was working through them. Likewise, I knew I could count on God no matter what circumstances I found myself in. I knew the strength I needed would come from God. I trusted. I was eager to find the very first opportunity to celebrate Mass, which I knew would strengthen my hope and restore my joy.

THE POSTURE OF FORGIVENESS

On the battlefield in Iraq during Lent 2011, three specific events formed me, and I administered three general absolutions.

The first was in the Green Zone, April 6. There are many uncomfortable moments on any battlefield, and one of those is being stuck in a vehicle convoy queue at a military gate trying to exit, as I was attempting to do when the alarm was given: "Second dog down!" A distinctive and quiet fear floats in the air inside you and among your traveling companions as vehicle engines are quickly turned off and personnel exit their vehicles and move quickly to a hardened bomb shelter. Bomb-sniffing dogs are used at the gates to help identify the presence of explosive materials in vehicles or on people trying to enter the military compounds. When a dog gives an alert, they sit. Sometimes the dog may just be tired from the prolonged hours of being on duty or dehydration from the intense heat, so sitting down could be a reasonable response. Hence, a second dog is always made available to verify the response of the first. If and when the second dog sits in the same space or area, you are almost 100 percent sure you have a hot situation unfolding. This was my experience with "second dog down." Our vehicle was third from the gate search location. We moved in an orderly fashion with deliberate haste to a hardened shelter for protection while an Explosive Ordinance Team arrived to defuse the situation. In the bunker, I did a quick inventory and realized that I had a fairly significant crowd of Catholics huddled together. I then began to administer the third form of the rite of reconciliation with general absolution.

The second event took place on the fifth Sunday of Lent, Basrah compound, April 10. "Incoming! Incoming! Incoming!" the siren and electronic voice alarms were both sounding. As a result, my final words during the Mass and the distribution of the Eucharist were, "Eat, drink…the Mass is quickly ended—move to the bunker now!" As the alarms were sounded, about sixty people in the chapel hit the floor. I was impressed as I stood there watching everyone covering their heads, plugging their ears, and opening their mouths to allow pressure to escape from the anticipated blast. Then I realized that I was standing and needed also to drop to the floor. We remained there while I gave general absolution. About two minutes later, we smartly moved outside to the bunkers near the chapel. Two of our soldiers in nearby sleeping tents were killed in that incident.

The third event took place on Good Friday, Basrah compound, April 22. Nine minutes into the liturgy of Good Friday and again we heard, "Incoming! Incoming! Incoming!" Again, we assumed the duck-and-cover positions—me, under the altar table, again, face down, ears plugged with fingers, and with mouth open. After about a good two- to four-minute silent pause, which to some of us felt like an eternity, the next electronic announcement came telling us to move quickly to the nearest bunker. We stood, and I once again quickly gave general absolution. Then, dismissing the crowd, I watched as about seventy people moved in an orderly fashion to concrete bunkers outside. First, I proceeded to the Blessed Sacrament room and took the ciborium filled with consecrated Hosts with me to the bunker. In the bunker, we continued the readings for Good Friday, prayed the Lord's Prayer, and distributed Holy Communion to those gathered. Twenty-five minutes later, the "all clear" was announced. We moved back into the wooden chapel for the veneration of the cross and dismissal. These multiple incoming rockets once again targeted our sleeping tents, and three more American GIs were killed that day. A sad day as we commemorated the "good" of this liturgical Good Friday.

I have learned one essential lesson from these three battlefield moments: None of us should wait until a "second dog down" alarm is given before we celebrate the sacrament of reconciliation!

Spiritually reflecting on these three experiences in Iraq, I share the early Christians' faith in God's victory in Jesus. With the help of Jesus, I still have some skirmishes to fight, but the final outcome is settled. Eternal Advent hope. I find it helpful, then, to think of my own death as the future coming of Jesus. I like the thought of the Risen Jesus as a kind of horizon that draws me to him, a kind of magnet attracting me to grow into him. I need faith-filled eyes to recognize Jesus in the enemy and a loving heart to meet his needs by meeting theirs. I am aware that Jesus is living in me and reaches out through me to love others. Jesus in me enables me to be good. Jesus lives also in others. In helping those who need me as priest, as chaplain, I am helping Jesus. I hope what they gain will be a richer understanding of God and a deeper relationship with this spirit of love. What a terrible waste war was then and is now.

The Posture of Prayer in Water

The Archdiocese for the Military Services was present in the Sinai desert in Egypt, on the day that a soldier received Christ through the sacraments of baptism and of confirmation. Father Jack Herron (army chaplain, LTC) had witnessed to him the joys of being a follower of Christ and the challenges to live as a witness in the world as a Roman Catholic. The soldier, Major Jack Burns, literally took the plunge into the sacrament of baptism when I fully immersed him in the waters of the Red Sea. Later that afternoon, I confirmed him with five others into the Catholic faith through the laying on of hands and anointing with the sacred chrism oils. There was great joy that day. I suspect that is what Teilhard de Chardin meant when he said, "Joy is the infallible sign of the presence of God." Wherever I see joy or whenever I feel it, I know that God is present. Perhaps joy is the best way I can call attention to the invisible Jesus within me and around me. Jesus lives in me and in my world. I am not the light, but I am to testify to the light. Jesus uses me to reflect his presence, hazy though I may be at times.

THE POSTURE OF SIMPLICITY

There is great joy in living the Christmas experience in one of our deployed military chapels with our women and men in uniform. Celebrating in a combat environment actually heightens the meaning as to why we pray and celebrate peace on earth. For sure, we all miss our loved ones back home during these special times of the year. But as the Archdiocese for the Military Services family, we find strength in being spiritually supported throughout the world. My thoughts around Christmastime while ministering on remote mountaintops far, far from the mainland of the US have always turned toward the simple Nativity scenes and holiday meal traditions found in our US Armed Forces chapels.

Our combat chapels on the ground and inside our ships may not be as elaborately decorated as those back in the mainland or on our garrison compounds overseas, but they all tend to take on a unique appearance. Most of our chapels in combat zones are simple plywood huts, such as the one I shared in 2012 in Iraq with His Excellency Matti Warda Bashar, a Chaldean bishop. There, we together venerated a small Nativity set along with the tabernacle of Our Lord. The diversity and the common bond that unites us as Catholics is strong in combat.

Many of our chapels are decorated very simply. Perhaps this is what draws my admiration and attention. Most everyone has a Nativity set displayed during the Christmas season. Some are plastic, some are wood, and others I have seen are even made out of cardboard, with the Holy Family and Magi figures drawn by magic-marker!

We prayed for peace in the world, but I was not sure we really thought that a world without war is possible. I grew up in the Vietnam War era and cheered for our troops and took for granted that war was a way to solve problems. Our military is part of the fabric of our country. We see nothing strange about someone who decides to make his career in the military while hoping never to go to war and instead become a true instrument of peace—not of destruction. But God promises to put an end to all wars. Jesus tells us that all who take the sword will perish by the sword, that we should turn the other cheek, that we should pray for our enemies. Do I really believe that what Jesus asks is sensible? Hope is possible only when the future is black. If we can see a logical way through our problems, there is no need for hope. The Christmas angels promised peace on earth. I want to be a person of hope.

THE POSTURE OF BEACH MINISTRY

Our archdiocese's spiritual contribution to the seventieth anniversary of the landing on Normandy beach was punctuated by several important events on location in France in June 2014. First, I was privileged to deliver the invocation prayer for the beginning of the memorial activities at the American cemetery on Omaha Beach, on the anniversary of D-Day. Following my invocation, US President Obama and French President Hollande spoke to the fifteen thousand invited guests, among whom were over four hundred veterans from the actual D-Day invasion. The next day, again on Omaha Beach, I offered a Mass at the American cemetery chapel. The prayers chosen for this occasion were from the Roman Missal, "For the Preservation of Peace and Justice." In my homily, I spoke about spiritual signs that signify peace and unity for our world and our appropriate responses as a nation and as individuals.

During the four days of ceremonies in Normandy, I had three notable conversations. The first was with Secretary Joseph Maxwell "Max" Cleland, an American politician from Georgia. Max is also a disabled US Army veteran of the Vietnam War, a recipient of the silver star and the bronze star for valorous actions in combat, and a former US senator. He was also administrator of Veterans Affairs. He continues to serve as secretary of the American Battle Monuments Commission. Senator Cleland lost both legs and his right arm in Vietnam. He reminded me of the words of General Pershing when he personally reflected on the importance of D-Day commemorations, saying, "Time will not dim the glory of their deeds." These words from a true and humble military leader are relevant for today's listener.

A second significant conversation was with Richard Courier of New York City, who landed on Omaha Beach, D-Day, at the age of eighteen. Today, he still proudly wears his army uniform and his purple heart medal. During our exchange of stories, he said, "Bishop, the only way I survived that day was by repeating the phrase 'God have mercy on my soul' and by keeping low on the ground. It was my faith that sustained me then and does so today."

A third exchange of stories happened with Sherwin Callander, who now lives in Madison, Alabama. He shared with me that knowing people back home "were praying for [him] on D-Day during the actual invasion was an encouragement and a strength to survive." He said he was not sure at the beginning of D-Day what he was fighting for, but now he understands what he was fighting against. Callander says that he now prays every day for our troops, just as others prayed for him when he wore the uniform seventy years ago.

I attended this monumental seventieth anniversary of D-Day because I believe our Church must be present alongside those who have sacrificed for the liberation of Europe. It is not only our duty to remember, but also an ever-present commitment in promoting peace and brotherhood today.

Conclusion: A Prayer Posture of Gratitude

I have been blessed and fortunate to experience multiple and various postures of prayer while serving God and country, and all with safe landings. Isaiah 11:6–9 promises a return to the harmony of paradise where even the animals get along with one another. The one who is coming will restore the original bliss in which we were created. Each human being will recognize God living in the wonderful variety of all human beings and come to live with them in loving harmony: "They shall not harm or destroy on all my holy mountain; / for the earth shall be filled with knowledge of the LORD, / as water covers the sea" (Isaiah 11:9).

"Peace be with you," Jesus says three times in chapter 20 of the Gospel according to St. John. This is his Easter gift to us. Earlier, in chapter 14, he said, "Peace I leave with you; my peace I give to you. Not as the world gives do I give it to you. Do not let your hearts be troubled or afraid" (John 14:27). The peace Jesus gives is not the absence of war. It is an inner peace that comes from the Spirit that the Risen Jesus breathes into me. The Spirit enables me to be still and, like breath, expands throughout my body and soul, my mind and will, bringing every part of me into harmony with every other part, making me feel together, at one with myself, at peace. This same Spirit fills all other people and all other creatures and brings us into harmony with one another. A deep spiritual tranquility comes from the growing awareness that the Spirit is breathing me into harmony with the divine and with myself and with all creation.

It is my wish that all of us will continue to pray for our sisters and brothers who wear our nation's uniform, as they too experience their postures of prayer. *Pro Deo et Patria!*

---

1. *The Jewish Study Bible*, editors Adele Berlin and Marc Zvi Brettler (New York: Oxford University Press, 2004), 788.
2. Scripture quotations are taken from *New American Bible*.

CHAPTER 35

In Search of Communion with Christ: Praying as a Seminarian

~ Michael Rubeling ~

One of the challenges of analyzing the experience of seminarians at prayer is the simple breadth and diversity of the men who are formed for the Catholic priesthood. Prayer directly parallels the man's journey from the call of the Lord to enter seminary to that moment when the hands of his bishop are laid upon his head at ordination. In the interval, the seminarian will experience all kinds of prayer, from liturgical to meditative, which in turn will help guide him through the spiritual adventure which is seminary formation. Nevertheless, the one common thread which informs the prayer of all seminarians is their goal: the priesthood. According to St. John Paul II, "[all seminary spiritual formation] should be structured according to the meanings and connotations which derive from the identity of the priest and his ministry."[1] This brief reflection on the prayer of seminarians will use these words as its guiding principle. It must also be noted that this reflection comes from the author's experiences as a diocesan seminarian, yet the principles and experiences mentioned here are often common to all those studying for the priesthood, whether diocesan or within a religious order. Though perhaps manifested differently in a diocesan seminary than in a religious novitiate, most men who join these communities have the common experience of shock as they try to adjust to the sheer amount of daily prayer, from Mass celebrated in community to the psalms recited in community to the rosary and stations of the cross and individual prayer time all done in community. For better or worse, seminarians know they are all brothers going through the same experiences!

When looking at the journey of a seminarian, especially seminarians learning how to pray, one is reminded of the twelve apostles as they were called and formed by Jesus to be his priests, then sent into the world to proclaim the Gospel. Indeed most, if not all, seminarians find a great kinship with the apostles and see themselves as following the Master to become "fishers of men." Just as the apostles asked Jesus to teach them how to pray, so too does the seminarian ask for guidance in prayer. In seminary, he lives with our Lord, learns who he is, and begins to pray with him. Within this formation, several forms of prayer are essential. In his apostolic decree on seminary formation, St. John Paul II highlights the threefold path of an authentic spiritual life centered on Jesus Christ: "A faithful mediation on the word of God, active participation in the

Church's holy mysteries and the service of charity to the 'little ones.'"[2] Contained within this threefold path are the basic elements of prayer for each and every seminarian: meditation on Scripture, the Liturgy of the Hours, the Eucharist and the other sacraments, pastoral ministry, and devotion to the Blessed Virgin Mary. The following reflection will examine each of these aspects of prayer in the journey of a young man to the Mass of ordination. Prayer and the interior life constitute the great adventure of seminary. It does not matter where a seminarian comes from or to which seminary he goes. The real journey is one of the heart in prayer. In this context, one feels the excitement in the heart of every seminarian as Jesus answers their question "Lord, where are you staying?" with the reply: "Come and see."

SACRED SCRIPTURE

Among those who hear the Lord's call to enter the seminary, some respond like Andrew, brimming with excitement to have found the Messiah, and others approach the call like St. Peter who responded in fear, "Depart from me, for I am a sinful man, O Lord" (Luke 5:8).[3] Some seminarians are enthusiastic, others reluctant. Though there are as many kinds of responses to the call as there are men who respond to it, each response has the quality of a search. "In a certain sense, the spiritual life of the person who is preparing for the priesthood is dominated by this search: by it and by the 'finding' of the Master, to follow Him, to be in communion with Him."[4] Among the many necessary aids to this search, to discernment, one of the most effective is sacred Scripture. Whether it be at Mass, on a discernment retreat, or perhaps just meditating on the Gospel in private, sacred Scripture provides a powerful way for a person to hear the call of our Lord. Scores of men have had the seed of a vocation planted in their hearts by hearing the accounts of God calling the apostles to himself. Jesus's command, Follow me, almost leaps off the page to someone whose heart is being tugged at by the Holy Spirit. Without a doubt, the "word of God is living and active" in the lives of those who are called to the holy priesthood (Hebrews 4:12).

After someone has taken the plunge and joined the seminary, his relationship with sacred Scripture continues to grow. *Lectio divina*, or the prayerful and meditative reading of sacred Scripture, becomes a daily part of the man's prayer life as he progresses in formation. Whether on retreat or in the chapel during an hour of silent prayer, the Gospels allow the seminarian to enter Christ's world and to spend time with him. This time of reading Scripture goes beyond that of the first call to follow the Lord. Instead, a man journeys with Jesus and begins to be formed by him. The seminarian often finds a great affinity with the apostles during this journey, this seeking. The triumphs and failures of the apostles are mirrored in the seminarian. Some men are haunted by past sins and may find great solace in the presence of St. Matthew among the apostles. The hearts of some men are drawn to the beloved disciple who was drawn not only into a special intimacy with our Lord and his mother, but also into the mystery of their suffering. However, the figure of St. Peter stands as the primordial archetype for the seminarian: honest and brash, enthusiastic and prideful, affirming Christ as savior in one moment, then rejecting the cross in the next. Both St. Peter and the seminarian venture into the deep, walking on the storms of life, both having to learn dependence on Jesus. Through *lectio divina*, a seminarian realizes his true identity as a son of God when he enters into Jesus's baptism in the Jordan. He experiences forgiveness with St. Peter, St. Mary Magdalene, and many others. And if he perseveres, the seminarian will begin to personally enter into the mystery of the Last Supper, the scene where Christ institutes the priesthood and gives the priest his most important prayer, the Holy Mass. The hope is that throughout their years of formation seminarians will delve deep into the pages of the Gospel in this search for intimacy with Jesus. To reverse the famous saying of St. Jerome, if one is to know Christ, one must know sacred Scripture.

As the seminarian approaches ordination, he will begin to see how his own prayerful reflection on sacred Scripture will be essential to his priestly duty to preach the Gospel. *Dei Verbum* states that: "All clerics, particularly priests of Christ and others who, as deacons or catechists, are officially engaged in the ministry of the word, should immerse themselves in the Scriptures by constant sacred reading and diligent study."[5] As is true for all the gifts one receives from God, the fruit of prayerful meditation on the Word of God is meant to be shared with others. The seminarian embraces this duty in a special way due to his future apostolic calling. Thus, the time spent with Jesus in Scripture, from the seminarian's call into the seminary itself to those moments of friendship with Jesus, will all inform his calling to preach the Gospel to those entrusted to his care.

LITURGY OF THE HOURS

After someone has entered seminary, the first form of prayer that confronts him in a drastically new way is the Liturgy of the Hours. On his very first day in the seminary, the seminarian will sit in the chapel with the rest of the seminary community and pray this prayer together. Little does he know about this practice of praying with the seminary community every day until he is ordained a priest. The first few encounters of praying the Liturgy of the Hours with the whole seminary community will most often leave the new seminarian confused, but after a while, he will pick up the rhythm of this prayer. He will eventually learn that the Liturgy of the Hours (also known as the breviary or the Divine Office) is the official daily prayer of the Church, whereby one prays the psalms with and for the Church. Although he does not know it at the beginning, the seminarian is entering into the prayers that Jesus Christ prayed during his earthly life and offered for the Church.[6] The newness of this prayer often obscures its depth to the seminarian at first, yet if he perseveres, he will find in it a special closeness with our Lord and his Church.

In order to learn how to pray the Liturgy of the Hours and foster the habit of praying it every day, seminarians often pray this prayer together, in community, in the morning and in the evening. Thus the seminarian's daily schedule is naturally bookended with these "hinges of the day."[7] This experience bonds seminarians together in several ways. Sometimes, when starting out, young seminarians will use the words of the psalms to make corny jokes, often to the groans of the older seminarians and priest faculty who have heard all these jokes before, and to the look of confusion of nonseminarians who have no idea why the joke is even supposed to be funny. However, beneath the superficial bond of simply praying together or making humorous light of the prayers themselves lies the reality that the words of sacred Scripture, the psalms, the daily prayer of Jesus himself, are becoming the common language of a group of men whose daily duty it will be to pray for the Church. After praying with the psalms and other parts of Scripture contained in the Liturgy of the Hours, the seminarian will eventually have Scripture on the tip of his tongue at all times. It will be the furniture of his mind, upon which everything in the house rests. And though many seminarians and priests can find the duty or obligation of praying the Hours difficult at first, one often finds that the words of the psalmist express the whole range of emotions found in the human condition.

An experienced Jesuit once advised a group of seminarians that "if you have had trouble saying your breviary, then that just shows that you have not suffered enough yet in your life. Suffering will make you understand the psalms, and how they are sincere, incredibly emotive prayers to almighty God."[8] Building upon this application of the psalms to one's personal experience, the breviary also bonds seminarians together by showing them a glimpse into the priest's role to pray always and to intercede for God's people. Even if the seminarian or priest finds praying the breviary to be the equivalent of chewing sand, he must realize that he does not pray it for himself. Rather, the seminarian prays the breviary now in order to prepare him to make the priestly promise "to celebrate faithfully the liturgy of the hours for the Church and for the whole world."[9] In preparing to become one who serves like Christ as a priest, the seminarian is following in the footsteps of the great high priest, Jesus Christ, who "is able for all time to save those who draw near to God through him, since he always lives to make intercession for them" (Hebrews 7:25). It is fitting that those preparing for the priesthood should also make such intercessions.

When he finally enters into pastoral ministry, the seminarian will see that praying the psalms is not merely a personal prayer. Rather he will see the deep emotions of the psalmist echoed in those he encounters at the hospital, in the celebration of a wedding or baptism or those who are in the various stages of seeking God. The seminarian will learn that he does not pray merely for himself, but rather for the sanctification of the whole world. Therefore, throughout his seminarian formation, whether he finds the Liturgy of the Hours pleasant or taxing, a seminarian is being led through this prayer into the deep mystery that is Christ's priesthood manifest on this earth.

Though the breviary has a primarily universal dimension, the seminarian will first encounter it on a personal level; thus, he often needs encouragement to see how it relates to his life in the present moment at the seminary. This reflection can offer one piece of encouragement to such a struggling seminarian. One of the blessings of the Liturgy of the Hours is the grace to instill holy order into the lives of those who are approaching the sacrament of Holy Orders. This is another way of expressing one of the essential purposes of the Liturgy of the Hours: the sanctification of the day.[10]

As mentioned above, most first year seminarians find the entrance into the rhythm of prayer in the seminary a very difficult adjustment. However, the seminarian must be reminded that the rhythm of prayer within a seminary is meant to foster a life of "intimate and unceasing union with God the Father through his Son Jesus Christ, in the Holy Spirit." In essence, the seminary is set up to enable a seminarian to abide with Christ, and Christ with the seminarian (see John 15:10). The fivefold structure of the breviary allows the seminarian to have a constant reminder of Christ's presence. When one feels the internal pull to pray the next set of psalms from the breviary, one should see in that obligation the eager desire of Jesus to be united with his friend. Each time one says "yes" in that moment of obligation, the Holy Spirit increases the flame of grace a little bit more in the depths of his heart. Duty and obligation eventually turn into virtue and love if one perseveres in his prayers. The key is showing up. The Holy Spirit does the rest! Here one sees the deconstruction and reconstruction that happens within the heart of a seminarian. Old habits are replaced with new ones, goodness is gradually elevated to holiness. If the seminarian is willing, God will replace his stony heart with the natural heart of Jesus Christ (see Ezekiel 36:26). The mundane, ordinary recitation of the Liturgy of the Hours is the way in which God will ignite the flame of love which will sustain a priest in the midst of his sometimes hectic pastoral ministry. This is the great challenge of the breviary, and its great reward!

HOLY MASS, ADORATION, AND PENANCE

Though the rhythm of a seminarian's day is dictated by the breviary, at the heart of a seminarian's prayer life should be participation in Holy Mass. Simply by living in a well-structured seminary, the seminarian almost intuitively learns that "the high point of Christian prayer is the Eucharist, which in its turn is to be seen as the *'summit and source' of the sacraments and the Liturgy of the Hours*."[11] Often the seminary structures its day with the celebration of Holy Mass at its center and the Liturgy of the Hours as the hinges of the day.[12] In his Apostolic Exhortation on the Formation of Priests, St. John Paul II observes that the whole of the priest's identity, his communion with God, the continual renewal of his spiritual life, his participation in the "new law" of the Holy Spirit written on his "new heart" and the foundation of his apostolic zeal, is contained in and finds fulfilment in the celebration of the Eucharist.[13] Thus the seminarian should see the Eucharist as central to the mission and identity of the priest who is "chosen from among men... to offer gifts and sacrifices for sins," in imitation of Christ himself (Hebrews 5:1). In a very personal statement on seminary formation, St. John Paul II declares:

> To be utterly frank and clear...: it is fitting that seminarians take part *every day* in the Eucharistic celebration...[and they should] be trained to consider the Eucharistic celebration as the essential moment of their day, in which they will take an active part and at which they will never be satisfied with a merely habitual attendance.[14]

Similar to the daily recitation of the hours, participation at daily Mass can be a struggle for new seminarians, especially if in their previous lives they did not have the habit of attending daily Mass. However, the Eucharist is so essential, so intimately connected with what the seminarian seeks, that he often very easily overcomes this difficulty and enters into the Holy Mass with a grateful and open heart. This personal love for the sacrament eventually gets extended on the day of ordination to actually participating in the beloved sacrament. On that day, a priest is commissioned to offer sacrifice for the sanctification of the world.[15] Through his formation, the seminarian deepens his conviction in the truth that there is no greater prayer, no greater action than the celebration of Holy Mass. For this sacred action does the priest exist, and consequently does the seminarian exist.

In recent years, adoration of the Blessed Sacrament has played a significant role in the vocation of many men who chose to enter the seminary and remains an integral part of their spiritual life. In the adoration of the Blessed Sacrament, or simply adoration, a priest or deacon exposes a consecrated Host in an ornate, often gold, monstrance[16] in order for the faithful to worship our Lord in this most august sacrament. The practice of adoration began in the early days of the Church, when the faithful expressed a desire to worship the Eucharistic Lord for a longer period of time than the mere elevation of the Host at Mass. The special part that adoration has played in the lives of many seminarians and priests is due in large part to the influence of St. John Paul II, who encouraged "the yearning to contemplate and bow in adoration before Christ [in the Eucharist],"[17] and Archbishop Fulton Sheen, who offered the traditional practice of a Holy Hour before the Blessed Sacrament as a concrete recommendation to priests "to make [them] worthy of the [supernatural] vocation to which [they are] called."[18]

Many people who discern a call to the priesthood today often have a devotion to Eucharistic Adoration. As a teenager, one young man started making a holy hour at the behest of his mother, who would drop him off at their parish's perpetual adoration chapel. At first, the young man would enter, quickly greet our Lord in prayer, and then promptly fall asleep with feet propped up. Years later, then a seminarian, the young man would reflect on the grace he received by just being there, making the choice to be present. With such a story, one is reminded of St. Thérèse of Lisieux, who herself would fall asleep in prayer at certain times, but was always confident in that fact that loving parents, like God the Father, love their children even when they are sleeping. Indeed, many seminarians (and priests) attribute their vocation to time spent before the Blessed Sacrament in adoration. Whether the man chooses to have a prayerful conversation with Jesus or to merely sit in his presence, there seems to be a special grace of intimacy that one receives during this time. A deep love for the Eucharistic Lord and the practice of solitude, both crucial for an authentic spiritual life, are cultivated within adoration. Here the seminarian speaks with his friend, and here that friendship is ever protected and grown.

Intimately connected with the seminarian's love for the Eucharist should be his discovery of "the beauty and joy of the sacrament of Penance."[19] If a seminarian has truly faced the depth of his sinfulness and unworthiness of the call to priesthood, then this love of penance will be fostered rather quickly. Yet the call to love this sacrament confronts many of the cultural hindrances that face all the faithful, especially seminarians. "From [penance] flow the sense of asceticism and interior discipline, a spirit of sacrifice and self-denial, the acceptance of hard work and of the cross." In short, this sacrament keeps priests and seminarians from the temptation to comfort and spiritual compliancy. Priests are instruments of God's love and mercy, and thus they must continually encounter that same love and mercy in their own spiritual lives. "If a priest were no longer to go to confession or properly confess his sins, his *priestly being* and his *priestly action* would feel its effects very soon, and this would also be noticed by the community of which he was the pastor."[20]

The seminarian's participation in the sacred mysteries of God, in the sacraments, prepares him to be transformed inwardly by them. At ordination, he will not merely administer the sacraments, but also live out in his body and heart the mysteries he celebrates. "The life of the ordained is the life of selfless outpouring, of laying down one's life for one's friends, of wounded love which knows no limit in its ability to embrace the other."[21] Without saying a word, the priest stands as a living testament to God's presence in the world.

SOLITUDE

For most seminarians first entering the seminary, one of the most surprising parts of their formation, both in life and in prayer, is that of silence and solitude. Seminarians recite the Liturgy of the Hours together, lift their voices in prayer at Holy Mass and say any number of vocal prayers as part of their personal devotions; however, silence and solitude are integral parts of their formation. St. John Paul II pointed out this reality: "A necessary training in prayer in a context of noise and agitation like that of our society is an education in the deep human meaning and religious value of silence as the spiritual atmosphere vital for perceiving God's presence and for allowing oneself to be won over by it."[22] Thus as formation in prayer deepens, a seminarian should begin to realize that amidst all the other aspects of formation and prayer, "[the] experience of extensive solitude—of being utterly alone with God—is crucial."[23]

Loneliness is one of the greatest fears of men entering the seminary, and to be quite honest, one of the greatest fears of those in the seminary. One truly experiences sacrifice in the renunciation of a wife and family through celibacy. It is a real cross that has both tremendous blessings and challenges. Similarly, as the seminarian steps deeper into his role as a public representative of the Church, he begins to experience the otherness, the separation that his future identity will entail. Prayerful solitude is God's gift to the seminarian and priest for exactly these kinds of struggles. In seminary, one should begin to foster a "monastic heart" that spends an ample amount of time with God.[24] This happens through holy hours spent in silence (both internally and externally), allowing *lectio divina* to lead to silence and simply listening to God in the small moments of the day. At first this experience of silence seems akin to standing close to a raging fire. "[Lengthy] periods of solitude are never easy; we sweat, we squirm, we blister, we burn in such a furnace."[25]

Solitude is incredibly difficult, and many men run from it. When one tries to pray in silence, many distracting and dark thoughts come rushing forward. When describing her prayer of recollection (found in the silence of one's heart), St. Teresa of Ávila says, "Let the soul try to cultivate the habit [of silent prayer], despite the fatigue entailed in recollecting itself and overcoming the body which is trying to reclaim its rights."[26] Today's cultural milieu, the former home of almost all seminarians, is one of noise and distraction. Although throughout his life a seminarian or priest will be tempted to see society as a source for something akin to wisdom, solitude will show him the shallowness of the modern world. Sure, "society is a book to read, even though a commonplace book. Solitude is a masterpiece."[27] The act of stepping away from that world presents a seminarian with an arduous transition to another kind of life. However, if he is able to take that step with the help of the Holy Spirit, "the monasticism of heart [fostered by solitude] develops and shapes a profoundly personal identity in God's love that will be continually needed to fan into flame the same fire of faith and zeal that burned in the heart of Jesus in the midst of his busy daily life."[28] In this sacred practice, one realizes that solitude is not loneliness, not idle, wasted time. Rather solitude begins to be seen for what it truly can be: fostering an intimate relationship with God. In the quiet of solitude is where a seminarian often transitions from merely loving Christ to being in love with Christ. Here is where loneliness is conquered, where one finds an anchor amidst the stormy situations of pastoral ministry and where a priest remains in constant contact with his Lord from which his whole identity flows!

In all the forms of prayer mentioned above, especially in silent prayer, the seminarian seeks to deepen his relationship with Christ in prayer, and also to progress in the spiritual life. The desire to grow in prayer is good in itself, but often seminarians do not know by what standards to gauge this growth, thus falling into a do-it-yourself model of prayer. Seeing the path to God as something to conquer and one's relationship with him as something obtained by sheer effort of will can often lead to discouragement and frustration. When faced with these challenges, this reflection can offer two pieces of advice. First, when he enters into prayer, particularly at first, a seminarian should be reminded that he should ask for and desire an affective experience of peace and joy, an evident sign of God's presence. These consolations or positive affective experiences go deeper than mere emotional elation and touch the depths of the soul.

For example, a person praying with the Gospel passage of Jesus's baptism in the Jordan River may receive a deep and abiding sense of God's love for him as a beloved son, which seems to come from nowhere and leaves in its wake an inexpressible peace.

In that moment, God has chosen to give a consolation to that person, and the person has, in turn, opened himself up to God's love. Notice it is a total gift of God, not merited, not earned, given freely out of love. This gift can be received by anyone who is open to it, because God desires to have a personal relationship with each of his children. A seminarian must know this truth and seek to live it out in his own life. Second, though a seminarian should desire these affective experiences, he should be led to focus on desiring not merely the gift, but rather the one who is the giver of these gifts. In other words, the aim of prayer is intimacy with God himself, not just with his gifts. This can only happen through the guidance of the Holy Spirit. Thus for all his striving, the person who enters into prayer is ultimately *dependent*, always *receiving* the grace to be led to God by the Holy Spirit.

Seminarians are often frustrated that they are not further along in the spiritual life. "I thought I would be holier this close to ordination" is a common sentiment among those who are close to that sacred day. What they fail to realize is that everything they have in the spiritual life, from where they are now to where they will go, is a complete gift of God! Spiritual formation is God's work alone. And these seminarians also do not often see the objective fact that God is always present to them as their creator and in them through divine grace.[29] "The soul who has the sense of the presence of God within it, possesses one of the most efficacious means of making prayer."[30] It is essential that the seminarian, or anyone who wishes for intimacy with Christ, must know that he always abides in the presence of almighty God. Whether the person experiences consolation or desolation, God is always present to him, and all the person needs to do to pray is turn to God in the silence of his heart. Relying on the truth of God's immanent presence, the seminarian's worries about progression in the spiritual life slowly dissipate. What is left is the concrete realization that Christ is present to them always, and that any growth in prayer should be left up to his good pleasure.[31]

MARIAN DEVOTION

"When Jesus saw his mother there, and the disciple whom he loved standing nearby, he said to her, 'Woman, behold your son!' Then he said to the disciple, 'Behold, your mother!'" (John 19:26–7). Mary's role in the life of a seminarian can be witnessed at Calvary. Each seminarian is the beloved disciple, the one whom Jesus loves and chooses to be his priest. He is also the one to whom he gives his mother in a special way. Mary herself has a special love for those men who will be conformed into the image of her son. If invited, she will gladly continually live in the home of her son, the seminarian.

For the seminarian, as for the rest of the faithful, the rosary is often one's first and primary encounter with the Blessed Virgin Mary. Whether kneeling in the chapel or taking a prayerful stroll around the seminary, praying the rosary allows Mary to gently guide the seminarian to Jesus. Some seminarians have Mary at the center of their spiritual life, consciously allowing her to guide them. Others, though their devotion to the Blessed Virgin may be less intentional, are always under her mantle. She is always present to seminarians, encouraging, guiding, supporting. In the mysteries of the rosary, one reflects on the life of Christ through her eyes. Through the rosary, one enters into the words of sacred Scripture and the mystery of the sacraments in a new way.

Among the multitude of graces that flow from the rosary, the grace of perseverance is particularly beneficial for those who journey along the road toward priesthood. The very practice of the rosary exercises the virtue of perseverance—Hail Marys said over and over again. Yet the end of each Hail Mary points to another kind of perseverance: "Holy Mary, Mother of God, pray for us sinners, now and at the hour of our death." The natural virtue of perseverance is being replaced with the supernatural. Through the prayers of Mary, the seminarian is asking for supernatural perseverance to weather the storms of life. Seminary has periods of intense struggle, and the temptation to leave can haunt many of the men who are truly called by the Lord. Mary's presence at these moments is indispensable. Even though he may not know it, the struggling seminarian always remains under Mary's mantle, and she remains present at whatever crosses her sons in the seminary might be enduring. For this reason, among so many others, devotion to the Blessed Virgin Mary is essential for every seminarian.

When the seminarian finally becomes a priest, he will imitate another dimension of Mary's life. As he administers the sacraments and serves the people of God, the priest will become aware that, like Mary who carried the Son of God in her womb and never stopped pointing to her divine Son, so too is the priest a *theotokos*, a "God-bearer." Even the simple act of wearing clerics or his habit witnesses to the world that God is among us. As the formation of seminary is left behind, the priest will need to follow the example of Mary in saying "yes" to the Lord's will in all things and always advising others to "do whatever he tells you."

Conclusion

While traveling along the road toward ordination, the seminarian holds fast to several forms of prayer which bring him into close contact with the one who calls him. The threefold path of the spiritual life, outlined by Church for the formation of her priests, allows the seminarian to encounter Christ in sacred Scripture, in God's holy mysteries, and in those whom he will serve in his ministry. Obviously, seminarians pray in other ways, and their interior lives are informed by other influences. However, the common experience of seminarians, and their primary foundation, come from these essential elements of prayer. Yet where does the prayer of a seminarian culminate? After the man has discerned, entered, embraced formation, lived like the apostles with Jesus in the community of the seminary, and even been ordained a priest, is there yet another level to which all his prayerful efforts point? The answer was given by Pope Francis on his visit to the United States.

On September 23, 2015, Pope Francis visited St. John Paul II College Seminary in Washington, DC. Though his stop at the seminary was one of many during his visit to the United States, for the men of the seminary, it was a profoundly moving and significant moment. After taking a tour of the seminary and posing for a picture with the seminarians, the Holy Father addressed his spiritual sons. He spoke from the heart, and for a moment, the whirlwind rush schedule seemed to slow. Coming to his central thought, Pope Francis told the men not simply to pray, but called them forward to a deeper level of intimacy with Christ Jesus. He said, "Dear brothers, do you adore? I know that you pray. I know that you serve. I know that you love. But do you adore?" Simple words, but a profound message. All the many hours spent in fervent prayer, every psalm recited and Mass celebrated, all holy hours and times of solitude lead to the Holy Father's call to "adore." This adoration springs not so much from the words or actions of the seminarian, but rather from the disposition of his heart. Adoring Christ Jesus within one's heart is the final destination of the prayer life of every seminarian, of every priest, and of every disciple.

---

1. John Paul II, *Pastores Dabo Vobis*, 45.
2. John Paul II, *Pastores Dabo Vobis*, 46. St. John Paul is referencing *Optatam Totius*, Vatican II's decree on priestly training. "[Seminarians] should be taught to seek Christ in faithful meditation on the word of God and in active participation in the sacred mysteries of the Church, especially the Eucharist and the Divine Office, to seek him in the bishop by whom they are sent and in the people to whom they are sent, especially the poor, little children, the weak, sinners and unbelievers. With the confidence of sons they should love and reverence the most blessed Virgin Mary, who was given as a mother to the disciple by Jesus Christ as he was dying on the cross" (*Optatam Totius*, 8).
3. All quotations from sacred Scripture are from the *Revised Standard Version*.
4. John Paul II, *Pastores Dabo Vobis*, 46
5. Second Vatican Council, Dogmatic Constitution on Divine Revelation (*Dei Verbum*), in *Vatican Council II*, vol. 1: *The Conciliar and Post Conciliar Documents*, ed. Austin Flannery (Northport, NY: Costello, 1998). This source is used for all Second Vatican Council documents in this chapter: CIC c. 840, 25.

6. Paul VI, "Apostolic Constitution Promulgation on the Divine Office," 1970, 3–4.
7. Second Vatican Council, The Constitution on the Sacred Liturgy (*Sacrosanctum Concilium*), 89.
8. From a conference given by Rev. Joseph Carola, SJ.
9. "Ordination of a Priest," in *The Rites of the Catholic Church: The Roman Ritual Revised by Decree of the Second Vatican Ecumenical Council and Published by Authority of Pope Paul VI and Pope John Paul II*. Study ed. vol. 2 (Collegeville, MN: Liturgical, 1991), 15.
10. See Second Vatican Council, *Sacrosanctum Concilium*, 88.
11. John Paul II, *Pastores Dabo Vobis*, 48.
12. Second Vatican Council, *Sacrosanctum Concilium*, 89.
13. See John Paul II, *Pastores Dabo Vobis*, 48.
14. John Paul II, *Pastores Dabo Vobis*, 48.
15. See "Ordination of a Priest," 15.
16. A monstrance is vessel used by the Church to show the Eucharist to the faithful. The Host is placed in the center of a gold stand (often resembling the sun) from which it can be seen and adored by the faithful.
17. John Paul II, *Pastores Dabo Vobis*, 48.
18. Fulton Sheen, *The Priest Is Not His Own* (San Francisco: Ignatius, 1963), 230.
19. John Paul II, *Pastores Dabo Vobis*, 48.
20. John Paul II, *Pastores Dabo Vobis*, 26.
21. Joseph Carola, *Conformed to Christ Crucified: Meditations on Priestly Life and Ministry* (Rome: Gregorian & Biblical, 2010), 35.
22. John Paul II, *Pastores Dabo Vobis*, 47.
23. George A. Aschenbrenner, *Quickening the Fire in Our Midst: The Challenge of Diocesan Priestly Spirituality* (Chicago: Jesuit Way, 2002), 65.
24. Aschenbrenner, 65.
25. Aschenbrenner, 66.
26. Gabriel of St. Mary Magdalen, *Divine Intimacy* (n.p.: Baronius, 1953), 440. Gabriel quotes St. Teresa of Ávila's *Way of Perfection* (chapter 28) when he describes her prayer of recollection. Due to the differences in translators' interpretations of St. Teresa, I have chosen to use Gabriel's choice of translation.
27. A.G. Sertillanges, *The Intellectual Life: Its Spirit, Conditions, Methods* (Washington, DC: Catholic University of America Press, 1987), 60.
28. Aschenbrenner, 65.
29. Gabriel of St. Mary Magdalen, 439.
30. Gabriel of St. Mary Magdalen, 440.
31. Francis de Sales, *The Art of Loving God: Simple Virtues for the Christian Life* (Manchester, NH: Sophia Institute, 1998), 15.

PART EIGHT

Liturgical Prayer and Praying during the Liturgical Seasons

This section opens with a treatment of the essential topic, Liturgical Prayer, by Joyce Ann Zimmerman. Beginning with a review of the history of the contemporary liturgical movement, she then focuses on four elements that are essential to grasp if we are to appreciate what liturgical prayer is. They include

- Liturgical prayer in relation to devotional prayer
- Liturgical prayer in relation to Christ
- Liturgical prayer's gains and losses since the Council
- Liturgical prayer as lived beyond its ritual expression

Zimmerman closes her chapter by looking at liturgical prayer as lived beyond its ritual expression. In doing this, she exclaims, "When liturgical prayer bursts forth from its ritual expression into our daily living, we ourselves are the faithful presence of the risen Christ through the power of the Holy Spirit. To that we join all the heavenly host in saying, 'Amen!'"

In Prayer in Ordinary Time, Peter Verity sets the stage beautifully by writing "Ordinary Time will only be routine and dull if we allow ourselves to think of it as the gap between the important high seasons of Christmas and Easter. If this is the case, we will never be able to make Ordinary Time what it truly is—the bedrock of our prayer, the foundation without which we will never be able to celebrate fully the great feasts." He then poses the question, "What can lift Ordinary Time out of these negative perceptions and make it what it should be?" In response, he reflects on the prayer opportunities in the Sunday and weekday liturgies of Ordinary Time and explores ideas for promoting new ways of thinking about this period. His goal is to "show how prayer becomes an adventure as it takes place in the midst of Ordinary Time," and I think readers will enjoy journeying with him. As Verity points out, "Both through the liturgy and in personal prayer these weeks [of Ordinary Time] are gifts of time to let

God work in us, and for us to respond generously to God." He helps us in this chapter to not miss this spiritual reality.

The final chapter in this section is a reflective piece on Prayer during the Advent, Christmas, Lenten, and Easter Seasons by Donal Neary. He brings us on a pilgrimage in prayer and reminds us that these important times in the liturgical year are not simply about the season but about ourselves as well. He helps us see Advent as "God's pilgrim promise" and shares with us "Advent people" such as Elizabeth, Zechariah, and the infant John to reflect upon and pray with. In "Praying at Christmas" he again helps us to join in the event with Mary, Joseph, the shepherds, Simeon, and Anna in a way that makes this celebratory time of year come alive in new ways. Then, he presents openings for us to explore Lenten spirituality by viewing the Sundays of Lent, the Triduum of Holy Week, and the forty Easter days with a new sense of intention and imagination that brings into play and has us hold closer to ourselves such figures as Mary Magdalene, Thomas, the disciples on the road to Emmaus, and the good shepherd. This chapter helps us look at these key seasons with a sense of creativity and reflection that leaves us wanting to read and reflect more when we encounter them again rather than to let them pass with merely a notice in our busy lives.

CHAPTER 36

Liturgical Prayer

~ Joyce Ann Zimmerman, CPPS ~

Many of us grew up at a time when prayer was simply prayer. We made few, if any, distinctions. Oh, yes, we knew Mass was an important prayer if for no other reason than that we were obliged to be there on Sundays and holy days of obligation, and we knew we were to go to confession regularly, and we knew babies were baptized as soon as possible, and we were confirmed sometime between the third and seventh grades, depending upon when the bishop was scheduled to come to the parish. We knew marriage was a sacrament, but we probably didn't think of it as prayer, except that most marriages took place within a nuptial Mass. Extreme unction was for the almost dead, a quick and short ritual with few people, if any, present except the dying person. We had no experience of holy orders at all unless a family member became a priest. And the Liturgy of the Hours? Well, we only knew that as the breviary that Father was obliged to pray. Certain terms we rather take for granted today were just not a part of our vocabulary. *Liturgy?* No. *Liturgical year?* No. *Paschal mystery?* No. *Liturgy of the Hours?* No. *Epiclesis?* No. *Anamnesis?* No. *Sign of peace?* No. And still other terms. No.

Much of our prayer in times gone by was more rote formulae than a prayerful, personal encounter with God. We prayed the Morning Offering when we got up, meal prayers, maybe the Angelus, the Angel of God prayer before going to bed. For many, the most enriching prayer was the rosary. We were faithful at benediction. Novenas and litanies were encouraged at certain times of the week or year. Our own private prayer tended to be petitionary prayer, during which we poured out our needs and desires, our hopes and dreams to a God who seemed far away.

The sincerity of all this prayer could never be questioned. People were, for the most part, faithful to what they understood was expected of them as prayerful Catholics. Many, many people lived holy lives, faithful to a deep prayer life. At the same time, they were largely oblivious to the richness they were missing. Liturgical prayer was simply a fixed time for our devotional prayer. Father prayed. The servers answered. The choir sang. A change began with the liturgical movement, initiated mainly in the large Benedictine monasteries of Europe and then spread beyond. The leaders of the liturgical movement had a very specific goal: to draw the laity into liturgical prayer, to help them understand it better, to promote participation. Pope St. Pius X gave much impetus to this movement. He lowered the age for receiving First Holy Communion, promoted frequent reception of Holy Communion and confession, and reformed sacred music. The liturgical movement continued to gain momentum throughout the first half of the twentieth century. Other changes were introduced, for example, singing vernacular hymns during Mass, the publication of daily missals containing both the Latin and vernacular translations of the Mass prayers, and a reform of the Holy Week liturgies.

It is no surprise, then, that the first document of the Second Vatican Council was *Sacrosanctum Concilium*.[1] Groundwork for this revolutionary document had been solidly laid. While some Catholics resisted the liturgical reforms required by this document (and some still do), by and large the new liturgy was well received. People were happy to pray in their own language. They were delighted to accept new responsibilities for liturgical ministries open to them, such as being hospitality ministers, lectors, extraordinary ministers of Holy Communion. Women could play a larger role during liturgy. Liturgy was discouraged as a time for personal devotions; those assembled were not to be "strangers or silent spectators" (SC, 48), and everyone was encouraged to embrace full, conscious, and active participation (see SC, 14, 30, 48). *Sacrosanctum Concilium*'s theology and pastoral sensitivity became hallmarks of other documents of the Council.[2] *Sacrosanctum Concilium* became a blueprint for renewal of the whole Church's life, placing liturgy squarely at the center.

To accomplish such a noble task, *Sacrosanctum Concilium* clearly called for liturgical education (see especially SC, 14–20). When the new rites were introduced a half century ago, education about the rites depended on the local churches and dioceses. Some did a better job of it than others. For all practical purposes, however, liturgical education (especially in any consistent or systematized way) has not been on the front burner of most parishes and dioceses. While liturgical topics are appropriate for homilies at Mass, rarely do we hear a preacher address the richness of the liturgical texts or elements.[3] Much is still to be accomplished to fulfill the vision of the Council Fathers for liturgical catechesis.

One step toward a robust liturgical catechesis is to have a firm grasp of what liturgical prayer is: liturgical prayer in relation to devotional prayer, liturgical prayer in relation to Christ, liturgical prayer's gains and losses since the Council, and liturgical prayer as lived beyond its ritual expression. These four considerations command our attention during the rest of this chapter.

To contrast liturgical and devotional prayer implies that they are separate realities. And they are. They are both prayer, to be sure. They are both very personal; we ourselves are involved in encountering God to give him praise, adoration, and thanksgiving. Both liturgical and devotional prayer are essential; we cannot live Gospel values as Jesus taught us without the strength and assurance that both of these prayers give us. They are both experiential, based on our daily interactions with people and events. This being said, the real telling is more in their contrast than in their sameness.

To begin, we might say that liturgical prayer is the relatively fixed, official celebrations of the seven sacraments and the Liturgy of the Hours. Liturgy is celebrated with a set ritual pattern; generally, there are no structural surprises in liturgy. We are familiar with it, we know what's coming next, we know what is expected of us. All of this because we have celebrated liturgy over and over again. We know its rhythms, words, gestures, responses, processions. While the origin of the word *liturgy* as the "work of the people" might lead us to think that liturgy is primarily our work, what we do for God; in fact, it is the other way around.[5] In liturgy God calls us, is present to us, acts on us. Our work during liturgy is to respond to this divine presence, to listen to God's promptings, and to surrender to God. Liturgical prayer does not end with the ritual, but continues into how we live our daily lives.[6]

Devotional prayer, we might say, is all prayer that is not liturgical prayer. For the average Catholic who is not present at daily Mass or who does not celebrate the Liturgy of the Hours, this means that the vast majority of prayer is actually devotional prayer. Prior to the Council, there were many more public devotional prayers in which the faithful participated. After the Council, many of these devotions fell by the wayside as we worked hard to immerse ourselves in the renewed liturgy. However, this was not the intent of the Council Fathers. Liturgical prayer and devotional prayer are not the same, but neither is it a matter of either/or. *Sacrosanctum Concilium* makes clear that both are essential:

> Popular devotions of the Christian people are to be highly endorsed, provided they accord with the laws and norms of the Church, above all when they are ordered by the Apostolic See.
>
> Devotions proper to particular Churches also have a special dignity if they are undertaken by mandate of the bishops according to customs or books lawfully approved.
>
> But these devotions should be so fashioned that they harmonize with the liturgical seasons, accord with the sacred liturgy, are in some way derived

from it, and lead the people to it, since, in fact, the liturgy, by its very nature far surpasses any of them.[7]

Almost every statement about liturgical and devotional prayer in the last fifty years has harkened back to this very important paragraph from *Sacrosanctum Concilium*. The Council Fathers could not be clearer in stating the value and dignity of devotional prayer, and no one could deduce from this paragraph that devotional prayer is to be ignored or expunged from the Church's life. At the same time, this paragraph makes clear that there is a hierarchy: liturgical prayer far surpasses devotional prayer.[8]

Liturgical prayer is the most important prayer we raise to God. As *Sacrosanctum Concilium* contends, "liturgy is the summit toward which the activity of the Church is directed; it is also the fount from which all her power flows" (SC, 10). Liturgical prayer flows to and from the Church; devotional prayer flows to and from liturgical prayer. Because of this, liturgical prayer is ecclesial prayer; it is prayer from, by, and for the Church. This is why liturgical prayer is fixed prayer, that is, the texts are a given. While presiders, homilists, and musicians make choices with respect to how liturgical prayer unfolds, those choices are limited within the overall structure of the rites of the Church. Rubrics (directions for how the liturgy unfolds) essentially do two things. First, they assure that there is a modicum of uniformity in the liturgy. We respond and sing as if we have one voice; we sit, stand, kneel, process as if we have one body; we pray united with Christ. Liturgy is not ours, but is a prayer of the whole Church. Second, rubrics protect us from the idiosyncrasies of overly zealous or personable or self-centered presiders. The prayer they are leading is not their prayer alone, but the prayer of the whole Church. Devotional prayer, on the other hand, may have a fixed text (such as the rosary or novenas), but only tradition dictates how we use that text or pray. We can replace devotional prayer texts with our own words. We can use our own words for the prayer. We are as free as our hearts prompt to say to God what we desire and take whatever time we need to listen to God in our prayer. As communal as liturgical prayer is by its very nature, so is devotional prayer necessarily individual and, yes, even idiosyncratic. In some respects, devotional prayer can be more immediately satisfying than liturgical prayer because it more immediately feeds our at-hand prayer needs.

So we come to another important distinction. While liturgical prayer is not meant to stifle us, strip us of emotion, or remove us from our everyday needs and concerns, neither is it directed to satisfying all our spiritual needs. Liturgical prayer ought not be devoid of feelings or prevent us from being ourselves or make us feel like our presence doesn't matter. Liturgical prayer is surely directed to our deepest spiritual need:

to encounter God in praise, adoration, and thanksgiving. However, liturgical prayer is larger than any one of us. Because it is a communal activity, something of our personal desires must be let go. Devotional prayer, on the other hand, can be largely directed to satisfying our affective needs. We tend to choose devotional prayer that takes us where we are in the moment and enables us to pour ourselves out to God. If we have a healthy devotional prayer life that satisfies our affective spiritual needs, then we do not come to liturgy looking for this kind of comfort. Liturgy, then, can do what it is supposed to do.

One of the most important challenges facing those preparing and celebrating liturgy today is how to enable liturgical prayer to touch the faithful in a multicultural situation. Few liturgical communities today are homogeneous. Gone are the days when we had a German parish on one corner, a Hungarian parish on another, a Polish parish on a third, and an Irish parish on a fourth corner. And this is good. Multicultural parishes aptly symbolize the diversity and universality of Christ's Church. A ghetto mentality betrays the inclusivity of the Gospel message. At the same time, we cannot ignore that a liturgical assembly will consist of people who, perhaps, speak different languages, live out of different cultural paradigms, and have different religious traditions concerning liturgy, festivals, and devotions. How do we celebrate in such cultural diversity?

If we are truly to be culturally sensitive, then celebrating genuine multicultural liturgy demands more than having more than one language spoken or sung during liturgy, having different kinds of processions, or sharing the sign of peace in different ways. The issue of culture runs far deeper than external manifestations. Culture might be described as

> an historically transmitted pattern of meanings embodied in symbols, a system of inherited conceptions expressed in symbolic forms by means of which [people] communicate, perpetuate, and develop their knowledge about and attitudes toward life.... Sacred symbols function to synthesize a people's ethos—the tone, character, and quality of their life, its moral and aesthetic style and mood, and their world view—the picture they have of the way things in sheer actuality are, their comprehensive ideas of order.[9]

Culture, then, informs how we approach life, view life, interpret life. It is not an add-on but is internal to us, part of our psyche, self, being. All prayer, then, is necessarily cultural. Devotional prayer is deeply cultural because we choose when, how, why, and what we pray. It is sporadic, that is, we pray when we are drawn to it, when we feel the need, when we have time, when we are ready, when we are free to give ourselves over to it. Liturgical prayer, however, presents unique challenges. First of all, it is communal. In this sense, liturgical prayer must be transcultural—it must embody the life approaches and attitudes of all who are present. It is inclusive by nature, even when the assembled body is very diverse. Second, it is a rhythmic given. Liturgical prayer happens daily, weekly, seasonally. It takes place at set hours for set purposes. Third, its very givenness cannot be empty or sterile. If liturgical prayer doesn't have the capacity to draw the faithful in, then it cannot be the prayer it is intended to be. There are no easy answers to the question of multicultural communities and encultur- ated prayer. But that cannot excuse those who plan, prepare, and celebrate liturgy in a given community from reflecting often and seriously on the challenges of culture. It demands that the members of the liturgical community discover and accept the rich diversity of the group. It means that there must be a good balance between communal liturgical prayer and communal devotional prayer, where the latter affords much more latitude for exploring and learning about the cultures of others.

One final distinction between liturgical and devotional prayer: Since we decide the when and what and why and how of devotional prayer, we are free to shape it to meet our affective prayer needs. Liturgical prayer, on the other hand, as a fixed ritual of the whole Church, shapes us. It transforms us into being more perfect members of Christ's Body. How liturgical prayer shapes us moves us to the next section. It shapes us because of liturgical prayer's relation to Christ.

LITURGICAL PRAYER IN RELATION TO CHRIST

The most distinctive characteristic of liturgical prayer is its relation to Christ. Liturgical prayer begins with, in, and from Christ and his saving event. Drawing on the Jewish practice of *zkr* (Greek: *anamnesis*, remember), every liturgical act remem- bers the entirety of the saving work of Jesus Christ. To remember in this specific context is not a matter of recall, of going back to some historical event to reflect on it and learn from it.[10] Jewish remembering is a making present, a doing in the here and now the saving act that is being remembered. Remembering actualizes a tradi- tion. In remembering, the past event becomes present, formative, and enduring. For example, when people of the Jewish faith celebrate Passover each spring, they are not simply recalling a past event of God leading them from slavery to freedom. No, they are celebrating *this year* the same act of God. They are celebrating God leading them from slavery to freedom here and now in their lives.

All liturgical prayer is an act of remembering. Specifically for us Christians, this prayer remembers Christ's saving mystery, the paschal mystery. As mystery, Christ's saving act can never be exhausted; we simply over time delve deeper and deeper into its richness and meaning. The word *paschal* probably derives from the Hebrew *pesach*, meaning a passing, a *transitus*. We have popularly come to understand the paschal mystery as Jesus's passing through death to risen life, that marvelous event we celebrate primarily from Good Friday to Easter Sunday. While that is surely a truism, the mystery is much deeper and broader. Moreover, the paschal mystery is not only about Christ, but it is also about us.

The notion of paschal mystery does not begin with Jesus's death, but with Jesus's Incarnation. His first passing over is from being the preexistent divine Son (see John 1:1–4) to being incarnated as a human in place and time. Our guiding scriptural passage here is that marvelous early Christian hymn as recorded in the Letter of Paul to the Philippians, the hymn to Christ's humility:

> Who, though he was in the form of God,
> > did not regard equality with God
> > as something to be exploited,
> but emptied himself,
> > taking the form of a slave,
> > being born in human likeness.
> And being found in human form,
> > he humbled himself
> > and became obedient to the point of death—
> > even death on a cross. (Philippians 2:6–8)[11]

Three words in this passage characterize Christ's relationship to his Father and our relationship to that same Father: self-emptying, humble, and obedient. These three words also characterize how we ought to approach liturgical prayer if we wish to identify with Christ in his paschal mystery. All three words can be summed up in a single act: self-giving. Christ's self-giving was total, even to the point of death. For this he was highly exalted (see Philippians 2:9); the Father raised him from death to risen life. His self-giving, however, did not end with his resurrection and ascension. He continues his self-giving during every liturgical prayer, the most sublime being his self-giving in the Eucharist. The reality of the paschal mystery continues in Christ's ongoing self-giving for our salvation. But this is not all that can be said about the paschal mystery.

St. Paul makes clear that at baptism we ourselves are plunged into this mystery:

> Do you not know that all of us who have been baptized into Christ Jesus were baptized into his death? Therefore we have been buried with him by

baptism into death, so that, just as Christ was raised from the dead by the glory of the Father, so we too might walk in newness of life. (Romans 6:3–4)

Christ's mystery of passing through death to life is our mystery. This mystery describes our own baptismal living. This is who we are and how we are to live as faithful followers of Christ. Our baptismal commitment identifies us with Christ and his saving mystery. His ascension is not an absence but, with the sending of the Spirit, a continued presence through us, made members of his body through baptism.

Liturgical prayer celebrates, makes present, and enacts the paschal mystery. *Sacrosanctum Concilium* makes this clear and, in so doing, helps us understand liturgy as a continuation of Christ's saving mystery:

> By a tradition handed down from the apostles and having its origin from the very day of Christ's resurrection, the Church celebrates the paschal mystery every eighth day, which, with good reason, bears the name of the Lord's Day or Sunday. For on this day Christ's faithful must gather together so that, by hearing the word of God and taking part in the eucharist, they may call to mind the passion, resurrection, and glorification of the Lord Jesus and may thank God.[12]

The *CCC* broadens this assertion of *Sacrosanctum Concilium* to apply it to all liturgy: "The Church celebrates in the liturgy above all the Paschal mystery by which Christ accomplished the work of our salvation" (SC, 1067). At liturgy, Christ's self-giving continues for our salvation, and we are invited into this obedient self-giving.

St. Paul has shown us how at baptism we are plunged into Christ's death so that we might rise to new life with him. In other words, we are plunged into Christ's paschal mystery. This is no less true of all celebrations of the sacraments and of the Liturgy of the Hours,[13] but "most of all in the divine sacrifice of the eucharist" (SC, 2), Christ's continuing self-giving sacrifice is so evident. The bread and wine are placed on the banquet table or altar of sacrifice; they will become for us the bread of life and our spiritual drink.[14] Bread and wine, our simple gifts, are substantially changed into the very Body and Blood of our Lord Jesus Christ. However, the Eucharist celebrates not only Christ's continued sacrifice, continued self-giving, but also our own. In the invitation to the prayer over the offerings (the *orate fratres*), the priest addresses us: "Pray, brethren (brothers and sisters), that my sacrifice and yours may be acceptable to God, the almighty Father" (RM, 29). The "my" here does not refer to the priest himself, but to the priest who is the visible presence of Christ, the head of his Church. The sacrifice is that of Christ. Then the invitation says, "and yours." Clearly, we ourselves are placed on the altar along with the bread and wine. We ourselves are offered to God for transformation through our full, conscious, and active participation—through our surrender to the action of the Holy Spirit.

The Holy Spirit acts on the gifts of bread and wine as well as ourselves for the transformation that is proper to the offering. This Spirit action is called an *epiclesis*, an invocation of the Holy Spirit. The *epiclesis* over the bread and wine from Eucharistic Prayer III begs that "by the same Spirit graciously make holy these gifts we have brought to you for consecration, that they may become the Body and Blood of your Son our Lord Jesus Christ" (RM, 109). Clearly it is the action of the Holy Spirit upon the gifts that effects the change. But this is not the only *epiclesis*.[15] There is a second one, sometimes called the "communion *epiclesis*," that occurs in the last part of the Eucharistic prayer. Again, from Eucharistic Prayer III: "Grant that we, who are nourished by the Body and Blood of your Son and filled with his Holy Spirit, may become one body, one spirit in Christ" (RM, 113). The language "may become" is included in both the *epiclesis* over the bread and wine and that over the people. The words describing what becomes are different—the bread and wine become the Body and Blood of the Risen Christ; we become more perfectly the body of Christ into which we were baptized. The effect, however, is the same. The bread and wine become the Body and Blood of Christ; we become more perfectly members of the body of Christ. St. Augustine long ago captured this mystery of our transformation at the Eucharistic celebration brilliantly when he wrote:

> If you are to understand what it means to be the Body of Christ, hear what Paul has to say: "Now you are the Body of Christ and individually members of it" (1 Corinthians 12:27). If you are the Body of Christ and members of it, then it is that mystery which is placed on the Lord's table: you receive the mystery, which is to say the Body of Christ, your very self. You answer "Amen" to who you are and in the answer you embrace yourself. You hear "Body of Christ" and answer "Amen". Be a member of Christ's Body, that your Amen will be true.[16]

Liturgical prayer is serious and dangerous business! When we surrender ourselves to the liturgical action, we give ourselves over to the action of the Holy Spirit. We become more than who we are. We are changed. We are conformed more perfectly to Christ, and in that identity we are called to commit ourselves to living the Gospel, to continuing Christ's saving mystery, to be as self-giving as Christ was. Liturgical prayer calls us to the same compassion and care, love and lovability, obedience and self-offering as Christ. Liturgical prayer enacts the paschal mystery of Christ. Our encounter with this mystery transforms us. This transformation is a distinctive characteristic of liturgical prayer. All liturgical prayer draws us into a deeper relationship with Christ and with our heavenly Father through the Holy Spirit. At liturgical prayer we are confronted with who we are to be and are given the means to become evermore perfectly members of the body of Christ.

Liturgical Prayer's Gains and Losses Since the Council

By far, there are many more gains than losses for liturgical prayer since the renewal called for by the Council. It is important for us to remember that liturgy is not our own to be shaped according to our own vision and needs. Liturgical prayer is the Church's greatest patrimony. It belongs to the whole Church. Any gains or losses affect the whole Church.

The gain for liturgical prayer of most import is the recovery of liturgy as enacting the paschal mystery. Not only identifying us with Christ's self-giving, this gain also shifts liturgical prayer away from its purpose being largely to receive graces to bringing about a deeper conformity to Christ. This gain moves the assembly's self-understanding away from being mere receptors of God's graces to being enlivened members of the body of Christ living the grace of identity with Christ. As Christ is active in liturgy, so are we. *Sacrosanctum Concilium*'s call for full, conscious, and active participation in Christ's continuing work of salvation means that liturgy is an ongoing presence of the Risen Christ. There is a shift from doing to being, from recipients to agents, from a focus on externals to an inner transformation. Liturgical prayer challenges us to be a presence of Christ for all we meet.

Another gain of the liturgical renewal is a greater sense of community, along with its attendant demand that we love and care for each other as Christ. Liturgical prayer is no longer an individual matter; we come together to gather with Christ our head to be Church made visible. A liturgical community has a deeper basis than merely doing for each other. We are a community, *cum* and *unus*, "one with," because we share the same identity and mission. Growing in the self-awareness of who we are as the Body of Christ, we cannot ignore the needs of others. Liturgical prayer urges solidarity with others. It urges action on behalf of others. It urges us to be toward others as Jesus was to his contemporaries and continues to be toward us.

Liturgical renewal has given us a deeper appreciation for how the liturgical year celebrates the mystery of Christ and how we enter into that mystery each year in a different way. The festivals on our calendar bring us in touch with the major events in Jesus's life and ministry. They bring us to reflect on the holy women and men who have gone before us and remain models of Gospel living. They help us to keep the Risen Christ at the center of our lives. Cyclic in nature, the liturgical year reminds us that the events of Christ's saving mission are not single, past events that are completed and finished, but continue in the Church's liturgical prayer and seasons. Each year we come around to a new celebration of a festival, we are different; we have grown in our self-understanding as Christ's Body and how we carry forward his saving mission.

We have gained a greater appreciation for the dynamic of God's word (see SC, 24, 50). A Liturgy of the Word is now required for every sacramental celebration (see *CCC* 1153–1155). The Liturgy of the Word is not simply a preamble to the sacramental action, but is an integral part of the whole celebration, the two being one single act of worship (see SC, 56). One of the monumental achievements of the liturgical renewal is the revised lectionary. Instead of a one-year cycle of readings with no regular proclamation of God's Word from the Old Testament, we now have a three-year cycle of readings with most Sundays proclaiming a First Reading from the Old Testament.[17] During Ordinary Time we have a sequential proclamation from one of the synoptic Gospels, which affords us a sense of the difference between these Gospels and the theology they intend to convey. [18] This revised lectionary helps us see the relationship between the two testaments. We are more clearly attuned to typology, whereby figures and events from the Old Testament foreshadow Christ and his saving mission. We have gained a greater sensitivity to our Jewish brothers and sisters and recognize that we share a common and ancient tradition.

While Gregorian chant continues to have a privileged place in the music tradition of the Church (see SC, 116), introduction of the vernacular (certainly a huge gain!) has opened up a whole sacred ministry of newly composed hymnody. Singing at liturgy is no longer simply the ministry of the choir. The choir supports the assembly's song. The whole assembly is a choir of voices being raised in praise and thanksgiving to God.[19]

The liturgical renewal promoted the recovery of the Liturgy of the Hours as the Church's daily prayer (see SC, 84, 88, 100). This beautiful prayer, which frames and punctuates the day with liturgical prayer (and, therefore, with the rhythm of the paschal mystery) can no longer be the sole domain of the clergy and those monastics required by their constitutions to pray it. Everyone, even in the privacy of their own homes, can join in this daily liturgical prayer. Publishers have made this prayer much more accessible to the people. The revised rite of the Liturgy of the Hours is now available to everyone in affordable formats in the vernacular. Some daily missalettes include a simplified morning and evening prayer for each day. Other resources are available which provide different styles and ways of celebrating this liturgical prayer both individually and communally. Some parishes celebrate this prayer in common, especially during the preparatory seasons of Advent and Lent, during the festal seasons of Christmas and Easter, and on solemnities.[20]

Many parishioners have a more active involvement in and ownership of the liturgy through their service as hospitality ministers (greeters, ushers), acolytes, lectors, cantors, liturgy coordinators, extraordinary ministers of Holy Communion, and in other ministries. Other gains include more liturgical ministries being opened to the laity. The introduction of the permanent diaconate has promoted more visible service in addressing various needs. Deacons and extraordinary ministers of Holy Communion have enabled receiving the Blessed Sacrament by the sick and home-bound to be more frequent. The introduction of the Rite of Christian Initiation of Adults (the RCIA) has made far richer the reception of new members into the Church community. All these and other gains: We are surely richer for them.

Admittedly, the renewal of liturgical prayer has not been all gain. We must admit to some losses. Perhaps the most serious loss is that we are sometimes a very divided Church: divided over whether to use the ordinary or extraordinary forms of the Eucharistic rite, over the kind of music to use, over enforcement of rubrics, over preaching styles, over how much silence to promote, over the kind of hospitality we desire, over use of incense, and so forth.[21] Often, the root of these divisions is a stubbornly continuing sense that liturgy must be what an individual wants. Instead, liturgy is of the whole Church, which implies that all of us must give a little in order to celebrate liturgy well as the one body of Christ.

In some liturgical communities, there has been a sense that the awe, reverence, and dignity that liturgical prayer demands has been lost. The tendency is to blame the revised liturgy, when the issue is really over how the renewed liturgy is implemented. A liturgy that is too self-referential (focusing on us rather than turning us as one body toward God) loses a sense of joining our praise with that of the whole heavenly host (see SC, 8). Sometimes the presiding priest draws too much attention to himself and away from the real focus of liturgy. This happens, for example, when too many personal comments are interspersed in the rite, when the presiding priest ad-libs the rite, when the legitimate options are not well chosen, when creativity is introduced into the rite that detracts from the flow of the rite, when the presider is overly nonchalant, and when rubrics are not respected. On the other hand, liturgical prayer that is too focused on rubrics, on getting it right instead of praying, can also lose much of its reverence and mystery.

We have lost the essential relationship between liturgical and devotional prayer and how they complement each other. All too many legitimate and helpful devotions have fallen into disuse. If we have a healthy and satisfying devotional prayer life, then we can more easily surrender ourselves to the demand of liturgy to let go of our own wants and needs to enter into the larger domain of the whole Church's prayer. Some of the urgency involved in celebrating the weekly Eucharistic liturgy, having infants baptized, participating in parish activities, as well as the closing of many parishes and Catholic schools, can all distract from an emphasis on liturgical renewal.

Yes, there have been both gains and losses after the onset of liturgical renewal. Sometimes it is good for us to sit back and weigh the gains and losses. What we will probably discover is that more good has happened than bad. We made a mistake after the Council, thinking that when we revised the liturgical rites and implemented them that renewal would be finished. Liturgical renewal has been happening since Christ himself said, "Do this in remembrance of me" (Luke 22:19). And it will continue until the Second Coming. It is helpful to keep in mind that liturgy is a dynamic rite. We are ever learning more and more about who Jesus is and about his mission. We will never exhaust learning how we participate through liturgy and life in his saving mission. And this open-endedness, this ongoing nature, is a positive thing. It is a constant reminder that Christ's mystery is rich and deep and can never be exhausted.

Liturgical Prayer as Lived Beyond Its Ritual Expression

It is no secret that the third edition of *The Roman Missal* is a fairly literal translation from the Latin *editio typica* (typical edition). The former sacramentary for the United States had a number of original texts; these have all been eliminated in this third edition for the US. It is interesting, however, that Pope Benedict XVI himself chose two new dismissals for our present *Roman Missal*. They are "Go and announce the Gospel of the Lord" and, "Go in peace, glorifying the Lord by your life" (RM, 144). Far more than simply putting his personal stamp on this new translation, Pope Benedict was emphasizing something that is extremely significant but that we often forget: While the ritual of Mass is completed, the Eucharistic action is never completed but is carried forth to be lived each moment of our day.

Liturgy is not simply a ritual ceremony but transforms us to live the mystery we have celebrated: "It is this mystery of Christ that the Church proclaims and celebrates in her liturgy so that the faithful may live from it and bear witness to it in the world" (*CCC* 1068). The *Catechism* goes on to quote from *Sacrosanctum Concilium* (2): "For it is in the liturgy, especially in the divine sacrifice of the Eucharist, that 'the work of our redemption is accomplished,' and it is through the liturgy especially that the faithful are enabled to express in their lives and manifest to others the mystery of Christ and the real nature of the true Church." Although the concluding rites are the briefest of the four major divisions of the Eucharistic liturgy, in some respects they are the longest; the dismissal moves us into our daily living, where we continue what we have celebrated. All liturgy concludes with a dismissal that is more than a signal that a rite has ended. It is an invitation to deepened Gospel living, being witnesses of Christ's risen presence among us, and a reminder of our baptismal commitment to embrace the faith we profess.

The paschal mystery is a rhythm of dying and rising, of self-giving and risen life. As we imitate in our own daily lives Christ's self-giving, we conform ourselves more perfectly to him. Becoming more like him, we share more deeply in his risen life. Here is the key: The paschal mystery that liturgy enacts is the same mystery we are to live. Our very lives are to be a rhythm of dying and rising, self-giving and risen life. In this sense, we might say that Gospel living is actually a kind of everyday liturgy. In liturgical prayer, we encounter Christ in his mystery, learn how to live better his mystery, and are sent forth as the embodiment of his mystery.

Liturgical prayer is compelling. It draws us into the mystery of who we are in Christ. We pass through the doors of the church; we bless ourselves with water reminding us of our baptismal identity and commitment; we surrender ourselves to being the liturgical assembly, the Church made visible; we enact the self-giving and saving mystery of Christ; and we are dismissed to live this mystery. We don't leave, we don't walk out the doors of the church, however, the same as we came in. With full, conscious, and active participation, we place ourselves into God's hands to be transformed into ever-more perfect images of the Risen Christ. Liturgy is God's work transforming us into a deeper share in divine life. We become a new creation. Not every liturgy makes this evident to us. Deep transformation comes slowly and often most imperceptibly. Immersing ourselves into the rhythm of the liturgical year, we embrace Christ's mystery. Through our surrender to the Holy Spirit's action within us, we ourselves become "a new heaven and a new earth" (Revelation 21:1).

The Revelation to John that concludes the New Testament is a marvelous description of the heavenly liturgy. Before the throne of the divine majesty, God's praises are sung "day and night without ceasing" (Revelation 4:8). The "Lamb standing as if it had been slaughtered" (Revelation 5:6) is present before the heavenly throne. The Lamb is also worshiped: "Worthy is the Lamb that was slaughtered / to receive power and wealth and wisdom and might / and honor and glory and blessing!" (Revelation 5:12). The Lamb opens the seals of the scrolls on which are written God's plan for creation and creatures. After the seventh seal "there was silence in heaven for about half an hour" (Revelation 8:1). This provocative and highly symbolic last book of the New Testament gives us a glimpse of where liturgical prayer leads those who are faithful followers of the Lamb. Liturgical prayer is an "already" experience of the "not yet" of the heavenly liturgy toward which we journey. We are sealed and belong to the Lamb, embodying the victory over death that has been won.[22]

Between the revelation of God's plan for us and the judgment of those worthy to be sealed, there is "silence in heaven for about half an hour" (Revelation 8:1). We might consider our earthly lives as being in this in-between awed and reverent silence before the full revelation of what is to be. Silence is not nothing, but is "the effect of absolute absorption in the presence of the Divine."[23] Liturgical prayer brings us to awed and reverent silence because in the silence our whole being can be surrendered, can be renewed, can be taken up into the divine being. In the silence, we experience ourselves as God intends us to be, as God wishes to gift us, as God chooses to relate to us. In the silence that is our lives, we ever stand before the throne of the divine majesty and the victorious Lamb, surrendering to the plan they have designed for us from the beginning of time. In liturgical prayer, we are privileged to have a foretaste of the heavenly liturgy, of eternal praise and thanksgiving, of definitive victory over evil and death. In liturgical prayer, we see our lives as they ought to be witnessing to faithful Gospel living, witnessing to the rhythm of the self-giving and exaltation proper to an appropriation into ourselves of the paschal mystery, choosing to model our lives after that of Jesus himself. When liturgical prayer bursts forth from its ritual expression into our daily living, we ourselves are the faithful presence of the Risen Christ through the power of the Holy Spirit. To that, we join all the heavenly host in saying, "Amen!" Our "amen" is a resounding act of worship repeated over and over again in our daily faithful "yes" to choosing God's will, and in doing so, we "will obtain the freedom of the glory of the children of God" (Romans 8:21). This is where liturgical prayer leads. It is God's free gift. And what a gift!

---

1. Second Vatican Council, *Sacrosanctum Concilium* (The Constitution on the Sacred Liturgy), December 4, 1963, in *The Liturgy Documents: Essential Documents for Parish Worship*, vol. 1, 5th ed. (Chicago: Liturgy Training, 2012); hereafter cited in the text as SC.
2. "Back to the sources" became the clarion call of the Council Fathers and the reforms they promoted. In addition to liturgy, this phrase was a driving force of *Dei Verbun* (The Dogmatic Constitution on Divine Revelation) November 18, 1965. In Austin Flannery, OP, ed., *Vatican Council II*, vol. 1, *The Conciliar and Post Conciliar Documents*, rev. ed. (Northport, NY: Costello, 1975); see especially no. 23.
3. See "The General Instruction of the Roman Missal" (Washington, DC: USCCB, 2011), 65. See also *Fulfilled in Your Hearing: The Homily in the Sunday Assembly* (Washington, DC: NCCB, 1982), 72 in *The Liturgy Documents*.
4. See the chart on page 22 in my *Worship with Gladness: Understanding Worship from the Heart* (Grand Rapids: Eerdmans, 2014), where I contrast for an ecumenical audience worship and liturgy, paralleling what I do in this section.

5. The *Catechism of the Catholic Church* says that in a Christian tradition *liturgy* means the participation of the People of God in "the work of God" (*CCC* 1069). The note given at the end of this quotation refers to John 17:4: "I glorified you on earth by finishing the work that you gave me to do." All Scripture quotations are from the NRSV.

6. This strong belief that liturgy spills over into daily living is taken up in the last section of this chapter.

7. SC, 13. That liturgical prayer supersedes devotional prayer is a point which comes back over and over again in the important document "Directory on Popular Piety and the Liturgy: Principles and Guidelines" (Vatican City: Congregation for Divine Worship and the Discipline of the Sacraments, 2001), 11, 13, 46, 50, 55. See also Peter C. Phan, ed., *Directory on Popular Piety and the Liturgy: Principles and Guidelines. A Commentary* (Collegeville, MN: Liturgical, 2005).

8. In the next section of this chapter, we explore why liturgical prayer stands at the pinnacle of a hierarchy of prayer.

9. Clifford Geertz, *The Interpretation of Cultures* (New York: Basic, 1973), 89. Specific to liturgy, see Anscar J. Chupungco, *Liturgical Inculturation: Sacramentals, Religiosity, and Catechesis* (Collegeville, MN: Liturgical, 1992), especially chapter 1, "A Definition of Terms," 13–31. Also, Mark R. Francis,CSV, *Liturgy in a Multicultural Community*, American Essays in Liturgy, ed. Edward Foley (Collegeville, MN: Liturgical, 1991), 11–13.

10. See H. Eising, "*zkr*" in G.J. Botterweck and H. Ringgren, eds., *Theological Dictionary of the Old Testament*, vol. 4, trans. David E. Green (Grand Rapids: Eerdmans, 1980), 66. For more on the Jewish notion of remembering, see B.S. Childs, *Memory and Tradition in Israel* (London: SCM, 1962).

11. All Scripture quotations are from the *New Revised Standard Version*.

12. SC, 106. In paragraph 6, SC makes the same point about baptism.

13. It goes beyond the scope of this chapter to trace how the paschal mystery is enacted in the other sacraments and Liturgy of the Hours.

14. United States Conference of Catholic Bishops, *The Roman Missal*, English translation according to the third typical edition (2011), 23 and 25; hereafter cited in the text as RM.

15. One of the great steps forward in the revision of the Eucharistic rite is the inclusion of a double *epiclesis* over the gifts and over the people in almost all of the Eucharistic prayers.

16. St. Augustine of Hippo, sermon 272 in scholarly editions. This is my translation.

17. A notable departure from this is the Sundays of Easter when the First Reading is taken from the Acts of the Apostles.

18. In Year A, we proclaim the Gospel from Matthew, in Year B from Mark, and in Year C from Luke. John's Gospel is proclaimed during festal seasons (especially Easter) and on many feast days.

19. See SC, especially 113. All of SC chapter 6 is on sacred music (see 112–121).

20. For a brief history, theology, pastoral practice, and suggestions for beginning Liturgy of the Hours, especially for a parish setting, see my *Morning and Evening: A Parish Celebration* (Chicago: Liturgy Training, 1996).

21. The ordinary form is the use of the third edition of *The Roman Missal* of 2011, in either the vernacular or in Latin. The extraordinary form is the use of *Missale Romanum* of 1962 of Pope St. John XXIII in Latin.

22. The sacramental anointing with holy chrism is called the *sphragis*, the sealing of the sacrament. We are marked for Christ and the fullness of life.

23. Joyce Ann Zimmerman, CPPS, *Silence: Everyday Living and Praying* (Chicago: Liturgy Training, 2010), 102.

CHAPTER 37

Prayer in Ordinary Time

~ Peter Verity ~

> Besides the times of year that have their own distinctive character, there remain in the yearly cycle thirty-three or thirty-four weeks in which no particular aspect of the mystery of Christ is celebrated, but rather the mystery of Christ itself is honoured in its fullness, especially on Sundays. This period is known as Ordinary Time.[1]
>
> —*Universal Norms for the Liturgical Year and Calendar*

Most commentators agree that the word *ordinary* in Ordinary Time, comes from the Latin word *ordinalis*, which means "showing order, denoting an order of succession." Ordinary Time is the counted weeks outside the other liturgical seasons. It is ordered, numbered, regular.

Described like that, Ordinary Time sounds unexciting. Synonyms for *ordinary* are commonplace, mediocre, everyday, conventional, average, routine, mundane, run of the mill, dull, drab, monotonous, boring, dreary. This would confirm the understanding of many that Ordinary Time is second rate and less important than the great penitential seasons of Advent and Lent and the high days and holy days of Christmas and Easter. This perception is exacerbated by the general practice in many parishes of promoting courses, discussion groups, and extra prayer meetings in Lent and Advent, thus giving the impression that these are the important times for prayer while the rest of the year, Ordinary Time, is not.

Ordinary Time will only be routine and dull if we allow ourselves to think of it as the gap between the important high seasons of Christmas and Easter. If this is the case, we will never be able to make Ordinary Time what it truly is—the bedrock of our prayer, the foundation without which we will never be able to celebrate fully the great feasts.

What can lift Ordinary Time out of these negative perceptions and make it what it should be? I suggest that our prayer in Ordinary Time is an adventure, a challenge which we ignore at our peril. *Adventure* evokes quite a different picture than *ordinary*. It implies stepping out into the unknown, going to a strange place, taking part in something exciting and dangerous. It includes exploration, discovery, and risk. There is nothing mundane or dreary about an adventure.

At the beginning of the Church, the Holy Spirit came down on the apostles, and the adventure began as they were empowered to live in a new way. It was not that the excitement of being with Jesus ended with the ascension and then everything went back to how it had been before. As the Acts of the Apostles and the letters of St. Paul bear witness, after Pentecost the real adventure of taking the Good News to the whole world began. For us too, Ordinary Time does not signal the end of interesting times, but rather the beginning of the excitement and adventure of real life.

I will begin by considering briefly the prayer opportunities in the Sunday and weekday liturgies of Ordinary Time. Later, I will explore one or two ideas for promoting new ways of thinking about the weeks and months of Ordinary Time and show how prayer becomes an adventure as it takes place in the midst of ordinary life.

THE SUNDAY LITURGY OF ORDINARY TIME

In the annual liturgical cycle, there are a total of thirty-three or thirty-four weeks of Ordinary Time in two separate periods. The first is from the end of the Christmas season on the Feast of the Baptism of the Lord to the beginning of Lent on Ash Wednesday. The second and longer period of Ordinary Time is from the Monday after Pentecost Sunday until the first Sunday of Advent. The number of weeks in each period varies from year to year depending on the date of Easter.

The Sunday at the end of Christmastide, immediately preceding the beginning of Ordinary Time, is the Feast of the Baptism of the Lord. Just as Jesus's baptism marked the beginning of his public ministry and the proclamation that the kingdom of God is very near (see Mark 1:15), so the celebration of the feast marks the time when the Church proclaims the dawn of Christ's presence in public life and the immanence of God's kingdom in the world.

Pentecost Sunday concludes the Lent and Easter seasons and immediately precedes the longer second part of Ordinary Time. Often called the birthday of the Church, it marks the beginning of the ministry of the apostles to take the Good News to the whole world, strengthened by the gift of the Holy Spirit.

The Baptism of the Lord and Pentecost are like bridges between the high celebrations of Christmas and Easter and the beginning or resumption of Ordinary Time. As we step onto each bridge, we look back with gratitude at the mysteries we have celebrated, and at the same time, we look forward to the new world, where we will put the mysteries into practice in daily life. We bring with us the memory of wonderful and mysterious events, eager for the opportunity to explore our everyday world in the light of what we have celebrated. Have the seasonal celebrations prepared us for the adventure of daily living where the sacred and the secular rub shoulders so closely?

In each year of the lectionary cycle, the Gospel readings for the second Sunday are intended to help us complete the transition into Ordinary Time. That each year this Gospel is from St. John is striking because the remainder of the Sunday Gospels, apart from special feasts and one exception in the year of Mark, come from the synoptic writers and follow in chronological sequence. What is the Church saying to us by placing these Johannine Gospel readings at the beginning of Ordinary Time? What spiritual message might we glean from this? The answer becomes clearer as we look at the Gospel passages for each of these second Sundays.

The Gospel for Year A tells the story of John the Baptist recognizing and pointing out the Lamb of God (John 1:29–34). Ordinary Time, which we are entering, is when the Risen Christ, the Lamb of God, walks in our midst, and we are challenged to recognize him and to point him out to others.

In Year B, the Gospel is the continuation of this passage (John 1:35–42).[2] The sentence, "Look, there is the Lamb of God," in verse 29 is repeated in verse 36, and in this second passage, the two disciples hear John the Baptist's message and ask Jesus where he lives. They are invited to "come and see"—as we are, too, when we enter into this Gospel story. They go with him and stay for the rest of the day. Is this an invitation for us to stay with Jesus for the remainder of Ordinary Time?

The Gospel in Year C is the wedding feast at Cana (John 2:1–12), where Mary says, "Do whatever he tells you." Hearing that command over the next thirty-four weeks and putting it into practice will be risky. Who knows what Jesus may ask us to do? Perhaps he will ask something that will change our hearts from the coldness of water to the richness of wine?

In each of the three years, therefore, the second Sunday of Ordinary Time provides a gateway into the life of prayer that will occupy us during the majority of weeks in the year. We are invited to look, to see where the Lamb of God is. We are invited to "come and see" where he lives and stay with him. We are invited to "do whatever he tells us." These three Gospel passages offer an agenda for spiritual development that can occupy us fully during our Ordinary Time and provide the way into a deepening prayer life in the weeks and months ahead.

As the Sunday Gospels unfold over the weeks of Ordinary Time, we are drawn further into the mystery of Christ. The universal norms quoted at the beginning of this chapter state that these are "thirty-three or thirty-four weeks in which no particular aspect of the mystery of Christ is celebrated, but rather the mystery of Christ itself is honoured in its fullness, especially on Sundays." The Gospel readings tell the story of the miracles, parables, sayings, and events of Jesus's life, and we are invited to make sense of them for ourselves in the light of the resurrection. Ordinary Time is when we can say, "Christ is risen; he is truly risen." It is happening now; it is not a past event. We are living in resurrection times. Ordinary Time is the era of the Church, a time when the struggle between good and evil continues but where the certainty of Christ's victory is assured. It is the time when the Risen Lord is unveiled in the midst of our world and our lives. It is Eucharistic time, when his presence comes in a special way into the daily events and circumstances of ordinary life.

This ongoing meditation on the pastoral ministry of Jesus in the Sunday Gospels of Ordinary Time uses all three of the Synoptics. Year A is from Matthew, beginning with the call of the first disciples on the third Sunday (Matthew 4:12–23), through the Beatitudes discourse of chapters 5 to 7 (fourth to ninth Sundays), to the call of Matthew himself (Matthew 9:9–13) on the tenth Sunday. The remaining Sundays use extracts from chapters 10 to 25 that include miracles, parables, and discourses from Jesus with explicit references to the implications of following him. Matthew's year ends with the parable of the last judgment, when the Son of Man will come in glory to separate the sheep and the goats (Matthew 25:31–46). The Sunday Gospels of Year A invite us to explore our discipleship of Christ as a community, the Church. What are we called to be? What will be the difficulties? How are we to renew the life of our local church if it has grown tired and weak? This living in the community of the church will be the focus of our prayer on the Sundays of Year A.

The Sunday Gospels in Year B are taken largely from Mark, although there is a significant section in the middle from John. Again they begin on the third Sunday with the call of the disciples (Mark 1:14–20). The readings continue until the sixteenth Sunday (Mark 6:30–34), when they break off abruptly just before Mark's version of the miracle of the loaves. Instead we are given five weeks from chapter 6 of John's Gospel, the discourse about the bread of life. The extracts from Mark resume on the twenty-second Sunday. The Gospel for the Feast of Christ the King is the dialogue between Pilate and Jesus from John 18:33–37, where Jesus admits, "Yes, I am a king. I was born for this, I came into the world for this: to bear witness to the truth; and all who are on the side of truth listen to my voice." In the Sunday Gospels of Year B, Mark's year, therefore, we are invited to ask ourselves, "Who Jesus is for us and how must we, his disciples, live?" Are we on the side of truth? Do we really listen to his voice? If we hear it, do we put it into practice?

We listen to Luke on the Sundays of Year C. The third Sunday recounts Jesus's own call in the synagogue at Nazareth when he reads from the scroll of the prophet Isaiah (Luke 4:14–21). The call of the first disciples comes two Sundays later on the fifth Sunday (Luke 5:1–11). There are no surprises as the extracts from Luke continue in sequence until the thirty-third Sunday. In the Gospel for the Feast of Christ the

King, Luke recalls the inscription hanging above Jesus on the cross, "The King of the Jews," and the contrasting responses of the two thieves crucified with him. In the Sunday Gospels of Year C, we hear some of our favorite stories and are drawn into the story of Jesus. Where is God's presence active in our daily lives? Do we recognize this? What is the story of our own faith and can we share it with others?

PRAYING THE DAILY LITURGY OF ORDINARY TIME

Although the Sunday Gospels provide the liturgical backbone to prayer in Ordinary Time, the daily Mass readings, the Divine Office, and other devotions are part of a rich tapestry which carries us along on our adventure.

The lectionary for daily Mass in Ordinary Time offers a breadth of Scripture readings to nurture our prayer. The weekday Gospel readings come from the Synoptics and are repeated every year. Mark is read from week one to week nine, Matthew from week ten to week twenty-one, and Luke from week twenty-two to the end of week thirty-four.

The First Readings of daily Mass are spread over a two-year cycle and cover many books from both the Old and New Testament. We immerse ourselves in the story, following the thread day by day. Books of the Bible are often grouped so that a theme develops over several weeks. For example, from the Old Testament, in Cycle 1 from week twelve until the end of week twenty, we follow the story of God's covenant with his people from the call of Abraham through the Exodus to the settlement in the Promised Land, ending with the books of Judges and Ruth. In Cycle 2, there is a ten-week section of readings from the prophets, beginning with the story of Elijah in First Kings (week ten) and including lengthy sections from Jeremiah, Ezekiel, and others. Other stories keep our interest too: Tobit (week nine), Ecclesiastes (week twenty-five), and Job (week twenty-six), to name just three.

Readings from the New Testament are similarly grouped, and the major letters of St. Paul are given plenty of space, First Corinthians from weeks twenty-one to twenty-three in Cycle 2 for example, and Romans from week twenty-eight to week thirty-two in Cycle 1. At the end of each Cycle, weeks thirty-three and thirty-four provide readings from apocalyptic literature, in Cycle 1 from 1 Maccabees and Daniel and in Cycle 2 from the book of Revelation.

Various feasts during Ordinary Time hold our interest. Outstanding among these are the feasts of the Sacred Heart, Corpus Christi, the Triumph of the Cross, the Assumption, and All Saints. Every week, we celebrate the feasts or memorials of diocesan, national, and worldwide saints. This liturgical treasury provides points of interest on our journey, staging posts for our adventure into the mystery of Christ's presence in our lives.

The liturgical color for the Sundays and weekdays of Ordinary Time is green, the color of springtime and luscious pastures, indicating hope and growth, harmony and fertility. Green is also the color of forward movement, inviting us to go into new territory, rather than to remain where we are. This is the adventure that faces us in Ordinary Time. Throughout our lives, Christ and his kingdom are unveiled, and ordinariness is transformed into God's order. There is nothing boring or routine about Ordinary Time!

In addition to the Eucharistic liturgy, many devotions can deepen our prayer during Ordinary Time. Special mention should be made of the Prayer of the Church, the Divine Office, which many laypeople as well as clergy use for prayer. The Office of Readings nourishes us with further Scripture readings and related patristic readings. Books of alternative patristic readings are becoming available and accepted in certain parts of the world.[3] Other devotions such as frequent Eucharistic Adoration, celebrations of saints on patronal feasts, pilgrimages and retreats are the bread and butter of prayer during Ordinary Time.

An extensive list of devotional recommendations can be found in *The Directory on Popular Piety and the Liturgy* (published by the Congregation for Divine Worship in 2001), in which many local and universal devotions are described. The directory stresses that authentic devotions point to the Eucharist. The section in the directory devoted to Ordinary Time highlights the Trinitarian character of prayer. Devotion to the Blessed Trinity has been central to popular piety in both private devotions and in the liturgy for many centuries, and its importance is emphasized by the feast of the Holy Trinity on the Sunday after Pentecost. In the section devoted to Ordinary Time,[4] the directory says,

> Most [of our pious practices] begin with the sign of the cross "in the name of the Father, and of the Son, and of the Holy Spirit," the same formula with which the disciples of Jesus are baptized (cf. Matthew 28:19), thereby beginning a life of intimacy with God, as sons of the Father, brothers of Jesus, and temples of the Holy Spirit. Other pious exercises use formulas similar to those found in the Liturgy of the Hours and begin by giving "Glory to the Father, Son, and Holy Spirit." Some pious exercises end with a blessing given in the name of the three divine Persons. Many of the prayers used in these pious exercises follow the typical liturgical form and are addressed to

the "Father, through Christ, in the Holy Spirit," and conserve doxological formulas taken from the Liturgy.

Together with the little doxology (Glory be to the Father, and to the Son, and to the Holy Spirit....) and the great doxology (Glory be to God in the highest), pious exercises addressed directly to the Most Blessed Trinity often include formulas such as the biblical Trisagion (Holy, Holy, Holy) and also its liturgical form (Holy God, Holy Strong One, Holy Immortal One, have mercy on us), especially in the Eastern Churches, in some Western countries as well as among numerous religious orders and congregations.

ORDINARY TIME AS "COME AND SEE" TIME

The thirty-three or thirty-four weeks of Ordinary Time are a gift of space and time which enables our spiritual life to mature and develop at its own proper pace. How are we to understand this and why is gradual development over time necessary?

All human beings need time for relationships to develop. When people fall in love or when a friendship is growing, quality time together allows the relationship to mature. Sometimes there are special celebrations or events, but to grow, the relationship also needs ordinary things, doing chores, idle time, being with the beloved in silence or absorbed in trivia. Because we live in a fast-moving world where time is at a premium, a conscious effort to find quality time together is necessary for healthy relationships to develop. In nature too, time is needed for growth. A seed planted in the ground takes time to develop into a plant; good wine needs time to mature in the oak barrels; a child spends nine months in its mother's womb. The seed of God's life deep within us needs the whole of our lives to grow to full maturity. It will do so throughout all the seasons of the year, but the particular gift of Ordinary Time is that it is extended time with fewer distractions and plenty of space for slow, steady maturity.

Pastorally and liturgically, the major seasons of Advent, Christmas, Lent, and Easter are rightly filled with activity and busyness. Pastors and others involved in parish leadership are especially occupied with preparing good liturgies, putting the final touches to the RCIA process, and providing extra activities to help people celebrate the seasons well. Outside church life, too, the weeks before Christmas and Easter are taken up with preparations for family celebrations and seasonal events in the community. The major seasons do not readily lend themselves to contemplative time. Ordinary Time, on the other hand, provides the extended space to be quietly with God, allowing our relationship with him to mature. Ordinary Time is time to spend with God, to allow him to be with us in everyday things for no other reason than because we want to be together. It is *being* time, rather than *doing* time; it is truly contemplative time.

Ordinary time is a gift to our prayer. It may feel like wasted time, but God is working in us, growth is happening, the seed is growing. We must be patient and let God do what God does in his time. There is mystery in the waiting. For God, a thousand years are like a day.

> [Jesus] said, "This is what the kingdom of God is like. A man throws seed on the land. Night and day, while he sleeps, when he is awake, the seed is sprouting and growing; how, he does not know. Of its own accord the land produces first the shoot, then the ear, then the full grain in the ear. And when the crop is ready, he loses no time: he starts to reap because the harvest has come." (Mark 4:26–29)

The gospels give many examples of people spending time with Jesus in order to let the relationship develop, such as the call of the disciples in John 1:39: "So they went and saw where he lived and stayed with him the rest of that day." The gospels also record Jesus's times of rest and recreation, as in Matthew 12:1: "Jesus took a walk one Sabbath day through the cornfields," and his invitation to the disciples in Mark 6:31, "You must come away to some lonely place all by yourselves and rest for a while." Perhaps the best-known example of spending time with Jesus is that of Mary in Luke 10:38–42: She knew the importance of putting aside her work in favor of sitting with Jesus and listening to him.

The Danger of Acedia

The greatest temptation which draws us away from this slow steady growth during Ordinary Time is acedia or listlessness. This is sometimes described as the noonday devil and has long been recognized in the monastic tradition as one of the worst enemies of the spiritual life. It is identified by the time of day when monks would be tired and less alert. The temptation to have a break or call it a day becomes very great. Tiredness and lethargy creep in and a person becomes careless, lazy, and perhaps even indifferent. Acedia was first recognized by the Desert Fathers and Mothers as a state of mind that beset those who were trying to progress in the spiritual life through long days and nights in solitude. In itself, it is not a sin but is a spiritual lethargy or disposition which can lead to sin. Acedia means people look elsewhere for meaning, believing that the grass on the other side is greener, searching here, there, and everywhere for new things. The simple ways of loving God and longing for greater intimacy become neglected.

An image of acedia in the Gospels is the barren fig tree in Matthew 21:19, "Seeing a fig tree by the road, [Jesus] went up to it and found nothing on it but leaves." There is also the parable of the bridesmaids with no oil in their lamps in Matthew 25:13, "So stay awake because you do not know either the day or the hour," and the parable of the talents with the condemnation of the man who hid his talent in Matthew 25:25: "So I was afraid, and I went off and hid your talent in the ground." A very familiar example of acedia is in the garden of Gethsemane. Mark's version (14:37) says, "He came back and found them sleeping, and he said to Peter, 'Simon, are you asleep? Had you not the strength to keep awake one hour?'"

For anyone who is lukewarm or faltering, Ordinary Time is the seedbed for acedia. As we go from day to day, week to week, month to month, the temptation to give up on prayer or put it off until another time can be very great. "We'll start again at Advent," we say, and in the meantime we busy ourselves with all the other important things of life. Acedia, which can attack anyone at any stage of the spiritual life, is the main enemy of *being*, which is the gift of Ordinary Time. Gifts are given to be used, not put on the shelf to gather dust.

Ordinary Time as "Hidden Treasure" Time

Ordinary Time is the season which reminds us how important it is to play our part in the drama of real human life. Prayer grows out of daily life and at the same time leads into it; the adventure of prayer takes place in the midst of normal everyday living. In front of the burning bush in Exodus 3:5, Moses is told, "Take the sandals off your feet, for the place where you are standing is holy ground." The present, the here and now, the Ordinary Time throughout the year, is our holy ground.

This is incarnational thinking, and it is at the heart of the adventure of Ordinary Time prayer. Many of the best stories are about a search for hidden treasure. They attract us because we sense there really is something hidden beneath the surface which we can't quite see. We feel a fascination in trying to unearth it, an adventure in the seeking. Jesus used the same idea in his parables to describe the kingdom of God.

> The kingdom of heaven is like a treasure hidden in a field which someone has found; he hides it again, goes off happy, sells everything he owns and buys the field.
>
> Again, the kingdom of heaven is like a merchant looking for fine pearls; when he finds one of great value he goes and sells everything he owns and buys it. (Matthew 13:44–46)

Prayer in Ordinary Time is the search for hidden treasure in the world about us and for the hidden treasure within ourselves as we sense the truth that there is something more to life than meets the eye. In the Catholic spiritual tradition, many writers have stressed the need to see the sacredness of everything. They tell us that although most of our time may be taken up with the mundane, finding God in the midst of it is what can make mundane things extraordinary. The daily events and surroundings of our lives are like the nectar collected by bees to work up into honey. The challenge and adventure of Ordinary Time comes when we realize that prayer can indeed produce honey from these ordinary everyday things.

Secular authors and poets also have tried to capture the sense of sacredness in ordinary events and situations. They describe heaven as being very near to us if only we could see it, of the need to pay close attention to the ordinary things surrounding us. This is sometimes described as mindfulness and is highly regarded for living in a healthy mental state. Some authors invite us to see an inner meaning in the events and circumstances of our world and then to tell others about how remarkable they are, the very word *remarkable* indicating something that can and should be remarked on. The hidden treasure is only a heartbeat away, and if we can penetrate through the veil that usually obscures this, we will be amazed. Paying attention to the presence of God in all creation is prayer. Put another way, prayer is discovering a beautiful color woven into the tapestry of our lives, intertwined with all the other colors and textures that are already there.

Why is this search for hidden treasure often so difficult? One reason is because we are so overwhelmed by the tasks and duties of daily life that we find it extremely difficult to stop and pay attention to God. We also feel we must get our own house in order first before inviting God in, although the truth is that God is happy with us as we are, warts and all. Not only that, but the wonder we discover is that God dwells in us—and we can never be worthy of that. When we accept ourselves as we are, and this can happen in our younger years or much later in life, we begin to see that the hidden treasure that we seek is the presence of God deep within us, the indwelling of the Holy Spirit. The space to let God reveal this to us is available in the weeks of Ordinary Time. Etty Hillesum, the Jewish mystic murdered in Auschwitz in 1943, wrote in her diaries, "There is a really deep well inside me. And in it dwells God. Sometimes I am there, too. But more often stones and grit block the well, and God is buried beneath. Then he must be dug out again."[5] The adventure of beginning to discover this will take more than thirty-four weeks; it will take a lifetime. But it is God's work, not ours, and we must let God do what God does in God's time.

Ordinary Time Is "Holy Saturday" Time

A good description of Ordinary Time is "Holy Saturday Time." For most people most of the time, life is like Holy Saturday. The desperate sufferings and difficulties which beset people at times of serious illness, bereavement, or loss of some kind are, for many, transient. Likewise, the moments of exhilaration, joy, and rapture are few and far between. Most of our lives are lived in the in-between times, the ordinary daily routine, doing the normal things of life. Karl Rahner described Holy Saturday as the symbol of everyday life in this way:

> [Holy Saturday] is, as it were, a symbol of everyday life which is a mean between the abysmal terror of Good Friday and the exuberant joy of Easter. For ordinary life is mostly in between the two, in the centre which is also a transition and can only be this…. Ordinariness, too, is a blessing. But this ordinariness of the in-between must be understood as a transition, the transition from Good Friday to Easter….
>
> The Holy Saturday of our life must be the preparation for Easter, the persistent hope for the final glory of God. If we live the Holy Saturday of our existence properly, this will not be a merely ideological addition to this common life as the mean between its contraries. It is realized in what makes our everyday life specifically human: in the patience that can wait, in the sense of humor which does not take things too seriously, in being prepared to let others be first, in the courage which always seeks for a way out of the difficulties.[6]

This Holy Saturday time should not be lived in a fantasy world of the future but, as Rahner points out, in all the human aspects of our everyday existence. Ordinary Time is not marking time, waiting for a better world in eternal life. It is actively participating in the events of life with the human values of patience, humor, service, love, and courage. Our prayer in Ordinary Time must relate to our daily life and be grounded in reality. It should focus on the present moment yet be aware that we are preparing the way for eternal life. Our receptivity of God's presence in everything will be at the heart of our prayer at all times, but Ordinary Time allows us the space to reflect on it in a more focused way.

There could be a misunderstanding here. Holy Saturday for some people is dead time, a time of waiting, a day to linger at the tomb dreaming of what might have been. But traditionally, Holy Saturday is the time of the harrowing of hell when Christ descended to the depths of the underworld, breaking the chains that bound humanity, reaching down to grasp Adam from the clutches of Satan and set humanity free from its bondage to sin and death. Holy Saturday is a time of activity when the adventure story reaches its climax and the final battle ends in triumph for good over evil. That is why Ordinary Time as Holy Saturday time is the present reality, not a time to sit back waiting for things to happen, but a time to actively participate in the ever-new human-divine story.

THE PASTOR'S ROLE IN ORDINARY TIME

Pastors, religious sisters, pastoral assistants, and catechists have the privilege of inviting people to draw closer to God using the opportunities given by Ordinary Time. After many years of experience as a pastor and as spiritual director in seminaries, I am convinced that the creative use of Ordinary Time is essential for the development of the spiritual life. If pastors and others really desire to see people mature on their spiritual journeys, Ordinary Time cannot be ignored or treated as second best. With careful planning and structure, resources can be made available to everyone so that they can honor the mystery of Christ in all its fullness while growing and maturing at their own pace.

Before looking briefly at programs for the whole parish, it is worth mentioning the value of one-to-one spiritual accompaniment. This does not mean that the pastoral leader has to be an expert in prayer and the spiritual life, rather it is a matter of one pilgrim walking with another over a long journey. Pastors and those who can make the time for the individual accompaniment of others, will find it both personally rewarding and pastorally effective. Unencumbered by the demands of the busy seasons, Ordinary Time provides the opportunity for regular spiritual accompaniment to be offered to individuals who are seeking to grow in their relationship with God.

In terms of parish activities, pastoral leaders have the space during Ordinary Time to develop creative ways of holding people's interest and exciting them with the adventure of the spiritual journey. At certain stages in the spiritual life, activities of prayer and spirituality are important for some, and they may benefit from a menu of prayers, devotions, and practices to keep them stimulated. These people will want to learn about different schools of prayer and to be allowed to experiment with devotions and pious practices. In time, each person will find what suits them best and will have picked up many useful techniques and expertise on the way. Suggestions from the pulpit about books, devotions, and prayers will always be welcome, as will recommendations about internet resources for improving prayer, although guidance will need to be given in how to discern the online nuggets from the dross. The "Directory of Popular Piety" from the Congregation for Divine Worship, as already mentioned, is a rich source of ideas for devotions and prayer.

Ordinary Time is also an opportunity to broaden people's prayer experience by encouraging them to pray with the Church in Morning and Evening Prayer from the Divine Office. This can be done in groups in the parish or in families or by individuals.

Pastoral leaders can promote this and teach people the practical skills and knowledge for making it successful. In addition, those who are keen to grow in the spiritual life may want spiritual reading to be made available perhaps through a spiritual book club, discussion group, or parish library.

An area that needs particular attention in our Catholic tradition is encouraging the use of Scripture for prayer. Ordinary Time gives the space to unfold the Word of God in the Scriptures, for example, in a short homily at every daily Mass. When a particular book is being read for several days at daily Mass, it is helpful to give people some background. Who wrote it and who was it written for? Why was it written? How do the circumstances relate to us today? A few words of background can help people understand the passages they are hearing and use them for prayer. The weeks of Ordinary Time can also be valuable for teaching about and encouraging people to pray using *lectio divina* and imaginative contemplation.

Advice and activity about prayer is necessary for those who are at the point on their spiritual journey where these things are important, but for those who have come to a time where prayer has become much quieter and who have realized that prayer is God's work, not theirs, more activity will simply be confusing. Their instinct is telling them they should be quieter, doing less in prayer themselves, and letting God do more.

In preaching to these people, encouragement and affirmation must be the guiding principles. Times of quiet prayer can be filled with darkness or dryness, and it is often in the darkness that the real adventure of prayer takes place. In preaching about prayer in Ordinary Time, pastoral leaders should not be afraid to talk of facing the darkness and telling people that it is a sign of God's presence. It is consoling for many people to hear the well-known story of Mother Teresa, who spent many years in darkness with regard to her prayer. The depth of desire for God will sustain people through the dryness that may be encountered in prayer during the long months of Ordinary Time.

To help people whose prayer is quieter, pastoral leaders need to find ways for them to be quiet with the Lord and to encourage them to be comfortable with silence and nonverbal communication. Ordinary Time gives the space to take part in courses, days of prayer, quiet days, and residential or nonresidential retreats. It may be possible to develop a habit of quiet days or quiet times in a parish to help people move away from customary busyness into a more contemplative space. In these quiet times, *lectio divina* with Scripture can be expanded to include prayerful reflection on creation, simply spending time looking at the beauty we find there, or with a work of art or a piece of music.

Encouragement to come to know God better is the key for everyone, and the preacher or teacher should aim to inspire this. Good preaching and teaching leads to enthusiasm for the great adventure of being loved by God and responding to God, of "thirsting" for God just as God "thirsts" for us.[7] Good preaching and teaching impassion people to seek opportunities for greater intimacy with God. If this desire fades, prayer in Ordinary Time will, at best, be a job to be done, and at worst, nonexistent.

When they preach, pastors can follow the example of Jesus by using parables from everyday life to teach people about the kingdom of God. Stories and parables from today's world will enhance our preaching and help people to pray in Ordinary Time. As Pope Francis wrote, "An attractive image makes the message seem familiar, close to home, practical and related to everyday life. A successful image can make people savor the message, awaken a desire and move the will towards the Gospel."[8] In talking to people, Jesus used ordinary language which was simple, clear and direct and we must do the same. Listen again to Pope Francis: "If we wish to adapt to people's language and to reach them with God's word, we need to share in their lives and pay loving attention to them."[9]

The role of the pastor in Ordinary Time will encompass all this: preaching, teaching, initiating pastoral activities, and making accessible the riches of resources available for people's spiritual development. Above all, he or she needs to be alert to the opportunities afforded by this space and time and then to have the enthusiasm and desire to use the time well.

CONCLUSION

Prayer in Ordinary Time is bedrock prayer, not second-class. Both through the liturgy and in personal prayer, these weeks are a gift of time to let God work in us and for us to respond generously to God. Ordinary Time is the season of prayer for everyone, and it takes place principally in the midst of daily life. It is a space of weeks and months each year for prayer to mature at a steady pace. Ordinary Time can transform our ordinary lives into an adventure of discovery, never-ending because it is the discovery of the infinite and eternal God and his wonderful love affair with each and every human being, as well as with family, church, and other communities. Ordinary time is a period when average people like you and me strive to become the extraordinary messengers of the Gospel that we have been commissioned to be through our baptism.

Let St. John Paul II have the last word:

We need heralds of the Gospel who are experts in humanity, who know the depth of the human heart, who can share the joys and hopes, the agonies and distress of people today, but who are at the same time contemplatives who have fallen in love with God. For this we need the saints of today.[10]

That is exactly what the space of Ordinary Time enables us to do.

1. Paul VI, Motu Proprio, *Mysterii Paschalis*, February 1969.

2. Quotations from the Bible throughout this article are taken from *The Jerusalem Bible* (London: Darton, Longman & Todd, 1966).

3. A two-year cycle of readings is used in some monasteries and in some parts of the world. For more information about this and for a free download of the second year of readings for the Office of Readings, the Catholic Study Centre at Durham University has details. Stephen Mark Holmes, "A Two Year Patristic Lectionary for the Divine Office," 2010, https://www.dur. ac.uk/theology.religion/ccs/patristiclectionary/history/.

4. *The Directory on Popular Piety and the Liturgy* (Vatican City: Congregation for Divine Worship, 2001), sections 157, 159, http://www.vatican.va/roman_curia/congregations/ccdds/documents/ rc_con_ccdds_doc_20020513_vers-direttorio_en.html.

5. *Etty: The Letters and Diaries of Etty Hillesum 1941–1942, Complete and Unabridged*, ed. Klaas A. D. Smelik, trans. Arnold J. Pomerans (Grand Rapids: Eerdmans, 2002) 91.

6. Karl Rahner, "Holy Saturday," *The Great Church Year: The Best of Karl Rahner's Homilies, Sermons and Meditation*, ed. Albert Raffelt, trans. Harvey Egan (New York: Crossroads, 1994), 168.

7. *CCC* 2560.

8. Pope Francis, *Evangelii Gaudium*, 157.

9. Pope Francis, *Evangelii Gaudium*, 158.

10. St. John Paul II, Address to the Symposium of the Council of the European Bishops' Conference, October 11, 1985.

CHAPTER 38

Prayer during the Advent, Christmas, Lenten, and Easter Seasons

~ Donal Neary, SJ ~

Praying the seasons of the Church's year is like a pilgrimage. We head off on a path that will bring us into varied terrain: waiting for a while, birth and new life, darkness and light, suffering and death on the way, and lightness and joy. A pilgrimage is a journey always of trust. When in a holy place, a pilgrim allows the place to pass through them, whereas a tourist simply passes through. These ways of entering into seasonal prayer introduce us to the big moments of the life of Jesus, which link into the big and ordinary moments of human life. Personal prayer brings the self to God, with all we are, how "we live and move and have our being" (Acts 17:28).[1]

As on a pilgrimage, so in prayer, nothing is unimportant. We may set off for a place, like Croagh Patrick in Ireland, to climb the mountain, to pray on the top, and to find that if we fall on the journey, we can find help, friendship, and support. And we thank God not for the success of reaching the top but for the compassion and active help we found. On a pilgrimage we give thanks for everything: for rain and sun, for tiredness and energy—all are part of the journey, as Paul says, always be grateful (1 Thessalonians 5:18).

Prayer is not just about seasons and about the self. It may be just silent presence in love to the one who loves totally. Content and ideas, as offered in these pages, can enhance a time of prayer and focus the mind and heart on our journeys. With a desire for a trusting Advent, a happy Christmas, a compassionate Lent, and a joyful Easter the following is offered.

JOURNEY

Our journey is our security.
Strange way of looking on life,
Normally we want our security to be where we are,
Our house, our family, our job, our love.
Our journey roots them, rather than the destination
As we are people who come from God and go to God,
And what could be more certain, mysterious or even frightening than that!
Our faith journey is somewhere to go,
Somewhere to move,

A space where time never stands still;
Our journey is God's pilgrim promise:
That God, the pilgrim from heaven
Walks always with his pilgrim people on earth.

Praying at Advent

From the view of spirituality, each season can link into different aspects of our life's journey. Advent takes us into the mystery of the unknown and the incomplete; Christmas opens to us new birth and childhood; Lent is the journey from darkness to light, death towards resurrection; and during Easter, we are on a journey of joy in our lives, from the resurrection into mission, into eternity.

A good icon for the Advent journey is the pilgrimage. Anything can happen on a pilgrimage; everything on a pilgrim journey leads to the goal. Hardships and joys are the context of every day; wrong turnings and mistakes are part of it also. Sharing the pilgrimage with others, accepting help and knowing that I am not in control, being able to say thanks for everything that happens, and connecting with others are essential. People who have done the Camino, the Lough Derg pilgrimage or Croagh Patrick in Ireland, the Catholic mission shrines in California, as well as journeys to many shrines in other parts of the world may identify with the first pilgrimage of Mary and Joseph for the birth of their child in Bethlehem.

The spirituality of Advent focuses us on the mystery of the unknown and the incomplete, connecting with the journey of Mary and Joseph. Our Christian life is the journey toward a destination but anything can happen on the way. Our Christian faith is contained in one big certainty that God is always with us. As we make the journey with God, nothing that happens can separate us. We discover ways of living with questions rather than finding answers, and the questions of the journey in prayer give foundations to the meaning of life.

"Always remember this: life is a journey. It is a path, a journey to meet Jesus," Pope Francis recently said.[2]

Some spiritualties present the journey as already over in the sense that we are expected to be perfect. But all of us have steps on our life's journey that have taken us off the right path, or experiences that tested our human growth and faith. We have struggled with faith doubts, sexual conflicts and orientation, and addiction; there have been marriage breakdowns and painful family contacts. People say, "I didn't marry to get divorced," or, "I didn't get ordained priest to leave," or, "I didn't plan that my daughter wouldn't talk to me anymore." All of this, too, is part of the journey, and the gaze of the journey is from God and Jesus, like an embryo inviting us to be loved and to grow. Even before birth, people such as John the Baptist in the womb, and Elizabeth the expectant mother, got the strength of his saving love. Pope Francis says,

> A journey in which we do not encounter Jesus is not a Christian journey.… To encounter Jesus also means allowing oneself to be gazed upon by him. "But, Father, you know," one of you might say to me, "you know that this journey is horrible for me, I am such a sinner, I have committed many sins… how can I encounter Jesus. And along the way Jesus comes and forgives us—all of us sinners, we are all sinners—even when we make a mistake, when we commit a sin, when we sin. We always encounter Jesus.[3]

A prayerful way of making the journey is presented in the *Spiritual Exercises* of St. Ignatius Loyola. In the meditation on the birth of the Lord, he invites us to take part personally in the journey. As always, he suggests the prayer of the imagination:

> It will be here (to imagine) how Our Lady went forth from Nazareth, about nine months with child, seated on an ass, and accompanied by Joseph and a maid taking an ox, to go to Bethlehem.
>
> See the place. It will be here to see with the sight of the imagination the road from Nazareth to Bethlehem; considering the length and the breadth, and whether such road is level or through valleys or over hills; likewise looking at the place or cave of the Nativity, how large, how small, how low, how high, and how it was prepared. (SE 112–3)[4]

Maybe you can enter into that journey with memories of your own life's journeys. What would this journey recall to you at this time of the year, this year at this time? What has happened to you on your journey of life as you notice Mary and Joseph making this most important journey of their lives? Would you have helped them or run away? You might think of them beginning the journey and what they might have feared. They would surely have made this journey in a group: Our life and faith journey is part of a community of family and others. You could play around with these questions prayerfully for Advent!

The Advent People in Luke 1

Elizabeth: We see the prayer of welcome to the Lord in a very human situation, in the pregnancies of Elizabeth and Mary. We see the prayer of amazement that the mother of the Lord would come, and the prayer of praise as they composed and prayed the Magnificat together.

Zechariah: We see the payer of doubt and pride. God will work my way! There is the good man whose religious practice and views were being challenged—the one who kept his faith even in doubt. The silent, confused believer.

The infant John: He was graced in the womb and born before Jesus. There is some indication that the meaning of his life was to be the announcer always that Jesus is near. Graced when he didn't know it, and announcing the one he was never sure of, maybe John is a saint for today.

Everything in the weeks up to Christmas can be reminders of the feast to come. The Christmas parties, the cards sent and received, the gifts we buy and the phone calls made—all are made because Jesus is near. As he is near now, he is near always. It can be a crowded time, so a five- or ten-minute time of prayer, an extra Mass, or a bit of sitting in silence can ensure we don't get lost in the preparations. Let everything in these weeks recall us to what is really happening in our waiting for the Lord.

A REFLECTION FOR ADVENT

Advent is waiting for the birth of Jesus,
but it's a strange waiting:
we are waiting each year for someone we know is here!
We recall in Advent
that the Lord Jesus has come among us,
is present all the time
and will come again in glory.
He is the child who is born each year,
for the world always needs its God and Savior
He is the child awaited each year,
for our lives are new each year,
and we need him in different ways at different stages of life,
and the world has different needs of God at different times.
We need the child of peace to be born
in our wars and violence,
the child of wisdom in our search for truth and meaning,
the child of gentleness in a world which can be harsh and greedy.
We need to know in Jesus
that birth and life
are among the most precious gifts of God,
and that in the birth of Jesus each year,
is the everlasting promise of God
to be with us.
And Advent looks ahead,
letting us see that the life of Jesus is never over,

that the truth of Jesus is always spoken,

that the love of Jesus is always real,

and that he will one day be seen in glory.

For we are people of Advent and Easter,

of waiting and of resurrection; we are people of earth

and heaven, as he is the Son of God and

Son of Mary,

and leads us through our life on earth

to the eternal glory of heaven.

PRAYING AT CHRISTMAS

At Christmas we remember human mysteries and realities such as birth, and trust in the future of the child and trust in marriage. We recall from the human birth of Jesus, the Incarnation, that God is in everything. It is a time of simple yet deep faith, and of memories. It is a deeply human mystery and touches many of our most relevant memories and longings. In prayer, we can identify with many of the people and situations in the infancy Gospels (Luke 1—2). This was very much the method popularized by St. Ignatius Loyola in his *Spiritual Exercises.*

St. Ignatius imagines the scene of the birth of Jesus. His immediate guidance on prayer is to put yourself in the crib. This is not exegesis or theology but sound practical spirituality. A well-known image of Ignatius is the one at Manresa, Spain. In it, Ignatius is at the crib, kneeling down, with the copy of the Jesuit constitutions beside him, offering this in some way to the Lord. Like the shepherds and the Magi, we go to the crib scene just as we are, each with our own gifts for God. Christmas invites us to become like a child, the child within you meeting the child Jesus. Bringing with us everything that is dear and everything that needs embracing. The embrace of birth is God's embrace of the whole person.

The spirituality of Christmas is strange in that we know how this child will be. We know his life story and we know the ending. We know that he has been part of our lives since our own early childhood, the one who helped and protected us many times. So we bring a full heart to the mysteries of Christmas.

PRAYING WITH THE CHRISTMAS PEOPLE IN THE GOSPELS

The people of these Christmas gospels touch into many experiences of the human heart. As you read the Gospel over this time, and as you often hear them in the liturgy, we can have some aspects of their lives in the background.

Mary: Let Mary remind you of your joy—memories of joy and joy now. She was as happy as any mother on the birth of her child. Prayer at Christmas includes many memories, as it is a time of remembering. There are two types of memory—recalling and reliving. The memory that relives remembers facts and feelings, while the memory of facts is about what happened and when. Reliving in memory can remember tones of voice, the smile with which something was said, the grief of someone's passing. All this is the memory for prayer. Reliving joy is like reliving moments of love. We can allow the feelings of love to renew this love. This is what Mary meant in her prayer: "The almighty has done great things for me" (Luke 1:49). We remember love in the past and it enlivens love in the here and now.

Joseph: Joseph reminds us of the prayer of trust. He took Mary on trust from God and knows that he will often be called on to trust again. When this trust was challenged in the future—like in the danger of going into Egypt with the child Jesus and Mary—he could allow the trust he knew from before the birth to remind him that God is with him now and always. Where is your trust when you are helped or challenged now? The prayer of knowing that with God all is well, and all will be well. "Joseph, do not be afraid to take Mary home as your wife" (Matthew 1:20).

The shepherds: They reveal to us the prayer of openness to God, however God might reveal himself. The prayer of knowing we don't have it all together but need to go to others to find greater faith. The prayer of being willing to be silent before the mystery and go home without too many answers but with a full heart.

The Magi: They show us the prayer of searching, of being willing to follow a dream to find meaning and God in life, and the prayer of discernment—of recognizing the star and knowing when we follow false stars. Theirs is the prayer of being open to change, to "going back by another way" (Matthew 2:12).

Simeon: He demonstrates the prayer of patience, knowing that the promises of God are not lightly made. And he is always new even in old age. His is the statement we often hear, "Now I can die happy." There are times when we just wait in prayer and in life. We recall times of waiting in the past and know that as God came near us then, he is with us now. (Luke 1:29–32)

Anna: Show us the prayer of silence: just waiting in prayer for what you want, and then being ready to welcome in the infant the God of all the world. (Luke 2:38)

The shepherds: At a crib in the church at the Shepherds' Fields in Bethlehem we see the wise men at the crib, and looking towards the door outside, which has in it a cross. Christmas can be a painful time for many people, and they find courage in the simple love of the Christ child who will know all the hardships of life.

Prayer always looks ahead. Even Christmas hints at the future of the child. The prayer of Christmas gives strength and renewal to the total Christian life. If we can keep Christmas for a day, why not keep it always?

St. Ignatius, in his *Spiritual Exercises* comments,

> The first Point is to see the persons; that is, to see Our Lady and Joseph and the maid, and, after His Birth, the Child Jesus, I making myself a poor creature and an unworthy slave, looking at them and serving them in their needs, with all possible respect and reverence, as if I found myself present; and then to reflect on myself in order to draw some profit. (*SE*, 114)

In prayer, we can picture the nativity scene: a poor room, Mary and Joseph, two young people, the child in the stone manger. The child warmed by straw. Some animals are near. You are watching. You know this scene well. You sense you have been here before. Where are you in it? Looking at the child? With Mary and Joseph? Mary is whispering that you go close to the child and give him affection. Stand, sit, or kneel there. Everyone is looking peaceful. What might this bring to mind for you? What do you remember of birth, Christmas? What is in your heart just now? Tell that to the infant Christ and end when you wish with a prayer in your own words, or end with a Hail Mary.

In the middle of the Christmas memories and celebrations, let everything remind you of what the season really means. Nothing is not sacred at Christmas: every mistletoe is the burning bush, every song is a shout of joy, and every child a new Incarnation. The reminders of Christmas may also be sad as we pray for loved ones gone before us, family and friends away from home, and sometimes we feel the general nostalgia of growing old. The child reminds us of youth, and the aged ones in the temple may remind us of old age. At every time of life, Christ is being born in us: this is the big truth of Christmas spirituality.

A CHRISTMAS REFLECTION

A manger in Palestine was a stone structure like a trough, storing food for the animals. They could come to eat straw from it, like cows drinking from a trough. Jesus's first bed was a food store! The manger was an appropriate resting place for him—a place of food, because he is food for the world. The baby needing food becomes the bread of life, the energy of the divine, the sustenance for the soul on the journey of life. He did that in his life, a man like us and God. He still does the same: feeding the soul with the words of the Gospel.

With the bread of the Eucharist, and with love each time, we look towards him and pray. At the back of our crib is a lighted cross. Greater love than this nobody has than to lay down life for others. The baby of Bethlehem is the man of the cross and the Christ of Easter.

Praying in Lent

The Lenten season focuses on the death and resurrection of the Lord, linking it with suffering and healing, death and new life, and a spirituality of the cross. The journey continues; the image of the pilgrimage may now focus more on the difficulties of the pilgrimage, especially the unexpected. Each of our journeys brings pain and suffering, but the Lenten spirituality is always in the light of what we know will later come: the resurrection and the mystery of Easter in our lives. It is the mystery of God being with us in the darkness of life. Pope Francis said: "God walks with all of humanity, the good people and the evil people because in this list there are saints and there are criminal sinners as well. There's so much sin here. But God is not frightened by this: He accompanies us. He walks with his people."[5] The major Lenten spirituality can be found in the classic Gospel readings of the liturgy: temptation, transfiguration, the well of living water, the care of the one born blind, and the raising to new life. This leads into the immense suffering of the passion and death of Jesus, to the quiet and momentous joy of the resurrection, our fourth week.

Themes for the Five Sundays of Lent

1. We make this desert journey to find ourselves again, and know we can be rolled off course. Like Jesus, we have a big goal in life, and we can be tempted away. Wealth, honor, and pride tempt us always. We might find ourselves living always in comfort, doing things to be thought well of, and thinking we are in charge of our lives. This can happen every day, but Jesus gives directions from the Scriptures to counteract this. (See Matthew 4:1–11.)

2. In this Lenten journey we are invited to move out of the comfort zone—to climb a mountain. To get away from the ordinary. To be open then to seeing things new, just like the apostles on Tabor saw the Lord in dazzling glory. Or, did they miss it? They were asleep some of the time. They draw us into what gives light to us in times of darkness and a foundation to life. Having known Jesus, what can go wrong? (See Matthew 17:9–12.)

3. Consider this searcher—this woman who came to the well. It was deep and she had to take time to draw meaning from the life (the living water). Lenten spirituality is to deepen our meaning in life, which is the big spiritual or religious quest today. She is us and she is everyone. She meets the kindly, human and suffering Lord. She knows she will find this meaning with him. (See John 4:5.)

4. Consider the man born blind who now can see. Maybe Lenten spirituality is to move us on annually to more of the real light in life. Can we find this in true love

and faithfulness, true prayer and true service of our neighbor? These are ways our blindness or deafness is lightened. Jesus is always the nonjudging one—there is no judgment on the woman nor on the blind man. We are all to be people through whom the glory of God can be seen. (See John 9.)

5. Lazarus is the man brought back to life. What this means can be confusing: was it to show the glory of God, a flashback to week two? Then, we saw Jesus as he really is. Now, we see ourselves as we really are, always people of life. Maybe Lazarus's being brought back to life is for the purposes of saying that death is never the end, although note that Lazarus is not raised from the dead, but restored to this life. It is a sort of great hope as we face into the horrors and the final freedoms of the next week, as we face into horrors, and darkness and messiness of life. (See John 11.)

Holy Week
We can highlight three main events for a prayerful approach to Holy Week.

Holy Thursday
In the washing of the feet, we come face to face with totally loving service, love unto death. A way of praying this mystery can be to recall ways in which you try to give this loving service to others: family, friends, community, neighborhood, and a concern for the suffering world, and the suffering of creation. We thank God for being able to do this, and know that in trying to serve others, we are joining in the washing of the feet. We might watch this scene in three gospels—entering into it, allowing Jesus to wash your feet, as he offers this love to us, and with him we wash the feet of others.

He washed the disciples' feet, even those of Judas, commencing from St. Peter, who, considering the majesty of the Lord and his own baseness, not wanting to consent, said, "Lord, you will never wash my feet." But St. Peter did not know that he was giving an example of humility, and for this he said, "I have given you an example that you may do as I did" (John 13:1–20).

Good Friday
In the background to prayer on the passion and death of Christ in the Ignatian tradition, we look at the suffering and death of Jesus and allow ourselves to really think, feel, and believe that this is God. God has become so much a part of us that he dies—not a death alone, but a cruel death. We respond in thanks, amazement, and in just wanting to be with him we are with him in any way we try—to accompany with compassion people suffering in our immediate and wider circles. We try to sympathize with him in his suffering.

We consider how the divinity hides itself, that is, how it could destroy its enemies and does not do it, and how it leaves the most sacred humanity to suffer so very cruelly. (SE 196) Another classic Ignatian picture imagines it this way:

Imagining Christ our Lord present and placed on the Cross, let me reflect with feeling, how from Creator He is come to making Himself man, and from life eternal is come to temporal death, and so to die for my sins. Likewise, looking at myself, what I have done for Christ, what I am doing for Christ, what I ought to do for Christ. And so, seeing Him such, and so nailed on the Cross, to go over that which will present itself. (SE 53)

HOLY SATURDAY

Praying Holy Saturday involves watching the taking down from the Cross, the anointing of Jesus's body, the laying in the tomb, and then the quiet and grief that must have come over the family, disciples, and friends of the Lord. This may be a day to think of those who have entered this other, new life before us. Another tradition is the visit of Jesus to the underworld, where he completed the work of the Old Testament, visiting the ones we had heard of so often: Adam and Eve, through Noah, and the prophets. It is hard to pray this except to see him from the time of his death being raised from death, and all the time offering to everyone the joy and consolation of his new life.

We often pray around the cross; this is a day to pray around the tomb, with the knowledge we have now that this tomb is empty, that nothing now can contain the love of Jesus. We will watch this in our prayer of the resurrection.

This is a quiet day. Prayer needs silence. What Mother Teresa says is true: "The fruit of Silence is prayer. The fruit of Prayer is faith. The fruit of Faith is love. The fruit of Love is service. The fruit of Service is peace." Little is said. Maybe today is watching Jesus beginning his walks of consolation, the risen pilgrim Lord. Say little, feel much. Carry the fruit of your prayer into Easter.

A REFLECTION: THE TWO PARADES OF HOLY WEEK INTO JERUSALEM FROM BETHANY ON THE SUNDAY

Jesus being acclaimed as a political savior.

People hoped he would triumph,

that his followers would put him into power

and all hoped he would get rid of the Romans.

The second, from Jerusalem outside the walls of the city on the following Friday

Like disgrace.

A man carrying his cross, crowned with thorns, mocked and bullied, tortured.

And about to be killed. Like the parade to a dishonored graveside.

He had all sorts of followers—like the camp followers, some terrorists,

the people on the make for themselves, or the ones who lasted till the end, like his mother, an aunt and a few of the followers.

The others were at a distance, they would come back,

and would follow later to the end.

Our hope is to be in that second parade.

Palms are for waving in triumph; they wither. The cross is forever, for all time.

The cross is his love, and as we follow in this parade, we show our willingness to console him in love to the end.

This is a holy week because a man like us, and one of the Trinity, gave his life in love for people as yet unborn.

Praying at Easter: Ignatius in the *Spiritual Exercises* says little in the Easter time except to quote the Scriptures and have us walk with Jesus who is sharing with his people his joy and peace. The classic gospels of the first four Sundays summarize Easter for us:

Mary Magdalene: Mary is the one weeping, the bereaved loving friend and disciple. Jesus just comes to her and by calling her by name, consoles her. Let the Risen Lord do the same for you. (See John 20:1–9).

Thomas: The one of doubts. An honest man who found it hard to believe. Somehow meeting Jesus just brought light to the doubts. Within this experience, he found faith and simply said the best creed of all times, "My Lord and my God." (See John 20:19–31).

Emmaus disciples: Sad and depressed, let down by everyone, they were walking home. They supported each other's sadness. The darkness took a long journey to let in the light. In the simple friendly sharing of bread, they knew that God was alive. The consolation of the presence in word and Eucharist. (See Luke 24:13–35).

The Good Shepherd: All the disciples were sent—Mary to those in Galilee, Thomas and company sent for forgiveness, the Emmaus pair back to the others who were hiding in Jerusalem, and now for all—the shepherd who finds us and asks us to shepherd others. (See John 10:1–10). As Fr. Kevin O'Brien explains,

> We marvel at how Jesus in the resurrected life—where his divinity is no longer hidden—does very human things: eating, talking, consoling, teaching, and enjoying the company of others. As with the mystery of the Incarnation, we see in the Resurrection how our divinity and humanity are not opposed but are an integral part of each other.[6]

The ministry of Easter time is consolation and mission. In all the Gospel scenes, watch Jesus consoling people. In John 21—he is waiting for them on the beach; he prepares food (a real human and ordinary service of consolation); he listens and empowers them with the catch of fish; and he sends them from their promise of love.

During these days, we might watch for moments when we feel the peace of the Lord and when we can spread this peace. We can feel the call like the apostles, the disciples, both men and women, felt from him, and to say "Yes, Lord; you know I love you" (John 21:15).

This leads into a life of finding God in all things, and of God finding us in all things. This, like the post-Easter Gospel readings will normally be gentle, peaceful, and inviting to us in our own personal gifts, talents, and faults, in the following of the Risen Lord. In finding the Lord, we find his creative love working in us all the time, calling us through the Advent journey of trust, the Christmas receiving of life, the Lenten path of compassion, the Easter movement toward joy and mission. We find in all of this the goodness inside ourselves, and if we find that in ourselves, we can trust that it is in everyone else.

CLOSING REFLECTION

God works from the goodness inside each of us—

The goodness that reaches out to others in help and to him in prayer.

He plants this goodness from the first moment,

Small beginnings from the bodies of father and mother

To grow, develop right through eternity.

Nourish that goodness—by working for good,

And in mindfulness, mediation, prayer, and community

And your goodness will bring good to the world and to others.

But first and even more so

Believe in the eternal goodness inside yourself!

---

1. All Scripture quotations are from *New Jerusalem Bible.*

2. Pope Francis, "Pastoral Visit to the Roman Parish of Saint Cyril of Alexandria," December 1, 2013, https://w2.vatican.va/content/francesco/en/homilies/2013/documents/papa-francesco_20131201_parrocchia-san-cirillo-alessandrino.html.

3. Pope Francis, "Pastoral Visit."

4. All quotations from the *Spiritual Exercises* are taken from Father Elder Mullan, SJ, *The Autograph* (New York: P. J. Kenedy & Sons, 1914), and are henceforward abbreviated SE, followed by the section number, in the text.

5. Susy Hodges, "Pope Francis: God Walks with All of Us, Saints and Sinners," Vatican Radio, September 8, 2015, http://en.radiovaticana.va/news/2015/09/08/pope_francis_god_walks_with_all_of_us,_saints_and_sinners/1170348.

6. Kevin O'Brien, SJ, *The Ignatian Adventure: Experiencing the Spiritual Exercises of Saint Ignatius in Daily Life* (Chicago: Loyola, 2011), 241.

PART NINE

Going Forward:
Creative and Brief Reflections on Prayer

In this final section, the creative and brief reflections offered are designed to remind us that prayer is simple, is an act of receiving love, is essential in the darkness, has a place in the active life, involves a spirit of gratitude, is a sacramental way of seeing the world, and yes, can be messy!

The opening chapter, The Easiest Prayer Ever, by James Martin, attests to prayer's simplicity. He calls us all to follow "five simple steps," and his goal is to help us see more clearly where God has been in our lives. By taking, in his words, "a backward look," we can discover patterns that we might have missed. He also points out that one of the most important goals of doing this is to become more open to recognizing —possibly for the first time—"responses" to our prayers that we previously felt went unanswered.

Following this brief chapter is one by Richard Rohr entitled, How Can Anyone Pray "Always"? He calls us to look again at how we view prayer. One of the ways he does this is to pose the following statement and question: "We have sought so many other ways to justify ourselves rather than owning our honest inability to be just, loving, and truly good. Is that perhaps what happens in real prayer?" The material in this brief but intense chapter is certainly meant to be prayed with, not simply read.

In Therese Borchard's Praying in the Darkness, she reflects on both spiritual darkness and clinical depression from a personal point of view and is sure to precipitate further discussion as to where and how prayer might play a role in both situations. In this regard, it is ideal material to discuss in a group or with one's spiritual director.

In Consideration: The Everyday Prayer of the Contemplative in Action, Joseph Tetlow has us reflect in a unique way on prayer in the Ignatian manner. Using consideration as a lens, he helps us walk through the *Spiritual Exercises* in a fresh manner. To accomplish this, he thematically looks at "what makes contemplatives in action," a recognition that the world is often "bleached by secularism," the intimate task of uncovering "the signs and times for each of us," and the importance of renewed emphasis on *lectio divina*. Tetlow's deep appreciation of the Ignatian approach and his creative way of reflecting on its use in our daily prayer life shines through.

Geraldine Fialkowski's Giving Voice to My Thanks: Praying with the Spirit of Gratitude, puts in front of us an essential element of the spiritual life. In her words, "If our spiritual journey consists in taking time on a daily basis to recognize and acknowledge the gifts of that day, we become more open to the many ways in which God is up front, personal, and central in our lives." Given this, Fialkowski speaks about the theme with such topics as "intentional gratitude," the role of being thankful in transformation, the relationship between gratitude and such important attitudes as hope, maintaining a healthy perspective, being mindful, and what she terms creatively as "an internal navigation system." Liberally using sacred Scripture, she helps us do something none of us can do enough (especially given today's self-centered and entitled cultural influences): revisit a prayer life that is centered on gratitude.

Kieran Scott's Praying with a Sacramental World offers us a fresh look at the dispositions needed to pray in a sacramental world. In doing this, he beautifully brings into play Celtic spirituality, nature mysticism, and mysticism within the Catholic tradition. As you read this chapter, you can begin to see why the Catholic sacramental imagination is so important to bring the other half of our soul alive rather than remain steeped in a left-brained, analytic approach to God and life. Reading about the three major characteristics of Celtic spirituality, reflecting on nature mysticism from inspirational writers like William Blake and Annie Dillard, and appreciating mysticism within our own tradition through the eyes of Jesuits Karl Rahner, Teilhard de Chardin, and Gerard Manley Hopkins is a joy. The chapter then aptly and helpfully closes with a section entitled Spiritual Exercises for Praying in a Sacramental World.

Finally, this section ends with a down to earth reflection by Kathy Coffey entitled Prayer in Chaos, Commotion, and Clutter. I think most of us can identify with the stress, anxieties, and daily hassles of life Coffey presents. But, as in the case of this handbook of *Prayer in the Catholic Tradition* as a whole, she doesn't leave us there but instead calls us to prayer in such ways as being open to receiving new "annunciations" in our own heart, and seeing prayer in ever transforming ways, such as, in Coffey's closing words, "reverently paying attention to and being grateful for [Christ's] actions hidden in our ordinary, chaotic, conflicted days."

CHAPTER 39

The Easiest Prayer Ever

~ James Martin, SJ ~

Plenty of people think they don't pray well. Or that they somehow pray wrong. Or that everyone else has an easier time praying.

With this in mind, let me introduce you to a kind of prayer that anyone can do. Whether you've been on dozens of retreats or are just beginning to incorporate prayer into your day, the examination of conscience can be a wonderful—and easy—support for your spiritual life.

Although many people had been using this prayer for centuries, it eventually came to be associated with St. Ignatius of Loyola, the sixteenth-century founder of the Jesuit Order, who popularized it. In addition to the Mass, St. Ignatius used to say, the examination of conscience is the one prayer that a Jesuit should never omit from his day. Many other Christians also find it invaluable for their own life with the Lord.

FIVE SIMPLE STEPS

In essence, the prayer is a review of the day. It can be done either once a day (usually before going to bed) or twice (usually at midday and evening). Traditionally, this prayer is broken up into five simple steps:

First, as with any prayer, you ask for God's grace in helping you to pray.

Second, you recall the things for which you are grateful from the past day. These can be big things—a healing conversation with a friend, an intimate moment with a spouse, an exciting new project at work. Or they might be as small as the feel of the sun on your face, a refreshing breeze, a funny moment in the office. You recall them and, as St. Ignatius said, savor them. Then you express your gratitude to God.

Third, you recall the events of the day, almost as if your day were a movie playing out in your head. You ask yourself: Where did I experience God's presence and accept God's invitation? And where did I turn away from God?

Fourth, you ask for forgiveness. Step three will probably reveal some sins that you committed (unless you're perfect!), so you ask the Lord to forgive you for them. You may also decide that you need to ask for forgiveness from someone or commit to seek out the sacrament of reconciliation.

Fifth, you ask for the grace to live the next day in God's love. And, says St. Ignatius, it is good to close the examination with an Our Father.

That's it: five simple steps. Normally, the examination takes only fifteen to twenty minutes, which makes it a prayer that is accessible to everyone.

BENEFITS OF THE BACKWARD LOOK

Essentially, this is a prayer that enables us to see where God has been. This is usually far easier than recognizing God in the present, since we're typically so distracted and preoccupied by our daily tasks.

In the Old Testament, God says to Moses, "You cannot see my face." How often that is the case with us! We, too, may feel unable to see God as the day's events are unfolding. But that same God then allows Moses to see him pass (see Exodus 33:20—34:7).

One way of thinking about this Bible passage is as a reminder that it is sometimes easier to see God in retrospect than in the moment. The examination allows us to do this at the close of every day; it encourages us to prayerfully reflect on the ways by which God communicates his presence in our daily lives. Jesuit theologian Walter Burghardt once wrote that prayer is a "long, loving look at the real." You might say that the examination of conscience provides this look as from a rearview mirror.

In time this backward look may reveal patterns. You may notice, for example, that you are constantly thanking God for a particular person. And over the days and weeks, you may begin to realize what a blessing that person has been. You may say to yourself, "I never fully recognized this before!" Eventually, your examination may make you so aware that you begin to appreciate your friend more in the present.

You may also find answers to prayers that you thought were going unanswered. Often we pray for something and, failing to receive it immediately, become disheartened. But the examination enables us to see more easily the gifts that God gives us, but which unfold over days, weeks, months, and even years. A friend likes to say that God is like a master carpenter in a very small town. When you need some carpentry work done, everyone will tell you, "There's only one man to see. He does the best work in town, but he takes a very long time!"

As you see more clearly, you may be carried away by gratitude for what is in your life. At the end of a tiring or frustrating day, I sometimes sit down to do my examination and suddenly remember a consoling moment—a kind comment or a bit of good news—and give myself the time to savor the moment and be grateful. The examination itself becomes a gift from God.

So, having a hard time finding God? Try the examination of conscience. You may not be able to see where God is. But you'll certainly be able to see where God was.

CHAPTER 40

How Can Anyone Pray "Always"?

~ *Richard Rohr, OFM* ~

"We cannot choose words to pray properly, so the Spirit expresses our pleas in a way beyond words—and God knows." Romans 8:26–27[1]

Over the centuries, the word *prayer* has been distorted and trivialized. As I read Jesus's attitude toward prayer in the Gospels, the use of the word in Paul's letters, the teachings of the desert fathers and mothers, and the Philokalia of Eastern Christianity, I am convinced that prayer is first of all referring to an inner state, a state of conscious, choice-filled, loving union with what is in front of us—which is to be in union with God! That is what makes something—anything—a prayer.

But most of us have absorbed the idea of prayer as an action, a behavior, a recitation, a time period, an attendance at, a social gathering in which the divine is mentioned, a private time in which we think devout thoughts—and almost always with the assumption that this somehow pleases God. I am sure it does, since God seems to be easily pleased—all opinion to the contrary. The biblical God is seeking and wanting union with us much more than we are seeking union with him or her. In fact, I think this is the theme of themes of the whole biblical text, or as Rabbi Abraham Joshua Heschel says, "God is seeking man."

Lest I fall into the dualistic thinking that I so often bemoan, I want to say that there can be true prayer in all of these actions or behaviors—whenever they proceed from—or lead to a state of conscious, loving union with what is. Then, and then alone, have we achieved the primary goal and the delicious fruit of prayer. As always, the pattern is both/and.

It is very important that this point is made at this time in history, because there are people of all religious denominations—including clergy—who appear to say prayers often and yet live very self-contained and self-satisfied lives of de facto hatred, racism, greed, classism, narcissism, and even terrorism. The very notion of prayer, I am afraid, can be easily used for egoic purposes and for the inflation of a superior self-image, as Jesus shows us in the Gospel Parable of the Pharisee and the Publican (Luke 18:9–14). The text tellingly states that the Pharisee prays "to himself," and "thanks God that he is not like" other people, who are supposedly inferior to him.

Prayer can be used to differentiate from and not be united with. The Pharisee is presented in complete counterpoint to the tax collector, who can only declare his foundational solidarity with all sinners and the universal need for divine mercy. This fully justifies him according to Jesus. It is quite obvious and yet still shocking when we realize that Jesus is not upset at sinners, but almost entirely at those who do not think they are sinners. The point cannot be made any clearer than here. Yet, one wonders how much Jesus's brilliant parable has really guided organized Christianity—in any of its denominational forms. We have sought so many other ways to justify ourselves rather than owning our honest inability to be just, loving, and truly good. Is that perhaps what happens in real prayer?

When Jesus goes into the desert for forty days (Matthew 4:1–11), he does not recite prayers or read the Hebrew Bible (the printing press had not been invented yet), yet it does appear from his thrice quoting of Deuteronomy that he had committed some biblical texts to memory. But here Satan knows and uses Scripture too, when he quotes Psalm 91 for his own dark purposes. Is there a message here? I surely think so (I am also aware that this is Matthew's or Luke's reading on Jesus's experience, but that is all we have to go on, and it does make a brilliant piece of theology that would seem to apply to the Jesus we know).

The Gospels speak variously of Jesus "leaving the house early" and "going apart to a lonely place to pray" (Mark 1:35, along with various formulations in Luke 4:42 and 5:16, and Matthew 14:23). Could it be that it is much easier to live in this state of conscious, loving union with God when there is nothing else competing for our attention? Nothing else demanding our emotions? I would expect that to be the case, and it is often the experience for many of us on retreat, especially extended retreats.

In both Jesus's desert initiation at the beginning of his ministry and his prayer in the garden of Gethsemane at the end, the emphasis seems to be that he goes alone and apart into nature—and not into temple or synagogue or any building humanly constructed. We are learning how important this is in the nature spirituality of people like Bill Plotkin and many other eco-theologians. Nature, the first Bible, might just be a major missing element in Christian spirituality and prayer. The Gospels make no mention of Jesus reciting any formula prayers, except at the Last Supper where he and his disciples likely sung the Hallel, or Psalms 113–118 (Matthew 26:30) at the close of the Passover meal. So neither was Jesus in reaction against social or liturgical prayer, yet it is certainly not his emphasis. This is quite interesting, given that later Orthodox and Catholic emphasis was clearly on public liturgy—and perhaps far too often this substituted for people and clergy who had no personal or conscious sense of loving union with God, but too often were trying to earn what they already had, by attending or performing such liturgies. Yet even such early stage bargaining can be, and often is, a starting point for authentic prayer. God is both humble and patient—and very enterprising.

It is interesting that the disciples ask Jesus for a formula, "just as John taught his disciples," to define their identity and their group (Luke 11:1). One could easily conclude that he had not taught them any spoken or common prayers up to that point. It seems that for a spiritual group to be a group at all, it always needs its public prayer by which to define itself to itself and to the larger world. This is good and surely how the Our Father functions for the entire Christian spectrum to this day. We also see how this same need is felt by 12-Step groups with the Serenity Prayer and by many Catholics with the rosary.

My arguable assumption is, that what we know to glibly call prayer, was in the early centuries of Christianity often referred to as "rest," "quieting," and eventually "contemplation"—a word that gained broad and authoritative coinage in both the Eastern and Western churches, considering that it is not as such in the Bible. In each case, it had much more to do with seeking an inner state, a place of communion, a nonargumentative mind that was referred to as "the peace that the world cannot give" or "the pearl of great price" by early commentators, especially in the desert and Eastern realms of Christianity.

We in the West must accept that when we split from the Eastern Church in 1054, we also split from much of the practical teaching—and emphasis—on the contemplative mind. This teaching held sway in the East, starting with the desert fathers and mothers, and organically developed into the doctrine of theosis (divinization), and this split of practice and theory lasted until the modern era. (I fully recognize that many false forms of contemplation, and almost entirely inward focused liturgies, also created a kind of quietism in the East that made many issues of mission to others and social justice largely invisible.) Both the East and West lost by separating from one another.

PRACTICE

All prayer is practicing for prayer. No one really knows how to pray, as Paul states in our epigraph at the beginning (Romans 8:26), and it is in this very experience of weakness and incapacity that the Spirit comes to pray in us, with us, and as us—with "groans unutterable" (Romans 8:27), which early on took the form of speaking in tongues (1 Corinthians 14:1–25) after the first Pentecost. Paul emphasizes that this early form of Christian prayer "does not feed the mind" or, in another translation, "my mind derives no fruit from it" (1 Corinthians 14:14). It was prayer at the prerational, transrational, or unconscious level, we might say today. It was done to us! Already we have something deeper, at least partially proceeding from forces beyond us, and thus many would say "Spirit led," which is something other than saying, thinking, memorizing, or reciting by ourselves. In fact, it is often called "babbling" or "praying in the Spirit," which appears to be somewhat embarrassing because it surely deflates the ego at least in the eyes of others. Although, the first time you surrender to it, it is a defeat to your own intelligence and common sense, too. No wonder it died out.

Luke's comment is significant in his ending to Matthew and Mark's excursus on what we call "intercessory prayer." He adds that the answer to every intercession is always the same: "How much will the heavenly father give the Holy Spirit to those who ask him [for anything]?" (Luke 11:13). So maybe prayer at its deepest level is not about getting something, problem solving, or resolving issues (although we are encouraged to trust in God for these things), but rather, all prayer is a radical receptivity to the Holy Spirit, which itself is inspired by that same Holy Spirit! We eventually know that God creates within us the desire—to desire—to pray for whatever we need or want. A divine and reverse Catch-22, you might say!

All we can do is pray that God can keep us open and completing the circuit of desire. God wants these good things for us more than we do, and any authentic Christian prayer is just seconding the divine motion. Again, we are merely practicing, continually learning, and forever surrendering to the divine mind. Letting go of our own small mind is the burden of all contemplative practice. And maybe this is why contemplative prayer died out too!

It is no surprise, therefore, that teachers of contemplative prayer, centering prayer, meditation, or the prayer of quiet, consistently prefer to use the words *practice* or *sitting* to describe what they do. Yet, it is not so much an action, a doing, as it is a non-doing. Prayer is not so much that the I is praying, as the profound and life-changing realization that prayer is happening through me. All I can do is gratefully be open to it and allow it to happen to me and through me and with me—and as me.

Prayer is also happening at rudimentary levels, in nature, in animals, in all growing and living things. How many of the psalms as well as the hymn in Daniel 3 speak easily of rivers "clapping their hands," fire and heat "praising," and animals and beasts "blessing the Lord"? This is not some New Age poetry; this is our poetry, our prose, and our gospel! How have we missed this? We defined prayer so supernaturally that we forgot how to do it naturally with what was all around us.

The act of praying might be the deepest meaning of something, in fact, the deepest meaning of being alive itself—and as in all of nature, elements, and animals, trusting and allowing the dying as a needed and important part of the life. It's only our humanity that wants to decide whether to join in with "the height, the length, the depth and the breadth" of things (Ephesians 3:18). The rest of creation seems to do itself quite naturally, spontaneously, and fully.

Prayer is saying "yes" to the paschal mystery at work in all things, and joyfully joining in with that flow—the movement of both death and resurrection equally—and thus allowing the very life of the Trinity, in whose pattern all things are created. This is already intimated in the first sentences of the Hebrew Bible in Genesis 1:1–2: God (Father), together with the Hovering Wind (Spirit), speaks the creative Word of Forms (Christ). History itself is one cosmic prayer spoken by God through this ongoing creation from the very beginning—each species "eagerly awaiting the full recognition [that they are each in their own way] children of God" (Romans 8:19). What else could fully good news mean? We humans are the free and blessed ones who can enjoy this daughterhood and sonship consciously and lovingly as we join in the one divine flow of praise, adoration, gratitude, and chosen solidarity with all that God is doing. Paul excitedly calls it "the great parade" or "the great triumph" (2 Corinthians. 2:14) that we are all invited to join. We are being prayed through, it seems, often without our even knowing it. But *you* can now know it, enjoy it, and pass it on.

In a very true sense, God is the only one praying, and we are all invited to join the Son, Jesus, in his one completely trustful and eternal "Yes" and his one eternal "Amen" (2 Corinthians 1:20) to that infinite prayer of God—and thus to all and every single thing that is. The indwelling Holy Spirit teaches us how to trust, enjoy, and suffer this flow. Thus all true prayer is in the Spirit and in Christ. We do not know how to do it by ourselves. This is surely what distinguishes Christian contemplation from other traditions and also what frees us from too much emphasis on any precise technique or undue asceticism. Jesus never emphasizes posture, fasting, timing, or gesture—only intention—which is why and how we can indeed "pray constantly" (1 Thessalonians 5:16), which before we never thought was possible. It is just this:

- God is the one who loves and prays through us,
- Jesus shares and participates in this flow with and in his Body (us!), and
- the Spirit keeps it all moving, dynamic, alive—and always flowing outward!

---

1. All Scripture quotations are from the author's own translations.

CHAPTER 41

Praying in the Darkness

~ *Therese J. Borchard* ~

One dark night,
Fired with love's urgent longings
—ah, the sheer grace!—
I went out unseen,
My house being now all stilled.

So begins the powerful poem "Dark Night" by Carmelite mystic John of the Cross.[1] John's practice was to speak, not of the dark night of the soul but only of dark night. His practice emphasizes the human experience of darkness in its many manifestations; that darkness occurs not only spiritually but emotionally and physically.

I memorized the poem my senior year at Saint Mary's College because I chose it as the topic of my senior project as a religious studies major, and my thesis advisor, the Carmelite expert Keith J. Egan, suggested that it would be more meaningful to write about if the words, through memorization, became part of me.

They, indeed, became part of me.

My paper argued that his poem could serve as a *locus theologicus* a place to do theology. And if theology is "faith seeking understanding," as St. Anselm of Canterbury defined it centuries ago, then it is logical and right that the dark night is a place where our faith seeks understanding.

That has been my experience and the experience of thousands that I speak with in my online depression communities.

The poem's story line is of a young woman in search of her lover. The theme is taken from the Song of Songs. John says that he composed the poem after the suffering of the dark night. Egan, who remains a close friend of mine to this day, says, "In the case of John of the Cross, the dark night comes from the human resistance, often unconscious, to God's lavish love. So the suffering brings about not anger or other kinds of suffering but love. Prayer is all about the discovery of being loved."[2]

I chose that thesis because I loved poetry and because I have always gravitated toward the Carmelite saints since I was named for Thérèse of Lisieux. Little did I know that I would suffer my own suicidal dark night twice after I defended that paper and go back to recite those stanzas, reminding myself that, as Egan said, "darkness is always for the sake of light and love. Darkness can transform us into loving people if we become free enough to accept God's love."

Of course, it is important to distinguish the spiritual dark night from clinical depression, even as it can be impossible to make that distinction, because many religious and spiritual people forego treatment, thinking that the pain they endure is necessary to purify their souls. Gerald May, MD, a retired psychiatrist and senior fellow in contemplative theology and psychology, discusses both in his book *The Dark Night of the Soul*. When a person is clinically depressed, he explains, she loses her sense of humor and the ability to see comedy in certain situations. The person is also too shut down to reach out to others who are in pain, to offer compassion to others. She can't see beyond her own discomfort. Clinical depression can render an energetic, sensitive person apathetic so that all her senses are disabled. Her very being seems to disappear beneath her illness.

With a dark night, the person stays intact, even though she is hurting. While a person in the midst of a dark night knows, on some level, there is a meaning to the pain, the depressed person is embittered and wants to be relieved immediately. "In accompanying people through dark-night experiences, I never felt the negativity and resentment I often felt when working with depressed people," explains Dr. May.[3]

Kevin Culligan, OCD, a psychologist and the former chair of the Institute of Carmelite Studies, also distinguishes between the dark night and clinical depression in his chapter in the book *Carmelite Spirituality*. He explains that a clinically depressed person has a loss of energy and pleasure in most things, including hobbies and sex. He will sometimes exhibit a dysphoric mood or psychomotor retardation. The person in the midst of a dark night experiences loss, too, but more as a loss of pleasure in the things of God. Culligan can often tell the difference between the two based on his response to the person with whom he's interacting. After listening to a depressed person, he often becomes depressed, helpless, and hopeless himself. He feels the rejection of self, as if the depression is contagious. In contrast, he is not brought down when people speak of a spiritual aridity.

I found the following paragraph in Culligan's chapter to be especially helpful:

> In the dark night of spirit, there is painful awareness of one's own incompleteness and imperfection in relation to God; however, one seldom utters morbid statements of abnormal guilt, self-loathing, worthlessness, and suicidal ideation that accompany serious depressive episodes. Thoughts of death do indeed occur in the dark night of the spirit, such as "death alone will free me from the pain of what I now see in myself," or "I long to die

and be finished with life in this world so that I can be with God," but there is not the obsession with suicide or the intention to destroy oneself that is typical of depression. As a rule, the dark nights of sense and spirit do not, in themselves, involve eating and sleeping disturbances, weight fluctuations, and other physical symptoms (such as headaches, digestive disorders, and chronic pain).[4]

Both Culligan and May agree that a person can at the same time experience *both* a dark night and clinical depression, that sometimes they are impossible to tease apart. "Since the dark night and depression so often coexist, trying to distinguish one from the other is not as helpful as it might first appear," writes May. "With today's understanding of the causes and treatment of depression, it makes more sense simply to identify depression where it exists and to treat it appropriately, regardless of whether it is associated with a dark-night experience."[5]

I am getting better at distinguishing what kind of depression is pure chemical response and what kind of depression would benefit from more contemplation and prayer, from remembering that God is an anxious lover awaiting our openness to his love. For example, when I eat anything made with sugar or white flour, I now know that I can expect suicidal thoughts that will last anywhere from forty-eight to ninety-six hours. My brain is on fire, inflamed, and there is little I can do but distract myself and remind myself that it is merely an allergic reaction. Those types of depression push me to God only in so far as I am reminded at how fragile I am, and that my delicate wiring must not rely on itself, but on God. However, there are other times, when I feel unlovable—rejected by a family member or colleague—when there is an aching sadness in my heart. At those times, John's words bring me hope and relief, that "the endurance of darkness leads to great light."

"You are writing about a darkness which is caused by medical or environmental or physical conditions," Egan explained to me recently. "John knows this kind of darkness, but mystical darkness is the liberation of what keeps us from discovering God's lavish love." For John, as for all of us, there are different kinds of darkness.

Is not all darkness capable of ending in the love John describes in the final stanza of his poem "Dark Night"?

I abandoned and forgot myself,
Laying my face on my Beloved;
All things ceased; I went out from myself,
Leaving my cares
Forgotten among the lilies.[6]

1. *The Collected Works of St. John of the Cross*, rev. ed., trans. Kieran Kavanaugh, OCD, and Otilio Rodriguez, OCD (Washington, DC: ICS, 1991), 358.
2. Quotations from Keith J. Egan in this essay are all from my notes of our personal conversations.
3. Gerald G. May, *The Dark Night of the Soul: A Psychiatrist Explores the Connection between Darkness and Spiritual Growth* (New York: HarperOne, 2005), 156.
4. Kevin Culligan, OCD, in *Carmelite Prayer: A Tradition for the 21st Century*, ed. Keith J. Egan (New York: Paulist, 2004), 130.
5. May, 156.
6. *The Collected Works of St. John of the Cross*, 359.

CHAPTER 42

Consideration: The Everyday Prayer of the Contemplative in Action

~ Joseph Tetlow, SJ ~

Jesus told his disciples to "consider the lilies of the field" and then shared some of his own considerations. St. Ignatius tells those making the thirty-day retreat to "consider" almost as many times as he tells them to "contemplate." In the *Contemplatio ad Amorem*, his directions suggest what consideration meant to him. Today, mature disciples who are intent on finding God in lives bleached with secularism make consideration their usual prayer. But most who pray this way do not know or understand its name; this leaves them misprizing their *lectio divina* and feeling that they ought to pray better. All of these developments are clear in stories told by people praying today.[1]

OPENING THE QUESTION

Joan has been married for sixty-six years. She is still active, but her spouse suffers dementia and is in a residence. Joan begins her day with prayer, starting with some prayers of devotion and reading a daily note by Cardinal Carlo Martini. Then she does a *lectio divina* on the Scripture of the day.[2] Some mornings, Joan will contemplate the incident in Jesus's life. But most of the time, she goes into her daily events, aware that God waits for her in whatever is coming.

For instance, one morning she wonders how long she will be able to drive to visit her spouse and asks God's help for herself and for him. She recalls an incident at Mass with her granddaughter. She felt joy and gratitude that the child, who has suffered a good deal, has been given a beautiful charism of compassion. She prays for her and thanks God for the charism. The gospels bring family and friends to mind and she is grateful to God. Ordinarily, Joan faces days busy with decisions and choices. This day, she prays for four people she is guiding through exercises in daily life (which Joan has been guiding for some thirty years).[3]

Joan's prayer is typical of those who have made the Spiritual Exercises and have chosen to keep finding God in all things, as we put it. The way she is praying is typically Ignatian, though we have not named it much lately. We have explained and explored Ignatian contemplation, the entering into an event with Jesus and his friends so as to share the experience with them. Many books explain and suggest help for the discernment of spirits and for managing the Ignatian examen.[4]

But the prayer of consideration? We have not given it much attention at all. Yet this prayer figures constantly in the prayer of *Spiritual Exercises*—an important reason for understanding it. The prayer is also the everyday prayer of the contemplative in action, those who live in the world and want to find God in all of it. This is a more urgent reason for understanding what the Ignatian tradition means by the prayer of consideration.

The Prayer of Consideration in the Spiritual Exercises

In his text, St. Ignatius directs us "to contemplate" an event in Jesus's life almost eighty times.[5] Then he directs us "to consider" it, or a call, or a truth about self and lifeworld —close to sixty times. The prayer continues through every part of the *Exercises*, beginning with the principle and foundation: "The consideration of our last end forms the entrance into the First Week."[6] This might seem dryly rational, but the prayer of consideration goes on to engage the imagination. In the first prayer on God's mercy and my sin, I "create with my imagination" a fantasy that my soul is exiled in a corruptible body, a mere animal.[7] Then I am to consider how I would experience that which moves me to disgust and loathing and revulsion from serving my body.

At times, Ignatius guides us to comparisons and contrasts. He instructs us to "consider who God is against whom I have sinned," and to compare God's infinite wisdom to my ignorance, His holiness to my unholiness, and so forth.[8] He calls on us to muse over something all day long. Describing different ways to be humble (obeying Commandments, living indifferently, yearning to be poor as Jesus was), he suggests that I consider them "at little stretches of time through the whole day."[9] This consideration moves me to "making the colloquy that will be explained [the triple colloquy]," and we turn to an elaborated prayer of petition.[10]

Consideration in the *Spiritual Exercises* generally leads to imagining how I will act in the future and to making a choice. When we hear the call of the King, for instance, we turn "to consider what answer good subjects of so liberal and kind a King ought to make."[11] In this instance and in others, ideas and thinking lead to affect and desiring. All along, the example of Jesus of Nazareth gives us a template, and we begin any serious choice "considering the example of Christ our Savior."[12]

Consideration regularly rises in the purest of contemplations. The Passion, for instance, we begin by contemplating Jesus sharing the Last Supper and washing his disciples' feet. But St. Ignatius adds that we are "to consider what Christ our Lord is suffering in His human nature…what he desires to suffer.… To consider how the divinity hides itself.… To consider that Christ suffers all this for my sins, and what I ought to do and suffer for Him."[13]

We are considering here the meaning of Christ's actions; adopting interpretations for myself are part of Ignatian consideration that certainly continues into daily finding God in all things. Ignatius makes that task emphatically clear in the contemplations on the Resurrection. To the scriptural events, Ignatius adds two points: "To consider the divinity, which seemed to hide itself during the passion, now appearing and manifesting itself so miraculously;" and to consider "the office of consoler that Christ our Lord exercises."[14] This moves us to interpret the meaning of Christ's work in the world.

Consideration in the *Contemplatio ad Amorem*

The *Contemplation to Attain the Love of God*, carefully read, gives further indications of what St. Ignatius meant by "consideration." He introduces the prayer with two affirmations about love. First, love is done, not just talked about or felt. Second, love consists in mutual sharing, the lover and the beloved both giving and accepting. This understanding of love defines the whole of this prayer.

Ignatius recommends the *Contemplation to Attain the Love of God* as a means of closure on the thirty-day retreat. When retreatants come to it, they have made some life-shaping decisions. A Jesuit priest had decided that he must pursue his gift as an artist. A laywoman had reenvisioned her life as one of service. A nun had decided she would remain in her congregation though it was dissolving around her. Anyone who has made the thirty-day retreat has come to some larger election and looks forward to the busyness of renewed daily life. This prayer throws open the broadest horizons of our understanding of human life and destiny, even while keeping us intimately attached to our lifeworld. The text of its four points show a clear progression in the prayer that Ignatius is recommending.[15]

In the first point, we are told to "recall to mind...creation, redemption...and the special favors I have received." Then we "reflect upon [ourselves], and consider, according to all reason and justice what [we] ought to offer the Divine Majesty." The gifts to be recalled begin, at least they usually do today, with the splendid colorful images of the universe. Most retreatants then come back to the earth—its beautiful mountains and plains, the oceans, and its teeming peoples.

Our consciousness, however, does not stay on gifts to the world in general: we are now to recall how I got to where I am now. I began the retreat with a growing realization that God creates me moment by moment. In that intimate communion, I have sinned and been taken back into God's grace. This recalling, reflecting, and considering leads me to be "moved by great feeling," and in that spiritual temper, "I will make this offering of myself"—the Suscipe.[16]

Note that the recalling, the reflecting on myself, and the considering are all done by a subject in the context of a concrete, ongoing experience. Read apart from the context of the *Exercises*, this could seem a mystical relationship between the lone individual and God. But here, this recalling embraces God's ongoing creating and redeeming. My reflecting is actually a sharing of consciousness and purposefulness with God, who is busy incessantly creating and redeeming.

The second point tells us to go directly to "reflect how God dwells in creatures," all the orders of creation as seen in Western thought as the Renaissance began, from elements through plants and animals to "bestowing intelligence" in human life.[17] We reflect on how "He dwells in me and gives me being, life....makes a temple of me, since I am created in the likeness and image of the Divine Majesty." The work here is to connect these images and ideas to myself-in-action.

From my reflection, I turn to the Suscipe again. The final sentence of the prayer I say is this: "Give me thy love and thy grace, for this is sufficient for me." The love and grace here are not abstract theological concepts; they are the retreatant's experience of love both in the prayer of the *Exercises* and in the real history of life. All has now been grasped as gift from God, even the failures and in a mysterious way, even my sins.

Those who enjoy greater spiritual freedom and generosity may go on to the mysticism of the rest of the Contemplation. For the third point guides retreatants to go directly "to consider," passing over recalling, pondering with affection, and reflecting on themselves.[18] The retreatants are to consider "how God works and labors for [them] in all creatures upon the face of the earth." Ignatius adds an unusual pleonasm, that is, "He conducts Himself as one who labors." Here is the God whom those who follow Ignatian spirituality are looking to find in all things. He is a busy God, and he pulls me after him into the work of loving, caring, creating, and redeeming. The consideration elicits marveling and feeling awed at the immensity and intensity of God's work. At this point, the retreatant is moved to reciprocate—that is, to think of what they are to do. The exercise has drawn into appreciative awareness their faith, their believing, and then enactment. As I say below, this seems to be what mature Christians mean by "discernment" today. Again, I make my offering.

The fourth and final point directs me "to consider all blessings and gifts as descending from above." Then Ignatius gives directions about what to consider: "Thus, my limited power comes from the supreme and infinite power above," and so do all my human endowments and enactments, "as the rays of light descend from the sun, and as the waters flow from their fountains, etc."[19] Clearly here, as in earlier points, Ignatius is moving us to use our imagination and our fantasy. Many find help in fantasizing a mirror standing out in a field and aimed directly at the sun. Looking into the mirror would blind us. Yet the mirror has no light of its own—all of its light is the sun's. The sun loses nothing, is filling the mirror with light, and yet the mirror is filled with light. So it is with us and God, who fills us with intelligence, freedom, creativity, joy, and much else, and remains the almighty God of gods.

What Makes Contemplatives in Action?

The retreatant who reaches this experience with depth and endurance finds that the result is "a state of heightened awareness where 'the fire of divine love' burns so intensely in him that 'a sincere impulse of love for God' motivates his every action."[20] This is the judgment of Juan de Polanco, Ignatius's secretary, confidant, and indispensable helper for long years. Polanco judged that anyone who prayed seriously through the *Exercises* would leave them having achieved four great objectives: liberation, illumination, discernment, and great passion to find God in all things. The more ardent live with what Bernard J. F. Lonergan calls "a universal antecedent willingness" to do whatever God seems to be about and is soliciting me to do with him. This is what doing God's will means. It is what Jesus of Nazareth meant when he said, "The Son can do nothing on his own, but only what he sees the Father doing; for whatever the Father does, the Son does likewise" (John 5:19).[21]

This prayer leads to discernment, to judgment, to decision, and to enactment based on the interplay of head, heart, and hands. This is a prayer for those who live and pray in the busyness of the marketplace, who "consider all blessings and gifts" not in some universal, generalized way, but in the concreteness of everyday life. It is also the prayer of Pope Francis—and of those who collaborate with him—that he expressed in his call to the Synod in Rome in October of 2015 to enter a "profound discernment to understand how the Lord wants his church."[22]

This is also the prayer of those who find their souls quite intensely incarnate, the mysticism of the soul exuberantly and unremittingly enfleshed. There were surely some who prayed this way before Ignatius, but a thread begins with him and flows down to today. This spirituality shaped the efforts of Roberto de Nobili and Matteo Ricci to enculturate the Good News into the flesh of India and China. It drove and drives Jesuits to keep inventing ways to form the young in both humanities and faith. The phylum leads to the Christian mysticism of Pierre Teilhard de Chardin and to the evangelical writings of Carlo Martini, whose pastoral appreciation of Word and world disallowed ignoring solidarity with the world around. "On the contrary, the Christian community located in this time and in this bit of history...is invited to be in harmony with that situation, weaving together Word and history so as to bring the Good News to today's peoples."[23]

And of course, the prayer and its mind-set and heart-set shine out of every page written by Pope Francis. The timbre of his having learned to love the way God loves resonates in sentences like this about Christ's presence in the world: "His flesh becomes visible in the flesh of the tortured, the crushed, the scourged, the malnourished, and the exiled…to be acknowledged, touched, and care for by us."[24]

THE USE OF THE PRAYER OF CONSIDERATION IN EVERYDAY LIFE

The reach of Teilhard's mysticism and Martini's scholarly grasp of Scripture's meaning is beyond most of us. The prayer of consideration is not. It governs our relationship with self and God until death. Jesuit Father Ed O'Brien, for instance, considered as he lay dying whether to give his body to science. Mindful of Jesus's selfless offering and of the Suscipe in which he had personally offered "all that I have and all that I am," he considered his body "the last thing I can give." So he offered his body to science for God's sake.

This braiding of Word and world gives shape to the prayer of consideration. As for the Word, it commonly begins in Scripture. In the *Spiritual Exercises*, Ignatius assigns three points for each of the mysteries of Jesus's life, beginning with the Annunciation and ending with the Ascension.[25] These were useful in his day, when no one had a Bible and many could not read. We can hardly expect to do the same when everyone has a Bible or two. So most directors simply give the retreatant the gospel citation, sometimes suggesting one thing or another to note particularly, but commonly leaving them to find in it what the Spirit is leading them to. For this reason, those in the Ignatian tradition find the *lectio divina* a natural form of prayer.

A WORLD BLEACHED BY SECULARISM

A pragmatic people, Americans also find consideration a natural form of prayer to weave Word and world in the prayer of our hearts. So what is our world? Take a hard look at the real situation most American Catholics (and Christians) find themselves in. Our daily life is hardly shot through with evangelical meaning. We make our way with some good habits and avoidance of most of the really sinful things about our culture. Not all of them, however: Serious Catholics who do not skip Mass on Sundays grimly embrace the slanderous and hateful opinions of current television commentators. Many of us might feel that members of the opposing political party are our enemies, and if we don't hate them, neither do we pray for them. Our political opinions are hardly untouched by fifty years of incessant claims that government is the problem. The media portray politicians as crooks. Who remembers while doing taxes the first pope's admonition, "For the Lord's sake accept the authority of every human institution" (1 Peter 2:13)? Most of our houses are, candidly, minor shrines to "unbridled consumerism."[26]

We may, at times, feel closer to God and feel that God is in our lives. Many of us faithfully pray. But every one of us has to struggle to make the living Word a steady companion in all our days. In this situation, when we do turn to Scripture, many of us do Bible study. Some might find peace of heart and personal integration by using centering prayer. But the sad truth is that Sunday Mass does little to fill the coming weekdays with joy and thanksgiving and zeal to make Jesus's name known. As Martini laments, "Our life could be filled with light by a prolonged and attentive contact with the Word. But instead we pass it by because we are resigned to live in darkness and are too lazy to do anything about it."[27]

Those who mean to find God in their lives and choose to do something about it found themselves eager to follow Vatican II and "read the signs of the times."[28] We also found it easy at first to understand the times as the vast processes like the Cold War, globalization, and the deepening of individualism, about which we could do little but pray. But that defined the work of the whole Church, as one theologian saw clearly: "The first responsibility of the church is to discern and respond with obedient faith to the work of the living God in the world."[29] So that remains the work of the Church assembled.

SIGNS AND TIMES FOR EACH OF US

The individual disciple has a more intimate task. We are to see that the Holy Spirit is constantly at work in each of us and in the life of the world around us. Pope John Paul II pointed out that "the call and demands of the Spirit resound in the very events of history."[30] He meant *our* history, not the world's, but seemed to open the doors to the grandeur of generality. Typically, Pope Francis brings it down to everyday life: "To believe that the Holy Spirit is at work in everyone means realizing that he seeks to penetrate every human situation and all social bonds."[31] Hence, the times of this discernment are the moments, days, and longer history of my own life caught up in my present self. These times are always filled with uncertainty and ambiguity. "The wisdom of discernment redeems the necessary ambiguity of life and helps us find the most appropriate means" to figure out the next good thing to do.

Then what are the signs that we are trying to read? In their turn, they are not global movements, ideological interpretations, or statistics and data. They are the doings, convictions, and feelings in and all around us. Berta Montes, for instance, is not looking for the signs given off by the millennials. She is prayerfully considering the signs of her son's faith being challenged by his experience in higher education.

She is looking for signs of what she might—or even must—do, herself. What she faces, we all face in some manner or other. For us, the signs are the holy demands that a situation may impose on us. I watched a lay colleague struggle whether he must resign from his tenured position in a university because of what he was convinced was unchristian behavior on its part. The signs may also be what our neighbor needs, particularly those whom God gave us as relatives. So Lisa Meier, a devout woman and a lawyer, has to figure out the signs of her spouse's deterioration to discern whether the Lord wants him at home or in a care facility. Then she has to decide what she is to do.

Hence, finding God in all things will bring us to consider what is happening right around us. And discerning what we are to do means considering even the historical development of the situation we are in. "Only in narrative form do you discern, not in a philosophical or theological explanation, which allows you rather to discuss."[32]

Sometimes these concrete, intimate signs of our own times, in our own lifeworld, are tightly connected with larger issues. The truly great-hearted are open to that— to learning and to being taught. The most urgent case recently has concerned the ecology. "Inasmuch as we all generate small ecological damage," Pope Francis wrote in *Laudato Si'*, "we are called to acknowledge 'our contribution, smaller or greater, to the disfigurement and destruction of creation.'"[33] This meant a lot to Joe Lipic, a very successful businessman and serious seeker of Jesus Christ. He considered it in his daily prayer (often done as he drives) and this has led to his strongly felt choice to use a lot less water, having listened to and heard both the world around him and the tradition as interpreted by recent pontiffs.

Considering the Use of *Lectio Divina*

Those who pray in the Ignatian tradition of consideration tend to continue praying daily with Scripture. As do many others, they apply some form of the *lectio divina*. There may seem to be little more to say about it by now. But in this context, it is important to point out that the *lectio divina* practiced in monastic life differs from its practice in everyday life. The purposes of *lectio*—to sanctify a life in community on the one hand and to sanctify a life in family and the marketplace on the other—differ in fact. I want to point out that the practice of *lectio* also differs, particularly among those who pray in the Ignatian tradition. So this is worth looking into.

Lectio Divina Monastica

In current writing, *lectio divina* is usually presented in its classical form and for its original purpose: to enter into a contemplative union with God. Fr. Luke Dysinger,

OSB, for instance, gives a lucid and encouraging description, one of the best I have found: "*Lectio divina* is a slow, contemplative praying of the Scriptures."[34] He then gives neat and freeing help on place, time, and coming to self-concentration. About the text, he suggests taking up the daily readings or perhaps praying through one of the Gospels.

This prayer, Fr. Dysinger points out, is fruitful everywhere, as it helps us identify a "spiritual rhythm" underlying our daily lives. He writes, "Within this rhythm, we discover an increasing ability to offer more of ourselves and our relationships to the Father, and to accept the embrace that God is continuously extending to us in the person of his son, Jesus Christ." He wisely notes that concerns and relationships and the distractions of everyday life "naturally intertwine with our meditations on the Scriptures." How are you to handle them? You are to understand them as "simply parts of yourself that, when they rise up during *lectio divina*, are asking to be given to God along with the rest of your inner self." Very instructively, he summarizes it this way: "*Lectio divina* has no goal other than that of being in the presence of God by praying the Scriptures."[35] This is a holy habit that many yearn for.

There remains much to say about it, but this expresses well the general practice of *lectio* urged today. It remains the *lectio divina monastica*. We might wonder whether the American individualists we described would be likely to make of it something like this: It leads me to be authentic and to remember that God loves me as I am. It leads me to keep mindful that God is always caring for me. As far as I can find, it is not likely today to lead me to remember that God loves me too well to leave me as I am. The ongoing conversion that all of us face does not figure large here. One devout (and anonymous) blogger reached for it by urging that we ask ourselves a question: "What does this Word mean for my life? What do I need to change?" But instead of guiding the one praying to look to changes in their daily lives, the blogger guides them to notice that we are giving an honest accounting of our lives and directing them more firmly "outward toward the Father, Son and Holy Spirit."[36]

What this *lectio* does not seem to do is move me to meditate or pray on what I am to do. It does not very explicitly draw us or weave into our communing with God the work of our hands: what we are doing, might do, must do, or must not do. Even when this *lectio monastica* is designedly presented as the prayer appropriate for a busy life, it encourages those remaining to focus on God and the individual praying. It might be useful to belabor this point because the limning of *lectio divina* seems to hold the field in popular writing, overshadowing a more action-focused asceticism and scriptural prayer.

One article among the hundreds in the current explosion of popular writing illustrates this. The writer of a lead article of *The Word Among Us* in July 2015 urges reflecting on our "personal operating system."[37]

> Clearly, Jesus challenged everyone's operating systems—and he wants to challenge ours as well. He wants to affect the way we think and act. He wants us to take on his own values and attitudes so that we can become more like him.

The operating system in a computer (the source of this metaphor) makes the computer's program work. Our personal system, then, would include the way we think, feel, and act. This is a clear attempt at asking what this event in Jesus's life says to me about the life I am now living. But the writer takes the *lectio* in another direction. He goes on to a meditation on the woman anointing Jesus's feet. His thoughts are about the woman loving and about Jesus teaching. Only at the end does he conclude that the woman did something great for love. "It's what will make us great in God's eyes as well." Notice that he seems to find no suggestions in this event of anything we might do for love of God beyond doing everything with a great love. This *lectio* shares in the *meditatio* and *oratio* that leads to *contemplatio*. Even in a booklet about daily life, it is the *lectio divina monastica*.

Lectio Divina Cotidiana

The form of the *lectio* in the Ignatian tradition differs, as the experience of Joan has shown. Its steps can be put this way: *lectio, consideratio, oratio, discretio*—which we take as *discernment*. The *meditatio* is replaced by *consideratio*, for meditating keeps us focused on the event in Jesus's life and what it means to us. Consideration, as I hope is clear, deliberately keeps our attention on braiding Word and world.

Then, the differences between the classical *discretio* and our current understanding of *discernment* highlight the changes introduced by a spirituality that seeks graced union with God acting now in the real world. Hence, the differences are worth noting. Origen, Tertullian, and Cassian meant a range of things by *discretio* and *diakrisis*, but they all refer to the spiritual ability to live aware of the movements of one's heart as one chooses among good things, an ability that allowed a monk to develop an interior spiritual life.[38] This *discretio* kept close to the monastic life, particularly to living with a *pater spiritualis*, a "spiritual director," who really directed and to whom obedience was essential. This is the monastic model.

For Catholics today, discernment adds a good deal to *discretio*. First, it lets us distinguish not only between or among good things, but helps us separate good from evil. The *Catechism of the Catholic Church* says this about the way current Catholics talk:

we apply discernment in the working of conscience—to judging what we are morally to do or not do.[39] Questions of conscience are not so frequent, yet mature disciples who have any interior life at all are discerning in all kinds of circumstances all the time. We are far more aware of the interplay of situation and prior conditioning, of subconscious motives, and even of the physical input into our awareness than were those monks who felt that all earthy impulses were the fault of their physical bodies. Current experience was summed up by then-Archbishop Jorge Bergoglio this way: "It's fundamental that one thinks what one feels and does; feels what one thinks and does; and does what one thinks and feels. You must use the language of the head, the heart, and the hands."[40] If we find this not intruding on our prayer but integral to it, we are moving in the direction of discernment.

This is the outcome of the *lectio divina cotidiana*, the quotidian form of prayer that belongs to those who pray regularly with the Gospels and pastoral letters, but whose prayer intricately and firmly weaves together family and marketplace busyness. It engages the prayer of consideration and it leads directly to what we today call "discernment" because it leads to the enactment of faith and belief. This is the hope of the contemplative in action: we do what we do, even when it is the most ordinary of things done today, charged with our belief that God is always acting within and around us and through us and that the consequences of what we do reach beyond the eulogy over our corpse.

FINALLY: CONSIDERING WORD AND WORLD

This leads us to the way those who are seeking God in all things apply *lectio divina* in their ordinary prayer. We consider our concrete experiences and feelings, our current thoughts and habits, and braid them with our convictions of evangelical truth and our commitments in Christ. The experience is clearly complex because it happens where supernatural grace and sinful nature intertwine and where our interior lives and enactments meet.

Consideration is like electricity. From a generator, electricity lights bulbs, boots up computers, and cranks up air conditioners. From our soul, considering makes present the truths of our faith, the convictions and commitments of our hearts, and cranks up whatever busyness we are engaged in now. Electricity brings the inert to action; the prayer of consideration elevates earthly human longing and living to our graced union with Christ.

This takes supernatural grace into the crowded streets. When a man with a "hungry" sign begs at a red light, I have already considered that Matthew 25 informs my conscience to give the needy whatever I can. So when I risk a traffic jam and raucous blaring horns to give him some money, I am not just helping a fellow human being or just contributing to his bondage in poverty. I am reaching out to help a man whom Christ loves and for whom he shed his blood.

This is considering the lilies of the field and the liberties and liabilities of secular urban life in the city of God.

1. These experiences are recounted with the approval of the men and women named.
2. *Lectio divina* here is understood as moving in four moments or manners of prayer: *lectio, meditatio, oratio, contemplatio.*
3. Like scores of men and women in Tacoma, St. Louis, Detroit, and elsewhere, Joan has collaborated in a program to bring Exercises in Daily Life to hundreds of others. The material used in her program is from Joseph Tetlow, SJ, *Choosing Christ in the World* (St. Louis: Institute of Jesuit Sources, 1989).
4. Publishing on discernment has slackened but continues on *examen*. See the recent work of Mark Thibodeaux, *Reimagining the Ignatian Examen: Fresh Ways to Pray from Your Day* (Chicago: Loyola, 2015). Books on the discernment of spirits are fewer. I am finishing a manuscript on current practice tentatively titled *Discernment: A Spirituality for the Twenty-First Century.*
5. St. Ignatius wrote and printed this text—some fifteen years after others had been guiding the *Exercises*—explicitly to help the one who gives them. The brief text of little more than thirty-two thousand words is not a prayer book.
6. Martin E. Palmer, SJ, tr. and ed., *On Giving the* Spiritual Exercises (St. Louis: Institute of Jesuit Sources, 1996), 311, 312.
7. *Spiritual Exercises*, 47. We have a far different attitude toward our flesh, instantiated by the ruminations on the theology of the body by St. John Paul II.
8. *Spiritual Exercises*, 59.
9. *Spiritual Exercises*, 164.
10. *Spiritual Exercises*, 147.
11. *Spiritual Exercises*, 94.
12. *Spiritual Exercises*, 135.
13. *Spiritual Exercises*, 195, 196, 197.
14. *Spiritual Exercises*, 223, 224. Ignatius adds here: "Compare it with the way in which friends are wont to console each other," always pressing us to think about our own lives.
15. *Spiritual Exercises*, 230–237. The Spanish title is *Contemplacion para alcanzar amor*, and a better if slightly ungrammatical translation would be "Contemplation to Learn to Love Like God."
16. The second of two prayers St. Ignatius wrote for the *Exercises*, 234. The other is "Eternal Lord of All Things," the prayer we say responding to our consideration of the call of the King.
17. *Spiritual Exercises*, 235.
18. *Spiritual Exercises*, 236.
19. *Spiritual Exercises*, 237.
20. James L. Connor, SJ, et al., *The Dynamism of Desire* (St. Louis: Institute of Jesuit Sources, 2006), 435. Connor is citing here the directory composed by Juan de Polanco.

21. All quotations from Scripture are taken from the *New Revised Standard Version.*

22. Antonio Spadaro, SJ, quoted in Cindy Wooden, "Pope Says Ministry to Divorced, Remarried Is Not Only Topic for Synod," Catholic News Service, www.catholicnews.com/services/english-news/2015/pope-says-ministry-to-divorced-remarried-is-not-only-topic-for-synod.cfm.

23. Carlo Martini, *Journeying with the Lord* (New York: Alba House, 1987), 349.

24. Pope Francis, *Misericordiae Vultus,* The Face of Mercy (Vatican City: Libreria Editrice Vaticana, 2015), 15.

25. *Spiritual Exercises,* 261–312.

26. *The Joy of the Gospel,* 60. "Today's economic mechanisms promote inordinate consumption, yet it is evident that unbridled consumerism combined with inequality proves doubly damaging to the social fabric."

27. Martini, 395.

28. We all once knew that this is *Gaudium et Spes,* 4. The phrase also occurred in St. John XXIII's deathbed message.

29. Luke Timothy Johnson, "A Modus Vivendi?" *Commonweal,* January 13, 2012, 17.

30. *Familiaris Consortio,* 4.

31. Pope Francis, *Lumen Fidei,* 178.

32. Pope Francis, *Lumen Fidei,* 178.

33. Pope Francis, *Laudato Si',* 8. The pope is citing Patriarch Bartholomew.

34. Rev. Luke Dysinger, OSB, "How to Practice Lectio Divina," BeliefNet.com. This ecumenical and even interfaith website is a fine instance of the millennials' needs and desires about the self. The images are all of men and women between about twenty and thirty-five. The only church I have seen mentioned is the United Methodist Church.

35. "How to Practice Lectio Divina: A Step-by-Step Guide to Praying the Bible," http://www.beliefnet.com/Faiths/Catholic/2000/08/How-To-Practice-Lectio-Divina.aspx#FPHgsLiM6sVufdQz.99.

36. The electronic reference for this blog has recently been deleted.

37. *The Word Among Us,* 34, no. 9, July 5, 2015.

38. Antony D. Rich, *Discernment in the Desert Fathers: Diakrisis in the Life and Thought of Early Egyptian Monasticism* (Milton Keynes, UK: Paternoster, 2007). Rich treats Origen, Evagrius Ponticus, and Cassian in separate chapters.

39. *CCC* 1978. Given principles of morality through synderesis, we apply them "in the given circumstances by practical discernment."

40. Rubin, Sergio, and Francesca Ambrogetti, *Pope Francis: Conversations with Jorge Bergoglio* (New York: Putnam's Sons, 2013), 57.

CHAPTER 43

Giving Voice to My Thanks:
Praying with the Spirit of Gratitude

~ Geraldine Fialkowski ~

If our spiritual journey consists in taking time on a daily basis to recognize and acknowledge the gifts of that day, we become more open to the many ways in which God is up front, personal, and central in our lives. We will discover that we begin to pay more attention to the ways God, in one way or another, is always present and rains down good things into our lives. Our spirit and hearts may come to live out a formula that goes something like this: God is the Giver of all good things. I receive many blessings from God. When I say, "Thank you," I am giving back to God.

Subsequently we are opening ourselves to be transformed in many good, life-enhancing ways. We learn to more readily identify the light in our lives and perhaps, as the saying goes, we come to see our difficulties as opportunities and possibilities. When we open ourselves to the experience of transformation, a hunger begins deep within us. We yearn for a deeper connection with the generous source of our being. The Song of Solomon 8:14 says, "Make haste my beloved, / and be like a gazelle / or a young stag / upon the mountains of spices!"[1] The process of deliberately attending to God's presence increases our sense of urgency to know and love God more, to make haste.

When we think about gratitude, we know that we are talking about both an attitude and an act of gratefulness. Gratitude also means grace and graciousness. In this consideration of gratitude, the terms *blessings*, *grace*, and *graciousness* will be used interchangeably. Ignatius of Loyola has said that the fundamental grace in our prayers is gratitude. He refers to gratitude as the "heart-set" which enables us to have an accurate "mind-set" on God, others, the world, and self.[2]

THE THANKSGIVING TABLE

> I wash my hands in innocence
>> and go around your altar O LORD,
> singing aloud a song of thanksgiving
>> and telling all your wondrous deed.
>
> —Psalms 26:6–7

Often there are times when we miss the psalmist's message. The older I get and, I hope, the wiser I become, it becomes clearer that gratitude needs to be the focal point of my own spiritual life, my prayer life. When I make gratitude an integral part of the way I operate daily in the world, I am paying attention to grace, to what is sacred in all that exists. This is because gratitude is the foundation for the altar the psalmist mentions. We pull our chairs to this altar or table, and in our gathering together, we understand that both our ordinary and extraordinary days have presented us with multiple occasions for giving voice to our thanks.

This altar of benevolence and abundant graciousness is with us here and now. Every day we gather around it and bring to the table our relationships with others, with God, and our experiences in the nitty-gritty of living. We bring the stories and events that we perceive as good, but also those stories that we do not believe as good or pleasant. Around this altar, all of our stories are welcome. Together we help each other identify God's presence and blessings. The psalmist encourages us to behold the "wondrous" beautiful universe and realize all is gift.

We gather too around the Eucharistic table. We do this as we celebrate our liturgy. The word *Eucharist* has its roots in the Greek language and we recall that it means "thanksgiving." As Catholics, the celebration of the Mass and the union, our communion with the real presence of Jesus Christ is at the essence of our faith. When we break the bread and drink the wine, Christ brings himself to us; he gives us his Body and Blood. Because we believe that we can share in Christ's life, in turn, we too bring ourselves to the altar. We give voice to our thanks by our participation in the breaking of the bread and the blessing of the wine. We discover that what God asks of us is that we be who we are.

The presence of Christ in the Eucharist and our celebration of his death and resurrection is a grace that we did not earn. We are the recipients of this profound act of love provided by Jesus. God has found us worthy. In his book *Our One Great Act of Fidelity*, Ronald Rolheiser's reflection on the Eucharist provides a perspective we sometimes overlook. He states that Jesus too offered himself in thanksgiving to God the Father.[3] It would seem that the prayer and practice of gratitude is an early and ancient one in our tradition.

In the Beginning

When we read the Genesis narrative of humankind's creation, we are made aware that it is about grace freely given. We are honored because we are made in the image of God. Not only that, we are further blessed because we are given personal freedom, autonomy, and free will. God who is the source of all these blessings is gracious and sustains us even when we use that freedom in ways that are unworthy of God's favor.

The first three chapters of Genesis leave no doubt that life is a gift. We did not do anything to earn our existence. Everything that God creates is good and there are opportunities every day wherein we can find God's benevolence at work. We are given an abundance of resources to facilitate our well-being and charged to show compassionate care for all that exists. Our Creator invites and challenges us to be cocreators and caretakers of this wondrous universe.

The Genesis accounts leave no doubt that God the Creator knows, values, and loves us. Blessings are bestowed upon us but not because we deserve them. Our response here needs to be one of humility and gratitude. Gratitude is expressed in the ways we choose to love and interact with others and our world. Our Creator God is not the one who holds on to our failures and clutches a debit sheet for a future accounting in the hereafter. God remains in love with us. "I have called you by name, you are mine," says Isaiah (43:1–5). This seems to make the case for a humble gratitude. We are God's!

Intentional Gratitude

The spiritual practice of gratitude is not only about saying thank you; it is about meaning thank you. We need to express gratefulness in such a way that we seek to pay it forward. Gratitude is connected to what mental health counselors often refer to as our "way of being." This refers to the ways in which we are present and interact with God, others, the universe, and ourselves. If our ways of being are holistic and healthy ones, we are persons who choose appropriate ways of self-care and are also other-centered. This means we give back by caring for others and the universe. We respect and honor all that is. A person who pays attention to God's presence and blessings in daily life does not take the Creator's gifts for granted. Gratitude then becomes a spiritual habit, a spiritual virtue.

Deborah Rollison notes, "Gratitude has been lauded throughout history as a virtue and a valuable emotional state."[4] She continues this idea with a declaration from Cicero who says, "Gratitude is not only the greatest of virtues, but the parent of all the others."[5] There is the understanding that when we become aware of how good life is for us, we often are motivated to demonstrate appreciation by passing some good along to others. This reminds me of a story.

My friend Megan told me that her family was so grateful that her husband Josh received a much needed, long desired pay raise. After her husband received his first paycheck that included the raise in salary, the family immediately increased their weekly contributions to their parish. This was a simple gesture but what was so revealing about it was Megan's perspective. She said, "Josh got a raise and so I gave God a raise too." Megan and Josh felt rewarded for Josh's hard work. They were aware that individuals do not always get kudos for hard work or good deeds. They were both surprised and grateful by their good fortune. The couple chose to see God as playing some part in this situation and did not hesitate to respond by their actions.

It is neither difficult nor complicated to incorporate gratitude prayers into our daily routines. When we intend to enhance our spiritual life and deliberately express our thanks, we become persons who choose to live life deeply. In my work with pastoral counselors in training, I often remind the counselors that in order to work with others in the process of healing it is very important that you have your own spiritual life. The students are encouraged to take some time throughout the day to check in with themselves and to check in with God. Students are reminded that this is a holy exercise that will nurture and attend to their body, spirit, and mind.

A grateful approach to our lives does not require that we study or memorize certain prayers. Being thankful is not a synonym for getting it right. If we wish to develop the virtue of gratitude and tighten up our spiritual way of being, then as the commercial says, we "just do it."

When my grandson Teddy was about nine years old, I was saying his night prayers with him. Rather than working with a "bless Mommy, bless Daddy" content, I urged Teddy to name three things from his day for which he might want to thank God. As I remember this, Teddy indeed did that. His evening prayer changed from "bless Mommy" to "thank you God for Mommy and Daddy, my sisters, and grandparents." For Teddy, that covered the agenda. I encouraged him to continue the practice of saying thank you for three things every night before he went to sleep. I shared that sometimes I said thanks for a Starbucks coffee or a full tank of gas. My motive was to help him to notice simple blessings in his everyday life. My hope was to help Teddy develop a habit of daily communication with God. About a month later, he phoned me to report on the score of an important lacrosse game in which he had played. After I duly complemented Teddy on his apparent athleticism, he said, "Oh yeah Grandmom, I remember sometimes to thank God for three good things. Tonight I am thanking God that I decked the guy on the other team and prevented a score. I am going to say thanks too because I was a starter in the game. That is for sure three things."

Yes, it was. He was grateful for three things and had thought about communicating that to God. I am unsure how thankful the other player was that he was "decked." Teddy, however, was paying attention to his gratitude list.

We can say that praying with gratitude is tied to our abilities to attend to the ordinariness and extraordinariness of our lives. To be conscious of how often we are blessed is connected to how and what we may perceive as actual blessings in our encounters and experiences. Consider both Megan's and Teddy's perceptions of gift.

Out of our commitment to be more consciously grateful may come for us the realization that God is willing to surprise us with something good. We may indeed come to learn that God does surprise us with blessings rather frequently and we are not paying attention.

We are challenged by St. Paul to take our gratitude to the point of action. He urges us to respond to grace with thanksgiving and praise. "Grace to you and peace from God our Father and the Lord Jesus Christ, who gave himself for our sins to set us free from the present evil age, according to the will of our God and Father, to whom be glory forever and ever. Amen" (Galatians 1:3–5). In Galatians 6:9–10, Paul continues this idea of first giving glory to God and then moving to some kind of action. "So, let us not grow weary in doing what is right, for we will reap at harvest time, if we do not give up. So then, whenever we have an opportunity, let us work for the good of all, and especially for those of the family of faith."

A client shared this story with me; it is an example of her extraordinary experience of gratitude in what was an ordinary experience for her. As she had done for a number of years, Jill was hosting Christmas dinner for her family. Three generations would be there, twenty-six relatives and ten of these were children under age eleven. Those attending would consist of parents, grandparents, siblings, spouses, nieces, nephews, and Jill's own offspring. As one might expect, Jill said there was an incredible, happy, loud din in the house and wrapping paper was everywhere. She reported her anxiety was high. The house was a mess and there were too many people in the kitchen. Eventually she moved to the entrance of the family room to announce that dinner was ready. Jill stopped for a minute and looked over the gathering. She looked and listened. Jill said her eyes filled with tears. She was overwhelmed with gratitude and quietly thanked God for all who were present for the dinner, for her ability to host them all. She said she had an epiphany. Her eyes were opened, and Jill realized that her family would not always be healthy or present. Being together in one place would not be a forever option. Even now, Jill says she thanks God that she did not miss that moment, the Christmas when she silently stopped, looked, and listened.

Gratitude and Transformation

Believe and hope in a God of surprises. When we allow ourselves to wonder and imagine that we can change our lives and that we possess a consciousness of God's graciousness and presence in all things, then we discover this imagining comes true. We are transformed. Our life is a thank-you. I once read that Gandhi was asked if he had a message for the world. Gandhi answered that his life was the message.[6] We too can live lives that are the message, a message that speaks to the truth that gratitude in practice makes life bearable, but even more than this, a joy. The Broadway show *Wicked* has a lyric that says, "Because I knew you, I have been changed for the good." Who will say that about us?

When we have the desire to live our lives in ways that reflect the good news that God cares for us and listens to our prayers, we are more likely to acknowledge God's availability in the routines of our daily lives. To do this, we need to work to become persons who show up in life, live deeply, and acknowledge that most of us struggle in order to come to terms with what we believe are our dark sides, our unacceptable selves. Anne Lamott, in her book *Traveling Mercies*, reminds us to "love the dark places inside."[7] These are the sides of ourselves that we do not love, that we fear others will see and not love. We even wonder how God could love us knowing these things about us.

Our personal struggle with coming to terms with what we sometimes call our "growing edges" in the counseling world, our imperfections, or even our faults are opportunities for us to accept ourselves at new levels and strengthen our belief and trust that God will always forgive us. God will not abandon us and will take us back. Believing that God loves us, warts and all, can lead us to experience gratitude in ways that can transform us.

Lamott provides this perspective of her own developing relationship with God. She quotes Eugene O'Neill: "Man is born broken. He lives by mending. The grace of God is glue."[8] Lamott points out that we are loved whether we are being "elegant" or not. She goes on to say that she asks God for help over and over again. This is what she believes God might say to her, "Well isn't that fabulous? Because I need your help too. So you go get that old woman over there some water and I'll figure out what we are going to do about your stuff."[9]

A habit of gratitude makes it easier to love ourselves even when we are not at our best. It helps us to love others when they are not at their best. This is because gratitude can help us to reframe what we are experiencing and see the goodness in the middle of what might seem hopeless. We might recall that there are others who said they would be praying for us. We hold on to the hope that there are possibilities that we can change and that some circumstances will change also. We remember that God needs us too. This desire to reframe darkness in ourselves, others, and the world is not about being a Pollyanna or a cockeyed optimist. It is about the belief that God's goodness is everywhere. We do not allow darkness to color our whole day or life. The desire to look at our darkness with new eyes is about hope and the ability to wonder what might be in store for us. "The heavens are telling the glory of God; / and the firmament proclaims his handiwork" (Psalm 19:1).

GRATITUDE AND HOPE

The following verse is a poignant reminder that we are not called to avoid the real world: "I believe that I shall see the goodness of the LORD / in the land of the living" (Psalm 27:13). The message of this psalmist is that we step up and engage in the land of the living. It is in this land we find God, a living God amidst the joys and sorrows.

We need not pretend that hurts do not hurt. In the present time, even if it does not seem like it at first, God's bounties for us abound. It may seem that this approach is one that says "yes" to adversity in our lives. The reality is that we will experience adversities and come face to face with our ability or lack of ability to control some circumstances. Saying yes to adversity and thanking God for it might not seem to be the most natural response on our part. Nor do our expressions of gratitude mean that when we thank God, we are blaming God for our problems. What is happening is that we are accepting the realities, good or bad, that are present in our lives.

The gratitude response is connected to hope. Hope happens when we recognize in tough times that these too will pass. Being honest with ourselves and others about what gives us pain helps us to live with the expectation that in time, God will surprise us. Brother David Steindl-Rast says, "The more the insight that life is surprising takes hold of us, the more our life will be a life of hope, a life of openness to surprise. And Surprise is a name of God."[10] We can choose to pay attention to the creative challenges that might be waiting for us when something appears to be too dark or difficult for us.

We who are honest about our difficulties often seek more information to support our ways of coping in adversity. We seek clarity about what is and realize that we might never know the why of our dilemmas, nor for sure how they will end. We have come to understand the Buddhist principle that all life is suffering is pretty much on the mark. Life is difficult. Nevertheless, we own our difficulties and proceed to mourn our losses and overcome hurdles. The resurrection of Jesus is our reality check.

Research in clinical psychology has indicated that there are lots of benefits for people who realize that they are grateful for many things. In her PhD dissertation, Deborah Rollison reported studies that found people who would record three blessings each week for a period of three weeks were more likely to have positive attitudes about their life in general. In addition, paying attention to the good things that happened also helped individuals to feel better emotionally and physically.[11]

There is an old song from the 1940s written by Johnny Mercer called "Accentuate the Positive." The lyrics are: "You got to accentuate the positive. Eliminate the negative. Latch on to the affirmative. Don't mess with Mr. In-between." Not bad advice.

A colleague of mine, Jack, shared the following experience with me. He found that his trip to work each morning was becoming a great source of stress for him. Daily, he traveled on a road that was one of the five busiest routes in the country. He believed that his morning classes were negatively affected by his mood when he arrived at the university. Jack even considered working at a different location and school. He began each morning commute with a sense of dread. After one particularly crazy traffic day, Jack admitted to himself that regardless of the hour he left for work on any given day he had no control over the road situation. Jack believed and felt that overall, most workdays would start badly, and there was little hope for his situation to be remedied. One morning when he was on the road and traffic was at a full stop, he inadvertently hit the CD button. Jack had intended to listen to news and sports. Classical music began to play as he waited, the motor idling. He waited with Bach, Chopin, and Beethoven. He later told me that he forgot to get stressed and realized he was so thankful for the radio, the music, and God's creation of musicians. Jack made a decision to look at a negative experience as one that held new possibilities for him. He said this changed him, his outlook on work, and his outlook for each day's drive.

In his book *Sharing Wisdom*, Robert Wicks notes that when working with people who have negative outlooks on life, it helps to remind them that when one is in a dark hallway, there seems to be no light in the house. However, if a person opens a door somewhere, one may discover there is some light in the house after all.[12] The ability to be grateful when circumstances are painful helps us to remember there is a sacred place within us that still has light. We can learn to appreciate what is but also imagine what might be. We can become more creative about finding that light behind the door or the music to diminish the traffic's snarl.

We hold on to our faith and the knowledge that God loves and desires us. God's longing for us is such a gift that, in return, our desire for him increases. "Set me as a seal upon your heart, / as a seal upon your arm; / for love is strong as death" (Song of Solomon 8:6). Many of us have experienced hopes, relationships, and dreams that have died. Yet when one works to see the blessings in the pain and expresses gratitude for them, this awareness can change us. At times the integration of gratitude into a tough situation may also transform the negative impact of this experience. We then may come to know that God is indeed set like a seal on our hearts.

GRATITUDE AND PERSPECTIVE

It is important that we think about the ways we normally view our lives, other people, and our world. Psychologists and counselors understand that clients' opinions of their environment and their own roles within their particular culture or society are important ingredients in terms of their spiritual, emotional, and physical health. What our worldview is, that is, how we see the world and the ways of people within it, all play a part in the ways we think, feel, and behave in our day to day existence. These are the types of questions that might help us to clarify what might be our view of the world.

- Do we perceive the world as a safe place?
- Are others in our relationship circle safe, trustworthy?
- Does God really care about us?
- Is life fair?

Depending on how we answer these questions, our lives might be more oriented to a belief in the overall goodness of life or one that is not so optimistic or hopeful. As Christians who profess belief in Jesus Christ, God incarnate, we are challenged to respond with prayer and the spirit of gratitude. We continue to walk daily in ways that see life as full of promise and potential, even when there are times that God seems to be absent.

Our perspective on the quality and course of our lives is not just a one-time, final, and forever thing. It seems each day demands that we choose our vision and attitude for getting along and living deeply and well. Shakespeare offers us a challenge that clarifies how relevant our world perspective is to how we cope with adversity or live with joy. In one of his tragedies, Shakespeare offers this perspective:

> Life's but a walking shadow, a poor player
> That struts and frets his hour upon the stage
> And then is heard no more. It is a tale
> Told by an idiot, full of sound and fury
> Signifying nothing.[13]

As faithful people who hold on to the truth that we have been redeemed, we choose to avoid this attitude. These are not images of being human that we want to embrace. We have, at the center of our hearts and prayer life, gratitude. When the roots of our spiritual lives are planted with seeds of hope and possibility, then life is comedy more often than not. This healthy perspective on life can yield great fruit. Comedies contain sadness, frustration, terror, and confusion in their plots. But the characters do not succumb to these ill fates, and in the end they discover other options, occasions for joy, and chances for new beginnings. We players who strut on the stage of life live with the spirit of gratitude, an ability to find blessings in adversity and God in dark spaces. Ralph Waldo Emerson comments, "All that I have seen teaches me to trust the Creator for all I have not seen."[14] Our faith assures us that all will ultimately be well because God is always near. Emily Dickinson writes,

> I know that He exists,
> Somewhere—in silence.
> He has hid his rare life
> From our gross eyes.[15]

GRATITUDE AND MINDFULNESS

This is a simple tool that I have offered to students and clients. I encourage them to take minisabbaticals throughout their day. A sabbatical in this case means that the students or clients choose to take a deliberate time out. This is not such an intrusive or time-consuming endeavor that those who attempt it would find it too cumbersome to arrange. This time out consists of a quiet moment, actually seconds (five to eight). I invite the students to breathe in deeply and thank God for one thing, then to exhale. That is it.

In a busy day, we need to pause and take some seconds to be mindful of God's goodness and presence in our lives. Of course, we would be better served if we were able to take more opportunities and more time for silence. For many of us, we allow the practicalities of our lives to create barriers for extended time-outs. You can probably guess, however, that once we begin to take a few, maybe three or four, minisabbaticals in our day, we long for more time to say thanks and more time to breathe deeply.

One of the great things about minisabbaticals is that we can accomplish these anywhere. For example, I have done them on an elevator at school or work, waiting at a red light, and even sometimes at a committee meeting. We can be mindful of God's graciousness as we eat our meals, even if there are others with us. Be present to everything. Choose to take the time to smell the fragrant apple, slowly sip the wine, listen to the music, and then breathe out and silently say, "Thank you." It will come as no surprise to hear that those who do this really like it: five seconds; deep breath; "Thank you, God"; exhale. If we are doing this, we are taking the time to live a more abundant lifestyle. We are choosing to direct our lives by prayer and to prayer.

In *A Cry for Mercy*, Henri Nouwen recalls a walk in a dark wood. He listens in the quiet place to the sounds and sees what is about him: birds, trees, clouds, and so on. Nouwen believes that everything speaks of God and that in stillness, he understands the Risen Christ to be present in the woods' gracious blessings and beauty. It is in the silence that Nouwen meets Christ who has been raised. The blessings in the dark wood tell Nouwen he is loved.[16] He showed up and was present to them.

AN INTERNAL NAVIGATION SYSTEM

We can imagine that we have a metaphorical inner GPS. It is a wonderful device to help us find a destination. It lets us know if we are taking a wrong turn in our life. When our hearts are set and our minds are focused on living a lifestyle that seeks to place gratitude smack in the center of our prayer life, then we want to program our inner GPS in that direction. Who we are being in daily life, that is, how we think and behave, sets the program for our personal GPS. If we choose to be proactive about our prayer life, to plan for some quiet time, to attend to the sacredness that is the here and now, then we have programmed our inner GPS for gratitude time. Our GPS will find the holy satellite and direct us to a space for silence, a space to breathe deeply and a space to rest in grace and be grateful. When it has become our habit to do this, to seek God in our daily routine, our inner GPS senses our longing and directs us to implement the strategy. If there are times we get lost and we become reactive to circumstances in our lives and therefore neglect to be proactive and take our time-outs, our internal GPS will notify us we have taken a detour. We can recalculate.

Grace was a graduate student in a research program. She was well educated, married, the mother of young children and employed full time as the director of religious education in a sizeable parish. Each evening before Grace closed her office, she made a priority list for the next day: it included the five things she needed to complete. These musts were placed front and center on her desk. She told herself that competency and efficiency meant that she successfully completed her to-do list. Day after day, she was able to complete only one or two of these priorities. It seemed that something always occurred to interrupt her agenda.

Grace was a compassionate, wise woman and an excellent listener. People were very comfortable telling her their concerns and stories. She could not convince herself to send them away and claim that she was too busy. Deep inside, Grace suspected that these conversations might be a very important part of her work. She was available to listen, albeit anxiously, because her agenda waited. When Grace told me about her frustration around not completing her daily priority list, I asked her if she thought that God had a different agenda for her day.

As she thought about that question, Grace's perspective changed over time. Her inner GPS was warning her that availability to others might be an OK direction for her to follow. Maybe Grace needed to recalculate. She began to see more of her workdays as opportunities rather than obstacles. She allowed her inner light to guide her through some foggy days. That light illuminated what might be the real priorities for a particular day.

Grace still had her own priorities for each day. However, she gave herself permission to be more flexible if the situation was warranted. She came to see the grace and blessing in what she initially perceived as interruption. Grace could see the humor in her situation, and it heightened her awareness of the need to control everything in her workday. She understood that this might not be the best direction for her. God's agenda might be a different one than Grace's. She worked on resetting her internal GPS and began to trust the satellite would lead. Victor Hugo, the author of *Les Miserables* said, "Sleep in peace. God is awake."[17]

SOME FINAL THOUGHTS ON GRATITUDE

Freud once talked about normal people as being those individuals who know how to love, work, and play.[18] I would agree and add to that. Many normal, or rather emotionally healthy, people are those who recognize the inner need to merge with their God, their source. St. Augustine reminds us, "Our hearts are restless until they rest in God."[19] We need a prayer life centered in gratitude.

In order to be more fully integrated persons (meaning healthy in mind, body, and spirit), we need to attend to the hungers inside of us. We are challenged to find meaning and purpose in our experiences, relationships, and the ordinariness of our day-to-day living. To address these hungers for meaning and purpose, we seek direction. There are a variety of routes we can choose to take, and our choices will help determine how restless or at peace we are. There are numerous road blocks and detours along our way. We learn how to love, work, play, and pray by trial and error. What is important is that we carry hope and faith along so we may discern the ways in which God is with us as we travel.

The directions for an integrated and healthy way of being in this life require us to acquire a heart-set and mind-set that is focused on saying thank you. If we do this, we will not miss too many opportunities to show up for others and express gratitude in word and action. When we appreciate moments of grace, we reciprocate gracefully.

If the center of our spiritual life is gratitude, we discover that adversity need not color all our experiences. Darkness does not have the last word. Resurrection and new life do. We exist because the Creator has called us into being and loves us. God's breath is our life force.

We always have choices, and Viktor Frankl reminds us that even if we cannot change a situation, we can choose how we will respond to it. We can choose to appreciate something about most things and respond accordingly.[20]

We want to behave as if we are God's beloved, because this is the truth. We find ourselves seeking alone time with God, and we desire to be fully alive and fully present in our time alone and our time with others. Steindl-Rast suggests that if we wish to be consistently awakened to the gratitude happenings in our lives, we need to be awake emotionally, intellectually, and intentionally.[21]

Let us intend to notice grace present everywhere and any time. Intend to take a minisabbatical and be grounded in what is here and now. Make a decision to find a light in experiences that feel like underground, sunless tunnels.

In his poem "The Ballad of the White Horse," G.K. Chesterton tells the tale of Alfred the Saxon. The Danes have made Alfred's life a misery. He is praying that God will send him a sign that England will not be defeated by the Norsemen. As he prays, on the opposite side of the river, he has a vision of Mary. Alfred asks her to reassure him that England will not be lost. Mary does not do this. In fact, she tells him that things will get three times darker than they are already ("thrice" darker).[22]

Poor Alfred. One would think a heavenly vision would mean good news. In a sense, it is that. Mary tells Alfred, "But the men signed of the cross of Christ / Go gaily in the dark."[23] Alfred is given a formula for life.

We are reminded that no matter how dark our dark times are, there will be light. To be grateful when things seem thrice darker is not an easy feat. Christ experienced darkness, and his cross is our guarantee that there is light at the end of the tunnel. His life was a thanksgiving. As we too practice over and over again the virtue of gratitude, we will ultimately find some light because it is present. The occasions for gratitude abound and are abundant. We know this because we are loved.

In *Positively Pooh*, A.A. Milne provides this snippet. "'Oh, Bear,' said Christopher Robin, 'how I love you.' 'So do I,' said Pooh."[24] When we believe and act and as people of faith, people who are determined to be grateful for all graces great and small, we are able to hear and see the ways in which God loves us and thus, respond in kind.

---

1. All Scripture quotations are taken from the *New Revised Standard Version*.

2. *Co-Laboring with the Living Lord: Ignatian Companions on Mission—A Year of Prayer*. The Maryland Province of the Society of Jesus, (2005–2006), 93.

3. Ronald Rolheiser, *Our One Great Act of Fidelity: Waiting for Christ in the Eucharist* (New York: Doubleday, 2011), 96–108.

4. Deborah G. Rollison, "Grace in Grateful: Exploring Gratitude's Potential Influence on Faith Maturity and Stress Related Growth," unpublished dissertation (Loyola University Maryland, 2011), 1.

5. Rollison, "Grace in Grateful," 1.

6. Drew Leder, *Spiritual Passages: Embracing Life's Sacred Journey* (New York: Putnam, 1997), 73.

7. Anne Lamott, *Traveling Mercies: Some Thoughts on Faith* (New York: Pantheon, 1999), 125.

8. Lamott, *Traveling Mercies*, 112.

9. Lamott, *Traveling Mercies*, 120.

10. Brother David Steindl-Rast, *Gratefulness, the Heart of Prayer: An Approach to Life in Its Fullness* (New York: Paulist, 1984), 123.

11. Rollison, "Grace in Grateful," 70.

12. Robert J. Wicks, *Sharing Wisdom: The Practical Art of Giving and Receiving Mentoring* (New York: Crossroad, 2000), 54.

13. William Shakespeare, *Macbeth*, act 5, scene 5, cited in Clyde F. Crews, *Ultimate Questions* (New York: Paulist, 1986), 29.

14. Ralph Waldo Emerson, *Thoughts on Modern Literature from Uncollected Prose* (n.p.: Dial Essays, 1840), http://www.emersoncentral.com.

15. Emily Dickinson, "I Know that He Exists—365," cited in Clyde F. Crews, *Ultimate Questions* (New York: Paulist, 1986), 33.

16. Henri J. M. Nouwen, *Prayers from the Genesee* (New York: Crown, 2013).

17. Paul Meurice, *The Letters of Victor Hugo* (New York: Houghton-Mifflin, 2014), XXI.

18. Jeremy E. Sherman, "Love, Work, Play: Physics, Organism and Romance in a Nutshell," *Psychology Today*, December 13, 2009, https//www.psychologytoday.com.

19. Augustine of Hippo, *The Confessions of St. Augustine*, cited in *Co-Laboring with the Lord: Ignatian Companions on a Mission—A Year of Prayer* (n.p.: The Maryland Province of the Society of Jesus, 2005–2006).

20. Viktor Frankl, *Man's Search for Meaning* (New York: Simon and Schuster, 1984), 75.

21. Brother David Steindl-Rast, *Gratefulness, The Heart of Prayer*, 140.

22. G. K. Chesterton, *The Ballad of the White Horse* (New York: John Lane, 1911).

23. Chesterton, *The Ballad of the White Horse*, 13.

24. A. A. Milne, *Positively Pooh: Timeless Wisdom from Pooh* (New York: Penguin Group, 1982), 124.

CHAPTER 44

Praying with a Sacramental World

~ Kieran Scott ~

"You are indeed Holy, O Lord, and all you have created rightly gives you praise."

—Eucharistic Prayer III

The Roman Catholic tradition, in many ways, is the most worldly of religions. In its narrowest sense, it is a religion of rules and regulations. However, in its broadest and deepest sense, it is a unique take on life, a holy vision, a sacramental way of seeing the world.

The Catholic tradition is the pursuit of a way. The good and the bad intermingle and have to be accepted daily in the pursuit of the way. The Catholic temptation, at times, has been to try to set things right—by leaping from a bottom story of sin to a higher story of redemption. In our attempt to make a good world, we have fallen into the temptation of refusing to accept the goodness of the created world, including our own pleasure and happiness. At its best and wisest, however, Catholicism is rooted in the goodness of creation. What needs doing is re-creation. We must transform what is *already* good into what is holy. Praying in a sacramental world is one way of pursuing the way, and the Catholic sacramental principle is the source of this prayerful outlook and practice.

Certain dispositions are needed to pray in a sacramental world. Celtic spirituality, nature mysticism, and mysticism within the tradition undergird and exemplify this prayerful way of being in the world and there are spiritual exercises available to help us pray in a sacramental world.

A Sacramental World

"Nothing is profane for those who know how to see."

—Teilhard de Chardin

The imagination plays a pivotal role in the cultivation of vision. It gives us new ways of perceiving the world. It lures us to discover another way of seeing. It renews our vision by teaching our eyes to see again. A Roman Catholic imagination is committed to a way of imagining existence rooted in a sacramental imagination. Thomas Groome writes, "Nothing is more significant to what makes us Catholic than the sacramental principle. It epitomizes a Catholic outlook on life in the world."[1] It is a distinctive way of seeing the world. It points to the presence of the divine in all things. Matthew Eggemeier writes, "The sacramental imagination views creation as a manifestation of the glory of God.... [It] is grounded in a distinctive relationship between God and creation…while God is transcendent to creation, God is also found in the immanence of creation."[2] It affirms the omnipresence of God's grace in the world. For Michael Himes, this is synonymous with an experience of the sacramentality of creation. Himes writes, "By sacrament I mean any person, place, thing, or event, any sight, sound, taste, touch, or smell, that causes us to notice the love which supports all that exists, that undergirds your being and mine and the being of everything about us. How many such sacraments are there? The number is virtually infinite."[3] The world and everything in it is seen as actual or potential carriers of the sacred. The sacred is mediated through matter—through the ordinary events and things of this world. We encounter "mystery through manners," as Flannery O'Connor would say.

The Catholic sacramental imagination offers intimations of eternity, signals of transcendent. It is an enchanted imagination. The miraculous is always present in the quotidian, even if elusively. It echoes the ancient psalmist praise, "The heavens are telling the glory of God" (Psalm 19:1).[4] This evokes a proper religious response of gratitude, praise, wonder, and thanksgiving. Religion here is an attempt to regard nothing in the world as alien or hostile to humanity. Religion is "the hallowing of the everyday" (Martin Buber), and creation is perceived as the primary sacrament. Religion and praying religiously are profound modes of presence and receptivity to our wondrous and wounded world.

CELTIC SPIRITUALITY

Celtic spirituality offers us a rich expression of sacramental imagination. "The Celtic approach to God," Ester de Waal writes, "opens up a world in which nothing is too common to be exalted and nothing is so exalted that it cannot be made common."[5] It renews our vision by teaching our eyes to see again, our ears to hear, our hands to handle. It teaches us to look for God within creation and to recognize the world— and everything in it—as a place of potential revelation. The whole of life is sacramental. All can be the Word of God.

Philip Newell notes, "The feature of Celtic spirituality that is probably most widely recognized, both within and outside the Church, is its creation emphasis…. This spirituality lent itself to listening for God at the heart of life…. It is a spirituality of deep and rich perspectives, with origins in the mystical traditions of the Old and New Testament."[6] The spiritual is seen coming through the physical. God is seen as the life within all life. This is not an elsewhere God, a creator who sets life in motion from afar and, then, steps back to watch from on high as life willy-nilly unfolds. No. This Creator God is the life force in the depths of all creation. Those who have eyes to see, let them see. Those who have ears to hear, let them hear. "Taste and see the goodness of the Lord." We are invited and called to listen within all things for the life and heartbeat of God. Celtic spirituality is part of an ancient stream of contemplative spirituality stretching back to the wisdom tradition of the Old Testament, St. John the Evangelist in the New Testament, and to the life of the early church in the British Isles.

There are three major characteristics of Celtic spirituality: the essential goodness of creation; good and bad, grace and sin, intermingle in life; and the immediacy of God's presence in the world.

The essential goodness of creation is the (methodological) starting point for Celtic seeing. It is a form of nature mysticism. The threads of heaven and the threads of earth are inseparably interwoven. The spirit is in the depths of matter. The material realm of creation is shot through with spirit. George MacLeod (1895–1991), founder of the Iona community, captures well this sense of the eternal "seeping through the physical." In his prayerful words, taken from "The Glory in the Grey," he writes,

> Almighty God,
> Sun behind all suns,
> Soul behind all souls,…
> Show to us in everything we touch and in everyone we meet
> the continued assurance of thy presence around us
> lest ever we should think thee absent.
> In all created things thou art there.
> In every friend we have
> the sunshine of thy presence is shown forth.
> In every enemy that seems to cross our path,
> thou art there within the cloud to challenge us to
> love.
> Show to us the glory in the grey.
> Awake for us thy presence in the very storm
> till all our joys are seen as thee
> and all our trivial tasks emerge as priestly
> sacraments
> in the universal temple of thy love.[7]

GOD IS THE LIFE WITHIN ALL LIFE.

The second characteristic of Celtic spirituality is the belief that good and bad are interwoven in our daily affairs. Even though creation is essentially good, and at its deepest level, bears the fingerprints of God, the world and its inhabitants are held down by forces of darkness. Echoing St. Paul, the whole world groans with labor pains to bring the new to birth (see Romans 8:22). Salvation means liberation from these evil forces that dominate us so that our essential goodness and the original blessings of the earth are set free. This sense of Christian realism and, at the same time, hopefulness saves Celtic spirituality from a naïve sense of romanticism. It prevents it from being hijacked and misinterpreted by those in search of an enchanted romantic perspective.

The third characteristic of a Celtic spirituality and its way of seeing is its sense of the immediacy of the presence of God in the whole world. It has a keen, mystical awareness. No ladder is needed to connect heaven and earth. Heaven is in the midst of earth. "So to look to God," Philip Newell notes,

> is not to look away from life but to look more deeply into it. Together with this emphasis on the presence of God at the heart of creation, of God being the heartbeat of life, there is also a sense of the closeness, the personal immediacy of God to us, a closeness not only of God but of the whole host of heaven, enfolding the earth and its people with love."[8]

This comes across in a striking manner in the famous "Breastplate Hymn," with its Christocentric focus, attributed to St. Patrick:

> Christ be with me, Christ within me,
> Christ behind me, Christ before me,
> Christ beside me, Christ to win me.
> Christ to comfort me and restore me,
> Christ beneath me, Christ above me,
> Christ in quiet, Christ in danger,
> Christ in hearts of all that love me,
> Christ in mouth of friend and stranger.

There is no great gap between Creator and creation. They are inseparably intertwined. Celtic spiritual awareness is to be aware of the presence of God in the flow of life—from the rising of the sun to its setting, in our work and play, in our rest and reformation, in the visible and invisible. God is closer to us than our very breath.

This way of seeing, historically at times, has been accused of violating religious orthodoxy. It has been indicted for crossing the border into pantheism, namely, that all is God. However, a Celtic spiritual way of seeing is not pantheism. It is panentheism; namely, it envisions a relationship whereby everything abides in God, who in turn encompasses everything. God is "above all and through all and in all" (Ephesians 4:6). God is the being on which all being rests, the light within all light, the good from which all goodness flows. The world is a theater of God's glory.

NATURE MYSTICISM

> To see the world in a grain of sand
> And a Heaven in a wild flower,
> Hold Infinity in the palm of your hand,
> And Eternity in an hour.

> —William Blake

For Blake, "If the doors of perception were cleansed, everything would be seen as it is, infinite." By minute attention to small and seemingly insignificant things, we can come to probe the mysteries of things that are far greater. Imaginatively seeing a sacramental world is not exclusive to explicit forms of traditional spirituality, nor is it confined to the four walls of the church. It has been seen and created by painters (Michelangelo), musicians (Handel), poets (Dante), and prose writers (Flannery O'Connor). A profound contemporary example of a "mysticism of open eyes" (Johan Baptist Metz) and a sacramental vision is the writings and prayerful poetry of Annie Dillard. Dillard's mystical excursion into the natural world opens up the sanctuary of God within the whole world. "It's all a matter of keeping my eyes open," she notes.[9] The real cathedral of God is the natural stuff of life.

In *Pilgrim at Tinker Creek*, Dillard describes two ways of seeing: seeing as "verbalization" and seeing as "letting go." Seeing as verbalization is active and assertive. "When I see this way," Dillard writes, "I analyze and pry. I hurl over logs and roll stones; I study the bank a square foot at a time, probing and tilting my head—Unless I call my attention to what passes before my eyes, I simply won't see it."[10] It does not merely go unnoticed but, for all practical purposes, unseen.

But there is another kind of seeing, Dillard asserts. It is a "kind of seeing that involves a letting go." "When I see this way," she reveals, "I sway transfixed and emptied.... When I see this way I see truly...I return to my senses."[11] This mode of seeing transcends a mere mechanical and instrumentalist approach to the world and opens the self to what is really given. Dillard notes, "The secret of seeing is, then, the pearl of great price.... But although the pearl may be found, it may not be sought...it is always, even to the most practiced and adept, a gift and a total surprise."[12] The only appropriate response is, "Alleluia." Matthew Eggemeier writes, "Dillard's writings witness to a self-emptying form of contemplative attention to the natural world."[13]

Dillard's way of seeing is rooted in a profoundly sacramental view of the world. The prayerful and gratitudinal quality of her writings shine forth in her work, *Holy the Firm*.[14] For Dillard, the firmament is holy. The biblical bush still burns, and we take off our shoes. Contemplatively attending to the goodness of creation represents a path to God. It is a form of prayer. It is *How to Pray Always (without Always Praying)*.[15] It is real presence. Our vocation, then, is to see the beauty of creation and the beautiful one from whom all blessings flow. God calls through the natural world, and the first human response is, "i thank You God for most this amazing day" (e. e. cummings).

Here is a nature mysticism of surrendering to beauty in order to experience the beauty of nature. This experience of letting go and being grasped by the beautiful is one of the clearest intuitions of the divine. The world is God's body. And when we *see* that way, we are praying with a sacramental world.

Mysticism within Tradition

The world is charged with the grandeur of God.

—Gerard Manley Hopkins

Karl Rahner, a very influential Roman Catholic theologian of the twentieth century, asserts, "In the days ahead, you will either be a mystic (one who has experienced God for real) or nothing at all."[16] A rich sense of nature mysticism runs through the Roman Catholic tradition. We see it in the classic phrase of Ignatius of Loyola ("see God in all things"), in the sacramental poetry of Gerard Manley Hopkins, and in the Christian mysticism of Teilhard de Chardin. Each affirms "The heavens are telling the glory of God" (Psalm 19:1). The fact that the world is simply there, in all its splendor and fragility, gives rise in each to wonder, awe, and religious sense of the loving power that quickens it. Each, with a contemplative human spirit, see the presence of the divine in nature. The earth is a sacred place. Through the religious spirit of (real) presence and receptivity to the world, we grow in realization of how deeply we humans are embedded in the earth. To do so, we must, in the words of Annie Dillard, let go of our way of seeing and return to our senses.

Teilhard de Chardin, a paleontologist, Jesuit priest and one of the twentieth century's great nature mystics, embodies these sentiments in his "Hymn to Matter":

Blessed be you, harsh matter, barren soil, stubborn rock: you who yield only to violence, you who force us to work if we would eat.

Blessed be you, perilous matter, violent sea, untameable passion: you who unless we fetter you will devour us.

Blessed be you, mighty matter, irresistible march of evolution, reality ever new-born; you who, by constantly shattering our mental categories, force us to go ever further and further in our pursuit of the truth.

Blessed be you, universal matter, immeasurable time, boundless ether, triple abyss of stars and atoms and generations: you who by overflowing and dissolving our narrow standards or measurement reveal to us the dimensions of God.

Without you, without your onslaughts, without your uprootings of us, we should remain all our lives inert, stagnant, puerile, ignorant both of ourselves and of God. You who batter us and then dress our wounds, you who resist us and yield to us, you who wreck and build, you who shackle and liberate, the sap of our souls, the hand of God, the flesh of Christ: it is you, matter, that I bless.[17]

For Teilhard, the world, and everything in it—every atom, pebble, flower, forest, desert, mountain, seashell—was a theophany, a visible manifestation of God. While in the Gobi Desert, in Mongolia, and without the elements of bread and wine to celebrate Eucharist, he sees the universe as the altar and the elements in it as Eucharistic offerings. Matter matters—it is a sacramental medium to the divine. When the priest raises his hands to consecrate the bread and wine at the church altar, Teilhard affirms, he is declaring all matter, all life, to be the Body and Blood of Christ. The world, symbolically, is in (the daily) bread and wine. These words come alive with new and richer meaning.

Blessed are you, Lord, God of all creation
Through your goodness we have this bread to offer,
Which earth has given and human hands have made.
It will become for us the bread of life.
Blessed be God forever.
Blessed are you, Lord, God of all creation.
Through your goodness we have this wine to offer,
Fruit of the vine and work of human hands.
It will become our spiritual drink.
Blessed be God forever.

The world is the host, and our appropriate religious response is to sing a hymn to the universe.

The Jesuit poet Gerard Manley Hopkins does just that throughout the corpus of his writings. His sacramental, poetic prayerfulness shines forth in his brilliant and revelatory poems, especially "Pied Beauty" and "God's Grandeur." For Rahner, Teilhard, and Hopkins, the world is not simply a stage to be (instrumentally) walked on, utilized or dominated. It is to be knelt on and surrendered to as we pray, "Holy the firm."

SPIRITUAL EXERCISES FOR PRAYING IN A SACRAMENTAL WORLD

Michael Himes observes, "The whole Catholic sacramental life is a training to be beholders."[18] This training can take multiple forms. Elizabeth Johnson suggests a trinity of practices and forms: contemplative, ascetic, and prophetic.[19]

First, the contemplative response is a training "to gaze on the world with eyes of love rather than with an arrogant, utilitarian stare."[20] It teaches us to "learn to appreciate the astonishing beauty of nature, to take delight in its intricate and powerful workings and to stand in awe of the never ending mystery of life and death played out in the predator-prey relationship. Nothing is too large (the farthest galaxies), nothing too small to escape our wonder."[21] This contemplative stance renders the world sacramental. It can also be profoundly countercultural.

Janet Ruffing describes our North American addiction to the demon of busyness.[22] She analyzes the erosion of leisure in our culture and business practices. With the invention of smart phones, e-mail, Facebook, Twitter, and so on, our islands of solitude have been invaded. Work is reduced to job. Time is money. Every moment of solitude or leisure is encroached on. The results, Ruffing notes, are "profoundly destructive to self-intimacy, intimacy with the Divine, interrelationships, reflective thought, the social fabric of our society, our care for the planet, and our own psychological and physical health."[23] When we are busy being busy, we deprive ourselves of moments of beauty, surprise, delight in what is before us. We become bushwhacked and spiritually blind.

There is an alternative, Ruffing suggests—an opposite state of mind and heart. "Traditionally," she writes, "this is called a contemplative attitude, creative leisure, recollection, or mindfulness."[24] This is when we do what we are doing with full attention. "We experience a sense of mindfulness, a feeling of undivided attention. We become centered, relaxed, and serenely present. We find ourselves able to delight in our day as it unfolds. We inhabit an enlarged contemplative awareness instead of a compulsive busyness."[25] With this contemplative training, we can become (mindfully) present and (restfully) receptive to the natural environment that envelops us.

The second response and training, Johnson suggests, is the ascetic. This is a discipline or asceticism of relinquishment. It calls for a discipline in using the things of the earth. This could also be a very countercultural way of life, where overconsumption and the wanton and reckless use of resources prevail.

Ascetical practices, at their wisest and best, seek to remove barriers that block our sensitivity to the presence and movement of the Spirit in our lives. Their true purpose is to make people fully alive to life and God. Training in detachment and self-abnegation are called for in light of the state of God's beloved creation. "There are whole new ways of engaging in ascetical practices," Johnson writes, "such as fasting, retreats and almsgiving. We can fast from shopping, contribute money and time to ecological works, endure the inconvenience of running an ecologically sensitive household and conduct business with an eye to the green bottom line as well as the red or black."[26] This earth-sensitive and earth-sensuous asceticism enables us to shed cumber, live more simply, with reverence for the earth and its creatures. It makes room for God, and, in the words of St. Paul, it enables us "to pray without ceasing" (1 Thessalonians 5:17).

The third form of spiritual training and response Elizabeth Johnson proposes is prophetic action on behalf of justice for the earth. "Who is my neighbor?" Brian Patrick asks. "The Samaritan? The outcast? The enemy? Yes, yes, of course. But it is also the whale, the dolphin, and the rainforest. Our neighbor is the entire community of life, the entire universe. We must love it all as our very self."[27]

The current destruction of our planet seen through sacramental eyes is a sacrilege. For Christians it bears the mark of deep sinfulness. It is flinging God's gift into his face. Wendell Berry notes, "To live we must daily break the bread and shed the blood of Creation. When we do this knowingly, lovingly, reverently, it is a sacrament. When we do it ignorantly, greedily, clumsily, destructively, it is a desecration."[28]

We have a moral imperative to act in favor of care, protection, and renewal of the earth. The critical challenge of our time, Pope Francis writes in his recent encyclical on the environment, is to develop a sustainable earth community.[29] This involves living a life of prophetic protest and resistance against the blasphemous behavior of ruining our beloved common home. "If nature is the new poor," Elizabeth Johnson writes, "then the Christian mandate of option for the poor and oppressed now includes the natural world."[30] Thou shalt not kill. Responsible stewardship is the moral goal to ensure vibrant life in community for all. It is the work of justice, the path to deification, and the avenue to praying with a sacramental world.

Melissa West asks, "What if all ground is holy? What if all bushes are burning, as well as trees, stones, creatures, our children, ourselves, and all the spaces in between."[31] For Christians with a sacramental imagination, the bushes still burn…all and all is on fire! The holy land is not so much a place as a process of seeing the spiritual depth in

the natural world. The human vocation is to hear this call and respond, praying the
Sanctus:

> Holy, holy, holy, Lord God of power and might,
>
> heaven and earth are full of your Glory.
>
> Hosanna in the highest.

1. Thomas Groome, *What Makes Us Catholic* (New York: HarperOne, 2003), 84.
2. Matthew Eggemeir, *A Sacramental—Prophetic Imagination* (Collegeville, MN: Liturgical, 2014), 8.
3. Michael Himes, "'Finding God in All Things': A Sacramental World View and Its Effects," in *As Leaven in the World: Catholic Perspectives on Faith, Vocation, and the Intellectual Life*, ed. T. Landy (Franklin, WI: Sheed & Ward, 2001), 91–103, 99.
4. All Scripture quotations are taken from the *New Revised Standard Version*.
5. Ester de Waal, "Living the Sacramental Principle," in *Catholic Spiritual Practices*, ed. Colleen Griffith and Thomas Groome (Brewster, MA: Paraclete, 2012), 63–67.
6. J. Philip Newell, *Listening for the Heartbeat of God* (New York: Paulist, 1997), 2–3.
7. George MacLeod, quoted in Newell, *Listening for the Heartbeat of God*, 87.
8. Newell, *Listening for the Heartbeat of God*, 48.
9. Annie Dillard, *Pilgrim at Tinker Creek* (New York: Bantam, 1974), 18.
10. Dillard, *Pilgrim at Tinker Creek*, 32.
11. Dillard, *Pilgrim at Tinker Creek*, 33–34.
12. Dillard, *Pilgrim at Tinker Creek*, 34–35.
13. Matthew Eggemeir, *A Sacramental—Prophetic Imagination*, 87.
14. Annie Dillard, *Holy the Firm* (New York: Harper & Row, 1977).
15. Silvio Fittipaldi, *How to Pray Always Without Always Praying* (Notre Dame, IN: Fides-Claretian, 1978).
16. In Brendan Manning, *The Furious Longing of God* (Colorado Springs: David C. Cook, 2009), 129.
17. Teilhard de Chardin, *Hymn of the Universe* (New York: Harper & Row, 1965), 63–64.
18. Michael Himes, "Finding God in All Things," 100.
19. Elizabeth Johnson, "God's Beloved Creation," *America*, 184, no. 13 (2001):10–12.
20. Johnson, "God's Beloved Creation," 10.
21. Johnson, "God's Beloved Creation," 10.
22. Janet Ruffing, "Resisting the Demons of Busyness," *Spiritual Life* 3, no. 1, (1996):1–8.
23. Ruffing, "Resisting the Demons of Busyness," 2.
24. Ruffing, "Resisting the Demons of Busyness," 4.
25. Ruffing, "Resisting the Demons of Busyness," 4.
26. Johnson, "God's Beloved Creation," 11.
27. Elizabeth Johnson, *Quest for the Living God* (New York: Continuum, 2007), 198.
28. Wendell Berry, quoted in Matthew Eggemeir, 102.
29. Pope Francis, *Laudato Si': On the Care of our Common Home* (Washington, DC: USCCB, 2015).
30. Elizabeth Johnson, "God's Beloved Creation," 12.
31. Melissa West, *If Only I Were a Better Mother* (Walpole, NJ: Stillpoint, 1992), 105.

CHAPTER 45

Prayer in Chaos, Commotion, and Clutter

~ Kathy Coffey ~

"In the name of the…" *Swipe dog food out of baby's mouth.*

"Father. And of the…" *"It's 55 degrees out. You cannot wear shorts simply to display the Batman bandage on your knee!"*

"Son." *Phone ringing. Shrill, frantic barking ensues.*

"And of …" *Unexplained, bone-rattling klunk.*

"the…" *"But you said I could have a snack!"*

"Holy Spirit." *Long sigh of frustration.*

Of course this scenario may be an exaggeration. But it's a glimpse of what many people, especially parents of young children, or those stressed by working multiple jobs, face when we religious sorts blithely encourage them to pray. The God who loves variety welcomes the disjointed conversation just as much as the serene voice. So it's perfectly natural and understandable when people ask in bewilderment, "Who has the time to pray? Or the quiet? Or the focus?"

Fair questions if prayer involves reading the right book, finding the rosary, or joining a group at church. Rarely do folks get the energy or uninterrupted stretches that many guidebooks seem to assume everyone has regularly. But another, perhaps more realistic, model emerges from John 13. There, amidst the commotion of a meal (pots and pans clanging, smells seeping from the kitchen, an argument between disciples—not in the quiet hush of a worship space), Jesus washes the feet of his friends. Verses 3–4, which precede this action, set the context: "Jesus, knowing that the Father had given all things into his hands and that he had come from God and was going to God, got up from the table, took off his outer robe, and tied a towel around himself" (John 13:3–4).[1] Notice the measured cadence, the surety, the practicality of his action. What is true for Jesus is true for us too: If we know we've come from God and are going to God, our lives are bracketed in security. What more do we need? We take the next step, put our hands to the next task with the passion and compassion of Christ. The banner of the new order isn't an ermine-trimmed scarlet cape. It's a towel.

If we think of prayer as being a matter of ritualized gesture, formulaic words, churchy settings, Sistine choirs, folded hands, and bent heads, how do we explain Jesus's action? Could we dare say it wasn't prayerful? Maybe he directs us beyond the stereotypes to a more practical form that can fit the busiest schedule: Transform the action with prayerful intent, see beneath the humdrum with deeper insight.

As John's Last Supper narrative continues, Peter motions to the beloved disciple seated beside Jesus, indicating he should ask him who will betray the master. The beloved disciple (thankfully not named so he or she can represent any of us) *leans back* on Jesus (John 13:23–25). That, says Beatrice Bruteau, is the stance of Christian prayer. At times we feel too exhausted, depleted, sick, or frustrated to pray. Then we need only rest on Jesus, just as we might lay our heads on someone's shoulder, and let him heal us. It doesn't require eloquence, brilliant insight, or heroic action. Nor does it demand a quiet church or hours of time. But it places us in the same relationship to Jesus as he is to his Father in John's prologue: "No one has ever seen God. It is God the only Son, who is close to the Father's heart, who has made him known" (John 1:18). Just as Jesus is close to the Father's heart, so we are close to his.

For an even homier image, picture a newborn who has just nursed, enjoys the bliss of being "milk drunk," and falls asleep on the mother's chest with drool spiraling down multiple chins. Thérèse of Lisieux wasn't worried about falling asleep at prayer, saying, "I know that children are just as dear to their parents whether they are asleep or awake."[2]

I've seen prayer from both sides now—the spacious tranquility of the retreat house, the realities of life with my four children and six grandchildren (all under age three). But from the former, I've learned the hidden prayerfulness of the latter. My point of identification with Christ is strongest in the arena of our shared motherhood. I borrow ideas on the motherhood of God from Julian of Norwich, who had no qualms about mixing up gender references. To her, action was more important: Jesus's maternal longing to feed all the children at the same table, his asking poignantly, "Have I done enough?" and dying in childbirth. Like the mother who would gladly take on the child's illness or broken ankle, he takes our suffering on himself. Motherhood is my only identity which lasts a lifetime; others, like those connected with career, fluctuate.

Catholic sacramentality means that just as a bite of bread or sip of wine feeds the soul, so too the most ordinary people, things, and actions camouflage the sacred. For instance, many years ago, a parent packed a child's lunch. Like 347 others, it was a sleepy, monotonous part of the morning routine. But something spectacular lurked in the lunch bag: those loaves and fishes would feed the multitude.

When the hungry family sits down to a long-awaited meal at the end of an exhausting day, does their casserole not hold the kindness of Eucharist? When there simply isn't time to read the day's Scriptures or withdraw for meditation, the activity itself is the prayer. Elizabeth Ann Seton, single mother of five and caretaker for many more children, understood the dilemma. She complained that if she tried to retreat for a moment, a dozen voices called, demanding her attention. So she adapted her prayer: "When I cannot get hours, I take minutes." The approach seems to have worked. She's the first US-born canonized saint.

A bit of Catholic jargon seems relevant here: the word *transubstantiation*. We may well balk at the strangeness of that hard-to-swallow mouthful of syllables. But as poet Denise Levertov reminds us, "Aren't there annunciations / of one sort or another / in most lives?"[3] So, too, do the events of our lives parallel those of Christ's and are turned into his breath and bone. Within his mystical body, nativities, epiphanies, travels, transfigurations, healings, crucifixions and resurrections don't stop with the last page of the Gospel, but are ongoing. Families know birth at the most literal level. Infant smallness and vulnerability evoke deep tenderness; hearts melt before such innocence. Babies' total dependence encourages adults to rise to the occasion, usually in the middle of the night. Who else could drag us out of bed or evoke such stalwart protection? Jesus knew human nature when he invited, "Whoever welcomes this child in my name welcomes me" (Luke 9:48).

There are also birth pains and births beyond the literal ones: coming to a new understanding, trying a different experience, moving to another location, making a friend, starting or deepening a relationship, taking a new job, engaging with unfamiliar cultures or ideas. If we're open and not calcified in our own thinking, we have frequent, broadening epiphanies: Slap-the-forehead moments of "Why didn't I see that before?" or "NOW I get it!"

The journey theme pervades Scripture—the Hebrew exodus, Jesus's final trip to Jerusalem—and later, pilgrimages became holy. But is there not a procession to school or work each morning, a relieved return home each evening, a high expectation of vacation trips? Why can we not see the holy aura surrounding the carpool or bus commute?

This Jesus who cured blindness with spit and muddy glop isn't likely to be deterred by the earthy. Nor does he seem the prissy sort to shield his ears from four-year-old scatology. Is he not then a vital part of healing in a hospital or home?

While we may not shine in dazzling white on a mountaintop, we go through many transfigurations as we mature. Few things are more transformative than a helpless infant becoming a toddler who talks, sings, laughs, follows a routine, and even with insufficient language, makes it precisely clear exactly what he or she wants. The mediocre student becomes an outstanding teacher, understanding firsthand the challenges some children confront. The self-centered young adult becomes a Jesuit, Vincentian, or Mercy Corps volunteer and gradually directs multiple talents to others. Or an itch turns to accomplishment, a note on a page soars into melody.

Crucifixion is no longer the capital punishment du jour. But ask anyone in grief or those in chronic pain: have they not felt the hammer blows, the sting of the nails? The parent of the addict, the child of the Alzheimer's patient, and the spouse of the alcoholic endures their personal Calvaries. If we can't see the little-r resurrections of our own lives (waking each morning, seeing a fresh angle to an old problem, energetically starting a new project, reconciling after an argument, planting seed in spring, recovering health after illness, finding a precious lost item), we may never appreciate resurrection with a capital R. Through lives that may seem undramatic, Christ dies again, is risen again, and comes again and again. Maybe prayer is reverently paying attention to and being grateful for his actions hidden in our ordinary, chaotic, conflicted days.

1. All quotations from Scripture are taken from the *New Revised Standard Version.*
2. "St. Thérèse of Lisieux (1873–1897)," Wisdom Line, www.goodnews.ie/wisdomlineenis.shtml.
3. Denise Levertov, "Annunciation," *The Stream and the Sapphire* (New York: New Directions, 1997), 59.

A BRIEF, FINAL NOTE FROM THE EDITOR

With this section we conclude a large volume with many wonderful, knowledgeable, talented, and prayerful voices writing on a vast array of topics on prayer. As was noted in the introduction, however, the topic of prayer in the Catholic tradition has so much more to offer. This has been, I hope, a good beginning to appreciate the treasures we have and how to begin or continue to mine them in ways that will help to fully enjoy one's life, share it freely with others, and to have God at our side and within us during each phase of the journey. Even though this handbook is, to my knowledge, the most extensive available, it is not complete. And so, while I hope this volume is a true support to adult Catholics and those who are called to minister to them, I have an equal hope that suggestions will arise on how we can expand this journey even more by adding other topics and voices in the future. That is my hope for this project and for those who it is designed to serve.

—RJW